CALVIN S. HALL

Professor of Psychology
Syracuse University

and

GARDNER LINDZEY

Professor of Psychology
University of Minnesota

Theories

of

Personality

Theories
of
Personality

NEW YORK · JOHN WILEY & SONS, INC.

London · Sydney

Library of Congress Catalog Card Number: 57–5915

PRINTED IN THE UNITED STATES OF AMERICA

To our teachers and friends

Gordon W. Allport

Henry A. Murray

Edward C. Tolman

Preface

In spite of the deepening interest of psychologists in personality theory, there is no single source to which the student can turn for a survey of existing theories of personality. The present volume is intended to correct this shortcoming. It provides compact yet comprehensive summaries of the major contemporary theories of personality written at a level of difficulty that is appropriate for undergraduate or graduate instruction. From this book the student can secure a detailed overview of personality theory and at the same time he can prepare himself to read original sources with more appreciation and greater facility. It is our hope that this volume will serve a function in the area of personality similar to that served by Hilgard's *Theories of Learning* in the area of learning.

What theories should be included in a volume on personality theory? Although it is not easy to specify precisely what a theory of personality is, it is even more difficult to agree as to what are the most important of these theories. As set forth in the first chapter, we are willing to accept any general theory of behavior as a theory of personality. In judging importance we have relied primarily upon our evaluation of the degree of influence the theory has had upon psychological research and formulation. Also involved in this complex judgment is the matter of distinctiveness. When two or more theories have appeared to us to be very similar, we have either treated them in a single chapter or selected one theory to focus upon to the exclusion of the others. Given these broad criteria of importance and distinctiveness, there will probably be little objection to the particular theories we have elected to include in the volume. There may be less unanimity, however, concerning our decision to omit certain theories from consideration. Notable among the omissions are McDougall's Hormic Theory, Role Theory, Guthrie's Contiguity Theory, Tolman's Purposive Behaviorism, and some of the recently developed positions such as David McClelland's, Julian Rotter's, and George Kelly's.

We originally planned to include both McDougall's Hormic Theory and Role Theory but limitations of space forced us to reduce the number of chapters and these were the theories we judged to be most expendable. Hormic Theory was omitted because its influence is somewhat more indirect than in the case of the other theories. Although we regard McDougall as a theorist of great importance, his contemporary impact is largely mediated by more recent theorists who have borrowed features of his theory. Role Theory, it seems to us, is less systematically developed than most of the other positions we elected to include. It is true that the theory contains a leading idea of considerable value and importance but this idea has not as yet been incorporated into a network of concepts which deal comprehensively with human behavior. Guthrie and Tolman were omitted in favor of Hull's reinforcement theory simply because there has been less extensive research application of these theories outside of the area of learning. McClelland, Rotter, and Kelly were not included because of their recency and because, in some respects, their positions resemble theories or combinations of theories that we have included.

Having decided upon what theories to include, we were still faced with the problem of how to organize and describe these positions. Some consistency in mode of presentation seemed desirable; yet at the same time we wished to preserve the integrity of the individual theories. Our compromise consisted of providing general categories in terms of which the theories could be described while permitting ourselves a good deal of latitude within these categories so as to present each theory in the manner that seemed most natural. Even these general categories were not adhered to rigidly. In some instances new ones were necessary in order to represent a particular theory adequately, and in one or two cases it seemed advisable to combine categories. Typically, however, each theory is introduced with an Orientation section which recounts briefly the personal history of the theorist, outlines the main lines of influence upon the theory, and provides a summary of the salient features of the theory. Next the reader will find a section on the Structure of Personality in which are included the concepts designed to represent the acquisitions or enduring portions of personality. Following this is a section on Dynamics of Personality which sets forth the motivational or dispositional concepts and principles espoused by the theorist. Then comes a section on Development of Personality which deals with growth and change as represented by the theory. A section on Characteristic Research and Research Methods follows, in which representative investigations and empirical techniques are presented. There is a concluding section entitled Current Status and Evaluation which outlines briefly the present state of the theory and summarizes the major contributions of the theory as well as the chief criticisms it has elicited. At the end of each chapter is a brief list of Primary Sources which represents the most important of the original sources concerning the theory. All of the publications referred to in the text are brought together in a final section at the end of each chapter entitled References.

We have attempted to present each theory in a positive light, dwelling upon those features of the theory that seem to us most useful and suggestive. Although we have included a brief critique of each theory it has not been our primary intention to evaluate these theories. Rather, we have attempted to present them in expository terms that will demonstrate what they are good for or what promise they hold for the individual who adopts them. The length of a chapter does not reflect our judgment of the relative importance of the theory. Each theory is written in what seemed to us the smallest number of pages necessary to represent its essential features accurately and comprehensively. The reader will observe that in some chapters there appears to be more detailed and personal information concerning the theorist and the development of his theory than in other chapters. This was determined solely by availability of information. In those instances where we knew a good deal about the theorist, we decided to include as much of this information as seemed vital even though this would result in some chapters appearing more personalized than others.

In the preparation of this volume we sought and received invaluable assistance from a number of colleagues. It is with deep gratitude and appreciation that we acknowledge the personal contribution made by many of the theorists whose work is presented here. They clarified our thinking upon a number of points and made numerous suggestions both as to form and content which greatly improved the manuscript. Whatever merit this book possesses must be attributed in large measure to the meticulous care with which each of the following theorists read and criticized the chapter devoted to his theory: Gordon W. Allport, Raymond B. Cattell, H. J. Eysenck, Kurt Goldstein, Carl Jung, Neal E. Miller, Gardner Murphy, Henry A. Murray, Carl Rogers, Robert R. Sears, and William Sheldon. In addition to illuminating comments concerning the chapter dealing with his own theory, Gordon Allport provided us with penetrating criticisms and generative suggestions concerning all of the remaining chapters. He also used many of the chapters in his undergraduate and graduate courses and provided us with the comments and suggestions of these students. We are greatly indebted not only to these Harvard and Radcliffe students but also to many students at Western Reserve University who read and commented upon the chapters. We are pleased to acknowledge our further indebtedness to the following individuals, each of whom read and improved by their suggestions one or more chapters in this book: John A. Atkinson, Raymond A. Bauer, Urie Bronfenbrenner, Arthur Combs, Anthony Davids, Frieda Fromm-Reichmann, Eugene L. Hartley, Ernest Hilgard, Robert R. Holt, Edward E. Jones, George S. Klein, Herbert McClosky, George Mandler, James G. March, A. H. Maslow, Theodore M. Newcomb, Helen S. Perry, Stewart E. Perry, M. Brewster Smith, Donald Snygg, S. S. Stevens, Patrick Suppes, John Thibaut, Edward C. Tolman, and Otto A. Will, Jr. We are indebted to Heinz and Rowena Ansbacher for providing us with page proof of their book *The Individual Psychology of Alfred Adler* prior to its publication. It was very helpful to us in writing the section on Adler's theory of personality. In the final preparation of the manuscript we received invaluable assistance from Virginia Caldwell, Marguerite Dickey, and Kenneth Wurtz.

The completion of this volume was greatly facilitated by a half-year leave of absence granted by Western Reserve University to Calvin S. Hall and by a fellowship at the Center for Advanced Study in the Behavioral Sciences granted to Gardner Lindzey. The writing was also facilitated by the permission granted Lindzey to use the facilities of the Dartmouth College Library during the summer of 1954.

Calvin S. Hall
Gardner Lindzey

Contents

1.

The Nature
of Personality Theory

The main purpose of this book is to present an organized summary of the major contemporary theories of personality. In addition to providing a digest of each theory we shall also discuss relevant research and give an over-all evaluation of the theory. Before proceeding with this task, however, something should be said about what personality theories are as well as how the various personality theories can be distinguished from one another. Further, there is an obligation to place these theories in a general context, relating them to what has gone on historically in psychology as well as locating them in the contemporary scene.

In this introductory chapter we shall commence with a very general and somewhat informal outline of the role of personality theory in the development of psychology, followed by a discussion of what is meant by the term personality and by the term theory. From these considerations it is an easy step to the question of what constitutes a personality theory. We shall also consider very briefly the relation between personality theory and other forms of psychological theory. In conclusion we shall present a number of dimensions by means of which personality theories can be compared with one another. These dimensions can be considered to represent the major theoretical issues in this area.

PERSONALITY THEORY AND THE HISTORY OF PSYCHOLOGY

A comprehensive view of the development of personality theory must surely begin with conceptions of man advanced by the great classical scholars such as Hippocrates, Plato, and Aristotle. An adequate account would also be obligated to deal with the contributions of dozens of thoughtful individuals, for example, Aquinas, Bentham, Comte, Hobbes, Locke, and Machiavelli, who lived in the intervening centuries and whose ideas are still to be detected in contemporary formulation. It is not our intention here to attempt any such general reconstruction. Our goal is much more limited. We shall merely consider in broad terms the general role personality theory has played in the development of psychology during the past six or seven decades.

To begin with, let us examine some relatively recent sources of influence upon personality theory. A tradition of clinical observation beginning with Charcot and Janet but including most importantly Freud, Jung, and McDougall has done more to determine the nature of personality theory than any other single factor. In a moment we shall examine some of the effects of this movement. A second path of influence stems from the Gestalt tradition and William Stern. These theorists were tremendously impressed with the unity of behavior and consequently were convinced that the segmental or fragmented study of small elements of behavior could never prove enlightening. As we shall discover, this point of view is deeply embedded in current personality theory. There is also the more recent impact of experimental psychology in general and learning theory in particular. From this avenue has come increased concern with carefully controlled empirical research and a better understanding of the nature of theory construction. A fourth determinant is represented by the psychometric tradition with its focus upon the measurement and study of individual differences. This source has provided increasing sophistication in measurement and the quantitative analysis of data. There are numerous other paths of influence upon personality theory including experimental genetics, logical positivism, and social anthropology but none of these seems, thus far, to have had such far-reaching implications as the four determinants we have just outlined.

The specific background out of which each of the theories presented in this book emerged is briefly discussed in the following chapters. General discussions of the development of contemporary personality theory will be found in Allport (1937), Boring (1950), MacKinnon (1944), MacKinnon and Maslow (1951), and Murphy (1949). The current status of personality theory and research is summarized in a series of chapters appearing in the *Annual Review of Psychology* (Bronfenbrenner, 1953; Child, 1954; Eysenck, 1952; MacKinnon, 1951; McClelland, 1956; Nuttin, 1955; Sears, 1950).

Let us turn now to some of the distinctive features of personality theory. Although this body of theory is manifestly a part of the broad field of psychology, still there are appreciable differences between personality theory and research and research and theory in other areas of psychology. These differences are particularly pronounced in regard to the early development of personality theory, and exist in spite of a great deal of variation among personality theories themselves. The individual differences between personality theories imply that almost any statement that applies with detailed accuracy to one theory of personality will be somewhat inaccurate when applied to certain other theories. In spite of this, there are modal qualities or central tendencies which inhere in most personality theories and it is upon these that we shall focus in our discussion.

Granted that there are important congruences in the streams of influence which determined the early paths of general psychology and of personality theory, still there are significant differences. It is true that Darwin was a potent factor in the development of both positions and it is also true that physiology of the nineteenth century had its influence upon personality theorists as well as a marked effect upon general psychology. Nevertheless the broad flavor of the factors influencing these two groups during the past three quarters of a century has been distinguishably different. While the personality theorist was drawing his leading ideas primarily from clinical experience, the experimental psychologist was paying heed to the findings of the experimental laboratory. Where the names Charcot, Freud, Janet, McDougall, and Stern are in the forefront of the work of early personality theorists, we find Helmholtz, Pavlov, Thorndike, Watson, and Wundt cast in a comparable role in experimental psychology. The experimentalists derived their inspirations and their values from the natural sciences while personality theorists remained closer to clinical data and their own creative reconstructions. One group welcomed intuitive feelings and insights but scorned the trappings of science with its restriction upon the imagination and its narrow technical skills. The other applauded the rigor and precision of delimited investigation and shrank in distaste from the unrestrained use of clinical judgment and imaginative interpretation. In the end it was clear that early experimental psychology had little to say concerning problems of interest to the personality theorist and that the personality theorist had little respect for problems of central importance to the experimental psychologist.

It is well known that psychology developed in the late nineteenth century as the offspring of philosophy and experimental physiology. The origin of personality theory owes much more to the medical profession and to the exigencies of medical practice. In fact, the early giants in this area (Freud, Jung, and McDougall) were not only trained in medicine but practiced as psychotherapists. This historical link between personality theory and practical application has remained evident throughout the development of psychology and provides an important distinction between this brand of theory and certain other types of psychological theory.

Consistent with what we have said thus far are two generalizations concerning personality theory. First, it is clear that *personality theory has occupied a dissident role in the development of psychology.* Personality theorists in their own times have been rebels. Rebels in medicine and in experimental science, rebels against conventional ideas and usual practices, rebels against typical methods and respected techniques of research, and most of all rebels against accepted theory and normative problems. The fact that personality theory has never been deeply embedded in the mainstream of academic psychology has had several important implications. On the one hand, it tended to free personality theory from the deadly grip of conventional modes of thought and preconceptions concerning human behavior. By being relatively uninvolved in the ongoing institution of psychology it was easier for personality theorists to question or reject assumptions which were widely accepted by psychologists. On the other hand, this lack of involvement also freed them from some of the discipline and the responsibility for reasonably systematic and organized formulation which was the heritage of the well-socialized psychologist.

A second generalization is that *personality theories are functional in their orientation.* They are concerned with questions that make a difference in the adjustment of the organism. They center about issues of crucial importance for the survival of the individual. At a time when the experimental psychologist was engrossed with such questions as the existence of imageless thought, the speed with which nerve impulses traveled, specifying the content of the normal-conscious-human-mind, deciding whether there was localization of function within the brain, the personality theorist was concerned with why it was that certain individuals developed crippling neurotic symptoms in the absence of organic pathology, the role of childhood trauma in adult adjustment, the conditions under which mental health could be regained, and the major motivations that underlay human behavior. Thus, it was the personality theorist, and only the personality theorist, who in the early days of psychology dealt with questions which to the average person seem to lie at the core of a successful psychological science.

The reader should not construe what has just been said as an indictment of general psychology and a eulogy of personality theory. It is still not clear whether the path to a comprehensive and useful theory of human behavior will proceed most rapidly from the work of those who have aimed directly at such a goal, or whether it will eventually owe more to the efforts of those who have focused upon relatively specific and delimited problems. The strategy of advance in an empirical discipline is never easy to specify and the general public is not usually considered an adequate final court for deciding what problems should be focused upon. In other words, while it is a statement of fact that personality theorists have dealt with issues which seem central and important to the typical observer of human behavior, it remains to be seen whether this willingness to tackle such issues will prove to advance the science.

As we have implied, there is no mystery concerning why personality theories were broader in scope and more practical in orientation than the formulations of most other psychologists. The great men of academic psychology in the nineteenth century were figures such as Wundt, Helmholtz, Ebbinghaus, Titchener, and Külpe who carried out their work within university settings with few pressures from the outside world. They were free to follow their own intellectual inclinations with little or no compulsion to deal with what others considered important or significant. In fact, they were largely able to define what was significant by their own values and activities. By contrast the early personality theorists were practitioners as well as scholars. Faced with the problems of everyday life, magnified by neurosis, it was natural that they should address themselves to formulations which had something to contribute to these problems. A set of categories for the analysis of emotions which could be applied by trained subjects in a laboratory setting was of scant interest to a therapist who daily observed the operation of emotions that were hampering, disabling, and even killing fellow humans. Thus, the strong functional flavor of personality theories, their concern with problems of significance to the survival of the organism, seems a natural outgrowth of the setting in which these theories developed.

It is clear that *personality theorists* have customarily *assigned a crucial role to the motivational process.* At a time when many psychologists ignored motivation or attempted to minimize the contribution ɔf such factors in their studies, the personality theorist saw in these same variables the key to understanding human behavior. Freud and McDougall were the first to give serious consideration to the motivational process. The wide gap between the arena of life and the theory developed by laboratory psychologists is pictured by McDougall as he justifies his attempts to develop an adequate theory of social behavior (which was more of a theory of personality than it was a theory of social behavior):

> The department of psychology that is of primary importance for the social sciences is that which deals with the springs of human action, the impulses and motives that sustain mental and bodily activity and regulate conduct; and this, of all the departments of psychology, is the one that has remained in the most backward state, in which the greatest obscurity, vagueness, and confusion still reign (McDougall, 1908, pp. 2–3).

Thus, variables that were primarily of nuisance value to the experimental psychologist became a matter for systematic study and focal interest on the part of the personality theorist.

Related to this interest in the functional and motivational is the personality theorist's conviction that *an adequate understanding of human behavior will evolve only from the study of the whole person.* Most personality psychologists insisted that the subject should be viewed from the vantage of the entire functioning person in his natural habitat. They pleaded strongly for the study of behavior in context, with each behavioral event examined and interpreted in relation to the rest of the individual's behavior. Such a point of view was a natural derivative of clinical practice where the entire person presented himself for cure and where it was indeed difficult to limit consideration to one sense modality or a limited array of experience.

If we accept the intent of most personality theorists to promote the study of the whole, unsegmented person, it is easy to understand why many observers have considered that *one of the most distinctive features of personality theory is its function as an integrative theory.* While psychologists in general have shown increased specialization, leading to the complaint that they were learning more and more about less and less, the personality theorist accepted at least partial responsibility for bringing together and organizing the diverse findings of specialists. The experimentalist might know a great deal about motor skills, audition, perception, or vision but he usually knew relatively little about the way in which these special functions related to one another. The personality psychologist was, in this sense, more concerned with reconstruction or integration than he was with analysis or the segmental study of behavior. From these considerations comes the somewhat romantic conception of the personality theorist as the individual who will put together the jigsaw puzzle provided by the discrete findings of separate studies within the various specialities that make up psychology.

In broad terms, then, *what has distinguished the personality theorist from the traditional psychological theorist?* He is more speculative and less tied to experimental or measuremental operations. The stiffening brush of positivism has spread much more lightly over the personality psychologist than over the experimental psychologist. He develops theories that are multidimensional and more complex than those fashionable within general psychology and, consistently, his theories tend to be somewhat more vague and less well specified than the experimentalist's theories. He is willing to accept any aspect of behavior which possesses functional significance as legitimate data for his theoretical mill whereas most experimental psychologists are content to fix their attention upon a limited array of observations or recordings. He insists that an adequate understanding of individual behavior can be achieved only when it is studied in a broad context which includes the total, functioning person. The personality theorist sees motivation, the "why" or underlying impellents of behavior, as *the* crucial empirical and theoretical problem whereas experimentalists see this as one of many problems and deal with it by means of a small number of concepts closely linked to physiological processes.

Thus far we have proceeded as though the reader and the writers were in good agreement concerning what the term personality means. Although this may be the case, it is by no means certain and before proceeding further it seems wise to examine the meaning of this term.

WHAT IS PERSONALITY?

There are few words in the English language which have such a fascination for the general public as the term personality. Although the word is used in various senses, most of these popular meanings fall under one of two headings. The first usage equates the term to social skill or adroitness. An individual's personality is assessed by the effectiveness with which he is able to elicit positive reactions from a variety of persons under different circumstances. It is in this sense that schools which specialize in glamorizing the American female intend the term when they refer to courses in "personality training." Likewise, the teacher who refers to a student as presenting a personality problem is probably indicating that his social skills are not adequate to maintain satisfactory relations with his fellow students and the teacher. The second usage considers the personality of the individual to inhere in the most outstanding or salient impression which he creates in others. A person may thus be said to have an "aggressive personality" or a "submissive personality" or a "fearful personality." In each case the observer selects an attribute or quality which is highly typical of the subject and which is presumably an important part of the over-all impression which he creates in others and his personality is identified by this term. It is clear that there is an element of evaluation in both usages. Personalities as commonly described are good and bad.

While the diversity in ordinary use of the word personality may seem considerable, it is overshadowed by the variety of meanings with which the psychologist has endowed this term. Allport (1937) in an exhaustive survey of the literature extracted almost fifty different definitions which he classified into a number of broad categories. Here we need concern ourselves with but a few of these definitions.

It is important initially to distinguish between what Allport calls biosocial and biophysical definitions. The *biosocial definition* shows a close correspondence with the popular use of the term as it equates personality to the "social stimulus value" of the individual. It is the reaction of other individuals to the subject which defines his personality. One may even assert that the individual possesses no personality but that provided by the response of others. Allport objects vigorously to the implication that personality resides only in the "responding-other" and suggests that a *biophysical definition* which roots the personality firmly in characteristics or qualities of the subject is much to be preferred. According to the latter definition, personality has an organic side as well as a perceived side and may be linked to specific qualities of the individual which are susceptible to objective description and measurement.

Another important type of definition is the rag-bag or *omnibus definition*. This definition embraces personality by enumeration. The term personality is used here to include everything about the individual and the theorist ordinarily lists the concepts he considers of primary importance in describing the individual and suggests that personality consists of these. Other definitions place primary emphasis upon the *integrative* or organizational function of personality. Such definitions suggest that personality is the organization or pattern that is given to the various discrete behaviors of the individual or else they suggest that the organization results from the personality which is an active force within the individual. Personality is that which gives order and congruence to all the different kinds of behavior in which the individual engages. A number of theorists have chosen to emphasize the function of personality in mediating the *adjustment* of the individual. Personality consists of the varied and yet typical efforts at adjustment which are carried out by the individual. In other definitions, personality is equated to the *unique* or individual aspects of behavior. In this case, it is a term to designate those things about the individual that are distinctive and set him apart from all other persons. Finally, some theorists have considered personality to represent the *essence* of man. These definitions suggest that personality refers to that part of the individual which is most representative of him, not only in that it differentiates him from other persons but, more important, because it is what he actually is. Allport's suggestion that "personality is what a man really is" illustrates this type of definition. The implication here is that personality consists of what, in the final analysis, is most typical and deeply characteristic of the person.

We could profitably spend much more time dealing with the problem of defining personality if it were not for the fact that in the ensuing chapters the reader will encounter many detailed definitions of personality in their natural context. Furthermore, it is our conviction that *no substantive definition of personality can be applied with any generality.* By this we mean simply that the way in which a given individual will define personality will depend completely upon his particular theoretical preference. Thus, if the theory places heavy emphasis upon uniqueness and the organized, unified qualities of behavior, it is natural that the definition of personality will include uniqueness and organization as important attributes of personality. Once the individual has created or adopted a given theory of personality, his definition of personality will be rather clearly implied by the theory. Thus, we submit that *personality is defined by the particular empirical concepts which are a part of the theory of personality employed by the observer.* Personality consists concretely of a set of values or descriptive terms which are used to describe the individual being studied according to the variables or dimensions which occupy a central position within the particular theory utilized.

If this seems an unsatisfactory definition to the reader, let him take consolation in the thought that in the pages to follow he will encounter a number of specific definitions any one of which will become his if he chooses to adopt that particular theory. In other words, what we have said is that it is impossible to define personality without coming to agreement concerning the theoretical frame of reference within which personality will be viewed. If we were to attempt a single substantive definition now, we would implicitly be settling many of the theoretical issues which it is the purpose of this book to explore.

WHAT IS A THEORY?

Just as everyone knows what a personality consists of, so everyone knows what a theory is. The most common conception is that a theory exists in opposition to a fact. A theory is an unsubstantiated hypothesis or a speculation concerning reality which is not yet definitely known to be so. When the theory is confirmed it becomes a fact. There is a grain of correspondence between this view and the usage we will advocate here for it is agreed that theories are not known to be true. There is also an element of disagreement as the common-sense view asserts that a theory will become true or factual when the appropriate data have been collected if these data are confirmatory. In our view, theories are never true or false although their implications or derivations may be either.

The passages to follow represent a relatively conventional summary of the thinking of methodologists or logicians of science. There is by no means complete agreement concerning all of the issues to be raised but the point of view presented is intended to be modal, although admittedly colored heavily by the teachings of logical positivism. The beginning student may find it a little difficult to grasp fully some of these ideas and it is only fair to indicate that an understanding of them is not essential in order to read and appreciate the remainder of the volume. On the other hand, if he is seriously interested in the field and has not yet immersed himself in this area of scholarship, the student would do well to acquaint himself with methodology much more extensively than he can hope to do in this brief section. There are a number of excellent sources which provide a detailed treatment of these matters (Cohen and Nagel, 1934; Conant, 1947; Feigl and Brodbeck, 1953; Feigl and Sellars, 1949; Frank, 1949; Hempel, 1952).

Let us commence by considering what a theory is and subsequently turn to the more important question of what are the functions of a theory. To begin with, a theory is a *set of conventions* created by the theorist. Viewing a theory as a "set of conventions" emphasizes the fact that theories are not "given" or predetermined by nature, the data, or any other determinant process. Just as the same experiences or observations may lead a poet or novelist to create any one of a multitude of different art forms, so the data of investigation may be incorporated in any of countless different theoretical schemes. The theorist in choosing one particular option to represent the events in which he is interested is exercising a free creative choice that is different from the artist's only in the kinds of evidence upon which it focuses and the grounds upon which its fruitfulness will be judged. We are emphasizing here the creative and yet arbitrary manner in which theories are constructed and this leads naturally to the observation that we can specify how a theory should be evaluated or appraised but we cannot specify how a theory should be constructed. There is no formula for fruitful theory construction any more than there is a formula for making enduring literary contributions.

The fact that a theory is a conventional choice, rather than something that is inevitable or prescribed by known empirical relations, emphasizes the lack of appropriateness of truth or falsity as attributes to be ascribed to a theory. A theory is only *useful or not useful* and these qualities are defined, as we shall see, primarily in terms of how efficiently the theory can generate predictions or propositions concerning relevant events which turn out to be verified (true).

Let us be somewhat more specific concerning what a theory is. Just what does a theory, in its ideal form, consist of? It should contain a cluster of relevant assumptions systematically related to each other and a set of empirical definitions!

The *assumptions* must be relevant in that they bear upon the empirical events with which the theory is concerned. If it is a theory of audition the assumptions must have something to do with the process of hearing; if it is a theory of perception the assumptions must bear upon the perceptual process. Ordinarily the nature of these assumptions represents the distinctive quality of the theory. The good theorist is the person who can ferret out useful or predictive assumptions concerning the empirical events within his domain. Depending upon the nature of the theory these assumptions may be very general or quite specific. A behavioral theorist might choose to assume that all behavior is motivated, that events taking place early in life are the most important determinants of adult behavior, that the behavior of different animal species is governed by the same general principles; or he might assume that increased anxiety leads to a decrement in motor performance or that a particular variable has a normal distribution within a given population. These assumptions may also vary in form from the precision of mathematical notation to the relative inexactness of most of the assumptions we have just used as illustrations.

Not only must the assumptions be stated clearly but also the assumptions and the elements within the theory must be explicitly combined and related to one another. That is, there must be rules for the systematic interaction between the assumptions and their embedded concepts. In order to give the theory logical consistency and permit the process of derivation, these internal relations must be clear. Without such specification it would be difficult or impossible to extract empirical consequences from the theory. Because of their similarity to the rules of grammar these statements are sometimes referred to as the *syntax* of the theory. We have already suggested that one might choose to assume that an increase in anxiety would lead to a decrement in motor performance. In addition, it might be assumed that an increase in self-esteem would lead to an improvement in motor performance. If we knew nothing more than this the relation between these two assumptions would be clearly indeterminant as we need to find out something about the relation between anxiety and self-esteem before we can make any predictions concerning what may take place under circumstances where both variables are involved. An adequate statement of the theoretical assumptions would provide the user of the theory with a clear specification of the relation between these two assumptions.

The *empirical definitions* (co-ordinating definitions) permit the more or less precise interaction of certain terms or concepts within the theory with empirical data. Thus, by means of these definitions the theory at certain prescribed places comes into definite contact with reality or observational data. These definitions are frequently called operational definitions as they attempt to specify operations by means of which the relevant variables or concepts can be measured. Emphasis upon empirical definitions is the mark of an investigative intent and it is safe to say that if a theory is eventually to make a contribution in an empirical discipline it must possess some means for empirical translation. On the other hand, it should be clear that these definitions exist on a continuum ranging from complete and exact specification to a very general and qualitative statement. Although the more precision the better, an early insistence upon complete specification can destroy many fruitful paths of inquiry. Defining intelligence as simply "what intelligence tests measure" or equating anxiety solely to certain physiological changes as measured by the galvanometer may be exact, but neither definition alone seems likely to lead to much productive thought or inquiry. The proper attitude toward empirical definitions is that they should be as precise as present conditions within the relevant field permit.

We have now seen, in general terms, of what a theory consists. The next question is, What does it do? First, and most important, it leads to the collection or *observation of relevant empirical relations not yet observed*. The theory should lead to a systematic expansion of knowledge concerning the phenomena of interest and this expansion ideally should be mediated or stimulated by the derivation from the theory of specific empirical propositions (statements, hypotheses, predictions) that are subject to empirical test. In a central sense, the core of any science lies in the discovery of stable empirical relationships between events or variables. The function of a theory is to further this process in a systematic manner. The theory can be seen as a kind of proposition mill, grinding out related empirical statements which can then be confirmed or rejected in the light of suitably controlled empirical data. It is only the derivations or propositions or ideas derived from the theory which are open to empirical test. The theory itself is assumed and acceptance or rejection of it is determined by its *utility*, not by its truth or falsity. In this instance, utility has two components—verifiability and comprehensiveness. *Verifiability* refers to the capacity of the theory to generate predictions which are confirmed when the relevant empirical data are collected. *Comprehensiveness* refers to the scope or completeness of these derivations. We might have a theory which generated consequences that were often confirmed but which dealt with only a few aspects of the phenomena of interest. Ideally the theory should lead to accurate predictions which deal very generally or inclusively with the empirical events which the theory purports to embrace.

It is important to distinguish between what may be called the systematic and the heuristic generation of research. It is clear that in the ideal case the theory permits the derivation of specific testable propositions and these in turn lead to specific empirical studies. However, it is also manifest that many theories, for example, Freud's and Darwin's, have had a great effect upon investigative paths without the mediation of explicit propositions. This capacity of a theory to generate research by suggesting ideas or even by arousing disbelief and resistance may be referred to as the *heuristic influence of the theory*. Both types of influence are of great importance and at the present stage of development within psychology are to be valued equally.

A second function which a theory should serve is that of permitting the *incorporation of known empirical findings* within a logically consistent and reasonably simple framework. A theory is a means of organizing and integrating all that is known concerning a related set of events. An adequate theory of psychotic behavior should be able to arrange all that is known concerning schizophrenia and other psychoses in an understandable and logical framework. A satisfactory learning theory must embrace in a consistent manner all of the dependable findings dealing with the learning process. Theories always commence with that which has thus far been observed and reported and in this sense begin in an inductive phase and are guided and to some extent controlled by what is known. However, if the theories did nothing more than make consonant and orderly what was presently known they would serve only a very minor function. Under such circumstances the dogged investigator would be justified in his conviction that theories are mere verbal fluff floating in the wake of the investigator who has done the real business of science. The empiricist who insists that theories are mere after-the-fact rationalizations of what the investigator has already reported fails to appreciate the main function of the theory which is to point out new and, as yet, unobserved relations. The productiveness of the theory is tested before the fact not after the fact.

Simplicity or, as it is sometimes called, parsimony is also of importance but only after matters of comprehensiveness and verifiability have been settled. It becomes an issue only under circumstances where two theories generate exactly the same consequences. As long as the theories differ in the derivations that can be made concerning the same empirical events, the choice of the theory should be decided in terms of the extent to which these predictions differ in verification. Thus, it is only when you have a tautology—two theories arriving at the same conclusions from different terms—that simplicity becomes an important question. Suffice it to say that there are few examples of such a state of affairs in science and none, to our knowledge, in psychology. Simplicity as opposed to complexity becomes, consequently, a matter of personal value or preference in personality theorizing, rather than an attribute which is necessarily to be prized or sought after.

Another function which a theory should serve is that of *preventing the observer from being dazzled by the full-blown complexity of natural or concrete events.* The theory is a set of blinders and it tells its wearer that it is unnecessary for him to worry about all of the aspects of the event he is studying. To the untrained observer any reasonably complex behavioral event seems to offer countless different possible means for analyzing or describing the event—and indeed it does. The theory permits the observer to go about abstracting from the natural complexity in a systematic and efficient maner. Abstract and simplify he will, whether he uses a theory or not, but if he does not follow the guide lines of an explicit theory the principles determining his view will be hidden in implicit assumptions and attitudes of which he is unaware. The theory specifies to the user a limited number of more or less definite dimensions, variables, or parameters which are of crucial importance. The other aspects of the situation can to a certain extent be overlooked from the point of view of this problem. A useful theory will detail rather explicit instructions as to the kinds of data that should be collected in connection with a particular problem. Consequently, as might be expected, individuals occupying drastically different theoretical positions may study the same empirical event and share little in the way of common observations.

A THEORY OF PERSONALITY

We have agreed that personality is defined by the particular concepts contained within a given theory that is considered adequate for the complete description or understanding of human behavior. We have also agreed that a theory consists of a set of related assumptions concerning the relevant empirical phenomena, and empirical definitions to permit the user to move from the abstract theory to empirical observation. By simple addition we have the implication that a theory of personality must be a set of assumptions relevant to human behavior together with the necessary empirical definitions. There is the further requirement that the theory must be relatively comprehensive. It must be prepared to deal with, or make predictions concerning, a wide range of human behavior. In fact, the theory should be prepared to deal with any behavioral phenomenon which can be shown to possess significance for the individual.

What has been said to this point possesses a formal validity which, however, cannot be sustained upon close scrutiny of existing theories of personality. Our discussion is of value in identifying the qualities toward which all theorists aspire and it also gives some idea of what, eventually, personality theories should look like. It is clear, nevertheless, that at the present time they do not look like this. A word should be said concerning the manner in which they fail to resemble the ideal both in structure and in function.

First of all, as we shall see, most of them lack explicitness. It is generally very hard to get at the assumptions or the axiomatic base of these theories. Personality theories are frequently packaged in a great mass of vivid word images which may serve very well as a means of persuading the reluctant reader but which frequently serve to cloak and conceal the specific assumptions which underlie the theory. In other words, most of the theories are not presented in a straightforward and orderly manner and many of them seem more oriented toward persuasion than exposition. Related to this lack of definiteness is a frequent confusion between that which is given or assumed and that which is stated empirically and open to test. As we have already agreed, it is only the derivations or the predictions generated by the theory which are open to empirical test. The remainder of the theory is assumed or given and is not to be judged on grounds of confirmation or disconfirmation but rather in terms of how successfully it generates verified propositions. In general, then, the distinction between the personality theory itself and its implications or derivations is very poorly maintained.

An inevitable consequence of the lack of explicitness concerning the nature of the assumptions underlying the theory is the existence of serious confusion in the process of deriving empirical statements from the theory. Thus, there is the possibility that different individuals using the same theory will arrive at conflicting derivations. Actually, the derivation process in most personality theories is haphazard, obscure, and inefficient. This is not only a reflection of the lack of explicitness of these theories but also of the fact that most personality theorists have been oriented toward after-the-fact explanation rather than toward the generation of new predictions concerning behavior. Finally, it is clear that although personality theories vary in how carefully they specify empirical definitions none of these theories achieves a very high standard in absolute terms.

The statements we have just made concerning the formal status of personality theories may seem sufficiently discouraging to warrant abandoning attempts to construct such theories at this time. Would it not be better at present to forget about theories and focus upon empirical tools and specific empirical findings? Emphatically no! Such a decision does not involve giving up inadequate theory for no theory but rather involves the substitution of implicit theory for explicit theory. There is no such thing as "no theory"; consequently, the moment we attempt to forget about theory "for the present" we are really using implicit, personally determined, and perhaps inconsistent assumptions concerning behavior and these unidentified assumptions will determine what will be studied and how. The observation of any concrete empirical event is carried out under the dictates of some "theory"—that is, certain things are attended to and certain things are overlooked—and one of the purposes of theorizing is to make explicit the rules determining this abstraction process. The possibility of improving upon the assumptions that are controlling research is eliminated the moment one gives up the attempt to define the theoretical base from which he operates.

Poor though personality theories may be when compared to the ideal, they still represent a considerable step forward when compared to the thinking of the naive realist who is convinced that he is embracing or viewing reality in the only way in which it can reasonably be viewed. Even though personality theories do not possess the degree of explicitness which one might wish, their mere existence makes it possible to work toward this goal in a systematic manner. In fact, it is clear that the present state of personality theory represents a considerable improvement over its formal status twenty years ago.

Granted that personality theories do not ordinarily permit as explicit a derivation process as we might wish, just what function do they serve for the individual who wields them? At the very least they represent a cluster of attitudes (assumptions) concerning behavior which in a broad way limits the kinds of investigation to be considered crucial or important. In addition to stimulating certain general kinds of research, they also provide specific parameters or dimensions which are considered important in the exploration of these problems. Thus, even if the theory does not provide an exact proposition for test it orients the theorist toward certain problem areas and tells him that particular variables are of central importance in studying these problems. Moreover, there is the heuristic value of these theories to be considered. Taken as a group, personality theories are highly provocative and, as we shall discover, they have led to large quantities of research even though relatively little of this has been the result of a formal derivation process. In other words, the capacity of these theories to generate ideas, to stimulate curiosity, to stir doubts, or to lead to convictions has resulted in a healthy flourishing of investigation in spite of their lack of formal elegance.

PERSONALITY THEORY AND OTHER PSYCHOLOGICAL THEORIES

Our discussion thus far has led us to the conclusion that a theory of personality should consist of a set of assumptions concerning human behavior together with rules for relating these assumptions and definitions to permit their interaction with empirical or observable events. At this point the question may reasonably be asked whether this definition in any way differentiates personality theories from other psychological theories. In answering this question it will be helpful to begin with a distinction between two types of psychological theory.

It is evident that certain psychological theories appear ready to deal with any behavioral event that can be shown to be of significance in the adjustment of the human organism. Other theories specifically delimit themselves to behavior as it occurs under certain carefully prescribed conditions. These theories profess an interest in only limited aspects of human behavior. A theory which attempts to deal with all behavioral phenomena of demonstrated significance may be referred to as a general theory of behavior and those theories that restrict their focus to certain classes of behavioral events are called single-domain theories.

Clearly, personality theories fall into the first category; they are general theories of behavior. This simple observation serves to separate personality theory from the bulk of other psychological theories. Theories of perception, audition, rote memory, motor learning, discrimination, and the many other special theories within psychology are single-domain theories and can be distinguished from personality theory on grounds of scope or comprehensiveness. They make no pretense at being a general theory of behavior and are content to develop concepts appropriate for the description and prediction of a limited array of behavioral events. Theories of personality, however, have generally accepted the challenge of accounting for or incorporating events of the most varied nature so long as they possess demonstrated functional significance for the individual.

The question remains whether there are not general theories of behavior which would not ordinarily be called personality theories. One possibility is that what has usually been called motivational theory may be a general theory of behavior and yet distinct from personality theory. Actually, insofar as the theory deals exclusively with the motivational process it is not a general theory, although, in fact, what are usually referred to as theories of motivation are also theories of personality, for example, psychoanalysis, hormic psychology, Murray's theory. As we shall discover, the motivational portion of theories of personality is of central importance to these theories. Thus, if the theory deals only with motivation it is a single-domain theory; if it is more embracive it is simply a type of personality theory.

A second possibility is that learning theory may in some instances be sufficiently generalized so that it constitutes a general theory of behavior. This is clearly the case and, as we shall see in detail later, a number of theorists have attempted to generalize learning theories so that they are comparable in comprehensiveness to any other general theory of behavior. In such instances, then, the theory of learning ceases to be merely a learning theory and becomes a personality theory or, if you like, a general theory of behavior. It is true that such generalized models possess certain distinctive characteristics which are reminiscent of their origin, but in intent and in logical properties they are no different from any other theory of personality.

This lumping together of theories which have had their origins in the animal laboratories and theories which originated in the therapist's chambers may appear forced to many observers. However, if we consider the theories from the point of view of what they intend to do and their general structure, rather than from the point of where they come from or the detailed assumptions they make about behavior, it is clear that any general theory of behavior is the same as any other. In this sense all general theories of behavior are personality theories and vice versa. Within this large group of theories, of course, many distinctions can be made and the following section will deal with a number of attributes in terms of which theories of personality can be differentiated or compared. One could set up numerous subgroups or classifications on the basis of these dimensions.

THE COMPARISON OF THEORIES OF PERSONALITY

It is evident that when bodies of formulation as numerous and complex as personality theories are examined there are many qualities in terms of which they can be compared and distinguished. Here we shall point to only a few of the more important of these to provide a basis for whatever generalizations may eventually seem worthwhile concerning the state of contemporary personality theory. These dimensions also serve to identify the main issues or options confronting the personality theorist today. The attributes divide naturally into those concerned with matters of formal adequacy and those concerned with the substantive nature of the theory.

FORMAL ATTRIBUTES. Here we are interested in how adequately the structure of the theory is developed and presented. There is a definite evaluative aura to each of these qualities as they represent an ideal and the closer the theory comes to reaching this ideal the more effectively it can be used.

The question of *clarity and explicitness* is of huge importance. This is a matter of how clearly and precisely the assumptions and embedded concepts that make up the theory are presented. In the limiting case the theory may be stated in terms of mathematical notation, with a precise definition of all but the primitive terms, so that the person who has been adequately trained can employ the theory with a minimum of ambiguity. Under such circumstances different individuals employing the theory independently will arrive at highly similar formulations or derivations. At the other extreme, we find theories presented with such a rush of vivid and complex description that it is extremely difficult for the individual who would employ the theory to be certain of just what its nature is. Under these circumstances there is little likelihood that individuals using the theory independently will arrive at the same formulations or derivations. It will become clear as we progress that there is no theory of personality that approaches very far toward the ideal of mathematical notation; still, granted the free use of verbal description, we shall find that there is considerable variation among personality theories in the clarity of their exposition.

A further question is the matter of *how well the theory is related to empirical phenomena.* Here we are concerned with the explicitness and practicality of the definitions proposed to translate theoretical conceptions into measuremental operations. At one extreme we find theories which prescribe relatively exact operations for assessing or measuring each of the empirical terms within the theory, whereas in other cases the theorist appears to assume that the name which he assigns to the concept is a sufficient defining operation by itself.

Perhaps this is an appropriate place to emphasize again our conviction that all matters of formal adequacy pale alongside the question of *what empirical research is generated by the theory.* However vague and poorly developed the theory, and however inadequate its syntax and empirical definitions, if it can be shown to have had a generative effect upon significant areas of research we would have to conclude that it passes the crucial test. Thus, the payoff question which overrides, and actually makes trivial, all questions of formal adequacy is the matter of how much important research the theory has produced. True, it is not easy to agree upon what is important research, particularly since importance will largely be determined by the theoretical position of the judge. It is also true that it is not always easy to say just what the process was which led to a particular investigation being conducted and thus the generative role of the theory may be difficult to assess. In spite of this there are clear and perceptible differences between theories of personality in the extent to which they have been translated into investigations which are of general interest.

SUBSTANTIVE ATTRIBUTES. While the formal attributes we have just described all present a normative or valued standard in terms of which each theory can be compared, the following attributes possess no such evaluative implication. They are neutral in regard to good and bad and merely reflect the particular assumptions concerning behavior which the theory embraces.

Differences between personality theories in content naturally reflect the major issues that currently exist in this area. Thus, in the following pages we shall not only be outlining dimensions which can be used for the comparison of personality theories but we shall also be pointing to the major options which face a theorist in this area. We could with perfect appropriateness label this section "issues in modern personality theory."

Older than the history of psychology is the question of whether man should be viewed as possessing *purposive or teleological qualities.* Some theories of behavior create a model of the individual in which goal-striving, purpose, and seeking are viewed as essential and central aspects of the individual's behavior. Other theories assume that the striving and seeking aspects of behavior are unimportant and believe that behavior can be accounted for adequately without such an emphasis. The latter theorists consider the subjective elements of striving and seeking as an epiphenomenon, accompanying behavior but not playing a determinant role in its instigation. Generally theories which minimize the importance of purpose or teleology are labeled "mechanistic" although this term has come to have a disparaging quality which is undesirable when, after all, we are simply considering matters of theoretical option.

Another ancient debate is concerned with the relative importance of conscious and *unconscious determinants of behavior.* In its archaic form this issue would be phrased in terms of the relative rationality or irrationality of man. The term unconscious is used here simply to refer to determinants of behavior of which the individual is unaware and unable to bring to awareness except under special conditions. Theories of personality range from those which explicitly reject any consideration of unconscious determinants of behavior, or refuse to accept the existence of such determinants, to the theories which consider them the most important or powerful determinants of behavior. A middle ground is occupied by those theorists who are willing to assign a central role to unconscious determinants in the behavior of disturbed or abnormal individuals while claiming that for the normal individual conscious motives are the ruling forces.

The relative importance of *hedonism, reward, or effect* is likewise a question which has engrossed students of human behavior for centuries. In its earlier formulations, such as those of the utilitarians, Bentham and J. S. Mill, it was a question of whether man was primarily motivated by seeking pleasure and avoiding pain. Its contemporary form is the "law of effect." This law states that only those responses that are accompanied by a reward or reinforcement will be retained or learned. In either case the question is one of how important are reward or pleasure as determinants of behavior. Again we find that theories vary from those in which the crucial role of reward is the dominant assumption to those that minimize the importance of reward or subsume its operation under other theoretical principles.

Just as some theorists place the law of effect at the core of their theory, so others consider the *principle of association* (contiguity) to be of first importance. These theorists consider that more important than the reward or effect that follows a given response is the exact stimulus configuration accompanying the response. In other words, it is the simultaneous or near-simultaneous occurrence of a stimulus and a response which leads to learning, rather than the reward or reinforcement which follows the response. Obviously these principles need not be mutually exclusive and, as we shall learn, there are theorists who have assigned to both principles a central role within the same theory.

A fundamental distinction between theories of personality has to do with the extent to which the *learning process*, or the modification of behavior, is a matter for detailed and explicit attention. Some personality theorists see in the understanding of the learning process the key to all behavioral phenomena whereas for other theorists learning is an important but secondary problem. Although no personality theorist would deny the significance of learning, we shall find that some theorists prefer to focus upon the acquisitions or outcomes of learning rather than on the process itself. This issue thus becomes a matter of disagreement between those who propose to deal primarily with the process of change and those who show themselves most interested in the stable structures or *acquisitions of personality* at a given time.

An issue as old as man's thoughts about man is the question of the relative importance of genetic or *hereditary factors* in determining behavior. Almost no one will deny that hereditary factors have some implications for behavior, but still there are many personality theorists who have dramatically undercut their importance, insisting that all of the major behavioral phenomena can be understood without recourse to the biological and genetic. In America the role of hereditary factors has generally been played down in favor of some brand of environmentalism but there is still considerable variation as to how much and how explicitly the various theorists are willing to deal with genetic factors.

An additional dimension in terms of which personality theories show considerable variation has to do with the relative importance of *early developmental experiences*. This is a question of whether the theory cedes a certain strategic and critical importance to events taking place in infancy and childhood which is not matched in importance by events taking place at later stages of development. As we shall discover, there are some theories which imply that the key to adult behavior is to be found in events that have taken place in the earliest years of development, while other theories state quite explicitly that behavior can be understood and accounted for solely in terms of contemporary or ongoing events. Related to this question is the extent to which theorists consider the personality structure at a given point in time to be autonomous or functionally distinct from the experiences that have preceded this point in time. For certain theorists the understanding of behavior in terms of *contemporaneous factors* is not only possible but the only defensible path to understanding. For others a reasonable understanding of the present must always depend partly upon some knowledge of events that have taken place in the past. Naturally those who emphasize the contemporaneous point of view are convinced of the functional independence of the personality structure at any particular point in time, while those who emphasize the importance of past or early experience are less convinced of the freedom of present structure from the influence of past events.

Closely related to the preceding issue is the question of the *continuity or discontinuity of behavior* at different stages of development. Most theories that emphasize the learning process and/or the importance of early developmental experiences tend to view the individual as a continuously developing organism. The structure that is observed at one point in time is related in a determined manner to the structure and experiences that occurred at an earlier point in time. Other theories tend to consider the organism as going through stages of development that are relatively independent and functionally separated from the earlier stages of development. The latter point of view may lead to the construction of drastically different theories for infant behavior and adult behavior.

A major difference between personality theories lies in the extent to which they embrace *holistic principles.* That is, do they consider it legitimate to abstract and analyze so that at a given time, or in a particular study, only a small part of the individual is being examined? The individuals who adopt a holistic position consider behavior to be understandable only in context, so that the total, functioning person together with the significant portions of his environment must be given simultaneous consideration if there is to be a fruitful outcome. Other theories accept the fact that the very nature of science and investigation necessitates analysis and these positions usually show no special concern over violation to the integrity of the whole organism which may be involved in segmental studies.

This emphasis upon the wholeness of the individual and his environment can be broken down into two rather distinct forms. The first is usually referred to as an *organismic position.* Here there is great stress upon the interrelatedness of everything the individual does, upon the fact that each act he performs can be understood only against the background provided by his other acts. Not only is there an implication that all behavior is essentially interrelated and not susceptible to techniques of analysis but also there is usually an interest in the organic underpinnings of behavior. Consequently, behavior should be viewed against the perspective provided by the individual's other acts as well as the perspective offered by accompanying physiological and biological processes. All of the person's behavior and his biological functioning make up an organic whole that is not to be understood if it is studied segmentally.

The second holistic position is usually referred to as a *field emphasis.* Here the theory is primarily concerned with the inextricable unity between a given behavioral act and the environmental context within which it occurs. To attempt to understand a given form of behavior without specifying in detail the "field" within which it occurs is to strive for understanding with a large proportion of the significant factors missing. Although behavior is partially a result of determinants that inhere in the individual, there are equally compelling forces which act upon the person from without. It is only when the individual's significant environment is fully represented that these forces acting outside of the person can be given their due. There is a strong tendency for theorists who emphasize the importance of the "field" to minimize the importance of hereditary factors as well as events taking place early in development. This is not a logical necessity but in practice most theorists who have focused strongly upon the environmental context of the individual have emphasized the present rather than the past and have been more interested in what is "out there" rather than what inheres in the individual.

Related to the issue of holism is the matter of *uniqueness* or individuality. Certain theories place a heavy emphasis upon the fact that each individual and, in fact, each act is unique and not to be duplicated by any other individual or act. They point out that there are always distinctive and important qualities which set off the behavior of any single individual from the behavior of all other persons. In general, the individual who strongly embraces a field or organismic point of view tends to stress uniqueness also. This follows naturally from the fact that if you broaden sufficiently the context which must be considered in connection with each behavioral event, the event will come to have so many facets that it is bound to display distinct differences in comparison to all other events. Some theories accept the fact that each individual is unique but propose that this uniqueness can be accounted for in terms of differences in the patterning of the same underlying variables. Other theories maintain that individuals cannot even be compared fruitfully in terms of common or general variables as these distort and misrepresent the individual's uniqueness. Personality theories vary from those that make no special mention of uniqueness to those where this is one of the most central assumptions.

We shall discover that certain personality theorists have centered their theoretical position about the importance of the *psychological environment* or the subjective frame of reference. This is a matter of emphasizing that the physical world and its events can affect the individual only as he perceives or experiences them. Thus, it is not objective reality which serves as a determinant of behavior but rather objective reality as it is *perceived* or assigned meaning by the individual. It is the psychological environment, not the physical environment, which determines the manner in which the individual will respond. In contrast, there are theoretical positions that assume a firm theory of behavior can never be built on the shifting sands of subjective report or the complicated inferences needed to infer "meaning" from physical events. Such theories maintain that greater progress can be achieved through largely overlooking individual differences in the manner in which the same objective event is experienced and focusing upon relations involving external and observable events.

A further distinction between personality theorists has to do with whether or not they find it necessary to introduce a *self-concept*. For certain theorists the most important single human attribute is the view or perception the individual has of himself and this self-viewing process is often seen as the key to understanding the multitude of puzzling behavioral events displayed by any single person. There are other theories where no such concept is elaborated and where the subject's perception of himself is considered of little general significance.

Personality theorists show great variation in the extent to which they explicitly emphasize cultural or *group membership determinants* of behavior. In some theories these factors are assigned a primary role in shaping and controlling behavior; in others the emphasis is almost exclusively upon determinants of behavior which operate independently of the society or cultural groups to which the individual is exposed. In general, theorists who are characterized by a heavy organismic emphasis tend to play down the role of group-membership determinants while those who emphasize the field within which behavior occurs are more sympathetic to the role of sociocultural or group-membership determinants. The extreme examples of this position, usually referred to as examples of cultural determinism, are found among anthropological and sociological theorists although psychological theorists also show considerable variation on this issue.

Related to the questions of hereditary determination and cultural determination is the more general question of how explicitly the personality theorist attempts to relate his theory to the theorizing and empirical findings in neighboring disciplines. This might be referred to as a question of *interdisciplinary anchoring*. Some personality theorists are relatively content to deal with behavioral phenomena in terms of psychological concepts and findings with little or no attention to what is going on in neighboring disciplines. Others feel that psychological theorizing should lean heavily upon the formulations and findings of other disciplines. The "other-oriented" personality psychologists can be neatly divided into two basic types: those who look toward the natural sciences (biology, physiology, neurology, genetics) for guidance and those who look toward the social sciences (sociology, anthropology, economics, history) for guidance.

Theories of personality show a great deal of variation in *the number of motivational concepts* they employ. In some cases one or two such concepts are considered to lie at the base of all behavior; for other theories there is an extremely large number of hypothesized motives; and for still others the number is theoretically limitless. There is also considerable difference between theories in how much attention is paid to primary or innate motives as opposed to secondary or acquired motives. Further, some theories provide a relatively detailed picture of the process whereby acquired motives develop while others show very little interest in the derivation or acquisition of motives.

We have now completed our list of dimensions for the comparison of theories of personality but we hope the reader will not put them from his mind. The very brief guide provided here can be given richer meaning and greater significance if these issues are considered while reading the chapters describing the individual theories of personality. It will also become clear that the most distinctive features of these theories have evolved from decisions concerning the issues we have just discussed. In the final chapter we shall reconsider these dimensions in the light of the specific theories of personality which by then will have been summarized.

This brings us to the close of our introductory discussion and we can now proceed to the essence of this volume—the theories of personality themselves. If the reader is to retain a lone thought from what has been said to this point, let it be the simple impression that personality theories are attempts to formulate or represent significant aspects of human behavior and that the fruitfulness of these theories is to be judged primarily by how effectively they serve as a spur to research.

BIBLIOGRAPHY

Allport, G. W. *Personality: a psychological interpretation.* New York: Holt, 1937.
Boring, E. G. *A history of experimental psychology.* 2nd Ed. New York: Appleton-Century-Crofts, 1950.
Bronfenbrenner, U. Personality. In C. P. Stone and D. W. Taylor (Eds.). *Annual review of psychology.* Vol. 4. Stanford, Calif.: Annual Reviews, 1953, pp. 157–182.
Child, I. L. Personality. In C. P. Stone and D. W. Taylor (Eds.). *Annual review of psychology.* Vol. 5. Stanford, Calif.: Annual Reviews, 1954, pp. 149–170.
Cohen, M. R., and Nagel, E. *An introduction to logic and scientific method.* New York: Harcourt, 1934.
Conant, J. B. *On understanding science.* New Haven: Yale Univ. Press, 1947.
Eysenck, H. J. Personality. In C. P. Stone and D. W. Taylor (Eds.). *Annual*

review of psychology. Vol. 3. Stanford, Calif.: Annual Reviews, 1952, pp. 151–174.

Feigl, H., and Brodbeck, May. *Readings in the philosophy of science*. New York: Appleton-Century-Crofts, 1953.

Feigl, H., and Sellars, W. *Readings in philosophical analysis*. New York: Appleton-Century-Crofts, 1949.

Frank, P. *Modern science and its philosophy*. Cambridge: Harvard Univ. Press, 1949.

Hempel, C. G. *Fundamentals of concept formation in empirical science*. Chicago: Univ. of Chicago Press, 1952.

McClelland, D. C. Personality. In P. R. Farnsworth and Q. McNemar (Eds.). *Annual review of psychology*. Vol. 7. Stanford, Calif.; Annual Reviews, 1956, pp. 39–62.

McDougall, W. *An introduction to social psychology*. Boston: Luce, 1908.

MacKinnon, D. W. The structure of personality. In J. McV. Hunt (Ed.). *Personality and the behavior disorders*. New York: Ronald Press, 1944, pp. 3–48.

MacKinnon, D. W. Personality. In C. P. Stone and D. W. Taylor (Eds.). *Annual review of psychology*. Vol. 2. Stanford, Calif.: Annual Reviews, 1951, pp. 113–136.

MacKinnon, D. W., and Maslow, A. Personality. In H. Helson (Ed.). *Theoretical foundations of psychology*. New York: Van Nostrand, 1951, pp. 602–655.

Murphy, G. *Historical introduction to modern psychology*. New York: Harcourt, 1949.

Nuttin, V. Personality. In C. P. Stone and D. W. Taylor (Eds.). *Annual review of psychology*. Vol. 6. Stanford, Calif.: Annual Reviews, 1955, pp. 161–186.

Sears, R. R. Personality. In C. P. Stone and D. W. Taylor (Eds.). *Annual review of psychology*. Vol. 1. Stanford, Calif.: Annual Reviews, 1950, pp. 105–118.

2.

Freud's Psychoanalytic Theory

When psychology emerged as an independent scientific discipline in Germany during the middle of the nineteenth century, it defined its task as the analysis of consciousness in the normal, adult human being. It conceived of consciousness as being made up of structural elements which were closely correlated with processes in the sense organs. Visual sensations of color, for example, were correlated with photochemical changes in the retina of eye, and tones with events taking place in the inner ear. Complex experiences resulted from the joining together of a number of elementary sensations, images, and feelings. The task of psychology was to discover the basic elements of consciousness and to determine how they formed compounds. Psychology was often referred to as mental chemistry.

Resistance to this kind of psychology came from many directions and for a variety of reasons. There were those who opposed the exclusive emphasis on structure and who insisted with considerable vigor that the outstanding characteristics of the conscious mind are its active processes and not its passive contents. Sensing and not sensations, thinking and not ideas, imagining and not images—these, it was asserted, should be the principal subject matter of the science of psychology. Others protested that conscious experience could not be dissected without destroying the very essence of experience, namely, its quality of wholeness. Direct awareness, they said, consists of patterns or configurations, and not of elements joined together. Another large and vocal group asserted that mind is not amenable to investigation by the methods of science because it is too private and too subjective. They urged instead that psychology be defined as the science of behavior.

Freud's attack upon the traditional psychology of consciousness came from quite a different direction. He likened the mind to an iceberg in which the smaller part showing above the surface of the water represents the region of consciousness while the much larger mass below the water level represents the region of unconsciousness. In this vast domain of the unconscious are to be found the urges, the passions, the repressed ideas and feelings—a great underworld of vital, unseen forces which exercise an imperious control over the conscious thoughts and deeds of man. From this point of view, a psychology which limits itself to the analysis of consciousness is wholly inadequate for understanding the underlying motives of man's behavior.

For over forty years, Freud explored the unconscious by the method of free association and developed what is generally regarded as the first comprehensive theory of personality. He mapped the contours of its topography, penetrated to the headwaters of its stream of energy, and charted the lawful course of its growth. By performing these incredible feats, he became one of the most controversial and influential figures in modern times.

Sigmund Freud was born in Moravia, May 6, 1856, and died in London, September 23, 1939. For nearly eighty years, however, he resided in Vienna and left that city only when the Nazis overran Austria. As a young man he decided that he wanted to be a scientist and with this goal in mind he entered the medical school of the University of Vienna in 1873 from which he graduated eight years later. Freud never intended to practice medicine but the scanty rewards of scientific work, the limited opportunities for academic advancement for a Jew, and the needs of a growing family forced him to enter private practice. In spite of his practice, he found time for research and writing, and his accomplishments as a medical investigator earned him a solid reputation.

Freud's interest in neurology caused him to specialize in the treatment of nervous disorders, a branch of medicine which had lagged behind in the forward march of the healing arts during the nineteenth century. In order to improve his technical skills Freud studied for a year with the famous French psychiatrist, Jean Charcot, who was using hypnosis in the treatment of hysteria. Although Freud tried hypnosis with his patients, he was not impressed by its efficacy. Consequently, when he heard about a new method that had been devised by a Viennese physician, Joseph Breuer, a method by which the patient was cured of his symptoms by talking about them, he tried it out and found it to be effective. Breuer and Freud collaborated in writing up some of their cases of hysteria which had been treated by the talking-out technique (1895).

However, the two men soon parted company over the importance of the sexual factor in hysteria. Freud felt that sexual conflicts were the cause of hysteria while Breuer held a more conservative view. Thereafter, Freud worked pretty much alone developing the ideas which were to form the foundation of psychoanalytic theory and which culminated in the publication of his first great work, *The interpretation of dreams* (1900). Other books and articles soon brought his views to the attention of physicians and scientists throughout the world, and it was not long before Freud was surrounded by a group of disciples from various countries, among them Ernest Jones of England, Carl Jung of Zurich, A. A. Brill of New York, Sandor Ferenczi of Budapest, Karl Abraham of Berlin, and Alfred Adler of Vienna. Jung and Adler later withdrew from the circle and developed rival viewpoints.

It is impossible within the brief space permitted us to cover even the highlights of Freud's intellectual and personal life: the early years as a medical student and investigator; the decisive influence of the great German physiologist, Ernst Brücke, who was one of the leaders in the Helmholtz School of Medicine and from whom Freud learned to regard man as a dynamic system subject to the laws of nature; his marriage to Martha Bernays and his lifelong devotion to her and to his six children, one of whom, Anna, followed her father's calling; the stimulating year with Charcot in Paris; his bizarre relationship with Wilhelm Fliess; his searching self-analysis begun in the 1890's and continuing throughout his life; the abortive attempt to account for psychological phenomena in terms of cerebral anatomy; the years of isolation from the medical community of Vienna; the invitation from G. Stanley Hall, the eminent American psychologist and president of Clark University, to address the meetings commemorating the founding of that university; the establishing of the International Psychoanalytic Association and the secession of such important disciples as Jung, Adler, Rank, and Stekel; the influence of World War I upon Freud's thinking and his thoroughgoing revision of the basic tenets of psychoanalytic theory; the application of psychoanalytic concepts in all fields of human endeavor; Freud's personal characteristics and the long torment of cancer of the jaw; and finally his melodramatic escape from the clutches of the Nazis. Fortunately, every nook and cranny of Freud's long life has been surveyed by the foremost English psychoanalyst, Ernest Jones, and brilliantly related in a three-volume biography (1953, 1955, —).

Nor does space permit us to list the published works of Freud. Beginning with *The interpretation of dreams* in 1900 and terminating in the posthumously published *Outline of psychoanalysis* in 1940, Freud's psychological writings fill twenty-four volumes in the definitive, standard English edition (1953–   ). For the reader who is unfamiliar with Freud's theory of personality, the following books are recommended: *The interpretation of dreams* (1900), *The psychopathology of everyday life* (1904), *A general introduction to psychoanalysis* (1917), *New introductory lectures on psychoanalysis* (1933), and *An outline of psychoanalysis* (1940).

In the following account of Freud's ideas we shall have to limit ourselves to those matters that pertain to Freud's theory of personality, and exclude from consideration the psychoanalytic theory of neurosis, which, in any event, has been covered so well by Otto Fenichel (1945), the techniques of psychoanalysis, and the far-flung applications of Freudian psychology in the social sciences, the arts, and the humanities. Nor shall we be able to take notice of the evolution of Freud's thinking with respect to the basic concepts of his personality theory; it will have to suffice to present Freud's final word on such concepts as we shall discuss. Regrettably, we cannot work in the contributions of his followers which have been numerous and in some instances represent substantial additions to psychoanalytic theory.

THE STRUCTURE OF PERSONALITY

The personality is made up of three major systems, the *id*, the *ego*, and the *superego*. Although each of these provinces of the total personality has its own functions, properties, components, operating principles, dynamisms, and mechanisms, they interact so closely with one another that it is difficult if not impossible to disentangle their effects and weigh their relative contribution to man's behavior. Behavior is nearly always the product of an interaction among these three systems; rarely does one system operate to the exclusion of the other two.

THE ID. The id is the original system of the personality; it is the matrix within which the ego and the superego become differentiated.

The id consists of everything psychological that is inherited and that is present at birth, including the instincts. It is the reservoir of psychic energy and furnishes all of the power for the operation of the other two systems. It is in close touch with the bodily processes from which it derives its energy. Freud called the id the "true psychic reality" because it represents the inner world of subjective experience and has no knowledge of objective reality.

The id cannot tolerate increases of energy which are experienced as uncomfortable states of tension. Consequently, when the tension level of the organism is raised, either as a result of external stimulation or of internally produced excitations, the id functions in such a manner as to discharge the tension immediately and return the organism to a comfortably constant and low energy level. This principle of tension reduction by which the id operates is called the *pleasure principle.*

In order to accomplish its aim of avoiding pain and obtaining pleasure, the id has at its command two processes. These are *reflex action* and the *primary process.* Reflex actions are inborn and automatic reactions like sneezing and blinking; they usually reduce tension immediately. The organism is equipped with a number of such reflexes for dealing with relatively simple forms of excitation. The primary process involves a somewhat more complicated psychological reaction. It attempts to discharge tension by forming an image of an object that will remove the tension. For example, the primary process provides the hungry person with a mental picture of food. This hallucinatory experience in which the desired object is present in the form of a memory image is called *wish-fulfillment.* The best example of the primary process in normal people is the nocturnal dream which Freud believed always represents the fulfillment or attempted fulfillment of a wish. The hallucinations and visions of psychotic patients are also examples of the primary process. Autistic or wishful thinking is highly colored by the action of the primary process. These wish-fulfilling mental images are the only reality that the id knows.

Obviously the primary process by itself is not capable of reducing tension. The hungry person cannot eat mental images of food. Consequently, a new or secondary psychological process develops, and when this occurs the structure of the second system of the personality, the ego, begins to take form.

THE EGO. The ego comes into existence because the needs of the organism require appropriate transactions with the objective world of reality. The hungry person has to seek, find, and eat food before the tension of hunger can be eliminated. This means that he has to learn to differentiate between a memory image of food and an actual perception of food as it exists in the outer world. Having made this crucial differentiation it is then necessary for him to convert the image into a perception which is accomplished by locating food in the environment. In other words, the person matches his memory image of food with the sight or smell of food as they come to him through his senses. The basic distinction between the id and the ego is that the former knows only the subjective reality of the mind whereas the latter distinguishes between things in the mind and things in the external world.

The ego is said to obey the *reality principle* and to operate by means of the *secondary process.* The aim of the reality principle is to prevent the discharge of tension until an object which is appropriate for the satisfaction of the need has been discovered. The reality principle suspends the pleasure principle temporarily because the pleasure principle is eventually served when the needed object is found and the tension is thereby reduced. The reality principle asks in effect whether an experience is true or false, that is, whether it has external existence or not, while the pleasure principle is only interested in whether the experience is painful or pleasurable.

The secondary process is realistic thinking. By means of the secondary process the ego formulates a plan for the satisfaction of the need and then tests this plan, usually by some kind of action, in order to see whether or not it will work. The hungry person thinks where he may find food and then proceeds to look in that place. This is called *reality testing.* In order to perform its role efficiently the ego has control over all of the cognitive and intellectual functions; these higher mental processes are placed at the service of the secondary process.

The ego is said to be the executive of the personality because it controls the gateways to action, selects the features of the environment to which it will respond, and decides what instincts will be satisfied and in what manner. In performing these highly important executive functions, the ego has to try to integrate the often conflicting demands of the id, the superego, and the external world. This is not an easy task and often places a great strain upon the ego.

It should be kept in mind, however, that the ego is the organized portion of the id, that it comes into existence in order to forward the aims of the id and not to frustrate them, and that all of its power is derived from the id. It has no existence apart from the id, and it never becomes completely independent of the id. Its principal role is to mediate between the instinctual requirements of the organism and the conditions of the surrounding environment; its superordinate objectives are to maintain the life of the individual and to see that the species is reproduced.

THE SUPEREGO. The third and last system of personality to be developed is the superego. It is the internal representative of the traditional values and ideals of society as interpreted to the child by his parents, and enforced by means of a system of rewards and punishments imposed upon the child. The superego is the moral arm of personality; it represents the ideal rather than the real and it strives for perfection rather than pleasure. Its main concern is to decide whether something is right or wrong so that it can act in accordance with the moral standards authorized by the agents of society.

The superego as the internalized moral arbiter of conduct develops in response to the rewards and punishments meted out by the parents. To obtain the rewards and avoid the punishments, the child learns to guide his behavior along the lines laid down by the parents. Whatever they say is improper and punish him for doing tends to become incorporated into his *conscience* which is one of the two subsystems of the superego. Whatever they approve of and reward him for doing tends to become incorporated into his *ego-ideal* which is the other subsystem of the superego. The mechanism by which this incorporation takes place is called *introjection*. The conscience punishes the person by making him feel guilty, the ego-ideal rewards the person by making him feel proud of himself. With the formation of the superego, self-control is substituted for parental control.

The main functions of the superego are (1) to inhibit the impulses of the id, particularly those of a sexual or aggressive nature, since these are the impulses whose expression is most highly condemned by society, (2) to persuade the ego to substitute moralistic goals for realistic ones, and (3) to strive for perfection. That is, the superego is inclined to oppose both the id and the ego, and to make the world over into its own image. However, it is like the id in being nonrational and like the ego in attempting to exercise control over the instincts. Unlike the ego, the superego does not merely postpone instinctual gratification; it tries to block it permanently.

In concluding this brief description of the three systems of the personality, it should be pointed out that the id, ego, and superego are not to be thought of as manikins which operate the personality. They are merely names for various psychological processes which obey different system principles. Under ordinary circumstances these different principles do not collide with one another nor do they work at cross purposes. On the contrary, they work together as a team under the administrative leadership of the ego. The personality normally functions as a whole rather than as three separate segments. In a very general way, the id may be thought of as the biological component of personality, the ego as the psychological component, and the superego as the social component.

THE DYNAMICS OF PERSONALITY

Freud was brought up under the influence of the strongly deterministic and positivistic philosophy of nineteenth century science and regarded the human organism as a complex energy system, which derives its energy from the food it consumes and expends it for such various purposes as circulation, respiration, muscular exercise, perceiving, thinking, and remembering. Freud saw no reason to assume that the energy which furnishes the power for breathing or digesting is any different, save in form, from the energy which furnishes the power for thinking and remembering. After all, as nineteenth century physicists were firmly insisting, energy has to be defined in terms of the work it performs. If the work consists of a psychological activity such as thinking, then it is perfectly legitimate, Freud believed, to call this form of energy *psychic energy*. According to the doctrine of the conservation of energy, energy may be transformed from one state into another state but can never be lost from the total cosmic system; it follows from this that psychic energy may be transformed into physiological energy and vice versa. The point of contact or bridge between the energy of the body and that of the personality is the id and its instincts.

INSTINCT. An instinct is defined as an inborn psychological representation of an inner somatic source of excitation. The psychological representation is called a *wish*, and the bodily excitation from which it stems is called a *need*. Thus, the state of hunger may be described in physiological terms as a condition of nutritional deficit in the tissues of the body whereas psychologically it is represented as a wish for food. The wish acts as a motive for behavior. The hungry person seeks food. Instincts are considered therefore to be the propelling factors of personality. Not only do they drive behavior but they also determine the direction that the behavior will take. In other words, an instinct exercises selective control over conduct by increasing one's sensitivity for particular kinds of stimulation. The hungry person is more sensitive to food stimuli, the sexually aroused person is more likely to respond to erotic stimuli.

Parenthetically, it may be observed that the organism can also be activated by stimuli from the external world. Freud felt, however, that these environmental sources of excitation play a less important role in the dynamics of personality than do the inborn instincts. In general, external stimuli make fewer demands upon the individual and require less complicated forms of adjustment than do the needs. One can always flee from an external stimulus but it is impossible to run away from a need. Although Freud relegated environmental stimuli to a secondary place, he did not deny their importance under certain conditions. For example, excessive stimulation during the early years of life when the immature ego lacks the capacity for binding large amounts of free energy (tension) may have drastic effects upon the personality, as we shall see when we consider Freud's theory of anxiety.

An instinct is a quantum of psychic energy or as Freud put it "a measure of the demand made upon the mind for work" (1905a, p. 168). All of the instincts taken together constitute the sum total of psychic energy available to the personality. As was previously pointed out, the id is the reservoir of this energy and it is also the seat of the instincts. The id may be considered to be a dynamo which furnishes psychological power for running the manifold operations of personality. This power is derived, of course, from the metabolic processes of the body.

An instinct has four characteristic features: a *source*, an *aim*, an *object*, and an *impetus*. The source has already been defined as a bodily condition or a need. The aim is the removal of the bodily excitation. The aim of the hunger instinct, for example, is to abolish the nutritional deficiency, which is accomplished, of course, by eating food. All of the activity which intervenes between the appearance of the wish and its fulfillment is subsumed under the heading of *object*. That is, object refers not only to the particular thing or condition which will satisfy the need but it also includes all of the behavior which takes place in securing the necessary thing or condition. For instance, when a person is hungry he usually has to perform a number of actions before he can reach the final consummatory goal of eating.

The impetus of an instinct is its force or strength which is determined by the intensity of the underlying need. As the nutritional deficiency becomes greater, up to the point where physical weakness sets in, the force of the instinct becomes correspondingly greater.

Let us briefly consider some of the implications that inhere in this way of conceptualizing an instinct. In the first place, the model which Freud provides is a tension-reduction one. The behavior of a person is activated by internal irritants and subsides as soon as an appropriate action removes or diminishes the irritation. This means that the aim of an instinct is essentially *regressive* in character since it returns the person to a prior state, one which existed before the instinct appeared. This prior state to which the personality returns is one of relative quiescence. An instinct is also said to be *conservative* because its aim is to conserve the equilibrium of the organism by abolishing disturbing excitations. Thus, we can picture an instinct as a process which repeats as often as it appears a cycle of events starting with excitement and terminating with repose. Freud called this aspect of an instinct *repetition compulsion*. The personality is compelled to repeat over and over again the inevitable cycle from excitation to quiescence. (The term repetition compulsion is also employed to describe perserverative behavior which occurs when the means adopted for satisfying the need are not completely appropriate. A child may perseverate in sucking its thumb when it is hungry.)

According to Freud's theory of instincts, the source and aim of an instinct remain constant throughout life, unless the source is changed or eliminated by physical maturation. New instincts may appear as new bodily needs develop. In contrast to this constancy of source and aim, the object or means by which the person attempts to satisfy the need can and does vary considerably during the lifetime of the person. This variation in object choice is possible because psychic energy is *displaceable;* it can be expended in various ways. Consequently, if one object is not available either by virtue of its absence or by virtue of barriers within the personality, energy can be invested in another object. If that object proves also to be inaccessible another displacement can occur, and so forth, until an available object is found. In other words, objects can be substituted for one another, which is definitely not the case with either the source or the aim of an instinct.

When the energy of an instinct is more or less permanently invested in a substitute object, that is, one which is not the original and innately determined object, the resulting behavior is said to be an *instinct derivative*. Thus, if the first sexual object choice of the baby is the manipulation of his own sex organs and he is forced to give up this pleasure in favor of more innocuous forms of bodily stimulation such as sucking his thumb or playing with his toes, the substitute activities are derivatives of the sexual instinct. The aim of the sexual instinct does not change one whit when a substitution takes place; the goal sought is still that of sexual gratification.

The displacement of energy from one object to another is the most important feature of personality dynamics. It accounts for the apparent plasticity of human nature and the remarkable versatility of man's behavior. Practically all of the adult person's interests, preferences, tastes, habits, and attitudes represent the displacements of energy from original instinctual object-choices. They are almost all instinct derivatives. Freud's theory of motivation was based solidly on the assumption that the instincts are *the* sole energy sources for man's behavior. We shall have a great deal more to say about displacement in subsequent sections of this chapter.

Number and kinds of instincts. Freud did not attempt to draw up a list of instincts because he felt that not enough was known about the bodily states upon which the instincts depend. The identification of these organic needs is a job for the physiologist, not the psychologist. Although Freud did not pretend to know how many instincts there are, he did assume that they could all be classified under two general headings, the *life* instincts and the *death* instincts.

The life instincts serve the purpose of individual survival and racial propagation. Hunger, thirst, and sex fall in this category. The form of energy by which the life instincts perform their work is called *libido*.

The life instinct to which Freud paid the greatest attention is that of sex, and in the early years of psychoanalysis almost everything the person did was attributed to this ubiquitous drive (Freud, 1905a). Actually, the sex instinct is not one instinct but many. That is, there are a number of separate bodily needs which give rise to erotic wishes. Each of these wishes has its source in a different bodily region which are referred to collectively as *erogenous zones.* An erogenous zone is a part of the skin or mucous membrane which is extremely sensitive to irritation and which when manipulated in a certain way removes the irritation and produces pleasurable feelings. The lips and oral cavity constitute one such erogenous zone, the anal region another, and the sex organs a third. Sucking produces oral pleasure, elimination anal pleasure, and massaging or rubbing genital pleasure. In childhood, the sexual instincts are relatively independent of one another but when the person reaches puberty they tend to fuse together and to serve jointly the aim of reproduction.

The death instincts, or, as Freud sometimes called them, the destructive instincts, perform their work much less conspicuously than the life instincts, and for this reason little is known about them, other than that they inevitably accomplish their mission. Every person does eventually die, a fact which caused Freud to formulate the famous dictum, "the goal of all life is death" (1920a, p. 38). Freud assumed specifically that the person has a wish, usually of course unconscious, to die. He did not attempt to identify the somatic sources of the death instincts although one may wish to speculate that they reside in the catabolic or breaking-down processes of the body. Nor did he assign a name to the energy by which the death instincts carry on their work.

Freud's assumption of a death wish is based upon the constancy principle as formulated by Fechner. This principle asserts that all living processes tend to return to the stability of the inorganic world. In *Beyond the pleasure principle* (1920a), Freud made the following argument in favor of the concept of the death wish. Living matter evolved by the action of cosmic forces upon inorganic matter. These changes were highly unstable at first and quickly reverted to their prior inorganic state. Gradually, however, the length of life increased because of evolutionary changes in the world but these unstable animate forms always eventually regressed to the stability of inanimate matter. With the development of reproductive mechanisms, living things were able to reproduce their own kind, and did not have to depend upon being created out of the inorganic world. Yet even with this advance the individual member of a species inevitably obeyed the constancy principle, since this was the principle that governed its existence when it was endowed with life. Life, Freud said, is but a roundabout way to death. Disturbed out of its stable existence, organic matter strives to return to a quiescent state. The death wish in the human being is the psychological representation of the constancy principle.

An important derivative of the death instincts is the *aggressive drive*. Aggressiveness is self-destruction turned outward against substitute objects. A person fights with other people and is destructive because his death wish is blocked by the forces of the life instincts and by other obstacles in his personality which counteract the death instincts. It took the Great War of 1914–1918 to convince Freud that aggression was as sovereign a motive as sex.

The life and death instincts and their derivatives may fuse together, neutralize each other, or replace one another. Eating, for example, represents a fusion of hunger and destructiveness which is satisfied by biting, chewing, and swallowing food. Love, a derivative of the sex instinct, can neutralize hate, a derivative of the death instinct. Or love can replace hate, and hate love.

Since the instincts contain all of the energy by which the three systems of the personality perform their work, let us turn now to consider the ways in which the id, ego, and superego gain control over and utilize psychic energy.

THE DISTRIBUTION AND UTILIZATION OF PSYCHIC ENERGY. The dynamics of personality consists of the way in which psychic energy is distributed and used by the id, ego, and superego. Since the amount of energy is a limited quantity there is competition among the three systems for the energy that is available. One system gains control over the available energy at the expense of the other two systems. As one system becomes stronger the other two necessarily become weaker, unless new energy is added to the total system.

Originally the id possesses all of the energy and uses it for reflex action and wish-fulfillment by means of the primary process. Both of these activities are in the direct service of the pleasure principle by which the id operates. The investment of energy in an action or image which will gratify an instinct is called an instinctual *object-choice* or *object-cathexis.*

The energy of the id is in a very fluid state which means that it can easily be shunted from one action or image to another action or image. The displaceable quality of this instinctual energy is due to the id's inability to form fine discriminations between objects. Objects that are different are treated as though they were the same. The hungry baby, for instance, will take up almost anything that it can hold and put it to its lips.

Since the ego has no source of power of its own it has to borrow it from the id. The diversion of energy from the id into the processes that make up the ego is accomplished by a mechanism known as *identification.* This is one of the most important concepts in Freudian psychology, and one of the most difficult to comprehend. It will be recalled from a previous discussion that the id does not distinguish between subjective imagery and objective reality. When it cathects an image of an object it is the same as cathecting the object itself. However, since a mental image cannot satisfy a need, the person is forced to differentiate between the world of the mind and the outer world. He has to learn the difference between a memory or idea of an object which is not present and a sensory impression or perception of an object which is present. Then, in order to satisfy a need, he must learn to match what is in his mind with its counterpart in the external world by means of the secondary process. This matching of a mental representation with physical reality, of something that is in the mind with something that is in the outer world, is what is meant by identification.

Since the id makes no distinction between any of the contents of the mind, whether they be perceptions, memory images, ideas, or hallucinations, a cathexis may be formed for a realistic perception as readily as for a wish-fulfilling memory image. In this way, energy is diverted from the purely autistic psychological processes of the id into the realistic, logical, ideational processes of the ego. In both cases, energy is used for strictly psychological purposes, but in the case of the id no distinction is made between the mental symbol and the physical referent whereas in the case of the ego this distinction is made. The ego attempts to make the symbol accurately represent the referent. In other words, identification enables the secondary process to supersede the primary process. Since the secondary process is so much more successful in reducing tensions, more and more ego cathexes are formed. Gradually the more efficient ego obtains a virtual monopoly over the store of psychic energy. This monopoly is only relative, however, because if the ego fails to satisfy the instincts, the id reasserts its power.

Once the ego has trapped enough energy it can use it for other purposes than that of gratifying the instincts by means of the secondary process. Some of the energy is used to bring the various psychological processes such as perceiving, remembering, judging, discriminating, abstracting, generalizing, and reasoning to a higher level of development. Some of the energy has to be used by the ego to restrain the id from acting impulsively and irrationally. These restraining forces are known as *anticathexes* in contradistinction to the driving forces or cathexes. If the id becomes too threatening, the ego erects defenses against the id. These defense mechanisms, which will be discussed in a later section, may also be used to cope with the pressures of the superego upon the ego. Energy, of course, is required for the maintenance of these defenses.

Ego energy may also be displaced to form new object-cathexes, so that a whole network of derived interests, attitudes, and preferences is formed within the ego. These ego-cathexes may not directly satisfy the basic needs of the organism but they are connected by associative links with objects that do. The energy of the hunger drive, for example, may fan out to include such cathexes as an interest in collecting recipes, visiting unusual restaurants, and selling chinaware. This spreading of cathexes into channels that are only remotely connected with the original object of an instinct is made possible by the greater efficiency of the ego in performing its fundamental job of gratifying the instincts. The ego has a surplus of energy to use for other purposes.

Finally, the ego as the executive of the personality organization uses energy to effect an integration among the three systems. The purpose of this integrative function of the ego is to produce an inner harmony within the personality so that the ego's transactions with the environment may be made smoothly and effectively.

The mechanism of identification also accounts for the energizing of the superego system. This, too, is a complex matter and takes place in the following way. Among the first object-cathexes of the baby are those of the parents. These cathexes develop early and become very firmly entrenched because the baby is completely dependent upon his parents or parent-substitutes for the satisfaction of his needs. The parents also play the role of disciplinary agents; they teach the child the moral code and the traditional values and ideals of the society in which the child is raised. They do this by rewarding the child when he does the right thing and punishing him when he does the wrong thing. A reward is anything that reduces tension or promises to do so. A piece of candy, a smile, or a kind word may be an effective reward. A punishment is anything that increases tension. It may be a spanking, a disapproving look, or a denial of some pleasure. Thus, the child learns to identify, that is, to match his behavior with the sanctions and prohibitions laid down by the parents. He introjects the moral imperatives of his parents by virtue of the original cathexes he has for them as need-satisfying agents. He cathects their ideals and these become his ego-ideal; he cathects their prohibitions and these become his conscience. Thus, the superego gains access to the reservoir of energy in the id by means of the child's identification with his parents.

The work performed by the superego is often, although not always, in direct opposition to the impulses of the id. This is the case because the moral code represents society's attempt to control and even to inhibit the expression of the primitive drives, especially those of sex and aggression. Being good usually means being obedient and not saying or doing "dirty" things. Being bad means being disobedient, rebellious, and lustful. The virtuous person inhibits his impulses, the sinful person indulges them. However, the superego can sometimes be corrupted by the id. This happens, for example, when a person in a fit of moralistic fervor takes aggressive measures against those whom he considers to be wicked and sinful. The expression of aggression in such instances is cloaked by the mantle of righteous indignation.

Once the energy furnished by the instincts has been channeled into the ego and the superego by the mechanism of identification, a complicated interplay of driving and restraining forces becomes possible. The id, it will be recalled, possesses only driving forces or cathexes whereas the energy of the ego and the superego is used both to forward and to frustrate the aims of the instincts. The ego has to check both the id and the superego if it is to govern the personality wisely, yet it must have enough energy left over to engage in necessary intercourse with the external world. If the id retains control over a large share of the energy, the behavior of the person will tend to be impulsive and primitive in character. On the other hand, if the superego gains control of an undue amount of energy, the functioning of the personality will be dominated by moralistic considerations rather than by realistic ones. The anticathexes of the conscience may tie up the ego in moral knots and prevent action of any sort, while the cathexes of the ego-ideal may set such high standards for the ego that the person is being continually frustrated and may eventually develop a depressing sense of failure.

Moreover, sudden and unpredictable shifts of energy from one system to another and from cathexes to anticathexes are common, especially during the first two decades of life before the distribution of energy has become more or less stabilized. These shifts of energy keep the personality in a state of dynamic flux. Freud was pessimistic about the chances of psychology ever becoming a very exact science because, as he pointed out, even a very small change in the distribution of energy might tip the scale in favor of one form of behavior rather than its opposite (Freud, 1920b). Who can say whether the man poised on the window ledge is going to jump or not, or whether the batter is going to strike out or hit a winning home run?

In the final analysis, the dynamics of personality consist of the interplay of the driving forces, cathexes, and the restraining forces, anticathexes. All of the conflicts within the personality may be reduced to the opposition of these two sets of forces. All prolonged tension is due to the counteraction of a driving force by a restraining force. Whether it be an anticathexis of the ego opposed to a cathexis of the id or an anticathexis of the superego opposed to a cathexis of the ego, the result in terms of tension is the same. As Freud was fond of saying, psychoanalysis is "a dynamic conception which reduces mental life to the interplay of reciprocally urging and checking forces" (1910b, p. 107).

ANXIETY. The dynamics of personality is to a large extent governed by the necessity for gratifying one's needs by means of transactions with objects in the external world. The surrounding environment provides the hungry organism with food, the thirsty one with water. In addition to its role as the source of supplies, the external world plays another part in shaping the destiny of personality. The environment contains regions of danger and insecurity; it can threaten as well as satisfy. The environment has the power to produce pain and increase tension as well as to bring pleasure and reduce tension. It disturbs as well as comforts.

The individual's customary reaction to external threats of pain and destruction with which it is not prepared to cope is to become afraid. The threatened person is ordinarily a fearful person. Overwhelmed by excessive stimulation which the ego is unable to bring under control, the ego becomes flooded with anxiety.

Freud recognized three types of anxiety: *reality* anxiety, *neurotic* anxiety, and *moral* anxiety or feelings of guilt (1926b). The basic type is reality anxiety or fear or real dangers in the external world; from it are derived the other two types. Neurotic anxiety is the fear that the instincts will get out of control and cause the person to do something for which he will be punished. Neurotic anxiety is not so much a fear of the instincts themselves as it is a fear of the punishment that is likely to ensue from instinctual gratification. Neurotic anxiety has a basis in reality, because the world as represented by the parents and other authorities does punish the child for impulsive actions. Moral anxiety is fear of the conscience. The person with a well-developed superego tends to feel guilty when he does something or even thinks of doing something that is contrary to the moral code by which he has been raised. He is said to feel conscience-stricken. Moral anxiety also has a realistic basis; the person has been punished in the past for violating the moral code and may be punished again.

The function of anxiety is to warn the person of impending danger; it is a signal to the ego that unless appropriate measures are taken the danger may increase until the ego is overthrown. Anxiety is a state of tension; it is a drive like hunger or sex but instead of arising from internal tissue conditions it is produced originally by external causes. When anxiety is aroused it motivates the person to do something. He may flee from the threatening region, inhibit the dangerous impulse, or obey the voice of conscience.

Anxiety which cannot be dealt with by effective measures is said to be traumatic. It reduces the person to a state of infantile helplessness. In fact, the prototype of all later anxiety is the *birth trauma*. The neonate is bombarded with stimuli from the world for which he is not prepared and to which he cannot adapt. The baby needs a sheltered environment until his ego has had a chance to develop to the point where it can master strong stimuli from the environment. When the ego cannot cope with anxiety by rational methods it has to fall back upon unrealistic ones. These are the so-called *defense mechanisms* of the ego which will be discussed in the following section.

THE DEVELOPMENT OF PERSONALITY

Freud was probably the first psychological theorist to emphasize the developmental aspects of personality and in particular to stress the decisive role of the early years of infancy and childhood in laying down the basic character structure of the person. Indeed, Freud felt that personality was pretty well formed by the end of the fifth year, and that subsequent growth consisted for the most part of elaborating this basic structure. He arrived at this conclusion on the basis of his experiences with patients undergoing psychoanalysis. Inevitably, their mental explorations led them back to early childhood experiences which appeared to be decisive for the development of a neurosis later in life. Freud believed that the child is father of the man. It is interesting in view of this strong preference for genetic explanations of adult behavior that Freud rarely studied young children directly. He preferred to reconstruct the past life of a person from evidence furnished by his adult recollections.

Personality develops in response to four major sources of tension: (1) physiological growth processes, (2) frustrations, (3) conflicts, and (4) threats. As a direct consequence of increases in tension emanating from these sources, the person is forced to learn new methods of reducing tension. This learning is what is meant by personality development.

Identification and *displacement* are two methods by which the individual learns to resolve his frustrations, conflicts, and anxieties.

IDENTIFICATION. This concept was introduced in an earlier section to help account for the formation of the ego and superego. In the present context, identification may be defined as the method by which a person takes over the features of another person and makes them a corporate part of his own personality. He learns to reduce tension by modeling his behavior after that of someone else. Freud preferred the term *identification* to the more familiar one *imitation* because he felt that imitation denotes a kind of superficial and transient copying behavior whereas he wanted a word that would convey the idea of a more or less permanent acquisition to personality.

We choose as models those who seem to be more successful in gratifying their needs than we are. The child identifies with his parents because they appear to him to be omnipotent, at least during the years of early childhood. As the child grows older, he finds other people to identify with whose accomplishments are more in line with his current wishes. Each period tends to have its own characteristic identification figures. Needless to say, most of this identification takes place unconsciously and not, as it may sound, with conscious intention.

It is not necessary for a person to identify with someone else in every respect. He usually selects and incorporates just those features which he believes will help him achieve a desired goal. There is a good deal of trial and error in the identification process because one is usually not quite sure what it is about another person that accounts for his success. The ultimate test is whether the identification helps to reduce tension; if it does the quality is taken over, if it does not it is discarded. One may identify with animals, imaginary characters, institutions, abstract ideas, and inanimate objects as well as with other human beings. Identification is also a method by which one may regain an object that has been lost. By identifying with a loved person who has died or from whom one has been separated, the lost person becomes reincarnated as an incorporated feature of one's personality. Children who have been rejected by their parents tend to form strong identifications with them in the hope of regaining their love. One may also identify with a person out of fear. The child identifies with the prohibitions of the parents in order to avoid punishment. This kind of identification is the basis for the formation of the superego.

The final personality structure represents an accumulation of numerous identifications made at various periods of the person's life, although the mother and father are probably the most important identification figures in anyone's life.

DISPLACEMENT. When an original object-choice of an instinct is rendered inaccessible by external or internal barriers (anticathexes), a new cathexis is formed unless a strong repression occurs. If this new cathexis is also blocked, another displacement takes place, and so on, until an object is found which yields some relief for the pent-up tension. This object is then cathected until it loses its power to reduce tension, at which time another search for an appropriate goal object is instituted. Throughout the series of displacements that constitute, in such large measure, the development of personality, the source and aim of the instinct remains constant; it is only the object that varies.

A substitute object is rarely if ever as satisfying or tension-reducing as the original object, and the less tension is reduced the more remote the displacement is from the original object. As a consequence of numerous displacements a pool of undischarged tension accumulates which acts as a permanent motivating force for behavior. The person is constantly seeking new and better ways of reducing tension. This accounts for the variability and diversity of behavior, as well as for man's restlessness. On the other hand, the personality does become more or less stabilized with age owing to the compromises that are made between the urging forces of the instincts and the resistances of the ego and superego.

As we have written in another place (Hall, 1954).

> Interests, attachments, and all the other forms of acquired motives endure because they are to some degree frustrating as well as satisfying. They persist because they fail to yield complete satisfaction. . . . Every compromise is at the same time a renunciation. A person gives up something that he really wants but cannot have, and accepts something second or third best that he can have (p. 104).

Freud pointed out that the development of civilization was made possible by the inhibition of primitive object-choices and the diversion of instinctual energy into socially acceptable and culturally creative channels (1930). A displacement which produces a higher cultural achievement is called a *sublimation*. Freud observed in this connection that Leonardo da Vinci's interest in painting Madonnas was a sublimated expression of a longing for intimacy with his mother from whom he had been separated at a tender age (1910a). Since sublimation does not result in complete satisfaction, any more than any displacement does, there is always some residual tension. This tension may discharge itself in the form of nervousness or restlessness, conditions which Freud pointed out were the price that man paid for his civilized status (1908).

The direction taken by a displacement is determined by two factors. These are (1) the resemblance of the substitute object to the original one, and (2) the sanctions and prohibitions imposed by society. The factor of resemblance is actually the degree to which the two objects are identified in the mind of the person. Da Vinci painted Madonnas rather than peasant women or aristocrats because he conceived of his mother as resembling the Madonna more than any other type of woman. Society acting through the parents and other authority figures authorizes certain displacements and outlaws others. The child learns that it is permissible to suck a lollipop but not to suck his thumb.

The ability to form substitute object-cathexes is the most powerful mechanism for the development of personality. The complex network of interests, preferences, values, attitudes, and attachments that characterize the personality of the adult human being is made possible by displacement. If psychic energy were not displaceable and distributive there would be no development of personality. The person would be merely a mechanical robot driven to perform fixed patterns of behavior by his instincts.

THE DEFENSE MECHANISMS OF THE EGO. Under the pressure of excessive anxiety, the ego is sometimes forced to take extreme measures to relieve the pressure. These measures are called defense mechanisms. The principal defenses are repression, projection, reaction formation, fixation, and regression (Anna Freud, 1946). All defense mechanisms have two characteristics in common: (1) they deny, falsify, or distort reality, and (2) they operate unconsciously so that the person is not aware of what is taking place.

Repression. This is one of the earliest concepts of psychoanalysis. Before Freud arrived at his final formulation of personality theory in terms of the id, ego, and superego, he divided the mind into three regions, consciousness, preconsciousness, and unconsciousness. The preconscious consisted of psychological material that could become conscious when the need arose. Material in the unconscious, however, was regarded by Freud as being relatively inaccessible to conscious awareness; it was said to be in a state of repression.

When Freud revised his theory of personality, the concept of repression was retained as one of the defense mechanisms of the ego. Repression is said to occur when an object-choice that arouses undue alarm is forced out of consciousness by an anticathexis. For example, a disturbing memory may be prevented from becoming conscious or a person may not see something that is in plain sight because the perception of it is repressed. Repression can even interfere with the normal functioning of the body. Someone may become sexually impotent because he is afraid of the sex impulse, or he may develop arthritis as a consequence of repressing feelings of hostility.

Repressions may force their way through the opposing anticathexes or they may find expression in the form of a displacement. If the displacement is to be successful in preventing the reawakening of anxiety it must be disguised in some suitable symbolic form. A son who has repressed his hostile feelings towards his father may express these hostile feelings against other symbols of authority.

Repressions once formed are difficult to abolish. The person must reassure himself that the danger no longer exists, but he cannot get such reassurance until the repression is lifted so that he can test reality. It is a vicious circle. That is why the adult carries around with him a lot of childish fears; he never gets a chance to discover that they have no basis in reality.

Projection. Reality anxiety is usually easier for the ego to deal with than is either neurotic or moral anxiety. Consequently, if the source of the anxiety can be attributed to the external world rather than to the individual's own primitive impulses or to the threats of his conscience, he is likely to achieve greater relief for his anxious condition. This mechanism by which neurotic or moral anxiety is converted into an objective fear is called projection. This conversion is easily made because the original source of both neurotic and moral anxiety is fear of punishment from an external agent. In projection, one simply says "He hates me" instead of "I hate him," or "He is persecuting me" instead of "My conscience is bothering me." Projection often serves a dual purpose. It reduces anxiety by substituting a lesser danger for a greater one, and it enables the projecting person to express his impulses under the guise of defending himself against his enemies.

Reaction formation. This defensive measure involves the replacement in consciousness of an anxiety-producing impulse or feeling by its opposite. For example, hate is replaced by love. The original impulse still exists but it is glossed over or masked by one that does not cause anxiety.

The question often arises as to how a reaction formation may be distinguished from a genuine expression of an impulse or feeling. For instance, how can reactive love be differentiated from true love? Usually, a reaction formation is marked by extravagant showiness—the person protests too much—and by compulsiveness. Extreme forms of behavior of any kind usually denote a reaction formation. Sometimes the reaction formation succeeds in satisfying the original impulse which is being defended against, as when a mother smothers her child with affection and attention.

Fixation and regression. In the course of normal development, as we shall see in the next section, the personality passes through a series of rather well-defined stages until it reaches maturity. Each new step that is taken, however, entails a certain amount of frustration and anxiety and if these become too great, normal growth may be temporarily or permanently halted. In other words, the person may become fixated on one of the early stages of development because taking the next step is fraught with anxiety. The overly dependent child exemplifies defense by fixation; anxiety prevents him from learning how to become independent.

A closely related type of defense is that of regression. In this case, a person who encounters traumatic experiences retreats to an earlier stage of development. For example, a child who is frightened by his first day at school may indulge in infantile behavior, such as weeping, sucking his thumb, hanging on to the teacher, or hiding in a corner. A young married woman who has difficulties with her husband may return to the security of her parents' home, or a man who has lost his job may seek comfort in drink. The path of regression is usually determined by the earlier fixations of the person. That is, a person tends to regress to a stage upon which he has been previously fixated. If he was overly dependent as a child, he will be likely to become overly dependent again when his anxiety increases to an unbearable level.

Fixation and regression are ordinarily relative conditions; a person rarely fixates or regresses completely. Rather his personality tends to include infantilisms, that is, immature forms of behavior, and predispositions to display childish conduct when thwarted. Fixations and regressions are responsible for the unevenness in personality development.

STAGES OF DEVELOPMENT. Freud believed that the child passes through a series of dynamically differentiated stages during the first five years of life, following which for a period of five or six years—the period of latency—the dynamics become more or less stabilized. With the advent of adolescence, the dynamics erupt again and then gradually settle down as the adolescent moves into adulthood. For Freud, *the first few years of life are decisive for the formation of personality.*

Each stage of development during the first five years is defined in terms of the modes of reaction of a particular zone of the body. During the first stage, which lasts for about a year, the mouth is the principal region of dynamic activity. The *oral* stage is followed by the development of cathexes and anticathexes around the eliminative functions, and is called the *anal* stage. This lasts during the second year and is succeeded by the *phallic* stage in which the sex organs become the leading erogenous zones. These three stages, the oral, anal, and phallic, are called the pregenital stages. The child then goes into a prolonged latency period, the so-called quiet years dynamically speaking. During this period the impulses tend to be held in a state of repression. The dynamic resurgence of adolescence reactivates the pregenital impulses; if these are successfully displaced and sublimated by the ego, the person passes into the final stage of maturity, the *genital* stage.

The oral stage. The principal source of pleasure derived from the mouth is that of eating. Eating involves tactual stimulation of the lips and oral cavity, and swallowing or, if the food is unpleasant, spitting out. Later when the teeth erupt the mouth is used for biting and chewing. These two modes of oral activity, incorporation of food and biting, are the prototypes for many later character traits that develop. Pleasure derived from oral incorporation may be displaced to other modes of incorporation such as the pleasure gained from acquiring knowledge or possessions. A gullible person, for example, is one who is fixated on the oral incorporative level of personality; he will swallow almost anything he is told. Biting or oral aggression may be displaced in the form of sarcasm and argumentativeness. By displacements and sublimations of various kinds, as well as by defenses against the primitive oral impulses, these prototypic modes of oral functioning provide the basis for the development of a vast network of interests, attitudes, and character traits.

Furthermore, since the oral stage occurs at a time when the baby is almost completely dependent upon his mother for sustenance, when he is cradled and nursed by her and protected from discomfort, feelings of dependency arise during this period. These feelings of dependency tend to persist throughout life, in spite of later ego developments, and are apt to come to the fore whenever the person feels anxious and insecure. Freud believed that the most extreme symptom of dependency is the desire to return to the womb.

The anal stage. After the food has been digested, the residue accumulates in the lower end of the intestinal tract and is reflexly discharged when the pressure upon the anal sphincters reaches a certain level. The expulsion of the feces removes the source of discomfort and produces a feeling of relief. When toilet training is initiated, usually during the second year of life, the child has his first decisive experience with the external regulation of an instinctual impulse. He has to learn to postpone the pleasure that comes from relieving his anal tensions. Depending upon the particular method of toilet training used by the mother and her feelings concerning defecation, the consequences of this training may have far-reaching effects upon the formation of specific traits and values. If the mother is very strict and repressive in her methods, the child may hold back his feces and become constipated. If this mode of reaction generalizes to other ways of be-

having, the child will develop a retentive character. He will become obstinate and stingy. Or under the duress of repressive measures the child may vent his rage by expelling his feces at the most inappropriate times. This is the prototype for all kinds of expulsive traits—cruelty, wanton destructiveness, temper tantrums, and messy disorderliness, to mention only a few. On the other hand, if the mother is the type of person who pleads with her child to have a bowel movement and who praises him extravagantly when he does, the child will acquire the notion that the whole activity of producing feces is extremely important. This idea may be the basis for creativity and productivity. Innumerable other traits of character are said to have their roots laid down in the anal stage.

The phallic stage. During this stage of personality development sexual and aggressive feelings associated with the functioning of the genital organs come into focus. The pleasures of masturbation and the fantasy life of the child which accompanies autoerotic activity set the stage for the appearance of the *Oedipus complex.* Freud considered the identification of the Oedipus complex to be one of his greatest discoveries. The Oedipus complex is named for the king of Thebes who killed his father and married his mother.

Briefly defined, the Oedipus complex consists of a sexual cathexis for the parent of the opposite sex and a hostile cathexis for the parent of the same sex. The boy wants to possess his mother and remove his father, the girl wants to possess her father and displace her mother. These feelings express themselves in the child's fantasies during masturbation and in the alternation of loving and rebellious actions toward his parents. The behavior of the three- to five-year-old child is marked to a large extent by the operation of the Oedipus complex, and although it is modified and suffers repression after the age of five it remains a vital force in the personality throughout life. Attitudes toward the opposite sex and toward people in authority, for instance, are largely conditioned by the Oedipus complex.

The history and fate of the Oedipus complex differ for males and females. To begin with, both sexes love the mother because she satisfies their needs and resent the father because he is regarded as a rival for the mother's affections. These feelings persist in the boy but change in the girl. Let us consider first the sequence of events which characterize the development of the male Oedipus complex.

The boy's incestuous craving for the mother and his growing resentment toward the father bring him into conflict with his parents, espe-

cially the father. He imagines that his dominant rival is going to harm him, and his fears may actually be confirmed by threats from a resentful and punitive father. His fears concerning what the father may do to him center around harm to his genital organs because they are the source of his lustful feelings. He is afraid that his jealous father will remove the offending organs. Fear of castration or, as Freud called it, *castration anxiety* induces a repression of the sexual desire for the mother and hostility toward the father. It also helps to bring about an identification of the boy with his father. By identifying with the father, the boy also gains some vicarious satisfaction for his sexual impulses toward the mother. At the same time, his dangerous erotic feeling for the mother is converted into harmless tender affection for her. Lastly, the repression of the Oedipus complex causes the superego to undergo its final development. In Freud's words, the superego is the heir of the male Oedipus complex. It is the bulwark against incest and aggression.

The sequence of events in the development and dissolution of the female Oedipus complex is more involved. In the first place, she exchanges her original love object, the mother, for a new object, the father. Why this takes place depends upon the girl's reaction of disappointment when she discovers that a boy possesses a protruding sex organ, the penis, while she has only a cavity. Several important consequences follow from this traumatic discovery. In the first place, she holds her mother responsible for her castrated condition which weakens the cathexis for the mother. In the second place, she transfers her love to the father because he has the valued organ which she aspires to share with him. However, her love for the father and for other men as well is mixed with a feeling of envy because they possess something she lacks. Penis envy is the female counterpart of castration anxiety in the boy, and collectively they are called the *castration complex*. She imagines that she has lost something valuable, while the boy is afraid he is going to lose it. To some extent, the lack of a penis is compensated for when a woman has a baby, especially if it is a boy baby.

In the girl the castration complex initiates the Oedipus complex by weakening her cathexis for the mother and instituting a cathexis for the father. Unlike the boy's Oedipus complex which is repressed or otherwise changed by castration anxiety, the girl's Oedipus complex tends to persist although it undergoes some modification due to the realistic barriers that prevent her from gratifying her sexual desire for the father. But it does not fall under the strong repression that the

boy's does. These differences in the nature of the Oedipus and castration complexes are the basis for many psychological differences between the sexes.

Freud assumed that every person is inherently bisexual; each sex is attracted to members of the same sex as well as to members of the opposite sex. This is the constitutional basis for homosexuality, although in most people the homosexual impulses remain latent. This condition of bisexuality complicates the Oedipus complex by inducing sexual cathexes for the same sex parent. Consequently, the boy's feelings for his father and the girl's feelings for her mother are said to be ambivalent rather than univalent in character. The assumption of bisexuality has been supported by investigations on the endocrine glands which show rather conclusively that both male and female sex hormones are present in each sex.

The emergence and development of the Oedipus and castration complexes are the chief events of the phallic period, and leave a host of deposits in the personality.

The genital stage. The cathexes of the pregenital periods are narcissistic in character. This means that the individual obtains gratification from the stimulation and manipulation of his own body and other people are cathected only because they help to provide additional forms of body pleasure to the child. During adolescence, some of this self-love or narcissism becomes channeled into genuine object choices. The adolescent begins to love others for altruistic motives and not simply for selfish or narcissistic reasons. Sexual attraction, socialization, group activities, vocational planning, and preparations for marrying and raising a family begin to manifest themselves. By the end of adolescence, these socialized, altruistic cathexes have become fairly well stabilized in the form of habitual displacements, sublimations, and identifications. The person becomes transformed from a pleasure-seeking, narcissistic infant into a reality-oriented, socialized adult. However, it should not be thought that the pregenital impulses are displaced by genital ones. Rather, the cathexes of the oral, anal, and phallic stages become fused and synthesized with the genital impulses. The principal biological function of the genital stage is that of reproduction; the psychological aspects help to achieve this end by providing a certain measure of stability and security.

In spite of the fact that Freud differentiated four stages of personality growth, he did not assume that there were any sharp breaks or abrupt transitions in passing out of one stage into another. The final organization of personality represents contributions from all four stages.

CHARACTERISTIC RESEARCH AND RESEARCH METHODS

The empirical data upon which Freud based his theories consisted principally of the verbalizations and expressive behavior of patients undergoing psychological treatment. Although Freud was schooled in the precise methods of nineteenth century science and had established a substantial reputation as a medical investigator before turning his attention to psychology, he did not employ experimental or controlled observational techniques in his investigations of the human mind. Freud was not a part of the movement of experimental psychology which had been initiated by Fechner in 1860 and developed into a science by Wundt during the following two decades. He was, of course, familiar with this movement and Fechner's philosophy influenced him, but Freud was not an experimental psychologist. He did not perform controlled psychological experiments, nor did he collect data and analyze them quantitatively as other psychologists of the nineteenth century were doing. One looks in vain for a table or graph in his extensive writings. Nor did Freud ever employ a diagnostic test or any other kind of objective appraisal of personality. His theories germinated as he listened to the facts and fancies verbalized by sick personalities.

Yet it would be a serious mistake to say that the verbalizations of people in treatment were the only ingredients out of which Freud fashioned his theories. Certainly as important as these raw data was the rigorously critical attitude that Freud brought to the analysis of his patients' free associations. Today we would say that he analyzed his raw material by the method of internal consistency. Inferences made from one part of the material were checked against evidence appearing in other parts, so that the final conclusions drawn from a case were based upon an interlocking network of facts and inferences. Freud proceeded in his work in much the same way as a detective assembling evidence or a lawyer summing up a case to the jury. Everything had to fit together coherently before Freud was satisfied that he had put his finger upon the correct interpretation. It should be remembered, moreover, that the material produced by one case who was seen five hours a week for as long as two or three years was of immense proportions, and that Freud had ample opportunity to check and recheck his hunches scores of times before deciding upon the final interpretation. By contrast, the subject in the typical psychological experiment performed under controlled conditions is observed or tested for only one or two hours on the average. Certainly two of Freud's most important contributions to research strategy were the intensive study of the single case and the use of the method of internal consistency for testing hypotheses.

Again and again Freud was forced to revise his theories because new discoveries could not be accounted for adequately by his current theories. Freud was reluctant to abandon a systematic position, once it had been formulated, but the history of the psychoanalytic theory of personality from its inception in the 1890's down to the late 1920's demonstrates quite conclusively that Freud's views were determined eventually by the weight of the evidence *as he saw it*. Although his close associates may have had some influence in shaping his ideas, it seems to be reasonably clear that the ultimate test of the validity of his theories was largely that of Freud's own self-criticism and his willingness to be guided by new evidence. The storm of indignant attacks upon psychoanalysis that began as soon as Freud had enunciated his theory of the sexual etiology of hysteria and which continued for the rest of his life did not influence his thinking. There were few times in life when he replied to his critics. Nor did the disaffection of some of his closest associates cause Freud to alter his theories. Freud seems to have been endowed with an abundance of intellectual autonomy, which is without doubt one of the prerequisites for greatness.

FREUD'S SCIENTIFIC CREDO. Freud's views on the way in which the scientist works to develop his science are succinctly set forth in one of his rare pronouncements on this topic. He writes:

The view is often defended that sciences should be built up on clear and sharply defined basal concepts. In actual fact no science, not even the most exact, begins with such definitions. The true beginning of scientific activity consists rather in describing phenomena and then in proceeding to group, classify and correlate them. Even at the stage of description it is not possible to avoid applying certain abstract ideas to the material in hand, ideas derived from various sources and certainly not the fruit of the new experience only. Still more indispensable are such ideas—which will later become the basal concepts of the science—as the material is further elaborated. They must at first necessarily possess some measure of uncertainty; there can be no question of any clear delimitation of their content. So long as they remain in this condition, we come to an understanding about their meaning by repeated references to the material of observation, from which we seem to have deduced our abstract ideas, but which is in point of fact subject to them. Thus, strictly speaking, they are in the nature of conventions; although everything depends on their being chosen in no arbitrary manner, but determined by the important relations they have to the empirical material—

relations that we seem to divine before we can clearly recognize and demonstrate them. It is only after more searching investigation of the field in question that we are able to formulate with increased clarity the scientific concepts underlying it, and progressively so to modify these concepts that they become widely applicable and at the same time consistent logically. Then, indeed, it may be time to immure them in definitions. The progress of science, however, demands a certain elasticity even in these definitions. The science of physics furnishes an excellent illustration of the way in which even those 'basal concepts' that are firmly established in the form of definitions are constantly being altered in their content (1915, pp. 60–61).

By choice, then, Freud preferred the more open, informal type of inductive theory-building which stays reasonably close to the empirical supports upon which it rests to the more formal deductive type of theory which starts with sharply defined concepts and carefully phrased postulates and corollaries from which testable hypotheses are derived and subsequently tested. Moreover, as this quotation shows, Freud was fully aware of the importance of the "prepared mind" of the scientist in enabling him to make maximum use of his empirical data. These "abstract ideas" might come from various sources; in Freud's case, from wide reading in the classics and other literature, from his hobby of archeology, from his observations as the father of six children, from everyday experiences of all kinds, and most of all, perhaps, from his lifelong habit of self-analysis.

Let us turn now to a consideration of some of the special data-collecting techniques employed by Freud. They were used, of course, in the therapeutic situation because this is where Freud gathered his data.

FREE ASSOCIATION AND DREAM ANALYSIS. After a brief tryout of the method of hypnosis (1887–1889) which was then very much in vogue, especially in France, Freud learned about a new method which had been used successfully by his friend and colleague, Dr. Joseph Breuer, in the treatment of a case of hysteria. This method which Breuer called catharsis or the "talking cure" consisted of the patient relating the details of the first appearance of each of his symptoms, following which the symptoms disappeared. Out of this method, Freud gradually evolved his own unique free-association method which Ernest Jones has called "one of the two great deeds of Freud's scientific life," the other being Freud's self-analysis.

In essence, the free-association method requires the patient to say everything that comes into consciousness, no matter how ridiculous or inappropriate it may sound. Unlike the cathartic method, the free-association method does not stop with the origin of symptoms; it allows—indeed it demands—that the patient talk about everything and anything that occurs to him, without restraint and without any attempt to produce a logical, organized, meaningful discourse. The role of the therapist is, to a great extent, a passive one. He sits and listens, prods occasionally by asking questions when the verbal flow of the patient dries up, but he does not interrupt the patient when he is talking. In order to reduce the influence of external distractions to a minimum, the patient ordinarily reclines on a couch in a quiet room.

Freud observed that when these conditions prevail, the patient eventually begins to talk about memories of early childhood experiences. These memories provided Freud with his first real insight into the formation of the personality structure and its subsequent development. This method of reconstructing the past from current verbalizations may be contrasted with the developmental method of observing the growth of personality from infancy to adulthood.

Perhaps Freud's most original insight about the undisciplined wanderings of his patients' verbalizations was that each statement is associated in some meaningful, dynamic manner with the preceding statement, so that a continuous chain of associations exist from first to last. Everything that the patient says is related, without exception, to what he has previously said. There may be numerous circumlocutions and verbal blockages, but eventually the history of the person's mind and its present organization will be divulged to the listener by following the chain of associations through the verbal maze.

The analysis of dreams is not a separate method from that of free association; it is a natural consequence of the instruction to the patient that he talk about everything that comes to his mind. Freud's early patients spontaneously recalled their dreams and then proceeded to give free associations to them. Freud soon realized that these reported dreams and the accompanying free associations were especially rich sources of information about the dynamics of human personality. As a result of this insight which he tested on his own dreams, Freud formulated the famous theory which states that the dream is an expression of the most primitive workings and contents of the human mind (1900). The primitive process which creates the dream Freud called the primary process. As we have seen, the primary process attempts to fulfill a wish or discharge a tension by inducing an image of the desired goal. By having his patients free-associate to their dreams, Freud was able to penetrate into the most inaccessible regions of the human mind and to discover the bedrock of personality.

FREUD'S CASE STUDIES. The vast amount of raw material from which Freud fashioned his theory of personality will never be known. The few case histories that Freud chose to publish represent only an infinitesimal fraction of the cases he treated. Professional ethics partially restrained Freud from presenting his cases to the world since there was always the danger that the identity of his patients might be guessed by a curious public.

Aside from the case histories appearing in *Studies in hysteria* (1895) which he wrote in collaboration with Breuer before psychoanalytic theory had taken definite shape in Freud's mind, he published only six accounts of cases. One of these, the so-called Schreber case (1911), was not a patient of Freud's. Freud based his analysis upon an autobiographical account of a case of paranoia written by Judge Daniel Schreber. Another case study concerned a phobia in a five-year-old boy, Little Hans (1909a), which was treated by the boy's father, himself a physician, under Freud's guidance and instructions. In the other four cases, Freud was the therapist. These are referred to as "Dora" (1905b), the "Rat Man" (1909b), the "Wolf Man" (1918), and a case of female homosexuality (1920b). Each of these cases was presented to bring out the salient features of one or more of Freud's theoretical concepts.

Dora was published, Freud says, in order to show how the analysis of dreams enables one to ferret out the hidden and repressed parts of the human mind and to demonstrate that hysterical symptoms are motivated by the sexual impulse. Following a fairly lengthy account of the background factors and the current clinical picture, Freud presents a detailed analysis of two of Dora's dreams. Much of the material consists of a verbatim account of Dora's free associations and Freud's interpretations, and gives a remarkably lucid picture of the exact manner in which dreams are interpreted. In this case history, as in the others, we see how Freud wove the patterned fabric of personality out of the tangled verbal threads of a suffering person, and we obtain glimpses of Freud's unusual talent for seeing relationships between widely disparate utterances. Operating on the assumption that everything that the person says or does is meaningful and fits into the total picture of the personality organization, Freud was a vigilant observer; the most commonplace statement or act was scrutinized for a deeper meaning.

Freud did not regard his talent for observation as being in any way unusual, as the following quotation indicates.

When I set myself the task of bringing to light what human beings keep hidden within them, not by the compelling power of hypnosis, but by observing what they say and what they show, I thought the task was a harder one than it really is. He that has eyes to see and ears to hear may convince himself that no mortal can keep a secret. If the lips are silent, he chatters with his finger tips; betrayal oozes out of him at every pore. And thus the task of making conscious the most hidden recesses of the mind is one which it is quite possible to accomplish (1905b, pp. 77–78).

Freud's remarkable ability to draw inferences of great significance from commonplace behavior is seen to best advantage in what is probably the most popular of all of his writings, *The psychopathology of everyday life* (1904). This book is replete with examples of the dynamic import of simple slips of the tongue, errors of memory, accidents, and mistakes of various kinds.

The case of Little Hans afforded Freud his first opportunity to verify his theory of infantile sexuality, which had been formulated on the basis of the adult memories, by observations made on a young child. Hans was afraid that a horse would bite him should he venture out in the street. From the careful notes kept by the boy's father, many of which are presented verbatim in the published account, Freud was able to show that this phobia was an expression of the two most important sexual complexes of early childhood: the Oedipus complex and the castration complex. The case of Little Hans exemplifies and corroborates the theory of infantile sexuality set forth by Freud in 1905.

In the case of the Rat Man, who suffered from the revolting obsession that his girl friend and his father would each be punished by having a potful of ravenous rodents fastened to their buttocks, Freud pieced together the involved dynamics and thought connections of an obsessional neurotic. Although the presentation is only fragmentary, this case clearly illustrates how Freud went about resolving the apparent contradictions, distortions, and absurdities in the disconnected ramblings of a sick personality, and made them into a logically coherent pattern. In reporting this case, Freud tells us that it is based upon notes made on the evening of the day of the treatment and not upon notes made during the analytic session. Freud was opposed to any note-taking by the therapist during the treatment period because he felt that the withdrawal of the therapist's attention would interfere with the progress of therapy. He believed in any event that the therapist would remember the important material and forget the trivial details.

Freud's analysis of the Schreber case was based upon Schreber's own account of his mental illness which was diagnosed as paranoia. Freud justified his use of this autobiographical book on the grounds that paranoia is a type of disorder in which the written case history is as satisfactory as personal acquaintance with the case. The characteristic symptom of paranoia is the tortuous delusional system which the patient constructs. Schreber's delusions consisted of thinking that he was the Redeemer and that he was being transformed into a woman. In an intricate analysis of these two delusions Freud showed that they were related, and that the motive power for both of them as well as for the other aspects of the case was that of latent homosexuality. In this case study, Freud set forth his famous hypothesis of the causal relationship between homosexuality and paranoia. Freud's penchant for deriving a generalization of far-reaching power from a mass of particular facts is beautifully portrayed in the Schreber case.

The Wolf Man is an account of an infantile neurosis which was brought to the surface during the analysis of a young man, and which was shown to be related dynamically to the present condition of the patient. Freud observed that the analysis of an experience which took place some fifteen years earlier has its advantages as well as its disadvantages when compared with the analysis of an event shortly after it occurs. The principal disadvantage is that of the unreliability of memory for early experiences. On the other hand, if one tries to analyze a very young child there is the drawback that he cannot express himself verbally. The Wolf Man is the adult counterpart of Little Hans and both approaches, the reconstructive and the genetic, are shown to be valuable sources of empirical evidence for the theories of psychoanalysis. The principal feature of this case history is a lengthy analysis of a dream of wolves which the patient remembered from his early childhood, and which was interpreted as being caused by the child's reaction to the *primal scene*, Freud's term for the child's observation or fantasy of seeing his parents engage in sexual intercourse.

The last case reported by Freud was one that he had to break off because the resistance of the patient to giving up her homosexuality was so strong that no progress could be made. Nevertheless, as the published case history shows, Freud was able to arrive at a complete understanding of the origin and development of homosexuality. Homosexuality in both sexes is due to two primary factors, an inherent bisexuality in all living things and a reversal of the Oedipus complex.

Instead of loving the father and identifying with the mother, this woman identified with the father and cathected the mother. In the case of male homosexuality, there would be an identification with the mother and a love for the father. This case also contains some of Freud's views on suicide, since the reason for the woman's coming to Freud in the first place was an attempt at self-destruction.

It is impossible to say with any assurance that these particular case histories which Freud chose to make public were the actual empirical sources for the theories that they exemplify, or whether they were merely convenient and clear-cut examples of theoretical formulations that had already taken shape in Freud's mind. It really does not make much difference whether the Schreber case, for example, was *the* case that revealed to Freud the dynamics of paranoia, or whether he had made the fundamental discovery on the basis of prior cases and merely applied them to this particular case. In any event, the type of material which Freud collected, the kind of techniques he employed, and the way in which he thought are revealed in these six case studies. Anyone who wishes to get close to the raw material with which Freud worked should read them.

One should not confuse these case histories with the application of psychoanalytic theory for the better understanding of literature and the arts or for the purposes of social criticism. Freud did not learn about sublimation from his study of the life of Leonardo da Vinci and he did not discover the Oedipus complex by reading Sophocles, Shakespeare, or Dostoevski. Nor did he fathom the basic irrationality of man's thinking by observing his religious or political behavior. The interpretation of a literary work or the analysis of a social institution using the insights of psychoanalytic theory may have helped to confirm the usefulness of the insights and even to validate their authenticity and universality, but the literary and artistic productions and the social institutions themselves did not constitute any part of Freud's empirical data.

FREUD'S SELF-ANALYSIS. The material dredged up from his own unconscious constituted an important source of empirical data for Freud. As related by Ernest Jones (1953), Freud began his own self-analysis in the summer of 1897 with the analysis of one of his dreams. From this searching self-scrutiny, Freud confirmed to his own satisfaction the theory of dreams and the theory of infantile sexuality. He found in his own personality those conflicts and contradictions and irrationalities that he had observed in his patients, and this experience perhaps more than any other convinced him of the essential correctness of his views. In fact, Freud was reluctant to accept the validity of any hypothesis until he had tested it out on himself. Freud continued his self-analysis throughout his life, reserving the last half hour of each day for this activity.

CURRENT STATUS AND EVALUATION

During Freud's lifetime, he was the master builder of psychoanalytic theory. He alone laid down the course of its development and assumed sole responsibility for its major revisions. If any of his disciples advanced theories of their own that deviated significantly from the main lines of Freud's thinking, they were banished from the official psychoanalytic family. A follower of orthodox psychoanalysis might contribute new ideas but they had to meet with Freud's approval and fall within the framework of his theory. Freud jealously guarded his most cherished achievement against assault from others.

Upon the death of Freud, his followers were faced with the difficult task of deciding what should be done regarding the future development of psychoanalytic theory. The course they chose as evidenced by their theoretical writings has been to amplify the undeveloped aspects of Freud's system, to make more explicit some of Freud's postulates, to sharpen the definitions of some of the basic concepts, to extend the range of phenomena covered by psychoanalytic explanations, and to employ other observational methods than that of the psychoanalytic interview to validate propositions derived from Freudian theory. In much of the recent literature contributed by psychoanalytic thinkers, the opening paragraphs are devoted to a presentation of what Freud has to say concerning the topic under consideration, which is then followed by the writer's amplification of the topic. Freud's writings are referred to as the primary authority, and quotations from them are sprinkled liberally throughout to justify the various points made by the writer. In spite of this strong allegiance to Freud on the part of his followers, and their understandable tendency to treat his published works as sacred writings, some new trends can be detected in the literature of psychoanalysis which has appeared during the last twenty years. We shall discuss five of these trends, They are (1) the elaboration of the ego as a more or less autonomous system of personality, (2) a greater emphasis upon noninstinctual determinants of personality, (3) observational studies of babies and children, (4) the experimental testing of psychoanalytic propositions, and (5) an increasing rapprochement of psychoanalysis and psychology.

Although Freud regarded the ego as the executive of the total personality, at least in the case of the healthy person, he did not grant it an autonomous position; it always remained subservient to the wishes of the id. In what was to be his final pronouncement on psychoanalytic theory (1940) Freud reiterated what he had said so many times before, "This oldest portion [the id] of the mental apparatus remains the most important throughout life" (p. 14). The id and its instincts express "the true purpose of the individual organism's life." There is no question as to how Freud felt regarding the relationship of the ego and the id: the id is the dominant member of the partnership.

The new thinking among psychoanalytic theorists is to play up the role of the ego in the total personality (Coriat, 1940; Hartmann, 1945, 1950; Hartmann, Kris, and Loewenstein, 1947; Rapaport, 1951b; French, 1952). Not only have they dealt with such problems as the development of the reality principle in childhood, the integrative or synthetic function of the ego, the auxiliary ego processes of perceiving, remembering, thinking, and acting, and the defenses of the ego, but there has also been put forward the concept of the autonomy of the ego. Discussion of the autonomous functions of the ego usually begins by quoting from one of Freud's last articles in which he wrote, "But we must not overlook the fact that id and ego are originally one, and it does not imply a mystical over-valuation of heredity if we think it credible that, even before the ego exists, its subsequent lines of development, tendencies and reactions are already determined" (Freud, 1937, pp. 343–344). Proceeding from this quotation such prominent theorists as Hartmann, Kris, and Loewenstein (1947) postulate that there is an undifferentiated phase early in life during which both the id and the ego are formed. In other words, the ego does not emerge out of an inborn id but each system has its origin in inherited predispositions and each has its own independent course of development. Moreover, they assert that the ego processes are operated by neutralized sexual and aggressive energy and that the aims of these processes may be independent of purely instinctual objectives. From these assumptions, a new "ego psychology" has been evolved, a psychology in which the ego is depicted as being a rational institution responsible for intellectual and social achievements and one whose functioning is not solely dependent upon the wishes of the id. It has its own sources of energy, its own motives and interests, and its own objectives. Such an ego psychology appears to constitute a radical break with psychoanalytic tradition.

The point has been made again and again by various critics of psychoanalysis that Freud placed too much weight upon heredity and maturation and too little upon the socially acquired features of personality. Consequently, there has been a noticeable tendency among current theorists identified with the psychoanalytic tradition to play down the role of the instincts and to bring to the fore psychological and social variables which are thought to shape personality. One finds in the literature, for example, a preference for the term "drive" over that of "instinct." The concept of the death instincts, but not that of aggression, is either ignored or openly rejected as being an untenable assumption. There is less discussion of such topics as the "instincts and their vicissitudes" or the libido theory and more of how personality traits are acquired through experience and as a result of social conditioning. Although the neo-Freudians (see Chapter IV) have taken the lead in "debiologizing" psychoanalysis, this trend is also noticeable in the writings of orthodox Freudians, especially those who favor an ego psychology.

In an influential paper on the genetic approach in psychoanalysis, Hartmann and Kris (1945) point out that Freud's thinking about the development of personality was conditioned primarily by the evolutionary doctrine and that consequently he was inclined to explain development in terms of the evolution of man. These writers believe that personality development can be explained more effectively in terms of the individual's life history. Furthermore, they feel such explanations are more amenable to empirical testing. Previously the empirical testing of genetic propositions employed the method of reconstructing the early experiences of a person from his adult memories which are revived during psychoanalytic treatment. Hartmann and Kris advocate supplementing these data with direct observations of infants and children. A large number of developmental studies have been made in recent years by psychoanalytically trained investigators, many of which are reported in the annual volumes of *The psychoanalytic study of the child* (Anna Freud *et al.*, 1945–).

Related to the interest in direct observations of the growing child is the increasing use of other nonanalytical methods for testing propositions derived from psychoanalytic theory (Ezriel, Farrell, and Stengel, 1951; Isaacs, Rickman, and Thouless, 1951). This trend reflects the attitude of some psychoanalysts and many psychologists that psychoanalysis should not depend exclusively on data secured from patients undergoing treatment for verification of its hypotheses but should test its hypotheses in the laboratory and other settings where the variables can be manipulated or controlled. The experimental literature which owes its existence either directly or indirectly to the stimulus of psychoanalytic theory has been reviewed by Sears (1943, 1944), Hilgard (1952), Masserman (1952), Kubie (1952), and Blum (1953). Animals as well as human subjects have been used in these studies (Levy, 1952).

As we observed earlier, psychoanalysis as a body of psychological theory developed apart from the main lines of general psychology. In fact, there has been a noticeable inclination to regard psychoanalysis and psychology as separate sciences, a state of affairs which confuses the average person because he cannot easily comprehend the nature of the difference between them. This way of thinking has become less common in recent years and the current tendency is to consider psychoanalysis as much a part of psychology as any other behavior theory is. This does not imply that all or even the majority of psychologists have become convinced of the validity or usefulness of psychoanalytic theory. Many of them, in fact, reject it. But they are no longer likely to see it as a theory which is alien to psychology, and reject it on that basis. Freud, of course, always identified psychoanalysis with psychology; at no time did he think that he was creating a rival discipline.

The increasing compatibility of psychoanalysis and psychology has been forwarded by a number of factors (Hall and Lindzey, 1954). There have been prominent molders of professional opinion on both sides of the fence who have helped to bring about greater unity of viewpoint. Kurt Lewin, Henry Murray, Else Frenkel-Brunswik, David Rapaport, Nevitt Sanford, and Ernest Hilgard are some of the psychologists who have taken a deep interest in psychoanalytic theory and have themselves carried on extensive studies instigated by psychoanalytic theory. Rapaport in an extremely important article (1951a) has drawn up a conceptual model of psychoanalysis which is closely interwoven with a number of psychological concepts. The psychoanalysts Ernst Kris, Heinz Hartmann, Thomas French, David Levy, and Erik Erikson, to name only a few, have taken a friendly interest in psychology and have encouraged closer relationships between the two fields. Symposia which include both psychologists and psychoanalysts interested in examining the mutual relations between the two fields are helping to bring about greater unity of thought (Frenkel-Brunswik, Richfield, Scriven, and Skinner, 1954; Pumpian-Mindlin, 1952).

Another factor has been the extent to which representatives of each tradition have begun to deal with overlapping empirical problems. Psychologists have become increasingly concerned with motivation which has led them to consider the relevance of Freud's theory while psychoanalysts involved in elaborating an ego theory have been forced to recognize the significance of some traditional psychological processes. The emergence of clinical psychology during and following the Second World War awakened many psychologists to the utility of psychoanalytic theory. Called upon to function as diagnosticians and therapists, they found in Freud the kind of assumptions and conceptions which helped them to deal more effectively with their cases. It was almost inevitable that there should be a feedback from the clinic to the laboratory, especially in view of the fact that the individual psychologist often functions as both clinician and experimentalist. Then, too, the impact of psychoanalysis upon the whole stream of modern thought has had a bandwagon effect from which psychologists have not been able to remain immune. As Freud's reputation grows in the world at large, it is difficult for psychologists not to claim him as their own.

It would be incorrect, however, to conclude that psychology and psychoanalysis have found an area of understanding. Psychoanalysis, at least in the United States, still maintains closer ties with medicine than it does with psychology. It is very difficult to become a recognized psychoanalyst without first completing medical school, in spite of the fact that Freud felt it was unnecessary to hold a medical degree to practice psychoanalysis (1926a). Psychoanalysts and psychologists have their own professional organizations, and they rarely encounter one another professionally. Nor do their paths cross very frequently at the level of graduate training. All of these factors plus an undisclosed amount of mutual suspicion and hostility work to keep the two groups apart.

No other psychological theory has been subjected to such searching and often such bitter criticism as has psychoanalysis. From every side and on every conceivable score, Freud and his theory have been attacked, reviled, ridiculed, and slandered. The only comparable case in modern science, in which both the theory and the theorist have been so ardently vilified, is that of Charles Darwin whose evolutionary doctrine shocked Victorian England. Freud's chief offenses consisted of ascribing lustful and destructive wishes to the baby, attributing incestuous and homosexual urges to all human beings, and explaining man's behavior in terms of sexual motivation. "Decent" people were infuriated by Freud's view of man and called him a libertine and a pervert.

It is not our intention to review the half-century of criticism that has been leveled at psychoanalysis. Much of it was scarcely more than the sound and fury of overwrought people. A lot of the criticism has been outdated by subsequent developments in Freud's thinking. And a sizable portion of the criticism, it can be seen now, was based upon misinterpretations and distortions of psychoanalysis. Moreover, to review the criticisms of psychoanalysis in an adequate manner would require a book at least as large as the present one. Instead, we shall discuss several types of criticisms which have been leveled repeatedly at psychoanalysis and which are still widely discussed.

One type of criticism asserts that there are grave shortcomings in the empirical procedures by which Freud validated his hypotheses. It is pointed out that Freud made his observations under uncontrolled conditions. Freud acknowledged that he did not keep a verbatim record of what he and the patient said and did during the treatment hour, but that he worked from notes made several hours later. It is impossible to say how faithfully these notes reflected the events as they actually occurred but judging from experiments on the reliability of testimony it is not unlikely that distortions and omissions of various kinds crept into the record. Freud's assumption that the significant material would be remembered and the trivial incidents forgotten has never been proved and seems improbable.

Critics of Freud's methods have also objected to his accepting at face value what a patient said without attempting to corroborate it by some form of external evidence. They believe he should have secured evidence from relatives and acquaintances, documents, test data, and medical information. However, Freud maintained that what was important for understanding human behavior was a thorough knowledge of the unconscious which could only be obtained from free association and dream analysis.

Given then what was surely an incomplete record and more than likely an imperfect one, Freud proceeded to draw inferences and reach conclusions by a line of reasoning that was rarely made explicit. For the most part what we find in Freud's writings is the end result of his thinking—the conclusions without the original data upon which they were based, without an account of his methods of analysis, and without any systematic presentation, either qualitative or quantitative, of his empirical findings. The reader is asked to take on faith the validity of his inductive and deductive operations. Consequently, it is practically impossible to repeat any of Freud's investigations with any assurance that one is proceeding in accordance with the original design. This may help to explain why other investigators have reached quite different conclusions, and why there are so many interpretations of ostensibly the same phenomenon.

Freud eschewed any quantifying of his empirical data which makes it impossible to weigh the statistical significance and reliability of his observations. In how many cases, for example, did he find an association between paranoia and homosexuality, between hysteria and fixation on the oral stage, between a wish and a phobia, between the primal scene and adult instability? How many cases of a particular type did he study and from what classes and backgrounds did these cases come? What measures and criteria were used for assigning a case to a particular clinical category? Did Freud ever check his interpretations against those of another competent psychoanalyst in order to establish the reliability of his judgment? These and numerous other questions of a similar nature trouble the quantitatively oriented psychologist.

Freud's disinclination to follow the conventions of full scientific reporting of his data leaves the door open for many doubts regarding the scientific status of psychoanalysis. Did Freud read into his cases what he wanted to find there? Were his inferences guided more by his biases than by the material at hand? Did he select only that evidence which was in agreement with his hypotheses and disregard negative instances? Were the free associations of his patients really free or were they telling Freud what he wanted to hear? Did Freud rear an elaborate theory of personality which was alleged to hold for all people on inferences drawn from the verbal utterances of a relatively small number of atypical patients? How much solid evidence did Freud really have to support his grandiloquent speculations? What safeguards did he employ against the insidious influence of subjectivism? Questions of this kind have cast doubts upon the validity of psychoanalytic theory.

Lawrence Kubie, a prominent psychoanalyst, has summarized the limitations of psychoanalysis as a basic science in the following way.

> In general, they [the limitations] can be summarized by saying that the basic design of the process of analysis has essential scientific validity, but that the difficulties of recording and reproducing primary observations, the consequent difficulty in deriving the basic conceptual structure, the difficulties in examining with equal ease the circular relationship from unconscious to conscious and from conscious to unconscious, the difficul-

ties in appraising quantitatively the multiplicity of variables, and finally the difficulty of estimating those things which increase and those things which decrease the precision of its hypotheses and the validity of its predictions are among the basic scientific problems which remain to be solved (1953, pp. 143–144).

Another type of criticism attacks the theory itself, and says in effect that the theory is "bad" because many parts of it do not have and cannot be made to have empirical consequences. For example, it is impossible to derive any empirical propositions from the postulation of a death wish. This being so, the death wish "remains shrouded in metaphysical darkness" and has no meaning for science. Although one may use the death wish to "explain" certain phenomena, such as suicide or accidents, such after-the-fact explanations mean very little. It is like betting on a horse after the race has been run. A good theory, on the other hand, is one that enables its user to predict in advance what is going to happen. Some people may prefer to bring together and organize a mass of apparently unrelated data under the single heading of the death wish, but preferences of this sort merely indicate the interests of the systematizer and not the "truth" of the heading. Used in this way, the death wish is scarcely more than a slogan.

Freudian theory is markedly deficient in providing a set of relational rules by which one can arrive at any precise expectations of what will happen if certain events take place. What exactly is the nature of the relationship between traumatic experiences, guilt feelings, repression, symbol formation, and dreaming? What connects the formation of the superego with the Oedipus complex? These and a thousand other questions have still to be answered regarding the tangled web of concepts and assumptions that Freud conjured up.

The theory stands silent on the knotty problem of how the interplay of cathexes and anticathexes are to be measured quantitatively. In fact, there is no specification of how one is to go about estimating, even in the roughest terms, differences in quantity. How intense does an experience have to be before it is traumatic? How weak must the ego be before it can be overridden by an instinctual impulse? In what ways do the various quantities interact with one another to produce a given result? And yet everything depends in the final analysis upon just such specifications. Lacking them no laws can be derived.

If one concedes that psychoanalytic theory is guilty of at least two serious faults, first that it is a "bad" theory and second that it has not been substantiated by scientifically respectable procedures (and also

mindful of the fact that many other criticisms might have been cited),
the question then arises as to why psychoanalytic theory is taken
seriously by anybody, and why it was not relegated to oblivion long
ago. How are we to account for its dominant and influential status
in the world today?

The fact of the matter is that all theories of behavior are pretty
poor theories and all of them leave much to be desired in the way of
scientific proof. Psychology has a long way to go before it can be
called an exact science. Consequently, the psychologist must select
the theory he intends to follow for reasons other than those of formal
adequacy and factual evidence.

What does psychoanalytic theory have to offer? Some people like
the picturesque language which Freud uses to project his ideas. They
are attracted by the skillful way in which he employs literary and
mythological allusions to put across fairly abstruse notions and his
talent for turning a phrase or creating a figure of speech in order to
illuminate a difficult point for the reader. His writing has an exciting literary quality which is rare among scientists. The style is
matched by the excitement of the ideas. Many people find Freud's
concepts fascinating and sensational. Of course, sex is an alluring
topic and has a sensation value even when it is discussed in scientific
works (*vide* Kinsey!). Aggression and destructiveness are almost as
absorbing as sex. It is only natural, then, that people are attracted
by Freud's writings.

But a fine literary style and an exciting subject matter are not the
main reasons for the great esteem in which Freud is held. Rather it is
because his ideas are challenging, because his conception of man is
both broad and deep, and because his theory has relevance for our
times. Freud may not have been a rigorous scientist nor a first-rate
theoretician, but he was a patient, meticulous, penetrating observer
and a tenacious, disciplined, courageous, original thinker. Over and
above all of the other virtues of his theory stands this one—it tries to
envisage a full-bodied individual living partly in a world of reality
and partly in a world of make-believe, beset by conflicts and inner
contradictions, yet capable of rational thought and action, moved
by forces of which he has little knowledge and by aspirations which
are beyond his reach, by turn confused and clearheaded, frustrated
and satisfied, hopeful and despairing, selfish and altruistic; in short, a
complex human being. For many people, this picture of man has an
essential validity.

BIBLIOGRAPHY

PRIMARY SOURCES

Freud, S. *The standard edition of the complete psychological works.* J. Strachey (Ed.). London: Hogarth Press, 1953– .

Freud, S. The interpretation of dreams. In *Standard edition.* Vols. IV and V. London: Hogarth Press, 1953. (First German edition, 1900.)

Freud, S. The psychopathology of everyday life. In *The basic writings of Sigmund Freud.* New York: Random House, 1938. (First German edition, 1904.)

Freud, S. Three essays on sexuality. In *Standard edition.* Vol. VII. London: Hogarth Press, 1953. (First German edition, 1905a.)

Freud, S. *A general introduction to psychoanalysis.* Garden City, N. Y.: Garden City Publishing Co., 1943. (First German edition, 1917.)

Freud, S. Beyond the pleasure principle. In *Standard edition.* Vol. XVIII. London: Hogarth Press, 1955. (First German edition, 1920a.)

Freud, S. *Inhibitions, symptoms, and anxiety.* London: Hogarth Press, 1936. (First German edition, 1926b.)

Freud, S. *New introductory lectures on psycho-analysis.* New York: Norton, 1933. (First German edition, 1933.)

Freud, S. *An outline of psychoanalysis.* New York: Norton, 1949. (First German edition, 1940.)

REFERENCES

Blum, G. S. *Psychoanalytic theories of personality.* New York: McGraw, 1953.

Breuer, J., and Freud, S. Studies on hysteria. In *Standard edition.* Vol. II. London: Hogarth Press, 1955. (First German edition, 1895.)

Coriat, I. The structure of the ego. *Psychoanal. Quart.,* 1940, 9, 380–393.

Ezriel, H., Farrell, B. A., and Stengel, E. The scientific testing of psychoanalytic findings and theory. *Brit. J. med. Psychol.,* 1951, 24, 26–51.

Fenichel, O. *The psychoanalytic theory of neurosis.* New York: Norton, 1945.

French, T. M. *The integration of behavior.* Vol. I. *Basic postulates.* Chicago: Univ. of Chicago Press, 1952.

Frenkel-Brunswik, Else, Richfield, J., Scriven, M., and Skinner, B. F. Psychoanalysis and scientific method. *Sci. Mon.,* 1954, 79, 293–310.

Freud, Anna *et al.* (Eds.). *The psychoanalytic study of the child.* New York: International Universities Press, 1945– .

Freud, Anna. *The ego and the mechanisms of defence.* New York: International Universities Press, 1946.

Freud, S. *The standard edition of the complete psychological works.* J. Strachey (Ed.). London: Hogarth Press, 1953– .

Freud, S. The interpretation of dreams. In *Standard edition.* Vols. IV and V. London: Hogarth Press, 1953. (First German edition, 1900.)

Freud, S. Psychopathology of everyday life. In *The basic writings of Sigmund Freud.* New York: Random House, 1938. (First German edition, 1904.)

Freud, S. Three essays on sexuality. In *Standard edition*. Vol. VII. London: Hogarth Press, 1953. (First German edition, 1905a.)

Freud, S. Fragment of an analysis of a case of hysteria. In *Collected papers*. Vol. III. London: Hogarth Press, 1933, pp. 13–148. (First published in German, 1905b.)

Freud, S. "Civilized" sexual morality and modern nervousness. In *Collected papers*. Vol. II. London: Hogarth Press, 1924, pp. 76–99. (First published in German, 1908.)

Freud, S. Analysis of a phobia in a five-year-old boy. In *Collected papers*. Vol. III. London: Hogarth Press, 1933, pp. 149–295. (First published in German, 1909a.)

Freud, S. Notes upon a case of obsessional neurosis. In *Collected papers*. Vol. III. London: Hogarth Press, 1933, pp. 296–389. (First published in German, 1909b.)

Freud, S. *Leonardo Da Vinci: a study in psychosexuality*. New York: Random House, 1947. (First German edition, 1910a.)

Freud, S. Psychogenic visual disturbance according to psycho-analytical conceptions. In *Collected papers*. Vol. II. London: Hogarth Press, 1924, pp. 105–112. (First published in German, 1910b.)

Freud, S. Psycho-analytic notes upon an autobiographical account of a case of paranoia (dementia paranoides). In *Collected papers*. Vol. III. London: Hogarth Press, 1933, pp. 390–472. (First published in German, 1911.)

Freud, S. Instincts and their vicissitudes. In *Collected papers*. Vol. IV. London: Hogarth Press, 1925, pp. 60–83. (First published in German, 1915.)

Freud, S. *A general introduction to psychoanalysis*. Garden City, N. Y.: Garden City Publishing Co., 1943. (First German edition, 1917.)

Freud, S. From the history of an infantile neurosis. In *Collected papers*.. Vol. III. London: Hogarth Press, 1933, pp. 473–605. (First published in German, 1918.)

Freud, S. Beyond the pleasure principle. In *Standard edition*. Vol. XVIII. London: Hogarth Press, 1955. (First German edition, 1920a.)

Freud, S. The psychogenesis of a case of homosexuality in a woman. In *Collected papers*. Vol. II. London: Hogarth Press, 1933, pp. 202–231. (First published in German, 1920b.)

Freud, S. *The question of lay analysis*. New York: Norton, 1950. (First German edition, 1926a.)

Freud, S. *Inhibitions, symptoms and anxiety*. London: Hogarth Press, 1936. (First German edition, 1926b.)

Freud, S. *Civilization and its discontents*. London: Hogarth Press, 1930. (First German edition, 1930.)

Freud, S. *New introductory lectures on psycho-analysis*. New York: Norton, 1933. (First German edition, 1933.)

Freud, S. Analysis terminable and interminable. In *Collected papers*. Vol. V. London: Hogarth Press, 1950, pp. 316–357. (First published in German, 1937.)

Freud, S. *An outline of psychoanalysis*. New York: Norton, 1949. (First German edition, 1940.)

Hall, C. S. *A primer of Freudian psychology*. Cleveland: World Publishing Co., 1954.

Hall, C. S., and Lindzey, G. Psychoanalytic theory and its applications in the social sciences. In G. Lindzey (Ed.). *Handbook of social psychology.* Vol. I. Cambridge: Addison-Wesley, 1954, pp. 143–180.

Hartmann, H. The mutual influences in the development of ego and id. In Anna Freud *et al.* (Eds.). *The psychoanalytic study of the child.* Vol. 7. New York: International Universities Press, 1945, pp. 9–30.

Hartmann, H. Comments on the psychoanalytic theory of the ego. In Anna Freud *et al.* (Eds.). *The psychoanalytic study of the child.* Vol. 5. New York: International Universities Press, 1950, pp. 74–96.

Hartmann, H., and Kris, E. The genetic approach in psychoanalysis. In Anna Freud *et al.* (Eds.). *The psychoanalytic study of the child.* Vol. I. New York: International Universities Press, 1945, pp. 11–30.

Hartmann, H., Kris, E., and Loewenstein, R. M. Comments on the formation of psychic structure. In Anna Freud *et al.* (Eds.). *The psychoanalytic study of the child.* Vol. 2. New York: International Universities Press, 1947, pp. 11–38.

Hilgard, E. R. Experimental approaches to psychoanalysis. In E. Pumpian-Mindlin (Ed.). *Psychoanalysis as science.* Stanford, Calif.: Stanford Univ. Press, 1952, pp. 3–45.

Isaacs, N., Rickman, J., and Thouless, R. H. Methodology and research in psychopathology. *Brit. J. med. Psychol.,* 1951, *24,* 1–25.

Jones, E. *The life and work of Sigmund Freud.* New York: Basic Books, Vol. 1, 1953; Vol. 2, 1955.

Kubie, L. S. Problems and techniques of psychoanalytic validation and progress. In E. Pumpian-Mindlin (Ed.). *Psychoanalysis as science.* Stanford, Calif.: Stanford Univ. Press, 1952, pp. 46–124.

Kubie, L. S. Psychoanalysis as a basic science. In F. Alexander and Helen Ross (Eds.). *20 years of psychoanalysis.* New York: Norton, 1953, pp. 120–154.

Levy, D. Animal psychology in its relation to psychiatry. In F. Alexander and Helen Ross (Eds.). *Dynamic psychiatry.* Chicago: Univ. of Chicago Press, 1952, pp. 483–507.

Masserman, J. H. Experimental approaches to psychoanalytic concepts. *Samiksa,* 1952, *6,* 243–261.

Pumpian-Mindlin, E. (Ed.). *Psychoanalysis as science.* Stanford, Calif.: Stanford Univ. Press, 1952.

Rapaport, D. The conceptual model of psychoanalysis. *J. Pers.,* 1951a, *20,* 56–81.

Rapaport, D. The autonomy of the ego. *Bull. Menninger Clin.,* 1951b, *15,* 113–123.

Sears, R. R. Survey of objective studies of psychoanalytic concepts. *Soc. Sci. Res. Council Bull.,* 1943, No. 51.

Sears, R. R. Experimental analyses of psychoanalytic phenomena. In J. McV. Hunt (Ed.). *Personality and the behavior disorders.* Vol. I. New York: Ronald Press, 1944, pp. 306–332.

3.

Jung's Analytic Theory

A strong personality like that possessed by Freud often attracts and then repels other strong personalities. Such is the history of Carl Jung's relationship to Freud and his ideas. Jung read Freud's *Interpretation of dreams* soon after it was published and proceeded to adduce proof for the validity of some of Freud's statements. In 1906 a regular correspondence began between Freud and Jung, and the following year Jung paid his first visit to Freud in Vienna. Their admiration for one another was very great, and Freud decided that Jung was to be his successor. When the International Psychoanalytic Association was founded in 1910, Jung became its first president, a position he held until 1914. In 1909, Freud and Jung traveled together to Clark University in Worcester, Massachusetts, both having been invited to deliver a series of lectures at the celebration of the twentieth year of the founding of the university. Three years later, however, the personal relationship between Freud and Jung began to cool until finally in early 1913 they terminated their personal correspondence, and a few months later their business correspondence. In April, 1914, Jung resigned his presidency of the association, and in August, 1914, he withdrew as a member. The break was then complete. Freud and Jung never saw one another again. (For accounts of Jung's association with Freud and the reasons for their breaking with one another see S. Freud, 1935, 1938; Jones, 1955; Jung, 1916; Weigert, 1942.)

Although the causes for the rupture in the once intimate relationship were complex and "overdetermined," involving as they did both personal and intellectual incompatibilities, one important reason was Jung's rejection of Freud's pansexualism. "The immediate reason was that Freud . . . identified his method with his sex theory, which I deemed to be inadmissable" (personal communication from Jung, 1954). Jung then proceeded to forge his own theory of psychoanalysis and his own method of psychotherapy, which became known as analytical psychology, the lines of which had been laid down before he met Freud and which he had been working on consistently during the period of his association with Freud (Jung, 1915).

Before discussing the salient and distinctive characteristics of Jung's viewpoint, let us briefly review some aspects of his life. Carl Gustav Jung was born in Kesswyl, a town on Lake Constance in the Canton of Thurgau, Switzerland, July 26, 1875, and grew up in Basel. His father was a pastor in the Swiss Reformed Church. Jung entered the University of Basel with the intention of becoming a classical philologist and if possible an archeologist, but a dream is supposed to have aroused his interest in the study of the natural sciences and thus incidentally in medicine. After obtaining his medical degree from the University of Basel he became an assistant in the Burghölzli Mental Hospital, Zurich, and the Psychiatric Clinic of Zurich and thus embarked upon a career in psychiatry. He assisted and later collaborated with Eugen Bleuler, the eminent psychiatrist who developed the concept of schizophrenia, and studied briefly with Pierre Janet, Charcot's pupil and successor in Paris. In 1909 he gave up his work at the Burghölzli and in 1913 his instructorship in psychiatry at the University of Zurich in order to devote full time to private practice, training, research, traveling, and writing. For many years he conducted a seminar in English for English-speaking students, and following his retirement from active teaching a training institute named for him was started in Zurich. In 1944 a chair of medical psychology was founded especially for Jung at the University of Basel, but poor health prevented him from occupying this professorship for more than a year. He lives in Zurich surrounded by his large family and continues to do research, write, and see a few patients. (Biographical material for Jung will be found in Current biography, 1943; Time, 1952, 1955; Frieda Fordham, 1953.)

Carl Jung is acknowledged to be one of the greatest living thinkers. For over a half century he has devoted himself with great energy and singularity of purpose to analyzing the far-flung and deep-lying processes of human personality. Now in his ninth decade of life, Jung is still actively engaged in research and writing. His writings are voluminous and the extent of his influence incalculable. He is known not only to psychologists and psychiatrists but to educated people in all walks of life. Many honors have been bestowed upon him, among them honorary degrees from Harvard University and Oxford University. He has often lectured in the United States and has many followers and admirers in this country. Next to Freud, Jung may well be considered the most outstanding modern psychologist.

Although Jung's theory of personality is usually identified as a psychoanalytic theory because of the emphasis that it places upon unconscious processes, it differs in some notable respects from Freud's theory of personality. Perhaps the most prominent and distinctive feature of Jung's view of man is that it combines teleology with causality. Man's behavior is conditioned not only by his individual and racial history (causality) but also by his aims and aspirations (teleology). Both the past as actuality and the future as potentiality guide one's present behavior. Jung's view of personality is prospective in the sense that it looks ahead to the person's future line of development and retrospective in the sense that it takes account of the past. To paraphrase Jung, "the person lives by aims as well as by causes." This insistence upon the role of destiny or purpose in human development sets Jung clearly apart from Freud. For Freud, there is only the endless repetition of instinctual themes until death intervenes. For Jung, there is constant and often creative development, the search for wholeness and completion, and the yearning for rebirth.

Jung's theory is also distinguished from all other approaches to personality by the strong emphasis that it places upon the racial and phylogenetic foundations of personality. Jung sees the individual personality as the product and container of its ancestral history. Modern man has been shaped and molded into his present form by the cumulative experiences of past generations extending far back into the dim and unknown origins of man as a separate species. The foundations of personality are archaic, primitive, innate, unconscious, and probably universal. Freud stresses the infantile origins of personality whereas Jung emphasizes the racial origins of personality. Man is born with many predispositions that have been bequeathed to him by his ancestors; these predispositions guide his conduct and determine in part what he will become conscious of and respond to in his own world of experience. In other words, there is a racially preformed and collective personality which reaches out selectively into the world of experience and is modified and elaborated by the experiences that it receives. An individual's personality is a resultant of inner forces acting upon and being acted upon by outer forces.

This great respect for man's racial past and the bearing that it has upon man today means that Jung, more than any other psychologist, has probed into man's history to learn what he can of the racial origins and evolution of personality. He has studied mythology, religion, ancient symbols and rituals, the customs and beliefs of primitive people, as well as dreams, visions, the symptoms of neurotics, and the hallucinations and delusions of psychotics, in his search for the roots and developments of human personality. His learning and erudition, both as to breadth of knowledge and depth of understanding, are probably unsurpassed among present-day psychologists.

THE STRUCTURE OF PERSONALITY

The total personality or psyche, as it is called by Jung, consists of a number of separate but interacting systems. The principal ones are the *ego,* the *personal unconscious* and its *complexes,* the *collective unconscious* and its *archetypes,* the *persona,* the *anima* or *animus,* and the *shadow.* In addition to these interdependent systems there are the *attitudes* of introversion and extraversion, and the *functions* of thinking, feeling, sensing, and intuiting. Finally, there is the *self* which is the fully developed and fully unified personality.

THE EGO. The ego is the conscious mind. It is made up of conscious perceptions, memories, thoughts, and feelings. The ego is responsible for one's feeling of identity and continuity, and from the viewpoint of the person himself it is regarded as being at the center of the personality.

THE PERSONAL UNCONSCIOUS. The personal unconscious is a region adjoining the ego. It consists of experiences that were once conscious but which have been repressed, suppressed, forgotten, or ignored and of experiences that were too weak in the first place to make a conscious impression upon the person. The contents of the personal unconscious, like those of Freud's preconscious material, are accessible to consciousness, and there is a great deal of two-way traffic between the personal unconscious and the ego.

Complexes. A complex is an organized group or constellation of feelings, thoughts, perceptions, and memories which exists in the personal unconscious. It has a nucleus which acts as a kind of magnet attracting to it or "constellating" various experiences.

Consider, for example, the *mother complex.* The nucleus is derived in part from racial experiences with mothers and in part from the child's experiences with his mother. Ideas, feelings, and memories relating to the mother are attracted to the nucleus and form a complex. The stronger the force emanating from the nucleus the more experiences it will pull to itself. Thus, someone whose personality is dominated by thoughts of his mother is said to have a strong mother complex. His thoughts, feelings, and actions will be guided by his conception of the mother, what she says and what she feels will mean a great deal to him, and her image will be uppermost in his mind. A complex may behave like an autonomous personality which has a mental life and a motor of its own (Jung, 1938, p. 14). It may seize control of the personality and utilize the psyche for its own ends, as Tolstoi is said to have been dominated by the idea of simplification and Hitler by the lust for power.

The nucleus and many of the associated elements are unconscious at any particular time, but any of the associations and even the nucleus itself may and often do become conscious.

THE COLLECTIVE UNCONSCIOUS. The concept of a collective or *transpersonal* unconscious is one of the most original and controversial features of Jung's personality theory. It is the most powerful and influential system of the psyche, and in pathological cases overshadows the ego and the personal unconscious.

The collective unconscious seems to be the storehouse of latent memory traces inherited from man's ancestral past, a past that includes not only the racial history of man as a separate species but his prehuman or animal ancestry as well. The collective unconscious is the psychic residue of man's evolutionary development, a residue that accumulates as a consequence of repeated experiences over many generations. It is almost entirely detached from anything personal in the life of an individual and it is seemingly universal. All human beings have more or less the same collective unconscious. Jung attributes the universality of the collective unconscious to the similarity of the structure of the brain in all races of men, and this similarity in turn is due to a common evolution.

Racial memories or representations are not inherited as such; rather we inherit the *possibility* of reviving experiences of past generations. They are predispositions which set us to react to the world in a selective fashion. These predispositions are projected on the world. For example, since human beings have always had mothers, every infant is born with the predisposition to perceive and react to a mother. The individually acquired knowledge of the mother is a fulfillment of an inherited potentiality that has been built into man's brain by the past experiences of the race. Just as man is born with the capacity for seeing the world in three dimensions and develops this capacity through experience and training, so man is born with many predispositions for thinking, feeling, and perceiving according to definite patterns and contents which become actualized through individualized experiences. Man is predisposed to be afraid of the dark or of snakes because it may be assumed primitive man encountered many dangers in the dark and was a victim of poisonous snakes. These latent fears may never develop in modern man unless they are strengthened by specific experiences, but nonetheless the tendency is there and makes one more susceptible to such experiences. Some ideas are easily formed, such as the idea of a Supreme Being, because the disposition has been firmly imprinted in the brain and needs very little reinforcement from individual experience to make it emerge into consciousness and influence behavior. These latent or potential memories depend upon inherent structures and pathways that have been engraved on the brain as a result of the cumulative experiences of mankind. To deny the inheritance of these primordial memories is to deny the evolution and inheritance of the brain.

The collective unconscious is the inherited, racial foundation of the whole structure of personality. Upon it are erected the ego, the personal unconscious, and all other individual acquisitions. What a person learns as a result of experiences is substantially influenced by the collective unconscious which exercises a guiding or selective influence over the behavior of the person from the very beginning of life. "The form of the world into which he is born is already inborn in him as a virtual image" (Jung, 1953a, p. 188). This virtual image becomes a concrete perception or idea by identifying itself with objects in the world that correspond to the image. One's experiences of the world are shaped to a large extent by the collective unconscious, although not completely so for otherwise there could be no variation and development.

The two unconscious regions of the mind, the personal and the collective, can be of immense service to man. "It [the unconscious] holds possibilities which are locked away from the conscious mind, for it has at its disposal all subliminal contents, all those things which have been forgotten or overlooked, as well as the wisdom and experience of uncounted centuries, which are laid down in its archetypal organs" (Jung, 1953a, p. 114). On the other hand, if the wisdom of the unconscious is ignored by the ego, the unconscious may disrupt the conscious rational processes by seizing hold of them and twisting them into distorted forms. Symptoms, phobias, delusions, and other irrationalities stem from neglected unconscious processes.

Archetypes. The structural components of the collective unconscious are called by various names: *archetypes, dominants, primordial images, imagos, mythological images,* and *behavior patterns.* An archetype is a universal thought form (idea) which contains a large element of emotion. This thought form creates images or visions that correspond in normal waking life to some aspect of the conscious situation. For example, the archetype of the mother produces an image of a mother figure which is then identified with the actual mother. In other words, the baby inherits a preformed conception of a generic mother which determines in part how the baby will perceive *his* mother. The baby's perception is also influenced by the nature of the mother and by the infant's experiences with her. Thus, the baby's experience is the joint product of an inner predisposition to perceive the world in a certain manner and the actual nature of that world. The two determinants usually fit together compatibly because the archetype itself is a product of racial experiences with the world, and these experiences are much the same as those that any individual living in any age and in any part of the world will have. That is to say, the nature of mothers—what they do—has remained pretty much the same throughout the history of the race, so that the mother archetype which the baby inherits is congruent with the actual mother with whom the baby interacts.

How does an archetype originate? It is a permanent deposit in the mind of an experience that has been constantly repeated for many generations. For instance, countless generations of men have seen the sun make its daily excursion from one horizon to the other. The repetition of this impressive experience eventually became fixed in the collective unconscious as an archetype of the sun-god, the powerful, dominating, light-giving, heavenly body that men deified and worshipped. Certain conceptions and images of a supreme deity are offshoots of the sun archetype.

In a similar manner, man has been exposed throughout his existence to innumerable instances of great natural forces—earthquakes, waterfalls, floods, hurricanes, lightning, forest fires, and so forth. Out of these experiences there has developed an archetype of energy, a predisposition to perceive and be fascinated by power and a desire to create and control power. The child's delight in firecrackers, the young person's preoccupation with "hot-rod" cars, and the adult's obsessive interest in releasing the hidden energies of atoms have their roots in the archetype of energy. Man is *driven* by this archetype to seek new sources of energies. Our present age of energy represents the ascendance of the energy archetype. That is, archetypes function as highly charged autonomous centers of energy that tend to produce in each generation the repetition and elaboration of these same experiences.

Archetypes are not necessarily isolated from one another in the collective unconscious. They interpenetrate and interfuse with one another. Thus, the archetype of the hero and the archetype of the wise old man may blend together to produce the conception of the "philosopher king," a person who is responded to and revered because he is both a hero leader and a wise seer. Sometimes, as seemed to be the case with Hitler, there is a fusion of the demon and hero archetypes so that one gets a satanic leader.

As we have already seen, the nucleus of a complex may be an archetype which draws experiences to it. The archetype can then penetrate into consciousness by way of these associated experiences. Myths, dreams, visions, rituals, neurotic and psychotic symptoms, and works of art contain a great deal of archetypal material, and constitute the best source of knowledge regarding archetypes. Jung and his associates have done a prodigious amount of work on archetypal representations in myths and dreams. (See, for example, Jung, 1954c; Jung and Kerenyi, 1949; Campbell, J., 1949; Neumann, E., 1954.)

There are presumed to be numerous archetypes in the collective unconscious. Some of the ones that have been identified are archetypes of birth, rebirth, death, power, magic, unity, the hero, the child, God, the demon, the old wise man, the earth mother, and the animal (Jung, 1954c, 1956).

Although all archetypes may be thought of as autonomous dynamic systems that can become relatively independent of the rest of the personality, some archetypes have evolved so far as to warrant their being treated as separate systems with the personality. These are the persona, the anima and animus, and the shadow.

THE PERSONA. The persona is a mask which is worn by the person in response to the demands of social convention and tradition and to his own inner archetypal needs. It is the role assigned to him by society, the part that society expects him to play in life. The purpose of the mask is to make a definite impression upon others and often, although not necessarily, conceals the real nature of the person. The persona is the *public* personality, those aspects which one displays to the world or which public opinion fastens on the individual as contrasted with the *private* personality which exists behind the social façade.

If the ego identifies with the persona, as it frequently does, the individual becomes more conscious of the part that he is playing than he is of his genuine feelings. He becomes alienated from himself and his whole personality takes on a flat or two-dimensional quality. He becomes a mere semblance of a man, a reflection of society instead of an autonomous human being.

The nucleus from which the persona develops is an archetype. This archetype, like all archetypes, originates out of the experiences of the race; in this case, the experiences consist of social interactions in which the assumption of a social role has served a useful purpose to man throughout his history as a social animal.

THE ANIMA AND THE ANIMUS. It is fairly well recognized and accepted that man is essentially a bisexual animal. On a physiological level, the male secretes both male and female sex hormones, as does the female. On the psychological level, masculine and feminine characteristics are found in both sexes. Homosexuality is just one of the conditions, but perhaps the most striking one, that has given rise to the conception of human bisexuality.

Jung ascribes the feminine side of man's personality and the masculine side of woman's personality to archetypes. The feminine archetype in man is called the *anima*, the masculine archetype in woman is called the *animus*. These archetypes, although they may be conditioned by the sex chromosomes and the sex glands, are the products of the racial experiences of man with woman and woman with man. In other words, by living with women throughout the ages man has become feminized; by living with man woman has become masculinized.

Not only do these archetypes cause each sex to manifest characteristics of the opposite sex but they also act as collective images which motivate each sex to respond to and understand members of the opposite sex. Man apprehends the nature of woman by virtue of his anima, and woman apprehends the nature of man by virtue of her animus. But the anima and animus may also lead to misunderstanding and discord if the archetypal image is projected without regard for the real character of the partner. That is, if a man tries to identify his idealized image of woman with an actual woman, and does not take into account sufficiently the discrepancies between the ideal and the real, he may suffer bitter disappointment when he realizes that the two are not identical. There has to be a compromise between the demands of the collective unconscious and the actualities of the external world in order for the person to be reasonably well adjusted.

THE SHADOW. The shadow archetype consists of the animal instincts which man inherited in his evolution from lower forms of life. Consequently, the shadow to begin with typifies the animal side of man's nature. As an archetype the shadow is responsible for man's conception of original sin; when it is projected outward it becomes the devil or an enemy.

The shadow archetype is also responsible for the appearance in consciousness and behavior of unpleasant and socially reprehensible thoughts, feelings, and actions. These then may either be hidden from public view by the persona or repressed into the personal unconscious. Thus the shadow-side of personality which owes its origin to an archetype permeates the private aspects of the ego and a large part of the contents of the personal unconscious as well.

The shadow with its vital and passionate animal instincts gives a full-bodied or three-dimensional quality to the personality. It helps to round out the whole person.

THE SELF. In his earlier writings Jung considered the self to be equivalent to the psyche or total personality. However, when he began to explore the racial foundations of personality and discovered the archetypes, he found one that represented man's striving for unity (Wilhelm and Jung, 1931). This archetype expresses itself through various symbols, the chief one being the *mandala* or magic circle. In his book *Psychology and alchemy* (1953b), Jung develops a psychology of totality based upon the mandala symbol. The main concept of this psychology of total unity is the *self*.

The self is the mid-point of personality, around which all of the other systems are constellated. It holds these systems together and provides the personality with unity, equilibrium, and stability.

> If we picture the conscious mind with the ego as its centre, as being opposed to the unconscious, and if we now add to our mental picture the process of assimilating the unconscious, we can think of this assimilation as a kind of approximation of conscious and unconscious, where the centre of the total personality no longer coincides with the ego, but with a point midway between the conscious and unconscious. This would be the point of a new equilibrium, a new centering of the total personality, a virtual centre which, on account of its focal position between conscious and unconscious, ensures for the personality a new and more solid foundation (Jung, 1953a, p. 219).

The self is life's goal, a goal that people constantly strive for but rarely reach. Like all archetypes, it motivates man's behavior and causes him to search for wholeness especially through the avenues provided by religion. True religious experiences are about as close to selfhood as most men will ever come, and the figures of Christ and Buddha are as highly differentiated expressions of the self archetype as one will find in the modern world. It is not surprising to learn that Jung discovered the self in his studies and observations of the religions of the Orient, in which the striving for unity and oneness with the world through various ritualistic practices such as Yoga is further advanced than in western religions.

Before a self can emerge it is necessary for the various components of the personality to become fully developed and individuated. For this reason, the archetype of the self does not become evident until the person has reached middle age. At this time, he begins to make a serious effort to change the center of personality from the conscious ego to one that is midway between consciousness and unconsciousness. This midway region is the province of the self.

The concept of the self is probably Jung's most important psychological discovery and represents the culmination of his intensive studies of archetypes.

THE ATTITUDES. Jung distinguishes two major attitudes or orientations of personality, the attitude of *extraversion* and the attitude of *introversion*. The extraverted attitude orients the person toward the external, objective world; the introverted attitude orients the person toward the inner, subjective world (1933a).

These two opposing attitudes are both present in the personality but ordinarily one of them is dominant and conscious while the other is subordinate and unconscious. If the ego is predominately extraverted in its relation to the world, the personal unconscious will be introverted.

THE FUNCTIONS. There are four fundamental psychological functions: *thinking, feeling, sensing,* and *intuiting.* Thinking is ideational and intellectual. By thinking man tries to comprehend the nature of the world and himself. Feeling is the value function; it is the value of things with reference to the subject. The feeling function gives man his subjective experiences of pleasure and pain, of anger, fear, sorrow, joy, and love. Sensing is the perceptual or reality function. It yields concrete facts or representations of the world. Intuition is perception by way of unconscious processes and subliminal contents. The intuitive man goes beyond facts, feelings, and ideas and constructs elaborate models of reality. Intuition enables one to get at the essence of reality (Jung, 1933a).

The nature of the four functions may be clarified by the following example. Suppose that a person is standing on the rim of the Grand Canyon of the Colorado river. If the feeling function predominates he will experience a sense of awe, grandeur, and breath-taking beauty. If he is controlled by the sensation function he will see the Canyon merely as it is or as a photograph might represent it. If the thinking function controls his ego he will try to understand the Canyon in terms of geological principles and theory. Finally, if the intuitive function prevails the spectator will tend to see the Grand Canyon as a mystery of nature possessing deep significance whose meaning is partially revealed or felt as a mystical experience.

That there are exactly four psychological functions is, Jung states, "a matter of empirical fact."

> But as the following consideration will show, a certain completeness is attained by these four. Sensation establishes what is actually given, thinking enables us to recognize its meaning, feeling tells us its value, and finally intuition points to the possibilities of the whence and whither that lie within the immediate facts. In this way we can orientate ourselves with respect to the immediate world as completely as when we locate a place geographically by latitude and longitude (Jung, 1933b, p. 107).

Thinking and feeling are called rational functions because they make use of reason, judgment, abstraction, and generalization. They enable man to look for lawfulness in the universe. Sensation and intuition are considered to be irrational functions because they are based upon the perception of the concrete, particular, and accidental.

Although a person has all four functions they are not necessarily equally well developed. Usually one of the four functions is more highly differentiated than the other three, and plays a predominant role in consciousness. This is called the *superior* function. One of the other three functions usually acts in an auxiliary capacity to the superior function. If the superior function is prevented from operating the auxiliary function automatically takes its place.

The least differentiated of the four functions is called the *inferior* function. It is repressed and unconscious. The inferior function expresses itself in dreams and fantasies. The inferior function also has an auxiliary function associated with it.

If the four functions are placed equidistant from each other on the circumference of a circle, the center of the circle represents the synthesis of the four fully differentiated functions. In such a synthesis there are no superior or inferior functions and no auxiliaries. They are all of equal strength in the personality. Such a synthesis can only occur when the self has become fully actualized. Since complete actualization of the self is impossible, the synthesis of the four functions represents an ideal goal towards which the personality strives.

INTERACTIONS AMONG THE SYSTEMS OF PERSONALITY. The various systems and the attitudes and functions that go to make up the total personality interact with each other in three different ways. One system may *compensate* for the weakness of another system, one system may *oppose* another system, or two or more systems may *unite* to form a synthesis.

Compensation may be illustrated by the interaction of the contrasting attitudes of extraversion and introversion. If extraversion is the dominant or superior attitude of the conscious ego, then the unconscious will compensate by developing the repressed attitude of introversion. This means that if the extraverted attitude is frustrated in some way, the unconscious inferior attitude of introversion will seize hold of the personality and exert itself. A period of intense extraverted behavior is ordinarily followed by a period of introverted behavior. Dreams are also compensatory so that the dreams of a predominantly extraverted person will have an introverted quality, and conversely, the dreams of an introvert will tend to be extraverted.

Compensation also occurs between functions. A person who stresses thinking and feeling in his conscious mind will be an intuitive, sensation type unconsciously. Likewise, the ego and the anima in a man and the ego and the animus in a woman bear a compensatory relationship to each other. The normal male ego is masculine while the anima is feminine and the normal female ego is feminine while the animus is masculine. In general, all of the contents of the conscious mind are compensated for by the contents of the unconscious mind. The principle of compensation provides for a kind of equilibrium or balance between contrasting elements which prevents the psyche from becoming neurotically unbalanced.

Virtually all personality theorists of whatever creed or persuasion assume that the personality contains polar tendencies that may come into conflict with one another. Jung is no exception. He believes that a psychological theory of personality must be founded on the principle of opposition or conflict because the tensions created by conflicting elements are the very essence of life itself. Without tension there would be no energy and consequently no personality.

Opposition exists everywhere in the personality; between the ego and the shadow, between the ego and the personal unconscious, between the persona and the anima or animus, between the persona and the personal unconscious, between the collective unconscious and the ego, and between the collective unconscious and the persona. Introversion opposes extraversion, thinking opposes feeling, and sensation opposes intuition. The ego is like a shuttlecock that is batted back and forth between the outer demands of society and the inner demands of the collective unconscious. As a result of this struggle a persona or mask develops. The persona then finds itself under attack from other archetypes in the collective unconscious. The woman in man, that is, the anima, invades the male's masculine nature and the animus chips away at the femininity of woman. The contest between the rational and irrational forces of the psyche never ceases. Conflict is a basic fact of life.

Must personality always be a house divided against itself? Jung believes not. Polar elements not only oppose one another, they also attract or seek one another. The situation is analogous to a husband and wife who quarrel with each other yet are held together by the very differences that provoke the disagreements. The union of opposites is accomplished by what Jung calls the *transcendent function* (see below). The operation of this function results in the synthesis of contrary systems to form a balanced, integrated personality. The center of this integrated personality is the *self*.

An example of interaction among the systems of personality. To illustrate the kinds of interactions that take place within the psyche, let us consider the relations between the anima and the other systems of personality. Jung says "the whole nature of man presupposes woman . . . his system is tuned in to woman from the start . . ." (Jung, 1953a, p. 188). The male infant, equipped with his archetype of woman, is instinctively attracted to the first woman he experiences, who is usually his mother. The establishing of a close relationship is nurtured, in turn, by the mother. However, as the child grows older these maternal bonds become restrictive and frustrating, if not actually dangerous to the child, so that the mother complex which has been formed in the ego is repressed into the personal unconscious.

At the same time that this development is taking place, feminine traits and attitudes which have been implanted in the ego by the anima are also repressed because they are alien to the role that society expects him to play as a male. In other words, his inborn femininity is repressed by a counterforce emanating from the persona and other archetypes.

As a result of these two acts of repression, the child's feelings for his mother and his femininity are driven from the ego into the personal unconscious. Thus, man's perception of women and his feelings and behavior toward them are directed by the combined forces of the personal and the collective unconscious.

The integrative task imposed upon the ego as a consequence of these vicissitudes of the mother archetype and the feminine archetype (the anima) is to find a woman who resembles the mother *imago* and who also fulfills the needs of his anima. If he chooses a woman who is at variance with either or both of these unconscious models, he is headed for trouble, because his conscious positive feelings for her will be disturbed by unconscious negative feelings. They will make him dissatisfied with her and he will blame her for various fancied faults and shortcomings without becoming aware of the real reasons for his discontent. If the transcendent function is operating smoothly it will unite all of his contradictory impulses and cause him to select a mate with whom he can be happy.

All of the important decisions in life require that due consideration be given unconscious as well as conscious factors if they are to be successful. Jung says that a great deal of maladjustment and unhappiness is due to a one-sided development of personality which ignores important facets of man's nature. These neglected facets create personality disturbances and irrational conduct.

For Jung, the personality is an exceedingly complex structure. Not only are there numerous components—the number of possible archetypes and complexes, for example, is legion—but the interactions between these components are intricate and involved. No other personality theorist has evolved such a rich and complex description of the structure of personality.

THE DYNAMICS OF PERSONALITY

Jung conceives of the personality or psyche as being a partially closed energy system. It is said to be incompletely closed because energy from outside sources must be added to the system, for example, by eating, and energy is subtracted from the system, for example, by performing muscular work. It is also possible for environmental stimuli to produce changes in the distribution of energy within the system. This happens, for instance, when a sudden change in the external world reorients our attention and perception. The fact that the personality dynamics are subject to influences and modifications from external sources means that the personality cannot achieve a state of perfect stabilization, as it might if it were a completely closed system. It can only become relatively stabilized (Jung, 1948, 1953a).

PSYCHIC ENERGY. The energy by which the work of the personality is performed is called *psychic energy*. Psychic energy is a manifestation of life energy which is the energy of the organism as a biological system. Psychic energy originates in the same manner as does all vital energy, namely, from the metabolic processes of the body. Jung's term for life energy is *libido* but he also uses libido interchangeably with psychic energy. Jung does not take a positive stand on the relation of psychic energy to physical energy but he believes that some kind of reciprocal action between the two is a tenable hypothesis.

Psychic energy is a hypothetical construct; it is not a concrete substance or phenomenon. Consequently it cannot be measured or sensed. Psychic energy finds concrete expression in the form of actual or potential forces. Wishing, willing, feeling, attending, and striving are examples of actual forces in the personality; dispositions, aptitudes, tendencies, inclinations, and attitudes are examples of potential forces.

Psychic values. The amount of psychic energy invested in an element of the personality is called the *value* of that element. Value is a measure of intensity. When we speak of placing a high value upon a particular idea or feeling, we mean that the idea or feeling exerts a considerable force in instigating and directing behavior. A person who values truth will expend a great deal of energy on the search for it. One who places great value upon power will be highly motivated to obtain power. Conversely, if something is of trivial value it will have little energy attached to it.

The absolute value of an idea or feeling cannot be determined, but its relative value can be. One simple although not necessarily accurate way of determining relative values is to ask a person whether he prefers one thing more than another. The order of his preferences can be taken as a rough measure of the relative strengths of his values. Or an experimental situation can be devised to test whether an individual will work harder for one incentive than for another. Observing someone closely for a period of time to see what he does yields quite a fair picture of his relative values. If he spends more time reading than he does playing cards, then it can be assumed that reading is more highly valued than card-playing.

The constellating power of a complex. Such observations and tests, useful though they may be for the determination of conscious values, do not shed much light upon the unconscious values. These have to be determined by evaluating the "constellating power of the nuclear element of a complex" (Jung, 1928). The constellating power of a complex consists of the number of groups of items that are brought into association by the nuclear element of the complex. Thus, if one has a strong patriotic complex it means that the nucleus, love of one's country, will produce constellations of experiences around it. One such constellation may consist of important events in the history of one's nation, while another may be a positive feeling towards national leaders and heroes. A very patriotic person is predisposed to fit any new experience into one of the constellations associated with patriotism.

What means are available for assessing the constellating power of a nuclear element? Jung discusses three methods; these are (1) direct observation plus analytical deductions, (2) complex indicators, and (3) the intensity of emotional expression.

Through observation and inference one can arrive at an estimate of the number of associations that are attached to a nuclear element. A person who has a strong mother complex will tend to introduce his mother or something associated with his mother into every conversation whether it is appropriate or not. He will prefer stories and movies in which mothers play a prominent role and he will make a great deal out of Mother's Day and other occasions on which he can honor his mother. He will tend to imitate his mother by adopting her preferences and interests, and he will be attracted to her friends and associates. And he will prefer older women to women his own age.

A complex does not always manifest itself publicly. It may appear in dreams or in some obscure form so that it is necessary to employ circumstantial evidence in order to discover the underlying significance of the experience. This is what is meant by analytical deduction.

A complex indicator is any disturbance of behavior which indicates the presence of a complex. It may be a slip of the tongue, for instance, when a man says "mother" when he intended to say "wife." It may be an unusual blockage of memory as happens when a person cannot remember the name of a friend because the name resembles that of his mother or something associated with his mother. Complex indicators also appear in the word association test.

Jung discovered the existence of complexes in 1903 by experiments using the word association test (Jung, 1918). This test, now so widely employed in the evaluation of personality (Levy, 1952; Rotter, 1951), consists of a standard list of words which are read one at a time to the person being tested. The subject is instructed to reply with the first word that enters his mind. If he takes an unusually long time to reply to a particular word, this indicates that the word is connected in some manner with a complex. Repetition of the stimulus word and an inability to respond at all are also complex indicators.

The intensity of one's emotional reaction to a situation is another measure of the strength of a complex. If the heart beats faster, the breathing becomes deeper, and the blood drains from the face, these are pretty good indications that a strong complex has been tapped. By combining physiological measures such as the pulse, respiration, and electrical changes in the conductivity of the skin with the word association test, it is possible to make a fairly accurate determination of the strength of a person's complexes.

THE PRINCIPLE OF EQUIVALENCE. Jung bases his view of psycho dynamics upon two fundamental principles, the principle of equivalence and that of entropy. The principle of equivalence states that if energy is expended in bringing about a certain condition, as for performing work, the amount expended will appear elsewhere in the system. Students of physics will recognize this principle as the first law of thermodynamics or the principle of the conservation of energy as propounded by Helmholtz. As applied to psychic functioning by Jung, the principle states that if a particular value weakens or disappears, the sum of energy represented by the value will not be lost from the psyche but will reappear in a new value. The lowering of one value inevitably means the raising of another value. For example, as the child's valuation of his family decreases, his interest in other people and things will increase. A person who loses his interest in a hobby will usually find that another one has taken its place. If a value is repressed, its energy can be used to create dreams or fantasies. It is possible, of course, for the energy lost from one value to be distributed among several other values.

In terms of the functioning of the total personality, the principle of equivalence states that if energy is removed from one system, for example the ego, it will appear in some other system, perhaps the persona. Or if more and more values are repressed into the shadow-side of personality, it will grow strong at the expense of the positive side of personality. Likewise, the de-energizing of the conscious ego is accompanied by the energizing of the unconscious. Energy is continuously flowing from one system of personality into other systems. These redistributions of energy constitute the dynamics of personality.

Of course, the principle of the conservation of energy cannot apply in any strict manner to a system like the psyche which is only partially closed. Energy is added to or subtracted from the psyche, and the rate at which it is added or subtracted can and probably does vary considerably. Consequently, the rise or fall of a value may be due not only to a transfer of energy from one part of the system to another but it may depend also upon the addition of energy from sources external to the psyche or by the subtraction of energy when muscular work is performed. One is invigorated mentally as well as physically after eating a meal or taking a rest, and one becomes mentally and physically tired after a period of work or exercise. It is these exchanges of energy between the psyche and the organism or the external world as well as the redistribution of energy within the psyche itself that are of great interest to Jung and to all dynamic psychologists.

THE PRINCIPLE OF ENTROPY. The principle of entropy or the second law of thermodynamics states, in effect, that when two bodies of different temperatures are placed in contact with one another heat will pass from the hotter to the colder body. Another example is that of the flow of water which is always in the direction of moving from a higher level to a lower level when a channel is available. The operation of the principle of entropy results in an equilibrium of forces. The warmer object loses thermal energy to the colder one until the two objects have the same temperature. At that point, the energy exchange stops and the two objects are said to be in thermal balance.

The principle of entropy as adapted by Jung to describe personality dynamics states that the distribution of energy in the psyche seeks an equilibrium or balance. Thus, to take the simplest case, if two values (energy intensities) are of unequal strength, energy will tend to pass from the stronger value into the weaker value until a balance is reached. However, since the psyche is not a closed system, energy may be added to or subtracted from either of the opposing values and upset the equilibrium. Although a permanent balance of forces in the personality can never be established, this is the ideal state towards which the distribution of energy always strives. This ideal state in which the total energy is evenly distributed throughout the various fully developed systems is the *self*. Consequently, when Jung asserts that self-actualization is the goal of psychic development he means among other things that the dynamics of personality move towards a perfect equilibrium of forces.

The directed flow of energy from a center of high potential to one of low potential is a fundamental principle governing the distribution of energy among the systems of personality. The operation of this principle means that a weak system attempts to improve its status at the expense of a strong system and in so doing creates tension in the personality. If the conscious ego, for example, is greatly overvalued relative to the unconscious, a great deal of tension will be generated in the personality by the attempt on the part of the energy to move from the conscious system into the unconscious. Likewise, the energy of the superior attitude, whether it be extraversion or introversion, tends to move in the direction of the inferior attitude. An overdeveloped extravert is under pressure to develop the introverted part of his nature. It is a general rule in Jungian psychology that any one-sided development of personality creates conflict, tension, and strain, and an even development of all the constituents of personality produces harmony, relaxation, and contentment.

However, as Jung points out, a state of perfect balance would be one in which no energy was being produced because the production of energy requires differences in potential between the various components of a system (1953a). A system runs down and stops when all parts of it are in even balance, or perfect entropy as it is called. Therefore, it is impossible for a living organism to reach complete entropy.

THE USE OF ENERGY. The total psychic energy available to the personality is used for two general purposes. Some of it is expended in performing work that is necessary for the maintenance of life and for the propagation of the species. These are the inborn, instinctive functions, as exemplified by hunger and sex. They operate according to natural biological laws. Any energy in excess of that needed by the instincts may be employed in cultural and spiritual activities. According to Jung, these activities constitute the more highly developed purposes of life. As the person becomes more efficient in satisfying his biological needs, more energy becomes available for the pursuit of cultural interests.

THE DEVELOPMENT OF PERSONALITY

The most salient feature of Jung's theory of personality, aside from his conception of the collective unconscious with its archetypes, is the emphasis that he places upon the forward-going character of personality development. Jung believes that man is constantly progressing or attempting to progress from a less complete stage of development to a more complete one. He also believes that mankind as a species is constantly evolving more differentiated forms of existence. "Every reduction, every digression from the course that has been laid down for the development of civilization does nothing more than turn the human being into a crippled animal" (Jung, 1916, p. 225).

What is the goal of development? Towards what end are man and mankind striving? The ultimate goal is summed up by the term *self-actualization*. Self-actualization means the fullest, most complete differentiation and harmonious blending of all aspects of man's total personality. It means that the psyche has evolved a new center, the *self*, which takes the place of the old center, the ego. All of evolution, as it manifests itself in psychic development, from the first primitive organisms down to the appearance of man, is a parade of progress. Progress did not stop with the creation of man; just as man represents an advance over all other species of animals, so does civilized man represent an improvement over primitive man. Even civilized man still has far to go before he will reach the end of his evolutionary journey. It is the future of man that Jung finds so interesting and challenging, and about which he has so much to say in his extensive writings (see especially Jung, 1954b).

CAUSALITY VERSUS TELEOLOGY. The idea of a goal that guides and directs man's destiny is essentially a teleological or finalistic explanation. The teleological viewpoint explains the present in terms of the future. According to this viewpoint, man's personality is comprehended in terms of where it is going, not where it has been. On the other hand, the present may be explained by the past. This is the viewpoint of causality which holds that present events are the consequences or effects of antecedent conditions or causes. One looks into man's past in order to account for his present behavior.

Jung maintains that both standpoints are necessary in psychology if a complete understanding of personality is sought (Jung, 1916, 1948). The present is not only determined by the past (causality) but it is also determined by the future (teleology). The psychologist in his quest for understanding has to be Janus-faced. With one face he looks into man's past, with the other he looks into man's future. The two views when combined yield a complete picture of man. "On the one side it [the mind] offers a picture of the precipitate of the past, and on the other side a picture of the germinating knowledge of all that is to come, in so far as the psyche creates its own future" (Jung, 1916, Chapter 13).

Jung admits that causality and teleology are merely arbitrary modes of thinking employed by the scientist for ordering and understanding natural phenomena. Causality and teleology are not themselves found in nature. Jung points out that a purely causal attitude is likely to produce resignation and despair in man since from the standpoint of causality he is a prisoner of his past. He cannot undo what has already been done. The finalistic attitude, on the other hand, gives man a feeling of hope and something to live for. Jung's psychology is essentially an optimistic one.

HEREDITY. Heredity is assigned an important role in Jungian psychology. In the first place, it is responsible for the biological instincts which serve the purposes of self-preservation and reproduction. The instincts constitute the animal side of man's nature. They are the links with his animal past. An instinct is an inner impulsion to act in a certain manner when a particular tissue condition arises. Hunger, for example, evokes food-seeking activities and eating. Jung's views on instincts are no different from those held by modern biology.

However, Jung deviates sharply from the position of modern biology when he asserts that there is, in addition to an inheritance of biological instincts, an inheritance of ancestral "experiences." These experiences, or to speak with greater accuracy, the potentiality of having the same order of experiences as one's ancestors, are inherited in the form of *archetypes*. As we have already seen, an archetype is a racial memory that has become a part of man's heredity by being frequently and universally repeated over many generations. By accepting the notion of cultural inheritance Jung aligns himself with the doctrine of acquired characters, a doctrine whose validity has been questioned by most contemporary geneticists.

STAGES OF DEVELOPMENT. Jung does not specify in detail, as Freud does, the stages through which the personality passes from infancy to adulthood. In the very early years, libido is invested in activities that are necessary for survival. Before the age of five, sexual values begin to appear, and reach their height during adolescence. In one's youth and early adult years, the basic life instincts and vital processes are in ascendance. The young person is energetic, vigorous, impulsive, and passionate, and he is still to a great extent dependent upon others. This is the period of life when the person is learning a vocation, getting married and having children, and establishing himself in the life of the community.

When an individual reaches the late thirties or early forties a radical transvaluation occurs. Youthful interests and pursuits lose their value and are replaced by new interests which are more cultural and less biological. The middle-aged person becomes more introverted and less impulsive. Wisdom and sagacity take the place of physical and mental vigor. His values are sublimated in social, religious, civic, and philosophical symbols. He is transformed into a spiritual man.

This transition is the most decisive event in a person's life. It is also one of the most hazardous because if anything goes amiss during the transference of energy the personality may become permanently crippled. This happens, for example, when the cultural and spiritual values of middle age do not utilize all of the energy formerly invested in instinctual aims. In that case, the excess energy is free to upset the equilibrium of the psyche. Jung has had a great deal of success treating middle-aged people whose energies have failed to find satisfying outlets.

PROGRESSION AND REGRESSION. Development may follow either a progressive, forward movement or a regressive, backward movement. By progression, Jung means that the conscious ego is adjusting satisfactorily both to the demands of the external environment and to the needs of the unconscious. In normal progression, opposing forces are united in a co-ordinated and harmonious flow of psychical processes.

When the forward-going movement is interrupted by a frustrating circumstance, the libido is thereby prevented from being invested in extraverted or environment-oriented values. As a consequence, the libido makes a regression into the unconscious and invests itself in introverted values. That is, objective ego values are transformed into subjective values. Regression is the antithesis of progression.

However, Jung believes that a regressive displacement of energy does not necessarily have a permanently bad effect upon adjustment. In fact, it may help the ego find a way around the obstacle and move forward again. This is possible because the unconscious, both personal and collective, contains the knowledge and wisdom of the individual and racial past which have either been repressed or ignored. By performing a regression the ego may discover useful knowledge in the unconscious that will enable him to overcome the frustration. Man should pay particular attention to his dreams because they are revelations of unconscious material. In Jungian psychology, a dream is regarded as a signpost that points the way forward to a useful compensation for a frustrated condition.

The interaction of progression and regression in development may be exemplified by the following schematic example. A young man who has detached himself from dependence upon his parents meets an insurmountable barrier. He looks to his parents for advice and encouragement. He may not actually return to his parents in a physical sense, but rather his libido may make a regression into the unconscious and reactivate the parental imagos that are located there. These parental images may then provide him with the knowledge and encouragement that he needs to overcome the frustration.

THE INDIVIDUATION PROCESS. That personality has a tendency to develop in the direction of a stable unity is a central feature of Jung's psychology. Development is an unfolding of the original undifferentiated wholeness with which man is born. The ultimate goal of this unfolding is the realization of selfhood.

In order to realize this aim it is necessary for the various systems of personality to become completely differentiated and fully developed. For if any part of the personality is neglected, the neglected and less well-developed systems will act as centers of resistance which will try to capture energy from more fully developed systems. If too many resistances develop the person will become neurotic. This may happen when the archetypes are not allowed to express themselves through the medium of the conscious ego or when the wrappings of the persona become so thick that they smother the rest of the personality. A man who does not provide some satisfying outlet for his feminine impulses or a woman who stifles her masculine inclinations is storing up trouble because the anima or animus under these conditions will tend to find indirect and irrational ways of expressing themselves. In order to have a healthy, integrated personality, every system must be permitted to reach the fullest degree of differentiation and development. The process by which this is achieved is called the *individuation process.*

THE TRANSCENDENT FUNCTION. When diversity has been achieved by the operation of the individuation process, the differentiated systems are then integrated by the *transcendent function.*

This function is endowed with the capacity to unite all of the opposing trends of the several systems and to work toward the ideal goal of perfect wholeness (selfhood). The aim of the transcendent function is the revelation of the essential man and "the realization, in all of its aspects, of the personality originally hidden away in the embryonic germplasm; the production and unfolding of the original, potential wholeness" (Jung, 1953a, p. 108). Other forces in the personality, notably repression, may oppose the operation of the transcendent function, yet in spite of any opposition the forward, unifying propulsion of development will take place, if not at a conscious level then at an unconscious one. The unconscious expression of a desire for wholeness is found in dreams, myths, and other symbolic representations. One such symbol that is always cropping up in myths, dreams, architecture, religion, and the arts is the mandala symbol. Mandala is a Sanskrit word meaning circle. Jung has made exhaustive studies of the mandala because it is the perfect emblem of complete unity and wholeness in Eastern and Western religions (Jung, 1939, 1953b; Wilhelm and Jung, 1931).

SUBLIMATION AND REPRESSION. Psychic energy is displaceable. This means that it can be transferred from one process in a particular system to another process in the same or different system. This transference is made according to the basic dynamic principles of equivalence and entropy. If the displacement is governed by the individuation process and the transcendent function it is called *sublimation*. Sublimation describes the displacement of energy from the more primitive, instinctive, and less differentiated processes to higher cultural, spiritual, and more differentiated processes. For example, when energy is withdrawn from the sex drive and invested in religious values, the energy is said to have been sublimated. Its form has been changed in the sense that a new type of work is being performed; in this case, religious work replaces sexual work.

When the discharge of energy either through instinctual or sublimated channels is blocked, it is said to be *repressed*. Repressed energy cannot just disappear; it has to go somewhere according to the principle of the conservation of energy. Consequently, it takes up its residence in the unconscious. By adding energy to unconscious material, the unconscious may become more highly charged than the conscious ego. When this happens, energy from the unconscious will tend to flow into the ego, according to the principle of entropy, and disrupt the rational processes. In other words, highly energized unconscious processes will try to break through the repression, and if they succeed, the person will behave in an irrational and impulsive fashion.

Sublimation and repression are exactly opposite in character. Sublimation is progressive, repression is regressive. Sublimation causes the psyche to move forward, repression causes it to move backward. Sublimation serves rationality, repression produces irrationality. Sublimation is integrative, repression is disintegrative.

However, Jung asks us to bear in mind that since repression is regressive it may enable the person to find the answers to his problems in his unconscious and thus move forward again.

SYMBOLIZATION. A symbol in Jungian psychology has two major functions. On the one hand, it represents an attempt to satisfy an instinctual impulse which has been frustrated; on the other hand, it is an embodiment of archetypal material. The development of the dance as an art-form is an example of an attempt to satisfy symbolically a frustrated impulse such as the sex drive. A symbolic representation of an instinctual activity can never be entirely satisfying, however, because it does not attain the real object and discharge all of the libido. Dancing does not take the place completely of more direct forms of sexual expression; consequently, more adequate symbolizations of thwarted instincts are constantly being sought. Jung believes that the discovery of better symbols, that is, symbols that discharge more energy and reduce more tension, enables civilization to advance to higher and higher cultural levels.

However, a symbol also plays the role of a resistance to an impulse. As long as energy is being drained off by a symbol, it cannot be used for impulsive discharge. When one is dancing, for example, one is not engaging in a direct sexual activity. From this standpoint a symbol is the same as a sublimation. It is a transmutation of libido.

The capacity of a symbol to represent future lines of personality development, especially the striving for wholeness, plays a highly significant role in Jungian psychology. It represents a distinctive and original contribution to the theory of symbolism. Jung returns again and again to a discussion of symbolism in his writings and has made it the subject of some of his most important books (1916, 1917, 1925, 1928, 1933a, 1938, 1939, 1953b). The essence of Jung's theory of symbolism is found in this quotation: "For the significance of a symbol is not that it is a disguised indication of something that is generally known but that it is an endeavor to elucidate by analogy what is as yet completely unknown and only in the process of formation" (Jung, 1917, p. 468).

Symbols are representations of the psyche. They not only express the stored-up racial and individually acquired wisdom of mankind but they can also represent levels of development that are far ahead of man's present status. Man's destiny, the highest evolution of his psyche, is marked out for him by symbols. The knowledge contained in a symbol is not directly known to man; he must decipher the symbol in order to discover its important message.

The two aspects of a symbol, one retrospective and guided by the instincts, the other prospective and guided by the ultimate goals of mankind, are two sides of the same coin. A symbol may be analyzed from either side. The retrospective type of analysis exposes the instinctual basis of a symbol, the prospective type reveals the yearnings of mankind for completion, rebirth, harmony, purification, and the like. The former is a causal, reductive type of analysis, the latter a teleological, finalistic type of analysis. Both are necessary for a complete elucidation of the symbol. Jung believes that the prospective character of a symbol has been neglected in favor of the view that a symbol is solely a product of frustrated impulses.

The psychic intensity of a symbol is always greater than the value of the cause that produced the symbol. By this is meant that there is both a driving force and an attracting force behind the creation of a symbol. The push is provided by instinctual energy, the pull by transcendental goals. Neither one alone suffices to create a symbol. Consequently, the psychic intensity of a symbol is the combined product of causal and finalistic determiners and is therefore greater than the causal factor alone.

CHARACTERISTIC RESEARCH AND RESEARCH METHODS

Jung has one of the most far-reaching and penetrating minds in modern psychology. He finds his facts everywhere: in ancient myths and modern fairy tales; in primitive life and modern civilization; in the religions of the Eastern and Western worlds; in alchemy, astrology, mental telepathy, and clairvoyance; in the dreams and visions of normal people; in anthropology, history, literature, and the arts; and in clinical and experimental research. In scores of articles and books, he has set forth the empirical data upon which his theories are based. Jung insists that he is more interested in discovering facts than he is in formulating theories. "I have no system, I talk of facts" (personal communication to the authors, 1954).

Since it is completely impossible to review the vast amount of empirical material that Jung has brought together in his numerous writings, we will have to resign ourselves to the presentation of a minute portion of Jung's characteristic research.

EXPERIMENTAL STUDIES OF COMPLEXES. Jung's first studies to attract the attention of psychologists made use of the word association test in conjunction with physiological measures of emotion (Jung, 1918). In the word association test, a standard list of words is read to the subject one at a time and he is instructed to respond with the first word that comes to mind. The time taken to respond to each word is measured by a stop watch. In Jung's experiments, changes in breathing were measured by a pneumograph strapped to the chest of the subject and changes in the electrical conductivity of the skin by a psychogalvanometer attached to the palm of the hand. These two measures give additional evidence of emotional reactions that may appear to specific words in the list since it is well known that breathing and skin resistance are affected by emotion.

Jung utilized these measures to uncover complexes in patients. A long period of delay in responding to the stimulus word plus respiratory and skin resistance changes indicates that a complex has been touched off by the word. For example, if a person's breathing becomes irregular, his resistance to an electric current decreases because of sweating of the palms, and his response to the word "mother" is unusually delayed, these factors suggest the presence of a mother complex. If other words related to "mother" are reacted to in a similar manner, it substantiates the existence of such a complex.

Jung's method has become standard diagnostic practice in clinical psychology.

CASE STUDIES. The case study, as we have already observed in discussing Freud, is the principal method employed by psychoanalysts for uncovering unconscious material and for discovering the way in which the strands of personality are woven together. Jung, like Freud, is a master of the case study technique. Using free associations and dreams as his basic data, Jung has employed his highly developed creative and critical abilities to unravel a number of complex cases. It is unnecessary to review these cases here because they follow much the same pattern as Freud's. Jung, however, has made two signal contributions to the case study method. These are (1) the dream series method, and (2) the method of active imagination.

The dream series method. Freud, it will be recalled, analyzed dreams one at a time by having the patient free-associate to each successive component of the dream. Then, by using the dream material and the free associations, Freud arrived at an interpretation of the meaning of the dream. Jung, while not disavowing this approach, has developed another method for interpreting dreams. In place of a single dream, Jung utilizes a series of dreams obtained from a person.

> . . . they [the dreams] form a coherent series in the course of which the meaning gradually unfolds more or less of its own accord. The series is the context which the dreamer himself supplies. It is as if not one text but many lay before us, throwing light from all sides on the unknown terms, so that a reading of all the texts is sufficient to elucidate the difficult passages in each individual one. . . . Of course, the interpretation of each individual passage is bound to be largely conjecture, but the series as a whole gives us all the clues we need to correct any possible errors in the preceding passages (1953b, p. 12).

In psychology, this is called the method of internal consistency, and is widely employed with qualitative material like dreams, stories, and fantasies. The use that Jung has made of it is displayed to advantage in his book *Psychology and alchemy* (1953b) in which an extremely long dream series is analyzed.

The method of active imagination. In this method, the subject is required to concentrate his attention on an impressive but unintelligible dream image, or on a spontaneous visual image, and observe what happens to the image. The critical faculties must be suspended and the happenings observed and noted with absolute objectivity. When these conditions are faithfully observed, the image will usually undergo a series of changes which bring to light a mass of unconscious material. The following example is taken from Jung and Kerenyi's *Essays on a science of mythology*, p. 229:

> I saw a white bird with outstretched wings. It alighted on the figure of a woman, clad in blue, who sat there like an *antique statue*. The bird perched on her hand, and in it she had a *grain of wheat*. The bird took it in its beak and flew into the sky again.

Jung points out that drawing, painting, and modeling can be used for representing the flow of images. In the foregoing example, the person painted a picture to accompany the verbal description. In the picture, the woman was portrayed as having large breasts which suggested to Jung that the vision represented a mother figure.

The fantasies produced by active imagination usually have better form than do nocturnal dreams because they are received by a waking consciousness rather than a sleeping one.

COMPARATIVE STUDIES OF MYTHOLOGY, RELIGION, AND THE OCCULT SCIENCES. Since the evidence for archetypes is difficult to secure from contemporary sources alone, Jung has devoted a great deal of attention to researches in mythology, religion, alchemy, and astrology. His investigations have taken him into areas that few psychologists have explored and he has acquired a vast amount of knowledge of such abstruse and complex subjects as Hindu religion, Taoism, Yoga, Confucianism, the Christian Mass, astrology, psychical research, primitive mentality, and alchemy.

The most impressive example of Jung's attempt to document the existence of racial archetypes is found in his extremely erudite book, *Psychology and alchemy* (1953b). Jung believes that the rich symbolism of alchemy expresses many, if not all, of the archetypes of man. In *Psychology and alchemy* he examines an extensive dream series collected from a patient (not one of Jung's) against the intricate tapestry of alchemical symbolism, and concludes that the same basic features appear in both. It is a *tour de force* of symbolical analysis which has to be read in its entirety in order to be appreciated. The few examples that we will present are merely to give the reader some idea of Jung's method.

The clinical material consists of over a thousand dreams and visions obtained from a young man. The interpretation of a selection of these dreams and visions occupies the first half of the book. The rest of the book is taken up with a scholarly account of alchemy and its relation to religious symbolism.

In one dream a number of people are walking to the left around a square. The dreamer is not in the center but stands at one side. They say that a gibbon is to be reconstructed (p. 119). The square is a symbol of the work of the alchemist which consisted of breaking down the original chaotic unity of the primal material into four elements preparatory to their being recombined into a higher and more perfect unity. Perfect unity is represented by a circle or mandala which appears in this dream as walking around a square. The gibbon or ape stands for the mysterious transforming substance of alchemy, a substance that transforms base material into gold. This dream signifies, therefore, that the patient must displace his conscious ego from the center of his personality in order to permit the repressed atavistic urges to be transformed. The patient can only achieve inner harmony by integrating all of the elements of his personality just as the alchemist could only reach his goal (which he never did) by the proper mixing of basic elements. In another dream, a glass filled with a gelatinous mass stands on a table before the dreamer (p. 168). The glass corresponds to the alchemical apparatus used for distillation and the contents to the amorphous substance which the alchemist hopes to turn into the *lapis* or philosopher's stone. The alchemical symbols in this dream indicate that the dreamer is trying or hoping to transform himself into something better.

When the dreamer dreams of water it represents the regenerative power of the alchemist's *aqua vitae;* when he dreams of finding a blue flower the flower stands for the birthplace of the *filius philosophorum* (the hermaphroditic figure of alchemy); and when he dreams of throwing gold coins on the ground he is expressing his scorn for the alchemist's ideal. When the patient draws a wheel Jung sees a connection between it and the alchemist's wheel which stood for the circulating process within the chemical retort by which the transformation of material was supposed to take place. In a similar vein, Jung interprets a diamond that appears in the patient's dream as the coveted *lapis* and an egg as the chaotic *prima materia* with which the alchemist began his labors.

Throughout all the dreams of the series, as Jung demonstrates, there are strong parallels between the symbols employed by the dreamer to represent his problems and his goals and the symbols devised by medieval alchemists to represent their endeavors. The striking feature of the dream series is the more or less exact portrayal in them of the material aspects of alchemy. Jung is able to point to exact duplications of objects in the dreams and in the illustrations found in old alchemical texts. He concludes from this that the personality dynamics of the medieval alchemist as projected into his chemical investigations and those of the patient are precisely the same. This exact correspondence of the images proves the existence of universal archetypes. Moreover, Jung, who has carried on anthropological investigations in Africa and other parts of the world, finds the same archetypes expressed in the myths of primitive races. They are also expressed in religion and art, both modern and primitive. "The forms which the experience takes in each individual may be infinite in their variations, but, like the alchemical symbols, they are all variants of certain central types, and these occur universally" (Jung, 1953b, p. 463).

CURRENT STATUS AND EVALUATION

Jungian psychology has a number of devoted admirers and proponents throughout the world. Many of these are practicing psychoanalysts who use Jung's method of psychotherapy and who have accepted his fundamental postulates regarding personality. Some are theoreticians who have elaborated Jung's ideas. Among these are Gerhard Adler (1948), Michael Fordham (1947), Mary Harding (1947), Erich Neumann (1954, 1955), Herbert Read (1945), Jolande Jacobi (1951), and Frances Wickes (1948). Jung himself, although in the ninth decade of his life, is still actively engaged in writing and seeing a few patients. Jung also has powerful lay supporters like Paul Mellon of the Pittsburgh Mellons, who is president of the Bollingen Foundation (named for Jung's country residence on Lake Zurich). The Bollingen Foundation sponsors the publication of Jungian books through the Pantheon Press. The most ambitious project of the Bollingen Foundation to date is the translation and publication of Jung's collected works in English under the editorial supervision of Read, Fordham, and Adler.

Jung's influence outside of the fields of psychiatry and psychology has been considerable. Arnold Toynbee, the historian, acknowledges that he is indebted to Jung for opening up "a new dimension in the realm of life." Philip Wylie, the writer, is a great admirer of Jung, as are Lewis Mumford, the author and critic, and Paul Radin, the anthropologist. Perhaps Jung's greatest impact has been upon modern religious thought (Progoff, 1953). Jung was invited to give the Terry lectures at Yale University on *Psychology and religion* (1938). Jung was severely criticized for supporting Nazism although he and his followers vigorously deny the charges and claim that Jung has been misrepresented (Harms, 1946; *Saturday Review*, 1949).

Jung has been attacked by psychoanalysts of the Freudian school beginning with Freud himself. Glover (1950), the English psychoanalyst, has made what is probably the most comprehensive assault upon analytical psychology. He ridicules the concept of archetypes as being metaphysical and incapable of proof. He believes that archetypes can be fully accounted for in terms of experience and that it is absurd to postulate racial inheritance. Glover says that Jung has no developmental concepts by which to explain the growth of the mind. Glover's principal criticism, however, and one that he reiterates a number of times, is that Jung's psychology is a retreat back to an outmoded psychology of consciousness. He accuses Jung of tearing down the Freudian concept of the unconscious and erecting a conscious ego in its place. Glover does not pretend to be impartial or detached in his evaluation of Jungian psychology. (For another comparison of the views of Freud and Jung, see Gray, 1949b.)

What influence has Jung's theory of personality had upon the development of scientific psychology? Very little that one can directly perceive, except for the word association test and the concepts of introversion and extraversion. The word association test was not original with Jung. Galton is usually credited with the invention of the test, and it was introduced into experimental psychology by Wundt. Consequently, when Jung lectured on the word association method at Clark University in 1909 it did not sound strange and alien to the psychologists in his audience. Moreover, Jung's studies on word association employed a quantitative, experimental methodology that was bound to win favor with psychologists who prided themselves on being scientific. The use of the word association test is discussed in a number of recent surveys of clinical psychology and projective techniques (Bell, 1948; Levy, 1952; Rotter, 1951).

It is less easy to account for psychology's interest in Jung's typology.

A number of tests of introversion-extraversion have been constructed, and there is a large psychological literature on the subject. By and large, the results indicate that people do not fall into the two classes of introverts and extraverts but that both attitudes are present in varying proportions in virtually all people. (For a critical and understanding discussion of introversion-extraversion see Murphy, 1947, Chapter 25).

Analytical psychology has not been subjected to the searching criticism accorded Freudian psychoanalysis by psychologists. Nor has it found a substantial place in the standard histories of psychology. Boring in his *History of Experimental Psychology* devotes six pages to Freud and four *lines* to Jung. Peters in his revision and abridgement of Brett's *History of Psychology*, after giving a rather full discussion of Freud, devotes a page each to Adler and Jung. He finds Jung's later work to be so mysterious as to be almost undiscussable. Flugel's *A Hundred Years of Psychology* spends more time on Jung but most of it has to do with the word association test and typology. Murphy's *Historical Introduction to Modern Psychology* devotes six pages to Jung as compared to a chapter of twenty-four pages given over to Freud, and those six pages come in a chapter entitled "The Response to Freud."

Why has psychology ignored Jung's analytical psychology when the world at large accords him so much respect and honor? One major reason is that Jung's psychology is based upon clinical findings rather than upon experimental investigations. It has appealed to the tough-minded experimentalist no more than Freudianism. In fact, Jung has had far less appeal than Freud because there is so much discussion of occultism, mysticism, and religion in Jung's writings that it apparently repels many psychologists. [This criticism infuriates Jung. He insists that his interest in the occult sciences of alchemy and astrology and in religion does not imply, in any sense, an acceptance of these beliefs. They are studied and appear in his writings because they provide evidence for his theory. Whether God exists or not is not for Jung to say; that most people believe in God is as true a fact as that water runs downhill. "God is an obvious psychic and non-physical fact, i.e., a fact that can be established psychically but not physically" (1954d, p. 169).] Moreover, he accepts such out-of-fashion ideas as acquired characters and teleology. As a consequence, Jung's theories seem to have stimulated very little interest among psychologists and even less research.

The fact that Jung is thought of as a psychoanalyst has also contributed to the neglect of his system by psychology. When one thinks of psychoanalysis one usually thinks of Freud and only secondarily of Jung and Adler. Freud's olympian stature in psychoanalysis diverts attention away from other luminaries in the field. The publication of Jung's collected works in English could change the situation although the simultaneous publication of Freud's collected writings may cancel out the effect.

Although Jung has not had much direct influence upon psychology, it may be that some recent developments in psychology owe more to Jung than is realized. Indirect influences are hard to evaluate because ideas that come into circulation may be due either to the influence of one man or they may arise more or less spontaneously in the minds of a number of men at about the same time due to the prevailing intellectual climate. It cannot be denied that many of Jung's ideas are now in common circulation, whether he is responsible or not. Take, for example, the conception of self-actualization. It or similar concepts are found in the writings of Goldstein, Rogers, Angyal, Murphy, Allport, and Maslow, to name only those psychologists whose views are presented in this book. In no instance do we find Jung being credited with developing the conception. This in itself does not mean that Jung has had no influence, whether directly or indirectly, upon these men. They may have borrowed from Jung unconsciously, or borrowed from other men who were influenced by Jung. Or consider the idea of development as proceeding from a global to a differentiated to an integrated state, which one finds in both Jung and Murphy. Did Jung influence Murphy (the opposite is not tenable since Jung's views were enunciated before Murphy's) or did Jung influence someone else who did influence Murphy or is there no connection between the two men other than their being contemporary figures living in Western civilization? There is no evidence one way or the other. Is the optimism that characterizes many recent views of men, for example, Rogers and Allport, a reflection of Jung's optimism or a reflection of the times? Has Jung's emphasis upon goal-directed behavior set the stage for other purposive theories, or is purpose as a theoretical concept fashionable right now because nineteenth century science was so mechanistic? These are hard questions to answer and we cannot answer them.

We feel fairly sure that what Jungian theory needs at this point is to be tested by the methods of scientific psychology. We have in mind not the clinical type of study (Adler, 1949; Fordham, 1949; Hawkey, 1947; Kirsch, 1949) nor type studies (Gray, 1947, 1948, 1949b) but a more experimental approach as found in the work of Bash (1952).

Bash placed his subjects in a sleeplike state and compared their responses to one of the Rorschach plates (IX) with their responses under normal conditions. A number of reversals occurred. Bash regards these reversals under the two conditions as confirmation of Jung's theory of the compensatory relationship between the conscious mind and the unconscious mind. When and if more studies of this type are done the status of Jung's theories among psychologists will tend to improve because psychologists favor theories that generate testable hypotheses and instigate research. It will take a good deal of ingenuity to formulate testable propositions regarding the concept of archetypes but the effort may prove to be very worthwhile.

Meanwhile, Jung continues to give birth to highly original ideas. In one of his more recent publications (Jung and Pauli, 1955), Jung proposes an acausal principle which he calls *synchronicity*. This principle applies to events that occur together in time but which do not cause one another, as, for example, when a thought corresponds with an objective event. Nearly everyone has experienced such coincidences. One is thinking of a person and the person appears, or one dreams about the illness or death of a friend or relative and later hears that it has actually happened. Jung points to the vast literature on mental telepathy, clairvoyance, and other types of paranormal phenomena as evidence for the principle of synchronicity. He believes that many of these experiences cannot be explained as chance coincidences; rather they suggest that there is another kind of order in the universe in addition to that provided by the principle of causality. He applies this principle to the concept of archetypes and argues that an archetype can fulfill itself psychically within the person and express itself physically in the objective world. The archetype does not cause both events but rather each event parallels the other. There is an acausal correspondence between the two manifestations. This principle of synchronicity would appear to be an improvement upon the notion that a thought *causes* the materialization of the thing thought about.

When all is said and done, Jung's theory of personality as developed in his prolific writings and as applied to a wide range of human phenomena stands as one of the most remarkable achievements in modern thought. The originality and audacity of Jung's thinking have few parallels in recent scientific history, and no other man aside from Freud has opened up more conceptual windows into what Jung would choose to call "the soul of man." His ideas merit the closest attention from every serious student of psychology.

BIBLIOGRAPHY

PRIMARY SOURCES

Jung, C. G. *Collected works.* Editorial committee: Herbert Read, Michael Fordham, and Gerhard Adler. Translator: R. F. C. Hull. In 18 volumes. Published jointly in England by Routledge and Kegan Paul, and in the United States by Pantheon Press. The entire edition constitutes No. XX in the Bollingen Series. This edition will contain revised versions of earlier works by Jung, works not previously translated, and works originally written in English. The following volumes have appeared to date:

Volume 5. *Symbols of transformation.* 1956. (A revised edition of the *Psychology of the unconscious.*)
Volume 7. *Two essays on analytical psychology.* 1953a.
Volume 12. *Psychology and alchemy.* 1953b.
Volume 16. *The practice of psychotherapy.* 1954a.
Volume 17. *The development of personality.* 1954b.

Jung, C. G. *Collected papers on analytical psychology.* New York: Moffat, Yard, 1917.
Jung, C. G. *Contributions to analytical psychology.* New York: Harcourt, 1928.
Jung, C. G. *Psychological types.* New York: Harcourt, 1933a.
Jung, C. G. *Modern man in search of a soul.* New York: Harcourt, 1933b.
Jung, C. G. *Psychology and religion.* New Haven: Yale Univ. Press, 1938.
Jung, C. G. *The integration of personality.* New York: Farrar and Rinehart, 1939.
Jung, C. G. *Über psychische Energetik und das Wesen der Traume.* Zurich: Rascher, 1948.
Jung, C. G. *Von den Wurzeln des Bewusstseins.* Zurich: Rascher, 1954c.

REFERENCES

Adler, G. *Studies in analytical psychology.* New York: Norton, 1948.
Adler, G. A discussion on archetypes and internal objects. III. A contribution of clinical material. *Brit. J. med. Psychol.,* 1949, *22,* 16–22.
Bash, K. W. Zur experimentellen Grundlegung der Jungschen Traumanalyse. (On the laying of an experimental foundation of Jung's dream analysis.) *Schweiz. Z. Psychol. Anwend.,* 1952, *11,* 282–295.
Bell, J. E. *Projective techniques.* New York: Longmans, 1948.
Campbell, J. *The hero with a thousand faces.* New York: Pantheon Press, 1949.
Current Biography. Carl Gustav Jung. 1943, pp. 359–362.
Fordham, Frieda. *An introduction to Jung's psychology.* London: Penguin Books, 1953.
Fordham, M. S. M. *The life of childhood.* London: Kegan Paul, 1947.
Fordham, M. S. M. A discussion on archetypes and internal objects. I. On the reality of archetypes. *Brit. J. med. Psychol.,* 1949, *22,* 3–7.
Freud, S. *An autobiographical study.* London: Hogarth Press, 1935.

Freud, S.   The history of the psychoanalytic movement.   In A. A. Brill (Ed.). *The basic writings of Sigmund Freud.*   New York: Random House, 1938.

Glover, E.   *Freud or Jung.*   New York: Norton, 1950.

Gray, H.   Jung's psychological types; meaning and consistency of the questionnaire.   *J. gen. Psychol.,* 1947, *37,* 177–185.

Gray, H.   Jung's psychological types in men and women.   *Stanford med. Bull.,* 1948, *6,* 29–36.

Gray, H.   Jung's psychological types; ambiguous scores and their interpretation. *J. gen. Psychol.,* 1949a, *40,* 63–88.

Gray, H.   Freud and Jung: their contrasting psychological types.   *Psychoanal. Rev.,* 1949b, *36,* 22–44.

Harding, Mary E.   *Psychic energy, its source and goal.*   New York: Pantheon Press, 1947.

Harms, E.   Carl Gustav Jung—defender of Freud and the Jews.   *Psychiat. Quart.,* 1946, *20,* 199–230.

Hawkey, M. L.   The witch and the bogey; archetypes in the case study of a child. *Brit. J. med. Psychol.,* 1947, *21,* 12–29.

Jacobi, Jolande.   *The psychology of C. G. Jung.*   Revised edition.   New Haven: Yale Univ. Press, 1951.

Jones, E.   *The life and work of Sigmund Freud.*   Vol. 2.   New York: Basic Books, 1955.

Jung, C. G.   *The theory of psychoanalysis.*   New York: Nervous and Mental Disease Publishing Co., 1915.

Jung, C. G.   *Analytical psychology.*   New York: Moffat, Yard, 1916.

Jung, C. G.   *Collected papers on analytical psychology.*   New York: Moffat, Yard, 1917.

Jung, C. G.   *Studies in word-association.*   London: Heinemann, 1918.

Jung, C. G.   *Psychology of the unconscious.*   New York: Dodd, 1925.

Jung, C. G.   *Contributions to analytical psychology.*   New York: Harcourt, 1928.

Jung, C. G.   *Psychological types.*   New York: Harcourt, 1933a.

Jung, C. G.   *Modern man in search of a soul.*   New York: Harcourt, 1933b.

Jung, C. G.   *Psychology and religion.*   New Haven: Yale Univ. Press, 1938.

Jung, C. G.   *The integration of personality.*   New York: Farrar and Rinehart, 1939.

Jung, C. G.   *Über psychische Energetik und das Wesen der Traume.*   Zurich: Rascher, 1948.

Jung, C. G.   *Collected works.*   Vol. 7.   *Two essays on analytical psychology.* New York: Pantheon Press, 1953a.

Jung, C. G.   *Collected works.*   Vol. 12.   *Psychology and alchemy.*   New York: Pantheon Press, 1953b.

Jung, C. G.   *Collected works.*   Vol. 17.   *The development of personality.*   New York: Pantheon Press, 1954b.

Jung, C. G.   *Von den Wurzeln des Bewusstseins.*   Zurich: Rascher, 1954c.

Jung, C. G.   *Answer to Job.*   London: Routledge and Kegan Paul, 1954d.

Jung, C. G.   *Collected works.*   Vol. 5.   *Symbols of transformation.*   New York: Pantheon Press, 1956.

Jung, C. G., and Kerenyi, C.   *Essays on a science of mythology.*   New York: Pantheon Press, 1949.

Jung, C. G., and Pauli, W. *The interpretation of nature and the psyche.* New York: Pantheon Press, 1955.

Kirsch, J. The role of instinct in psychosomatic medicine. *Amer. J. Psychother.,* 1949, *3,* 253–260.

Levy, S. Sentence completion and word association tests. In D. Brower and L. E. Abt (Eds.). *Progress in clinical psychology.* Vol. 1. New York: Grune and Stratton, 1952, pp. 191–208.

Murphy, G. *Personality.* New York: Harper, 1947.

Neumann, E. *The origins and history of consciousness.* New York: Pantheon Press, 1954.

Neumann, E. *The great mother.* London: Routledge and Kegan Paul, 1955.

Progoff, I. *Jung's psychology and its social meaning.* New York: Julian, 1953.

Read, H. E. *Education through art.* New York: Pantheon Press, 1945.

Rotter, J. B. Word association and sentence completion methods. In H. H. Anderson and Gladys L. Anderson (Eds.). *An introduction to projective techniques.* New York: Prentice-Hall, 1951, pp. 279–311.

Saturday Review. Various writers. 1949, *32,* July 9, p. 25; July 16, pp. 21, 23; July 30, pp. 6–8; Sept. 10, p. 27; Oct. 15, pp. 23–25.

Time. Biographical sketch of Carl Gustav Jung. 1952, *60,* 37.

Time. The old wise man. 1955, *65,* 62–70.

Weigert, E. V. Dissent in the early history of psychoanalysis. *Psychiatry,* 1942, *5,* 349–359.

Wickes, Frances G. *The inner world of man.* New York: Holt, 1948.

Wilhelm, R., and Jung, C. G. *The secret of the golden flower.* New York: Harcourt, 1931.

4.

Social Psychological Theories: Adler, Fromm, Horney, and Sullivan

The psychoanalytic theories of personality formulated by Freud and Jung were nurtured by the same positivistic climate that shaped the course of nineteenth century physics and biology. Man was regarded primarily as a complex energy system which maintains itself by means of transactions with the external world. The ultimate purposes of these transactions are individual survival, propagation of the species, and an ongoing evolutionary development. The various psychological processes that constitute the personality serve these ends. According to the evolutionary doctrine some personalities are better fitted than others to perform these tasks. Consequently, the concept of variation and the distinction between adjustment and maladjustment conditioned the thinking of the early psychoanalysts. Even academic psychology was swept into the orbit of Darwinism and became preoccupied with the measurement of individual differences in abilities and with the adaptive or functional value of psychological processes.

At the same time, other intellectual trends which were at variance with a purely biophysical conception of man were beginning to take shape. During the later years of the nineteenth century, sociology and anthropology began to emerge as independent disciplines and their rapid growth during the present century has been phenomenal. While sociologists studied man living in a state of advanced civilization and found him to be a product of his class and caste, his institutions and folkways, anthropologists ventured into remote areas of the world where they found evidence that human beings are almost infinitely malleable. According to these new social sciences, man is chiefly a product of the society in which he lives. His personality is social rather than biological.

Gradually, these burgeoning social and cultural doctrines began to seep into psychology and psychoanalysis and to erode the nativistic and physicalistic foundations of these sciences. A number of followers of Freud who became dissatisfied with his myopia regarding the social conditioners of personality withdrew their allegiance from classical psychoanalysis and began to refashion psychoanalytic theory along lines dictated by the new orientation developed by the social sciences. Among those who provided psychoanalytic theory with the twentieth century look of social psychology are the four people whose ideas form the content of the present chapter—Alfred Adler, Karen Horney, Erich Fromm, and Harry Stack Sullivan. Of these four, Alfred Adler may be regarded as the ancestral figure of the "new social psychological look" because as early as 1911 he broke with Freud over the issue of sexuality, and proceeded to develop a theory in which social interest and a striving for superiority became two of its most substantial conceptual pillars. Later, Horney and Fromm took up the cudgels against the strong instinctivist orientation of psychoanalysis and insisted upon the relevance of social psychological variables for personality theory. Finally, Harry Stack Sullivan in his theory of interpersonal relations consolidated the position of a personality theory grounded in social processes. Although each of the theories has its own distinctive assumptions and concepts, there are numerous parallels among them which have been pointed out by various writers (James, 1947; Ruth Munroe, 1955; and H. L. and R. R. Ansbacher, 1956).

Our choice of the major figure for this chapter, Harry Stack Sullivan, is dictated primarily by our belief that he brought his ideas to a higher level of conceptualization and consequently has been a more pervasively influential theorist. Sullivan was considerably more independent of prevailing psychoanalytic doctrines; although he earlier used the Freudian framework, in his later work he developed a theoretical system which deviated markedly from the Freudian one. He was profoundly influenced by anthropology and social psychology. Both Horney and Fromm, on the other hand, kept well within the province of psychoanalysis in their thinking; Adler, although a separatist from the Freudian school, continued to show the impact of his early association with Freud throughout his life. Horney and Fromm are usually referred to as revisionists or neo-Freudians. Neither of them engaged in developing a new theory of personality; rather they regarded themselves as renovators and elaboraters of an old theory. Sullivan was much more of an innovator. He was a highly original thinker who attracted a large group of devoted disciples and developed what is sometimes called a new school of psychiatry.

ALFRED ADLER

Alfred Adler was born in Vienna in 1870 of a middle-class family and died in Aberdeen, Scotland, in 1937 while on a lecture tour. He received a medical degree in 1895 from the University of Vienna. At first he specialized in ophthalmology and then, after a period of practice in general medicine, he became a psychiatrist. He was one of the charter members of the Vienna Psychoanalytic Society and later its president. However, Adler soon began to develop ideas which were at variance with those of Freud and others in the Vienna Society, and when these differences became acute he was asked to present his views to the society. This he did in 1911 and as a consequence of the vehement criticism and denunciation of Adler's position by other members of the society, Adler resigned as president and a few months later terminated his connection with Freudian psychoanalysis (Colby, 1951; Jones, 1955; H. L. and R. R. Ansbacher, 1956).

He then formed his own group, which came to be known as Individual Psychology and which attracted followers throughout the world. During the First World War, Adler served as a physician in the Austrian army and after the war he became interested in child guidance and established the first guidance clinics in connection with the Viennese school system. He also inspired the establishment of an experimental school in Vienna which applied his theories of education.

In 1935 Adler settled in the United States where he continued his practice as a psychiatrist and served as Professor of Medical Psychology at the Long Island College of Medicine. Adler was a prolific writer and published a hundred books and articles during his lifetime. *The practice and theory of individual psychology* (1927) is probably the best introduction to Adler's theory of personality. Shorter digests of Adler's views appear in the *Psychologies of 1930* (1930) and in the *International Journal of Individual Psychology* (1935). Heinz and Rowena Ansbacher recently edited and annotated an extensive selection of passages from Adler's writings (1956) which is the best single source of information about Adler's Individual Psychology. Phyllis Bottome has written a book-length biography of Adler (1939). Adler's ideas are promulgated in the United States by the American Society of Individual Psychology with branches in New York, Chicago, and Los Angeles and through its journal, *The American Journal of Individual Psychology.*

In sharp contrast to Freud's major assumption that man's behavior is motivated by inborn instincts and Jung's principal axiom that man's conduct is governed by inborn archetypes, Adler assumed that man is motivated primarily by social urges. Man is, according to Adler, inherently a social being. He relates himself to other people, engages in co-operative social activities, places social welfare above selfish interest, and acquires a style of life which is predominantly social in orientation. Adler did not say that man becomes socialized merely by being exposed to social processes; social interest is inborn although the specific types of relationships with people and social institutions which develop are determined by the nature of the society into which a person is born. In one sense, then, Adler is just as biological in his viewpoint as are Freud and Jung. All three assume that man has an inherent nature which shapes his personality. Freud emphasized sex, Jung emphasized primordial thought patterns, and Adler stressed social interest. This emphasis upon the social determinants of behavior which had been overlooked or minimized by Freud and Jung is probably Adler's greatest contribution to psychological theory. It turned the attention of psychologists to the importance of social variables and helped to develop the field of social psychology at a time when social psychology needed encouragement and support, especially from the ranks of psychoanalysis.

Adler's second major contribution to personality theory is his concept of the creative self. Unlike Freud's ego which consists of a group of psychological processes serving the ends of inborn instincts, Alder's self is a highly personalized, subjective system which interprets and makes meaningful the experiences of the organism. Moreover, it searches for experiences which will aid in fulfilling the person's unique style of life; if these experiences are not to be found in the world the self tries to create them. This concept of a creative self was new to psychoanalytic theory and it helped to compensate for the extreme "objectivism" of classical psychoanalysis, which relied almost entirely upon biological needs and external stimuli to account for the dynamics of personality. As we shall see in other chapters, the concept of the self has played a major role in recent formulations regarding personality. Adler's contribution to this new trend of recognizing the self as an important cause of behavior is considered to be a very significant one (H. L. and R. R. Ansbacher, 1956).

A third feature of Adler's psychology which sets it apart from classical psychoanalysis is its emphasis upon the uniqueness of personality. Adler considered each person to be a unique configuration of motives, traits, interests, and values; every act performed by the person bears the stamp of his own distinctive style of life. In this respect, Adler belongs to the tradition of William James and William Stern who are said to have laid the foundation for personalistic psychology.

Adler's theory of the person minimized the sexual instinct which in Freud's early theorizing had played an almost exclusive role in the dynamics of behavior. To this Freudian monologue on sex, Adler added other significant voices. Man is primarily a social and not a sexual creature. He is motivated by social and not by sexual interest. His inferiorities are not limited to the sexual domain, but may extend to all facets of his being, both physical and psychological. He strives to develop a unique style of life in which the sexual drive plays a minor role. In fact, the way in which he satisfies his sexual needs is determined by his style of life and not vice versa. Adler's dethroning of sex was for many people a welcome relief from the monotonous pansexualism of Freud.

Finally, Adler made consciousness the center of personality. Man is a conscious being; he is ordinarily aware of the reasons for his behavior. He is conscious of his inferiorities and conscious of the goals for which he strives. More than that, he is a self-conscious individual who is capable of planning and guiding his actions with full awareness of their meaning for his own self-realization. This is the complete antithesis of Freud's theory which had virtually reduced consciousness to the status of a nonentity, a mere froth floating on the great sea of the unconscious.

MAJOR CONCEPTS

Alfred Adler, like other personality theorists whose primary training was in medicine and who practiced psychiatry, began his theorizing in the field of abnormal psychology. He formulated a theory of neurosis before broadening his theoretical scope to include the normal personality, which occurred during the 1920's (H. L. and R. R. Ansbacher, 1956). Adler's theory of personality is an extremely economical one in the sense that a few basic concepts sustain the whole theoretical structure. For that reason, Adler's viewpoint can be rather quickly sketched under a few general rubrics. These are (1) fictional finalism, (2) striving for superiority, (3) inferiority feelings and compensation, (4) social interest, (5) style of life, and (6) the creative self.

FICTIONAL FINALISM. Shortly after Adler dissociated himself from the circle that surrounded Freud, he fell under the philosophical influence of Hans Vaihinger whose book *The psychology of "as if"* (English translation, 1925) had been published in 1911. Vaihinger propounded the curious and intriguing notion that man lives by many purely fictional ideas which have no counterpart in reality. These fictions, for example, "all men are created equal," "honesty is the best policy," and "the end justifies the means," enable man to deal more effectively with reality. They are auxiliary constructs or assumptions and not hypotheses which can be tested and confirmed. They can be dispensed with when their usefulness has disappeared.

Adler took over this philosophical doctrine of idealistic positivism and bent it to his own design. Freud, it will be recalled, laid great stress upon constitutional factors and experiences during early childhood as determiners of personality. Adler discovered in Vaihinger the rebuttal to this rigid historical determinism; he found the idea that man is motivated more by his expectations of the future than he is by experiences of the past. These goals do not exist in the future as a part of some teleological design—neither Vaihinger nor Adler believed in predestination or fatality—rather they exist subjectively or mentally here and now as strivings or ideals which affect present behavior. If a person believes, for example, that there is a heaven for virtuous people and a hell for sinners this fiction, it may be presumed, will exercise considerable influence on his conduct. These fictional goals were, for Adler, the subjective causation of psychological events.

Like Jung, Adler identified Freud's theory with the principle of causality and his own with the principle of finalism.

> Individual Psychology insists absolutely on the indispensability of finalism for the understanding of all psychological phenomena. Causes, powers, instincts, impulses, and the like cannot serve as explanatory principles. The final goal alone can explain man's behavior. Experiences, traumata, sexual development mechanisms cannot yield an explanation, but the perspective in which these are regarded, the individual way of seeing them, which subordinates all life to the final goal, can do so (1930, p. 400).

This final goal may be a fiction, that is, an ideal which is impossible to realize but which is nonetheless a very real spur to man's striving and the ultimate explanation of his conduct. Adler believed, however, that the normal person could free himself from the influence of these fictions and face reality when necessity demanded, something that the neurotic person is incapable of doing.

STRIVING FOR SUPERIORITY. What is the final goal toward which all men strive and which gives consistency and unity to personality? By 1908, Adler had reached the conclusion that aggression was more important than sexuality. A little later, the aggressive impulse was replaced by the "will to power." Adler identified power with masculinity and weakness with femininity. It was at this stage of his thinking (circa 1910) that he set forth the idea of the "masculine protest," a form of overcompensation that both men and women indulge in when they feel inadequate and inferior. Later, Adler abandoned the "will to power" in favor of the "striving for superiority," to which he remained committed thereafter. Thus, there were three stages in his thinking regarding the final goal of man: to be aggressive, to be powerful, and to be superior.

Adler makes it very clear that by superiority he does not mean social distinction, leadership, or a pre-eminent position in society. By superiority, Adler means something very analogous to Jung's concept of the self or Goldstein's principle of self-actualization. It is a striving for perfect completion. It is "the great upward drive."

> I began to see clearly in every psychological phenomenon the striving for superiority. It runs parallel to physical growth and is an intrinsic necessity of life itself. It lies at the root of all solutions of life's problems and is manifested in the way in which we meet these problems. All our functions follow its direction. They strive for conquest, security, increase, either in the right or in the wrong direction. The impetus from minus to plus never ends. The urge from below to above never ceases. Whatever premises all our philosophers and psychologists dream of—self-preservation, pleasure principle, equalization—all these are but vague representations, attempts to express the great upward drive (1930, p. 398).

Where does the striving for superiority or perfection come from? Adler says that it is innate; that it is a part of life; in fact, that it is life itself. From birth to death, the striving for superiority carries the person from one stage of development to the next higher stage. It is a prepotent dynamic principle. There are no separate drives, for each drive receives its power from the striving for completion. Adler acknowledges that the striving for superiority may manifest itself in a thousand different ways, and that each person has his own concrete mode of achieving or trying to achieve perfection. The neurotic person, for example, strives for self-esteem, power, and self-aggrandizement—in other words, for egoistic or selfish goals—whereas the normal person strives for goals that are primarily social in character.

Precisely how do the particular forms of the striving for superiority come into being in the individual? In order to answer this question it is necessary to discuss Adler's concept of inferiority feelings.

INFERIORITY FEELINGS AND COMPENSATION. Very early in his career, while he was still interested in general medicine, Adler put forth the idea of organ inferiority and overcompensation (English translation, 1917). At that time, he was interested in finding the answer to the perennial question of why people, when they became sick or suffer some affliction, became sick or afflicted in a particular region of the body. One person develops heart trouble, another lung trouble, and a third lumbago. Adler suggested that the reason for the site of a particular affliction was a basic inferiority in that region, an inferiority which existed either by virtue of heredity or because of some developmental abnormalty. He then observed that a person with a defective organ often tries to compensate for the weakness by strengthening it through intensive training. The most famous example of compensation for organ inferiority is that of Demosthenes who stuttered as a child and became one of the world's greatest orators. Another more recent example is that of Theodore Roosevelt who was a weakling in his youth and developed himself by systematic exercise into a physically stalwart man.

Shortly after he had published his monograph on organ inferiority Adler broadened the concept to include any feelings of inferiority, those that arise from subjectively felt psychological or social disabilities as well as those that stem from actual bodily weakness or impairment. At this time, Adler equated inferiority with unmanliness or femininity, the compensation for which was called "the masculine protest." Later, however, he subordinated this view to the more general one that feelings of inferiority arise from a sense of incompletion or imperfection in any sphere of life. For example, the child is motivated by his feelings of inferiority to strive for a higher level of development. When he reaches this level, he begins to feel inferior again and the upward movement is initiated once more. Adler contended that inferiority feelings are not a sign of abnormality; they are the cause of all improvement in man's lot. Of course, inferiority feelings may be exaggerated by special conditions such as pampering or rejecting the child, in which case certain abnormal manifestations may ensue, such as the development of an inferiority complex or a compensatory superiority complex. But under normal circumstances, the feeling of inferiority or a sense of incompleteness is the great driving force of mankind. In other words, man is pushed by the need to overcome his inferiority and pulled by the desire to be superior.

Adler was not a proponent of hedonism. Although he believed that inferiority feelings were painful he did not think that the relief of these feelings was necessarily pleasurable. Perfection, not pleasure, was for him the goal of life.

SOCIAL INTEREST. During the early years of his theorizing when he was proclaiming the aggressive, power-hungry nature of man and the idea of the masculine protest as an overcompensation for feminine weakness, Adler was severly criticized for emphasizing the selfish drives of man and ignoring his social motives. Striving for superiority sounded like the war cry of the Nietzschean superman, a fitting companion for the Darwinian slogan of survival of the fittest.

Adler, who was an advocate of social justice and a supporter of social democracy, enlarged his conception of man to include the factor of social interest (1939). Although social interest takes in such matters as co-operation, interpersonal and social relations, identification with the group, empathy, and so forth, it is much broader than all of these. In its ultimate sense, social interest consists of the individual helping society to attain the goal of a perfect society. "Social interest is the true and inevitable compensation for all the natural weaknesses of individual human beings" (Adler, 1929b, p. 31).

The person is embedded in a social context from the first day of life. Co-operation manifests itself in the relationship between the infant and the mother, and henceforth the person is continuously involved in a network of interpersonal relations which shape his personality and provide concrete outlets for his striving for superiority. Striving for superiority becomes socialized; the ideal of a perfect society takes the place of purely personal ambition and selfish gain. By working for the common good, man compensates for his individual weakness.

Adler believed that social interest is inborn; that man is a social creature by nature, and not by habit. However, like any other natural aptitude, this innate predisposition does not appear spontaneously but has to be brought to fruition by guidance and training. Because he believed in the benefits of education Adler devoted a great deal of his time to establishing child guidance clinics, to improving the schools, and to educating the public regarding proper methods of rearing children.

It is interesting to trace in Adler's writings the decisive although gradual change that occurred in his conception of man from the early years of his professional life when he was associated with Freud to his later years when he had achieved an international reputation. For the young Adler, man is driven by an insatiable lust for power and domination in order to compensate for a concealed deep-seated feeling of inferiority. For the older Adler, man is motivated by an innately given social interest which causes him to subordinate private gain to public welfare. The image of the perfect man living in a perfect society blotted out the picture of the strong, aggressive man dominating and exploiting society. Social interest replaced selfish interest.

STYLE OF LIFE. This is the slogan of Adler's personality theory. It is a recurrent theme in all of Adler's later writings (for example, 1929a, 1931) and the most distinctive feature of his psychology. Style of life is *the* system principle by which the individual personality functions; it is the whole that commands the parts. Style of life is Adler's chief idiographic principle; it is the principle that explains the uniqueness of the person. Everyone has a style of life but no two people develop the same style.

Precisely what is meant by this concept? This is a difficult question to answer because Adler had so much to say about it and because he said different and sometimes conflicting things about it in his various writings. Then, too, it is difficult to differentiate it from another Adlerian concept, that of the *creative self*.

Every person has the same goal, that of superiority, but there are innumerable ways of striving for this goal. One person tries to become superior through developing his intellect, while another bends all of his efforts to achieving muscular perfection. The intellectual has one style of life, the athlete another. The intellectual reads, studies, thinks; he lives a more sedentary and more solitary life than the active man does. He arranges the details of his existence, his domestic habits, his recreations, his daily routine, his relations to his family, friends, and acquaintances, his social activities, in accordance with his goal of intellectual superiority. Everything he does he does with an eye to this ultimate goal. All of a person's behavior springs from his style of life. He perceives, learns, and retains what fits his style of life, and ignores everything else.

The style of life is formed very early in childhood, by the age of four or five, and from then on experiences are assimilated and utilized according to this unique style of life. His attitudes, feelings, apperceptions become fixed and mechanized at an early age, and it is practically impossible for the style of life to change thereafter. The person may acquire new ways of expressing his unique style of life, but these are merely concrete and particular instances of the same basic style that was found at an early age.

What determines the individual's style of life? In his earlier writings, Adler said that it is largely determined by the specific inferiorities, either fancied or real, that the person has. The style of life is a compensation for a particular inferiority. If the child is a physical weakling, his style of life will take the form of doing those things which will produce physical strength. The dull child will strive for intellectual superiority. Napoleon's conquering style of life was determined by his slight physical stature, and Hitler's rapacious craving for world domination by his sexual impotence. This simple explanation of man's conduct which appealed to so many of Adler's readers and which was widely applied in the analysis of character during the 1920's and 1930's did not satisfy Adler himself. It was too simple and too mechanistic. He looked for a more dynamic principle and found the creative self.

THE CREATIVE SELF. This concept is Adler's crowning achievement as a personality theorist. When he discovered the creative self all of his other concepts were subordinated to it; here at last was the prime mover, the philosopher's stone, the elixir of life, the first cause of everything human for which Adler had been searching. The unitary, consistent, creative self is sovereign in the personality structure.

Like all first causes, the creative self is hard to describe. We can see its effects, but we cannot see it. It is something that intervenes between the stimuli acting upon the person and the responses he makes to these stimuli. In essence, the doctrine of a creative self asserts that man makes his own personality. He constructs it out of the raw material of heredity and experience.

> Heredity only endows him with certain abilities. Environment only gives him certain impressions. These abilities and impressions, and the manner in which he 'experiences' them—that is to say, the interpretation he makes of these experiences—are the bricks which he uses in his own 'creative' way in building up his attitude toward life. It is his individual way of using these bricks, or in other words his attitude toward life, which determines this relationship to the outside world (Adler, 1935, p. 5).

The creative self is the yeast that acts upon the facts of the world and transforms these facts into a personality that is subjective, dynamic, unified, personal, and uniquely stylized. The creative self gives meaning to life; it creates the goal as well as the means to the goal. The creative self is the active principle of human life, and it is not unlike the older concept of soul.

In summary, it may be said that Adler fashioned a humanistic theory of personality which was the antithesis of Freud's conception of man. By endowing man with altruism, humanitarianism, co-operation, creativity, uniqueness, and awareness, he restored to man a sense of dignity and worth that psychoanalysis had pretty largely destroyed. In place of the dreary materialistic picture which horrified and repelled many readers of Freud, Adler offered a portrait of man which was more satisfying, more hopeful, and far more complimentary to man. Adler's conception of the nature of personality coincided with the popular idea that man can be the master, and not the victim, of his fate.

CHARACTERISTIC RESEARCH AND RESEARCH METHODS

Adler's empirical observations were made largely in the therapeutic setting and consist for the most part of reconstructions of the past as remembered by the patient and appraisals of present behavior on the basis of verbal reports. There is space to mention only a few examples of Adler's investigative activities.

ORDER OF BIRTH AND PERSONALITY. In line with his interest in the social determiners of personality, Adler observed that the personalities of the oldest, middle, and youngest child in a family were likely to be quite different (1931, pp. 144–154). He attributed these differences to the distinctive experiences that each child has as a member of a social group.

The first-born or oldest child is given a good deal of attention until the second child is born; then he is suddenly dethroned from his favored position and must share his parents' affections with the new baby. This experience may condition the oldest child in various ways, such as hating people, protecting himself against sudden reversals of fortune, and feeling insecure. Oldest children are also apt to take an interest in the past when they were the center of attention. Neurotics, criminals, drunkards, and perverts, Adler observes, are often first-born children. If the parents handle the situation wisely by preparing the oldest child for the appearance of a rival, the oldest child is more likely to develop into a responsible, protective person.

The second or middle child is characterized by being ambitious. He is constantly trying to surpass his older sibling. He also tends to be rebellious and envious but by and large he is better adjusted than either his older or younger sibling.

The youngest child is the spoiled child. Next to the oldest child he is most likely to become a problem child and a neurotic maladjusted adult.

This theory has been tested a number of times but most of the findings do not lend support to it (Jones, 1931).

EARLY MEMORIES. Adler felt that the earliest memory a person could report was an important key to understanding his basic style of life (1931). For example, a girl began an account of her earliest memory by saying, "When I was three years old, my father . . ." This indicates that she is more interested in her father than in her mother. She then goes on to say that the father brought home a pair of ponies for an older sister and her, and that the older sister led her pony down the street by the halter while she was dragged along in the mud by her pony. This is the fate of the younger child—to come off second best in the rivalry with an older sibling—and it motivates her to try to surpass the pacemaker. Her style of life is one of driving ambition, an urge to be first, a deep feeling of insecurity and disappointment, and a strong foreboding of failure.

A young man who was being treated for severe attacks of anxiety recalled this early scene. "When I was about four years old I sat at the window and watched some workmen building a house on the opposite side of the street, while my mother knitted stockings." This recollection indicates that the young man was pampered as a child because his memory includes the solicitous mother. The fact that he is looking at others who are working suggests that his style of life is that of a spectator rather than a participant. This is borne out by the fact that he becomes anxious whenever he tries to take up a vocation. Adler suggested to him that he consider an occupation in which his preference for looking and observing could be utilized. The patient took Adler's advice and became a successful dealer in art objects.

Adler used this method with groups as well as individuals and found that it was an easy and economical way of studying personality.

CHILDHOOD EXPERIENCES. Adler was particularly interested in the kinds of early influences that predispose the child to a faulty style of life. He discovered three important factors: (1) children with inferiorities, (2) spoiled children, and (3) neglected children. Children with physical or mental infirmities bear a heavy burden and are likely to feel inadequate in meeting the tasks of life. They consider themselves to be, and often are, failures. However, if they have understanding, encouraging parents they may compensate for their inferiorities and transform their weakness into strength. Many prominent men started life with some organic weakness for which they compensated. Over and over again Adler spoke out vehemently against the evils of pampering for he considered this to be the greatest curse that can be visited upon the child. Pampered children do not develop social feeling; they become despots who expect society to conform to their self-centered wishes. Adler considered them to be potentially the most dangerous class in society. Neglect of the child also has unfortunate consequences. Badly treated in childhood, as adults they become enemies of society. Their style of life is dominated by the need for revenge. These three conditions—organic infirmity, pampering, and rejection—produce erroneous conceptions of the world and result in a pathological style of life.

ERICH FROMM

Erich Fromm was born in Frankfurt, Germany, in 1900 and studied psychology and sociology at the Universities of Heidelberg, Frankfurt, and Munich. After receiving a Ph.D. degree from Heidelberg in 1922, he was trained in psychoanalysis in Munich and at the famous Berlin Psychoanalytic Institute. He came to the United States in 1933 as a lecturer at the Chicago Psychoanalytic Institute and then entered private practice in New York City. He has taught at a number of universities and institutes in this country. Not only have his books received considerable attention from specialists in the fields of psychology, sociology, philosophy, and religion but also from the general public.

The essential theme of all of Fromm's writings is that man feels lonely and isolated because he has become separated from nature and from other men. This condition of isolation is not found in any other species of animal; it is the distinctive human situation. The child, for example, gains freedom from the primary ties with his parents with the result that he feels isolated and helpless. The serf eventually secured his freedom only to find himself adrift in a predominantly alien world. As a serf, he belonged to someone and had a feeling of being related to the world and to other people, even though he was not free. In this book, *Escape from freedom* (1941), Fromm develops the thesis that as man has gained more freedom throughout the ages he has also felt more alone. Freedom then becomes a negative condition from which he tries to escape.

What is the answer to this dilemma? Man can either unite himself with other people in the spirit of love and shared work or he can find security by submitting to authority and conforming to society. In the one case, man uses his freedom to develop a better society; in the other, he acquires a new bondage. *Escape from freedom* was written under the shadow of the Nazi dictatorship and shows that this form of totalitarianism appealed to people because it offered them a new security. But as Fromm points out in subsequent books (1947, 1955), any form of society that man has fashioned, whether it be that of feudalism, capitalism, fascism, socialism, or communism, represents an attempt to resolve the basic contradiction of man. This contradiction consists of man being both a part of nature and separate from it, of being both an animal and a human being. As an animal he has certain physiological needs which must be satisfied. As a human being he possesses self-awareness, reason, and imagination. These two aspects constitute the basic conditions of man's existence. *"The understanding of man's psyche must be based on the analysis of man's needs stemming from the conditions of his existence"* (1955, p. 25).

What are the specific needs that rise from the conditions of man's existence? They are five in number: the need for relatedness, the need for transcendence, the need for rootedness, the need for identity, and the need for a frame of orientation. The need for relatedness stems from the stark fact that man in becoming man has been torn from the animal's primary union with nature. "The animal is equipped by nature to cope with the very conditions it is to meet" (1955, p. 23) but man with his power to reason and imagine has lost this intimate interdependence with nature. In place of those instinctive ties with nature which animals possess man has to create his own relationships, the most satisfying being those which are based upon productive love. Productive love always implies mutual care, responsibility, respect, and understanding.

The urge for transcendence refers to man's need to rise above his animal nature, to become a creative person instead of remaining a creature. If his creative urges are thwarted, man becomes a destroyer. Fromm points out that love and hate are not antithetical drives; they are both answers to man's need to transcend his animal nature. Animals can neither love nor hate, but man can.

Man desires natural roots; he wants to be an integral part of the world, to feel that he belongs. As a child, he is rooted to his mother but if this relationship persists past childhood it is considered to be an unwholesome fixation. Man finds his most satisfying and healthiest roots in a feeling of brotherliness with other men and women. But man wants also to have a sense of personal identity, to be a unique individual. If he cannot attain this goal through his own creative effort, he may obtain a certain mark of distinction by identifying himself with another person or group. The slave identifies with the master, the citizen with his country, the worker with his company. In this case, the sense of identity arises from belonging to someone and not from being someone.

Finally, man needs to have a frame of reference, a stable and consistent way of perceiving and comprehending the world. The frame of reference that he develops may be primarily rational, primarily irrational, or it may have elements of both.

For Fromm these needs are purely human and purely objective. They are not found in animals and they are not derived from observing what man says he wants. Nor are these strivings created by society; rather they have become embedded in human nature through evolution. What then is the relation of society to the existence of man? Fromm believes that the specific manifestations of these needs, the actual ways in which man realizes his inner potentialities, are determined by "the social arrangements under which he lives" (1955, p. 14). His personality develops in accordance with the opportunities that a particular society offers him. In a capitalistic society, for example, he may gain a sense of personal identity by becoming rich or develop a feeling of rootedness by becoming a dependable and trusted employee in a large company. In other words, man's adjustment to society usually represents a compromise between inner needs and outer demands. He develops a social character in keeping with the requirements of the society.

From the standpoint of the proper functioning of a particular society it is absolutely essential that the child's character be shaped to fit the needs of society. The task of the parents and of education is to make the child want to act as he has to act if a given economic, political, and social system is to be maintained. Thus, in a capitalistic system the desire to save must be implanted in people in order that capital is available for an expanding economy. A society which has evolved a credit system must see to it that people will feel an inner compulsion to pay their bills promptly. Fromm gives numerous examples of the types of character that develop in a democratic, capitalistic society (1947).

By making demands upon man which are contrary to his nature, society warps and frustrates man. It alienates him from his "human situation" and denies him the fulfillment of the basic conditions of his existence. Both capitalism and communism, for example, try to make man into a robot, a wage slave, a nonentity, and they often succeed in driving him into insanity, antisocial conduct or self-destructive acts. Fromm does not hesitate to stigmatize a whole society as being sick when it fails to satisfy the basic needs of man (1955).

Fromm also points out that when a society changes in any important respect, as occurred when feudalism changed into capitalism or when the factory system displaced the individual artisan, such a change is likely to produce dislocations in the social character of people. The old character structure does not fit the new society, which adds to man's sense of alienation and despair. He is cut off from traditional ties and until he can develop new roots and relations he feels lost. During such transitional periods, he becomes a prey to all sorts of panaceas and nostrums which offer him a refuge from loneliness.

The problem of man's relations to society is one of great concern to Fromm, and he returns to it again and again. Fromm is utterly convinced of the validity of the following propositions: (1) man has an essential, inborn nature, (2) society is created by man in order to fulfill this essential nature, (3) no society which has yet been devised meets the basic needs of man's existence, and (4) it is possible to create such a society.

What kind of a society does Fromm advocate? It is one

> . . . in which man relates to man lovingly, in which he is rooted in bonds of brotherliness and solidarity . . . ; a society which gives him the possibility of transcending nature by creating rather than by destroying, in which everyone gains a sense of self by experiencing himself as the subject of his powers rather than by conformity, in which a system of orientation and devotion exists without man's needing to distort reality and to worship idols (1955, p. 362).

Fromm even suggests a name for this perfect society: Humanistic Communitarian Socialism. In such a society everyone would have equal opportunity to become fully human. There would be no loneliness, no feelings of isolation, no despair. Man would find a new home, one suited to the "human situation."

KAREN HORNEY

Karen Horney was born in Hamburg, Germany, September 16, 1885, and died in New York City, December 4, 1952. She received her medical training at the University of Berlin and was associated with the Berlin Psychoanalytic Institute from 1918 to 1932. She was analyzed by Karl Abraham and Hans Sachs, two of the pre-eminent training analysts in Europe at that time. Upon the invitation of Franz Alexander, she came to the United States and was Associate Director of the Chicago Psychoanalytic Institute for two years. In 1934 she moved to New York where she practiced psychoanalysis and taught at the New York Psychoanalytic Institute. Becoming dissatisfied with orthodox psychoanalysis, she and others of similar convictions founded the Association for the Advancement of Psychoanalysis and the American Institute of Psychoanalysis. She was Dean of this institute until her death.

Horney conceives of her ideas as falling within the framework of Freudian psychology, not as constituting an entirely new approach to the understanding of personality. She aspires to eliminate the fallacies in Freud's thinking—fallacies which have their root, she believes, in his mechanistic, biological orientation—in order that psychoanalysis may realize its full potentialities as a science of man. "My conviction, expressed in a nutshell, is that psychoanalysis should outgrow the limitations set by its being an instinctivistic and a genetic psychology" (1939, p. 8).

Horney objects strongly to Freud's concept of penis envy as the determining factor in the psychology of women. Freud, it will be recalled, observed that the distinctive attitudes and feelings of women and their most profound conflict grew out of their feeling of genital inferiority and their jealousy of the male. Horney believes that feminine psychology is based on lack of confidence and an overemphasis of the love relationship, and has very little to do with the anatomy of her sex organs. Regarding the Oedipus complex, Horney feels that it is not a sexual-aggressive conflict between the child and his parents but an anxiety growing out of basic disturbances, for example, rejection, overprotection, and punishment, in the child's relationships with his mother and father. Aggression is not inborn as Freud stated, but is a means by which man tries to protect his security. Narcissism is not really self-love but self-inflation and overevaluation owing to feelings of insecurity. Horney also takes issue with the following Freudian concepts: repetition compulsion, the id, ego, and superego, anxiety, and masochism (1939). On the positive side, Horney asserts that Freud's fundamental theoretical contributions are the doctrines of psychic determinism, unconscious motivation, and emotional, nonrational motives.

Horney's primary concept is that of basic anxiety, which is defined as

. . . the feeling a child has of being isolated and helpless in a potentially hostile world. A wide range of adverse factors in the environment can produce this insecurity in a child: direct or indirect domination, indifference, erratic behavior, lack of respect for the child's individual needs, lack of real guidance, disparaging attitudes, too much admiration or the absence of it, lack of reliable warmth, having to take sides in parental disagreements, too much or too little responsibility, overprotection, isolation from other children, injustice, discrimination, unkept promises, hostile atmosphere, and so on and so on (1945, p. 41).

In general, anything that disturbs the security of the child in relation to his parents produces basic anxiety.

The insecure, anxious child develops various strategies by which to cope with his feelings of isolation and helplessness (1937). He may become hostile and seek to avenge himself against those who have rejected or mistreated him. Or he may become overly submissive in order to win back the love that he feels he has lost. He may develop an unrealistic, idealized picture of himself in order to compensate for his feelings of inferiority (1950). He may try to bribe others into loving him, or he may use threats to force people to like him. He may wallow in self-pity in order to gain people's sympathy.

If he cannot get love he may seek to obtain power over others. In that way, he compensates for his sense of helplessness, finds an outlet for hostility, and is able to exploit people. Or he becomes highly competitive, in which the winning is far more important than the achievement. He may turn his aggression inward and belittle himself.

Any one of these strategies may become a more or less permanent fixture in the personality; a particular strategy may, in other words, assume the character of a drive or need in the personality dynamics. Horney presents a list of ten needs which are acquired as a consequence of trying to find solutions for the problem of disturbed human relationships (1942). She calls these needs "neurotic" because they are irrational solutions to the problem.

1. *The neurotic need for affection and approval.* This need is characterized by an indiscriminate wish to please others and to live up to their expectations. The person lives for the good opinion of others and is extremely sensitive to any sign of rejection or unfriendliness.

2. *The neurotic need for a "partner" who will take over one's life.* The person with this need is a parasite. He overvalues love, and is extremely afraid of being deserted and left alone.

3. *The neurotic need to restrict one's life within narrow borders.* Such a person is undemanding, content with little, prefers to remain inconspicuous, and values modesty above all else.

4. *The neurotic need for power.* This need expresses itself in craving power for its own sake, in an essential disrespect for others, and in an indiscriminate glorification of strength and a contempt for weakness. People who are afraid to exert power openly may try to control others through intellectual exploitation and superiority. Another variety of the power drive is the need to believe in the omnipotence of will. Such people feel they can accomplish anything simply by exerting will power.

5. *The neurotic need to exploit others.*

6. *The neurotic need for prestige.* One's self-evaluation is determined by the amount of public recognition received.

7. *The neurotic need for personal admiration.* A person with this need has an inflated picture of himself and wishes to be admired on this basis, not for what he really is.

8. *The neurotic ambition for personal achievement.* Such a person wants to be the very best and drives himself to greater and greater achievements as a result of his basic insecurity.

9. *The neurotic need for self-sufficiency and independence.* Having been disappointed in his attempts to find warm, satisfying relationships with people, the person sets himself apart from others and refuses to be tied down to anyone or anything. He becomes a lone wolf.

10. *The neurotic need for perfection and unassailability.* Fearful of making mistakes and of being criticized, the person who has this need tries to make himself impregnable and infallible. He is constantly searching for flaws in himself so that they may be covered up before they become obvious to others.

These ten needs are the sources from which inner conflicts develop. The neurotic's need for love, for example, is insatiable; the more he gets the more he wants. Consequently, he is never satisfied. Likewise, his need for independence can never be fully satisfied because another part of his personality wants to be loved and admired. The search for perfection is a lost cause from the beginning. All of the foregoing needs are unrealistic.

In a later publication (1945), Horney classifies these ten needs under three headings: (1) moving toward people, for example, need for love, (2) moving away from people, for instance, need for independence, and (3) moving against people, for example, need for power. Each of these rubrics represents a basic orientation toward others and oneself. Horney finds in these different orientations the basis for inner conflict. The essential difference between a normal and a neurotic conflict is one of degree. ". . . the disparity between the conflicting issues is much less great for the normal person than for the neurotic" (1945, p. 31). In other words, everyone has these conflicts but some people, primarily because of early experiences with rejection, neglect, overprotection, and other kinds of unfortunate parental treatment, possess them in an aggravated form.

While the normal person can resolve these conflicts by integrating the three orientations, since they are not mutually exclusive, the neurotic person, because of his greater basic anxiety, must utilize irrational and artificial solutions. ① He consciously recognizes only one of the trends and denies or represses the other two. ② Or he creates an idealized image of himself in which the contradictory trends presumably disappear, although actually they do not. In a later book (1950), Horney has a great deal more to say about the unfortunate consequences that flow from the development of an unrealistic conception of the self and from attempts to live up to this idealized picture. The search for glory, feelings of self-contempt, morbid dependency upon other people, and self-abasement are some of the unhealthy and destructive results that grow out of an idealized self. ③ A third solution employed by the neurotic person for his inner conflicts is to externalize them. He says, in effect, "I don't want to exploit other people, they want to exploit me." This solution creates conflicts between the person and the outside world.

All of these conflicts are avoidable or resolvable if the child is raised in a home where there is security, trust, love, respect, tolerance, and warmth. That is, Horney, unlike Freud and Jung, does not feel that conflict is built into the nature of man and is therefore inevitable. Conflict arises out of social conditions. "The person who is likely to become neurotic is one who has experienced the culturally determined difficulties in an accentuated form, mostly through the medium of childhood experience" (1937, p. 290).

HARRY STACK SULLIVAN

Harry Stack Sullivan is the creator of a new viewpoint which is known as the *interpersonal theory of psychiatry*. Its major tenet as it relates to a theory of personality is that personality is "the relatively enduring pattern of recurrent interpersonal situations which characterize a human life" (1953, p. 111). Personality is a hypothetical entity which cannot be isolated from interpersonal situations, and interpersonal behavior is all that can be observed as personality. Consequently, it is vacuous, Sullivan believes, to speak of the individual as the object of study because the individual does not and cannot exist apart from his relations with other people. From the first day of life, the baby is a part of an interpersonal situation, and throughout the rest of his life he remains a member of a social field. Even a hermit who has resigned from society carries with him into the wilderness memories of former personal relationships which continue to influence his thinking and acting.

Although Sullivan does not deny the importance of heredity and maturation in forming and shaping the organism, he feels that that which is distinctly human is the product of social interactions. Moreover, the interpersonal experiences of a person may and do alter his purely physiological functioning, so that even the organism loses its status as a biological entity and becomes a social organism with its own socialized ways of breathing, digesting, eliminating, circulating, and so forth.

For Sullivan, the science of psychiatry is allied with social psychology, and his theory of personality bears the imprint of his strong preference for social psychological concepts and variables. He writes,

> The general science of psychiatry seems to me to cover much the same field as that which is studied by social psychology, because scientific psychiatry has to be defined as the study of interpersonal relations, and this in the end calls for the use of the kind of conceptual framework that we now call *field theory*. From such a standpoint, personality is taken to be hypothetical. That which can be studied is the pattern of processes which characterize the interaction of personalities in particular recurrent situations or fields which "include" the observer (1950, p. 92).

Harry Stack Sullivan was born on a farm near Norwich, New York, on February 21, 1892, and died on January 14, 1949, in Paris, France, on his way home from a meeting of the executive board of the World Federation for Mental Health in Amsterdam. He received his medical degree from the Chicago College of Medicine and Surgery in 1917, and served with the armed forces during the First World War. Following the war he was a medical officer of the Federal Board for Vocational Education and then became an officer with the Public Health Service. In 1922 Sullivan went to Saint Elizabeth's Hospital in Washington, D. C., where he came under the influence of William Alanson White, a leader in American neuropsychiatry. From 1923 until 1930 he was associated with the Medical School of the University of Maryland and with the Sheppard and Enoch Pratt Hospital in Towson, Maryland. It was during this period of his life that Sullivan conducted investigations of schizophrenia which established his reputation as a medical scientist. In 1933 he became president of the William Alanson White Foundation, serving in that office until 1943. In 1936, he helped found and became director of the Washington School of Psychiatry, which is the training institution of the foundation. The journal *Psychiatry* began publication in 1938 to promote Sullivan's theory of interpersonal relations. He was its coeditor and then editor until his death. Sullivan served as consultant for the Selective Service System in 1940–1941; he was a participant during 1948 in the UNESCO Tensions Project established by the United Nations to study tensions affecting international understanding; and he was appointed a member of the international preparatory commission for the International Congress of Mental Health in the same year. Sullivan was a scientific statesman as well as a prominent spokesman for psychiatry, the leader of an important school for training psychiatrists, a remarkable therapist, an intrepid theorist, and a productive medical scientist. By his vivid personality and original thinking, he attracted a number of people who became his disciples, students, colleagues, and friends.

Aside from William Alanson White, the chief influences on Sullivan's intellectual development were Freud, Adolph Meyer, the social philosopher, George Mead, the cultural anthropologists, Edward Sapir and Ruth Benedict, and the sociologist, Leonard Cottrell. Sullivan felt particularly close to Edward Sapir who was one of the pioneers in advocating a closer working relationship between anthropology, sociology, and psychoanalysis. Sullivan began to formulate his theory of interpersonal relations in 1929 and had consolidated his thinking by the mid-1930's.

During his lifetime Sullivan published only one book setting forth his theory (1947). However, he kept detailed notebooks and many of his lectures to the students of the Washington School of Psychiatry were recorded. These notebooks and recordings, as well as other unpublished material, have been turned over to the William Alanson White Psychiatric Foundation. Two books based upon the Sullivan papers have recently been published. *The interpersonal theory of psychiatry* (1953) consists mainly of a series of lectures given by Sullivan in the winter of 1946–1947 and represents the last complete account of his theory of interpersonal relations. The other book, *The psychiatric interview* (1954), is based upon two lecture series that Sullivan gave in 1944 and 1945. Other books compiled from the Sullivan papers are to be published soon. Patrick Mullahy, a philosopher and disciple of Sullivan, has edited several books dealing with the theory of interpersonal relations. One of these, *A study of interpersonal relations* (1949), contains a group of papers by people associated with the Washington School and the William Alanson White Institute in New York City. All of the articles were originally printed in *Psychiatry*, including three by Sullivan. Another book entitled *The contributions of Harry Stack Sullivan* (1952) consists of a group of papers presented at a memorial symposium by representatives of various disciplines, including psychiatry, psychology, and sociology. This book contains a succinct account of interpersonal theory by Mullahy and a complete bibliography of Sullivan's writings through 1951. A similar digest of Sullivan's views also appears in Mullahy's book, *Oedipus—myth and complex* (1948). Sullivan's interpersonal theory has been treated at length by Dorothy Blitsten (1953). In spite of Sullivan's own sparse presentation of interpersonal theory in published form during his lifetime, his systematic position is being thoroughly expounded by a number of very literate and dedicated followers.

THE STRUCTURE OF PERSONALITY

Sullivan insists repeatedly that personality is a purely hypothetical entity which cannot be observed or studied apart from interpersonal situations. The unit of study is the interpersonal situation and not the person. The organization of personality consists of interpersonal events rather than intrapsychic ones. Personality only manifests itself when the person is behaving in relation to one or more other individuals. These people do not need to be present; in fact they can even be illusory or nonexistent figures. A person may have a relationship with a folk hero like Paul Bunyan or a fictional character like Anna Karenina or with his ancestors or with his as yet unborn descendants. Perceiving, remembering, thinking, imagining, and all of the other psychological processes are interpersonal in character. Even nocturnal dreams are interpersonal, since they usually reflect the dreamer's relationships with other people.

Although Sullivan grants personality only hypothetical status, nonetheless he asserts that it is a dynamic center of various processes which occur in a series of interpersonal fields. Moreover, he gives substantive status to some of these processes by identifying and naming them and by conceptualizing some of their properties. The principal ones are *dynamisms, personifications,* and *cognitive processes.*

DYNAMISMS. A dynamism is the smallest unit which can be employed in the study of the individual. It is defined as "the relatively enduring pattern of energy transformations, which recurrently characterize the organism in its duration as a living organism" (1953, p. 103). An energy transformation is any form of behavior. It may be overt and public like talking, or covert and private like thinking and fantasying. Because a dynamism is a pattern of behavior that endures and recurs, it is about the same thing as a habit. Sullivan's definition of pattern is quaintly phrased; he says it is "an envelope of insignificant particular differences" (1953, p. 104). This means that a new feature may be added to a pattern without changing the pattern just as long as it is not significantly different from the other contents of the envelope. If it is significantly different it changes the pattern into a new pattern. For example, two apples may be quite different in appearance and yet be identified as apples because their differences are not important. However, an apple and a banana are different in significant respects and consequently form two different patterns.

The dynamisms which are distinctively human in character are those which characterize one's interpersonal relations. For example, one may behave in a habitually hostile way toward a certain person or group of persons, which is an expression of a dynamism of malevolence. A man who tends to seek out lascivious relationships with women displays a dynamism of lust. A child who is afraid of strangers has a dynamism of fear. Any habitual reaction towards one or more persons, whether it be in the form of a feeling, an attitude, or an overt action, constitutes a dynamism. All people have the same basic dynamisms but the mode of expression of a dynamism varies in accordance with the situation and the life experience of the individual.

A dynamism usually employs a particular zone of the body such as the mouth, the hands, the anus, and the genitals by means of which it interacts with the environment. A zone consists of a receptor apparatus for receiving stimuli, an effector apparatus for performing action, and a connecting apparatus called *eductors* in the central nervous system which connects the receptor mechanism with the effector mechanism. Thus, when the nipple is brought to the baby's mouth it stimulates the sensitive membrane of the lips which discharges impulses along nerve pathways to the motor organs of the mouth which produce sucking movements.

Most dynamisms serve the purpose of satisfying the basic needs of the organism. However, there is an important dynamism which develops as a result of anxiety. This is called the dynamism of the self or the self-system.

The self-system. Anxiety is a product of interpersonal relations, being transmitted originally from the mother to the infant and later in life by threats to one's security. In order to avoid or minimize actual or potential anxiety, the person adopts various types of protective measures and supervisory controls over his behavior. He learns, for example, that he can avoid punishment by conforming to his parents' wishes. These security measures form the self-system which sanctions certain forms of behavior (the good-me self) and forbids other forms (the bad-me self).

The self-system as the guardian of one's security tends to become isolated from the rest of the personality; it excludes information that is incongruous with its present organization and fails thereby to profit from experience. Since the self guards the person from anxiety, it is held in high esteem and is protected from criticism. As the self-system grows in complexity and independence, it prevents the person from making objective judgments of his own behavior and it glosses over obvious contradictions between what the person really is and what his self-system says he is. In general, the more experiences the person has with anxiety, the more inflated his self-system becomes and the more it becomes dissociated from the rest of his personality. Although the self-system serves the useful purpose of reducing anxiety, it interferes with one's ability to live constructively with others. Sullivan believes that the self-system is a product of the irrational aspects of society. By this he means that the young child is made to feel anxious for reasons that would not exist in a more rational society; he is forced to adopt unnatural and unrealistic ways of dealing with his anxiety. Although Sullivan recognizes that the development of a self-system is absolutely necessary for avoiding anxiety in modern society, and perhaps in any kind of society which man is capable of fashioning, he also acknowledges that the self-system as we know it today is "the principal stumbling block to favorable changes in personality" (1953, p. 169).

PERSONIFICATIONS. A personification is an image that an individual has of himself or of another person. It is a complex of feelings, attitudes, and conceptions that grows out of experiences with need-satisfaction and anxiety. For example, the baby develops a personification of a good mother by being nursed and cared for by her. Any interpersonal relationship which involves satisfaction tends to build up a favorable picture of the satisfying agent. On the other hand, the baby's personification of a bad mother results from experiences with her that evoke anxiety. The anxious mother becomes personified as the bad mother. Ultimately, these two personifications of the mother along with any others that may be formed, such as the seductive mother or the overprotective mother, fuse together to form a complex personification.

These pictures that we carry around in our heads are rarely accurate descriptions of the people to whom they refer. They are formed in the first place in order to cope with people in fairly isolated interpersonal situations, but once formed they usually persist and influence our attitudes towards other people. Thus a person who personifies his father as a mean and dictatorial man may project this same personification onto other older men, for example, teachers, policemen, and employers. Consequently, something that serves an anxiety-reducing function in early life may interfere with one's interpersonal relations later in life. These anxiety-fraught pictures distort one's conceptions of currently significant people. Personifications of the self such as the good-me and the bad-me follow the same principles as personifications of others. The good-me personification results from interpersonal experiences which are rewarding in character, the bad-me personification from anxiety-arousing situations. And like personifications of other people, these self-personifications tend to stand in the way of objective self-evaluation.

Personifications which are shared by a number of people are called *stereotypes.* These are consensually validated conceptions, that is, ideas which have wide acceptance among the members of a society and are handed down from generation to generation. Examples of common stereotypes in our culture are the absent-minded professor, the unconventional artist, and the hard-headed businessman.

Cognitive Processes. Sullivan's unique contribution regarding the place of cognition in the affairs of personality is his threefold classification of experience. Experience, he says, occurs in three modes; these are *prototaxic, parataxic,* and *syntaxic.* Prototaxic experience "may be regarded as the discrete series of momentary states of the sensitive organism" (1953, p. 29). This type of experience is similar to what James called the "stream of consciousness," the raw sensations, images, and feelings that flow through the mind of a sensate being. They have no necessary connections among themselves and possess no meaning for the experiencing person. The prototaxic mode of experience is found in its purest form during the early months of life and is the necessary precondition for the appearance of the other two modes.

The parataxic mode of thinking consists of seeing causal relationship between events that occur at about the same time but which are not logically related. The eminent Czech writer, Franz Kafka, portrays an interesting case of parataxic thinking in one of his short stories. A dog who lived in a kennel surrounded by a high fence was urinating one day when a bone was thrown over the fence. The dog thought, "My urinating made that bone appear." Thereafter whenever he wanted something to eat he lifted his leg. Sullivan believes that much of our thinking does not advance beyond the level of parataxis; that we see causal connections between experiences that have nothing to do with one another. All superstitions, for instance, are examples of parataxic thinking.

The third and highest mode of thinking is the syntaxic, which consists of consensually validated symbol activity, expecially of a verbal nature. A consensually validated symbol is one which has been agreed upon by a group of people as having a standard meaning. Words and numbers are the best examples of such symbols. The syntaxic mode produces logical order among experiences and enables people to communicate with one another.

In addition to this formulation of the modes of experience, Sullivan emphasizes the importance of foresight in cognitive functioning. "Man, the person, lives with his past, the present and the neighboring future all clearly relevant in explaining his thought and action" (1950, p. 84). Foresight depends upon one's memory of the past and interpretation of the present.

Although dynamisms, personifications, and cognitive processes do not complete the list of the constituents of personality, they are the chief distinguishing structural features of Sullivan's system.

THE DYNAMICS OF PERSONALITY

Sullivan, in common with many other personality theorists, conceives of personality as an energy system whose chief work consists of activities that will reduce tension. Sullivan says there is no need to add the term "mental" to either energy or tension since he uses them in exactly the same sense as they are used in physics.

TENSION. Sullivan begins with the familiar conception of the organism as a tension system which theoretically can vary between the limits of absolute relaxation, or euphoria as Sullivan prefers to call it, and absolute tension as exemplified by extreme terror. There are two main sources of tension: (1) tensions that arise from the needs of the organism, and (2) tensions that result from anxiety. Needs are connected with the physiochemical requirements of life; they are such conditions as lack of food or water or oxygen which produce a disequilibrium in the economy of the organism. Needs may be general in character, such as hunger, or they may be more specifically related to a zone of the body, such as the need to suck. Needs arrange themselves in a hierarchical order; those lower down on the ladder must be satisfied before those higher on the ladder can be accommodated. One result of need reduction is an experience of satisfaction. "Tensions can be regarded as needs for particular energy transformations which will dissipate the tension, often with an accompanying change of 'mental' state, a change of awareness, to which we can apply the general term, _satisfaction_" (1950, p. 85). The typical consequence of prolonged failure to satisfy the needs is a feeling of apathy which produces a general lowering of the tensions.

Anxiety is the experience of tension that results from real or imaginary threats to one's security. In large amounts, it reduces the efficiency of the individual in satisfying his needs, disturbs interpersonal relations, and produces confusion in thinking. Anxiety varies in intensity depending upon the seriousness of the threat and the effectiveness of the security operations that the person has at his command. Severe anxiety is like a blow on the head; it conveys no information to the person but instead produces utter confusion and even amnesia. Less severe forms of anxiety can be informative. In fact, Sullivan believes that anxiety is the first greatly educative influence in living. Anxiety is transmitted to the infant by the "mothering one" who is herself expressing anxiety in her looks, tone of voice, and general demeanor. Sullivan admits that he does not know how this transmission takes place, although it is probably accomplished by some kind of empathic process whose nature is obscure. As a consequence of this mother-transmitted anxiety, other objects in the near surroundings become freighted with anxiety by the operation of the parataxic mode of associating contiguous experiences. The mother's nipple, for example, is changed into a bad nipple which produces avoidance reactions in the baby. The infant learns to veer away from activities and objects that increase anxiety. When the baby cannot escape anxiety, he tends to fall asleep. This dynamism of somnolent detachment, as Sullivan calls it, is the counterpart of apathy, which is the dynamism aroused by unsatisfied needs. In fact, these two dynamisms cannot be objectively differentiated. Sullivan says that one of the great tasks of psychology is to discover the basic vulnerabilities to anxiety in interpersonal relations rather than to try to deal with the symptoms resulting from anxiety.

ENERGY TRANSFORMATIONS. Energy is transformed by performing work. Work may be overt actions involving the striped muscles of the body or it may be mental such as perceiving, remembering, and thinking. These overt or covert activities have as their goal the relief of tension. They are to a great extent conditioned by the society in which the person is raised. "What anyone can discover by investigating his past is that patterns of tensions and energy transformations which make up his living are to a truly astonishing extent matters of his education for living in a particular society" (1950, p. 83).

Sullivan does not believe that instincts are important sources of human motivation nor does he accept the libido theory of Freud. An individual learns to behave in a particular way as a result of interactions with people, and not because he possesses innate imperatives for certain kinds of action.

THE DEVELOPMENT OF PERSONALITY

Sullivan was very assiduous in spelling out the sequence of interpersonal situations to which the person is exposed in passing from infancy to adulthood, and the ways in which these situations contribute to the formation of personality. More than any other personality theorist, with the possible exception of Freud, Sullivan viewed personality from the perspective of definite stages of development. Whereas Freud held the position that development is largely an unfolding of the sex instinct, Sullivan argued persuasively for a more social-psychological view of personality growth, one in which the unique contributions of human relationships would be accorded their proper due. Although Sullivan did not reject biological factors as conditioners of the growth of personality, he did subordinate them to the social determiners of psychological development. Moreover, he was of the opinion that sometimes these social influences run counter to the biological needs of the person and have detrimental effects upon his personality. Sullivan was not one to shy away from recognizing the deleterious influences of society. In fact, Sullivan, like other social-psychological theorists, was a sharp, incisive critic of contemporary society.

STAGES OF DEVELOPMENT. Sullivan delineates six stages in the development of personality prior to the final stage of maturity. These six stages are typical for Western European cultures and may be different in other societies. They are (1) infancy, (2) childhood, (3) the juvenile era, (4) preadolescence, (5) early adolescence, and (6) late adolescence.

The period of infancy extends from birth to the appearance of articulate speech. It is the period in which the oral zone is the primary zone of interaction between the baby and his environment. Nursing provides the baby with his first interpersonal experience. The feature of the environment which stands out during infancy is the object which supplies food to the hungry baby, either the nipple of the mother's breast or the nipple of the bottle. The baby develops various conceptions of the nipple depending upon the kinds of experiences he has with it. These are: (1) the good nipple which is the signal for nursing and a sign that satisfaction is forthcoming, (2) the good but unsatisfactory nipple because the baby is not hungry, (3) the wrong nipple because it does not give milk and is a signal for rejection and subsequent search for another nipple, and (4) the bad nipple of the anxious mother which is a signal for avoidance.

Other characteristic features of the infantile stages are (1) the appearance of the dynamisms of apathy and somnolent detachment, (2) the transition from a prototaxic to a parataxic mode of cognition, (3) the organization of personifications such as the bad, anxious, rejecting, frustrating mother and the good, relaxed, accepting, satisfying mother, (4) the organization of experience through learning and the emergence of the rudiments of the self-system, (5) the differentiation of the baby's own body so that the baby learns to satisfy his tensions independently of the mothering one, for example, by thumbsucking, and (6) the learning of co-ordinated moves involving hand and eye, hand and mouth, and ear and voice.

The transition from infancy to childhood is made possible by the learning of language and the organization of experience in the syntaxic mode. Childhood extends from the emergence of articulate speech to the appearance of the need for playmates. The development of language permits, among other things, the fusion of different personifications, for instance, the good and bad mother, and the integration of the self-system into a more coherent structure. The self-system begins to develop the conception of gender: the little boy identifies with the masculine role as prescribed by society, the little girl with the feminine role. The growth of symbolic ability enables the child to play at being a grownup—Sullivan calls these as-if performances *dramatizations*—and to become concerned with various activities both overt and covert which serve the purpose of warding off punishment and anxiety—Sullivan calls these *preoccupations*.

One dramatic event of childhood is the *malevolent transformation*, the feeling that one lives among enemies. This feeling, if it becomes strong enough, makes it impossible for the child to respond positively to the affectionate advances of other people. The malevolent transformation distorts the child's interpersonal relations and causes the child to isolate himself. He says, in effect, "Once upon a time everything was lovely, but that was before I had to deal with people." The malevolent transformation is caused by painful and anxious experiences with people, and may lead to a regression to the less threatening stage of infancy.

Sublimation, which Sullivan defines as "the unwitting substitution for a behavior pattern which encounters anxiety or collides with the self-system, of a socially more acceptable activity pattern which satisfies parts of the motivational system that caused trouble" (1953, p. 193), appears during childhood. The excess of tension which is not discharged by sublimation is expended in symbolic performances, for instance, in nocturnal dreams.

The juvenile stage extends throughout most of the grammar-school years. It is the period for becoming social, for acquiring experiences of social subordination to authority figures outside of the family, for becoming competitive and co-operative, for learning the meaning of ostracism, disparagement, and group feeling. The juvenile learns to be inattentive to external circumstances that do not interest him, to supervise his behavior by internal controls, to form stereotypes in his attitudes, to develop new and more effective modes of sublimation, and to distinguish more clearly between fantasy and reality.

One great event of this period is the emergence of a conception of orientation in living.

> One is oriented in living to the extent to which one has formulated, or can easily be led to formulate (or has insight into), data of the following types: the integrating tendencies (needs) which customarily characterize one's interpersonal relations; the circumstances appropriate to their satisfaction and relatively anxiety-free discharge; and the more or less remote goals for the approximation of which one will forego intercurrent opportunities for satisfaction or the enhancement of one's prestige (1953, p. 243).

The relatively brief period of preadolescence is marked by the need for an intimate relationship with a peer of the same sex, a chum in whom one can confide and with whom one can collaborate in meeting the tasks and solving the problems of life. This is an extremely important period because it marks the beginning of genuine human relationships with other people. In earlier periods, the interpersonal situation is characterized by the dependence of the child upon an older person. During preadolescence, the child begins to form peer relationships in which there are equality, mutuality, and reciprocity between the members. Without an intimate companion, the preadolescent becomes the victim of a desperate loneliness.

The main problem of the period of early adolescence is the development of a pattern of heterosexual activity. The physiological changes of puberty are experienced by the youth as feelings of lust; out of these feelings the lust dynamism emerges and begins to assert itself in the personality. The lust dynamism involves primarily the genital zone, but other zones of interaction such as the mouth and the hands also participate in sexual behavior. There is a separation of erotic need from the need for intimacy; the erotic need takes as its object a member of the opposite sex while the need for intimacy remains fixated upon a member of the same sex. If these two needs do not become divorced, the young person displays a homosexual rather than a heterosexual orientation. Sullivan points out that many of the conflicts of adolescence arise out of the opposing needs for sexual gratification, security, and intimacy. Early adolescence persists until the person has found some stable pattern of performances which satisfies his genital drives.

"Late adolescence extends from the patterning of preferred genital activity through unnumbered educative and eductive steps to the establishment of a fully human or mature repertory of interpersonal relations as permitted by available opportunity, personal and cultural" (1953, p. 297). In other words, the period of late adolescence constitutes a rather prolonged initiation into the privileges, duties, satisfactions, and responsibilities of social living and citizenship. The full complement of interpersonal relations gradually takes form and there is a growth of experience in the syntaxic mode which permits a widening of the symbolic horizons. The self-system becomes stabilized, more effective sublimations of tensions are learned, and stronger security measures against anxiety are instituted.

When the individual has ascended all of these steps and reached the final stage of adulthood, he has been transformed largely by means of his interpersonal relations from an animal organism into a human person. He is not an animal, coated by civilization and humanity, but an animal that has been so drastically altered that he is no longer an animal but a human being—or, if one prefers, a human animal.

DETERMINERS OF DEVELOPMENT. Although Sullivan firmly rejects any hard and fast instinct doctrine he does acknowledge the importance of heredity in providing certain capacities, chief among which are the capacities for receiving and elaborating experiences. He also accepts the principle that training cannot be effective before maturation has laid the structural groundwork. Thus, the child cannot learn to walk until the muscles and bony structure have reached a level of growth which will support him in an upright position. Heredity and maturation provide the biological substratum for the development of personality, that is, the capacities and predispositions and inclinations, but the culture operating through a system of interpersonal relations makes manifest the abilities and the actual performances (energy transformations) by which the person reaches the goal of tension reduction and need-satisfaction.

The first educative influence is that of anxiety which forces the young organism to discriminate between increasing and decreasing tension and to guide his activity in the direction of the latter. The second great educational force is that of trial and success. Success, as many psychologists have pointed out, tends to stamp in the activity which has led to gratification. Success may be equated with the earning of rewards—a mother's smile or a father's praise; failure with punishments—a mother's forbidding look or a father's words of disapproval. One may also learn by imitation and by inference; for the latter type of learning Sullivan adopts the name proposed by Charles Spearman: eduction of relations.

Sullivan does not believe that personality is set at an early age. It may change at any time as new interpersonal situations arise because the human organism is extremely plastic and malleable. Although the forward thrust of learning and development predominates, regressions can and do occur when pain, anxiety, and failure become intolerable.

CHARACTERISTIC RESEARCH AND RESEARCH METHODS

Harry Stack Sullivan, in common with other psychiatrists, acquired his empirical knowledge of personality by working with patients suffering from various types of personality disorders but chiefly with schizophrenics and obsessional cases. As a young psychiatrist, Sullivan discovered that the method of free association did not work satisfactorily with schizophrenics because it aroused too much anxiety. Other methods were tried but these also proved to provoke anxiety which interfered with the communication process between patient and therapist. Consequently, Sullivan became interested in studying the forces that impede and facilitate communication between two people. In so doing, he found that the psychiatrist was much more than an observer; he was also a vital participant in an interpersonal situation. He had his own apprehensions, such as his professional competence and his personal problems, to deal with. As a result of this discovery Sullivan developed his conception of the therapist as a *participant observer.*

The theory of interpersonal relations lays great stress on the method of participant observation, and relegates data obtained by other methods to at most a secondary importance. This in turn implies that skill in the face to face, or person to person *psychiatric interview* is of fundamental importance (1950, p. 122).

THE INTERVIEW. The psychiatric interview is Sullivan's term for the type of interpersonal, face to face situation that takes place between the patient and the therapist. There may be only one interview or there may be a sequence of interviews with a patient extending over a long period of time. Sullivan defines the interview as "a system, or series of systems, of *interpersonal processes,* arising from participant observation in which the interviewer derives certain conclusions about the interviewee" (1954, p. 128). How the interview is conducted and the ways in which the interviewer reaches conclusions regarding the patient form the subject matter of Sullivan's book, *The psychiatric interview* (1954).

Sullivan divides the interview into four stages: (1) the formal inception, (2) reconnaissance, (3) detailed inquiry, and (4) the termination.

The interview is primarily a vocal communication between two people. Not only what the person says but how he says it—his intonations, rate of speech, and other expressive behavior—are the chief sources of information for the interviewer. He should be alert to subtle changes in the patients vocalizations, for example, changes in volume, because these clues often reveal vital evidence regarding the patient's focal problems and attitudinal changes towards the therapist. In the inception, the interviewer should avoid asking too many questions but should maintain an attitude of quiet observation. He should try to determine the reasons for the patient's coming to him and something as to the nature of his problems.

Sullivan is very explicit about the role of the therapist in the interview situation. He should never forget that he is earning his living as an expert in the area of interpersonal relations, and that the patient has a right to expect he is going to learn something which will benefit him. The patient should feel this from the very first interview, and it should be continually reinforced throughout the course of treatment. Only by having such an attitude will the patient divulge information from which the interviewer can reach the proper conclusions regarding the patterns of living which are causing trouble for the patient. Obviously, the psychiatrist should not use his expert knowledge to obtain personal satisfaction or to enhance his prestige at the expense of the patient. The interviewer is not a friend or enemy, a parent or lover, a boss or employee, although the patient may cast him in one or more of these roles as a result of distorted parataxic thinking; the interviewer is an expert in interpersonal relations.

The period of reconnaissance centers about finding out who the patient is. The interviewer does this by means of an intensive interrogatory into the past, present, and future of the patient. These facts about the patient's life fall under the heading of personal data or biographical information. Sullivan does not advocate a hard-and-fast, structured type of questioning which adheres to a standard list of questions. On the other hand, Sullivan insists that the interviewer should not let the patient talk about irrelevant and trivial matters. The patient should learn that the interview is serious business and that there should be no fooling around. Nor should the interviewer ordinarily make notes of what the patient says at any time during the course of treatment because note-taking is too distracting and tends to inhibit the communication process.

Sullivan does not believe that one should start with any formal prescription to the effect "say everything that comes into your mind." Rather the therapist should take advantage of the patient's memory lapses during the interrogatory to teach him how to free-associate. In this way, the patient not only learns how to free-associate without becoming alarmed by this unfamiliar mode of discourse but he also experiences the usefulness of the free-association technique before he has been given any formal explanation of its purpose.

By the end of the first two stages of the interview process the psychiatrist should have formed a number of tentative hypotheses regarding the patient's problems and their origins. During the period of *detailed inquiry*, the psychiatrist attempts to ascertain which of several hypotheses is the correct one. He does this by listening and by asking questions. Sullivan suggests a number of areas which should be inquired into—such matters as toilet training, attitude toward the body, eating habits, ambition, and sexual activities—but here again he does not insist upon any formal prospectus which should be rigidly followed.

As long as everything runs smoothly the interviewer is not likely to learn anything about the vicissitudes of interviewing, chief of which is the impact of the interviewer's attitudes upon the patient's capacity for communication. But when the communication process deteriorates, the interviewer is forced to ask himself, "What did I say or do which caused the patient to become anxious?" There is always a good deal of reciprocity between the two parties—Sullivan's term for it is *reciprocal emotion*—and each is continually reflecting the feelings of the other. It is incumbent upon the therapist to recognize and to control his own attitudes in the interest of maximum communication. In other words, he should never forget his role as an expert participant observer. A series of interviews is brought to termination by the interviewer making a final statement of what he has learned, by prescribing a course for the patient to follow, and by assessing for the patient the probable effects of the prescription upon his life.

It is quite apparent from reading Sullivan's sage remarks on interviewing that he considers it to be an immense challenge to the accuracy of observation of the participant observer. The reader may be interested in contrasting the type of interviewing advocated by Sullivan with the wide variety of interviewing procedures discussed by the Maccobys (1954) and with the techniques of clinical interviewing set forth in the recent book, *The clinical interview* (1955), edited by Felix Deutsch and William Murphy.

Sullivan's principal research contribution in psychopathology consists of a series of articles on the etiology, dynamics, and treatment of schizophrenia. These studies were conducted for the most part during his period of association with the Sheppard and Enoch Pratt Hospital in Maryland and were published in psychiatric journals during the years 1924 to 1931. They reveal Sullivan's great talents for making contact with and understanding the mind of the psychotic. Empathy was a highly developed trait in Sullivan's personality, and he used it to excellent advantage in studying and treating the victims of schizophrenia. For Sullivan, these victims are not hopeless cases to be shut away in the back wards of mental institutions; they can be treated successfully if the psychiatrist is willing to be patient, understanding, and observant.

Sullivan was also instrumental in stimulating other psychiatrists and social scientists to carry on research related to interpersonal theory. Many of these studies are reported in the journal *Psychiatry*, which was founded largely to promote and advance Sullivan's ideas. Three recent books which owe a great deal to Sullivan may be mentioned here. In *Communication, the social matrix of psychiatry*

(1951), Ruesch and Bateson apply Sullivan's concepts to problems of human relations and to the interrelations between culture and personality. Frieda Fromm-Reichmann in her influential book, *Principles of intensive psychotherapy* (1950), has elaborated many of Sullivan's ideas regarding the therapeutic process. The recent study of a mental hospital by Stanton and Schwartz (1954) depicts very clearly the kinds of interpersonal situations that exist in an institution and the effect of these situations upon the patients and personnel alike.

Of the four theorists presented in this chapter, Sullivan's interpersonal theory has probably been the greatest stimulus to research. One reason for this is that Sullivan employed a more objective language in describing his theory, a language which helped to span the gap between theory and observation. Sullivan kept his conceptual constructions quite closely tied to empirical observation, with the result that he seemed to be describing at close quarters the behavior of real people. In spite of the abstractness of his thought, he did not become so abstruse as to lose touch with concrete, one might almost say everyday, conduct of individuals. Interpersonal theory is a down-to-earth proposition mill which invites and encourages empirical testing.

CURRENT STATUS AND EVALUATION

The four theories which have been presented in this chapter belong together because they all emphasize the influence of social variables in shaping personality. All of them, in one way or another, constitute a reaction against the instinctivist position of Freudian psychoanalysis, yet each of the theorists acknowledges his indebtedness to the seminal thinking of Freud. They have all stood on Freud's shoulders, and have added their own cubits to his towering height. They have invested personality with social dimensions equal if not superior in importance to the biological dimensions provided by Freud and Jung. Moreover, these theories have helped to place psychology in the sphere of the social sciences.

In spite of the common ground which they occupy each theory stresses somewhat different clusters of social variables. Erich Fromm devotes most of his attention to describing the ways in which the structure and dynamics of a particular society mold its members so that their social character fits the common values and needs of that society. Karen Horney, although she recognizes the influence of the social context in which a person lives, dwells more upon the intimate factors within the family setting which shape personality. In this respect, Sullivan's interpersonal theory resembles Horney's views more than it does Fromm's. For Sullivan the human relationships of infancy, childhood, and adolescence are of paramount concern, and he is most eloquent and persuasive when he is describing the nexus between the "mothering one" and the baby. Adler, on the other hand, roams widely throughout society looking for factors that are relevant to personality and finds them everywhere.

Although all four theories strenuously oppose Freud's instinct doctrine and the fixity of human nature, none of the four adopts the radical environmentalist position that an individual's personality is created solely by the conditions of the society into which he is born. Each theory, in its own way, agrees that there is such a thing as human nature which the baby brings with him, largely in the form of fairly general predispositions or potentialities rather than as specific needs and traits. These generalized potentialities as exemplified by Adler's social interest and Fromm's need for transcendence are actualized in concrete ways by means of the formal and informal educative agencies of the society. Under ideal conditions, these theories agree, the individual and society are interdependent; the person serves to further the aims of the society and society in turn helps man to attain his goals. In short, the stand adopted by these four theorists is neither exclusively social or sociocentric nor exclusively psychological or psychocentric; it is truly social-psychological in character.

Furthermore, each theory not only asserts that human nature is plastic and malleable but also that society is equally plastic and malleable. If a particular society does not fulfill the demands of human nature it can be changed by man. In other words, man creates the kind of society he thinks will benefit him the most. Obviously, mistakes are made in developing a society and once these errors have become crystallized in the form of social institutions and customs it may be difficult to change them. Yet each theorist was optimistic regarding the possibility of change, and each in his own way tried to bring about fundamental changes in the structure of society. Adler supported social democracy, pressed for better schools, started child guidance centers, urged reforms in the treatment of criminals, and lectured widely on social problems and their cures. Fromm and Horney through their writings and talks have pointed the way to a better society. Fromm, in particular, has spelled out some of the basic reforms that need to be made in order to achieve a sane society. Sullivan was actively engaged in trying to bring about social amelioration through the medium of international co-operation at the time of his death. All four of them in their professional capacities as psychotherapists had extensive experiences with the casualities of an imperfect social order; consequently, they spoke from personal knowledge and practical experience in their roles as critics and reformers.

Another assumption which each theory makes is that anxiety is ③ socially produced. Man is not by nature "the anxious animal." He is made anxious by the conditions under which he lives—by the specter of unemployment, by intolerance and injustice, by the threat of war, by hostile parents. Remove these conditions, say our theorists, and the wellsprings from which anxiety gushes forth will dry up. Nor is man by nature destructive as Freud believed. He may become destructive when his basic needs are frustrated, but even under conditions of frustration other avenues such as submission or withdrawal may be taken.

All of the theories with the exception of Sullivan's also underscore ④ the concepts of the unique individual and the creative self. In spite of attempts by society to regiment people, each person manages to retain some degree of creative individuality. Indeed, it is by virtue of man's inherent creative powers that he is able to effect changes in society. People create different kinds of societies on different parts of the globe, and at different times in history, in part, because people are different. Man is not only creative; he is also self-conscious. He knows what he wants and he strives consciously to· reach his goals. The idea of unconscious motivation is not accorded much weight by these social-psychological theorists.

In general, the theories developed by Adler, Fromm, Horney, and Sullivan enlarged the scope of Freudian psychology by providing room for the social determinants of personality. A number of critics, however, have disparaged the originality of these social-psychological theories. They say that such theories merely elaborate upon one aspect of classical psychoanalysis, namely, the ego and its defenses. Freud saw clearly that personality traits often represented the person's habitual defenses or strategies against inner and outer threats to the ego. The needs, trends, styles, orientations, personifications, dynamisms, and so forth, in the theories treated in this chapter are accommodated in Freudian theory under the heading of ego-defenses. Therefore, these critics conclude, nothing new has been added to Freud, and a great deal has been subtracted. By reducing personality to the single system of the ego, the social-psychological theorist has cut the personality off from the vital springs of human behavior, springs that have their ultimate sources in the evolution of man as a species. By enlarging upon the social character of man's personality, they have alienated man from his great biological heritage.

A criticism which is sometimes voiced against the conception of man evolved by Adler, Fromm, and Karen Horney (it does not apply to Sullivan) is that it is too sugar-coated and idealistic. In a world which has been torn apart by two great wars and the threat of a third one, not to mention the many other forms of violence and irrationality that men display, the picture of a rational, self-conscious, socialized man strikes one as being singularly inappropriate and invalid. One can, of course, blame society and not man for this deplorable state of affairs, and this is what these theorists do. But then they say, or at least imply, that rational man created the kind of social arrangements which are responsible for his irrationality and unhappiness. This is the great paradox of these theories. If man is so self-conscious, so rational, and so social, why has he evolved so many imperfect social systems?

Another less devastating criticism, but one which carries more weight with psychologists as distinguished from psychoanalysts, is the failure of these social-psychological theories to specify the precise means by which a society molds its members. How does a person acquire his social character? How does he learn to be a member of society? This evident neglect of the learning process in theories which depend so heavily upon the concept of learning to account for the ways in which personality is formed is considered to be a major omission. Is it enough just to be exposed to a condition of society in order for that condition to affect the personality? Is there a mechanical stamping in of socially approved behavior and an equally mechanical stamping out of socially disapproved behavior? Or does the person react with insight and foresight to the social milieu, selecting those features which he thinks will produce a better organization of personality and rejecting other features which he feels are inconsistent with his self-organization? For the most part these theories stand silent on the nature of the learning process, in spite of the fact that learning has been a central topic in American psychology for a good many years.

Although these social-psychological theories have not stimulated a great deal of research in comparison with some other theories, they have served to foster an intellectual climate in which social-psychological research could flourish and has done so. Social psychology is no longer the stepchild of psychology. It is a large and exceedingly active component part in the science of psychology. Adler, Fromm, Karen Horney, and Sullivan are not solely responsible for the rise of social psychology, but their influence has been considerable. Each of them has contributed in no small measure to the picture of man as a social being. This is their great value in the contemporary scene.

BIBLIOGRAPHY

PRIMARY SOURCES

Adler, A. *The practice and theory of individual psychology*. New York: Harcourt, 1927.
Adler, A. Individual Psychology. In C. Murchison (Ed.). *Psychologies of 1930*. Worcester, Mass.: Clark Univ. Press, 1930, pp. 395–405.
Ansbacher, H. L., and Rowena R. (Eds.). *The Individual-Psychology of Alfred Adler*. New York: Basic Books, 1956.
Fromm, E. *Escape from freedom*. New York: Rinehart, 1941.
Fromm, E. *Man for himself*. New York: Rinehart, 1947.
Fromm, E. *The sane society*. New York: Rinehart, 1955.
Horney, Karen. *Neurotic personality of our times*. New York: Norton, 1937.
Horney, Karen. *New ways in psychoanalysis*. New York: Norton, 1939.
Horney, Karen. *Self-analysis*. New York: Norton, 1942.
Horney, Karen. *Our inner conflicts*. New York: Norton, 1945.
Horney, Karen. *Neurosis and human growth*. New York: Norton, 1950.
Sullivan, H. S. *The interpersonal theory of psychiatry*. New York: Norton, 1953.

REFERENCES

Adler, A. *Study of organ inferiority and its psychical compensation*. New York: Nervous and Mental Diseases Publishing Co., 1917.
Adler, A. *Practice and theory of individual psychology*. New York: Harcourt, 1927.
Adler, A. *The science of living*. New York: Greenberg, 1929a.
Adler, A. *Problems of neurosis*. London: Kegan Paul, 1929b.
Adler, A. Individual Psychology. In C. Murchison (Ed.). *Psychologies of 1930*. Worcester, Mass.: Clark Univ. Press, 1930, pp. 395–405.
Adler, A. *What life should mean to you*. Boston: Little, 1931.
Adler, A. The fundamental views of Individual Psychology. *Int. J. Indiv. Psychol.*, 1935, *1*, 5–8.
Adler, A. *Social interest*. New York: Putnam, 1939.
Ansbacher, H. L., and Rowena R. (Eds.). *The Individual-Psychology of Alfred Adler*. New York: Basic Books, 1956.
Blitsten, Dorothy R. *The social theories of Harry Stack Sullivan*. New York: The William-Frederick Press, 1953.

Bottome, Phyllis. *Alfred Adler; a biography.* New York: Putnam, 1939.

Colby, K. M. On the disagreement between Freud and Adler. *Amer. Imago,* 1951, 8, 229–238.

Deutsch, F., and Murphy, W. F. *The clinical interview.* New York: International Universities Press, 1955.

Fromm, E. *Escape from freedom.* New York: Rinehart, 1941.

Fromm, E. *Man for himself.* New York: Rinehart, 1947.

Fromm, E. *The sane society.* New York: Rinehart, 1955.

Fromm-Reichmann, Frieda. *Principles of intensive psychotherapy.* Chicago: Univ. of Chicago Press, 1950.

Horney, Karen. *Neurotic personality of our times.* New York: Norton, 1937.

Horney, Karen. *New ways in psychoanalysis.* New York: Norton, 1939.

Horney, Karen. *Self-analysis.* New York: Norton, 1942.

Horney, Karen. *Our inner conflicts.* New York: Norton, 1945.

Horney, Karen. *Neurosis and human growth.* New York: Norton, 1950.

James, W. T. Karen Horney and Erich Fromm in relation to Alfred Adler. *Indiv. Psychol. Bull.,* 1947, 6, 105–116.

Jones, E. *The life and work of Sigmund Freud.* Vol. 2. New York: Basic Books, 1955.

Jones, H. E. Order of birth in relation to the development of the child. In C. Murchison (Ed.). *Handbook of child psychology.* Worcester, Mass.: Clark Univ. Press, 1931, pp. 204–241.

Maccoby, Eleanor E., and Maccoby, N. The interview: a tool of social science. In G. Lindzey (Ed.). *Handbook of social psychology.* Vol. I. Cambridge: Addison-Wesley, 1954, pp. 449–487.

Mullahy, P. *Oedipus—myth and complex.* New York: Hermitage House, 1948.

Mullahy, P. (Ed.). *A study of interpersonal relations.* New York: Hermitage House, 1949.

Mullahy, P. (Ed.). *The contributions of Harry Stack Sullivan.* New York: Hermitage House, 1952.

Munroe, Ruth. *Schools of psychoanalytic thought.* New York: Dryden Press, 1955.

Ruesch, J., and Bateson, G. *Communication, the social matrix of psychiatry.* New York: Norton, 1951.

Stanton, A. H., and Schwartz, M. S. *The mental hospital.* New York: Basic Books, 1954.

Sullivan, H. S. *Conceptions of modern psychiatry.* Washington, D. C.: William Alanson White Psychiatric Foundation, 1947.

Sullivan, H. S. Tensions interpersonal and international: a psychiatrist's view. In H. Cantril (Ed.). *Tensions that cause war.* Urbana, Ill.: Univ. of Illinois Press, 1950, pp. 79–138.

Sullivan, H. S. *The interpersonal theory of psychiatry.* New York: Norton, 1953.

Sullivan, H. S. *The psychiatric interview.* New York: Norton, 1954.

Vaihinger, H. *The philosophy of "as if."* New York: Harcourt, 1925.

5.

Murray's Personology

Unique among personality theorists is the sophistication in biological science, clinical practice, and academic psychology which Henry A. Murray brings to his theoretical efforts. As a rich integrative force for these diverse talents Murray possesses a brilliant writing style nurtured by a deep and enduring interest in literature and the humanities. The theory that has evolved from these sources shows a considerable respect for the determinant importance of biological factors, a full appreciation for the individual complexity of the human organism, and an interest in representing behavior in such a manner that controlled investigation is a natural outcome of these formulations.

The focus of this theory is upon the individual in all his complexity and this point of view is highlighted by the term "personology" which was introduced by Murray (1938) as a label for his own efforts and those of others who were primarily concerned with a full understanding of the individual case. He has emphasized consistently the organic quality of behavior, indicating that a single segment of behavior is not to be understood in isolation from the rest of the functioning person. In contrast to many other theorists who share this belief, Murray is perfectly willing to engage in the abstraction necessary to permit various kinds of specialized study—always insisting that the task of reconstruction must be engaged in after analysis is completed. A further contrast to most holistic theorists is his "field" orientation: his insistence that the environmental context of behavior must be thoroughly understood and analyzed before an adequate account of individual behavior is possible. Not only has Murray placed general emphasis upon the importance of environmental determinants but, more distinctively, he has developed an elaborate set of concepts designed to represent these environmental forces.

The past or history of the individual is fully as important in Murray's view as the present individual and his environment. His theory shares with psychoanalysis the assumption that events taking place in infancy and childhood are crucial determinants of adult behavior. A further similarity between this position and psychoanalysis lies in the considerable importance attributed to unconscious motivation and the deep interest displayed in the subjective or free, verbal report of the individual, including his imaginative productions.

In many ways the most distinctive feature of this theory is its highly differentiated and carefully specified treatment of motivation. Murray's scheme of motivational concepts has seen wide usage and has been of great influence. A further unusual feature of the theory is the consistent emphasis upon the coexisting and functionally linked physiological processes which accompany all psychological processes. His concept of "regnancy," which we shall discuss later, serves to keep the theorist continuously oriented toward the brain as the locus of personality and all its component parts. Murray has often emphasized the importance of detailed description as a necessary prelude to complicated theoretical formulation and investigation. Consistent with this point of view is his deep interest in taxonomy and the exhaustive classifications which he has established for many aspects of behavior.

Murray has made serious efforts to effect a compromise between the often conflicting demands of clinical complexity and investigative economy. He has devised means of representing, at least in part, the tremendous diversity of human behavior; and at the same time he has focused upon the task of constructing operations for assessing variables that occupy a central role in this theoretical scheme. This twofold emphasis has led naturally to narrowing the gap between clinical practice and the psychological laboratory.

We have now seen the broad outlines of Murray's personology, but what of the man who constructed this theory? Henry Murray was born in New York City on May 13, 1893, and received his education at Groton School and Harvard College, securing his A.B. from the latter institution in 1915 with a major in history. Following graduation from Harvard he enrolled in the Columbia College of Physicians and Surgeons where he graduated at the head of his class in 1919. In 1920 he received an M.A. in biology from Columbia and served briefly as an instructor in physiology at Harvard University following which he served a two-year surgical interneship at Presbyterian Hospital in New York. He then joined the staff of the Rockefeller Institute for Medical Research in New York City where as an assistant he carried on embryological research for two years. Following this came a period of study at Cambridge University where he conducted biochemical research which led to his securing a Ph.D. in biochemistry from Cambridge in 1927. It was during this interval of European study that his interests first began to turn seriously toward psychology. This intellectual evolution is best described in Murray's own words:

At college a bud of interest in psychology was nipped by the chill of Professor Münsterberg's approach. In the middle of his second lecture I began looking for the nearest exit. There was more bread (and fewer stones) in biology and chemistry, and afterwards in medicine. During my fourth year at the College of Physicians and Surgeons, while waiting for calls to deliver babies in Hell's Kitchen, I completed a modest study of 25 of my classmates, in which 40 anthropometric measures were correlated with 30 traits. Here I had the symphony of the endrocrines in mind. Later, as an interne in a hospital, I spent more time than was considered proper for a surgeon, inquisitively seeking psychogenic factors in my patients. Whatever I succeeded in doing for some of them—the dope fiend, the sword-swallower, the prostitute, the gangster—was more than repaid when, after leaving the hospital, they took me through their haunts in the underworld. This was psychology in the rough, but at least it prepared me to recognize the similarity between downtown doings and uptown dreams. . . . Then psychology was put aside, and did not come up again until I began to wonder, after several years of research in biochemistry and physiology, why some of the men with whom I was associated at the Rockefeller Institute clung so tenaciously to diametrically opposing views about the simplest phenomena. In the hope of shedding light on conceptual preferences as functions of personality, I sent out a long questionnaire to fifty creative thinkers (mostly scientists); and still puzzled, I took courses in philosophy with Professor Morris Cohen and later at Cambridge with Professor Broad. But it was Jung's book, *Psychological Types*, which, by providing a partial answer to my question, started me off in earnest toward psychology. There were besides this, another book, a woman, some German music and several other fructifying influences that made me feel and think at once, instead of separately.

On the crest of a wave I visited Dr. Jung in Zurich supposedly to discuss abstractions; but in a day or two to my astonishment enough affective stuff erupted to invalid a pure scientist. This was my first opportunity to weigh psychoanalysis in a balance; and I recommend it as one method of measuring the worth of any brand of personology. Take your mysteries, your knottiest dilemmas, to a fit exponent of a system and judge the latter by its power to order and illumine your whole being. . . . In 1925 . . . I had no scales to weigh out Dr. Jung, the first full-blooded, spherical—and Goethian, I should say—intelligence I had ever met, the man whom the judicious Prinzhorn called "the ripest fruit on the tree of psycho-analytical knowledge." We talked for hours, sailing down the lake and smoking before the hearth of his Faustian retreat. "The great floodgates of the wonder-world swung open," and I saw things that my philosophy had never dreamt of. Within a month a score of bi-horned problems were resolved, and I went off decided on depth psychology. I had *experienced* the unconscious, something not to be drawn out of books (Murray, 1940, pp. 152–153).

Thus, deeply interested in psychology Murray returned to this country and the Rockefeller Institute where he remained for one year as an associate before accepting in 1927 an invitation to come to Harvard University as an instructor in psychology. This unconventional choice of an unusual man, untrained in academic psychology, by a distinguished, traditional department of psychology was arranged by Morton Prince who had just founded the Harvard Psychological Clinic. The clinic was endowed with the explicit provision that it be devoted to the study and teaching of abnormal and dynamic psychology and Prince, searching for a young and promising scholar to guide the future of the clinic, selected Murray. In 1928 Murray was made an assistant professor and director of the Psychological Clinic, and in 1937 he was made an associate professor. He was one of the charter members of the Boston Psychoanalytic Society and by 1935 had completed his training in psychoanalysis under Franz Alexander and Hans Sachs. A fascinating account of his training analysis and his attitudes toward psychoanalysis is contained in a symposium concerning psychologists and psychoanalysis (Murray, 1940).

During the roughly fifteen years that transpired before war interrupted, the Harvard Psychological Clinic, under the intellectual and spiritual leadership of Henry Murray, was the scene of an intensely creative theoretical and empirical enterprise. Murray gathered about him a group of able young students whose joint efforts to formulate and investigate the human personality were exceedingly fruitful. The *Explorations in personality* volume (1938) contains a partial record of the generativeness of this era but the most important outcomes were carried away in the form of values, conceptions, and intentions by individuals such as Donald W. MacKinnon, Saul Rosenzweig, R. Nevitt Sanford, Silvan S. Tomkins, and Robert W. White. Here at the Clinic for the first time psychoanalytic theory was given a serious academic audience and earnest efforts were made to devise means of translating the brilliant clinical insights of Freud into experimental operations which would permit some degree of empirical confirmation or rejection. Not only did Murray create a sense of excitement and imminent discovery among his own students but also the clinic opened its doors to mature scholars from a variety of fields (Erik Homburger Erikson, Cora DuBois, Walter Dyk, H. Scudder McKeel) so that there was a marked interdisciplinary aura to the enterprise.

In 1943 this era came to a close as Murray left Harvard to join the Army Medical Corps where as a major, and subsequently lieutenant colonel, he established and directed an assessment service for the Office of Strategic Services. His organization was given the difficult task of screening candidates for complex, secret, and dangerous missions. The activities of this group have been summarized in *Assessment of men* (1948). His work with the Army led to his being awarded the Legion of Merit in 1946. In 1947 he returned to Harvard on a part-time basis as a lecturer on clinical psychology in the newly formed Department of Social Relations and in 1950 he was appointed professor of clinical psychology. He established the Psychological Clinic Annex at Harvard University in 1949 where he and a few colleagues and graduate students have since conducted further studies of personality.

As the preceding paragraphs make clear, Murray is not a person whose intellectual antecedents are easy to specify. The number and diversity of theoretical exemplars to which he has been exposed are so great that we can hope to do no more than select a few of the more prominent. Clearly psychoanalysis, in the broadest sense of the term, has had a great deal to do with his intellectual development. In a direct and personal sense Jung, Alexander, and Sachs have all influenced him and Freud, primarily through his writing, has had great impact. The depth of the influence of psychoanalysis upon Murray's view of behavior is clearly revealed in the following passage:

> I can hardly think myself back to the myopia that once so seriously restricted my view of human nature, so natural has it become for me to receive impressions of wishes, dramas and assumptions that underlie the

acts and talk of everyone I meet. Instead of seeing merely a groomed American in a business suit, travelling to and from his office like a rat in a maze, a predatory ambulating apparatus of reflexes, habits, stereotypes, and slogans, a bundle of consistencies, conformities, and allegiances to this or that institution—a robot in other words—I visualize (just as I visualize the activity of his internal organs) a flow of powerful subjective life, conscious and unconscious; a whispering gallery in which voices echo from the distant past; a gulf stream of fantasies with floating memories of past events, currents of contending complexes, plots and counterplots, hopeful intimations and ideals. To a neurologist such perspectives are absurd, archaic, tender-minded; but in truth they are much closer to the actualities of inner life than are his own neat diagrams of reflex arcs and nerve anastomoses. A personality is a full Congress of orators and pressure-groups, of children, demagogues, communists, isolationists, war-mongers, mugwumps, grafters, log-rollers, lobbyists, Caesars and Christs, Machiavellis and Judases, Tories and Promethean revolutionists. And a psychologist who does not know this in himself, whose mind is locked against the flux of images and feelings, should be encouraged to make friends, by being psychoanalyzed, with the various members of his household (Murray, 1940, pp. 160–161).

Murray's medical and biological research and training have contributed to the deep respect he has consistently shown for the importance of physical and biological factors in behavior. His experience in medical diagnosis has had an obvious outcome in his belief that personality should ideally be assessed by a team of specialists and that in this assessment the subject's statements about himself should be given serious audience. His interest in the taxonomy or classification of behavior, as well as his conviction that the careful study of individual cases is an essential to future psychological progress, are also highly congruent with his medical background. His detailed awareness of the great literary creations of our own and past eras, and particularly his expert knowledge of Melville and his works, have provided him with an inexhaustible source of ideas concerning man and his potentialities for good and evil. The exquisite mind of Alfred North Whitehead provided a model of logical and synthetic thought, while the truculent but brilliant Lawrence J. Henderson served as a model of rigor and critical orientation. His thinking has absorbed much from academic psychologists with Lewin and McDougall as perhaps the most significant of these sources of influence. Cultural anthropology, with Clyde Kluckhohn as the most important agent, also contributed its share to his thinking. From such a complex lineage it is no wonder that the evolved product is an elaborate and many-sided structure.

It is clear to all who have known him that Henry Murray's talent and devotion to the study of the human personality are only partially revealed in his published works. His casual remarks and free-ranging speculations concerning an endless variety of topics, which were so integral a part of lunches at the Psychological Clinic, have provided fruitful research ideas for dozens of his students and colleagues. Unfortunately not all of these messages fell on fertile ground and one can only regreat that the spoken word has not been preserved to enrich the written record. Murray's tendency to reveal only occasional fruits of his intellect is clearly demonstrated in the publications that have stemmed from his twenty-five years of intensive study of Herman Melville. These years of dedicated scholarship have earned him a reputation among students of Melville that is without parallel and yet he has thus far published but two papers dealing with this engrossing topic. One is a brilliant analysis of the psychological meaning of *Moby Dick* (Murray, 1951c), about which we shall have more to say later, and the other an introduction to and penetrating analysis of *Pierre* (Murray, 1949b), one of Melville's most intriguing and baffling novels.

Granted the inadequacy of the written record, we find that Murray's psychological theorizing and research are best represented in *Explorations in personality* (1938), which summarizes the thought and research of the Psychological Clinic staff at the end of its first decade of existence. A partial record of some of the subsequent research is contained in *A clinical study of sentiments* (1945), which was written with his long-time collaborator Christiana Morgan. The major changes that his theoretical convictions have undergone during the subsequent years are best represented in a chapter written jointly with Clyde Kluckhohn (1953), a chapter published in *Toward a general theory of action* (1951a), and an article published in *Dialectica* (1951b). The *Manual of Thematic Apperception Test* (1943) serves as the best introduction to this personality instrument, devised jointly with Christiana Morgan (Morgan and Murray, 1935), which has become one of the most important and widely used empirical tools of the clinician and personality investigator. The great sensitivity and ingenuity which Murray has shown in developing means of appraising and analyzing man's capacities and directional tendencies are vividly revealed in *Assessment of men* (1948).

Murray's theoretical writings have occasionally pointed to the importance for human beings of variety or change and Murray is consistent with his theory, in at least this instance, for his theoretical ideas are constantly being overhauled and recast. Thus, what follows may accurately represent the main themes of Murray's thought but it almost certainly will be inaccurate in regard to some of the details of his present position.

THE STRUCTURE OF PERSONALITY

The nature of personality and its acquisitions and attainments have occupied a considerable portion of Murray's theoretical attention. His views on the structure of personality have been heavily influenced by psychoanalytic theory and yet in many respects they are strikingly differentiated from an orthodox Freudian view. Here we shall consider Murray's definition of personality and the concepts he has elaborated in the attempt to represent the nature of personality.

DEFINITION OF PERSONALITY. Although Murray has proposed many definitions of personality at different times the major elements of these definitions are contained in the following illustrations:

> The term "personality" has been reserved for the hypothetical structure of the mind, the consistent establishments and processes of which are manifested over and over again (together with some unique or novel elements) in the internal and external proceedings which constitute a person's life. Thus personality is not a series of biographical facts but something more general and enduring that is inferred from the facts (Murray and Kluckhohn, 1953, p. 30).
>
> Personality is the governing organ of the body, an institution, which, from birth to death, is ceaselessly engaged in transformative functional operations (Murray, 1951a, p. 436).

These definitions contain several important components. First, they make clear the abstract nature of personality, the fact that it is a construction of the theorist which, although related to specific empirical events, is not simply a summary of these events. The individual's personality will clearly vary depending upon the theorist who is representing or formulating it. Second, there is the implication that the individual's personality refers to a series of events which in the ideal case span his entire lifetime. This longitudinal emphasis is expressed more strongly in the phrase "the history of the personality *is* the personality" which appears time and again throughout Murray's writing. Third, the definitions imply that personality should reflect the enduring and recurrent elements of behavior as well as the novel and unique. Fourth, personality is the organizing or governing agent of the individual. It is the personality which produces order and integration among the disparate impulses and constraints to which the individual is exposed.

The conception of personality as an organizing and integrating force readily suggests the question of what the major functions of personality are. Murray has described these as follows:

. . . the general functions of personality are to exercise its processes, to express itself, to learn to generate and reduce insistent need-tensions, to form serial programs for the attainment of distant goals, and, finally, to lessen or resolve conflicts by forming schedules which more nearly permit the frictionless appeasement of its major needs (Murray and Kluckhohn, 1953, p. 39).

To this list Murray subsequently adds the functions of adjusting aspiration levels so to increase the likelihood of their being attained and controlling behavior so as to conform to social expectation.

The major revelant theme in Murray's writings thus far omitted is the emphasis upon the physiological ground of personality. Consistent with his experience in biological science Murray has chosen to stress the biological processes accompanying or underlying all of the events with which the psychologist concerns himself. In fact he has suggested that:

Personality may be biologically defined as the governing organ, or superordinate institution, of the body. As such, it is located in the brain. No brain, no personality (Murray, 1951b, p. 267).

Thus, Murray throughout all of his writings has chosen to anchor personality firmly in the brain, pointing out that all we know of the physiological processes necessary for behaviorial function indicates that the brain must be the seat of the organizing and executive functions—the personality.

. . . since all complex adaptive behavior is evidently co-ordinated by excitations in the brain, the unity of the organism's development and behavior can be explained only by referring to organizations occurring in this region. It is brain processes, rather than those in the rest of the body, which are of special interest to the psychologist (Murray, 1938, p. 45).

As we shall see later, not only the personality but all of the specific variables employed in representing personality are considered to have their accompanying brain processes.

In spite of this insistence upon giving the personality a locus in the brain, we find Murray convinced that the psychologist must make his advances independently of contributions from physiology and neurology. He feels that:

. . . the behaviors of human personalities are on a different level from physiological phenomena, and hence should be studied and conceptualized in their own right without waiting for more "basic" sciences to provide a complete formulation (Murray and Kluckhohn, 1953, p. 4).

Thus, Murray's attempts at a definition of personality make clear that he is strongly oriented toward a view which gives adequate weight to the past of the organism, to the organizing function of personality, to the recurrent and novel features of the individual's behavior, to the abstract or conceptual nature of personality, and to the physiological processes underlying the psychological.

PERSONALITY AS A PARTIAL FORMATION. Murray has emphasized that properly one should speak of formulation rather than diagnosis when describing what the psychologist does in portraying a personality. Diagnosis implies a fixed component or identity in terms of which the individual is compared whereas what the personality psychologist actually does is ". . . an exercise in constructive conceptualization, hypothetical and tentative, a step, at best, in the direction of a typology" (Murray, 1951b, p. 276). Thus, the term formulation emphasizes the fact that personality description is still in part an artistic process with few firm guide lines and rules of procedure. It also points to the abstract nature of the process and, consistent with Murray's definition of personality, reminds the user that the personality formulated is in part determined by the particular theorist or the theoretical constructs employed.

Not only must a personality description be considered a formulation rather than a description but also this formulation is always incomplete or partial, designed to serve certain particular functions rather than to predict all behavior at all times. A complete formulation would require so much detail and would be so cumbersome as to be impractical.

PROCEEDINGS AND SERIALS. The basic data of the psychologist are proceedings, which are subject-object interactions, or subject-subject interactions, of sufficient duration to include the significant elements of any given behaviorial sequence. In Murray's words:

. . . proceedings are the things which we observe, and try to represent with models, and to explain, the things which we attempt to predict, the facts against which we test the adequacy of our formulations (Murray, 1951b, pp. 269–270).

Although in certain settings it is possible to define a proceeding exactly, for example, a verbal response and its reply, it is usually possible to provide only a very general definition. In this spirit Murray suggests that, "Ideally, the duration of a proceeding is determined

by 1) the initiation, and by 2) the completion, of a dynamically significant pattern of behavior . . ." (Murray, 1951b, p. 269).

This conception of the basic unit of the psychologist as consisting
of proceedings reflects Murray's conviction that behavior is inextricably
caught in a time dimension. Thus, the proceeding is a compromise
between the practical limitations imposed by the intellect and techniques of the investigator and the empirical given that behavior exists
in a time dimension. Murray suggests that proceedings can be classified in terms of whether they are *internal* (daydreaming, problem-
solving, planning in solitude) or *external* (interacting with persons or
objects in the environment).

In a recent unpublished work, Murray has emphasized that at any
single moment an individual may be engaged in a multitude of proceedings. He may be watching television, talking to a friend, drinking, listening for the sound of a waking child, petting his dog, scowling
at his wife, all during the same short period of time. Thus, if the
individual's behavior is examined closely one will usually discover a
number of *overlapping proceedings* occurring simultaneously. The
term *durance* is used to designate a temporal unit of living including
all of the overlapping proceedings, a unit which embraces the natural
complexity of the person's existence. The concept of durance makes
clear that the single proceeding is ordinarily an abstraction from the
complexity of ongoing behavior and represents only one trend or
aspect among many. It is possible to divide the individual's life into
long durances (childhood, adolescence, old age) or into *short durances* (responding to a stimulus for one minute, a traumatic experience of ten minutes' duration).

For many purposes the representation of behavior in terms of proceedings is perfectly adequate. However, under some circumstances it
is necessary to include in a single unit or formulation behavior taking
place over a longer period of time. This longer functional unit of
behavior is referred to as a *serial.*

. . . a directionally organized intermittent succession of proceedings may
be called a *serial.* Thus, a serial (such as friendship, a marriage, a career
in business) is a relatively long functional unit which can be formulated
only roughly. One must obtain records of critical proceedings along its
course and note such indices of development as changes of disposition,
increase of knowledge, increase of ability, improvement in the quality of
the work accomplished, and so forth. No one proceeding in the serial can
be understood without reference to those which have led up to it and
without reference to the actor's aims and expectations, his design for the
future (Murray, 1951b, p. 272).

Thus, representation of behavior in terms of serials is made necessary because certain proceedings are so intimately related to one another that it is impossible to study them separately without destroying their full meaning.

SERIAL PROGRAMS AND SCHEDULES. A very important function for the individual is served by *serial programs, which are orderly arrangements of subgoals that stretch into the future perhaps for months or years and which, if all goes well, will lead eventually to some desired end state.* Thus, the individual aspires to the goal of becoming a medical doctor but intervening between his present situation and this goal are years of study and special training. If he develops a set of subgoals, each of which plays a part in bringing him closer to his medical degree, this would be referred to as a serial program.

Likewise of importance are *schedules which represent devices for reducing conflict among competing needs and goal objects by arranging for expression of these tendencies at different times.* By means of a schedule the individual may give a maximum of expression to his various aims. If he is efficient at constructing schedules he can greatly diminish the quantity and intensity of his conflicts.

Murray has recently subsumed serial programs and schedules under the term *ordination which includes the process of plan-making as well as the outcome of the process*—an established program or schedule. According to Murray's present views, ordination is a higher mental process on the same level as cognition. The aim of cognition is a complete conceptual understanding of the environment, but once the external situation has been sufficiently understood, the process of ordination asserts itself in order to arrange policy-making and planning of strategy and tactics.

ABILITIES AND ACHIEVEMENTS. In contrast to many personality psychologists, Murray has shown a consistent interest in ability and achievement and considers these qualities an important part of the personality. These components of the individual serve a central function in mediating between dispositions to action and the end results toward which these dispositions are oriented. In virtually all of his personality research subjects have been appraised in terms of a variety of different areas of ability and achievement: physical, mechanical, leadership, social, economic, erotic, and intellectual.

ESTABLISHMENTS OF PERSONALITY. Even if we accept personality as an ever-changing phenomenon, still there are certain stabilities or structures that appear over time and which are crucial to an understanding of behavior. In representing these mental structures, Murray borrows the terms ego, id, and superego from psychoanalysis but introduces certain distinctive elements in his development of these concepts.

Murray agrees with Freud in conceiving of the *id* as the repository of primitive and unacceptable impulses. Here is the origin of energy, the source of all innate motives, the unseeing and unsocialized self. More than this, insists Murray, the id includes impulses which are acceptable to the self and society. In making clear his difference with orthodox psychoanalytic theory on this score he states:

> In due time it became apparent to other analysts, if not to Freud, that the concept of id could not be limited to unacceptable dispositions. In infancy, for example, when the ego system is non-existent or at best very rudimentary, the mind is a hive of involuntary spontaneities, emotions, and needs, many of which are not only acceptable to the child and its mother during these early years, but continue to be acceptable and, what is more, culturally encouraged throughout life. It would not be proper to say that respiration, ingestion of food, defecation, expressions of affection, endeavors to master the environment, and so forth, had their sources in the ego. . . . It seems best to think of the id as consisting of all the basic energies, emotions, and needs (value-vectors) of the personality, some of which are wholly acceptable . . . when expressed in a culturally approved form, towards a culturally approved object, in a culturally approved place, at a culturally approved time (Murray and Kluckhohn, 1953, p. 24).

Not only does the id contain impulses toward both good and evil but the strength of these tendencies varies between individuals. Thus the task facing different individuals in controlling or directing their id tendencies is by no means of equal difficulty.

We have already seen that in Murray's theory the id is not wholly wicked and asocial. Further, the *ego* is not solely an inhibitor and repressor. Not only must the ego hold back or repress certain impulses or motives but more importantly it must arrange, schedule, and control the manner in which other motives are to appear. The ego, consistent with psychoanalytic theory, is viewed as the central organizer or integrator of behavior. Part of this organization, however, is intended to facilitate or promote the expression of certain id impulses. The strength and effectiveness of the ego is an important determinant of the individual's adjustment.

The *superego* in Murray's theory, as in Freud's, is considered to be a cultural implant. It is an internalized subsystem which acts within the individual to regulate behavior in much the same manner that agents outside the individual once acted. These agents, typically the parents, acted as surrogates of the culture so that internalizing their prescriptions represents a move in the direction of internalizing cultural prescriptions. The nature of the superego is determined in large part by the kinds of experiences involving parents and authority figures to which the individual is exposed. Murray suggests that in addition to this important source of influence, however, there is also the impact of peer groups as well as the significant contribution of literary and mythological figures. The standards acquired from these sources become internalized and act as a source of reward or punishment depending upon how well the action of the individual meets these standards.

Intimately related to the superego is the *ego-ideal* which consists of an idealized picture of the self—an aspired self, or a set of personal ambitions toward which the individual strives.

> One of the important establishments of personality is the ego ideal, an integrate of images which portrays the person "at his future best," realizing all his ambitions. More specifically, it is a set of serial programs, each of which has a different level of aspiration. Ego ideals run all the way from the Master Criminal to the Serene Sage. They are imaginatively created and recreated in the course of development in response to patterns offered by the environment—mythological, historical, or living exemplars. Thus the history of the ideal self may be depicted as a series of imaginative identifications, of heroes and their worship (Murray and Kluckhohn, 1953, p. 40).

The ego-ideal may be entirely divorced from the superego, as in the case of the individual who aspires to be a Dillinger, or it may be closely related, so that the individual moves toward personal ambitions in a manner conforming exactly with the sanctions of his society. If the superego is dominant and the ego-ideal is suppressed, the person may attempt to serve "God's will" or the "welfare of the society" at the expense of giving up all personal ambition.

It is important to note that Murray's conception of the superego and ego-ideal provides more latitude for alteration and development in the years subsequent to childhood than does the orthodox psychoanalytic view. Murray also indicates that a prime function of the superego is the instigation of time-place-mode-object formulae for the expression of various needs. That is, the individual internalizes from his exemplars prescriptions as to *when* a given need should be expressed, *where* it should be expressed, *how* it should be expressed, and toward *which objects* it should be directed. It is less a matter of the individual being totally unable to express certain needs than it is a matter of his being able to express these needs only under sanctioned circumstances.

In normal development the relation between these three institutions changes so that where once the id ruled supreme, the superego and eventually the ego come to have determinant roles. In the happiest of instances a benign superego and a strong and ingenious ego combine to permit adequate expression of id impulses under circumstances that are culturally approved.

THE DYNAMICS OF PERSONALITY

It is in the representation of man's striving, seeking, desiring, wishing, and willing that Murray's contributions to psychological theory have been most distinctive. One might fairly say that his position is primarily a motivational psychology. This focusing upon the motivational process is perfectly congruent with Murray's conviction that the study of man's directional tendencies holds the key to understanding human behavior. ". . . the most important thing to discover about an individual . . . is the superordinate *directionality* (or directionalities) of his activities, whether mental, verbal, or physical" (Murray, 1951b, p. 276). Murray's interest in directionality has led to the most complex and carefully delineated system of motivational constructs that can be found on the contemporary psychological scene. His taxonomic interests are clearly revealed here in the patient and absorbed classifying of the elements of human behavior in terms of their underlying determinants or motives.

Murray is certainly not the first person to place heavy emphasis upon the importance of motivational analysis. However, his formulations possess several distinctive elements. While the prevailing tides in psychology have flowed in the direction of simplicity and a small number of concepts, Murray has insisted that an adequate understanding of human motivation must rest upon a system that employs a sufficiently large number of variables to reflect, at least partially, the tremendous complexity of human motives in the raw. He also has made serious efforts to provide empirical definitions for his variables which, if imperfect, at least far exceed the operational effectiveness of most of the preceding schemes in the field of human motivation. The result of these efforts is a set of concepts which makes a bold attempt to bridge the gap between clinical description and the demands of empirical research.

In considering Murray's theory of motivation we shall begin with a discussion of the *need* concept, which from the beginning has been the focus of his conceptual efforts, and follow this with a discussion of such related concepts as *press, tension reduction, thema, need integrate, unity-thema,* and *regnancy.* Finally we shall turn to his related *value* and *vector* concepts which represent a more recent turn in his theorizing.

NEED. Although the concept of need has been widely used in psychology, no other theorist has subjected the concept to so careful an analysis nor provided such a complete taxonomy of needs as has Murray. The detail of Murray's analysis of this concept is suggested by his definition:

> A need is a construct (a convenient fiction or hypothetical concept) which stands for a force . . . in the brain region, a force which organizes perception, apperception, intellection, conation and action in such a way as to transform in a certain direction an existing, unsatisfying situation. A need is sometimes provoked directly by internal processes of a certain kind . . . but, more frequently (when in a state of readiness) by the occurrence of one of a few commonly effective press [environmental forces]. . . . Thus, it manifests itself by leading the organism to search for or to avoid encountering or, when encountered, to attend and respond to certain kinds of press. . . . Each need is characteristically accompanied by a particular feeling or emotion and tends to use certain modes . . . to further its trend. It may be weak or intense, momentary or enduring. But usually it persists and gives rise to a certain course of overt behavior (or fantasy), which . . . changes the initiating circumstance in such a way as to bring about an end situation which stills (appeases or satisfies) the organism (Murray, 1938, pp. 123–124).

We find from this definition that the concept of need, as was true for the concept of personality, is ceded an abstract or hypothetical status but is nevertheless linked to underlying physiological processes in the brain. It is also conceived that needs may be either internally aroused or set into action as a result of external stimulation. In either case the need produces activity on the part of the organism and maintains this activity until the organism-environment situation has been altered so as to reduce the need. Some needs are accompanied by particular emotions or feelings, and they are frequently associated with particular instrumental acts which are effective in producing the desired end state.

Murray states that the existence of a need can be inferred on the basis of: (1) the effect or end result of the behavior, (2) the particular pattern or mode of behavior involved, (3) the selective attention and response to a particular class of stimulus objects, (4) the expression of a particular emotion or affect, and (5) the expression of satisfaction when a particular effect is achieved or disappointment when the effect is not achieved (1938, p. 124). Subjective reports regarding feelings, intentions, and goals provide additional criteria. Given the general definition and the above criteria for inferring or classifying needs, Murray, following the intensive study of a small number of subjects, arrived at a tentative list of twenty needs. Although this list has been subjected to considerable modification and elaboration the original twenty needs remain highly representative. These variables were presented in *Explorations in personality* (1938) with an outline of pertinent facts concerning each need, including questionnaire items for measuring the need, accompanying emotions, and illustrations of the need. The twenty needs are briefly listed and defined in Table 1.

TABLE 1

ILLUSTRATIVE LIST OF MURRAY'S NEEDS *

Need	Brief Definition
n Abasement	To submit passively to external force. To accept injury, blame, criticism, punishment. To surrender. To become resigned to fate. To admit inferiority, error, wrongdoing, or defeat. To confess and atone. To blame, belittle, or mutilate the self. To seek and enjoy pain, punishment, illness, and misfortune.
n Achievement	To accomplish something difficult. To master, manipulate, or organize physical objects, human beings, or ideas. To do this as rapidly and as independently as possible. To overcome obstacles and attain a high standard. To excel oneself. To rival and surpass others. To increase self-regard by the successful exercise of talent.
n Affiliation	To draw near and enjoyably co-operate or reciprocate with an allied other (an other who resembles the subject or who likes the subject). To please and win affection of a cathected object. To adhere and remain loyal to a friend.
n Aggression	To overcome opposition forcefully. To fight. To revenge an injury. To attack, injure, or kill another. To oppose forcefully or punish another.
n Autonomy	To get free, shake off restraint, break out of confinement. To resist coercion and restriction. To avoid or quit activities prescribed by domineering authorities. To be independent and free to act according to impulse. To be unattached, irresponsible. To defy convention.
n Counteraction	To master or make up for a failure by restriving. To obliterate a humiliation by resumed action. To overcome weaknesses, to repress fear. To efface a dishonor by action. To search for obstacles and difficulties to overcome. To maintain self-respect and pride on a high level.

TABLE 1 *(Continued)*

Need	Brief Definition
n Defendance	To defend the self against assault, criticism, and blame. To conceal or justify a misdeed, failure, or humiliation. To vindicate the ego.
u Deference	To admire and support a superior. To praise, honor, or eulogize. To yield eagerly to the influence of an allied other. To emulate an exemplar. To conform to custom.
a Dominance	To control one's human environment. To influence or direct the behavior of others by suggestion, seduction, persuasion, or command. To dissuade, restrain, or prohibit.
n Exhibition	To make an impression. To be seen and heard. To excite, amaze, fascinate, entertain, shock, intrigue, amuse, or entice others.
n Harmavoidance	To avoid pain, physical injury, illness, and death. To escape from a dangerous situation. To take precautionary measures.
n Infavoidance	To avoid humiliation. To quit embarrassing situations or to avoid conditions which may lead to belittlement: the scorn, derision, or indifference of others. To refrain from action because of the fear of failure.
n Nurturance	To give sympathy and gratify the needs of a helpless object: an infant or any object that is weak, disabled, tired, inexperienced, infirm, defeated, humiliated, lonely, dejected, sick, mentally confused. To assist an object in danger. To feed, help, support, console, protect, comfort, nurse, heal.
n Order	To put things in order. To achieve cleanliness, arrangement, organization, balance, neatness, tidiness, and precision.
n Play	To act for "fun" without further purpose. To like to laugh and make jokes. To seek enjoyable relaxation of stress. To participate in games, sports, dancing, drinking parties, cards.
n Rejection	To separate oneself from a negatively cathected object. To exclude, abandon, expel, or remain indifferent to an inferior object. To snub or jilt an object.
n Sentience	To seek and enjoy sensuous impressions.
n Sex	To form and further an erotic relationship. To have sexual intercourse.
n Succorance	To have one's needs gratified by the sympathetic aid of an allied object. To be nursed, supported, sustained, surrounded, protected, loved, advised, guided, indulged, forgiven, consoled. To remain close to a devoted protector. To always have a supporter.
n Understanding	To ask or answer general questions. To be interested in theory. To speculate, formulate, analyze, and generalize.

* Adapted from Murray, 1938, pp. 152–226.

Types of needs. Thus far, we have seen how Murray defines need, we have examined the criteria he provides for their identification, and we have seen a typical list of needs. In addition to this it is important to consider the basis for distinguishing between different types of needs. First of all, there is the distinction between primary and secondary needs. The primary or *viscerogenic needs* are linked to characteristic organic events and typically refer to physical satisfactions. Illustrative of these are the needs for air, water, food, sex, lactation, urination, and defecation. The secondary or *psychogenic needs* are presumably derived from the primary needs and are characterized by a lack of focal connection with any specific organic processes or physical satisfactions. Illustrative of these are the needs for acquisition, construction, achievement, recognition, exhibition, dominance, autonomy, and deference.

Second, we have the distinction between *overt needs* and *covert needs,* that is, manifest needs and latent needs. Here we are differentiating between those needs that are permitted more or less direct and immediate expression and those that are generally restrained, inhibited, or repressed. One might say that overt needs typically express themselves in motor behavior while covert needs usually belong to the world of fantasy or dreams. The existence of covert needs is in large part the outcome of the development of internalized structures (superego) that define proper or acceptable conduct. Certain needs cannot be given free expression without violating the conventions or standards that have been taken over from society by means of the parents and these needs often operate at a covert level.

Third, there are *focal needs* and *diffuse needs.* Some needs are closely linked to limited classes of environmental objects whereas others are so generalized as to be applicable in almost any environmental setting. Murray points out that unless there is some unusual fixation a need is always subject to change in the objects toward which it is directed and the manner in which these are approached. That is, the sphere of environmental events to which the need is relevant may be broadened or narrowed and the instrumental acts linked to the need may be increased or decreased. If the need is firmly attached to an unsuitable object this is called a *fixation* and is customarily considered pathological. However, as Murray indicates, the inability of the need to show any enduring object preference may be just as pathological as a fixation.

Fourth, there are *proactive needs* and *reactive needs.* The pro-

active need is one that is largely determined from within, one that becomes "spontaneously kinetic" as the result of something in the person
rather than something in the environment. Reactive needs on the
other hand are activated as a result of, or in response to, some environmental event. The distinction here is largely that between a
response elicited by appropriate stimulation and a response produced
in the absence of any important stimulus variation. Murray uses these
concepts also to describe interaction between two or more persons
where usually one individual can be identified as the *proactor* (initiates
the interaction, asks the questions, in general provides the stimulus to
which the other must respond) and another individual can be identified as the *reactor* (reacts to the stimuli provided by the proactor).

Fifth, there is the distinction between *process activity, modal needs,*
and *effect needs.* American psychologists with their conventional emphasis upon function and utility have consistently emphasized effect
needs—needs which lead to some desired state or end result. Murray,
however, has insisted upon the equal importance of process activity
and modal needs—tendencies to perform certain acts for the sake of
the performance itself. The random, unco-ordinated, nonfunctional
operation of various processes (vision, hearing, thought, speech, and
so forth) which occurs from birth on is called process activity. This
is "sheer function pleasure," doing for the sake of doing.

> More basic and elementary than integrated goal-directed activities are
> the somewhat anarchic, unco-ordinated medley of tentative, short-lived
> mental processes which characterize the stream of consciousness during
> periods of rest and day dreaming, at one extreme, and during periods of
> intense emotional excitement or lunacy, at the other. For these spontane-
> ous, random, ungoverned, but yet expressive cacophonies of energy we
> have proposed the term "process activity." This is pure Being, a state
> in which the mind moves in its own inherent manner for its own intrinsic
> pleasure. We have only to conceptualize a free, irresponsible and playful
> release of vitality, enjoyed for its own sake (Murray and Kluckhohn, 1953,
> p. 37).

Modal needs, on the other hand, involve doing something with a certain degree of excellence or quality. It is still the activity which is
sought and enjoyed but it is now rewarding only when it is performed with a certain degree of perfection. These needs are satisfied by:

> . . . excellence of form (musical patterns, logical clarity and coherence,
> gracious social manners, executive efficiency as an art, verbal eloquence,
> beauty of physique and movement) and are different from process needs

insofar as they require *perfected* expressions, most of which can be achieved only by diligent application and discipline (Murray, 1951a, p. 446).

Interrelation of needs. It is evident that needs do not operate in complete isolation from each other and the nature of this interaction or mutual influence is of crucial theoretical importance. Murray accepts the fact that there exists a hierarchy of needs with certain tendencies taking precedence over others. The concept of *prepotency* is used to refer to needs which "become regnant with the greatest urgency if they are not satisfied" (Murray, 1951a, p. 452). Thus, in situations where two or more needs are aroused simultaneously and motivate incompatible responses, it is the prepotent need (such as pain, hunger, thirst) which ordinarily will be translated into action as prepotent needs cannot be postponed. A minimal satisfaction of such needs is necessary before other needs can operate. In his investigation of personality Murray has habitually employed a set of concepts to represent *conflict* involving important needs. Thus, it is customary in his research to secure estimates for each subject of the intensity of conflict in certain key areas, for example, autonomy versus compliance, achievement versus pleasure.

Under certain circumstances multiple needs may be gratified by a single course of action. In instances where the outcome of different needs is behaviorally the same Murray speaks of *fusion* of needs. Another important kind of relation among needs is referred to by the concept of *subsidiation.* A subsidiary need is one which operates in the service of another; for instance, the individual may show aggressive needs but these may be serving only to facilitate acquisitive needs. In any instance where the operation of one need is merely instrumental to the gratification of another we speak of the first need as subsidiary to the second. Tracing chains of subsidiation can be of great value in revealing the dominant or root motives of the individual.

We have now examined in a tentative fashion the manner in which Murray chooses to represent the motivation of the individual. However, these personal motivations are intimately linked with events taking place outside of the individual and it remains for us to scrutinize the manner in which Murray proposes to represent these significant environmental happenings. One may justifiably question the decision to consider environmental events in a section devoted to "dynamics of behavior." However, the motivational state of the individual and the operant environmental forces are so closely intertwined in Murray's view that it would be a serious distortion to separate them in our treatment here.

PRESS. Just as the concept of "need" represents the significant determinants of behavior within the person so the concept of "press" represents the effective or significant determinants of behavior in the environment. In simplest terms a press is a property or attribute of an environmental object or person which facilitates or impedes the efforts of the individual to reach a given goal. Press are linked to persons or objects that have direct implications for the efforts of the individual to satisfy his need strivings. "The *press* of an object is what it can *do to the subject* of *for the subject*—the power that it has to affect the well-being of the subject in one way or another" (1938, p. 121). By representing the environment in terms of press the investigator hopes to extract and classify the significant portions of the world in which the individual lives. Clearly we know a great deal more about what an individual is likely to do if we have a picture not only of his motives or directional tendencies but also a picture of the way in which he views or interprets his environment. It is this later function which the press concepts are designed to fulfill.

Murray has developed various lists of press for particular purposes. Representative of these is the classification contained in Table 2 which was designed to represent significant childhood events or influences. In practice these press are not only identified as operating in a given individual's experience but they are also assigned a quantitative rating to indicate their strength or importance in the individual's life.

It is important to distinguish between the significance of environmental objects as they are perceived or interpreted by the individual (*beta press*) and the properties of those environmental objects as they exist in reality or as objective inquiry discloses them (*alpha press*). The individual's behavior is most closely correlated with the beta press but it is nevertheless important to discover situations in which there is a wide discrepancy between the beta press to which the individual is reacting and the alpha press which actually exist.

Cathexis and sentiment. Murray adopts the conventional Freudian term "cathexis" for referring to the capacity of an environmental object to attract or repel the individual. A positive cathexis is said to exist if the individual likes or is attracted to a given object while a negative cathexis exists when an object arouses dislike and avoidance. In cases where an object is both attractive and repellent the individual is said to be ambivalent toward the object.

TABLE 2

ABBREVIATED LIST OF PRESS *

1. p Family Insupport
   a. Cultural Discord
   b. Family Discord
   c. Capricious Discipline
   d. Parental Separation
   e. Absence of Parent: Father,
      Mother
   f. Parental Illness: Father, Mother
   g. Death of Parent: Father, Mother
   h. Inferior Parent: Father, Mother
   i. Dissimilar Parent: Father,
      Mother
   j. Poverty
   k. Unsettled Home
2. p Danger or Misfortune
   a. Physical Insupport, Height
   b. Water
   c. Aloneness, Darkness
   d. Inclement Weather, Lightning
   e. Fire
   f. Accident
   g. Animal
3. p Lack or Loss
   a. of Nourishment
   b. of Possessions
   c. of Companionship
   d. of Variety
4. p Retention, Withholding Objects

5. p Rejection, Unconcern, and Scorn
6. p Rival, Competing Contemporary
7. p Birth of Sibling
8. p Aggression
   a. Maltreatment by Elder Male,
      Elder Female
   b. Maltreatment by Contempo-
      raries
   c. Quarrelsome Contemporaries
9. p Dominance, Coercion, and Pro-
   hibition
   a. Discipline
   b. Religious Training
10. p Nurturance, Indulgence
11. p Succorance, Demands for Ten-
    derness
12. p Deference, Praise, Recognition
13. p Affiliation, Friendships
14. p Sex
    a. Exposure
    b. Seduction; Homosexual, Heter-
       osexual
    c. Parental Intercourse
15. p Deception or Betrayal
16. p Inferiority
    a. Physical
    b. Social
    c. Intellectual

* Adapted from Murray, 1938, pp. 291–292.

The concept of "sentiment" represents a different way of viewing the same phenomenon. Where cathexis refers to the capacity *of the object* to attract or repel, sentiment refers to the tendency *within the individual to be attracted to or repelled by certain objects.* Murray defines a sentiment as: "a more or less enduring disposition . . . in a personality to respond with a positive or a negative affect to a specified entity" (Murray and Morgan, 1945). When an investigator is primarily interested in the object he normally uses the concept of cathexis, but when his focus is upon the individual the concept of sentiment is ordinally preferred.

The *Clinical study of sentiments* (Murray and Morgan, 1945) reports an intensive study of eleven subjects focused about sentiments toward war, religion, parents, and sex. One might fairly say that in this study Murray extends the concepts of cathexis and sentiment so that they can be applied to any person, object, or thought with which an individual can have transactions. He also considers the relation of cathexis and sentiment to other traditional psychological concepts and proposes a number of attributes and distinctions relative to the study and understanding of these aspects of behavior.

TENSION REDUCTION. We have already seen that Murray conceives of the individual as set into action by a complex set of motives. Further, he grants that when a need is aroused the individual is in a state of tension, and satisfaction of the need involves reduction of the tension. Finally, the organism will learn to attend to objects and perform acts that it has found in the past to be associated with tension reduction.

Although this conventional formulation meets with Murray's approval he contends that it is an incomplete picture. Not only does the individual learn to respond in such a manner as to reduce tension and thus experience satisfaction but also he learns to respond in such a manner as to develop tension so that it can later be reduced.

It is important to note that it is not a tensionless state, as Freud supposed, which is generally most satisfying to a healthy organism, but the *process* of reducing tension, and, other factors being equal, the degree of satisfaction is roughly proportional to the amount of tension that is reduced per unit of time. . . . A tensionless state is sometimes the ideal of those who suffer from chronic anxiety or resentment or a frustrated sex drive; but, as a rule, the absence of positive need-tensions—no appetite, no curiosity, no desire for fellowship, no zest—is very distressing. This calls our attention to the fact that the formula, tension → reduction of tension, takes account of only one side of the metabolic cycle. It covers catabolism, but not anabolism (which is the synthetic growth process by which tissues and potential energies are not only restored but, during youth, actually increased). The principle of homeostasis represents conservation but not construction. . . . These considerations lead us to submit tentatively a more inclusive formula: generation of tension → reduction of tension. This formula represents a temporal pattern of states instead of an end state, a way of life rather than a goal; but it applies only to the positive need systems. The conservative systems that are directed towards withdrawals, avoidances, defenses, and preventions, are adequately covered by the reduction-of-tension formula (Murray and Kluckhohn, 1953, pp. 36–37).

Thus, satisfaction or pleasure accompanies tension reduction and the individual may increase this satisfaction by increasing the amount of tension he has to reduce. One should note that this formulation applies only to effect needs. In process activity and modal needs the satisfaction is intrinsic to the activity and may be just as intense at the beginning or middle as at the end.

Murray accepts the proposition that man acts in such a way as to *intend* the increase of satisfaction and decrease of tension. However, this is only an intention or belief on the actor's part and it does not always turn out that the act which he believes will reduce tension, and lead to satisfaction, is successful in attaining this goal. Moreover, man is not motivated to increase satisfaction *in general; it is always a specific tension relevant to a particular need which he is attempting to reduce.* Satisfaction is thus largely an outcome or result of need states and their behavioral consequences. As Murray suggests, "Need, then, is the fundamental variable, and degree of satisfaction (hedone) the best indicator of its state of progress" (Murray and Kluckhohn, 1953, p. 18).

THEMA. A thema is simply a molar and interactive behavioral unit. It includes the instigating situation (press) and the need that is operating. Thus, it deals with the interaction between needs and press and permits a more global and less segmental view of behavior. By means of this concept the theorist can represent the situations that instigate or lead to the operation of particular needs, as well as the outcome or resultants of the operation of these needs.

Themas vary from simple formulations of a single subject-object interaction to more general and cruder formulations of longer transactions, and include formulations that represent the combination of a number of simple themas (*serial themas*). The thema as an analytic unit is a natural outcome of Murray's conviction that interpersonal relations should be formulated as a *dyadic unit*. That is, the theorist must represent not only the subject who is his focus of interest but he must also represent fully the nature of the person with whom the subject is interacting. He must show an equal concern for the details of both subject and object if he is to fully understand the nature and determination of behavior (cf. Sears, pp. 453–456 of this volume).

NEED INTEGRATE. Although needs are not necessarily linked to specific objects in the environment, it often happens that with experience the individual comes to associate particular objects with certain needs. Likewise particular modes of response, or means of approaching or avoiding these objects, may be acquired and associated with the need. When this integration of the need and the image or thought of the environmental object, as well as instrumental acts, has taken place, Murray speaks of a *need integrate*. A need integrate is a well-established "thematic disposition"—a need for a certain kind of inter-action with a certain kind of person or object. Under circumstances where a need integrate exists the arousal of the need will ordinarily lead the person to seek in an appropriate way the environmental object corresponding to the image that was a part of the need integrate.

UNITY-THEMA. The unity-thema is essentially the single pattern of related needs and press, derived from infantile experience, which gives meaning and coherence to the largest portion of the individual's behavior. It operates largely as an unconscious force. It is not always possible to discover a unity-thema, although one can usually arrive at a developmental formulation which sheds light upon all or most of the individual's behavior and without which it would not be possible to bring much order to his behavior. Murray refers to a man's unity-thema as the "key to his unique nature" and suggests:

> A *unity-thema* is a compound of interrelated—collaborating or conflicting— dominant needs that are linked to press to which the individual was exposed on one or more particular occasions, gratifying or traumatic, in early childhood. The thema may stand for a primary infantile experience or a subsequent reaction formation to that experience. But, whatever its nature and genesis, it repeats itself in many forms during later life (1938, pp. 604–605).

REGNANT PROCESSES. A regnant process is the physiological accompaniment of a dominant psychological process. We have already seen in Murray's definition of personality, as well as in our discussion of the need concept, that he places great emphasis upon the importance of the physiological or neurological processes which underlie the phenomena of interest to the psychologist. This clear intention of locating or referring all psychological processes to brain function led to the development of a specific concept (regnancy) designed to keep this brain-personality identity in the forefront of the theorist's attention. In defining this concept Murray suggests:

> It may prove convenient to refer to the mutually dependent processes that constitute dominant configurations in the brain as *regnant* processes; and, further, to designate the totality of such processes occurring during a single moment (a unitary temporal segment of brain processes) as a *regnancy*. . . . To a certain extent the regnant need dominates the organism (1938, p. 45).

Murray also makes clear that all conscious processes are regnant but that not all regnant processes are conscious. Thus, consciousness is just one property of a dominant psychological process, and this may or may not be present in a given instance.

Consistent with this emphasis upon physiological factors is Murray's willingness to accept constitutional factors as playing an important role in determining behavior. Although this point of view is not given heavy emphasis in his writings it is clear from many statements, for example, the suggestion that certain constitutional types may be expected to find cultural prescriptions more difficult to conform to than other types, or the implication that individuals vary in the strength of their id tendencies, that he considers constitutional and genetic factors to play an important role in behavior.

VECTOR-VALUE SCHEME. One of the marked shortcomings of the concepts of need and press as they have been elaborated above is the fact that they do not show sufficient respect for the embeddedness of behavior, for the extent to which given needs are linked with specific press and other needs. True, there are the concepts of subsidiation, need integrate, and thema; but these are sometimes difficult to apply and, in any case, they are efforts to remedy an evil introduced by the original method of analysis. Recently Murray has made serious efforts to represent more adequately this interaction among the determinants of behavior. Specifically, he has reasoned that needs always operate in the service of some value, or with the intent of bringing about some end state and, therefore, this value should be made a part of the analysis of motives:

> Since observation and experience testify to the fact that aggression, as well as every other kind of action, has an effect (function) which can be best defined in terms of some valued entity (its construction, conservation, expression, or reproduction), the naming of the valued entity in conjunction with the named activity should contribute a good deal to our understanding of the dynamics of behavior (1951b, p. 288).

In this recent scheme Murray proposes that behavioral tendencies be represented in terms of vectors which represent broad "physical or psychological directions of activity." The values which the vectors serve are represented by a series of value concepts. Although the scheme is not completely worked out Murray has provided tentative lists of values and vectors. The vectors consist of rejection, reception, acquisition, construction, conservation, expression, transmission, expulsion, destruction, defendance, and avoidance. The values consist of body (physical well-being), property (useful objects, wealth), authority (decision-making power), affiliation (interpersonal affection), knowledge (facts and theories, science, history), aesthetic form (beauty, art), and ideology (system of values, philosophy, religion). In practice it is intended that these vectors and values be arranged in a matrix of intersecting rows and columns so that each cell in the matrix will represent behavior that corresponds to a particular vector in the service of a particular value. Although the development of these concepts is far from complete Murray has demonstrated the operation of these values and vectors in the form of such a matrix with each cell containing examples or illustrations of behavioral events which typify the operation of such a vector in the service of that value.

THE DEVELOPMENT OF PERSONALITY

We have now examined the elaborate set of concepts developed by Murray to represent the dispositions or striving of the individual and we have also viewed the concepts with which he proposes to represent significant environmental events. Thus, it is now possible to represent the individual at any point in time as a complex integrate of needs and press or vectors and values, as well as personality structures, abilities, achievements, and sentiments. However, we have also learned that the "history of the organism is the organism," and this clearly indicates that representing the individual at a single point in time is not sufficient. The longitudinal study of the individual is a matter of prime importance and Murray has a good deal to say about the path of psychological development.

The variables we have already considered can, of course, be applied at any point in development. In addition to these concepts, however, Murray has elaborated and refined the psychoanalytic conception of "complex" so as to represent a particularly important set of early childhood experiences. Although Murray's treatment of development is heavily flavored by psychoanalytic theorizing, he introduces novel dimensions into his use of these conceptions and has been particularly inventive in devising means of measuring some of the important variables.

In discussing development we shall begin with a consideration of the infantile complexes and follow this with a brief summary of Murray's position in regard to several theoretical issues including sociocultural determinants, uniqueness of the individual, the role of unconscious factors, and the socialization process.

INFANTILE COMPLEXES. If we accept the fact that events taking place early in the individual's life are of unusual importance as determinants of adult behavior we find an empirical dilemma posed by the fact that these events take place, for the most part, prior to the development of language. Consequently, the usual methods of appraisal or measurement are inappropriate and the investigator must depend upon external observation of the child and vague reconstructions which the individual can make after language has developed. Utilization of these two sources of data has led to the isolation of certain areas of experience as possessing particular importance for the development of the child and subsequently the adult. Murray suggests that these are:

> . . . five highly enjoyable conditions or activities, each of which is terminated, frustrated or limited (at some point in development) by external forces: (1) the secure, passive and dependent existence within the womb (rudely interrupted by the painful experience of birth); (2) the sensuous enjoyment of sucking good nourishment from the mother's breast (or from a bottle) while lying safely and dependently in her arms (brought to a halt by weaning); (3) the free enjoyment of the pleasurable sensations accompanying defecation (restricted by toilet training); (4) the pleasant sense impressions accompanying urination . . . ; and (5) the thrilling excitations that arise from genital friction (prohibited by threats of punishment) (1938, pp. 361–362).

All of these areas have been indicated by the psychoanalyst as posing special problems for the growing child. Murray's contributions here represent an elaboration and clarification of the orthodox Freudian views.

In cases where the effects of these infantile experiences upon later behavior are clear and extensive we speak of a *complex.* Actually it is presumed that all individuals have "complexes" of varying severity and it is only in extreme cases that this implies abnormality. In Murray's terms a complex is "An enduring integrate (derived from one of the above-mentioned enjoyed conditions) that determines (unconsciously) the course of later development . . ." (1938, p. 363).

Murray defines and provides rough specification for the measurement of five complexes: claustral, oral, anal, urethral, and castration. Each represents the outcome of happenings involving one of the five areas of pleasurable experience outlined above.

The *claustral complexes* represent residuals of the uterine or prenatal experience of the individual. This area of experience has been dealt with by analysts including Freud and Rank. Murray brought together and systematized these ideas, elaborated upon them, and added a suitable label. He suggests that under this general heading there are three specific types of complex:

> . . . 1) a complex constellated about the wish to reinstate the conditions similar to those prevailing before birth; 2) a complex that centres about the anxiety of insupport and helplessness; and 3) a complex that is anxiously directed against suffocation and confinement (1938, p. 363).

Having provided a general specification of the complexes Murray proceeds to provide detailed symptoms or criteria in terms of which each of the three types of claustral complex may be identified. The *simple claustral complex* (reinstatement of uterine conditions) is characterized by: cathexis for claustra (womblike enclosures), nurturant or motherly objects, death, the past, and resistance to change, needs for passivity, harmavoidance, seclusion, and succorance. Thus, the overall picture is of a passive, dependent person who is oriented toward the past and generally resistant to novelty or change. The *fear of insupport complex* manifests itself in fear of open spaces, falling, drowning, earthquake, fire, and family insupport. The *egression complex* is concerned with escaping or departing and displays itself in cathexis for open spaces and fresh air, need to move and travel, cathexis for change, claustrophobia, and a strong need for autonomy. Thus, the individual who displays this complex is in most respects the opposite of the person displaying the simple claustral complex.

The oral complexes represent derivatives of early feeding experiences and again we find that Murray has proposed three specific subcomplexes, all of which involve the mouth but each of which implies a distinctive kind of activity. The *oral succorance complex* involves oral activity in combination with passive and dependent tendencies. The existence of this complex can be inferred from oral automatisms such as sucking; cathexis for oral objects such as the nipple, breast, or thumb; compulsive eating and drinking; need for passivity and succorance; cathexis for words, nurturant objects; and inhibited aggressive needs. The *oral aggression complex* combines oral activity with aggression and is manifested in oral automatisms such as biting; cathexis for solid oral objects (meat, bones); strong aggressive needs; ambivalence toward authority figures; projection of oral aggression (seeing the environment as full of biting aggressive objects); need for harmavoidance; phobia for biting objects; and stuttering. The *oral rejection complex* involves spitting out and disgust over oral activities and objects. More specifically it is revealed in a negative cathexis for certain foods, low need for food, fear of oral infection or injury, need to reject, need for seclusion and autonomy, and dislike for nurturant objects.

The *anal complexes* are derived from events associated with the act of defecating and bowel training. Murray suggests, following Freud and Abraham, that there are two specific complexes here, one concerned primarily with the tendency to expel and the other with the tendency to retain. The *anal rejection complex* includes diarrhoea and cathexis for faeces and further involves need for aggression, particularly involving disorder and dirtying or smearing; anal theory of birth, need for autonomy, anal sexuality. The *anal retention complex* involves an underlying cathexis for faeces but this is concealed behind an apparent disgust, prudishness, and negative reaction to defecation. This complex also is associated with the anal theory of birth and anal sexuality as well as the need for autonomy, although in this instance the autonomy is displayed through resistance to suggestion rather than seeking for independence or freedom. There is a strong need for order and cleanliness, and also a need to retain possessions. This complex, of course, restates the famous Freudian trilogy of "parsimony, cleanliness, and obstinacy" which were suggested as typifying the "anal character."

Originally Murray (1938) considered the *urethral complex* of rather minor importance. He indicated initially that the complex involved bed-wetting, urethral soiling, and urethral erotism. Postwar research has convinced him of the central importance for many individuals of this area of experience, and he has since provided a further description of the complex as well as a series of empirical devices for assessing it, although as yet this material has not been published. He has also suggested that the syndrome be called the *Icarus complex* after the mythological figure who flew too near the sun against his father's advice, with the result that his artificial wings melted and he plunged to his death. A detailed case history of an *American Icarus* has been published (Murray, 1955). In his recent formulations he has indicated that the individual who is an Icarian typically displays such qualities as cathexis for fire, a history of enuresis, a craving for immortality, strong narcism, and a lofty ambition which dissolves in the face of failure.

The *castration complex* is also given less attention in Murray's early writing than the first three complexes. He suggests that the complex should be given a more limited meaning or significance than that commonly assigned to it by the psychoanalysts:

> To us it seems better to confine the term castration complex to its literal meaning; anxiety evoked by the fantasy that the penis might be cut off. This complex occurs often enough, but it does not seem possible that it is the root of all neurotic anxiety. It usually comes as a resultant of the fantasies associated with infantile masturbation (1938, p. 385).

Space limitations have forced us to omit the detailed discussion Murray provides of the experiential links between the attributes we have listed as diagnostic of the various complexes. These clusters of variables represent the distillates of considerable research and in his presentation they are further cemented by logical and theoretical considerations. In Murray's investigations of personality it has been customary to rank or rate each subject in terms of the importance of each of these complexes as a determinant of his behavior.

SOCIOCULTURAL DETERMINANTS. Murray, in marked contrast to most theorists who have drawn heavily from psychoanalytic theory, has deliberately assigned a major role in development to environmental factors. We have already seen that in distinction to most students of motivation he has developed an elaborate set of concepts (press) designed to represent the environment of the individual. Further, he has made frequent reference to the fact that the path of development cannot be adequately understood without a full picture of the social setting in which the process evolves. Consistently, his concepts of "proceeding" and "thema" imply an interactionist belief—a conviction that full understanding of behavior will follow only when both subject and object are adequately represented. All of these considerations make clear that Murray accepts and accentuates the importance of a "field" view of behavior.

While his field emphasis preceded the period during which he and Clyde Kluckhohn have been professionally associated, there is little doubt that collaboration with his anthropologist friend has served to cement his field convictions and to produce a somewhat more explicit consideration of institutional and cultural variables. The following statement by Murray and Kluckhohn bears strong testimony to Murray's convictions in this area.

> A person is an emergent entity *of* and *in* a certain physical, social, and cultural milieu. He cannot be properly represented in isolation from his locale, or from the culture of the group of which he is a member, or from his status (role) in the structure of that group. Basically, every person is a social person, an interdependent part of a system of human interactions (1953, p. 6).

Society is believed to exert a tremendous influence upon the individual. Thus, it is important to represent the significant elements in the environment not only through concepts such as press but also through variables related to the cultural milieu of the individual.

UNIQUENESS. In spite of his attention to general categories of analysis Murray has always taken the essential uniqueness of each person, and even of each behavioral event, as self-evident facts. His respect for naturalistic observation and his creative and intuitive literary talents make it easy for him to grasp and express compellingly the individuality and elusive complexity of each subject or event. In his words:

> Every proceeding leaves behind it some trace of its occurrence—a new fact, the germ of an idea, a re-evaluation of something, a more affectionate attachment to some person, a slight improvement of skill, a renewal of hope, another reason for despondency. Thus, slowly, by scarcely perceptible gradations—though sometimes suddenly by a leap forward or a slide backward—the person changes from day to day. Since his familiar associates also change, it can be said that every time he meets with one of them, both are different. In short, every proceeding is in some respects unique (Murray and Kluckhohn, 1953, p. 10).

It is this respect for the complexity and uniqueness of the individual which has led Murray to develop such a manifold and complicated scheme of variables for dealing with human behavior. Further, this awareness has led him to examine small numbers of subjects intensively while shunning studies that would involve securing no more than two or three measures for each subject studied.

Thus, we find that Murray shows full respect for the individuality and uniqueness of behavior and has taken strong measures to give this quality adequate conceptual representation. However, he also accepts the necessity of abstraction in the process of empirical investigation and he has not hesitated to engage in operations which involve dealing with components of behavior in terms of common or general variables. He would insist, nevertheless, that the results of such segmental studies could be adequately interpreted only when the investigator knew a great deal about each individual subject.

UNCONSCIOUS PROCESSES. Among academic psychologists Murray was among the first to accept the insidious and pervasive role of unconscious determinants of behavior (Murray, 1936). As we have observed, in his first major theoretical statement (1938) he made clear that not all regnant processes have conscious correlates and, naturally enough, those that do not, determine behavior without the individual's awareness. Not only is the individual unaware of certain tendencies that influence his behavior but, more important, some of these tendencies are actively defended against or warded off from consciousness. Thus, Murray not only accepts the role of unconscious determinants of behavior but also recognizes the operation of the Freudian mechanisms of repression and resistance.

The distinction between latent and overt needs, which we have already mentioned, and the importance which Murray attributes to the infantile complexes make clear that his theory assigns a central role to unconscious processes even in the normal individual. It is true, however, that he places a somewhat less extreme emphasis upon unconscious determinants than does orthodox psychoanalytic theory.

THE SOCIALIZATION PROCESS. Murray has suggested that the human personality is a compromise between the individual's own impulses and the demands and interests of other people. These demands of other people are represented collectively by the institutions and cultural patterns to which the individual is exposed, and the process whereby his own impulses are compromised by these forces is referred to as the socialization process. Conflicts between the individual and the approved patterns of his social milieu are customarily solved by means of the individual conforming to the group patterns in some manner. Only occasionally and in unusual individuals is it possible for the person to bring about a change in the cultural patterns which will ease the conflict with his own impulses. For the most part it is the personality that is more malleable and therefore the conflict is usually reduced by altering the person.

The exact aims of socialization vary from one society to another but there are certain general aims which hold true across different societies:

> Beginning in the nursery, the process of socialization continues throughout life. Among other things, what must be learned are: the power to inhibit, or to moderate, the expression of unacceptable needs; the ability to transfer cathexis from a prohibited goal-object to an acceptable substitute; the habitual and automatic use of a large number of approved action patterns (methods, manners, and emotional attitudes); and the ability to adapt to schedules (to do things at the proper time, keep appointments, etc.) (Murray and Kluckhohn, 1953, p. 45).

All of these things are necessary if the individual is to live comfortably with himself and with his fellow man.

An essential element in achieving the above goals is the development of an adequate superego. As we have already seen, by internalizing aspects of the authority figures to whom he has been exposed, the person develops an internal structure which serves to reward and punish him when he is behaving appropriately or inappropriately in terms of the culture pattern as interpreted by these authority figures. This implies that the parents, as the most important authority figures, are the chief agents of the socialization process. The effectiveness of the parents in rewarding approved and punishing disapproved patterns of behavior will largely determine the success of this developmental process. An important component of the parent's role as socializer is the effectiveness with which he develops a mutually affectionate relationship with the child so that mere approval or disapproval can serve as significant motivating conditions in controlling the child's behavior.

Murray points out that in the well-socialized individual it is legitimate to speak of a *need for roleship, that is, a need to be a member of an existing group or groups and to have a defined and accepted role and status within the group.* Thus, the tendency on the part of the individual to conform to the decrees of his society is, in part, accounted for by means of this general need to belong to and participate in a functioning group.

Socialization is not without its negative qualities. An individual can be oversocialized, and conceivably an entire society may be exposed to socialization processes that are debilitating rather than preparatory for a fruitful life. As Murray suggests, man is fundamentally an animal and to the extent that socialization denies this fundamental, biological nature it may destroy the creative spontaneity and vigor which are essential to the most important kinds of human advances.

CHARACTERISTIC RESEARCH AND RESEARCH METHODS

We have already pointed out that Murray's research has been distinguished primarily by its originality and this very fact makes it singularly difficult to characterize in a representative fashion the investigations he has inspired and conducted. Before turning to the difficult task of selecting representative investigations to summarize, let us examine very briefly several distinctive qualities of Murray's general approach to personality research. The interested reader will find several papers in which Murray has outlined his conception of how personality research should be pursued (Murray, 1947, 1949b).

INTENSIVE STUDY OF SMALL NUMBERS OF NORMAL SUBJECTS. The large-scale study of human behavior, in which findings consist of group tendencies or over-all relations which may characterize very poorly any single individual within the group, represents a limited avenue to understanding human behavior. Murray is convinced, with the wisdom of the naturalist and clinician, that an adequate understanding of behavior must follow a complete and detailed study of individual subjects. Just as case study has provided indispensable assistance in the growth and development of medical science, so the future of psychology is linked to the willingness of investigators to take the time and effort to understand thoroughly individual cases.

Group relations are important only when accompanied by a careful inquiry into the deviations within the group, and conditions which cause or accompany these deviations. To report a finding which characterizes 80 per cent of a specified group is of little value unless some explanation can be provided for the failure of the other 20 per cent to fit into this pattern. Murray's consistent emphasis on this point is one of his principal contributions to research methods.

If we are interested in the individual subject and also concerned with reasons for subjects representing exceptions to general relationships, it is clear that we must secure a very large amount of information concerning each subject with which we deal. Thus, it is inevitable that Murray's position should lead him to the intensive study of his subjects and this, of course, has the natural result of reducing the number of subjects who can be studied at any one time and the total number of studies that can be carried out by any one investigator in a given number of years.

The contrast between Murray's interests in human behavior and the interests of many academic psychologists is adeptly highlighted in the following passage:

At first I was taken aback, having vaguely expected that most academic psychologists would be interested in Man functioning in his environment. But not at all: almost everyone was nailed down to some piece of apparatus, measuring a small segment of the nervous system as if it were isolated from the entrails. I was in the position, let us imagine, of a medical student who suddenly discovers that all his instructors are eye, ear, nose and throat specialists. The phenomena that intrigued me were not mentioned, since these were not susceptible to exact experimental validation, a standard that rules out geology, paleontology, anthropology, embryology, most of medicine, sociology, and divine astronomy. If my chief aim had been to "work with the greatest scientific precision" I would never have quit electrolytes and gases. I had changed because of a consuming interest in other matters, in problems of motivation and emotion. To try to work these out on human subjects was to become a "literary" or applied psychologist, a practitioner of mental hygiene, outside and looking in upon the real psychologists who, I concluded, were obsessed by anxious aims to climb the social scale of scientists and join the elect of this day's God at any cost. What else could account for their putting manners (appliances and statistics) so far ahead of ends (importance of the problems studied)? No matter how trivial the conclusions, if his coefficients were reliable, an experimenter was deemed pure and sanctified (Murray, 1940, p. 154).

As Murray points out, this was an initial impression which has since been moderated. But the core complaint remains: psychologists all too often are not interested in the full range of human behavior.

A further distinctive quality of his research has been its emphasis upon the study of *normal individuals*. In general, the intensive study of individual cases has been reserved for the clinical setting where the pathology of the patient has made him a subject of particular interest or else the demands of diagnostic or therapeutic expediency have necessitated extensive information. Thus, Murray's choice of the normal subject as the focus of his research provided a natural complement to the case histories available from psychiatric settings.

He was also one of the pioneers in *interdisciplinary co-operation in personality research*. The Harvard Psychological Clinic staff habitually included representatives of psychiatry, psychology, anthropology, and other disciplines, in an era when this was anything but commonplace.

THE DIAGNOSTIC COUNCIL. Murray has placed great emphasis upon the importance of the observer or the psychologist as an instrument in psychological research. Although we may use rating scales, category sets, or psychological tests to appraise personality, still, at the base of all these instruments is the sensitive observation of the investigator or clinician. Because of the root status of the observer Murray is convinced that more attention should be paid to his frailties and more serious efforts directed at improving his powers of observation. These considerations have led him to refer to the psychologist himself as the most important "instrument of precision" in psychological research.

One evident means of placing checks upon, and improving the quality of, observation is to have multiple observers all examining the same data from a different perspective. Thus, using a number of investigators to study the same individual, or individuals, offers unique rewards in the form of canceling out limitations posed by the biases of particular observers or the limitations offered by specialized sets of data. Not only is the end result of such group observation presumably superior to individual observation but the members of the group should sharpen and improve their powers of observation as a result of the corrective function of the observations of others.

These considerations led Murray to devise the *diagnostic council* which involves many observers all studying the same subjects from different points of view, and with the opportunity for a final discussion and synthesis of the information secured from these different vantage points. After a period of individual observation during which each investigator studies the subjects through his own specialized techniques there is a conference for each subject. At this time every investigator presents his data and their interpretation with a full opportunity for the observations and interpretations of other observers to support or suggest modifications in the report. A single investigator has primary responsibility for assembling and presenting the synthesis of each case but each member of the council is given an unlimited opportunity for contributing to this final product.

INSTRUMENTS OF PERSONALITY MEASUREMENT. Among contemporary psychologists there is no one who has made more significant contributions to personality assessment than Murray. He has devised a very large number of ingenious devices for the measurement of personality, only a small number of which have been systematically exploited. The volumes, *Explorations in personality* and *Assessment of men,* provide ample illustration of the ingenuity and diversity of the instruments which he has devised or been influential in developing. One of these, the *Thematic Apperception Test,* has become, next to the *Rorschach Test,* the most widely used projective technique in current use.

Almost all of Murray's instruments have been congruent with his fundamental conviction that an ultimate understanding of human behavior will derive not from the study of lower organisms or the study of humans under highly restricted conditions but rather from the complex study of individual behavior. That is, Murray has argued for the collection of rich and multiform data which can be expected to reflect a wide range of behavioral tendencies and capacities. He is convinced that one of the natural advantages of the psychologist is the fact that he deals with a talking organism and that this should be capitalized upon fully. In contrast to the biologist, the zoologist, or the physicist, the psychologist deals with a subject who can tell a great deal about internal processes that operate, about external events that are attended to, about the major determinants of behavior. It is true that these reports must be assessed carefully, and that they cannot always be taken at their face value, but nevertheless they represent a crucial beginning in the attempt to unravel the secrets of human behavior.

Given this interest in subjectivity it is quite natural that Murray should have pioneered in developing personality instruments which explore the full mental content of the subject. His instruments typically do not limit the response alternatives of the subject by means of predetermined categories but rather they permit and encourage a full and subjective exposition on the part of the subject. Imagination and fantasy are permitted full participation by these techniques. They provide the investigator with a fullness of data which is at the same time richly promising and complexly discouraging.

PERSONALITY EXPLORATIONS. In order to give the reader some impression of the diversity of Murray's research we have elected to summarize three studies that are *not* part of a program of research. These investigations illustrate the originality and adeptness with which Murray has made forays into a variety of important areas of personality research. The first study is a pioneer investigation of the influence of emotional factors upon perception, the second is an intriguing inquiry concerning the possible clairvoyance of dreams, the third an application of psychological principles in the attempt to understand a literary masterpiece, *Moby Dick.*

The effect of fear upon judgments of personality. Murray set out in this study, making ingenious use of a natural setting, to explore the extent to which an individual's ascription of personality characteristics to others was influenced by his own emotional state. The data for the study were collected during a week-end house party given by his daughter for four girl friends. As part of the entertainment it was planned that the children would play a game called "murder." The game is played in complete darkness and involves an initial drawing of lots at which time one of the participants is assigned the role of detective and another (secretly) the role of murderer. After the drawing the participants go off in the dark except for the detective. The murderer then kills one of the players by touching him, whereupon the victim announces his demise by shouting, and the participants are reassembled. It is then the task of the detective to decide who committed the crime by questioning the players. They must all tell the truth except for the murderer who is free to deceive as much as he wishes. As the five subjects were only eleven years old and as four of them were in a strange and darkened house it seemed a plausible hypothesis that this experience would arouse fear in the subjects. That the game was successful in this respect is attested to by several observations. First, some of the subjects volunteered the fact that they had been frightened during the game. Second, and more convincing, is the fact that one of the girls awakened during the night following the game with the conviction that there had been burglars ransacking the house and that she had watched them. Although no such event had taken place, two of the other girls eventually came to believe her story and on the following evening insisted upon numerous precautions to protect them during the night from the imaginary burglars.

The effects of this fear-arousing experience were assessed by having the subjects make judgments of the goodness (benevolence) or badness (maliciousness) of thirty photographs taken from a newsweekly. The thirty photographs were divided into two series of fifteen pictures each, with the two series roughly matched with each other in terms of the positive and negative appearance of the face. One series (half the pictures) was administered under neutral conditions on the same day but prior to the game of murder. The second series was administered under neutral conditions on the day following the experiment. The entire series of pictures was administered immediately following two games of murder as the experimental test. The girls were asked to rate each picture on a nine-point scale ranging from (1) extremely good (generous, kind, loving, and tender) to (9) extremely bad (cruel, malicious, and wicked).

The results of the study showed a clear tendency for the girls to rate the pictures as more malicious or bad immediately following the fear-arousing game than they did at the time of either control rating. Thus, the findings of the study provide a strong confirmation for the belief that the emotional state of the individual influences his judgments of the personality of others. Characteristically, Murray, in reporting this study, deals in great detail with the individual differences in the subjects' response, relating these to personality characteristics of the girls as well as to particular observations made during the study.

In discussing these findings Murray distinguishes between two principal types of projection. The first is commonly referred to as *complementary projection* and refers to the tendency on the part of the subject to perceive or understand his environment in such a manner as to make it congruent with or justify his needs, affects, and impulses. The second is called *supplementary projection*. In this case the subject endows objects or persons in the environment with attributes which he himself possesses and which in the usual case are unacceptable to him. The results of Murray's study clearly exemplify complementary projection as the subjects perceived their environments as more malicious which was a complement to their increased fearfulness.

Clairvoyance of dreams. It is a common belief that dreams sometimes provide an accurate account of events that have occurred in distant places or under circumstances where the dreamer could have no direct sensory information concerning the event. While this is a testable hypothesis, and one that would be of great significance if it were verified, it is not easy to secure suitable data. Further, it is a sufficiently unconventional question so that most psychologists would shy away from it. Murray, however, in a highly imaginative investigation (Murray and Wheeler, 1937), undertook to explore the possible clairvoyant function of dreams through securing a large number of dreams about an event of national interest prior to the time at which the outcome of this event was known.

The event was the kidnaping of the Lindbergh baby. Several days after the kidnaping and prior to the solution of the case, Murray had a notice placed in a Boston paper indicating that the Harvard Psychological Clinic was interested in securing dreams that related to the Lindbergh kidnaping. The notice was immediately reprinted in papers across the country with the result that before the baby had been discovered the investigators had received 1300 dreams pertaining to the case.

In the attempt to test the clairvoyance of the dreams they took as facts the objective conditions surrounding the discovery of the baby's body. Medical examination indicated that the child had died instantly from a fractured skull. The body was discovered in a shallow grave which was located in a wood near a road within several miles of the Lindbergh home. The sleeping gown which the child had been wearing when he was kidnaped was not with the body when it was found.

With this objective standard in mind, the investigators proceeded to read carefully all 1300 dreams in the attempt to identify dreams that showed any correspondence with the known facts. They found a large number of dreams which reflected current newspaper speculation concerning the possible whereabouts of the baby, for example, that he was concealed on a boat at sea, but only about 5 per cent of the dreams indicated that the baby was dead and of these only seven (less than 1 per cent) involved conditions corresponding even in a general way to those described above.

The authors point out that in only 4 out of 1300 dreams was there specific indication of the three central items of death, burial in a grave, and location among trees. Further, they suggest that the possibilities in connection with these events are by no means unlimited, for instance, the baby must be either dead or alive, if he is dead he must be above the ground, below the ground, or in the water. Thus, although there is no means for estimating chance or a random performance satisfactorily, it seems exceedingly unlikely that the 4 dreams out of 1300 which came close to the target represent an improvement over chance. The authors conclude, "The findings do not support the contention that distant events and dreams are causally related." (Murray and Wheeler, 1937, p. 313)

The meaning of Moby Dick. The most fascinating of Murray's recent investigations is contained in a paper entitled *In Nomine Diaboli* (Murray, 1951c) which, summarizing the results of years of careful study, presents a psychological interpretation of the meaning of *Moby Dick* as intended by Melville. This interpretation rests upon a complex combination of sophistication in psychological theory, detailed knowledge of Melville and his work, and an intimate familiarity with the novel *Moby Dick.* It is impossible to do full justice to this paper here, for an integral part of the analysis lies in the style with which Murray expresses his ideas and the detail in which each interpretation is anchored firmly in multiple supporting observations.

The predictable reservations of a student of literature for the methods of psychology are expressed in an early passage of this paper:

> The habit of a psychologist is to break down the structure of each personality he studies into elements, and so in a few strokes to bring to earth whatever merit that structure, as a structure, may possess. Furthermore, for reasons I need not mention here, the technical terms for the majority of these elements have derogatory connotations. Consequently, it is difficult to open one's professional mouth today without disparaging a fellow-being. Were an analyst to be confronted by that much-heralded but still missing specimen—the normal man—he would be struck dumb, for once, through lack of appropriate ideas.
>
> If I am able to surmount to some extent any impediments of this origin, you may attribute my good fortune to a providential circumstance. In the procession of my experiences *Moby Dick* anteceded Psychology, that is, I was swept by Melville's gale and shaken by his appalling sea dragon before I had acquired the all-leveling academic oil that is poured on brewed-up waters, and before I possessed the weapons and tools of science—the conceptual lance, harpoons, cutting irons, and what-nots—which might have reduced the "grand hooded phantom" to mere blubber. Lacking these defenses I was whelmed. Instead of my changing this book, this book changed me (pp. 436–437).

We see revealed in this passage not only Murray's deep and enduring interest in *Moby Dick* but also a conviction Murray has long felt concerning the nature of psychological theory. He suggests with convincing phrases that psychological theory is at its best in dealing with the worst of behavior and somewhat at a loss when confronted with the positive and creative aspects of behavior. Thus, Murray's own theoretical position has understandably given somewhat more emphasis to positive and self-determining aspects of behavior than has been true of most other psychological theories.

Murray also deals with the question of whether it may not be that there is no "meaning" to *Moby Dick*. That is, it may be that the artist created the story simply as a vivid narrative of the sea so that there is no "meaning," conscious or unconscious, implied by the story other than that which is manifest. Murray rejects this point of view chiefly on the ground of statements by Melville which make clear that in writing this book he had a definite intention of creating an underlying meaning.

The bulk of the paper is devoted to developing and documenting several hypotheses concerning the significance of characters within this story. The first hypothesis states in simplest terms that Captain Ahab represents Satan or the Devil and his forces of evil. In psychological terms Ahab represents the primitive and largely evil forces of the id. This hypothesis is supported with characteristic care and attention to detail in a series of passages typified by the following:

> That it was Melville's intention to beget Ahab in Satan's image can hardly be doubted. He told Hawthorne that his book had been broiled in hellfire and secretly baptized not in the name of God but in the name of the Devil. He named his tragic hero after the Old Testament ruler who "did more to provoke the Lord God of Israel to anger than all the Kings of Israel that were before him." King Ahab's accuser, the prophet Elijah, is also resurrected to play his original role, though very briefly, in Melville's testament. We are told that Captain Ahab is an "ungodly, god-like" man who is spiritually outside Christendom. He is a well of blasphemy and defiance, of scorn and mockery for the gods—"cricket-players and pugilists" in his eyes. Rumor has it that he once spat in the holy goblet on the altar of the Catholic Church at Santa. "I never saw him kneel," says Stubb. He is an "anaconda of an old man." His self-assertive sadism is the linked antithesis of the masochistic submission preached by Father Mapple (Murray, 1951c, pp. 441–442).

The second hypothesis is that Moby Dick is the antithesis of the unbridled forces of evil—the superego. As such, the whale represents not only the moral forces within the individual but also the conventional institutions of Melville's society.

> Stated in psychological concepts, Ahab is captain of the culturally repressed dispositions of human nature, that part of personality which psychoanalysts have termed the "Id." If this is true, his opponent, the White Whale, can be none other than the internal institution which is responsible for these repressions, namely the Freudian Superego. This then is my second hypothesis: Moby Dick is a veritable spouting, breaching, sounding whale, a whale who, because of his whiteness, his mighty bulk and beauty, and because of one instinctive act that happened to dismember his assailant, has received the projection of Captain Ahab's Presby-

terian conscience, and so may be said to embody the Old Testament Calvinistic conception of an affrighting Deity and his strict commandments, the derivative puritan ethic of nineteenth-century America, and the society that defended this ethic. Also, and most specifically, he symbolizes the zealous parents whose righteous sermonizings and corrections drove the prohibitions in so hard that a serious young man could hardly reach outside the barrier, except possibly far away among some tolerant, gracious Polynesian peoples. The emphasis should be placed upon that unconscious (and hence inscrutable) wall of inhibition which imprisoned the puritan's thrusting passions. "How can the prisoner reach outside," cries Ahab, "except by thrusting through the wall? To me, the White Whale is that wall, shoved near to me. . . . I see in him outrageous strength, with an inscrutable malice sinewing it." As a symbol of a sounding, breaching, white-dark, unconquerable, New England conscience what could be better than a sounding, breaching, white-dark, unconquerable sperm whale? (pp. 443–444)

These then are the major revelations of Murray's analysis. To secure an adequate impression of the strength and beauty of Murray's interpretations it is necessary to refer to the original article.

Some may question whether this is in fact psychological research. Certainly there is no control group, no distribution of numbers, no index of reliability, no statistical analysis. In spite of these ritual violations, however, Murray has asked an interesting psychological question and has arrayed evidence that bears upon this question. Further, in the process of presenting the question and his findings, he employed assumptions concerning human behavior that are an integral part of the theory we have just expounded. Most important of all is the fact that these passages contain speculations and generalizations concerning human behavior that are almost certain to have a generative effect upon the reader. There are few experimentalists within psychology who could not profit from exposure to the kinds of ideas so vividly and provocatively presented in this paper.

CURRENT STATUS AND EVALUATION

We have already seen that Murray's theoretical conceptions undergo a constant process of re-examination and modification. In fact, as this chapter is written his theory is being at least partially recast. Even in the face of this constant flux, however, certain elements stand firm. At no time has his deep interest in the motivational process wavered nor has he shown any inclination to desert his descriptive and taxonomic activities. Similarly, his theory has always emphasized the importance of unconscious sources of motivation and has throughout stressed the relation of psychological process to brain process. Thus, although it seems likely that future developments may drastically change the theory in some respects, it also seems likely that certain core emphases will remain constant.

Murray's formulations have been found useful not only by his students but also by many other investigators and clinicians interested in studying personality. His concepts of need and press have had a wide usage, particularly among clinicians and investigators who have used the Thematic Apperception Test. Few persons who have been concerned with the details of classifying human behavior have failed to gain something from the several important classifications which Murray has proposed. As we have indicated, his influence upon the current methods or procedures for assessing personality has been profound. Both in the development of specific instruments and in the presentation of a point of view his work has had a great deal to do with contemporary developments in this area. Fully as important as these substantive contributions has been Murray's capacity to intrigue, excite, and inspire his students and colleagues. The enthusiasm and conviction with which he has imbued his students is undoubtedly responsible to a considerable extent for the fact that they have played such an important role in the development of personality research.

Which of the features of his theoretical position have been of most influence? Perhaps the most distinctive component in Murray's position, as suggested earlier, is the careful and sensitive treatment of the motivational process. There has been a strong tendency on the part of recent personality theorists to deal with motivation through one of two rather simple paths. The first path assigns all behavior to a remarkably small number of cardinal motives so that everything can be viewed as stemming from these master motives. The second path assumes that the number of motives is legion and that each individual is driven by motives which are so complex and so uniquely different from those of other individuals that it is not possible to specify motives which can be usefully applied to more than one person. This alternative denies the utility of any attempt at a general classification of motives. Murray's position is clearly between these easy extremes. He grants the complexity of human motivation and firmly avers his conviction that the process cannot be represented adequately in terms of two, three, four, or five general motives. However, he insists that there are motives of sufficient generality that can be used fruitfully to represent the behavior of all or most individuals within specified groups. Thus, he faces realistically the task of developing a set of constructs which will do justice to the complexity of human behavior, but at the same time will be carefully specified so that they can be used repeatedly by different investigators. The result, as we have seen, is a classification of motives that is probably more widely useful than any other comparable classification.

Murray's theory and his research have played a crucial role in promoting a more serious interest in psychoanalytic theory on the part of academic psychologists. In the era when Murray first came to the Harvard Psychological Clinic psychoanalysis was largely an alien and a trespasser within the domain of psychology. The subsequent twenty-five years have found Freud firmly ensconced as one of the intellectual giants of our field, and this shift is in no small part attributable to the importance of Murray's example.

As we have seen, his theory possesses the unique feature of a simultaneous emphasis upon the importance of the past of the organism and the present context within which behavior takes place. In a psychological world where most theorists have self-consciously developed a preoccupation with the contemporary field, or else have turned to the past of the organism as the sole key to understanding behavior, it is decidedly healthy to have one position where both of these classes of determinants are given their due. His interest in the field or environment within which behavior takes place led to the distinctive system of press concepts which permits the investigator to represent the perceived environment as well as the objective environment. It is one thing to speak generally of the importance of the environment and quite another thing to undertake the grim and exacting task of specifying categories in terms of which the significant aspects of the environment can be represented. Murray is one of a remarkably small number of theorists who have undertaken this task.

The negative aspects of Murray's theory are in many respects the mirror image of the positive. To a considerable extent the main criticisms of the theory are closely related to the originality, the incorporativeness, and the complexity of the theory. We have already agreed that the most serious allegation which can be leveled against any theory is the charge that it does not lead to research. The critic may maintain that in Murray's system there is definitely a set of concepts, and a related set of empirical definitions, but that there is *no* set of explicitly stated psychological assumptions linked to these concepts in such a manner as to produce testable consequences. Certainly it is true, as the studies we have briefly sampled reveal, that the research which Murray and his students have done is not to be considered in any direct way the consequence of his theory. His investigations have not been focused on testing predictions which derive explicitly from his theoretical position. In defense of the theory it must be admitted that its assumptions and concepts do provide a general point of view concerning behavior which clearly has a lot to do with the specific manner in which particular research problems are approached. Further, the defined variables are applicable to most or many such problems. One may claim with considerable justice that these functions are about all that most personality theories are equipped to do at present.

Some critics have felt that the theory is so broadly incorporative as to lose the power or vigor that would attach to a more limited and specialized point of view. Thus, the very qualities which make the theory complex and at the same time protect it against many of the usual criticisms that are raised against personality theories might combine to reduce the effectiveness of the theory as a compelling point of view. It is as though the theory says so much that no single thing is said with a salience and conviction that makes it stand out from the rest of the theory, or that makes the theory itself stand out from others.

In spite of the breadth and diversity of Murray's theoretical formulations it is clear that he has devoted more of his attention to the motivational process than he has to the learning process. This has led some critics to believe that Murray's theory suffers from an inability to account for the manner in which motives become transformed and develop. Although his classification of motives is uniquely useful, and his methods for measuring motivation of central importance, he has relatively little to say concerning the exact process whereby these motives develop.

Murray's patience and skill as a taxonomist have led him to create so many fine distinctions and detailed classifications that some observers feel that he has been unnecessarily complex in his approach to the study of behavior. It is certainly true that the number of different categories he has developed, coupled with his tendency to change or modify these frequently, and his further tendency to introduce new terms for describing these concepts produce considerable confusion in the casual reader. While one may maintain that the task of a taxonomist is to represent reality accurately and not necessarily to make his reader happy, it must be admitted that many of Murray's variables have not seen extensive and prolonged application to empirical data.

In general Murray's writings and his research are not fashionable within the existing psychological world. There is too much of the poet and too little of the positivist in his make-up. He is at home with his imagination, he is willing to speculate freely about issues that offer no immediate possibility for empirical translation, and he is willing to make his unbridled speculations public. None of these are qualities that lead to immediate acceptance on the part of professionals who are still sensitive concerning their suspended position between the natural sciences and the humanities. There is a strong tendency for the experimentalist to dismiss as mere subjectivity the problems and issues raised by his contemporaries who do not choose to be bound by manipulable method and technique. Thus, understandably, many investigators have considered Murray's writings irreverent in the respect they show for experimental technique and distressing in the complex considerations which they introduce as necessary for an adequate understanding of human behavior.

In any final appraisal of Murray's contributions one must combine the theory, the man, and his research. There can be no doubt that this combination has introduced a note of vivid originality into an area of research sorely in need of such qualities. In the long run one of the great enemies of empirical and theoretical progress is the fixation upon stable but trivial events, and there has been no more ruthless critic of trivial investigation and formulation in personality research than Henry Murray.

BIBLIOGRAPHY

PRIMARY SOURCES

Murray, H. A. (and collaborators). *Explorations in personality*. New York: Oxford, 1938.

Murray, H. A. Toward a classification of interaction. In T. Parsons and E. A. Shils (Eds.). *Toward a general theory of action*. Cambridge: Harvard Univ. Press, 1951a, pp. 434–464.

Murray, H. A. Some basic psychological assumptions and conceptions. *Dialectica*, 1951b, 5, 266–292.

Murray, H. A., and Kluckhohn, C. Outline of a conception of personality. In C. Kluckhohn, H. A. Murray, and D. Schneider (Eds.). *Personality in nature, society, and culture*. 2nd Ed. New York: Knopf, 1953, pp. 3–52.

Murray, H. A., and Morgan, Christiana D. A clinical study of sentiments. *Genet. Psychol. Monogr.*, 1945, 32, 3–311.

REFERENCES

Morgan, Christiana D., and Murray, H. A. A method for investigating fantasies. *Arch. Neurol. Psychiat.*, 1935, *34*, 289–306.

Murray, H. A. The effect of fear upon estimates of the maliciousness of other personalities. *J. soc. Psychol.*, 1933, *4*, 310–329.

Murray, H. A. Basic concepts for a psychology of personality. *J. gen. Psychol.* 1936, *15*, 241–268.

Murray, H. A. (and collaborators). *Explorations in personality.* New York: Oxford, 1938.

Murray, H. A. What should psychologists do about psychoanalysis? *J. abnorm. soc. Psychol.*, 1940, *35*, 150–175.

Murray, H. A. *Manual of Thematic Apperception Test.* Cambridge, Mass: Harvard Univ. Press, 1943.

Murray, H. A. Problems in clinical research: round table. *Amer. J. Orthopsychiat.*, 1947, *17*, 203–210.

Murray, H. A. Introduction. In H. Melville. *Pierre, or the ambiguities.* New York: Farrar Straus, 1949a, pp. xiii–ciii.

Murray, H. A. Research planning: a few proposals. In S. S. Sargeant (Ed.). *Culture and personality.* New York: Viking Fund, 1949b, pp. 195–212.

Murray, H. A. Toward a classification of interaction. In T. Parsons and E. A. Shils (Eds.). *Toward a general theory of action.* Cambridge: Harvard Univ. Press, 1951a, pp. 434–464.

Murray, H. A. Some basic psychological assumptions and conceptions. *Dialectica*, 1951b, *5*, 266–292.

Murray, H. A. *In Nomine Diaboli, New Eng. Quart.*, 1951c, *24*, 435–452. (*Princeton Univ. Library Chronicle*, 1952, *13*, 47–62.)

Murray, H. A. American Icarus. In A. Burton and R. E. Harris (Eds.). *Clinical studies in personality.* Vol. 2. New York: Harper, 1955, pp. 615–641.

Murray, H. A., and Kluckhohn, C. Outline of a conception of personality. In C. Kluckhohn, H. A. Murray, and D. Schneider (Eds.). *Personality in nature, society, and culture.* 2nd Ed. New York: Knopf, 1953, pp. 3–52.

Murray, H. A., and Morgan, Christiana D. A clinical study of sentiments. *Genet. Psychol. Monogr.*, 1945, *32*, 3–311.

Murray, H. A., and Wheeler, D. R. A note on the possible clairvoyance of dreams. *J. Psychol.*, 1937, *3*, 309–313.

Office of Strategic Services Assessment Staff. *Assessment of Men.* New York: Rinehart, 1948.

Wolf, R., and Murray, H. A. An experiment in judging personalities. *J. Psychol.*, 1937, *3*, 345–365.

6.

Lewin's Field Theory

The older sciences of physics and chemistry have often influenced the course of newer sciences like psychology by furnishing them ways of thinking about and conceiving of natural phenomena. As new viewpoints develop in physics and chemistry it is almost inevitable, considering the basic unity of all sciences, that they should be taken over by the less mature sciences and applied in their special provinces. It is not surprising, therefore, that the so-called field concept of physics, initiated by the work of Faraday, Maxwell, and Hertz on electromagnetic fields in the nineteenth century and culminating in Einstein's powerful theory of relativity in the twentieth century, has had an impact on modern psychological thought. It should be pointed out, however, as Deutsch does (1954), that it is the *method* of representing reality and not the actual physical concepts and facts themselves that has been incorporated into psychology.

The first important manifestation of the influence of physical field theory in psychology appeared in the movement known as Gestalt psychology which was initiated by three German psychologists, Max Wertheimer, Wolfgang Köhler, and Kurt Koffka, in the years immediately preceding the First World War. The chief tenet of Gestalt psychology is that the way in which an object is perceived is determined by the total context or configuration in which the object is embedded. Relationships among components of a perceptual field rather than the fixed characteristics of the indivdual components determine perception.

206

Kurt Lewin was associated with Wertheimer and Köhler at the University of Berlin in the years following World War I. Born in Prussia in 1890, Lewin attended the Universities of Freiberg, Munich, and Berlin from which he received his doctorate in 1914. After serving in the German army for four years, he returned to the University of Berlin as an instructor and a research assistant in the Psychological Institute. In 1926, he was appointed professor of philosophy and psychology. At the time of Hitler's rise to power, Lewin was a visiting professor at Stanford University. He returned briefly to Germany to get his family and settle his affairs; this done, he established his permanent residence in the United States. He was professor of child psychology at Cornell University for two years, 1933–1935, before being called to the University of Iowa as professor of psychology in the Child Welfare Station. In 1945, Lewin accepted an appointment as professor and director of the Research Center for Group Dynamics at Massachusetts Institute of Technology. He died in Newtonville, Massachusetts, February 12, 1947, at the age of 56.

Lewin is considered by many of his peers to be one of the most brilliant figures in contemporary psychology (G. W. Allport, 1947; Tolman, 1948). His theoretical writings (Lewin, 1935a, 1936a, 1938, 1951) and his experimental work have left an indelible mark upon the development of psychology. Lewin stood first and foremost for the application of field theory in all branches of psychology. For Lewin, field theory is not a new system of psychology limited to a specific content; it is a set of concepts by means of which one can represent psychological reality (1936a, pp. 6–7). These concepts should be broad enough to be applicable to all kinds of behavior, and at the same time specific enough to represent a definite person in a concrete situation.

The principal characteristics of Lewin's field theory may be summarized as follows: (1) behavior is a function of the field which exists at the time the behavior occurs, (2) analysis begins with the situation as a whole from which are differentiated the component parts, and (3) the concrete person in a concrete situation can be represented mathematically. Lewin also emphasizes underlying forces as determiners of behavior and expresses a preference for psychological as opposed to physical or physiological descriptions of the field. A field is defined as "the totality of coexisting facts which are conceived of as mutually interdependent" (Lewin, 1951, p. 240).

The concepts of field theory have been applied by Lewin to a wide variety of psychological and sociological phenomena including infant and child behavior (Lewin, 1951, Chapter X), adolescence (1951, Chapter VI), feeblemindedness (1935a, Chapter VII), minority group problems (1935b, 1946), national character differences (1936b), and group dynamics (Lewin, 1948). Lewin, like so many other personality theorists, was not an ivory-tower thinker who turned aside from the problems of the world. A person of broad humanitarian sympathies and democratic values, he attempted rather directly to ameliorate some of the problems facing mankind by undertaking the type of investigation which is known as action research. Action research has as its objective the changing of social conditions. Examples of action research performed by Lewin and his associates will be found in Bavelas and Lewin (1942) and Lewin (1943, 1946, 1947, 1948).

In the present chapter, we shall focus our attention upon Lewin's theory of the structure, dynamics, and development of the person. We shall have to consider the psychological environment as well, since the person and his environment are interdependent regions of the *life space*, which is Lewin's term for the total psychological field.

THE STRUCTURE OF PERSONALITY

The first step in defining the person as a structural concept is to represent him as an entity set apart from everything else in the world. This setting apart can be done in words as a dictionary definition does, for example, a person is an individual human being (Webster), or it can be done by making a spatial representation of the person. Because spatial representations can be treated mathematically and ordinary verbal definitions cannot be, Lewin prefers to define his structural concepts spatially. In this way, Lewin attempts to mathematize his concepts from the very beginning. One important advantage of this type of scientific strategy according to Lewin is that mathematical representations require precise formulation whereas verbal definitions are more likely to be inexact and ambiguous. Furthermore, mathematical representations can be made to divulge important information by performing various mathematical operations on them. Unknowns can be solved for, rational equations connecting different concepts can be written, and functional relationships can be formulated. Words, on the other hand, only lead to more words. Mathematics, Lewin reminds us, is the proper language of scientific discourse, although the type of mathematics employed by Lewin for representing psychological concepts is not the kind with which most people are familiar. Lewin's mathematics is nonmetrical in character and describes spatial relationships in other than Euclidean terms. It is essentially a mathematics for describing interconnections and inter-communications among spatial regions without regard to size or shape.

The separation of the person from the rest of the universe is accomplished by drawing an enclosed figure. The boundary of the figure defines the limits of the entity known as the person. Everything lying inside the boundary is *P* (the person); everything lying outside the boundary is non-*P*. It does not make any difference whether the figure drawn is a circle, a square, a triangle, an octagon, or an irregular shape just as long as it is completely bounded.

Before proceeding let us pause to consider what has been conceptualized by representing the person as an enclosed figure. Since absolute size and shape are irrelevant properties of the representation, the only significant feature of Figure 1 is that it portrays a completely

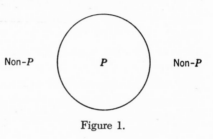

Figure 1.

bounded area lying within a larger area. Thus it follows that two properties of the person are conceptualized by drawing a circle on a piece of paper. These are (1) separation from the rest of the world by means of a continuous boundary, and (2) inclusion in a larger area. The first property is that of *differentiation*, the second of the *part-whole relationship*. In short, the person is represented as being separated from yet included within a larger totality. Such a conception is not at variance with common sense since the skin or the individual's garments are visible boundaries which set him off from the larger universe through which he moves and of which he is so evident a part.

THE PSYCHOLOGICAL ENVIRONMENT. Were we only interested in the person and not in the world of which he is a part, we could restrict our attention to the properties of the area circumscribed by the circle and ignore the boundary and its hinterland. To proceed in this manner, however, would be to overlook the important interactions between the person and his environment.

The next step, then, in the representation of psychological reality is to draw another bounded figure which is larger than and encloses the person. The shape and size of this enclosing figure are not important as long as it fulfills the two conditions of being bigger than and including the person. For this representation Lewin prefers a figure that is roughly elliptical in form. An additional qualification is also necessary. The new figure cannot share any part of the boundary of the circle which represents the person. There must be a space left between the boundary of the person and the boundary of the larger figure. Aside from this restriction, the circle may be placed anywhere inside the ellipse. The sizes of the two forms relative to one another are immaterial.

We now have a picture of a circle enclosed by but not touching an ellipse. The region between the two perimeters is the *psychological environment, E.* The total area within the ellipse, including the circle, is the *life space, L.* The space outside the ellipse represents the non-

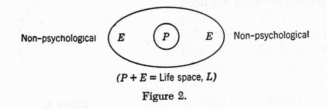

(P + E = Life space, L)

Figure 2.

psychological aspects of the universe. For the sake of convenience, we shall call this region the physical world, although it is not restricted to physical facts alone. There are, for example, social facts as well in the nonpsychological world.

Although this simple exercise in drawing figures may appear to be inconsequential, it is absolutely indispensible for an understanding and appreciation of Lewin's theory. It is essential, Lewin maintains, to start with an over-all picture of psychological reality, a picture of the greatest general validity, and then proceed, step by step, to differentiate out of this broad panorama the details by which a precise understanding of the concrete psychological situation can be achieved. For it is Lewin's contention that if the general picture of psychological reality is inaccurate, the more detailed picture cannot be correct.

The circle-in-the-ellipse is not merely an illustration or a teaching device; it is a faithful representation of the most general structural concepts of Lewin's theory, namely, the person, the psychological environment, and the life space. The circle-in-the-ellipse is a map or conceptual representation of reality, and like any map its function is to guide its user through unfamiliar territory and in so doing to acquaint him with new facts about reality.

THE LIFE SPACE. Although we began with the person and subsequently surrounded him with a psychological environment, it would have been more in keeping with Lewin's rule of going from the general to the particular to have started with the life space and differentiated from it the person and the environment. For the life space is the psychologist's universe; it is the whole of psychological reality. It contains the totality of *possible* facts which are capable of determining the behavior of an individual. It includes *everything* that has to be known in order to understand the concrete behavior of an individual human being in a given psychological environment at a given time. Behavior is a function of the life space. $B = F(L)$. "The task of dynamic psychology is to derive univocally the behavior of a given individual from the totality of the psychological facts that exist in the life space at a given moment" (Lewin, 1936a).

The fact that the life space is surrounded by the physical world does not mean that the life space is a part of the physical world. Rather, the life space and the space beyond it are differentiated and separate regions of a larger totality.

Figure 3.

Whether this larger totality, the universe, is finite or infinite, chaos or cosmos, is of no concern to psychology except in one very important respect. Facts that exist in the region outside and adjacent to the boundary of the life space, a region which Lewin calls "the foreign hull of the life space," can materially influence the psychological environment. That is, nonpsychological facts can and do alter psychological ones. Lewin has suggested that the study of the facts in the foreign hull be called "psychological ecology" (1951, Chapter VIII). The first step in making a psychological investigation is to establish the nature of the facts which exist at the boundary of the life space since these facts help to determine what is and what is not possible, what might or might not happen in the life space. Lewin did this before he undertook to investigate the food habits of people and how they might be changed (1943; 1951, Chapter VIII).

Facts in the psychological environment can also produce changes in the physical world. There is two-way communication between the two realms. Consequently, it is said that the boundary between the life space and the outer world is endowed with the property of *permeability*. A boundary resembles a permeable membrane or screen more than it does a wall or rigid barrier. Parenthetically, it should be noted that the physical world cannot communicate directly with the person, nor can the person communicate directly with the outer world. A fact must exist in the psychological environment before it can influence or be influenced by the person. This is evident from the diagram which depicts the person as being completely surrounded by the region of the psychological environment.

The implication of a permeable boundary between the life space and the physical world is of far-reaching significance. Since a fact in the nonpsychological world may radically change the whole course of events in the life space, prediction from a knowledge of psychological laws alone is usually futile. One can never be sure beforehand that a fact from the foreign hull may not penetrate the boundary of the life space and turn everything topsy-turvy in the psychological environment. A chance meeting, an unexpected telephone call, an automobile accident, have been known to change the course of one's life. Therefore, as Lewin emphasizes, it is more feasible for a psychologist to try to understand the momentary, concrete psychological situation by describing and explaining it in field-theoretical terms than it is for him to attempt to predict how a person is going to behave at some future time.

Another property of the life space should be noted. Although the person is surrounded by his psychological environment, he is not a part of or included in the environment. The psychological environment stops at the perimeter of the circle just as the nonpsychological world stops at the perimeter of the ellipse. However, the boundary between the person and the environment is also a permeable one. This means that environmental facts can influence the person, $P = F(E)$, and personal facts can influence the environment, $E = F(P)$. Before considering the nature of this influence, a further differentiation within the structure of the person and of the environment must be made.

THE DIFFERENTIATED PERSON. Up to this point, the person has been represented as an empty circle. Such a representation would be appropriate if the person were a perfect unity, which he is not. Lewin maintains that the structure of the person is heterogeneous not homogeneous, that it is subdivided into separate yet intercommunicating and interdependent parts. To represent this state of affairs, the area within the circle is divided into zones.

One proceeds in the following manner. First, divide the person into two parts by drawing a concentric circle within the larger circle. The outer part represents the *perceptual-motor region* (P-M), the central part represents the *inner-personal region* (I-P). The inner-personal region is completely surrounded by the perceptual-motor area, so that it has no direct contact with the boundary separating the person from the environment.

The next step is to divide the inner-personal region into cells. The cells adjacent to the perceptual-motor region are called *peripheral* cells, *p*; those in the center of the circle are called *central* cells, *c*. Lewin is not explicit regarding the differentiation of the perceptual-motor area into smaller regions. He feels that the motor system acts

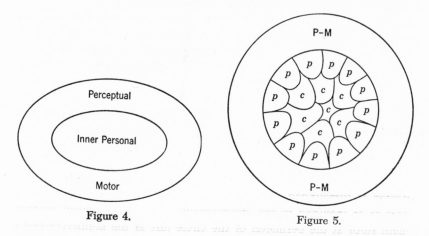

Figure 4.   Figure 5.

as a unit since it can ordinarily perform only one action at a time. Similarly, the perceptual system usually functions in a unified manner, that is, a person can attend to and perceive only one thing at a time. It is clear, however, that the motor system should be separated from the perceptual system because they are independent systems. How this separation is to be conceptualized spatially is not divulged. Perhaps the best solution and one that Lewin apparently adopts is to leave the perceptual-motor system unstructured, with the understanding that when the direction of influence is from the environment to the person the region surrounding the inner-personal sphere represents perceptual processes, and when the direction of influence is from the person to the environment this same region stands for the motorium. This would agree with the common-sense view that input involves perception and output involves motor action.

We now have an accurate conceptual representation of the structure of the person. The person is defined as a differentiated region in the life space. Now let us consider the environment.

THE DIFFERENTIATED ENVIRONMENT. A homogeneous or undifferentiated environment is one in which all the facts are equally influential upon the person. In such an environment the person would have perfect freedom of movement since there would be no barriers to impede him. Such complete freedom of movement obviously does not represent the true state of affairs. Therefore, it is necessary to subdivide the environment into part regions.

There is one difference between the differentiation of the environment and the differentiation of the person. It is not necessary to distinguish between different *kinds* of environmental regions. The environment does not contain anything comparable to a perceptual-motor stratum or an inner-personal sphere. All of the regions of the environment are alike. Consequently, any crisscross pattern of lines will serve our present purpose. It should be pointed out, however, that in the concrete representation of a particular person in a concrete psychological situation at a given moment the exact number and relative positions of the environmental subregions, as well as the precise number and relative positions of the inner-personal sphere, must be known if one is to understand behavior. A complete and accurate structural analysis reveals the totality of possible psychological facts in the momentary situation. Dynamical analysis, which is the topic of the next section of this chapter, tells us which of the possible facts will actually determine the behavior.

Figure 6.

CONNECTIONS BETWEEN REGIONS. The life space is now represented by a differentiated person surrounded by a differentiated environment. This differentiation has been accomplished by drawing lines which serve as boundaries between regions. It is not intended, however, that these boundaries should represent impenetrable barriers which divide the person and the environment into independent and unconnected regions. Permeability, as we have already pointed out, is one of the properties of a boundary. Since this is so, the life space consists of a network of interconnected systems.

What is signified by saying that regions are connected? In order to answer this question, let us assume that each of the subregions of the environment contains one psychological fact, and that the same fact does not appear in more than one region at the same time. (Lewin's use of the word *fact* in this context may sound strange to some ears. A fact, for Lewin, is not only an observable thing like a chair or a football game; it is also something that may not be directly observable but which can be inferred from something that is observable. In other words, there are empirical or phenomenal facts and hypothetical or dynamic facts. Anything, either sensed or inferred, is a fact in Lewin's eyes. An event, on the other hand, is the result of the interaction of several facts. A chair and a person are each facts, but a person seating himself on a chair is an event.) Two regions are said to be connected when a fact in one region is in communication with

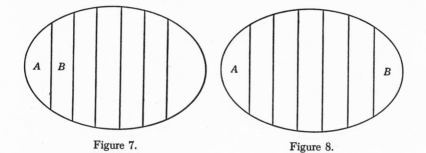

Figure 7.   Figure 8.

a fact in another region. For example, the person is said to be connected with the environment because a fact in the environment can alter, modify, displace, intensify, or minimize facts within the person. In ordinary language, the environment can change the person, and vice versa. Lewin also says that two regions are connected when the facts of one region are accessible to the facts of another region. Accessibility is the spatial counterpart of influence.

Our immediate problem, then, is how to represent the extent of influence or accessibility between regions. There are several ways of doing this. One way is to place the regions close together when the influence of one upon the other is great (Figure 7), and to place them far apart when the influence is weak (Figure 8). The number of regions intervening between A and B represents the extent of their influence upon one another. This type of representation may be called the *nearness-remoteness* dimension.

For example, a region that is buried deeply in the central portion of the inner-personal stratum may be many cells away from the perceptual-motor area. Under these circumstances an environmental fact will have a difficult time getting to the remote central region, and likewise a fact embedded in the central region will have little or no communication with the environment. They will be relatively independent of one another. On the other hand, a peripheral region of the inner-personal sphere which adjoins the perceptual-motor system may be very accessible to environmental facts.

Two regions may be very close together, even to the extent of sharing a common boundary, and yet not influence or be accessible to each other at all. The degree of connectedness or interdependence is not only a matter of the number of boundaries that must be crossed; it also depends upon the strength of the resistance offered by the boundary. If the resistance is very great then it does not make any

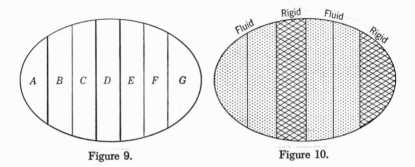

Figure 9.   Figure 10.

difference how close together the regions are; they will have very little influence upon one another. On the other hand, two regions may be far apart and still exert considerable influence upon each other if all of the intervening boundaries are very weak.

The resistance of a boundary, or its permeability, is represented by the width of the boundary line. A very thin line represents a weak boundary, a very thick line represents an impermeable boundary (Figure 9). This type of representation may be called the *firmness-weakness* dimension.

A boundary is not necessarily equally permeable from both sides. That is to say, a fact in region A may influence a fact in region B but a fact in region B may have virtually no influence over a fact in region A. There is no way to represent this difference in accessibility except to make two drawings, one in which the boundary line is thin, the other in which the boundary line is thick. This is conceptually proper since the influence of A upon B is a psychologically different situation from that of B's influence on A.

A third way of representing the interconnections between regions is to take into account the nature of the medium of a region. The medium of a region is its floor or surface quality. Lewin has distinguished several properties of the medium, the most important of which is the *fluidity-rigidity* dimension. A fluid medium is one that responds quickly to any influence that is brought to bear upon it. It is flexible and pliant. A rigid medium resists change. It is stiff and inelastic (Figure 10). Two regions that are separated from each other by a region whose surface quality is extremely rigid will not be able to communicate with one another. It is analogous to a person trying to cross a swamp or make his way through heavy underbrush.

By utilizing the concepts of nearness-remoteness, firmness-weakness,

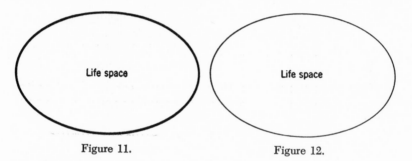

Figure 11.   Figure 12.

and fluidity-rigidity, most of the possible interconnections in the life space can be represented. Let us take a few concrete examples. In Figure 11, the boundary of the life space is thick, while in Figure 12 the boundary is thin. Figure 11 depicts a situation in which the outside world has little influence on the life space and the life space has little influence on the outside world. The person is encapsulated in his psychological environment; his contacts with physical reality are slight. One thinks of a deteriorated schizophrenic or a person who is asleep and dreaming. Figure 12 portrays just the opposite situation. The life space and the outer world are closely connected. Changes in the outer world affect the state of the life space and changes in the life space affect the outer world. This is the picture of a person whose psychological environment is closely attuned to the physical world. The slightest change in the "foreign hull" is immediately reflected in a change in the psychological environment.

Figures 13 and 14 show an inaccessible and an accessible person. One is firmly insulated from his environment by a thick wall, the other has free and easy exchanges with the psychological environment,

Figure 15 portrays a more complexly structured person. Cells p_1

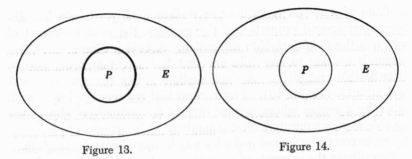

Figure 13.   Figure 14.

and p_2 are closely connected, while p_2 and p_3 are cut off from one another by an impermeable boundary. Region c has little or no accessibility to any other region. It is as though this area were dissociated from the rest of the person. The crosshatched cell is impervious to influence because of the turgid quality of its surface, while the dotted area is easily influenced. Region p_4 is remotely connected to p_1, p_2, and p_3. Figure 16 portrays a complexly structured psychological environment.

It should be kept in mind that these drawings represent momentary situations. There is nothing fixed or static about them, and they are constantly changing as a result of dynamic forces. One cannot characterize the person as being thus and so for any long period of time. A firm boundary can suddenly dissolve, a weak boundary grow tough. Regions that were far apart may come close together. A stiff medium softens while a pliant medium hardens. Even the number of regions can increase or decrease from moment to moment. Consequently, spatial representations are continually going out of date because psychological reality is forever changing. Lewin does not put much stock in fixed traits, rigid habits, or other constants of personality. Concepts of this sort are characteristic of Aristotelian thinking which Lewin deplores (1935a, Chapter I).

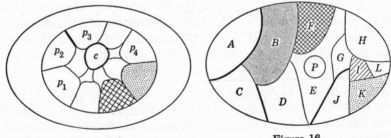

Figure 15.   Figure 16.

THE NUMBER OF REGIONS. What determines how many regions there will be in the life space? The number of regions is determined by the number of separate psychological facts that exist at any given moment of time. When there are only two facts, the person and the environment, there are only two regions in the life space. If the environment contains two facts, for example, the fact of play and the fact of work, then the environment has to be divided into a play area and a work area. If there are a number of different kinds of play facts, for instance, the fact of playing football, the fact of playing chess, and the fact of playing darts, then the play area must be divided into as many subregions as there are separate play facts. Similarly, there may be different kinds of work facts each of which has to have its own separate region. Should it not make any difference to the person whether he plays football or chess or darts, just as long as he plays something, there will only be one play area and not three. For a person who is overcome by terror, the whole psychological environment may be filled with the one fact of terror. All other facts may disappear, leaving a perfectly homogeneous environment. As the person begins to regain his composure, he may see that one part of his environment offers security. At this moment, the environment becomes differentiated into a safe area and a danger area. In short, a new region is differentiated out of the life space whenever a new fact comes into existence; a region disappears whenever a fact disappears or merges with another fact. A psychological fact is co-ordinated with a psychological region.

The number of regions in the person is also determined by the number of personal facts that exist. If the fact of feeling hungry is the only one that exists, then the inner-personal sphere will consist of only one region. But if in addition to the fact of hunger there is also a need to finish a given job, the inner-personal region has to be divided into two regions.

As we shall see later, the principal facts of the inner-personal region are called *needs*, while the facts of the psychological environment are called *valences*. Each need occupies a separate cell in the inner-personal region and each valence occupies a separate region in the psychological environment.

THE PERSON IN THE ENVIRONMENT. Earlier when we were discussing the placing of the person in the environment, we said it did not make any difference where the circle was placed inside the ellipse just as long as their two boundaries did not touch. This holds true only for an undifferentiated, homogeneous environment where all the facts are in one and the same region, that is, where all the facts are identical. As soon as the environment becomes differentiated into bounded regions, then it makes considerable difference where the circle is placed. For whatever region it is placed in, the facts of that region are closer to and have more influence on the person than do the facts of any other region. An understanding of a concrete psychological situation requires, therefore, that we know where the person is in his psychological environment. Physically he may be sitting in a schoolroom, but psychologically he may be replaying a baseball game on the playground. Some facts that exist in the schoolroom, such as what the teacher is saying, may not impinge upon him at all, whereas others, for example, a note from a girl sitting at the next desk, may easily divert his thoughts from the ball game.

LOCOMOTION AND COMMUNICATION. The way in which the regions that make up the life space are interconnected represents the degree of influence or accessibility between regions. Precisely how does this influence or accessibility express itself? In the preceding example of the boy who is accessible to the note from the girl but inaccessible to what the teacher is saying, accessibility means that the boy can move more easily into the region of the girl than into the region of the teacher. When the girl performs the action of passing the boy a note, he may move out of the baseball region and into her region. He has performed what Lewin calls a *locomotion*. Two regions are closely connected, accessible to one another, and mutually influential, if locomotions may be made easily between the regions.

A locomotion in the psychological environment does not mean that the person has to make a physical movement through space; in fact, most of the locomotions that are of interest to the psychologist involve very little physical movement. There are social locomotions such as joining a club, vocational locomotions such as being promoted, intellectual locomotions such as solving a problem, and many other types of locomotions.

We now see that an important property of the psychological environment is that it is a region in which locomotion is possible. "One can treat everything as environment in which, toward which, or away from which the person as a whole can perform locomotions" (Lewin, 1936a, p. 167). In performing a locomotion, the person traverses a path through the environment. The direction of the path and the regions through which it passes are determined in part by the strength of the boundaries and the fluidity of the regions, and in part by dynamic factors yet to be discussed.

The influence, then, of environmental regions upon one another is expressed by the ease with which the person can move from one region to another. Is locomotion also the mode by which regions of the person reveal their influence upon one another? Lewin says not. "The person himself cannot . . . be considered as a medium within which an object carries out locomotions from one part region to another" (1936a, p. 168). Regions of the person are said to *communicate* with one another. The perceptual region communicates with the peripheral cells of the inner-personal region, and they in turn communicate with the more centrally located cells. Inner-personal cells can communicate with one another and with the motor sphere. Which regions will communicate with one another and the path by which the communication is transmitted through a number of regions are determined in part by such structural features as the width of the boundaries and the nature of the medium, and in part by dynamic factors.

Locomotion and communication are said to be events since they result from an interaction of facts. A fact, it will be recalled, is represented by a region. Accordingly, an event represents an interaction between two or more regions. Lewin says that in deriving an event, for example, a locomotion or a communication, from the life space three principles should be followed. The first one which is called the *principle of relatedness* has already been mentioned. It states that an event is always the result of an interaction between two or more facts. One fact alone cannot cause an event. It is necessary to have at least two facts, for example, the person and the environment, before there can be any locomotion. The second principle, that of *concreteness, says that only concrete facts can have effects*. A concrete fact is one that actually exists in the life space. Potential or possible facts, that is, facts which may come into existence sometime in the future but which do not exist now, cannot be the cause of present events. Closely related to the principle of concreteness is the *principle of contemporaneity, which states that only present facts can produce present behavior*. Facts that once existed but no longer do cannot influence the present. The facts of infancy or childhood can have no bearing upon the behavior of the adult unless those facts have managed to remain in some sort of existence throughout the intervening years (Lewin, 1936a, pp. 18–36).

RESTRUCTURING OF THE LIFE SPACE. Locomotion and communication are not the only events that may occur as the result of one fact (region) impinging upon another fact (region). Other consequences may follow. The number of regions may be increased or decreased depending upon whether new facts are added or old facts are subtracted from the life space. The position of regions relative to each other may be altered. Two regions that were far apart may draw closer and regions that were close together may draw apart. Changes in the boundary may occur. A permeable boundary may become firm, a strong boundary may become weak. Finally, there may be alterations in the surface qualities of regions. A fluid region may stiffen up, a rigid region relax. All of these structural changes or events may be subsumed under the general heading, *restructuring of the life space* (Lewin, 1951, p. 251).

LEVELS OF REALITY. Thus far in our discussion of Lewin's structural concepts two dimensional spatial representations have sufficed. However, a third dimension is necessary in order to give a complete representation of the life space. This third dimension is co-ordinated with the concept of degrees of reality and unreality. Reality consists of an actual locomotion whereas unreality consists of an imaginary locomotion. There are various degrees or levels between actuality and pure imagination. For example, a person can join a club, change his job, or work out a problem, or he can plan to do these things, or he can daydream about doing them. Planning or thinking is an intermediate level between the most realistic level of performance and the most unrealistic level of pure fantasy.

By and large, locomotions are easier to make as one moves up the ladder towards unreality; the boundaries become less firm and the surface qualities of the regions become more fluid.

Lewin believes that the concept of levels of reality applies not only to the structure of the environment but also to the structure of the person. Although he does not elaborate on this point, it appears that he means that communications between regions of the person can be more or less realistic. For example, an inner-personal cell may actually affect the motor region or it may do so in an imaginary way. A person may speak his mind or he may only daydream about doing so.

THE TIME DIMENSION OR PERSPECTIVE. Although neither the past nor the future can affect present behavior, according to the principle of contemporaneity, the person's attitudes, feelings, and thoughts about the past and the future may have considerable influence upon his conduct. The hopes of the future may be much more important to a person than the hardships of the present. Just as expectations of things to come may lighten current burdens so may shadows from the past darken the present. The present, therefore, must be represented as containing both a psychological past and a psychological future (Lewin, 1951, pp. 53–56). This dimension may be long or short. It may be well-defined or hazy. Its structure may be simple or complex, and its boundaries may be weak or firm.

RÉSUMÉ. The principal structural concepts discussed in this section are a *life space* consisting of a *person* surrounded by a *psychological environment*. The person is differentiated into a *perceptual-motor region* and an *inner-personal region*. The inner-personal region is subdivided into a group of *peripheral cells* and *central cells*. The psychological environment is also differentiated into *regions*. The life space is surrounded by a *foreign hull* which is part of the nonpsychological or objective environment.

Regions of the person and of the environment are separated by *boundaries* which possess the property of *permeability*. The regions of the life space are *interconnected* so that a *fact* in one region can influence a *fact* in another region. When such an influence occurs between two facts it is called an *event*. The degree of connectedness or the extent of the influence between regions is determined by the *firmness* of the boundaries, the number of regions *intervening*, and the *surface qualities* of the regions.

Regions of the environment are said to be connected when the person can perform a *locomotion* between the regions. Regions of the person are said to be connected when they can *communicate* with one another.

Two other dimensions of the life space are those of *reality-unreality* and *past-future*.

Lewin represents (defines) the foregoing concepts in spatial terms so that they may be handled by a branch of mathematics known as topology. Topology deals with spatial relations. It is not concerned with size or shape, nor with magnitudes, distances, and other conventional characteristics of space. Topology involves such spatial relationships as "being included in," "part-whole," and "connectedness and disconnectedness." Since Lewin represents his structural concepts topologically he calls this part of his system *topological psychology* (1936a).

In order to represent dynamic concepts such as direction, distance, and force, Lewin had to invent a new kind of space which he called *hodological*. Hodology is the science of paths. A path is the same as a locomotion.

We turn now to a discussion of Lewin's dynamic concepts which taken together constitute what Lewin calls *vector psychology*.

THE DYNAMICS OF PERSONALITY

A structural representation of the life space is like a road map. A good road map contains all of the information one needs to know in order to plan any sort of a trip just as a good structural representation of the person and his environment contains all of the facts one needs to know in order to account for any possible kind of behavior. But just as a road map cannot tell us what trip a person will actually decide to take, neither can a detailed picture of the life space tell us how a person is going to behave. Structural or topological concepts alone cannot explain concrete behavior in an actual psychological situation. For this kind of understanding dynamic concepts are needed.

Lewin's principal dynamic concepts are energy, tension, need, valence, and force or vector.

ENERGY. Lewin, in common with most personality theorists, assumes that the person is a complex energy system. The kind of energy that performs psychological work is called *psychical energy*. Since Lewin's theory is exclusively psychological in character, it is not necessary for him to deal with the question of the relation of psychical energy to other kinds of energy.

Psychical energy is released when the psychic system (the person) attempts to return to equilibrium after it has been thrown into a state of disequilibrium. Disequilibrium is produced by an increase of tension in one part of the system relative to the rest of the system, either as a result of external stimulation or internal change. When tension throughout the system becomes equalized again, the output of energy is halted and the total system comes to rest.

TENSION. Tension is a state of the person, or speaking more precisely, it is a state of an inner-personal region relative to other inner-personal regions. When Lewin refers to the dynamic properties of a region or cell of the inner-personal sphere, he calls the region a *system*.

Tension has two important conceptual properties. The first property is that a state of tension in a particular system tends to equalize itself with the amount of tension in surrounding systems. If system *a*, for example, is in a state of high tension, and if the surrounding systems, *b, c, d, e*, and *f*, are in a state of low tension (Figure 17), then tension will tend to pass from *a* into *b, c, d, e*, and *f* until there is an equality of tension throughout the whole system (Figure 18).

The psychological means by which tension becomes equalized is called a *process*. A process may be thinking, remembering, feeling,

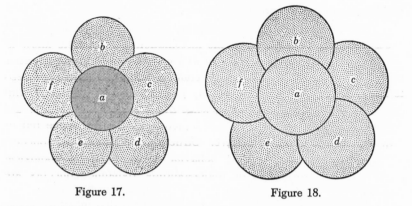

Figure 17.   Figure 18.

perceiving, acting, or the like. For instance, a person who is faced with the task of solving a problem becomes tense in one of his systems. In order to solve the problem and thereby reduce the tension he engages in the process of thinking. Thinking continues until a satisfactory solution is found, at which time the person returns to a state of equilibrium. Or the intention may be one of remembering a name. The memory process goes into action, recalls the name, and enables the tension to subside.

Although tension always moves towards a condition of equilibrium, this conceptual property applies only to the system as a whole, and not necessarily to all of the part systems. A part system may actually become more and more tense during the time that the whole system is returning to a balanced condition. This happens when a person has to take a circuitous route in solving a problem. During the detour, tension may mount in one of the subregions although the over-all process will eventually bring the person back to a state of equilibrium. For example, someone may undertake a task, knowing full well that he will have to endure increasing tension, but at the same time he anticipates that the end result will be a more perfect balance of forces.

A state of equilibrium does not mean that the system is without tension. Probably no organism can achieve a completely tension-free state and remain alive. Equilibrium means either that the tension throughout the total system is equalized or that a subsystem in which an unequal amount of tension exists is firmly walled off and isolated from the other inner-personal systems (Figure 19). Such a tense system may remain segregated for a long period of time and constitute a more or less permanent reservoir of energy. There may be a number of such firmly segregated tense systems in the personality, which furnish a continuous supply of energy for the operation of psychological processes.

A person who has established an equilibrium on a high tension level differs appreciably from a person who has established an equilibrium on a low tension level. In the former case, the pressure on the motoric will be greater and there is likely to be a continual seepage of energy into the motoric. Such a person will show a great deal of diffuse, restless activity.

A second conceptual property of tension is that it exerts pressure upon the boundary of the system. If the boundary is particularly firm, the diffusion of tension from one system to adjacent systems will be impeded, but if the boundary is weak tension will flow readily from one system into other systems. Ordinarily, a particular tension system shares its boundary with more than one other tension system. In such cases, the resistance of one part of the boundary may be weaker than that at other parts of the boundary. This will permit tension to pass in certain directions more freely than in other directions. In other words, dynamic communication between systems is a variable condition. Tension system *a* may be in close communication with tension system *b* so that exchanges of energy are easily made, whereas *a* may be remotely connected with *c, d, e,* and *f* so that exchanges of energy are difficult to make (Figure 20).

Figure 19.

Dynamically speaking, a boundary is a region of resistance or a barrier. As a barrier it corresponds to a restraining force. Does the boundary itself have the property of being a tension system? Lewin thinks not. It is more likely that the force exerted at the region of the boundary of *a* against the force which is generated within *a* is determined by the states of tension in the surrounding systems. That is, the opposing force is really the tension being exerted on the boundary from adjacent systems (Figure 21).

NEED. An increase of tension or the release of energy in an innerpersonal region is caused by the arousal of a need. A need may be a physiological condition such as hunger, thirst, or sex; it may be a

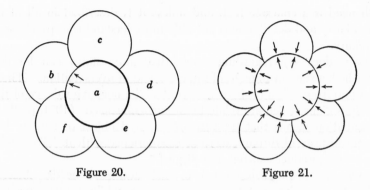

Figure 20.   Figure 21.

desire for something such as a job or a spouse; or it may be an intention to do something such as completing a task or keeping an appointment. A need is, therefore, a motivational concept and is equivalent to such terms as motive, wish, drive, and urge.

Lewin refrains from systematically discussing the nature, source, number, and kinds of needs because he is not at all satisfied with the concept. He feels that eventually the term *need* will be dropped from psychology in favor of a more suitable concept, one that is more observable and measurable. Nor does he feel that it is worthwhile to set forth a list of needs as so many psychologists do. In the first place, the list would be of almost infinite length, and in the second place, the only thing that really matters in the description of psychological reality is to represent those needs that actually exist in the momentary situation. These are the only needs that are producing effects. On an abstract level, it may be said that everyone is capable of feeling hungry but it is only when the hunger drive is actually disturbing the equilibrium of a person that it has to be taken into account.

It is apparent that Lewin is extremely pluralistic in his conception of needs. There are as many needs as there are specific and distinguishable cravings. One can have a need for the kind of rare beefsteak that is served in only one particular restaurant or a need to hear a particular movement of a Sibelius symphony played by a specific orchestra. Lewin does not attempt to reduce a number of specific needs down to one general need, for as he says

The problem of the emergence of needs lies at the crossroad of cultural anthropology, developmental psychology, and the psychology of motivation. Its investigation has been hampered by premature speculative attempts to systematize needs into a few categories (1951, p. 280).

Each need is a concrete fact, and unless it is described in all of its particularity and detail, one is not able to understand true psychological reality.

Lewin does say regarding needs that three states can be distinguished, a state of hunger, of satiation, and of oversatiation. "These states correspond to a positive, a neutral, and a negative valence of the activity regions which are related to a particular need" (1951, p. 282). Oversatiation means that the formerly desired object or activity has become distasteful through continued experience with it. Too much of anything produces surfeit and disgust.

Lewin also distinguishes between needs and quasi needs. A need is due to some inner state, such as hunger, while a quasi need is equivalent to a specific intention, like satisfying one's hunger by eating at a particular restaurant. Lewin feels that the needs of a person are determined to a large extent by social factors (1951, p. 289).

TENSION AND MOTORIC ACTION. Thus far, we have been concerned primarily with the internal dynamics of tension systems, that is, with the dynamic interdependence and communication between systems. What is the relation of tension to action? One might conjecture that energy flowing from an inner-personal region into the motoric would result directly in a psychological locomotion. Lewin, however, rejects such a position. Tension pressing on the outer boundary of the person cannot cause a locomotion. Therefore, instead of linking need or tension directly to action by way of the motoric, he links need with certain properties of the environment which then determine the kind of locomotion that will occur. This is a very ingenious way of connecting motivation with behavior.

Two additional concepts are required in order to accomplish this purpose. They are *valence* and *force*.

VALENCE. A valence is a conceptual property of a region of the psychological environment. It is the value of that region for a person. There are two kinds of value, positive and negative. A region of positive value is one that contains a goal object which will reduce tension when the person enters the region. For example, a region that contains food will have a positive valence for a person who is hungry (Figure 22). A region of negative value is one that will increase tension. For a person who is afraid of dogs any region that contains a dog will have a negative valence (Figure 23). Positive valences attract, negative valences repel.

A valence is co-ordinated with a need. This means that whether a particular region of the environment has a positive or negative value

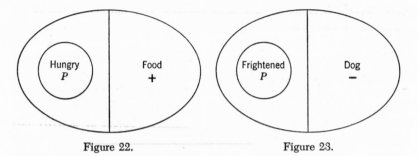

Figure 22. Figure 23.

depends directly upon a system in a state of tension. Needs impart values to the environment. They organize the environment into a network of inviting and repelling regions. However, this network of valences depends also upon alien factors which do not fall within the scope of psychological laws. The presence or absence of the needed objects themselves obviously plays an important part in structuring the psychological environment. Whether food is present and recognizable, what kind of food it is and in what quantity, its availability and its proximity to objects that possess negative valence, are all nonpsychological factors that influence the valence of a region for a hungry person.

A valence is a variable quantity; it may be weak, medium, or strong. The strength of a valence depends upon the strength of the need plus all of the nonpsychological factors mentioned above.

A valence is not a force. It steers the person through his psychological environment but it does not supply the motive power for the locomotion. As we have already seen, neither does a system in a state of tension produce a locomotion. Another concept is needed. This is the concept of *force* or *vector*.

FORCE OR VECTOR. A locomotion occurs whenever a force of sufficient strength acts upon a person. A force is co-ordinated with a need, but it is not a tension. A force exists in the psychological environment while a tension is a property of an inner-personal system.

The conceptual properties of force are direction, strength, and point of application. These three properties are represented mathematically by a *vector*. The direction in which the vector points represents the direction of the force, the length of the vector represents the strength of the force, and the place where the tip of the arrow impinges upon the outer boundary of the person represents the point of application. A vector is always drawn on the outside of a person (Figure 24) and never inside because psychological forces are properties of the environment and not of the person.

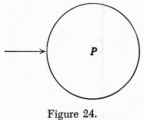

Figure 24.

If there is only one vector (force) acting upon a person, then there will be a locomotion or a tendency to move in the direction of the vector. If two or more vectors are pushing the person in several different directions, the resulting locomotion will be the resultant of all of the forces.

Now we can see the relation of valence to vector. A region which possesses a positive valence is one in which the forces acting upon the person are directed toward this region. A region of negative valence is one in which the vectors are pointing in the opposite direction. In other words, the direction of a vector is directly determined by the location of a region with either positive or negative valence. The strength of a vector is related to the strength of a valence, to the psychological distance between the person and the valence, and to the relative potency of other valences.

Parenthetically, it may be observed that the concept of need is the one concept with which all of the other dynamical constructs are coordinated. A need releases energy, increases tension, imparts value, and creates force. It is Lewin's central or nuclear concept around which the other concepts cluster.

LOCOMOTION. We are now in a position to represent the specific path that a person will transcribe in moving through his psychological environment. For example, a child passes a candy store, looks in the window, and wishes he had some candy. The sight of the candy arouses a need, and this need does three things. It releases energy and thereby arouses tension in an inner-personal region (the candy-wanting system). It confers a positive valence upon the region in which the candy is located. It creates a force which pushes the child in the direction of the candy.

Let us say that the child has to enter the store and buy the candy. This situation can be represented by Figure 25. Suppose, however, that the child does not have any money; then the boundary between him and the candy will be an impassable barrier. He will move as close to the candy as possible, perhaps putting his nose against the window, without being able to reach it (Figure 26).

He may say to himself, "If I had some money, I could buy some candy. Maybe mother will give me some money." In other words,

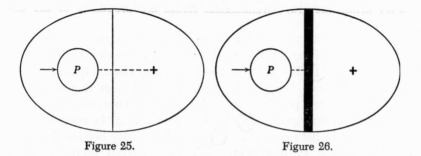

Figure 25.   Figure 26.

a new need or quasi need, the intention to get some money from his mother, is created. This intention, in turn, arouses a tension, a vector, and a valence which are represented in Figure 27. A thin boundary has been drawn between the child and the mother on the assumption that he has to go home, find his mother, and ask her for money. Another thin boundary has been drawn between the mother and the candy to represent the effort required to return to the store and make a purchase. The child moves to the candy by way of the mother.

If the mother refuses to give the child any money, he may think of borrowing it from a friend. In this case, the region containing the mother is surrounded by an impenetrable barrier, and a new path through the region containing the friend to the candy is transcribed (Figure 28).

This topological representation could be endlessly complicated by introducing additional environmental regions and boundaries of varying degrees of firmness, and additional needs with their co-ordinate tension systems, valences, and vectors.

In general, it may be said that any locomotion can be fully accounted for by the concepts of need, tension, force, valence, barrier.

Figure 27.   Figure 28.

the properties of the medium, the dimension of reality-unreality, and the time perspective.

DYNAMICAL RESTRUCTURING OF THE PSYCHOLOGICAL ENVIRONMENT. The dynamics of the psychological environment can change in four different ways. ①) The value of the region may change quantitatively, for example, from less positive to more positive, or it may change qualitatively, from positive to negative. New valences can appear and old ones can disappear. ②) Vectors may change in strength or in direction or in both respects. ③) Boundaries may become firmer or weaker, appear or disappear. ④) The material properties of a region, for instance, its fluidity or rigidity, may be altered.

Restructuring of the psychological environment may take place as a result of changes in the tension systems of the person, as a result of a locomotion, or as a result of cognitive processes. Cognitive restructuring occurs when the person discovers a new way of solving a problem (insight), remembers something that he has forgotten, or perceives something about his environment that he has not noticed before. Restructuring can also result from the intrusion of alien factors from the foreign hull into the psychological environment.

RETURN TO EQUILIBRIUM. The ultimate goal of all psychological processes is to return the person to a state of equilibrium. This goal can be reached in a number of ways, depending upon the particular process that is engaged. Although some of the processes have been described in the preceding discussion, it may be helpful to list all of them at this time.

Disequilibrium is defined as a state of unequal tension throughout the various systems of the person. For the sake of simplicity, let us assume that one inner-personal system is in a condition of heightened tension and all of the others have a low tension level. One way in which an equilibrium can be reached is for the tension of system *a* to diffuse throughout all of the other systems until the tension throughout the inner-personal sphere is equalized. Assuming that no energy is lost from the inner-personal sphere, the consequence of this diffusion is to raise the tension level of the total system and to increase the pressure on the boundary between the inner-personal stratum and the perceptual-motor stratum. Assuming that this process is repeated again and again, the result will be an accumulation of tension in the inner-personal sphere. Such a person is said to be under great inner tension. When the boundary of the inner-personal region is no longer able to resist the pressure on it, there will be a sudden breakthrough of energy into the motorium which will produce agitated behavior. This describes what takes place when a person has a temper tantrum or a fit.

If the boundary between the inner-personal system and the perceptual-motor area is fairly permeable, the tension can be dissipated in restless activity. This is a fairly primitive mode of tension reduction which is seen chiefly during infancy. As the baby becomes hungrier, for example, he becomes more restless. Restlessness, it is said, helps one blow off steam.

The most prevalent method of returning to a state of equilibrium is by performing an appropriate locomotion in the psychological environment. An appropriate locomotion is one which brings the person into the region of a satisfying goal object. For instance, if a person is in a state of tension because he is unemployed, then finding a job will remove the tension. In such cases, perceptual and motor processes are instrumental in bringing about relief from tension. It may be necessary, of course, to restructure the environment in order to reach the desired goal, and this restructuring may involve complicated and time-consuming cognitive processes. A man who aspires to be president may spend years manipulating the environment before he is successful. Or he may never be successful, in which case he will remain in a permanent state of disequilibrium.

Tension may be reduced and equilibrium restored by a substitute locomotion. This process requires that two needs be closely interdependent so that the satisfaction of one need discharges the tension from the other need system. We will have more to say about this topic in a later section of this chapter.

Finally, tension may be reduced by purely imaginary locomotions. A person who imagines that he has performed some difficult feat or occupies a pre-eminent position gains a kind of vicarious satisfaction from merely daydreaming about success. We are even provided with a number of ready-made daydreams in the form of novels, plays, and movies.

Résumé. In this section, Lewin's principal dynamic concepts, those of need, psychical energy, tension, force or vector, and valence, have been presented and discussed. These dynamical constructs taken in conjunction with the structural constructs discussed in the last section determine the specific locomotions of the individual and the way in which he structures his environment. Locomotions and restructurings serve the purpose of reducing tension by satisfying needs.

THE DEVELOPMENT OF PERSONALITY

Although Lewin does not reject the idea that heredity and maturation play a role in development, nowhere in his writings does he discuss their possible influence in any detail, nor does he assign them any place in his conceptual representations. This is in keeping with Lewin's preference for a purely psychological theory. Since heredity and maturation fall within the realm of biological facts and consequently exist outside the life space along with physical and social phenomena, Lewin ignores them. On rare occasions, he intimates that organic changes can and do influence psychological development. In discussing the period of adolescence, for example, he observes that changes in the functions and structure of the body profoundly influence the psychic structure in the direction of greater uncertainty and instability (1951, Chapter VI).

Nor does Lewin have a learning theory as that term is usually understood in American psychology. He describes the kinds of changes that take place in behavior and ascribes them to such constructs as cognitive restructuring, differentiation, organization, integration, and motivation (1951, Chapter IV).

It is interesting to recall, however, that Lewin's earliest experimental work consisted of research on associative learning. Frequency of repetition and contiguity between the stimulus words to be associated were thought to be, at that time, important determinants of learning. Lewin discovered, however, that the items to be associated had to belong to the same tension system in order for a connection to be formed between them. Lewin's finding cast doubt upon the validity of associationistic theories of learning. Hilgard presents a fine account of this phase of Lewin's scientific work (1956, Chapter 8).

Moreover, Lewin has written an extensive paper on reward and punishment (1935a, Chapter IV) but his ideas on this subject have very little connection with such hedonistic formulations as those of the law of effect (Thorndike) or the principle of reinforcement (Hull). Lewin was interested in reward and punishment, not as habit-makers or habit-breakers, but as devices for controlling behavior in the concrete, momentary situation. Reward and punishment do not, in Lewin's analysis, stamp in or stamp out associations as Thorndike used to say; rather, they cause changes in the vectors, valences, and boundaries of the psychological environment and in the tension systems of the person. Lewin acknowledges that reward and punishment may lead to a transformation in the valence of the thing itself, although this is accomplished when the reward or punishment is embedded in a larger interest situation.

Nor should one overlook the fact that Lewin and his students, notably Zeigarnik (1927), made a large contribution to our understanding of memory when they demonstrated that interrupted tasks were remembered better than completed ones. But all of this work does not constitute a theory of learning. We agree with Hilgard, who has made an analysis of Lewin's ideas as they bear upon the psychology of learning (1948, Chapter 8), that although many of Lewin's formulations are relevant to a theory of learning they do not constitute such a theory. Nor did Lewin ever claim that they did.

BEHAVIORAL CHANGES. In his important paper, *Regression, retrogression and development* (1951, Chapter V), Lewin discusses some of the behavioral changes that occur during development, following which he tries to show how these changes can be represented by means of field constructs.

Variety. It is pretty obvious that as one grows older the variety of his activities, emotions, needs, information, and social relationships increases, at least up to a certain age. Thereafter, the versatility of his behavior may show a contraction.

Organization. Not only do activities become more versatile with age; they also show important changes in organization. A given unit of behavior displays increasing complexity. A young child can carry on a relationship with one other child at a time, but an older child can have relationships with a number of children at the same time. Behavior also becomes more hierarchical in structure. For example, a young child may play with blocks just for the pleasure he derives from the activity, but as he grows older playing with blocks may become a means to other goals as well, such as the desire for approval or the need to outdo another child. Behavior may also become more complicated in the sense that an older child can engage in several activities during a period of time. He can be crayoning a picture, talking to a friend, be interrupted to run an errand for his mother, return to his crayoning, talk with another friend, answer the phone, and return to his crayoning. The young child is a good deal more distractible. He does one thing at a time, and when that is interrupted he is not likely to return to it.

Extension of areas of activities. The older child has more freedom of movement than the baby. He can do things, for example, cross the street, go to school, visit friends, that the younger child cannot do. Furthermore, time becomes more extended with age. The young child is pretty much a creature of the present; for him the future and to a lesser degree the past do not exist. As he grows older, he begins to think about the past, make plans for the future, and see the present as consisting of a larger block of time.

Interdependence of behavior. It is a matter of common observation that the behavior of the infant involves diffuse reactions of the whole body. Lewin calls this behavior an example of *simple interdependence* or an *undifferentiated state.* With increasing maturity, specialized and independent forms of action become differentiated out of mass activity. The simple unity of infantile behavior yields to a plurality of actions. Some integration takes place when independent actions become organized hierarchically but real integration is achieved only through what Lewin calls *organizational interdependence.* Organizational interdependence consists of combining and integrating separate activities or needs into a larger whole. Playing the piano, building a tree house, or writing a story involves the bringing together of a lot of separate activities. Lewin points out that mass activity decreases with age, hierarchical organization increases with age, and the degree of unity based on organizational interdependence fluctuates with age.

Degree of realism. A person customarily becomes more oriented to reality as he grows older. The young child does not readily distinguish between what is real and what is imaginary. Not until he learns to differentiate between them can he develop a sense of reality.

DEVELOPMENTAL CONCEPTS. Having set forth some of the important changes that take place during development, namely, changes in variety, complexity, extensity, organization, integration, and realism, Lewin then proceeds to conceptualize these changes. The constructs he uses are the same as those discussed in preceding sections of this chapter, since behavior and development are both deemed to be functions of the same structural and dynamics factors (Lewin, 1951, p. 238).

Differentiation. This is one of the key concepts in Lewin's theory of personality development and applies to all aspects of the life space. It is defined as an increase in the number of parts of a whole. For example, the number of regions in the inner-personal sphere increases with age. Compare the child and the adult in Figure 29. The adult has many more differentiated tension systems than the child. In a similar manner, the psychological environment becomes increasingly differentiated with age. The time dimension becomes differentiated into a remote past, a near past, a present, a near future, and a far future. Increasing maturity also brings an increasing differentiation of the reality-unreality dimension. By the time a person gets to be an adult he has learned to distinguish not only between the true and the false but also between different degrees of possibility and probability.

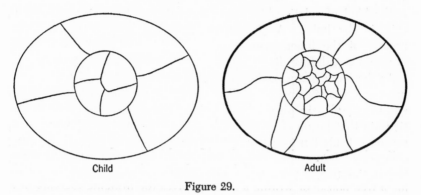

Child   Adult

Figure 29.

Boundary properties. Greater differentiation of the person and the psychological environment obviously means an increase in the number of boundaries. But not all boundaries are alike. They vary in strength. In general, the boundaries of the child are less firm than those of the adult. For example, the boundary between the child and his psychological environment is weaker than that between the adult and his environment. This accounts for the fact that the child is more subject to influences from the environment and that he can discharge inner tensions more easily than the adult can. The child is more a part of his environment. As a matter of fact, during the very early weeks of life, there may be virtually no boundary at all between the infant and his psychological environment. The weakness of the boundaries in the inner-personal sphere of the child means that one need can substitute more easily for another need than is the case with the adult. A similar weakness of boundaries in the reality-unreality dimension and the time perspective is also characteristic of the child.

Integration. Differentiation and changing boundary properties can account for many of the facts of development, but they cannot explain the increasing organization and integration of behavior with age. Another concept is necessary, which Lewin calls *organizational interdependence.* In order to appreciate what is meant by this concept, it may help to contrast it with the simple interdependence of regions. Consider, for example, two neighboring and interdependent tension systems, *a* and *b*. When *a* is thrown into a state of heightened tension, energy flows from *a* into *b* until a state of equal tension exists between the two systems. Similarly, if the tension level of *b* is raised, energy will flow into *a*. The influence is mutual and reciprocal. This is the kind of relationship between tension systems that appears to exist in the baby. A disturbance in one region spreads to other regions of the inner-personal sphere and out through the motoric in a massive, diffuse discharge. The hungry baby is restless all over.

As the baby matures, the influence of neighboring tension systems upon one another appears to lose the characteristics of being mutual and reciprocal. In place of simple interdependence, the type of relationship that becomes established is that of leader and led. Tension system *a* leads tension system *b* in such a manner as to help *a* discharge its tension without necessarily leading to any final equality between the two. A simple example of this organizational interdependence is the way in which an inner-personal region can subordinate the motoric to its objectives, or when an inner-personal region regulates and controls what will be perceived.

Moreover, in organizational interdependence tension does not diffuse from region to region on the basis of proximity alone. Selectivity develops so that systems which are remote from one another may dominate or lead each other. A whole hierarchy of dominant-subordinate relationships can become established; region *a* may rule region *b*, *b* may rule *c*, and so on. This would explain, among other things, the ability of an older person to organize and execute a complicated plan of action, an ability in which children seem to be deficient.

Lewin likens the organizational unity of a person to an organization with one head. When the one head breaks up into several heads, unity decreases; when a new central head emerges, unity increases. Thus, the unity of the adult person waxes and wanes instead of developing in a straight-line manner.

STAGES OF DEVELOPMENT. Lewin does not discuss this subject at any length. Development is, for him, a continuous process in which it is difficult to recognize discrete stages. He does say that important developmental changes occur around the age of three, that this is followed by a period of relative stability until adolescence which is a period of dynamic reorganization culminating finally in the stability of adulthood (1951, Chapter VI). He also points out that the first regions to become differentiated in the baby are those that have to do with eating and elimination.

Lewin believes that the use of an age scale for describing development is not really adequate for understanding psychological growth. The age scale will eventually have to be dropped in favor of degrees of differentiation, organization, integration, and the like. Moreover, psychology must address itself to the task of discovering the coexisting and dynamically related facts which represent the conditions for the change at the time the change takes place. It is not enough to say that six-year olds do things that three-year olds do not do. One must account for the change using the concepts of field theory

REGRESSION. Any theory of development must take into account the regressions that occur from time to time. Lewin has made some important contributions, both theoretical and experimental, to our understanding of regression (1951, Chapter V). In the first place, he distinguishes between retrogression and regression. Retrogression refers to a return to an earlier form of behavior in the life history of the person whereas regression refers to any change to a more primitive form of behavior, regardless of whether the person himself had ever behaved in that way previously. It is much easier to study regression than retrogression, as these terms are defined, because it is not necessary to establish whether the behavior took place previously in the lives of the subjects. Moreover, in studying regression, the experimenter can make use of age norms that have been established for various activities. For example, if two-year-old children play with toys in certain ways, while four-year-old children play with toys in different ways, one can ask under what conditions will four-year olds regress to the play level of two-year olds. Lewin and his associates have performed such experiments and have found that frustration is one factor which produces regression (Barker, Dembo, and Lewin, 1941).

RÉSUMÉ. Lewin's theoretical analysis of development employs such field concepts as differentiation, changes in boundary conditions, organization, and integration. In general, it may be said that with increasing maturity there is greater differentiation both of the person and of the psychological environment, increasing firmness of boundaries, and a more complicated network of hierarchical and selective relationships among the tension systems. For Lewin, development of behavior is a function of the person and the psychological environment.

CHARACTERISTIC RESEARCH AND RESEARCH METHODS

One widely acknowledged criterion of a "good" theory is the measure of its fruitfulness in stimulating research. In this respect, Lewin's theory is a very "good" theory indeed. Few other theories of personality have been responsible for generating so much experimentation. Lewin himself, although he is known as a brilliant theoretician, was always a working scientist. He took the lead in formulating empirical tests of many of his basic hypotheses, and his great enthusiasm for research has been transmitted to many generations of students in Germany and in the United States. The series of articles in the *Psychologische Forschung* between 1926 and 1930 is one of the most distinguished group of empirical studies in the psychological literature. Moreover, Lewin's ideas and his genius for devising simple and convincing demonstrations of his theoretical conceptions have acted as catalysts for many psychologists who were never personally associated with him. It is impossible to estimate the number of investigations that bear the imprint of Lewin's influence. Their number is surely legion. Whatever may be the fate of Lewin's theory in the years to come, the body of experimental work instigated by it constitutes an enduring contribution to our knowledge of personality.

The empirical investigations of Lewin and his many associates have always been theory-oriented. That is, experiments were undertaken to test propositions suggested by field theory; they were never done purely for the sake of collecting facts. A particular fact was only of significance to Lewin as it shed light upon the validity of a general principle or law.

The studies growing out of Lewin's conception of tension systems are a case in point. It will be recalled that the inner-personal sphere of personality consists of a number of regions or cells. Each cell is separated from its neighboring cells by boundaries whose chief property is that of offering resistance to the diffusion of energy from one cell into adjacent cells. The firmness of the boundaries can and does vary, with the result that a region may be in closer communication with one region than another. This means that when the tension level of a cell is increased by a need or intention, energy can pass more readily into a neighboring region where the barrier is weak than into one where the barrier is strong. This much is theory. How can it be tested in the crucible of empirical investigation?

Lewin devised the following experimental strategy (1935a, pp. 180–193). Suppose, for example, that a child is given an opportunity to build something with blocks. An intention to build a house, let us say, is induced in the child. An intention, it will be recalled, is coordinated with an inner-personal region in a state of tension. Before the child has an opportunity to complete the task and thus discharge the tension completely, he is interrupted and given another type of play material, such as some plasticine. A new intention, for instance, to model a horse, is induced which means conceptually that a second inner-personal region is thrown into a state of tension. The child is allowed to complete the second project. Then he is given an opportunity to return to the unfinished task of building a house out of blocks. If he does not resume the interrupted task, it indicates that the tension in the first system has been discharged by the completion of the second task. The second task is said to be a substitute for the first task. On the other hand, if the child resumes the interrupted task, it indicates that the tension in the block-building system has not been drained off by the completed activity of modeling a horse. That is, the completed activity has no substitute value for the interrupted activity. Each of these results can be depicted by the following conceptual representations (Figure 30).

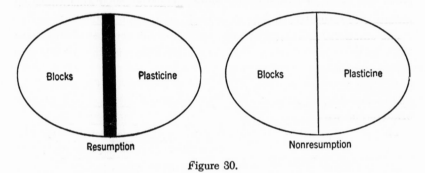

Figure 30.

In the left-hand figure, the two regions are separated by a strong, impermeable boundary, which prevents the discharge of tension from the blocks system by way of the plasticine system. The tension remaining in the blocks system causes the child to resume building with blocks. In the right-hand figure, the boundary is weak and the tension in the blocks system can be easily drained off through the plasticine system. Since no tension remains in the blocks system after the plasticine horse has been completed, the child has no desire to return to the blocks. The experimental design also requires that a control group, in which the children are interrupted but are given no substitute task, be used. The purpose of the control group is to make sure that at the time of interruption there actually is some tension in the system. Otherwise, no test of the substitute value of the completed task would be possible.

Experimental investigations that make use of this basic design are called studies of substitution. One of the earliest of the substitution experiments performed under the influence of Lewin's field theory was done by Kate Lissner (1933). She sought to determine what there was about the tasks themselves that had a bearing upon the substitute value of one task for another. She found, as might be expected, that the more similar the two tasks were, the greater was the substitutibility of one for the other. For example, if the interrupted task consisted of modeling a horse and the substitute task of modeling a snake, the amount of resumption was much less than if the substitute task consisted of drawing a picture or stringing beads. Unfortunately, there are no very good criteria for determining beforehand the amount of similarity between tasks. Two tasks may seem to be very much alike to an observer and yet be quite different in the eyes of the person doing them, or two tasks may appear to be very dissimilar and yet be very much alike to the performer. Lissner also discovered that if the substitute task is difficult it will have greater substitute value than if it is easy, other things being equal. Task difficulty is also hard to judge before the actual test is made. What is difficult for one person may be easy for another.

Another one of Lewin's students, Mahler (1933), found that the higher the degree of reality of the second task, the more substitute value it will have for the first task. Thus, if a child is interrupted in the middle of drawing a picture and is then permitted to tell how he would complete it if given the opportunity, there is less going back to the original task than if he is told to think about or imagine how he would have finished it. Talking about an activity is assumed to be more realistic than thinking about it. However, as Sliosberg's work (1934) indicates, the degree to which the less real can be substituted for the more real depends upon the character of the situation. In a relaxed, play situation a fantasy may be as satisfying as actual motor activity, while in a more serious context the fantasy may have no substitute value whatsoever.

Köpke (cited in Lewin, 1935a, p. 185) has used the substitution experimental design for testing a special application of Lewin's theory of the person. Lewin suggested that the boundaries between the cells of the inner-personal sphere of the feeble-minded child should be firmer than those of the normal child. If this hypothesis is correct, there should be less substitutibility of tasks among retarded children than among normal ones. This is confirmed by Köpke's findings. Even with very similar tasks such as drawing a picture of a cat on red paper, and drawing the same animal on green paper, feeble-minded children nearly always went back and finished the first task after they had completed the second task. This difference between the boundary properties of normal children and morons is illustrated in the following figure (Figure 31).

The heavier boundaries of the feeble-minded child's inner-personal region indicate that there is less communication between tension systems than is the case in the normal child. There are more cells in the representation of the normal child because Lewin postulates that the normal child is more differentiated than the moron. For other differences between the retarded and the normal child see Lewin (1935a, Chapter VII).

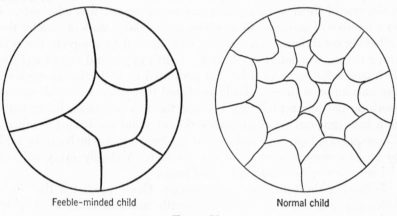

Feeble-minded child   Normal child

Figure 31.

Perhaps the most ambitious and carefully formulated investigation of substitution based upon Lewin's theory and experimental design was carried out by Mary Henle (1942). Henle has numerous criticisms to make of previous studies of substitution, the most relevant for our purposes being the circularity involved in Lissner's interpretation of her findings. Henle makes the point that it adds very little if anything to our knowledge of substitutibility to say that one task has substitute value for another task because the two systems are in dynamic communication, when one has to find out by empirical test whether one task will actually be a substitute for another task. In other words, to explain results after the results have been obtained is not a real test of the theory, since explanations based upon other theories might work just as well. One must be able to *predict* in advance what one expects to find if the theory is to have any unique explanatory power. Accordingly, Henle addresses herself to the significant problem of finding some principles by which one can predict beforehand what tasks will and what tasks will not substitute for each other.

Henle selected principles from the Gestalt theory of perception and learning. Gestalt theory asserts that such structural factors as similarity, proximity, homogeneity, closure, and figure-ground relationships are important in producing perceptual organization and in determining what is learned. Henle asks whether these principles may not be operative in task substitution.

Accordingly, she devised the following experiment based upon the principles of homogeneity and proximity. A series of five homogeneous tasks, one of them solving paper and pencil mazes, was administered to a number of subjects, all of whom were college students, under the following conditions. The subject was allowed to complete the first three mazes, was interrupted on the fourth maze, and completed the fifth one, following which he was permitted to go back and work on the uncompleted maze. Henle predicted that subjects would resume work on the interrupted task because the two last tasks, being units in a homogeneous series of mazes, do not stand out from the others. Consequently, tasks four and five do not form a pair which can be said to be in communication with one another. Virtually every subject did resume work on the interrupted maze.

Following the same line of reasoning, Henle predicted that in a heterogeneous series in which the fourth and fifth tasks were quite different from the first three, there should be less resumption than there was in the homogeneous series. This prediction was not borne out. For example, when the first three tasks consisted of making mosaic designs, and the interrupted fourth and the completed fifth tasks consisted of working jigsaw puzzles, the amount of resumption was similar to that for the homogeneous series. Henle acknowledges that failure to predict the results correctly in the second experiment nullifies the purported confirmation of the hypothesis by the first experiment, since the two predictions were made on the basis of the same principles.

Henle was puzzled by the results of the second experiment because in a previous one in which two tasks alone were used instead of a series of tasks, a fairly high proportion of the subjects did *not* resume the interrupted task. Why should there be this difference? Henle suggests three possibilities. In the first place, the interruption of a task in a series of tasks may make the interrupted task stand out from the other four. By becoming segregated, the interrupted task would lose its dynamic communication with the others. When there are only two tasks, the interrupted one does not stand out as much and maintains its relationship with the completed task. As a result there would be greater substitute value when only two tasks were used. If this is the reason, then the following procedure should elicit the required proof. Five tasks were used. The first three were alike and the last two were alike, thus constituting a heterogeneous series. Tasks one, three, and four were interrupted, so that task four, which was to be tested for amount of resumption, did not stand out by being interrupted since tasks one and three were also interrupted. The results were the same as those found when only task four was interrupted. That is, most of the subjects resumed work on the interrupted fourth task after completing the fifth one. Apparently, interruption by itself does not make a task stand out and cause the tension system to lose its dynamic connection with neighboring systems.

A second possible factor that might have caused a disparity in the results for a series of tasks versus a pair of tasks was the greater attractiveness (valence) of the tasks used in the series compared to those used in pairs. It may be, Henle suggests, that substitutes will be accepted less readily when the subject is very much interested in the interrupted task. To test this conjecture, Henle used pairs of tasks varying in relative valence. One pair consisted of highly preferred tasks, a second pair of medium valence, and a third pair of low interest value. The results plainly showed that the greatest degree of resumption took place for the task of highest valence, the lowest for the task of little valence, and a moderate amount of resumption for the task of medium valence. A strong valence inhibits communication between tension systems and reduces substitute value. Or it may be that a task of high valence has greater tension behind it which is not sufficiently drained off by the completion of the second task, as would be the case with a task of low valence and correspondingly low tension. In either case, the contradictory results obtained for a pair of tasks of low valence versus a series of tasks of high valence would be explained by the difference in valence. Consequently, in planning experiments on structural factors such as proximity and similarity it is necessary to use tasks of equal valence in the different experimental conditions.

The third factor that Henle thought might have produced different results between the experiment using a pair of tasks and the experiment employing a series of five tasks is that of *success*. Her argument regarding the influence of success runs as follows. A subject tends to view an interrupted task as being more difficult than a completed one. When he has an opportunity to complete a number of tasks, as he does when a series of five is presented, he gains confidence in his ability to do the work. Consequently, he tends to go back and complete the interrupted task. When there are only two tasks, he does not have an opportunity to build up much self-confidence by experiencing success and so he is less likely to resume the difficult interrupted task.

Henle investigated the relevance of this factor in the following way. Subjects were allowed to complete three mazes of increasing difficulty, followed by an interrupted maze and a completed one. Practically all of the subjects returned to work on the interrupted maze. When the first three mazes were so simple that they did not provide the subjects with feelings of success, a much smaller number of subject resumed the interrupted task.

Having determined that task valence and task difficulty were important variables in substitution experiments, Henle proceeded to keep these two factors constant while varying the conditions of task homogeneity and task proximity.

A series of heterogeneous tasks consisting of three letter cancellation tests which were completed and two mosaic design tests, one of which was interrupted and the other completed, resulted in a great deal less resumption of the interrupted task than when a series of homogeneous tasks, for example, all letter cancellation tests or all mosaic design tests, was administered. Heterogeneity of tasks permits the last two to stand out and become dynamically interdependent, whereas homogeneity prevents communication from developing.

In order to test for the factor of proximity, the following two series of three tasks were used. In the first series, the sequence was task one completed, task two interrupted, and task three completed. Tasks two and three were similar and task one was different. In this series, the interrupted task was next to a similar completed task. Seventy-five per cent of the subjects did *not* resume the interrupted task. This result shows that task three has a very high substitute value for task two. In the second series, the sequence was task one interrupted, task two completed, and task three completed. Tasks one and three were similar and two was different. In this series, the interrupted task was separated from its similar completed task. Only 36 per cent of the subjects did *not* resume the interrupted task. The results of these two sets of experiments confirm the hypothesis that the boundary between two tension systems is made more permeable under conditions of task heterogeneity and task proximity.

The foregoing studies of substitution constitute only a small segment of the experimental work that has been instigated by Lewin's field theory. It is quite impossible to do justice to all of the research within the limits of a single chapter. We can only point out some of the areas of research which bear directly upon Lewin's theory of personality, and trust that the reader will acquaint himself with them. They are level of aspiration (Lewin, Dembo, Festinger, and Sears, 1944), interrupted activities (Katz, 1938; Zeigarnik, 1927), psychological satiation (Karsten, 1928), regression (Barker, Dembo, and Lewin, 1941), and conflict (Lewin, 1951, pp. 260–268). A convenient survey of the experimental work done by Lewin and his associates will be found in Lewin's chapter in the *Manual of child psychology* (1954).

CURRENT STATUS AND EVALUATION

One indication of the vitality of a scientific viewpoint is the amount of controversy it arouses between proponents of the system and its critics. Watson's behaviorism, psychoanalysis, Hull's behavior theory, and Tolman's purposive behaviorism are examples of viewpoints that have divided psychologists into rival camps, and in each case the theory has exercised considerable influence upon the course that psychology has taken.

Lewin's field theory has been the object of considerable controversy for the past twenty years. During that time it has attracted a devoted group of adherents who, since the death of Lewin, have been carrying on the work that he started, especially in the study of group processes. Many of those who were associated with Lewin in the Research Center for Group Dynamics at Massachusetts Institute of Technology are now working together at the University of Michigan. As Deutsch points out (1954), group dynamics has become an integral part of social psychology.

Lewin's theory of the person has not fared as well. Lewin himself during the later years of his life devoted his energies largely to the study of group processes and to action research (Lewin, 1948). He became interested in applying field theory throughout the social sciences. Consequently, there have been no important advances in Lewin's theory of the person since the early 1940's. Many of his concepts, however, have become assimilated into the main stream of psychology. Vector, valence, tension system, barrier, and life space are no longer strange words to the ears of psychologists.

One significant innovation in studies which have a field theoretical orientation is the increased attention that is being paid to the influence of nonpsychological factors on the life space. Escalona and Leitch, for example (Escalona, 1954), in their studies of infant behavior show how such constitutional factors as sensitivity to various stimuli, physical activity, and tension tolerance affect the psychological environment of the child. An impressive investigation of psychological ecology is being carried out by Barker, Wright, and their associates at the University of Kansas (Barker and Wright, 1951). Their aim is to describe the behavior settings of all of the children in a small midwestern town in the United States. Escalona says that these two studies indicate that "topologists have broadened their realm by concerning themselves not only with the nature of the psychological situation but also with its genesis and its development through time" (1954, p. 982).

The criticisms of Lewin's field theory may be subsumed under four headings.

Lewin's topological and vectorial representations do not divulge anything new about the behavior they are supposed to explain. This objection has been formulated in various ways by different critics. Some like Garrett (1939) allege that Lewin's representations are cumbersome portrayals of fairly simple psychological situations; they are nothing more than pictorial analogies or illustrative metaphors (Brolyer, 1936–37). London (1944) says that they are pictures of what is already known, that they do not add any new knowledge or insights. In Lindzey's review (1952) of Lewin's *Field theory in social science* he notes Lewin's tendency to employ after-the-fact illustrations more often than before-the-fact predictions made on the basis of propositions deduced from the basic theory. Householder (1939) also observes that Lewin formulates no laws and gives no account of the operations required for determining the constants of the equations from which predictions of the behavior of an individual in a given situation might be made. Spence (1944) denies that Lewin's experimental work has anything to do with his theory. "Lewin sets up a most attractive program for theory. Taken in conjunction with his interesting experiments the illusion is nicely created that there is some connection between them."

Tolman raises the same question in his appreciative article on Lewin at the time of his death. "Is it true as I have heard asserted—or as I myself have at times been tempted to believe—that the proper conceptualization of a given life space is possible only after the behaviors which are supposed to result from it have already been observed?" (Tolman, 1948, p. 3). More charitable than other critics, Tolman avers that the fault lies in Lewin's failure to make explicit certain steps in his thinking. Heidbreder (1937) in a very thoughtful review of

Lewin's *Principles of topological psychology* asserts that Lewin did not intend that his topological diagrams should serve as models of reality. Rather, they are graphic methods of representing the logical structure of the relationships themselves. Heidbreder goes on to say that topological concepts may be peculiarly adapted to portray compactly and conveniently the complex network of relationships in a psychological situation.

Lewin has this to say about the criticism that his representations are merely pictures of known facts and do not permit one to predict in advance what behavior will occur.

> Not infrequently it has been stated that theories which merely explain known facts are of no particular value. I cannot agree with this view. Particularly if the theory combines into one logical system known facts which previously had to be treated by separate theories; it would have a definite advantage as an organizational device. Besides, agreement with the known facts proves the adequacy of this theory at least to a certain degree (Lewin, 1951, p. 20).

But then Lewin goes on to admit the validity of the criticism.

> It is true, however, that it is a clearer test of the adequacy of the theory if one can make predictions from it and prove these predictions experimentally. The reason for this difference seems to be that empirical data generally allow for quite a range of different interpretations and classifications and that therefore *it is usually easy to invent a variety of theories covering them* [our italics] (1951, p. 20).

In the italicized portion of the last sentence, Lewin has put his finger on the reason why after-the-fact explanations are criticized and why a rigorous scientific methodology insists that empirical predictions should be made beforehand in order to test a theory.

Psychology cannot ignore the objective environment. This criticism of Lewin's field theory has been raised by Leeper (1943), Brunswik (1943), and Tolman (1948). The argument runs as follows. The life space is not a closed psychological system. On the one hand, the life space is influenced by the external world, and on the other hand, the life space produces changes in the objective world. In order to have an adequate psychological theory it is necessary, therefore, to formulate a "set of principles whereby such and such individual and group life-space configurations will produce such and such behaviors, [and] a set of principles whereby the independent variables of environmental situation and given personality make-up will produce such and such inner and outer life spaces" (Tolman, 1948, pp. 3–4). Tolman believes that Lewin's theory falls down especially in not conceptualizing how the external environment produces changes in the life space. Failure to provide such principles means that Lewin's field theory falls into the trap of subjectivism from which only intuition can rescue it. That is, one has to intuit what is in the life space instead of discovering by scientific operations the independent variables in the environment that produce a given life space. If one knows the independent variables that are responsible for producing a life space, one can predict and control the life space in an objective fashion.

Lewin's answer to this criticism consists of two parts. In the first place, he states that he does take into account those aspects of the objective environment that are affecting the life space of the person at the time (1951, pp. 57 ff.). It certainly seems to be true that when Lewin and his colleagues are doing research they specify the independent variables and the stimuli from the nonpsychological environment in much the same manner as any experimentalist does.

Secondly he proposes an area of investigation, psychological ecology, that will study the relation between psychological and nonpsychological factors (1951, Chapter VIII). Apparently, it is to be the main task of this discipline to make predictions about what variables in the objective environment are likely *at some future time* to influence the life space of the individual. Valuable as this new program may be for long-range predictions of what might happen in the unspecified future, it does not seem to answer the objection of Leeper, Brunswik, and Tolman. What they want is a conceptualization of the environmental factors, here and now, that are affecting the life space. What are the mediation processes by which physical and social facts are transformed into psychological facts?

A different criticism but one that is related to the problem of the relation of the physical world to the life space has recently been elaborated by Floyd Allport (1955). Allport believes that Lewin has confused the physical with the psychological, or as Allport prefers to call the life space, "the phenomenological" (direct awareness). In Lewin's writings, locomotions are sometimes physical, sometimes "mental"; boundaries are sometimes actual barriers in the external world and sometimes they are inner barriers. Lewin's model confuses the inner world of phenomenology with the outer world of physics, and the result, Allport avers, is a hopeless muddle. Allport feels that this muddle is inevitable if one adopts a field theoretical approach because of the great temptation to include within the same field factors that lie within the person (phenomenology) and factors that lie outside the person (physicalism). Only by keeping the two sets of factors conceptually separate to begin with is it possible to find the laws by which they interact with one another.

Lewin does not take into account the past history of the individual. Leeper (1943) and Garrett (1939), in particular, raise this objection. They feel that in order to have a complete explanation of any present behavior it is necessary to look into the individual's past for causative factors. This criticism carries considerable weight with those psychologists who believe that the person is a product of heredity, maturation, and learning.

It is true that Lewin's principle of contemporaneity seems to exclude the past, but Lewin denies that historical causation should be excluded from psychology. Concerning this matter Lewin writes as follows:

> This principle [the principle of contemporaneity] has been stressed by the field theorists from the beginning. It has been frequently misunderstood and interpreted to mean that field theorists are not interested in historical problems or in the effect of previous experiences. Nothing can be more mistaken. In fact, field theorists are most interested in developmental and historical problems and have certainly done their share to enlarge the temporal scope of the psychological experiment from that of the classic reaction time experiment, which last only a few seconds, to experimental situations, which contain a systematically created history throughout hours or weeks (1951, pp. 45–46).

Lewin misuses physical and mathematical concepts. Although Lewin has taken great pains to point out that he has merely adopted the method of field theory as expounded in physics and not its content, and that he uses those aspects of topology that are appropriate for psychological representations, nevertheless he has been severely scolded for an undiscriminating and incorrect use of physical and mathematical concepts (London, 1944). The objection appears to be that words like force, vector, valence, tension system, path, boundary, space, region and other terms used by Lewin are taken out of their context in physics, chemistry, and mathematics and are misapplied as psychological constructs. Valence in psychology, for example, does not mean the same thing as it means in chemistry. Moreover, as both Leeper (1943) and Cantril (1935) have indicated, Lewin does not always define his terms carefully, which can and has led to confusion. For if the borrowed term is not rigorously defined in its new setting, its old meaning is apt to persist.

Probably the most trenchant criticism that has been made of Lewin's field theory is that it pretends to offer a mathematical model of behavior from which specific predictions can be made, when in fact no such predictions can be formulated. In the eyes of many mathematical psychologists, Lewin's so-called mathematical model has no utility whatsoever in generating testable propositions. Whatever mathematical manipulations Lewin indulged in, he performed after the observations had been made. In other words, he made his equations fit the data, rather than deriving equations deductively from his theory which could then be tested by observational techniques. Discovering a way of expressing one's findings in mathematical terms is an interesting exercise in translating verbal statements into numerical or nonmetrical ones, but it does not have any relevance for the development of a useful theory. Lewin's field theory is not a mathematical one despite the topological language used in setting forth the theory.

On the positive side, psychologists have found much to commend in Lewin's work. There is, first of all, the tremendous amount of investigatory activity that has been stimulated by Lewin's ideas. He opened many new doors for the psychologist, doors that have led into regions of the personality and social behavior which were previously closed to the experimenter. The work on substitution, level-of-aspiration, the effects of interruption on memory, regression, conflict, and group dynamics was initiated by Lewin. The importance of many of these psychological phenomena had been established by the observations of psychoanalysts but it remained for Lewin to provide a congenial theoretical atmosphere and to devise methods by which the phenomena could be investigated. The problem of human motivation, in particular, which had proved to be an intransigent area for research except for the experimental studies of biological drives in lower animals has become a vital area of experimentation, thanks to Lewin.

Lewin possessed the valuable talent of being able to make explicit and concrete some of the more implicit and elusive assumptions regarding personality. He saw, for example, the necessity of spelling out in detail the basic assumptions made by psychoanalytic theorists regarding the substitution of one activity for another. When this was done in terms of an organization of segregated tension systems whose boundaries possessed the property of permeability the way was provided for experimental attack. In a similar manner, the rather involved question of psychological conflict which has always played a central role in psychoanalytic theory was worked over by Lewin and emerged as a clear statement of what conflict is and how it may be studied experimentally. This capacity for fairly rigorous and clarifying thinking about significant concepts was one of Lewin's strong points, and he illuminated many problems that had languished in the shade of incomplete conceptualization and fuzzy theorizing. He was convinced that the science of psychology, if it was to be of use to man, would have to penetrate and explore experimentally the significant dimension of man's conduct. Although Lewin could be abtruse in his theorizing, he rarely failed to get down ultimately to concrete cases and practical prescriptions for research.

Moreover, he clearly recognized that a theory which would encompass the vital aspects of man's behavior would have to be multidimensional in scope. In other words, it would have to be a field theory, one that embraced a network of interacting variables rather than pairs of variables. It was this field emphasis that was needed in the 1920's and 1930's to counteract the influence and prestige of an oversimplified and naive stimulus-response psychology. While Gestalt psychology was assaulting and overwhelming the ramparts of structural psychology which stood for mental analysis into elements, Lewin's topological and vector psychology was vying with a rather barren form of behaviorism which reduced man's conduct to simple stimulus-response connections. Furthermore, the type of field theory that Lewin espoused was thoroughly psychological in character, which contrasted sharply with the more physical and physiological orientation of behaviorism, and even with the physicalistic bias of Gestalt psychology. Lewin's theory helped to make a subjective frame of reference scientifically respectable at a time when objectivism was the dominant voice in psychology. The so-called inner determinants of conduct, such things as aspirations, values, and intentions, had been summarily cast out by an "objective" psychology in favor of conditioned reflexes, rote learning, and the automatic stamping in and out of stimulus-response bonds. Behaviorism had almost succeeded in reducing man to an automaton, a mechanical puppet who danced to the tune of external stimuli or jerked to the promptings of internal physiological drives, a robot bereft of spontaneity and creativity, a hollow man.

Lewin's theory was one of those that helped to revive the conception of man as a complex energy field, motivated by psychological forces, and behaving selectively and creatively. The hollow man was replenished with psychological needs, intentions, hopes, and aspirations. The robot was transformed into a living human being. The crass and dreary materialism of behaviorism was replaced by a more humanistic picture of man. While "objective" psychology tailored many of its empirical propositions to be tested on dogs, cats, and rats.

Lewin's theory led to research on human behavior as expressed in more or less natural settings. Children at play, adolescents in group activities, workers in factories, housewives planning meals, these were some of the natural life situations in which hypotheses derived from Lewin's field theory were empirically tested. With such vital research being done under the persuasive aegis of field theory, it is not surprising that Lewin's viewpoint became widely popular. The heuristic power of the theory, irrespective of its formal adequacy or its pretensions of being a mathematical model, justifies the high esteem in which Lewin's field theory is held in contemporary psychology.

BIBLIOGRAPHY

PRIMARY SOURCES

Lewin, K. *A dynamic theory of personality.* New York: McGraw, 1935a.
Lewin, K. *Principles of topological psychology.* New York: McGraw, 1936a.
Lewin, K. The conceptual representation and measurement of psychological forces. *Contr. psychol. Theor.*, 1938, *1*, no. 4.
Lewin, K. *Resolving social conflicts; selected papers on group dynamics.* Gertrude W. Lewin (Ed.). New York: Harper, 1948.
Lewin, K. *Field theory in social science; selected theoretical papers.* D. Cartwright (Ed.). New York: Harper, 1951.

REFERENCES

Allport, F. H. *Theories of perception and the concept of structure.* New York: Wiley, 1955.
Allport, G. W. The genius of Kurt Lewin. *J. Pers.*, 1947, *16*, 1–10.
Barker, R. G., Dembo, Tamara, and Lewin, K. Frustration and regression: an experiment with young children. *Univ. Ia. Stud. Child Welf.*, 1941, *18*, no. 1.
Barker, R. G., and Wright, H. F. *One boy's day.* New York: Harper, 1951.
Bavelas, A., and Lewin, K. Training in democratic leadership. *J. abnorm. soc. Psychol.*, 1942, *37*, 115–119.
Brolyer, C. R. Review of Lewin's *Principles of topological psychology. Character and Pers.*, 1936–37, *5*, 257–258.
Brunswik, E. Organismic achievement and environmental probability. *Psychol. Rev.*, 1943, *50*, 255–272.
Cantril, H. Review of Lewin's *A dynamic theory of personality. J. abnorm. soc. Psychol.*, 1935, *30*, 534–537.
Deutsch, M. Field theory in social psychology. In G. Lindzey (Ed.). *Handbook of social psychology.* Cambridge: Addison-Wesley, 1954, pp. 181–222.
Escalona, Sibylle. The influence of topological and vector psychology upon current research in child development: an addendum. In L. Carmichael (Ed.). *Manual of child psychology.* New York: Wiley, 1954, pp. 971–983.

Lewin's Field Theory 255

Garrett, H. E. Lewin's "topological" psychology: an evaluation. *Psychol. Rev.*, 1939, *46*, 517–524.

Heidbreder, Edna. Review of Lewin's *Principles of topological psychology*. *Psychol. Bull.*, 1937, *34*, 584–604.

Henle, Mary. An experimental investigation of dynamic and structural determinants of substitution. *Contr. psychol. Theor.*, 1942, *2*, no. 3.

Hilgard, E. R. *Theories of learning.* 2nd Ed. New York: Appleton-Century-Crofts, 1956.

Householder, A. J. Review of Lewin's *Principles of topological psychology*. *J. gen. Psychol.*, 1939, *54*, 249–259.

Karsten, Anitra. Psychische Sättigung. *Psychol. Forsch.*, 1928, *10*, 142–154.

Katz, Evelyn. Some factors affecting resumption of interrupted activities by pre-school children. *Inst. Child Welf. Monogr. Ser.*, 1938, no. 16.

Leeper, R. W. Lewin's topological and vector psychology; a digest and critique. *Univ. Ore. Publ. Stud. Psychol.*, 1943, no. 1.

Lewin, K. *A dynamic theory of personality.* New York: McGraw, 1935a.

Lewin, K. Psycho-sociological problems of a minority group. *Character and Pers.*, 1935b, *3*, 175–187.

Lewin, K. *Principles of topological psychology.* New York: McGraw, 1936a.

Lewin, K. Some social-psychological differences between the United States and Germany. *Character and Pers.*, 1936b, *4*, 265–293.

Lewin, K. The conceptual representation and measurement of psychological forces. *Contr. psychol. Theor.*, 1938, *1*, no. 4.

Lewin, K. Forces behind food habits and methods of change. *Bull. Nat. Res. Counc.*, 1943, *108*, 35–65.

Lewin, K. Action research and minority problems. *J. soc. Issues*, 1946, *2*, 34–46.

Lewin, K. Frontiers in group dynamics. II. Channels of group life; social planning and action research. *Hum. Relat.*, 1947, *1*, 143–153. (Reprinted in K. Lewin. *Field theory in social science*, Chapter VIII.)

Lewin, K. *Resolving social conflicts; selected papers on group dynamics.* Gertrude W. Lewin (Ed.). New York: Harper, 1948.

Lewin, K. *Field theory in social science; selected theoretical papers.* D. Cartwright (Ed.). New York: Harper, 1951.

Lewin, K. Behavior and development as function of the total situation. In L. Carmichael (Ed.). *Manual of child psychology.* New York: Wiley, 1954, pp. 918–970. (Reprinted in K. Lewin. *Field theory in social science*, Chapter X.)

Lewin, K., Dembo, Tamara, Festinger, L., and Sears, Pauline S. Level of aspiration. In J. McV. Hunt (Ed.). *Personality and the behavior disorders.* New York: Ronald Press, 1944, pp. 333–378.

Lindzey, G. Review of Lewin's *Field theory in social science*. *J. abnorm. soc. Psychol.*, 1952, *47*, 132–133.

Lissner, Kate. Die Entspannung von Bedürfnissen durch Ersatzhandlungen. *Psychol. Forsch.*, 1933, *18*, 218–250.

London, I. D. Psychologists' misuse of the auxiliary concepts of physics and mathematics. *Psychol. Rev.*, 1944, *51*, 266–291.

Mahler, Wera. Ersatzhandlungen verschiedenen Realitätsgrades. *Psychol. Forsch.*, 1933, *18*, 27–89.

Sliosberg, Sara. Zur Dynamik des Ersatzes in Spiel- und Ernstsituationen. *Psychol. Forsch.*, 1934, *19*, 122–181.

Spence, K. W. The nature of theory construction in contemporary psychology. *Psychol. Rev.*, 1944, *51*, 47–68.

Tolman, E. C. Kurt Lewin, 1890–1947. *Psychol. Rev.*, 1948, *55*, 1–4.

Zeigarnik, Bluma. Über das Behalten von erledigten und unerledigten Handlungen. *Psychol. Forsch.*, 1927, *9*, 1–85.

7.

Allport's Psychology
of the Individual

Two decades ago most of the best minds in psychology
were pushing relentlessly toward increasing rigor and
quantification or else were earnestly seeking to track unconscious motives to their hidden lair. In the very midst of these trends Gordon
Allport serenely pursued his own way, advocating the importance of
the qualitative study of the individual case and emphasizing conscious
motivation. This reluctance to swim with contemporary currents of
thought has resulted at times in Allport's formulations seeming archaic
or old-fashioned, but on other occasions he has appeared to champion
new and radical ideas. In spite of his occasional iconoclasm, he represents, perhaps better than any other contemporary theorist, the
synthesis of traditional psychological thought and personality theory.

His systematic position represents a distillation and elaboration of
ideas that are in part derived from such highly reputable sources as
Gestalt psychology, William Stern, William James, and William
McDougall. From Gestalt theory and Stern has come a distrust of
the customary analytic techniques of natural science and a deep interest in the uniqueness of the individual, as well as the congruence
of his behavior. James is reflected not only in Allport's brilliant writing style, a wide-ranging, relatively humanistic orientation toward
human behavior, and an interest in the self but also in certain doubts
concerning the ultimate power of psychological methods to represent
adequately and to understand completely the enigma of human be-

havior. Similar to McDougall's position is Allport's heavy emphasis upon the importance of motivational variables, his ready acceptance of the important role played by genetic or constitutional factors, and his prominent use of "ego" concepts. In addition to these focal influences it is clear from Allport's writings that he deeply respects the message of the past and he consistently shows a full awareness of, and sympathy for, the classical problems that psychologists in and out of the laboratory have struggled with during the past seven decades.

Allport, one of four sons of a physician, was born in Indiana in 1897 but grew up in Cleveland where he received his early education in public schools. He completed his undergraduate work at Harvard University at the same time that his older brother Floyd was a graduate student in psychology at the same university. It is interesting to note that in spite of the brothers' early collaboration and the fact that each has made substantial contributions to psychology, there is little communality in their present theoretical views. After securing an A.B. in 1919 with a major in economics and philosophy, Allport spent a year at Robert College in Istanbul teaching sociology and English. He then returned to Harvard and completed the requirements for the Ph.D. in psychology in 1922. During the next two years he studied in Berlin, Hamburg, and Cambridge, England. This extensive experience in foreign academic settings must have played some part in developing the stout interest in international affairs that has been so evident in Allport's activities during the past twenty years. It also led to Allport serving for a decade or more as one of the chief interpreters of German psychology in America. Returning from Europe he accepted an appointment as instructor in the Department of Social Ethics at Harvard University. Again there seems to be a continuity between this first American teaching appointment and Allport's persistent concern with problems imbued with social and ethical implications. At the end of two years he accepted an appointment as assistant professor of psychology at Dartmouth College; he remained there four years before returning to Harvard where he has continued until the present. He was one of the central figures in the interdisciplinary movement that led to the formation of the Department of Social Relations at Harvard University, in the attempt to effect a partial integration of psychology, sociology, and anthropology.

Against the background of these many years of college teaching, it should come as no surprise that in much of his professional writing Allport displays a deliberate didactic intent. In contrast to most technical writers, whose primary goal appears to be the construction of irreproachable statements that defy the efforts of the critic to find a tooth-hold, Allport seems much more interested in expressing issues in a salient, provocative fashion. This sometimes leads to overstatement or else to focusing upon a particular issue to the relative exclusion of other pertinent questions. Thus, it might be said that Allport is one of the most hotly criticized of psychological theorists, but in the same breath it should be mentioned that questions Allport has raised have usually become matters of general concern to psychologists.

During his career Allport has received many professional honors, including election as president of the American Psychological Association, president of the Eastern Psychological Association, and president of the Society for the Psychological Study of Social Issues. In addition, he served for twelve years as editor of the influential *Journal of Abnormal and Social Psychology*. The breadth and diversity of his scholarly work are clearly revealed in the books he has written: *Studies in expressive movement* (with P. E. Vernon), 1933; *The psychology of radio* (with H. Cantril), 1935; *Personality: A psychological interpretation*, 1937a; *The use of personal documents in psychological science*, 1942; *The psychology of rumor* (with L. Postman), 1947; *The individual and his religion*, 1950b; *The nature of personality: Selected papers*, 1950a; *The nature of prejudice*, 1954; *Becoming: Basic considerations for a psychology of personality*, 1955. In addition, he has coauthored two widely used psychological tests: *The A-S Reaction Study* (with F. H. Allport), 1928; and *A study of values* (with P. E. Vernon), 1931, revised edition (with P. E. Vernon and G. Lindzey), 1951.

How can we characterize Allport's theoretical convictions? To begin with, his writings reveal an unceasing attempt to do justice to the complexity and uniqueness of individual human behavior. In spite of the dazzling complexity of the individual, the main trends in his nature display an underlying congruence or unity. Furthermore, for the normal individual at least, conscious determinants of behavior are of overwhelming importance. The congruence of behavior and the importance of conscious motives lead Allport naturally to an emphasis upon those phenomena often represented under the terms *self* and *ego*. Consistent with this emphasis upon rational factors is Allport's conviction that the individual is more a creature of the present than the past. His concept of "functional autonomy," to be discussed later, represents a deliberate attempt to free the theorist or investigator from unnecessary preoccupation with the history of the organism. In broad terms, his is a view of man in which positive, conscious elements of motivation are emphasized, and behavior is seen as internally consistent and determined by contemporary factors.

For Allport there is a discontinuity between normal and abnormal, child and adult, animal and man. Theories such as psychoanalysis may be highly effective as representations of disordered or abnormal behavior; however, they are of little utility in any attempt to account for normal behavior. In similar vein, theories that provide a perfectly adequate conceptualization of the infant or young child are not adequate as representations of adult behavior. Allport has consistently opposed extensive borrowing from the natural sciences. His belief is that methods of study and theoretical models that have proved useful in the physical sciences may only be misleading in the study of complex human behavior. This conviction is most clearly revealed in a discussion (Allport, 1947) of the various kinds of models currently popular in psychological theorizing. He considers the mechanical model, the animal model, and the model of the child, and concludes that none of these provides an adequate base from which to construct a useful theory of human behavior. Consistent with this distrust of borrowing is his belief that premature emphasis upon the importance of operationism, a detailed concern for specifying the measurement operations implied by each empirical concept, can serve to impede progress in psychology.

The application of psychological method and findings in an "action setting," where an effort is made to bring about the amelioration of some undesirable social condition, represents a deep and enduring interest for Allport. For many years he has inveighed against encapsulating psychology within the walls of the laboratory, and his work in the fields of prejudice and international relations are among the more fruitful examples of the application of psychology to social issues. It is interesting to note that with many other theorists who have emphasized strongly the uniqueness and individuality of human behavior there is an underlying pessimism on Allport's part concerning the ultimate power of psychological method and theory to unravel the mystery of human behavior. The enigma posed by the complex individual is too great to be completely understood through the earth-bound methods and conceptions of the psychologist. Thus, although Allport accepts the importance and inevitability of an experimental approach to psychological problems, he maintains reservations concerning the eventual success of this effort.

As we have indicated, a basic consistency of viewpoint is to be found in Allport's writing. However, he himself does not claim to be a systematist. He asserts that his work is oriented always toward empirical *problems* rather than toward the achievement of theoretical or methodological unity. To him personality is a riddle to be solved in the most adequate way possible with the tools available in the middle of the twentieth century; so, too, the other problems he has set himself: rumor, radio, prejudice, the psychology of religion, the nature of attitudes, and other topics of human interest. To all these problem areas he applies concepts in a somewhat eclectic manner, striving for what to him seems the most adequate account that can be achieved in our present state of knowledge. Thus, questions of the formal adequacy of his theory are of no great significance to him.

THE STRUCTURE AND DYNAMICS OF PERSONALITY

In the preceding chapters we have usually considered separately the structure of personality and the dynamics of personality. However, in the case of Allport's theory, this distinction seems largely inapplicable. Personality structure is primarily represented in terms of traits, and, at the same time, behavior is motivated or driven by traits. Thus, structure and dynamics are, for the most part, one and the same.

Gordon Allport's eclecticism is nowhere better reflected than in the rich variety of concepts he is willing to accept as playing some useful role in the description of human behavior. He considers concepts as segmental as specific reflexes and as broad as cardinal traits or the proprium (self) to possess some importance in understanding behavior, and he sees the processes referred to by these concepts as operating within the organism in a hierarchical fashion so that the more general usually takes precedence over the more specific. In the most detailed statement of his theory, Allport (1937) suggests that each of the following concepts possesses some utility: conditioned reflex, habit, attitude, trait, self, and personality.

Although all of the above concepts are acknowledged and conceded a certain importance, the major emphasis of the theory is upon traits, with attitudes and intentions given an almost equivalent status. Indeed, Allport's theory is often referred to as a trait psychology. Within this theory, traits occupy the position of the major motivational construct. What the need is to Murray, the instinct to Freud, the sentiment to McDougall, the trait is to Allport. Before proceeding to a more detailed consideration of the trait concept, let us examine Allport's definition of personality.

PERSONALITY, CHARACTER, AND TEMPERAMENT. For Allport definitions are not matters to be treated lightly. Before arriving at his own
definition of *personality* he lists and discusses half a hundred proposals by various authorities in the field. He classifies these in terms
of whether they refer to: *a.* etymology or early history of the term; *b.*
theological meanings; *c.* philosophical meanings; *d.* juristic meanings;
e. sociological meanings; *f.* external appearance; *g.* psychological meanings. After this detailed summary and critique, Allport attempts to
combine the best elements of the previous definitions while avoiding
their major shortcomings. First, he suggests that one might briefly
define personality as "what a man really is." However, he agrees that
this is too abbreviated to be very helpful and proceeds to the better
known definition:

> Personality is the dynamic organization within the individual of those
> psychophysical systems that determine his unique adjustments to his en-
> vironment (1937a, p. 48).

Certain aspects of this definition merit special emphasis. The phrase
"dynamic organization" emphasizes the fact that personality is constantly developing and changing, although at the same time there is
an organization or system that binds together and relates the various
components of personality. The term "psychophysical" reminds the
reader that personality is "neither exclusively mental or exclusively
neural. The organization entails the operation of both body and
mind, inextricably fused into a personal unity" (1937a, p. 48). The
word "determine" makes clear that personality is made up of determining tendencies that play an active role in the individual's behavior.
"Personality *is* something and *does* something. . . . It is what lies
behind specific acts and *within* the individual" (1937a, p. 48).

What has been said thus far makes it clear that for Allport personality is not merely a construct of the observer, nor is it something that
exists only when there is another person to react to it. Far from this,
personality has a real existence involving neural or physiological concomitants. An important element in the above definition is the word
"unique," which points to the heavy emphasis that Allport's theory
places upon individuality. No two individuals make exactly the same
adjustments to their environment, and thus no two individuals have
the same personality. With the phrase "adjustments to his environment" Allport indicates his conviction that it is personality that mediates between the individual and his physical and psychological environment, sometimes submitting to it, sometimes mastering it. Thus,

personality is of crucial functional or adaptive significance. The care and detail with which Allport has developed his definition of personality are reflected in the frequency with which other theorists and investigators have borrowed from it.

Although the terms personality and *character* have often been used interchangeably, Allport shows that traditionally the word character has implied some code of behavior in terms of which the individual or his acts are appraised. Thus, in describing an individual's character the word "good" or "bad" is often employed. Allport suggests that character is an ethical concept and states that: "Character is personality evaluated, and personality is character devaluated" (1937a, p. 52).

Temperament and personality have also frequently been confused. However, here again there is a clear basis for distinguishing between them in terms of common usage. Temperament ordinarily refers to those dispositions that are closely linked to biological or physiological determinants and which consequently show relatively little modifiability with development. The role of heredity is naturally somewhat greater here than in the case of some other aspects of personality. For Allport, then, temperament is a special subsection within the broader domain of personality. His definition follows:

> Temperament refers to the characteristic phenomena of an individual's emotional nature, including his susceptibility to emotional stimulation, his customary strength and speed of response, the quality of his prevailing mood, and all peculiarities of fluctuation and intensity in mood; these phenomena being regarded as dependent upon constitutional make-up, and therefore largely hereditary in origin (1937a, p. 54).

Given these important distinctions, it is now possible to consider those concepts that are more uniquely a part of Allport's theory.

TRAIT. The trait is a determining tendency or a predisposition to respond. Allport defines the trait as

> . . . a generalized and focalized neuropsychic system (peculiar to the individual), with the capacity to render many stimuli functionally equivalent, and to initiate and guide consistent (equivalent) forms of adaptive and expressive behavior (1937a, p. 295).

Important to note in this definition are the emphasis upon individuality and the implication that the tendency is not narrowly linked to a small number of specific stimuli or responses. The reference to "neuropsychic systems" points to the affirmative answer provided by Allport to the question of whether traits are "really there." Contrasting the biosocial viewpoint (treating traits as existing only in the observations made by some person other than the subject) with the biophysical viewpoint (which holds that traits are not dependent upon the observer but have real existence in the subject) he clearly adopts the second point of view. In lectures, he has suggested that traits are "the ultimate realities of psychological organization," and in his writing he has elaborated this as follows:

> A trait . . . has more than nominal existence; it is independent of the observer, it is *really there*. . . . this view does not hold that every trait-name necessarily implies a trait; but rather that behind all confusion of terms, behind the disagreement of judges, and apart from errors and failures of empirical observation, there are none the less *bona fide* mental structures in each personality that account for the consistency of behavior (1937a, p. 289).

It is necessary not only to indicate what this concept refers to but also to distinguish it from related concepts. Traits and *habits* are both determining tendencies but the trait is more general both in the situations appropriate to it and in the responses to which it leads. Actually, the trait, to a considerable extent, represents the outcome of combining or integrating two or more habits. Somewhat more difficult is the distinction between trait and *attitude*. Both, for Allport, are predispositions to respond; both may be unique; both may initiate or guide behavior; and both are the joint outcome of genetic factors and learning. Nevertheless, there remain certain distinctions between the two concepts. First, the attitude is linked to a specific object or class of objects while the trait is not. Thus, the generality of the trait is almost always greater than that of the attitude; in fact, as the number of objects increases to which the attitude refers, it comes to resemble a trait more and more. The attitude may vary in generality from highly specific to the relatively general, while the trait must always be general. Second, the attitude usually implies evaluation (acceptance or rejection) of the object toward which it is directed while the trait does not. In summarizing this, Allport suggests:

> Both *attitude and trait* are indispensable concepts. Between them they cover virtually every type of disposition with which the psychology of personality concerns itself. Ordinarily *attitude* should be employed when the disposition is bound to an object of value, that is to say, when it is aroused by a well-defined class of stimuli, and when the individual feels toward these stimuli a definite attraction or repulsion (1937a, p. 295).

It is of interest that Allport's publications dealing with attitudes (Allport, 1935, 1937a) have been of signal importance in shaping developments in this central area of social psychology.

Finally, Allport distinguishes between traits and *types* in terms of the extent to which they are tailored to the individual. A man can be said to possess a trait but not a type. Types are idealized constructions of the observer, and the individual can be fitted to them, but only at the loss of his distinctive identity. The trait can represent the uniqueness of the person whereas the type must conceal it. Thus, for Allport, types represent artificial distinctions that bear no close resemblance to reality, and traits are true reflections of what actually exists.

Individual and common traits. Essential to an understanding of Allport's theory is his distinction between individual and common traits. He insists that in reality no two individuals ever have exactly the same trait. Although there may be similarities in the trait structures of different individuals, there are always unique features to the way in which any particular trait operates for any one person that distinguish it from all similar traits in other persons. Thus, in the most important sense, all traits are individual traits—unique and applicable only to the single individual. The reader should note that our earlier discussion and definition of traits is strictly applicable *only* to individual traits.

Granted that no trait can be observed in more than a single person, still Allport admits that because of the community of common influences involved in a shared culture and species similarities, individuals do develop ". . . a limited number of *roughly comparable* modes of adjustment" (1937a, p. 298). Thus, the investigator may construct measures that get at common aspects of individual traits and that possess a certain crude predictive power—these are the common or nomothetic traits. Of course, they will not do justice to the unique individuality of each person, but for the sake of efficiency and convenience such a procedure may be justified. Much of Allport's own research has focused about such an approach, as his use of *A Study of Values* and the *A-S Reaction Study* make clear. In summarizing his convictions in this area, Allport states:

> In the strict sense of the definition of traits only the individual trait is a true trait: (a) because traits are always in individuals and not in the community at large, and (b) because they develop and generalize into dynamic dispositions in unique ways according to the experiences of each individual. The common trait is not a true trait at all, but is merely a measurable aspect of complex individual traits (1937a, p. 299).

One might reason that common traits should be given an entirely different label in order to distinguish them from the individual trait.

Allport argues against this because the term has been widely used in both senses and because the two usages point to the two major approaches to the study of personality. The common trait reminds the investigator of those aspects of personality in terms of which individuals can be usefully compared. In general, Allport feels that the study of common traits can be helpful as long as the investigator does not deceive himself into thinking that such concepts accurately represent the individual.

Cardinal traits, central traits, and secondary traits. As we have indicated, traits represent generalized predispositions to behavior. There remains the question of whether all traits possess roughly the same degree of generality, and if not, how to distinguish between the varying degrees. Allport suggests a distinction between cardinal, central, and secondary traits. He says of a cardinal trait that:

> It is so dominant that there are few activities that cannot be traced directly or indirectly to its influence. . . . No such trait can for long remain hidden; an individual is known by it, and may even become famous for it. Such a master quality has sometimes been called *the eminent trait, the ruling passion, the master-sentiment,* or *the radix* of a life (1937a, pp. 337–338).

This variety of trait is relatively unusual and not to be observed in every person. More typical are the *central traits, which represent tendencies that are highly characteristic of the individual, often called into play, and very easy to infer.* In a recent book Allport (1955) has suggested that the number of central traits by which a personality can be fairly accurately known is surprisingly few—perhaps five or ten. The *secondary trait* is more limited in its occurrence, less crucial to a description of the personality, and more focalized in the responses it leads to, as well as the stimuli to which it is appropriate.

There are certain traits that may be considered *expressive*. These dispositions color or influence the form of behavior, but are not in most people motivational (as are interests, values, and long-range intentions). Illustrative of expressive traits are ascendance, expansiveness, and persistence. No matter what end the individual pursues he may display these traits. It is also possible to consider certain traits as *attitudinal traits*. As the distinction that Allport makes between traits and attitudes implies, these are traits whose influence is limited to certain specific areas of life.

Here arises the question of whether traits serve to guide or direct behavior only, or whether they also have a role in initiating or instigating behavior. There is no simple answer to this question. Some traits are clearly more impelling, have a more crucial motivational role, than others. Thus, among traits there is considerable variation in the extent to which they exert driving influences upon the individual. Further, we may reason that in one sense there is always a previous stimulation that is related to the activation of the trait, for example, an external stimulus or an internal state of some sort must always precede the operation of the trait. However, it is clear that most traits are not pallid reflectors of external stimuli. In fact, the individual actively seeks stimuli that make appropriate the operation of the trait. The person with a marked trait of sociability does not wait for a suitable situation in which to express this trait; rather he creates situations in which he can interact with people.

A further consideration is the *independence of traits*. To what extent do they exist as systems of behavior that operate without regard for other systems? Is the operation of a particular trait always conditioned by and relative to other traits and their state? Allport argues that the trait is identifiable not by its rigid independence but rather by its focal quality. Thus, it tends to have a center around which its influence operates, but the behavior it leads to is clearly influenced simultaneously by other traits. There is no sharp boundary that delimits one trait from another. This interrelatedness governs the functioning of individual traits. The arbitrarily defined independence of common traits, as in some psychometric studies, represents one of their important shortcomings as accurate representatives of real behavior. This intertwining of the various traits also accounts in part for the fact that it is not possible to devise completely satisfactory methods for classifying traits.

It is clear that the inferences involved in identifying a trait imply *consistency*. Thus, by definition, a trait is known only by virtue of certain regularities or consistencies in the manner in which an individual behaves. Allport is quick to point out that his theory of traits does not necessitate a complete consistency. The mere fact that there are multiple, overlapping traits simultaneously active suggests that apparent inconsistencies in the organism's behavior may be expected relatively frequently. Further, the fact that the traits are uniquely and individually organized implies that they may include elements that would appear inconsistent when viewed from a normative or external viewpoint. Thus, we may observe apparent inconsistency in behavior which actually reflects a uniquely organized internal consistency. It is less the observance of exact correspondence or consistency in behavior that is implied by Allport's theory than it is the existence of a subtle congruence that unites, frequently in a fashion difficult to detect, the various behavioral manifestations of the individual. It is not implied that every (or any) personality is perfectly integrated. Dissociation and repression may exist in every life. But there is ordinarily more consistency than the customary methods of psychological investigation are equipped to discover.

An interesting and useful outgrowth of Allport's interest in traits is his painstaking categorization of roughly eighteen thousand terms taken from an unabridged dictionary. In collaboration with Odbert (1936) these terms were classified primarily in terms of whether they represented authentic traits of personality, present activities (temporary states), or evaluative terms.

INTENTIONS. More important than all of the searching into the past or the history of the organism is the simple question of what the individual intends or is striving for in the future. The hopes, wishes, ambitions, aspirations, plans of the person are all represented under this general heading of intention, and here one of the characteristic differences between Allport and most other contemporary personality theorists is manifested. It is the contention of this theory that what the individual is trying to do (and by and large it is accepted that he can tell us what he is trying to do) is the most important key to how he will behave in the present. Whereas other theorists turn to the past for the key that will unlock the riddle of present behavior, Allport turns to the intended future. In this respect, he shows a strong similarity to certain views of Alfred Adler and Carl Jung, although there is no reason to believe that there was any direct influence from these sources.

THE PROPRIUM. Although Allport has been called an "ego" or even a "self" psychologist, this characterization is only partially accurate. In 1943 (*The ego in contemporary psychology*) and again in 1955 (*Becoming: Basic considerations for a psychology of personality*) he reviewed the many meanings of ego and of self in psychological writing. In his earlier basic text (1937a) he largely avoided the problems raised by these concepts; but finally came to ask directly the crucial question, "Is the concept of self necessary?" His answer is guarded. Anxious to avoid the confusion and special connotations of these terms, he proposes that all of the self- or ego-functions that have been described be called propriate functions of the personality. These (including bodily sense, self-identity, self-esteem, self-extension, rational thinking, self-image, propriate striving, and the function of knowing) are all true and vital portions of personality. They have in common a phenomenal warmth and a "sense of importance." Together they might be said to comprise "the proprium." It is in this region of personality that we find the root of the consistency that marks attitudes, intentions, and evaluations. The proprium is not innate, but develops in time. Bodily sense, self-identity, self-esteem, are about all that the three-year-old child has achieved; other propriate functions develop later.

By approaching the riddle of the self in this manner, Allport hopes to avoid the question-begging position of many theorists to whom the self or ego is like a homunculus, a "man within the breast" who does the organizing, pulls the strings, and administers the personality system. He admits the importance of all psychological functions that have been ascribed to self and ego, but wishes at all costs to avoid the factotum or "agent" type of theory. To him, self and ego may be used adjectivally to indicate the propriate functions within the total sphere of personality (many functions are not propriate but merely "opportunistic") but he believes neither term needs to be used as a substantive. There is no ego or self that acts as an entity distinct from the remainder of personality.

FUNCTIONAL AUTONOMY. Thus far we have outlined the major constructs Allport uses in representing personality, and at the same time we have discussed what appear to him the most important motivational forces operating within the individual. However, this picture of individual motivation is far from complete. In particular, we have given no adequate picture of the *contemporaneity of motivation.* We have seen that the individual reaches out into the future and that his goals are all important as determinants of his present behavior. But at the same time we have understood that traits are learned, they appear with development, and if this is so, does not the past of the organism play an important role in determining what the individual is now motivated to do? Are traits then so different from other motives that are seen as growing out of primitive or vegetative drives and early experience?

For Allport, the answer is "yes." The key to why they are different is contained in the principle of *functional autonomy.* This is easily the best known and most controversial of the concepts introduced by Allport. In many respects it stands at the center of his system, for a number of the distinctive features of his theory derive quite naturally from this position. The principle simply states that a given activity or form of behavior may become an end or goal in itself, in spite of the fact that it was originally engaged in for some further reason. Any behavior, complex or simple, although it may originally have derived from organic or segmental tensions, may be capable of sustaining itself indefinitely in the absence of any biological reinforcement.

The reader should carefully distinguish the principle of functional autonomy from the common notion that a given behavior may be continued for a motive different from the one originally giving rise to the behavior; for example, the hunter initially hunts in order to eat, but when there is ample food he hunts to express his inborn aggression. This formulation still refers the behavior back to a more primitive or pre-existing motive, which is just what Allport wishes to avoid. Functional autonomy implies that the hunter would continue to hunt even in the absence of all instrumental significance, that is, even if there were no aggression or other more basic needs served by this act. A hunter may simply "like" hunting.

In presenting this view, Allport (1937a, 1937b) indicates that it echoes certain earlier formulations; for example, Woodworth's (1918) well-known dictum that mechanisms may be transformed into drives, Stern's (1935) assertion that phenomotives may become genomotives, and Tolman's (1935) suggestion that "means-objects" may "set up in their own right." One might suggest that such current formulations as Harlow's (1950) "manipulation drive," and "partial irreversibility" as proposed by Solomon and Wynne (1954), are intended to account for phenomena quite similar to those that played an important role in leading to the concept of functional autonomy.

In justification of the concept, Allport points to observations from a number of areas, all of which suggest a tendency on the part of an organism to persist in a particular response even though the original reason for engaging in the response is no longer present. He points to the circularity of child behavior and of neurotic behavior among adults, the repetitive elements in the Zeigarnik effect (the observation that incompleted tasks tend to be remembered better than completed tasks), the frequently observed temporal regularities or rhythms in behavior of both animals and men, the motivating power of acquired interests and values that appear to have no anchoring in fundamental motives. There is also some evidence drawn from comparative psychology. A study by Olson (1929) revealed that when collodion was placed on the ears of rats they scratched continuously in an attempt to remove the foreign substance. Moreover, long after the collodion was removed and when there was no longer any evidence of skin irritation, they continued to scratch and with no apparent reduction in rate. Thus, the scratch began as a functional attempt to cope with a physical state but with sufficient repetition it appeared to become an integral part of the organism's behavior in spite of the fact that it no longer served a biological function. Some of the important research conducted recently by Selye (1952) and his collaborators suggests similarly that adaptive responses may set up in their own right even to the detriment of the organism. Similar to this are studies by Anderson (1941a, 1941b, 1941c, 1941d) of what he called "externalization of drive." In these studies rats were taught to navigate runways at high rates of speed under strong hunger drive and rewarded with food at the end of the runway. After a very large number of reinforced trials, the rats did not appear to show ordinary extinction of the response when placed in the same situation under low drive or in a satiated state; that is, even though they were no longer hungry they continued to travel through the runways at the same rapid rate. Thus, we again have the spectacle of an organism performing an act for clear biological reasons, and yet when these reasons are removed the behavior continues without apparent interruption. Anderson would reason that this phenomenon results from the fact that aspects of the stimulus situation have been conditioned to provide secondary reward; Allport would say, according to the principle of functional autonomy, that the behavior is continued simply because it had been repeated so often that it became an end or motive in itself, a part of the rat's "style of life."

Following Allport's original statement of this principle, he was vigorously attacked by Bertocci (1940) who raised several serious questions. First of all, asked Bertocci, is it in fact true that any form of behavior if repeated often enough will become autonomous? Are there no limits or conditions to be placed on this generalization? Second, if any form of behavior is potentially capable of becoming an enduring motive, what is to prevent the individual from developing a kind of psychological anarchy in which conflicting and antithetical motives are built into the organism and tear him asunder?

Such questions as these led Allport to clarify and expand his position, and to embrace a form of ego psychology. He recognized that the examples of functional autonomy just listed include, in effect, two types of autonomous conduct. One is the sheerly *perseverative behavior* of animals as well as of men. Patterns of motor adjustment, scratching, observance of rhythms, and other acts that seem to outlive their biological usefulness and to resist extinction—these constitute one type. The other is the motivating power that lies in acquired interests, values, sentiments, and the total life style. The latter range of phenomena Allport came to call *propriate motives* (Allport, 1955); the former are "opportunistic" patterns that are found in all personalities, but are not centrally bound to the proprium (that is, are not "ego-involved"). Propriate patterns provide the organizing forces in personality, and explain why the individual does not break up into bits and pieces of unrelated motivation, as Bertocci predicted.

Once again we mention that Allport does not invoke the ego as a puppeteer who somehow magically manipulates motives and their conflicts to achieve unity of personality. Consistency is conferred not by a "little man within the breast" but through the gradual integration of dynamic patterns, composed of central traits, intentions, propriate striving, self-images, or such other functional units as may be empirically identified in a personality after careful investigation by all available methods.

The fact that the proprium is a developmental phenomenon, derived from primitive states and past experience, does seem to imply a direct link with the past, in spite of functional autonomy. As the forms of behavior that will become autonomous are determined by an organization that owes much to the past of the organism, it appears that the past retains a central role. In the end, however, the most important issue here seems to be whether or not mature, adult motivations retain a functional tie to their origins in infancy or biology. Whatever ambiguity may exist concerning the exact status of the concept of functional autonomy, it is clear that Allport contends strongly that for most adult motives there is no longer any functional relation to the historical roots of the motive.

A further question that is often asked of this principle is whether all adult motives are functionally autonomous. The answer is "no." There are infantilisms and other kinds of motivation that retain their historical links with their early beginnings. However, the extent to which an individual's motivations are autonomous is a measure of the maturity of the individual. The more his present motives are linked to the past and to underlying biological states, the more immature he is and the less he has evolved from a childish state.

Clearly the most important question that can be asked of any concept is what will it do for the person who utilizes it. The consequences of functional autonomy are clear, and it is in terms of these that the psychologist should decide whether he wishes to embrace the concept or not. Most important is the fact that *it permits a relative divorce from the past of the organism.* If the ongoing motives do not depend completely upon more basic or primary motives for their continuance, then the investigator may legitimately turn away from the past of the individual and focus upon the present and the future. The history of the individual becomes a matter of relative indifference if he is at present driven by desires and intentions that are independent of what motivated the individual at earlier periods. A further significant consequence of this principle is that it makes more or less inevitable the great, dazzling, unique *individuality* that is so much emphasized in Allport's theory. If potentially any form of instrumental behavior can become an end in itself, we know that there is sufficient heterogeneity of behavior and environmental demand to lead to a bewildering complexity and uniqueness in motives. Insofar as the individual's adult motivational structure is freed from whatever communality may have existed at birth, we can expect that the motives of different individuals will show little similarity.

The essence of what we have just said is aptly summarized by Allport in the following passage:

The principle of functional autonomy holds (1) that . . . motives are contemporary, that whatever drives must drive now; that the "go" of a motive is not bound functionally to its historical origins or to early goals, but to present goals only; (2) that the character of motives alters so radically from infancy to maturity that we may speak of adult motives as *supplanting* the motives of infancy; (3) that the maturity of personality is measured by the degree of functional autonomy its motives have achieved; even though in every personality there are archaisms (infantilisms, regressions, reflex responses), still the cultivated and socialized individual shows maturity to the extent he has overcome early forms of motivation; (4) that the differentiating course of learning (reflecting ever more diversified environmental influence), acting upon divergent temperaments and abilities, creates individualized motives. The dynamic structure of every personality is unique, although similarities due to species, culture, stages of development, climate, may produce certain resemblances that justify—so long as they are admitted to be approximations—the use of universal dimensions for the purposes of comparing individuals in reference to a norm, or for the purpose of constructing convenient "types" according to the special interests of the investigator. While not denying the possible existence of instincts in infancy—or even the persistence of some instinctive (or reflex) forms of activity throughout life—still the principle of functional autonomy regards the *developed* personality as essentially a post-instinctive phenomenon (1940a, p. 545).

THE DEVELOPMENT OF PERSONALITY

Thus far we have seen what personality is composed of and have examined in broad terms the dispositions that set behavior in action. In this section we are concerned with the way in which these structures emerge and the differences in the manner in which the individual is represented at various developmental stages. It is already clear from our discussion of functional autonomy that this theory proposes important changes between infancy and adulthood.

THE INFANT. Let us begin with the individual at birth. Where Allport is a radical when dealing with adult behavior, he is an archconservative when discussing infant behavior. In fact, until the child has lived the first two or three years of his life, Allport's formulations have little in the way of surprise value. It is only with the development of self-identity that things begin to assume a new and unexpected appearance. This is getting ahead of our story, however; let us return to the neonate as seen by this theory.

Allport considers the newborn infant almost altogether a creature of heredity, primitive drive, and reflex existence. He has not yet developed those distinctive attributes that will appear later as a result of transactions with the environment. Significantly, Allport does not consider the neonate to possess a personality. At birth the infant is innately endowed with certain physique and temperament potentialities, although fulfillment of these must wait upon growth and maturation. In addition, he is able to respond with some highly specific reflexes, such as sucking and swallowing, to rather clearly delimited kinds of stimulation. Finally, he displays mass action or gross undifferentiated responses in which most or all of the individual's muscular apparatus seems to be involved.

Given this equipment, how is the child set into action or motivated? Initially, Allport assumes that there exists a general stream of activity which is the original source of motivated behavior. At this point in development, the child is largely a creature of segmental tensions and pleasure-pain feelings. A biological model of behavior or a theory that rests heavily upon the importance of reward, the law of effect, or the pleasure principle, is perfectly acceptable as a guide for the earliest years of life. Thus, motivated by the need to minimize pain and to maximize pleasure and with these conditions determined largely by the reduction of visceral, segmental tensions, the child proceeds to develop.

In spite of the fact that the individual at birth lacks the distinctive qualities that later will go to make up his personality, this state is altered very early and in a gradual manner. Even in the first year of life, Allport considers that the infant begins to show distinctive qualities, for example, differences in motility and emotional expression, that tend to persist and merge into the more mature modes of adjustment learned later. Thus, some of the infant's behavior is recognizable as a forerunner of subsequent patterns of personality. Allport concludes that at least by the second half of the first year the infant is definitely beginning to show distinctive qualities that presumably represent enduring personality attributes.

TRANSFORMATION OF THE INFANT. The process of development takes place along multiple lines. A wide variety of mechanisms or principles is considered appropriate by Allport to describe the changes that take place between infancy and adulthood. He discusses specifically differentiation, integration, maturation, imitation, learning, functional autonomy, and extension of self. He even accepts the explanatory role of psychoanalytic mechanisms and trauma although these processes do not have a central theoretical role in what he calls *normal* personality.

In respect to learning theory, Allport is completely eclectic. He holds that all the myriad observations that investigators have made, all the conclusions they have reached, and all the resulting theories of learning are probably true in a sense and to a degree. Thus, conditioning, reinforcement theory, and habit hierarchy are valid principles, especially when applied to animal, infant, and opportunistic learning. They are inadequate to account for propriate learning which requires such principles as identification, closure, cognitive insight, self-image, and subsidiation to active ego-systems. Allport himself has made no systematic contribution to the theory of learning. Rather he has proposed functional autonomy as a basic fact in human motivation that must eventually be accounted for in terms of principles of learning which have not yet been adequately co-ordinated into a sufficiently broad theoretical scheme. Perhaps his chief contribution to the subject is his sharp criticism of theories of learning (for example, Allport, 1946b) that claim more universal validity than he will concede.

Thus, we have an organism that at birth is a creature of biology, transformed into an individual who operates in terms of a growing ego, a widening trait structure, and a kernel of future goals and aspirations. Crucial to this transformation is, of course, the role played by functional autonomy. This principle makes clear that what is initially a mere means to a biological goal may become an autonomous motive that directs behavior with all the power of an innately endowed drive. In large part because of this discontinuity between the early and the later motivational structure of the individual, we have essentially two theories of personality. The one, a biological or tension-reduction model, is adequate at birth and becomes gradually less adequate until, with growing awareness of the self, the individual develops motives that bear no close relation to those that had previously motivated behavior. At this point a reorientation is necessary if we are to represent the individual adequately.

THE ADULT. We now have, in the mature individual, a person whose major determinants of behavior are a set of organized and congruent traits. These traits have arisen in a variety of means from the sparse motivational equipment that characterized the newborn infant. The exact path of development for these tendencies is of no special interest because they are no longer, according to the principle of functional autonomy, deriving their motive power from primitive sources, whatever they may have been. As Allport puts it: "What drives behavior, drives now," and we need not know the history of the drive in order to understand its operation. To a considerable extent the functioning of these traits is conscious and rational. The normal individual knows, as a rule, what he is doing and why he does it. His behavior fits into a congruent pattern and at the core of this pattern lie the functions Allport terms propriate. A full understanding of the adult cannot be secured without a picture of his goals and aspirations. His most important motives are not echoes of the past but rather beckonings from the future. In most cases, we will know more about what a person will do if we know his conscious plans than if we know his repressed memories.

Allport grants that the picture we have just outlined is somewhat idealized. Not all adults achieve full maturity. There are grown individuals whose motivations still smack of the nursery. Not all adults seem to guide their behavior in terms of clear, rational principles. However, the extent to which they avoid unconscious motivation and the degree to which their traits are independent of childish origins represents a measure of their normality and maturity. It is only in the seriously disturbed individual that we will find adults acting without knowing why they act, whose behavior is more closely linked to events that took place in childhood than to events taking place in the here and now or in the future.

In contrast to most personality theorists, the bulk of whose interest is focused on the negative side of the adjustment register, Allport considers at some length the qualities that make for more than an "adequate" or "normal" adjustment. The *mature personality* must possess first of all an *extension of the self*. That is, his life must not be tied narrowly to a set of activities that are closely linked to his own immediate needs and duties. He should be able to participate in and enjoy a wide variety of different activities. His satisfactions and frustrations should be many and diverse, rather than few and stereotyped. An important part of this extension of the self involves projection into the future—planning, hoping. For maturity, the individual must also possess *self-objectification.* Allport considers that there are two main components to this attribute, *humor and insight.* It is clear that what we mean by insight is the capacity of the individual to understand himself, even though it is by no means clear just how to secure an adequate standard against which to compare the individual's beliefs. A sense of humor implies not only the capacity to find enjoyment and laughter in the customary places but also an ability to maintain positive relations to oneself and loved objects, at the same time being able to see incongruities and absurdities connected with them. Finally, maturity implies that the individual possess a unifying *philosophy of life.* Although an individual should be able to be objective and even amused about the ordinary events in his life, there should nevertheless be an underlying thread of complete seriousness that gives purpose and meaning to everything he does. Religion represents one of the most important sources of unifying philosophies, although this is by no means the only source of such integrating themes.

CHARACTERISTIC RESEARCH AND RESEARCH METHODS

In considering Allport's research, it is important to distinguish between that which has some direct bearing upon his theoretical convictions and that which has grown out of other orientations such as his concern with "action" research. Likewise his use and development of methods of measuring personality has been only in part dictated by his theoretical convictions. In spite of his pleas for "idiographic" methods and studies, much or most of his own work has been "nomothetic." In this section we shall begin with a consideration of the distinction between idiographic and nomothetic, follow this with a discussion of direct and indirect methods of measuring personality, and finally discuss studies of expressive behavior as the best example of investigation that mirrors central aspects of his theoretical position.

IDIOGRAPHIC VERSUS NOMOTHETIC. Allport has emphasized that the investigator may choose to study behavior in terms of general principles, universal variables, and a large number of subjects; or he may elect to focus on the individual case, using methods and variables that are adequate to the individuality of each person. In labeling these two approaches to the study of behavior, Allport borrowed from the German philosopher Windelband the terms idiographic (individual) and nomothetic (universal). There is a place in psychology for both approaches, argues Allport, but the emphasis, particularly in American psychology, has been so overwhelmingly upon nomothetic methods that a drastic reorientation is needed. This reorientation is particularly urgent as the individual or idiographic approach is eventually the more desirable and will lead to better prediction and understanding. In contrasting idiographic and nomothetic prediction, Allport suggests:

> . . . psychology will become *more* scientific, i.e. better able to make predictions, when it has learned to evaluate single trends in all their intrinsic complexity, when it has learned how to tell what will happen to *this* child's IQ if we change his environment in a certain way . . . (1940b, p. 17).

Consistently, in discussing the contributions that the study of literature has to make to psychology, he suggests that one of the most important things a psychologist can learn is ". . . how to keep a sustained interest in one individual person for a *long* period of time" (1938, p. 9). A further reflection of this conviction is his admonition that ". . . as long as psychology deals only with universals and not with particulars, it won't deal with much—least of all human personality" (1946a, p. 66).

This emphasis upon the idiographic approach, study of the individual case, is a logical outgrowth of several features of Allport's theoretical position. First of all, his emphasis upon the uniqueness of each person places a heavy obligation upon the investigator to select methods of study that will not conceal and blur this individuality. Second, and closely related, is the emphasis upon the importance of individual traits as the primary determinants of behavior. If these traits are the "real" units of personality, and if they are characteristic of only a single person, then clearly the most effective approach to the study of behavior will be a method of studying the individual.

All of this leaves unanswered the question of the feasibility of idiographic methods. Allport (1942) believes that these methods are intrinsically no more difficult to employ than nomothetic, but the weight of psychological opinion seems to be against him on this issue. Even in his own work, he has more frequently used nomothetic methods than idiographic.

Perhaps the best illustration of a method that permits the maintenance of individuality is the use of matching techniques in the manner employed by Allport and Vernon (1933) in their studies of expressive behavior. This approach encourages the investigator to examine relationships without having to reduce the data to analytic units for comparison; for example, a life history can be compared directly to an artistic production. The development of the Q technique by Stephenson (1953) and the work in intraindividual correlation by one of Allport's students, A. L. Baldwin (1942, 1950), represent developments that permit the investigator to approach the study of the individual case with somewhat more efficiency than was possible in the past. Allport's interest in personal documents (1942) is of course intimately related to this emphasis upon the idiographic approach to behavior.

It seems fair to say, in summary, that Allport, consistent with his theoretical position, has strongly urged psychologists to devote more of their time and energy to the study of the individual case than has been their custom. Further, it appears that this emphasis has met with considerable favor on the part of contemporary psychologists, so that what was once a deviant position is today widely accepted.

DIRECT AND INDIRECT MEASURES OF PERSONALITY. The past two decades in American psychology have seen an unprecedented expansion in and development of indirect methods of assessing personality. The main impact of psychoanalytic theory was felt in academic psychology during this period and naturally led to an increased interest in instruments that seemed sensitive to unconscious motives and conflicts. In the face of this trend, projective techniques became enormously popular, while techniques of self-report, including the interview and questionnaire, waned in their popularity. In Allport's words:

At no point do these [projective] methods ask the subject what his interests are, what he wants to do, or what he is trying to do. Nor do the methods ask directly concerning the subject's relation to his parents or to authority figures. They infer this relationship entirely by assumed identification. So popular is this indirect, undercover approach to motivation that many clinicians and many university centers spend far more time on this type of diagnostic method than on any other. . . . it is probably true that most psychologists prefer to assess a person's needs and conflicts by going the long way around. The argument, of course, is that everyone, even a neurotic, will accommodate himself fairly well to the demands placed upon him by reality. Only in an unstructured projective situation will he reveal his anxieties and unmasked needs. . . . this uncompromising statement . . . seems to mark the culmination of a century-long era of irrationalism, and therefore of distrust. Has the subject no right to be believed? . . . This prevailing atmosphere of theory has engendered a kind of contempt for the "psychic surface" of life. The individual's conscious report is rejected as untrustworthy, and the contemporary thrust of his motives is disregarded in favor of a backward tracing of his conduct to earlier formative stages. The individual loses his right to be believed. And while he is busy leading his life in the present with a forward thrust into the future, most psychologists have become busy tracing it backward into the past. . . . It is not the well-integrated subject, aware of his motivations, who reveals himself in projective testing. It is rather the neurotic personality, whose façade belies the repressed fears and hostilities within. Such a subject is caught off guard by projective devices; but the well-adjusted subject gives no significantly different response (1953, pp. 108–110).

Allport's position on this issue is altogether consistent with the importance he attributes to conscious, rational determinants of behavior. His conviction that the normal individual behaves in terms of known, reasonable motives leads him to the assertion that projective techniques have a unique contribution to make only in the case of the neurotic or disturbed individual, where the importance of unconscious motives may, in fact, be considerable. Allport maintains that direct and indirect methods will give a consistent picture in the case of the normal individual, whereas there may be considerable discrepancy between direct and indirect methods for the seriously maladjusted individual. He generalizes:

. . . a normal, well-adjusted individual with strong goal-directedness may on projective tests do one of two things: 1) either give material identical with that of conscious report—in which case the projective method is not needed; or 2) give no evidence whatever of his dominant motives (1953, p. 111).

He concludes that indirect methods may reveal important unconscious determinants of behavior, but only if compared with the yield of direct methods. It follows that indirect methods should never be used except in conjunction with direct methods. For the normal person direct methods give a much fuller and more useful picture of the motivational structure of the subject than does the indirect method. Not to be overlooked in a comparison of these methods is the vastly greater efficiency and simplicity of the direct methods.

Allport's construction and use of questionnaire methods is consistent with the point of view we have just outlined. On the other hand, it must be remembered that his stress upon the use of personal documents as an approach to personality and his studies of expressive behavior represent contributions to the indirect assessment of personality.

STUDIES OF EXPRESSIVE BEHAVIOR. Beginning in the early 1930's Allport and his collaborators have carried out a series of investigations concerned with demonstrating the significance and consistency of expressive behavior. In defining this area of study, Allport distinguishes between two components that are present in every human response. First, there is the adaptive or coping component, which is primarily concerned with the functional value of the act, the effect which it produces, or the end to which it leads. Second, there is the expressive component, which refers to the manner or style in which the act is performed. Millions of individuals perform the same adaptive acts, but no two individuals carry out these acts with exactly the same flavor or style. Considering the emphasis in Allport's theory upon the individual and unique elements in behavior, it seems fitting that he should be deeply interested in expressive behavior—the personal or idiosyncratic component that appears in even the most stereotyped responses.

Not only does Allport's theory seem to lead naturally to an interest in expressive behavior; it also promises that the study of this aspect of behavior will be of general significance. If all of the individual's behavior is congruent and interrelated, then even the most trivial individual acts must be related to central aspects of the individual's make-up. Consequently, we may study the inconspicuous expressive acts in order to obtain information about the most central aspects of behavior. In comparing expressive and adaptive components, Allport states:

> The expressive portion of conduct results, then, from deep-lying determinants, functioning, as a rule, unconsciously and without effort. The adaptive portion, on the other hand, is a more limited system, circumscribed by the purpose of the moment, closely dependent upon the stimulus and upon voluntary effort or upon habits of skill. The *reason* for a present act of conduct is to be sought in the present desires and intentions of the individual (though these in turn may arise from deep-lying personal traits and interests); but the *style of execution* is always guided directly and without interference by deep and lasting personal dispositions (1937a, p. 466).

Thus, Allport, in consonance with his theory, studies expressive aspects of behavior as a means of securing ready access to important sources of motivation and conflict in the individual.

The style of behavior is not determined solely by personality factors. Allport accepts the role of sociocultural determinants, temporary states or moods, organic conditions and other variables. The contributions of these multiple factors do not lessen the importance of expressive behavior as a source of evidence concerning personality; they serve only to make somewhat more complex the empirical task of the investigator or diagnostician. Expressive behavior may be classified in terms of the type of act involved, for example, facial expression, gait, voice, and handwriting. Allport argues that one should not attend to any one type of expressive behavior exclusively, since all are of significance and add to our knowledge of the individual.

The most extensive of Allport's investigations in this area was carried out in collaboration with Philip E. Vernon (Allport and Vernon, 1933) and was aimed particularly at the problem of consistency of expressive movement. In one part of this investigation, a group of twenty-five subjects of rather heterogeneous composition was studied in three different sessions, each session separated by a period of about four weeks. During each session, the subject responded to a large number of different tests providing measures of: speed of reading and counting; speed of walking and strolling; length of stride; estimation of familiar sizes and distances; estimation of weights; strength of handshake; speed and pressure of finger, hand, and leg tapping; drawing squares, circles, and other figures; various handwriting measures; muscular tension, and so forth. In addition, observer ratings were secured for various measures, such as voice intensity, speech fluency, amount of movement during natural speech, and neatness of appearance. It is obvious that the investigators had an extremely large number of derived measures that they were able to use in their analysis.

In their study of consistency, Allport and Vernon began by examining the repeat-reliability (consistency of measure on two different occasions) of the various expressive measures. In general, these reliabilities appeared to be reasonably high, the intercorrelations being roughly equivalent to repeat-reliabilities for conventional psychological measuring instruments. In the face of this consistency, the authors conclude: "Single habits of gesture, as we have measured them, are stable characteristics of the individuals in our experimental group" (1933, p. 98). Next they examined the relation between scores for the same tasks performed by different muscle groups, left and right side of the body, arms and legs, and so forth, and found about an equal amount of consistency. This finding is of considerable importance, as it tends to suggest a general or central integrating factor that produces a consistent style no matter what peripheral manifestation is chosen.

The most difficult of the group comparisons that the investigators attempted was the intercorrelation of the major variables from all of their tasks. A total of thirty-eight measures was intercorrelated. The first impression gained from the matrix of correlations was that the intercorrelations were more often positive than would be expected by chance. Thus, the initial evidence suggests that there is some generality underlying the individual scores. The data did not permit application of conventional factor analysis, so the investigators performed a kind of cluster analysis in which they identified groups of correlations or factors consisting of those variables that showed significant intercorrelations. They concerned themselves not only with the statistical significance but also with the psychological meaningfulness of the cluster in question.

In the end there appeared to be three group factors that accounted for most of the intercorrelations observed. The first of these was called the "areal group factor" and included such variables as: area of total writing, area of blackboard figures, area of foot squares, overestimation of angles, length of self-rating checks. This appears to be a kind of "motor expansiveness." The second cluster was called the "centrifugal group factor" and included such variables as: overestimation of distance from body with legs, extent of cubes, verbal speed, underestimation of weights, underestimation of distances toward the body with hands. The authors are less content with this factor than with the previous one, but they conclude: "The group factor is based chiefly on the centrifugal-centripetal measures. . . . Thus the group factor may be interpreted as a general 'outward-tendency,' freedom and 'extroversion' of expressive movement, the reverse of shut-in, restrained, and pedantic motility" (1933, p. 112). The third cluster was called the "group factor of emphasis" and included such measures as: voice intensity, movement during speech, writing pressure, tapping pressure, overestimation of angles, pressure of resting hand. The investigators conclude that this is a relatively heterogeneous factor but that a common factor of emphasis seems to underlie most of the measures. They suggest: "Mere physical pressure or tension would seem to be significant only as part of a wider and more psychological tendency to make emphatic movements" (1933, p. 112).

Allport and Vernon, not completely satisfied with their group comparisons, followed this analysis with four case histories in which the subjects' expressive movements are examined in the context of their known personalities. They say: ". . . we are forced to the striking conclusion that virtually no measurements contradict the subjective impression of the personalities. The measures faithfully record what common sense indicates. Even measures which do not correspond statistically fit into the picture in such a way as to be readily intelligible and psychologically congruent" (1933, p. 180). Further, it was found that judges were able to match, with more than chance success, handwriting samples and kymographic curves (indicating the pressure exerted while writing) with personality sketches. They make an interesting final statement: "There are degrees of unity in movement, just as there are degrees of unity in mental life and in personality. It is surely not unreasonable to assume that insofar as personality is organized, expressive movement is harmonious and self-consistent, and insofar as personality is unintegrated, expressive movement is self-contradictory" (1933, p. 182).

Allport and Vernon report two additional studies, both focused about graphology, one carried out by Edwin Powers, and the other executed by the authors in collaboration with D. B. Lucas, a professional graphologist, and June E. Downey, a well-known psychologist. In the study by Powers, an attempt was made to examine the extent to which handwriting permitted accurate judgments of personality. He was not interested in a detailed analysis of the handwriting, but rather in over-all judgment of the sort involved in *matching the handwriting samples to personality sketches*. The subjects were ten male adults of highly heterogeneous composition. The handwriting samples consisted of a forty-word passage that was copied by the subject using his own pen and writing in his usual manner. The personality sketches were roughly 250 words in length and were prepared by three psychologists in collaboration. In each case, at least one of the psychologists was intimately acquainted with the person to be described. Three groups of judges were employed in the study: 143 male undergraduates; 25 college faculty members and wives of faculty members; 17 professional graphologists. The number of correct matches to be expected by chance alone was one out of ten. All three of the groups exceeded this figure with the college students averaging 1.77 correct matches, the faculty group averaging 1.80, and the professional graphologists averaging 2.41. Thus, the untrained judges did better than chance, but more poorly than the trained judges. These results are considered to provide moderate evidence for the congruence of handwriting, an expressive form of behavior, with the general psychological make-up of the individual.

In the second graphology study, a group of twenty-three undergraduate males, who had been studied extensively through the use of conventional psychological measures, as well as through ratings secured from various observers, provided a number of handwriting samples. These handwriting samples were then given to two collaborators (Downey and Lucas) who prepared personality sketches based solely upon a knowledge of the individual's handwriting. The experimenter then attempted to identify the personality sketches through his detailed knowledge of the subjects, working with the entire group of subjects, as well as with small subgroups. Using either method, his success in identifying the subjects correctly exceeded chance, although in absolute terms the accuracy was not great.

After a final consideration of the positive findings of their investigations, Allport and Vernon conclude:

> From our results it appears that a man's gesture and handwriting both reflect an essentially stable and constant individual style. His expressive activities seem not to be dissociated and unrelated to one another, but rather to be organized and well-patterned. Furthermore, the evidence indicates that there is a congruence between expressive movement and the attitudes, traits, values, and other dispositions of the "inner" personality. Although the question of the organization of the personality as a whole is beyond the scope of this volume, it is clear that the foundations for an adequate solution of this important problem cannot be supplied by the anarchic doctrine of specificity but only by the positive and constructive theories of consistency (1933, p. 248).

A related series of studies was carried out by one of Allport's students, Stanley Estes (1938), who in six experiments examined the ability of 323 judges to appraise the personalities of 15 male subjects when they were permitted to examine motion picture records of the nonverbal behavior of the subjects in several settings. In the first experiment, a group of social workers rated the subjects on twenty-three personality variables using a six-point rating scale. The ratings were compared with independent measures derived from the intensive study of these subjects. For almost all of the variables, the combined ratings of the judges were more accurate than would be expected by chance alone. A comparison of the ten best and ten poorest judges revealed a marked difference between subjects in the accuracy with which they were able to interpret the behavior. In the second and third studies, groups of college undergraduates and summer school students were given word lists and asked to check the ten words that best characterized each of the subjects whose expressive behavior was observed. Their judgments were compared with criterial judgments made by five clinical psychologists. Again judges, on the average, did better than chance, and again there was considerable variation among judges in their accuracy. In the fourth study, a group of adults was asked to match the expressive behavior records with brief personality sketches based upon case histories of the subjects. On an average, there were twice as many correct matchings as would be expected by chance. There was the usual variability among judges in their accuracy and also considerable individual differences among the subjects in the accuracy with which they could be judged. These results also indicated that the members of the group who were college teachers and psychologists were significantly less accurate in their ratings than the other members of the group; and individuals who had an active interest in painting and dramatics were significantly more accurate than the remaining members of the group. In the fifth and sixth studies, two additional groups of students were again asked to match samples of expressive behavior with personality sketches. Once again, the judges were able to match the sketches and expressive behavior with greater than chance success.

The combined findings of the six studies make clear that expressive behavior *does* permit inferences concerning personality that are more accurate than could be expected by chance. Further, in some of the studies it appeared that the judges did better when they were permitted to make over-all judgments of the sort involved in matching experiments than when they were asked to rate specific attributes. The results also suggest that some subjects are easier to judge than others and that some personality characteristics are easier to evaluate than others. Finally, there was a consistent difference between judges in their skill in making personality inferences from expressive behavior, with the more skillful being generally less conceptual in their thinking and more interested in painting and dramatics, as well as being less self-consciously analytical in making their judgments.

A series of studies by Allport and Cantril (1934) attempted to assess the extent to which judges could estimate personality accurately on the basis of voice alone. Over 600 judges were employed in the judgment of 16 speakers. Three different techniques of judging were used: personality sketches, matching speakers to personality descriptions, and rating speakers on attributes that were independently measured. The attributes judged included: physical and expressive features, like age, height, complexion, appearance in photographs and handwriting; as well as interests and traits, for example, vocation, political preference, extroversion, ascendance.

The results of these studies were consistent in indicating that judges were able to relate the voice with personality characteristics and with certain physical characteristics with better than chance accuracy. A comparison of judgments based on the natural voice with those based on the radio voice revealed that under both conditions the judges were able to do better than chance, but that the natural voice led to slightly more accurate ratings than the radio voice. An examination of the different personal characteristics that were assessed revealed that the judges were both more consistent and more accurate in their estimates of interests and traits as opposed to physical features and handwriting. The authors conclude from this: "Not only are the more highly organized traits and dispositions judged more consistently than such outer characteristics as physique and appearance, but they are also judged more *correctly*" (Allport and Cantril, 1934, p. 51).

Another student of Allport's, C. W. Huntley (1940), conducted several interesting studies designed to examine expressive behavior with special reference to self-esteem. These studies grew out of the work of Werner Wolff (1933, 1943) and represent an attempt to examine some of Wolff's findings under carefully controlled experimental conditions. In the two studies that Huntley conducted, he asked the subjects to take a series of tests and during the test sessions managed to record without the subjects' awareness a number of "forms of expression." These included photographs of the back of the hands of the subjects and their profiles, as well as samples of their handwriting and voices. Six months after the original session, the subjects were recalled and asked to judge samples of their own and others' forms of expression. They were not told, of course, that any of the samples were their own. In each trial, they were presented with four samples: two from the opposite sex, one from the same sex, and the remaining sample the subject's own. The subject was then asked to give a free personality characterization of the owner of each sample and also asked to rank the samples in order of his preference for them, or else he was asked to rate each sample in terms of a series of specified attributes: originality, attractiveness, intelligence, and so forth. The two major findings concern recognition of own forms of expression and the evaluative reaction to recognized and unrecognized own forms. Huntley's study concurred with Wolff's in showing a surprisingly low incidence of complete recognition of samples of own expression. Further, the results of these studies showed that when the individual evaluated his own samples without recognizing them as his own there was a strong tendency to be extreme in the reaction. The evaluation was sometimes negative, but usually positive, and very seldom neutral. When there was a partial or dubious recognition of the samples as own, the judgments became markedly more favorable, and where there was complete recognition, the judgments tended to become neutral. There were also marked individual differences in the self-judgments, with some subjects being consistently extreme while others were moderate. More recently, some of Wolff's and Huntley's findings have been re-examined by Lindzey (Lindzey, Prince, and Wright, 1952) who was also a student of Allport's.

Allport, generalizing from the results of his own and others' investigations, states:

> The expressive features of the body are not independently activated. Any one of them is affected in much the same way as any other. Hence, to a degree Lavater is justified in saying that "one and the same spirit is manifest in all."
> The consistency, however, is never found to be perfect. One channel of expression is not an exact replica of all others. If this were so, mono-symptomatic methods of psychodiagnostics would be fully justified. The complete personality would be betrayed equally well in every feature. Handwriting would tell the whole story, so too would the eyes, the hands, or the limbs. The amount of agreement that has been demonstrated does not justify so simple an interpretation of the case.
> The unity of expression turns out, as we would indeed expect, to be entirely a question of degree, just as the unity of personality itself is a matter of degree. The expressive features of the body should not be expected to reflect more consistency than the personality itself possesses (nor should they be expected to reflect *less*). Expression is patterned in complex ways precisely as personality itself is patterned. There are major consistencies and secondary consistencies, much congruence and some conflict and contradiction. Psychodiagnostics must then proceed as any other branch of the psychology of personality proceeds, to the study of *complex* phenomena at a *complex* level (1937a, pp. 480–481).

CURRENT STATUS AND EVALUATION

In contrast to many theorists, Allport has never developed a school of followers, although traces of his influence may be found in the work of former students such as A. L. Baldwin, J. S. Bruner, H. Cantril, D. G. McGranahan, and M. B. Smith. Most of the developments in his theory have depended upon Allport's own contributions, which have been continuous over the past twenty years. Beginning with an interest in an appropriate unit for the description of personality that led to his conception of the trait, and a simultaneous concern over the developmental transformation that motives undergo, which culminated in the concept of functional autonomy, he has progressively modified the theory so as to place increasing emphasis upon intentionality and ego (propriate) functions. At the present moment, the theory is in the process of undergoing a general restatement as Allport revises his major publication in this area (Allport, 1937a).

Although few psychologists have embraced this theory in its total form, it has nevertheless had considerable influence. One bit of evidence for the theory's utility is supplied by a questionnaire circulated by the Division of Clinical and Abnormal Psychology of the American Psychological Association (Schafer, Berg, and McCandless, 1951). This questionnaire was sent to practicing clinical psychologists and asked them to indicate what personality theorist was of most direct value to them in their day-to-day clinical work. The overwhelming majority of the respondents mentioned Freud as being most influential, but the second most frequently mentioned theorist was Allport.

One of the most interesting current developments in connection with this theory is the manner in which it has become of interest to psychoanalytic theorists. Allport's emphasis upon active propriate (ego) functions and the concept of functional autonomy are highly congruent with recent developments in psychoanalytic ego psychology. Thus, in spite of the fact that he has been one of the most unremitting critics of orthodox psychoanalysis, Allport has, in the end, proved to be one of the most fashionable of psychological theorists among psychoanalysts.

Whatever the ultimate systematic status of this theory, it is clear that its plentiful novel features must have consequences for future developments in psychological theorizing. In an area where there are so few well-established regularities and where the major variables almost certainly are not yet clearly identified, it seems important to maintain a healthy diversity in the theoretical positions guiding research. From this point of view, Allport has occupied a crucial role in psychological theorizing, as his views give persuasive emphasis to problems and concepts often neglected in contemporary psychological theory.

One of the striking phenomena of the past sixty years in psychology has been the demise and subsequent rebirth of self and ego concepts. Perhaps no other psychologist has had so influential a role in restoring and purifying the ego concept as Allport. Not only has he placed the concept in historical context but he has also attempted persistently to show the functional necessity of employing some such concept in a discriminating way in any attempt to represent normal, complex, human behavior. A further novel feature of Allport's position has been his emphasis upon the importance of conscious determinants of behavior, and, as a corollary to this, his advocacy of direct methods of assessing human motivation. As we have already indicated, this position has been distinctly unpopular among contemporary psychologists, and yet it is a point of view that should be represented if we are to avoid a one-sided approach to our subject matter. More in keeping with current modes in psychology is the ardent plea that

Allport has made for the detailed study of the individual case. Although others have shared this conviction, Allport, with his monograph on the use of personal documents in psychology (1943), his stress upon idiographic methods, and his publication of case histories as editor of the *Journal of Abnormal and Social Psychology*, is clearly one of the most important figures in a movement that has led to current acceptance of the individual case as a legitimate object of psychological investigation.

We have already mentioned the fact that Allport represents one of the few theorists who provides an effective bridge between academic psychology and its traditions on the one hand and the rapidly developing field of clinical and personality psychology on the other hand. This continuity not only serves to enrich each of the subdisciplines with the insights of the other but also helps to maintain an intellectual continuity that is important for the long-term development of psychology. A final novelty in Allport's position is contained in his emphasis upon the future and the present to the relative exclusion of the past. With the influence of psychoanalysis so pervasive, it is easy for the investigator or practitioner to forget about the importance of situational and ongoing determinants of behavior in favor of historical determination. Consequently, it has indeed been helpful to have Allport's writings as a constant reminder that the past is not the whole of the functioning individual.

So much for the positive side of the register. Let us examine the negative. In many respects, this theory is singularly vulnerable to criticism, and there has been no dearth of active critics, such as Bertocci (1940), Coutu (1949), Seward (1948), and Skaggs (1945). As we suggested earlier, Allport has usually been more concerned with presenting his viewpoint vividly and effectively than in protecting himself from criticism. The formal inadequacy of the theory has led to much negative comment. Just what is the axiomatic base of his position? What is assumed and what open to empirical test? Just how are the assumptions made by the theory interrelated, and where are the careful empirical definitions that permit the investigator to translate concepts into observation terms? Intimately related to these questions, but vastly more important, is the issue of the variety and quantity of investigation to which the theory has led. It must be admitted that, with the possible exception of the field of expressive behavior, this theory has not been an efficient generator of propositions for empirical test. Like most other personality theories, it is more at home when attempting to account for known relations than it is in attempting to make predictions about unobserved events. Thus, although Allport's own writings and investigations have led to a large amount of related research, for example, prejudice, social and religious attitudes, and rumor, we must admit that his theory falls down sadly as a formal device for generating research.

Many psychologists feel that one reason the theory has difficulty in making predictions is that the concept of functional autonomy is not susceptible to empirical demonstration, let alone to making predictions about unobserved events. We have already referred to some embarrassment created for this concept when the notion of propriateness is introduced as a criterion for determining what becomes autonomous. The basis of functional autonomy is a failure to observe the expected extinction or dropping out of a given response, and no matter how long we observe a given response that has failed to extinguish, there is always the possibility of criticism. The detractor may say we should have watched longer in order to observe extinction, or he may account for the apparent autonomy of the response in terms of some underlying motivation that is not adequately understood by the investigator. It is always possible to account for any concrete example of functional autonomy in terms of other theoretical formulations, but so, too, can examples of other theoretical principles be accounted for in terms of alternative principles. Perhaps the most serious criticism of this principle is that Allport provides no adequate account of the process or mechanism underlying functional autonomy. He tells us that the phenomenon takes place but provides no satisfactory explanation of how or why it takes place.

Another feature of the theory that has come under heavy critical fire is Allport's assumption of partial discontinuity between normal and abnormal, and between infant and adult. Most psychologists are so firmly convinced that we have gained increased knowledge of normal behavior from studying abnormal subjects that any attempt to imply that the abnormal is discontinuous from the normal seems nothing short of heretical. In fact, the extent to which psychologists have borrowed conceptions developed through observation of lower animals makes the assumption of discontinuities within the human species all the more difficult to accept. Consistent with his view of normal, adult, human behavior as distinct from abnormal, child or lower animal behavior is Allport's preference for a model of man that emphasizes positive or normatively prized aspects of behavior. The influence of psychoanalysis and comparative psychology has been so strong that a theory which insists upon emphasizing socially acceptable motives rather than primitive needs, such as sex and aggression, sounds mildly Victorian at present. Allport himself would say that he does not deny the importance of biological or of unconscious motives but wishes to give due place to the role of socialized motives and rational processes, which he believes a transitory era of irrationalism has neglected. However that may be, many critics of the theory maintain that Allport's position represents man in terms that are altogether too similar to those which the man in the street himself uses in accounting for his behavior.

No contemporary psychologist can dwell heavily upon "uniqueness" without incurring the wrath of many of his colleagues who are oriented toward abstracting and measuring behavior. What Coutu (1949) has called "the fallacy of the unique personality" represents a major disagreement between Allport's beliefs and those of most contemporary social scientists. It is their conviction that individuality can be accounted for in terms of adequate common or general principles and that to focus upon the individual and unique at psychology's present state of development can only lead to sterile speculation.

A further objection to the theory, intimately related to its failure to generate empirical propositions, is the theory's inability to specify a set of dimensions to be used in studying personality. Individual traits, by definition, cannot be stated in a general form, and consequently, the investigator, if he takes the idiographic approach, must begin anew the task of devising variables for each subject he undertakes to study. Obviously, this is a discouraging state of affairs for the person interested in research.

Finally, those among contemporary psychologists who are impressed with the contribution of sociocultural determinants to behavior—and this is a sizable group—find no easy way to give these factors adequate representation in Allport's theory. They maintain that the theory gives full attention to the interrelatedness of all behavior, but fails to recognize the interrelatedness of behavior and the environmental situation within which it operates. Allport gives too much credit to what goes on inside the organism and not enough credit to the seductive and constraining impact of external forces.

In any attempt at an over-all evaluation of this systematic position, it is wise to remember that in the past Allport has not considered himself immune to criticism. His current emphasis upon propriate (ego) functions and intentions reflects the vigorous and legitimate criticism that his earlier formulations elicited from Bertocci and others. Thus, it should come as no surprise if in the future we find Allport's theory giving a more serious audience to environmental determinants of behavior, early childhood experiences, and other factors suggested by cumulating empirical findings. On the other hand, it would indeed be regrettable, as well as unlikely, if the theory came to reflect current emphases so precisely that its distinctive features were lost.

BIBLIOGRAPHY

PRIMARY SOURCES

Allport, G. W. *Personality: A psychological interpretation.* New York: Holt, 1937a.

Allport, G. W. *The nature of personality: Selected papers.* Cambridge, Mass.: Addison-Wesley, 1950a. (Includes the most important of Allport's papers published prior to this date.)

Allport, G. W. *Becoming: Basic considerations for a psychology of personality.* New Haven: Yale Univ. Press, 1955.

REFERENCES

Allport, G. W. Attitudes. In C. C. Murchison (Ed.). *A Handbook of Social Psychology.* Worcester, Mass.: Clark Univ. Press, 1935, pp. 798–844.

Allport, G. W. *Personality: A psychological interpretation.* New York: Holt, 1937a.

Allport, G. W. The functional autonomy of motives. *Amer. J. Psychol.,* 1937b, 50, 141–156.

Allport, G. W. Personality: A problem for science or a problem for art? *Revista de Psihologie* (Cluj, Rumania), 1938, 1, 1–15.

Allport, G. W. Motivation in personality: Reply to Mr. Bertocci. *Psychol. Rev.,* 1940a, 47, 533–554.

Allport, G. W. The psychologist's frame of reference. *Psychol. Bull.,* 1940b, 37, 1–28.

Allport, G. W. *The use of personal documents in psychological science.* New York: Soc. Sci. Res. Council, Bull. 49, 1942.

Allport, G. W. The ego in contemporary psychology. *Psychol. Rev.,* 1943, 50 451–478.

Allport, G. W. Geneticism *versus* ego-structure in theories of personality. *Brit. J. educ. Psychol.,* 1946a, 16, 57–68.

Allport, G. W. Effect: A secondary principle of learning. *Psychol. Rev.,* 1946b, 53, 335–347.

Allport, G. W. Scientific models and human morals. *Psychol. Rev.,* 1947, 54, 182–192.

Allport, G. W. *The nature of personality: Selected Papers.* Cambridge, Mass.:

Addison-Wesley, 1950a. (Includes the most important of Allport's papers published prior to this date.)

Allport, G. W. *The individual and his religion.* New York: Macmillan, 1950b.

Allport, G. W. The trend in motivational theory. *Amer. J. Orthopsychiat.,* 1953, *23,* 107–119.

Allport, G. W. *The nature of prejudice.* Cambridge, Mass.: Addison-Wesley, 1954.

Allport, G. W. *Becoming: Basic considerations for a psychology of personality.* New Haven: Yale Univ. Press, 1955.

Allport, G. W., and Allport, F. H. *A-S reaction study.* Boston: Houghton, 1928.

Allport, G. W., and Cantril, H. Judging personality from voice. *J. soc. Psychol.,* 1934, *5,* 37–55.

Allport, G. W., and Cantril, H. *The psychology of radio.* New York: Harper, 1935.

Allport, G. W., and Odbert, H. S. Trait-names: A psycho-lexical study. *Psychol. Monogr.,* 1936, *47,* no. 211, 1–171.

Allport, G. W., and Postman, L. *The psychology of rumor.* New York: Holt, 1947.

Allport, G. W., and Vernon, P. E. *A study of values.* Boston: Houghton, 1931. (Rev. ed. with P. E. Vernon and G. Lindzey, 1951.)

Allport, G. W., and Vernon, P. E. *Studies in expressive movement.* New York: Macmillan, 1933.

Anderson, E. E. The externalization of drive: I. Theoretical considerations. *Psychol. Rev.,* 1941a, *48,* 204–224.

Anderson, E. E. The externalization of drive: II. The effect of satiation and removal of reward at different stages in the learning process of the rat. *J. genet. Psychol.,* 1941b, *59,* 359–376.

Anderson, E. E. The externalization of drive: III. Maze learning by non-rewarded and by satiated rats. *J. genet. Psychol.,* 1941c, *59,* 397–426.

Anderson, E. E. The externalization of drive: IV. The effect of pre-feeding on the maze performance of hungry non-rewarded rats. *J. comp. Psychol.,* 1941d, *31,* 349–352.

Baldwin, A. L. Personal structure analysis: A statistical method for investigating the single personality. *J. abnorm. soc. Psychol.,* 1942, *37,* 163–183.

Baldwin, A. L. Statistical problems in the treatment of case histories. *J. clin. Psychol.,* 1950, *6,* 6–12.

Bertocci, P. A. A critique of G. W. Allport's theory of motivation. *Psychol. Rev.,* 1940, *47,* 501–532.

Coutu, W. *Emergent human nature.* New York: Knopf, 1949.

Estes, S. G. Judging personality from expressive behavior. *J. abnorm. soc. Psychol.,* 1938, *33,* 217–236.

Harlow, H. F., Harlow, Margaret K., and Meyer, D. R. Learning motivated by a manipulation drive. *J. exp. Psychol.,* 1950, *40,* 228–234.

Huntley, C. W. Judgments of self based upon records of expressive behavior. *J. abnorm. soc. Psychol.,* 1940, *35,* 398–427.

Lindzey, G., Prince, Blanche, and Wright, H. K. A study of facial asymmetry. *J. Pers.,* 1952, *21,* 68–84.

Olson, W. C. *The measurement of nervous habits in normal children.* Minneapolis: Univ. of Minnesota Press, 1929.

Schafer, R., Berg, I., and McCandless, B. Report on survey of current psychological testing practices. Supplement to Newsletter, Division of clin. abn. Psychol., Amer. Psychol. Ass., 1951, *4*, no. 5.

Selye, H. *The story of the adaptation syndrome.* Montreal: Acta, 1952.

Seward, J. P. The sign of a symbol: A reply to Professor Allport. *Psychol. Rev.,* 1948, *55*, 277–296.

Skaggs, E. B. Personalistic psychology as science. *Psychol. Rev.,* 1945, *52*, 234–238.

Solomon, R. L., and Wynne, L. C. Traumatic avoidance learning: The principles of anxiety conservation and partial irreversibility. *Psychol. Rev.,* 1954, *61*, 353–385.

Stephenson, W. *The study of behavior: Q-technique and its methodology.* Chicago: Univ. of Chicago Press, 1953.

Stern, W. *Allgemeine Psychologie auf personalistischer Grundlage.* The Hague: Nijhoff, 1935. (Engl. translation by H. D. Spoerl. *General psychology: from the personalistic standpoint.* New York: Macmillan, 1938.)

Tolman, E. C. Psychology versus immediate experience. *Phil. Sci.,* 1935, *2*, 356–380.

Wolff, W. The experimental study of forms of expression. *Character & Pers.,* 1933, *2*, 168–176.

Wolff, W. *The expression of personality.* New York: Harper, 1943.

Woodworth, R. S. *Dynamic psychology.* New York: Columbia Univ. Press, 1918.

8.

Organismic Theory

Ever since Descartes in the seventeenth century split the individual into two separate yet interacting entities, body and mind, and Wundt in the nineteenth century, subscribing to the tradition of British associationism, atomized the mind by reducing it to the elementary particles of sensations, feelings, and images, there have been recurrent attempts to put the mind and the body back together and to treat the organism as a unified, organized whole. One notable attempt which has attracted a large following within recent years is known as the organismic or holistic viewpoint. This viewpoint has found expression in the psychobiology of Adolf Meyer (Meyer, 1948; Rennie, 1943), in the new medical orientation which is called psychosomatics (Dunbar, 1954), and in the fundamental work of Coghill on the development of the nervous system in relation to behavior (1929). The most important medical forerunner of the organismic concept is Hughlings Jackson, the preeminent English neurologist (1931). Jan Smuts, the great South African statesman and soldier, is recognized as the leading philosophical proponent of organismic theory and his notable book *Holism and evolution* (1926) has been very influential. General Smuts coined the word *holism* from the Greek root *holos* meaning complete, whole, entire. In psychology, organismic theory has been expounded by J. R. Kantor (1924, 1933, 1947), R. H. Wheeler (1940; see also Hilgard, 1948), Heinz Werner (1948), Gardner Murphy (see

Chapter 13), and Carl Rogers (see Chapter 12). Organismic theory drew nourishment from John Dewey's epoch-making article, *The reflex arc concept in psychology* (1896). Aristotle, Goethe, Spinoza, and William James have been mentioned as providing the seedbed from which organismic theory germinated. Although not all of these authors presented full-fledged organismic theories, their concepts are pointed in that direction.

Closely related to the organismic point of view is the Gestalt movement initiated by Wertheimer, Koffka, and Köhler, who in the years just prior to the First World War led a revolt against the type of mental analysis then being performed by Wundt and his followers. This movement stood for a new kind of analysis of conscious experience. Starting with the perceptual field as a whole, they proceeded to differentiate it into figure and background and then studied the properties of each of these components and their mutual influences. In the area of learning, they replaced the doctrine of association with the concept of insight. A person learns a task as a meaningful whole rather than in a piecemeal fashion. Although Gestalt psychology has had a tremendous influence upon modern thought and is certainly congenial to organismic theory, it cannot be regarded, strictly speaking, as an organismic psychology. The reason for this is that Gestalt psychology as developed by Wertheimer, Koffka, and Köhler has tended to restrict its attention to the phenomena of conscious awareness and has said very little about the organism or personality as a whole. Organismic theory has borrowed many of its concepts from Gestalt psychology, and the two viewpoints are on the friendliest terms. Organismic psychology may be regarded as the extension of Gestalt principles to the organism as a whole.

The leading exponent of organismic theory today is Kurt Goldstein, the eminent neuropsychiatrist. Largely as a result of his observations and investigations of brain-injured soldiers during World War I, and his earlier studies of speech disturbances, Goldstein came to the conclusion that any particular symptom displayed by a patient could not be understood solely as the product of a particular organic lesion or disease but had to be considered as a manifestation of the total organism. The organism always behaves as a unified whole and not as a series of differentiated parts. Mind and body are not separate entities, nor does the mind consist of independent faculties or elements and the body of independent organs and processes. The organism is a single unity. What happens in a part affects the whole. The psychologist studies the organism from one perspective, the physiologist from another. However, both disciplines need to operate within the framework of organismic theory because any event, be it psychological or physiological, always occurs within the context of the total organism unless it has become artificially isolated from this context. The laws of the whole govern the functioning of the differentiated parts of the whole. Consequently, it is necessary to discover the laws by which the whole organism functions in order to understand the functioning of any member component. This is the basic tenet of organismic theory.

The principal features of organismic theory as they pertain to the psychology of the person may be summarized as follows.

(1) Organismic theory emphasizes the unity, integration, consistency, and coherence of the normal personality. Organization is the natural state of the organism; disorganization is pathological and is usually brought about by the impact of an oppressive or threatening environment, or, to a lesser degree, by intraorganic anomalies.

(2) Organismic theory starts with the organism as an organized system and proceeds to analyze it by differentiating the whole into its constituent members. A member is never abstracted from the whole to which it belongs and studied as an isolated entity; it is always considered to have membership character in the total organism. Organismic theorists believe that it is impossible to understand the whole by directly studying isolated parts and segments because the whole functions according to laws that cannot be found in the parts. The atomistic viewpoint is felt to be particularly cumbersome because after the organism has been reduced to its elements it is then necessary to postulate an "organizer" which integrates the elements into an organized whole. Organismic theory does not require an "organizer" because organization is built into the system from the beginning and the integrity of the organism is not permitted to be lost or destroyed by analysis.

(3) Organismic theory assumes that the individual is motivated by one sovereign drive rather than by a plurality of drives. Goldstein's name for this sovereign motive is *self-actualization* or *self-realization* which means that man strives continuously to realize his inherent potentialities by whatever avenues are open to him. This singleness of purpose gives direction and unity to one's life.

(4) Although organismic theory does not regard the individual as a closed system, it tends to minimize the primary and directive influence of the external environment on normal development and to

stress the inherent potentialities of the organism for growth. The organism selects the features of the environment to which it will react and save in rare and abnormal circumstances the environment cannot force the individual to behave in a manner that is foreign to his nature. If the organism cannot control the environment it will try to adapt itself to it. In general, organismic theory feels that the potentialities of the organism, if allowed to unfold in an orderly way by an appropriate environment, will produce a healthy, integrated personality, although malignant environmental forces may at any time destroy or cripple the person. There is nothing inherently "bad" in the organism; it is made "bad" by an inadequate environment. On this point, organismic theory has much in common with the views of the French philosopher, Jean Jacques Rousseau, who believed that natural man is good but that he can be and often is perverted by an environment which denies man the opportunity to act and develop in accordance with his nature.

(5) Organismic theory frequently makes use of the principles of Gestalt psychology but it feels that the preoccupations of the Gestaltists with isolated functions of the organism such as perception and learning provide too narrow a base for understanding the total organism. Organismic theory has broadened the base by including within its scope everything that the organism is and does. Although there is much in organismic theory to remind one of Lewin, nevertheless Lewin's topology is strictly psychological in character and does not include the whole biological organism.

(6) Organismic theory feels that there is more to be learned from a comprehensive study of one person than from an extensive investigation of an isolated psychological function abstracted from many individuals. For this reason, organismic theory has tended to be more popular with clinical psychologists who are concerned with the total person than it has been with experimental psychologists who are primarily interested in separate processes or functions, like perception and learning.

In the present chapter, we shall present first an account of organismic theory as developed by Kurt Goldstein and some typical examples of the research his theory has led to. We shall then consider another important formulation of the organismic point of view made by Andras Angyal which differs in some major respects from that of Goldstein's. Two other versions of organismic theory, one by Abraham Maslow, the other by Prescott Lecky, will be touched upon briefly.

GOLDSTEIN'S ORGANISMIC THEORY

Kurt Goldstein received his training in neurology and psychiatry in Germany and rose to a position of eminence as a medical scientist and professor before migrating to the United States in 1935 after the Nazis came to power. He was born in Upper Silesia, then a part of Germany but now a part of Poland, November 6, 1878, and earned a medical degree at the University of Breslau, Lower Silesia, in 1903. He served an apprenticeship with several outstanding medical scientists for several years prior to accepting a teaching and research position at the Psychiatric Hospital in Koenigsberg. During his eight years in this post he did a great deal of research and wrote numerous papers which established his reputation and led to his appointment at the age of thirty-six as professor of neurology and psychiatry and director of the Neurological Institute of the University of Frankfurt. During the First World War, he became director of the Military Hospital for Brain-Injured Soldiers and was instrumental in establishing an institute for research on the after-effects of brain injuries. It was in this institute that Goldstein made the fundamental studies which laid the basis for his organismic viewpoint. In 1930 he went to the University of Berlin as professor of neurology and psychiatry and also served as director of the Department of Neurology and Psychiatry at Moabit Hospital. He gave up these posts and went to Amsterdam in 1933 where he completed his most important book, *Der aufbau des organismus*, which was translated into English under the title, *The organism* (1939). Coming to the United States in 1935 he worked for a year at the New York Psychiatric Institute, following which he became chief of the Laboratory of Neurophysiology at Montefiore Hospital, New York City, and clinical professor of neurology at the College of Physicians and Surgeons of Columbia University. During this period he lectured on psychopathology in the Department of Psychology at Columbia and was invited to give the William James lectures at Harvard University which were published under the title, *Human nature in the light of psychopathology* (1940). During the war years he was clinical professor of neurology at Tufts Medical School in Boston and published a book on the aftereffects of brain injuries in war (1942). In 1945 he returned to New York City to engage in the private practice of neuropsychiatry and psychotherapy. He is currently associated with Columbia University and the New School for

Social Research. His most recent book is on language and language disturbances (1948), an area in which he has done research throughout his professional life. In his later years Goldstein has become more and more identified with the field of psychology and has exerted considerable influence upon the thinking of psychologists. He has been closely identified with Gestalt psychology especially through his work with Gelb (1920) on figure-ground relationships in visual perception, although he does not regard himself as a Gestalt psychologist and is critical of some of its tenets (Chapter VIII, 1939). (This biographical material was taken largely from Freiman, 1954.)

THE STRUCTURE OF THE ORGANISM

The organism consists of differentiated members which are articulated together; these members do not become detached and isolated from one another except under abnormal or artificial conditions, for example, strong anxiety. The primary organization of organismic functioning is that of figure and ground. A figure is any process that emerges and stands out against a background. In terms of perception, it is that which occupies the center of attentive awareness. When, for instance, a person is looking at an object in a room, the perception of the object becomes a figure against the background of the rest of the room. In terms of action, the figure is the principal, ongoing activity of the organism. When one is reading a book, the reading is the figure which stands out from such other activities as twisting one's hair, chewing one's pencil, hearing the rumble of voices in the next room, and breathing. A figure has a definite boundary or contour which encloses it and separates it from the surroundings. The background is continuous; it not only surrounds the figure but extends behind it. It is like a carpet on which an object has been placed or the sky against which an airplane is seen. A member part of the organism may stand out as figure against the background of the whole organism and still retain its membership in the structure of the total organism.

What causes a figure to emerge from the background of the total organism? It is determined by the task which the nature of the organism at the time requires. Thus, when a hungry organism is confronted by the task of getting food, any process which will aid in performing the task becomes elevated as a figure. It may be a memory of where food has been found in the past, a perception of food objects in the environment, or an activity which will produce food. However, if the organism should change, for example, when a hungry person becomes frightened, a new process will emerge as figure which is appropriate to the task of dealing with the fear. New figures emerge as the tasks of the organism change.

Goldstein distinguishes between natural figures which are functionally embedded in a background consisting of the totality of the organism and unnatural figures which have become isolated from the total organism and whose background is also an isolated part of the organism. These unnatural figures are produced by traumatic events and by repetitive drill under conditions that are meaningless to the person. Goldstein believes that many psychological experiments which are designed to study isolated stimulus-response connections bear little or no relation to the natural behavior of the organism and so provide little useful knowledge of the laws by which the organism functions.

By what criteria can a natural, embedded figure be distinguished from an unnatural, isolated one? Goldstein says that the figure is a natural one if it represents a preference on the part of the person and if the behavior which is called forth is orderly, flexible, and appropriate to the situation. It is an unnatural one if it represents a task that is imposed upon the person and if the resulting behavior is rigid and mechanical. A person in a deep hypnotic trance who performs various actions at the suggestion of the hypnotist often behaves unnaturally because behavior is cut off by the dissociated state of hypnosis from his normal personality. They do not represent his preferences but those of the hypnotist, and they are often completely inappropriate to the situation. He is an automaton rather than a person. A young child who has been taught the words of a song and sings them without knowing what he is singing exemplifies the kind of automatic behavior which Goldstein characterizes as being an unnatural figure.

Although Goldstein emphasizes the flexible and plastic nature of natural processes as against the rigid character of unnatural processes, he recognizes that preferred activities may remain fairly constant throughout life without losing their intimate relationship to the whole organism. Traits and habits do not necessarily become precipitated out and lose touch with the total matrix in which they are embedded. In fact, Goldstein attributes many constancies to the organism such as sensory thresholds, motor performances, intellectual characteristics, emotional factors, and the like. These constants are inborn and operate as selective agents for behavior. However, the constants are also shaped and molded by experience and training to a certain extent so that their concrete manifestations always bear the imprint of the culture in which the person has been raised.

Although Goldstein does not have much to say regarding the structure of the organism aside from differentiating between figure and ground, he does point out that there are three different kinds of behavior. These are the *performances* which are voluntary, consciously experienced activities, *attitudes* which are feelings, moods, and other inner experiences, and *processes* which are bodily functions that can be experienced only indirectly (1939, pp. 307 ff.).

Another structural distinction that Goldstein makes great use of is that between concrete and abstract behavior. Concrete behavior consists of reacting to a stimulus in a fairly automatic or direct manner while abstract behavior consists of action upon the stimulus by the organism. For example, in concrete behavior one perceives the stimulus configuration and reacts to it as it appears at the moment whereas in abstract behavior the person thinks about the stimulus pattern, what it means, its relation to other configurations, how it can be used, and what its conceptual properties are. The difference between concrete and abstract behavior is the difference between a direct reaction to a stimulus and reacting to it after thinking about the stimulus. These two kinds of behavior depend upon contrasting attitudes toward the world, which will be discussed in the section on Characteristic Research and Research Methods.

THE DYNAMICS OF THE ORGANISM

The main dynamic concepts presented by Goldstein are (1) the equalization process or the centering of the organism, (2) self-actualization, and (3) "coming to terms" with the environment.

EQUALIZATION. Goldstein postulates an available energy supply which is fairly constant and which tends to be evenly distributed throughout the organism. This constant, evenly distributed energy represents the "average" state of tension in the organism, and it is to this average state that the organism always returns or tries to return following a stimulus that changes the tension. This return to the "average" state is the equalization process. For example, a person hears a sound coming from his right and turns his head in that direction. The turning of the head equalizes the distribution of energy in the system which has been unbalanced by the sound. Eating when hungry, resting when tired, and stretching when cramped are other familiar examples of the equalization process.

The goal of a normal, healthy person is not simply to discharge tension but to equalize it. The level at which tension becomes balanced represents a centering of the organism. This center or organismic Plimsoll line is one which enables the organism to perform most effectively its work of coping with the environment and of actualizing itself in further activities according to its nature. Full centering or complete balance is an ideal holistic state and is probably rarely achieved.

The principle of equalization explains the consistency, coherence, and orderliness of behavior in spite of disturbing stimuli. Goldstein does not believe that the sources of disturbance are primarily intraorganic except under abnormal and catastrophic circumstances which produce isolation and inner conflict. In an adequate environment, the organism will always remain more or less in balance. Energy redistributions and imbalance of the system result from environmental interferences and sometimes from inner conflict. As a result of maturation and experience, the person develops preferred ways of behaving which keep the interferences and conflicts to a minimum and preserve the balance of the organism. An individual's life becomes more centered and less subject to the fortuitous changes of the inner and outer world as he grows older.

SELF-ACTUALIZATION. This is Goldstein's master motive; in fact, it is the only motive that the organism possesses. What appear to be different drives such as hunger, sex, power, achievement, and curiosity are merely manifestations of the sovereign purpose of life, to actualize oneself. When a person is hungry he actualizes himself by eating; when he craves power he actualizes himself by obtaining power. The satisfaction of any particular need is in the foreground when it is a prerequisite for the self-realization of the total organism. Self-actualization is the creative trend of human nature. It is the organic principle by which the organism becomes more fully developed and more complete. The ignorant person who desires knowledge feels an inner emptiness; he has a sense of his own incompleteness. By reading and studying, his desire for knowledge is fulfilled and the emptiness disappears. A new person has been created, thereby, one in whom learning has taken the place of ignorance. His desire has become an actuality. Any need is a deficit state which motivates the person to replenish the deficit. It is like a hole that demands to be filled in. This replenishment or fulfillment of a need is what is meant by self-actualization.

Although self-actualization is a universal phenomenon in nature, the specific ends towards which people strive vary from person to person. This is so because people have different innate potentialities that shape their ends and direct the lines of their individual development and growth as well as different environments and cultures to which they must adjust and from which they must secure the necessary supplies for growth.

How can an individual's potentialities be determined? Goldstein says that this can best be done by finding out what the person prefers and what he does best. His preferences correspond to his potentialities. This means that if we are to know what a person is trying to actualize we must familiarize ourselves with what he likes to do and what he has a gift for doing. The baseball player is actualizing those potentialities which are developed by playing baseball, the lawyer those potentialities which are realized by the practice of law.

In general, Goldstein stresses conscious motivation over unconscious motivation. The unconscious, in his eyes, is the background into which conscious material recedes when it is no longer useful for self-realization in a definite situation and from which it emerges when it again becomes suitable and appropriate for self-realization. "All the peculiarities which Freud enumerates as characteristic for the unconscious, correspond completely to the changes which normal behavior undergoes through isolation by disease" (1939, p. 323).

"COMING TO TERMS" WITH THE ENVIRONMENT. Although Goldstein as an organismic theorist emphasizes the inner determinants of behavior and the principle that the organism finds the environment which is most appropriate for self-actualization, he does not adopt the extreme position that the organism is immune to the events in the external world. He recognizes the importance of the objective world both as a source of disturbance with which the individual must cope and as a source of supplies by means of which the organism fulfills its destiny. That is, the environment intrudes upon the organism by stimulating or overstimulating it so that the organic equilibrium is upset, while on the other hand the upset organism searches in the environment for what it needs in order to equalize the inner tension. In other words, there is an interaction between the organism and the environment.

The person has to come to terms with the environment both because it affords the means by which self-actualization can be achieved and because it contains obstructions in the form of threats and pressures which hinder self-realization. Sometimes the threat from the environment may be so great that the individual's behavior becomes frozen by anxiety and he is unable to make any progress toward the goal. At other times, self-actualization may be hampered because the environment lacks those objects and conditions that are necessary for actualization.

Goldstein tells us that a normal, healthy organism is one "in which the tendency towards self-actualization is acting from within, and overcomes the disturbance arising from the clash with the world, not out of anxiety but out of the joy of conquest" (1939, p. 305). This moving statement suggests that coming to terms with the environment consists primarily of mastering it. If this cannot be done, then the person has to accept the difficulties and adjust himself as best he can to the realities of the outer world. If the discrepancy between the organism's goals and the realities of the environment is too great, the organism either breaks down or has to give up some of its aims and try to actualize itself on a lower level of existence.

Goldstein has provided a concise summary of his views regarding the organization and dynamics of the organism in the following passage.

There is a continuous alteration as to which "part" of the organism stands in the foreground . . . and which in the background. The foreground is determined by the task which the organism has to fulfill at any given moment, i.e. by the situation in which the organism happens to find itself, and by the demands with which it has to cope.
The tasks are determined by the "nature" of the organism, its "essence," which is brought into actualization through environmental changes that act upon it. The expressions of this actualization are the performances of the organism. Through them the organism can deal with the respective environmental demands and actualize itself. The possibility of asserting itself in the world, while preserving its character, hinges upon a specific *kind of "coming to terms" of the organism with its environment*. This has to take place in such a fashion that each change of the organism, caused by environmental stimuli, *is equalized after a definite time*, so that the organism regains that "average" state which corresponds to its nature, which is "adequate" to it. *Only when this is the case is it possible that the same environmental events can produce the same changes*, can lead to the same effects and to the same experiences. Only under this condition can the organism maintain its constancy and identity. If this equalization towards the average or adequate state did not occur, then the same environmental events would produce diverse changes in the organism. Thereby, the environment would lose its constancy for the organism, and would alter continually. An ordered course of performances would be impossible. The organism would be in a continual state of disquiet, would be endangered in its existence, and *actually would be continuously "another"* organism. This, however, is actually not the case. On the contrary we can observe that the performances of the organism show a *relatively great constancy*, with fluctuations around a con-

stant mean. If this relative constancy did not exist it would not even be possible to recognize an organism as such; we could not even *talk of a specific organism* (1939, pp. 111–112).

THE DEVELOPMENT OF THE ORGANISM

Although the concept of self-actualization suggests that there are patterns or stages of development through which the person progresses, Goldstein does not have much to say concerning the course of growth, save for some generalities to the effect that behavior becomes more even and orderly and more fitted to the environment as the person grows older. Goldstein hints that there are tasks which are peculiar to certain age levels but he does not specify what these tasks are or whether they are the same for all individuals. The importance of heredity is also implied but its relative contribution is not made explicit. Nor does Goldstein present a theory of learning. He does talk about the "reorganization" of old patterns into new and more effective patterns, the "repression of attitudes and urges which are in opposition to the development of the *whole* personality," the acquisition of preferred ways of behaving, the emergence of figure from background, the fixation of patterns of behavior by traumatic stimuli or by repetitive practice with isolated stimuli, adjustmental shifts, and substitute formations, but these notions are not brought together into a systematic theory of learning. They are most congenial to a Gestalt theory of learning.

Goldstein does say that if a child is exposed to situations with which he can cope, he will develop normally through maturation and training. As new problems arise he will form new patterns to deal with them. Reactions that are no longer useful for the goal of self-actualization will drop out. However, if the conditions of the environment are too arduous for the child's capacities, he will develop reactions that are not consistent with the principle of self-actualization. In this case, the process tends to become isolated from the person's pattern of life. Isolation of a process is the primary condition for the development of pathological states. For example, man is neither aggressive nor submissive by nature, but in order to fulfill his nature he sometimes has to be aggressive and at other times submissive, depending upon circumstances. However, should a strong, fixated habit of either aggression or submission be formed it will tend to have a disruptive influence upon personality by asserting itself at inappropriate times and in ways that are contrary to the interests of the whole person.

CHARACTERISTIC RESEARCH AND RESEARCH METHODS

As an investigator trained in medicine and practicing the medical specialty of neuropsychiatry, Kurt Goldstein has spent his long productive life studying symptoms and behavior patterns not as isolated events but as reactions that are embedded in and are expressions of the total organism. For Goldstein, a symptom is not simply a manifestation of changes in a specific function or structure of the organism; it is also to be considered as a form of adjustment made by the sick or defective person. In his study of the aphasias or language disturbances, for example, he rejects the theory that aphasia is the result of a lesion in a particular area of the brain and maintains instead that since *"language is a means of the individual to come to terms with the outer world and to realize himself"* (1948, p. 23) *"it follows that every individual speech-performance is understandable only from the aspect of its relation to the function of the total organism in its endeavor to realize itself as much as possible in the given situation"* (1948, p. 21).

THE MEANING OF SYMPTOMS. In connection with his studies of language disturbances Goldstein distinguishes four groups of symptoms according to their origin. These are (1) direct symptoms, (2) indirect or depending symptoms, (3) symptoms due to catastrophic conditions and protective mechanisms against catastrophe, and (4) symptoms due to fatigue and perseveration.

Direct symptoms are those that result from a systematic disintegration of the function involved. Goldstein calls this disintegration *dedifferentiation* because it represents a developmental regression to an earlier, less differentiated condition of the organism. For example, damage to the cortex of the brain causes a rise in the thresholds of the sense organs so that brain-injured patients respond more slowly to stimuli. A person who fails a task when it is presented rapidly may succeed when it is administered at a slower rate. Brain-injured patients are more distractible because external conditions play a much greater role in determining their behavior than they do for normal people. Consequently, their symptoms may stem from an inability to concentrate rather than from any specific type of brain lesion. There is also a blurring of the contours between figure and ground so that it is more difficult for the brain-injured person to make the appropriate discriminations among environmental objects. Words, instead of standing out as patterns, tend to merge into the background. Finally, there is an impairment of the abstract attitude which Goldstein holds responsible for so many of the symptoms displayed by brain-injured cases. The abstract attitude is required in order to carry on any kind of abstract or conceptual thinking, a type of thinking which is especially important for language behavior. The person reverts to the more primitive concrete attitude in which he is bound to and cannot transcend the particular, concrete characteristics of the stimulus objects.

In addition to the type of direct symptom that results from the dedifferentiation of function, there are also symptoms that arise from the isolation of an undamaged area of the brain from a damaged one with which it was formerly closely associated. In the case of both dedifferentiation and isolation, the appearance of a symptom depends upon a general modification of the total organism, or at least upon changes in extensive areas of the cortical field rather than upon narrowly circumscribed lesions.

A second class of symptoms is produced by the effect of changes in the damaged area on other parts of the nervous system. The defective part disturbs the function of any other part of the nervous system with which it has a functional or dependent relationship. Goldstein points out the very interesting fact that the complete destruction of a functional unit, such as vision, may disturb the functioning of the total organism less than a partial destruction does. The reason for this is that the completely blind person is forced to depend upon his other senses whereas the partially blind person is constantly trying to come to terms with the environment through an imperfect sensory system with the result that his total performance usually suffers.

The most interesting symptoms, from the standpoint of psychology, are those that arise from the tendency of the organism to avoid failure. In this connection Goldstein observes that a symptom is usually a variable condition. Sometimes a patient can perform an intellectual task; at other times he cannot. The reason for this variation is often to be found in the patient's attitude toward his ability to perform the task successfully. If he feels that he cannot do a simple mathematical problem, he may not even try because he does not want to fail. On another occasion, he may approach a similar problem with confidence and perform creditably. Goldstein reminds us that the injured person is more sensitive regarding his abilities than is the normal individual, and that the need to avoid failure is greater. Since his defective condition makes failure more probable, the sick person tends to withdraw from many situations which he might be able to adjust to satisfactorily if he would only try. The environment or life space of the brain-injured person tends to shrink, and he tends to develop a routine type of existence in his shrunken environment.

Finally, there are symptoms resulting from fatigue and perseveration. Fatigue is not simply related to the amount of work performed but is also likely to appear when the task is one that appears to the patient to be beyond his ability. In other words, fatigue serves as a kind of protective mechanism which allows the patient to escape from a stressful situation. Perseveration, or the tendency to repeat a performance that the patient is able to do, is another means by which the person can avoid catastrophe.

STUDIES OF BRAIN-INJURED CASES. Beginning with his observations on soldiers who had received head wounds during the First World War, Goldstein has conducted numerous investigations on the effects of injury to the brain. These studies, most of which were published in Germany, have been brought together and summarized in his book *After-effects of brain injuries in war* (1942). This book is based on the observations of nearly two thousand patients, some of whom were seen more or less continuously for ten years, and it gives an account of the neurological and psychological symptoms of patients suffering from brain damage, methods of testing psychological functions, and the treatment of this type of patient. Throughout this book, as well as in his other published writings, Goldstein maintains a consistent organismic point of view, which illuminates and explains the behavior of brain-injured patients. For example, one marked feature of the behavior of these patients is their orderliness and neatness. They spend a great deal of time keeping their possessions in order and seeing that everything is shipshape. They are very good hospital patients because they quickly adapt themselves to routine activities and readily become absorbed in housekeeping tasks. Goldstein found that this behavior was a symptom resulting from their defect. By devoting their full attention to routine tasks, the patients were able to avoid the unusual and unexpected situation. Such situations may have catastrophic effects on the behavior of the patient. In other words, their routine orderliness is an expression of the struggle of the changed personality to cope with the defect by avoiding situations that can no longer be mastered or adjusted to. Indeed, much of the behavior of the brain-injured person is compensatory in character and permits him to come to terms with the world in the best possible way under the given circumstances.

Goldstein observes that the organism is very resilient and quickly adapts itself to any localized damage as long as the person feels that he can come to terms with his environment and is not thrown off balance by undue pressures from the external world. One patient was not able to recognize visually even the simplest form, yet he learned to read. He could differentiate between light and dark so that by following or tracing the border between the dark spots of the letters and the light area of the background, he could make out the words and read them. The motor images produced by the kinesthetic tracing of the dark spots took the place of visual images. This substitution was made unconsciously and the patient was not aware of how he did it. In this case, as in so many others, motivation plays an important role. A patient will make an effort to realize himself as much as possible in the environment if there is some incentive for doing so.

The organismic viewpoint regarding symptoms has practical implications as well as theoretical ones. In testing a brain-injured patient, for example, it is essential to employ tests and to administer them in such a way as to reveal the modifications in his abilities that are the direct result of the damage and to distinguish these symptoms from those that arise as secondary reactions to the defect. One important reason for making this distinction is that the kind of training and therapy that is employed depends upon knowing what symptoms can be more or less directly remedied and what symptoms have to be altered by working on the personality as a whole. In the one case, a visual defect may be improved by specific training in the visual function; in the other case, an apparent visual defect may be removed by methods that increase the self-confidence of the patient.

The careful analysis of the meaning of a symptom also requires an intensive study of all aspects of the person's functioning. It is not enough ordinarily to give a patient a battery of tests which yield a set of numerical scores or pluses and minuses. The examiner must be alert to qualitative features of the patient's performance as well and pay heed to even the slightest clues that may shed light upon his behavior. He must not depend entirely upon diagnostic tests, useful as these may be, for understanding the patient. He must also observe the patient in his daily life under more or less natural conditions, for the patient's success and failure in meeting the common problems of daily existence are the ultimate tests of his abilities. This is why Goldstein favors the intensive study of a single case over a fairly long period of time.

SINGLE CASE STUDIES. The intensive study of one person is exemplified by a case of a brain-damaged, middle-aged man observed by Goldstein and his colleagues (Hanfmann, Rickers-Ovsiankina, and Goldstein, 1944) over a period of years. This man lived in an institution and his daily behavior in this setting as well as his performance in standardized test and interview situations were observed and recorded. He could find his way around the hospital quite well but this ability depended upon his recognition of fairly concrete objects rather than upon any generalized frames of reference. For example, he recognized the testing room because unlike the other rooms it had three windows in it. However, he had to open a number of doors before he found the correct one because he had no spatial orientation which would tell him where the room with the three windows was located. He learned to follow other patients to the shop where he worked and to the dining hall but if he got separated from them he became lost. He could recognize his own bedroom because he had tied a string to the bedpost. Someone watching him might think that he was fairly well oriented in space and time but a closer familiarity with his conduct would show otherwise.

He was usually sociable and friendly when he was with people but he did not form any kind of permanent attachment to another person. The reason for this was that he could not remember or recognize the same person from one day to the next. Only by a careful analysis of his total behavior was it revealed that his inability to form stable relations with others and be a permanent part of a group was due to a lack of recognition of characteristics which could be remembered rather than a distaste for social relations or a desire not to become involved intimately with another person.

He had great trouble listening to someone read or tell a story, not because he was distractible or because he lacked comprehension but because he could not distinguish between reality and fiction. If the story started out "Once there was a little boy," he began looking around for the boy and when he could not find him he became quite agitated. Everything that he experienced was regarded as existing here and now. Not only did he fail to differentiate between fact and fiction but he also could not understand what was meant by past, present, and future.

Once he was shown a picture of an animal and was asked to identify it. When he could not decide whether it was a dog or a horse, he spoke directly to the picture, saying "Are you a dog?" When the picture did not reply he became very angry. When he was given a mirror he looked behind it for the person he saw in the mirror and became excited when he did not find a person there. The casual observer might think that this patient was highly excitable and emotionally unstable from watching his behavior in various situations, when actually he was a fairly mild man whose excitement was brought on by threatening conditions of an environment which to a normal person would not have been threatening at all. When one does not possess any stable, dependable frames of reference regarding space and time, fact and fiction, object and subject, the world is bound to be an unpredictable and highly frustrating place.

Although he could not understand the principle of a mirror when it alone was shown to him, he behaved in an appropriate manner when he was given a comb along with a mirror. He took the comb, looked in the mirror, and combed his hair in quite a natural manner. This behavior showed that he had no abstract concept of a mirror as such but he did know how to use it for performing a concrete task. Another example of this same type of behavior was his failure to distinguish between a ball and an egg until he had discovered by trying them out that the ball was throwable whereas the egg was breakable and edible. He had no abstract concept of an egg and a ball. In fact, his capacity for abstract behavior was almost totally lacking, and it was this impairment of the abstract attitude that accounted for so much of his unusual behavior.

Another case studied intensively by the method of organismic theory was that of an eleven-year-old boy, a so-called "idiot savant" (Scheerer, Rothman, and Goldstein, 1945). In spite of his serious intellectual deficiency in some respects this boy could perform amazing feats of computation. Given the date of one's birthday he could rapidly tell what day of the week it fell on for any specified year. He was also regarded as a musical genius because he could reproduce any piece he heard on the piano. Actually, however, a more careful analysis of his behavior revealed that his lightning calculations and his musical performances were merely mechanical reproductions. There was nothing creative about them. Given the native endowment for counting and playing by ear, he concentrated all of his energy in actualizing these two potentialities. He learned as a very young child that these were satisfying ways for coming to terms with the world and so they became his preferred performances. He had practically no ability for dealing with symbols, concepts, words, shapes, and other abstractions. His social relationships were virtually non-existent although he had learned to say polite things in a robot fash-

ion.   His deficiencies all stem from a defect of the abstract attitude.
The authors make the point that the "concept of abstract attitude
should serve as a methodological frame of reference . . . for understanding of these symptoms from a unitary point of view" (p. 29).

ABSTRACT VERSUS CONCRETE BEHAVIOR.   Goldstein's most important
psychological studies have been made on abstract and concrete behavior.   He and his associates have developed a number of tests for
diagnosing the amount of impairment of the abstract attitude (Goldstein and Scheerer, 1941, 1953).   These tests are widely used in
clinical practice, especially for assessing the presence and amount
of brain damage.   Goldstein strongly urges the examiner who uses
these tests not to restrict himself to the mechanical adding up of
passes and failures but to take note of the qualitative aspects of the
patient's behavior during testing as well.   Goldstein feels that these
qualitative features may be even more enlightening than the numerical
scores earned by the patient.

A detailed analysis of impairment of the abstract attitude produced
by injury to the frontal lobes reveals the following deficiencies. (1)
The patient is unable to separate the outer world from inner experience.   For example, the brain-injured patient cannot be induced
to repeat the sentence "The sun is shining" when it is actually raining
outside.   (2) He cannot assume a set to do something willfully and
consciously.   When asked to set the hands of a clock to a certain
hour, he cannot do it although he can recognize what time it is when
presented with a clock.   (3) He has no sense of spatial relations.
He can point correctly to the source of a sound but he cannot say
what direction it is coming from.   (4) He cannot shift from one task
to another.   When asked to call out a series of numbers starting with
one he can do so, but when he is asked to start with a number other
than one he is lost.   (5) He is unable to hold a discrimination in
mind for any length of time.   For example, when he is instructed to
cross out a particular letter in a printed passage he begins correctly
but soon shifts to crossing out every letter.   (6) He lacks the ability
to react to an organized whole, to break the whole up into parts, and
to synthesize them again.   This defect prevents him from telling any
sort of organized story to a picture.   He can only enumerate the
individual items in a picture.   (7) He cannot abstract the common
properties of a series of objects or form any part-whole relationships.
This means that he is unable to understand an analogy like "shoe is
to foot as what is to hand?"   (8) The brain-injured person is unable
to plan ahead, to take into account the probability of something
happening in the future, or to think in symbolic terms.   He may be

able to find his way around in a fixed environment but he cannot draw a map or give a verbal account of how he gets from one place to another.

A defect in the abstract attitude produces changes in the personality as a whole and cuts across all forms of behavior. The abstract attitude is not a synthesis of lower mental functions but represents an entirely new mental set in which the factor of conscious will is one of its most essential features. Lacking this attitude, the person is qualitatively different from the normal person.

Goldstein's empirical studies of abstract and concrete behavior illustrate the organismic dictum that whatever happens in one part of the organism affects the whole organism. In the case of a severe injury to the frontal lobes the effects are particularly massive. Injuries to other tissues or organs may be less dramatic and less obvious in their effects on the whole person, but whatever happens, happens to and affects the whole person.

In this brief survey of Goldstein's research activities we have not been able to do justice to the richness of his empirical data; nor has it been possible to convey to the reader the full measure of his insights into the reasons for man's conduct. We have merely tried to give some idea of the type of research strategy employed by a representative organismic theorist. This strategy may be summarized in the following set of directions to the investigator who wishes to conduct research in the organismic manner. (1) Study the whole person. (2) Make intensive studies of individual cases using tests, interviews, and observations under natural conditions. Do not depend upon just one type of evidence. (3) Try to understand the behavior of the person in terms of such system principles as self-actualization, coming to terms with the environment, abstract versus concrete attitudes rather than as specific responses to specific stimuli. (4) Use both qualitative and quantitative methods in the collection and analysis of the data. (5) Do not employ experimental controls and standardized conditions which destroy the integrity of the organism and make the behavior unnatural and artificial. (6) Always bear in mind that the organism is a complex structure and its behavior is the resultant of a vast network of determiners.

ANGYAL'S ORGANISMIC THEORY

Angyal, like Goldstein, feels that there is a need for a new science which will not be primarily psychological, sociological, or physiological in character but which will embrace the person as a whole.

Unlike Goldstein, however, Angyal insists that it is impossible to differentiate the organism from the environment because they interpenetrate one another in such a complex manner that any attempt to unravel them tends to destroy the natural unity of the whole and to create an artificial distinction between organism and environment.

Andras Angyal is known primarily to psychologists for his important book, *Foundations for a science of personality* (1941). Educated at the University of Vienna where he was awarded a Ph.D. in 1927 and at the University of Turin where he received an M.D. in 1932, Angyal came to the United States in 1932 as a Rockefeller fellow in the Department of Anthropology of Yale University. For a number of years he was engaged in research at Worcester State Hospital, Massachusetts, serving as Director of Research from 1937 to 1945. He left this post to enter private practice as a psychiatrist in Boston.

THE STRUCTURE OF THE BIOSPHERE

Angyal has coined a new term, the *biosphere,* to convey his conception of a holistic entity which includes both the individual and the environment "not as interacting parts, not as constituents which have independent existence, but as aspects of a single reality which can be separated only by abstraction" (1941, p. 100). The biosphere does not refer exclusively to somatic processes as the name suggests but includes the psychological and social as well. The psychological domain consists of the symbolic functions of the organism, that is, perceiving, thinking, remembering, imagining, and the like; the social domain consists of man's interactions with society.

Although the biosphere is an indivisible whole, it possesses an organization which consists of systems structurally articulated with one another. It is the task of the organismic scientist to identify those lines of demarcation within the biosphere which are prescribed by the natural structure of the whole itself. These lines of division constitute the real holistic units of the biosphere.

The largest and most basic division that can be made in the biosphere is that between the organism which is called the *subject* and the environment which is called the *object.* The organism constitutes one pole of the biosphere and the environment constitutes the other pole, and the whole dynamics of life consists of the interactions between these two poles. Angyal maintains that neither organismic processes nor environmental events alone reflect reality but rather that *biospheric occurrences, which are bipolar in character, are the reality* with which the biological and social scientist must deal.

"Instead of studying the 'organism' and the 'environment' and their interaction, we propose to study life as a unitary whole and endeavor to describe the organization and dynamics of the biosphere" (1941, pp. 100–101).

Angyal acknowledges that it is possible to distinguish between processes that fall more under the domination of organismic government from those that are more environmentally governed, although processes can never be exclusively one or the other. They are always biospheric.

BIOSPHERIC SYSTEMS. The holistic units of the biosphere are called systems. Angyal prefers system analysis to the more usual type of relationship analysis that is employed in psychology for the following reasons.

(1) A system may include as many members as are necessary to explain a given phenomenon whereas a relationship involves only two members. Angyal feels that the reduction of a complex structure like that of the biosphere to pairs of related members tends to destroy its natural coherence and unity and oversimplify the kinds of connections that exist in the biosphere.

(2) The components of a system are connected with one another by virtue of their respective positions in the system whereas the members of a relationship are connected by virtue of possessing some common property such as color or form. Two red objects are related to one another by their redness, but the parts of a machine are organized in terms of their respective positions in the whole machine. Angyal feels that position is more important than attribute for organismic analysis. In a power system, such as a government or other institution, the position of each person in the system is far more important than any specific relationship that a person may possess with other members of the system.

(3) The members of a system need have no direct connection with one another but the two members of a relationship must be directly connected. This necessity for direct connection limits the kind of analysis that can be made using relations. For instance, two citizens of the same country may have absolutely no direct relation to one another yet as holistic units living within the same political region they are governed by the same laws and customs.

For these reasons Angyal believes that systems, not relations, are the true holistic units of the biosphere. In a paper on the holistic approach in psychiatry (1948) Angyal states that system analysis consists of two steps, (1) the location of the context in which a given phenomenon belongs, and (2) the determination of its position in this context. When these two steps are taken the phenomenon is said to be properly defined and fully explained. (For a further discussion of the theory of systems in biology and psychology see Bertalanffy, 1950a, 1950b; Krech, 1950.)

One important property of a system is its rigidity or plasticity. In a rigid system the parts have fixed positions and are relatively immovable whereas in a plastic system the parts are more flexible and can shift about to form new constellations within the system. As might be expected, events produced by a rigid system are highly standardized and uniform whereas those produced by a plastic system have a broad range of functional variation. The processes that go on in a rigid system are likely to be quite localized happenings which have little impact upon surrounding systems; those of a plastic system tend to spread into neighboring systems. Rigid systems tend to be associated with a high degree of environmental stability and plastic systems with a low degree of environmental stability. The operations of a rigid system run off more automatically and with less conscious control than those of a plastic system. Both kinds of systems are found in the biosphere in varying degrees. Sensory-neuromuscular functions, for example, tend to be fairly plastic and visceral functions tend to be fairly rigid.

A system consists of parts which are either fully differentiated or still embedded in the whole in an undifferentiated state. Differentiation of parts out of the whole occurs when a complex operation requires a division of labor among the parts of the system. In a highly differentiated whole the parts are more individualized and possess greater relative autonomy. Since this state of affairs tends to produce disunity and disintegration in the system and will eventually destroy the system if allowed to go unchecked, there has to be a counterbalancing principle. This principle which is integrative in nature co-ordinates the differentiated part functions under the general system principle of *self-expansion*. A system expands by successive stages of differentiation and integration, although the tendency of any system is to be conservative with respect to differentiation and to permit it only when it is absolutely essential.

A part of a whole has to have two characteristics; it must be relatively complete in itself and it has to occupy a position in a system which does not require the mediation of intermediary systems for its maintenance. In other words, it has to be relatively autonomous and independent without becoming isolated from the system.

THE DIMENSIONS OF PERSONALITY STRUCTURE. There are three main dimensions within the biosphere. These are called vertical, progressive, and transverse. The *vertical* dimension extends from overt behavior at the surface of the biosphere down into the central core of the biosphere. Occurrences that lie near the surface are the concrete or behavioral expressions of deeper processes. An act of aggression, for example, is the expression of an underlying attitude of hostility and this attitude in turn can be traced to even deeper lying and more generalized attitudes. Surface behavior changes more easily than do the deeper processes. The goal of surface behavior is to create a biospheric condition which represents the satisfaction of a need in the core of personality. As a rule, gratification cannot be achieved with one behavior act; rather a succession of acts is required. A series of acts which brings the person closer and closer to a final goal constitutes the *progressive* dimension. The points along this dimension are defined in terms of the distance from the goal. The *transverse* dimension consists of the co-ordination of discrete acts into a larger, better integrated, and more effective behavior unit. Accordingly any behavior act can be described as an expression of underlying processes, as a phase in a means-end organization, and as a co-ordination of discrete acts. For example, the taking of an examination which represents an overt activity on the surface of the biosphere fulfills the deeper need to prove one's intellectual adequacy. At the same time, it is a step along the progressive dimension towards the ultimate goal of becoming a fully educated person. It also represents the co-ordination of many discrete facts which have been learned during the course of study.

THE SYMBOLIC SELF. Angyal observes that man is capable of developing ideas about himself as an organism because many of his organic processes become conscious. The sum total of these self-conceptions constitutes his symbolic self. However, Angyal warns us that the symbolic self is not always a reliable representation of the organism, that what a person thinks about himself rarely yields a true picture of reality. Consequently, if the individual's behavior is governed by the symbolic self, that is, if he behaves according to the image he has of himself, his behavior may not be appropriate to the real needs of the organism. "The relative segregation of the symbolic self within the organism is perhaps the most vulnerable point of the human personality organization" (1941, p. 121), because the symbolic self may falsify and distort the reality of the biosphere.

In conclusion it may be said that the totality of all of the components organized by position in the general pattern of the biosphere constitute the structure of personality.

THE DYNAMICS OF THE BIOSPHERE

The energy of the biosphere is supplied by the tensions that arise between the environmental pole and the organismic pole. These tensions arise because the environment pulls in one direction and the organism in another. These opposite directional trends of the organism and the environment within the biosphere are called *autonomy* and *homonomy* respectively. The trend toward autonomy consists of the expansion of the organism by assimilating and mastering the environment. It is analogous to an egoistic drive in which the person strives to satisfy his cravings and advance his interests by bending the environment to his needs. The trend toward autonomy is expressed through a number of specific channels, for instance, the desire for superiority, for acquisition, for exploration, and for achievement. The trend toward homonomy motivates the person to fit himself to the environment and to share and participate in something that is larger than his individual self. He submerges his individuality by forming a harmonious union with the social group, with nature, or with a supernatural, omnipotent being. Homonomy expresses itself through such specific motives as the desire for social status, attention, love of nature, religious sentiments, and patriotism.

In a more recent presentation of his views, Angyal (1951, 1952) has called these directional trends of the biosphere, self-determination versus self-surrender.

> The total function of personality is patterned according to a double orientation of self-determination . . . self-surrender. . . . These two tendencies of the human being, the tendency to increase his self-determination in his expanding personal world, and the tendency to surrender himself willingly to a superordinate whole, can be summed up by saying that the human being comports himself *as if he were a whole of an intermediate order*. By this I mean a "part-Gestalt," like, for example, the cardiovascular system, or the central nervous system, each of which is a *whole*, an organization of many parts, but at the same time a *part* with regard to its superordinate whole, the body. The human being is both a *unifier*, an organizer of his immediate personal world, and a *participant* in what he conceives as the superordinate whole to which he belongs (1952, p. 133).

Although autonomy or self-determination and homonomy or self-surrender may appear to be opposed to one another, they are really two phases of a more inclusive trend of the biosphere, that of *self-expansion*. The person is an open system with an input phase and an output phase. The input phase consists of assimilating the environment, which is the basis for autonomy, and the output phase consists of productivity, which is the basis for homonomy. Both phases are necessary for the full development of the individual. The person develops himself by incorporating things from the environment and he expands his environment by making personal contributions to it. He both takes and gives and in so doing he expands the whole biosphere which, it will be remembered, includes both the organism and the environment. The trends toward increased autonomy and increased homonomy, that is, toward self-expansion, constitute the chief system principle of the biosphere.

SYSTEM DYNAMICS. A tension may arise either in part of a system and spread to the whole or it may arise in the whole and affect all of the parts. However, a tension change in a part cannot directly affect a distant region; there is always a continuous spread outward from the affected part to adjacent ones like the concentric rings of waves that are made by throwing a stone in a pool of water. This spread of tension from its source into adjacent regions is a basic law of system dynamics.

As has already been mentioned, a part is differentiated out of the whole when a new function is required. Parts of a system are, therefore, to be regarded as functional units. However, a given function or part may participate in more than one system. A motor skill may be used in several co-ordinated activities such as typing, playing the piano, driving a car, and so forth. In fact, the organism operates economically by utilizing a relatively small number of part functions in a great variety of larger functional systems. A system is assembled out of a number of parts by the mechanism of *setting*. Thus, when a person begins a new job a number of different abilities, skills, and traits are assembled together from various systems to aid him in performing the work. The dissolution of a system that has already been set and the formation of a new system is accomplished by the mechanism of *shifting*. Setting and shifting are the principal mechanisms for any kind of organized activity.

Although these mechanisms are highly efficient in providing for the kind of action that is both need-satisfying and relevant to the conditions of the environment, there is bound to be interference and competition between systems when they try to use the same parts simultaneously. Various consequences may follow from this competition between systems. If one system is stronger, that is, has more energy, than the other system, the stronger system still has to deal with the pressure exerted upon it by the weaker system. As a result various pressure symptoms may develop, such as neurasthenia, fatigue, nervousness, and general anxiety. When the interfering system is more forceful, although still not as dominant as the other system, it may intrude itself into the activities of the stronger system and cause errors, accidents, and confusion in the performance. When the two systems are about equal in strength, they will invade one another in a reciprocal manner. Generalized confusion and a disintegration of behavior are symptoms of mutual invasion by competing systems. System interference becomes pathological when the interfering system is persistent so that strong resistances have to be mobilized against it by the dominant system. Inhibited tendencies may find expression in phantasy, dreams, somatic symptoms, acting out behavior, and the like.

The integrity of the biosphere may also be disturbed by the *segregation* of systems so that they lose their power to communicate with one another. Segregation may take place along any one of the three dimensions of personality. *Vertical* segregation consists of a dissociation between the outer expression and deeper tendencies which results in superficial behavior, pretending, overconformity, and the like. This type of segregation produces something analogous to Jung's persona. When there is segregation along the dimension of *progression* one may speak of *frustration*. Frustration prevents closure of the means-end continuum by reaching an appropriate goal. Segregation in the *transverse* dimension manifests itself in lack of co-ordination and in dissociated acts.

When one or more part processes impede or disturb the total functioning of the organism, the relationship between the part and the whole is said to be *bionegative*. Thus, anxiety is bionegative when the person is trying to solve an intellectual problem.

The environment may traumatize the organism in one of two ways. It may actively interfere with the autonomy of the organism, or it may be deficient with respect to that which will satisfy the organism's needs. The former are called *positive* traumata, the latter *scarcity* traumata. Angyal points out that one has to distinguish between the direct causal effects of a disturbing agent and the organism's reaction to these effects. The organism may be reacting to the by-products of its own reactions with further adjustive attempts. An example of this would be the person's attempts to deal with anxiety rather than with the environmental threat which caused the anxiety in the first place.

To summarize, then, the dynamics of the biosphere consists of the stresses and strains that occur between the two poles, one representing the organism which strives for autonomy and self-determination and the other representing the environment which pulls in the direction of homonomy and self-surrender. As a result of these pushes and pulls, the biosphere tends to become larger.

THE DEVELOPMENT OF PERSONALITY

Angyal views personality as an extended "temporal Gestalt" or pattern in which past, present, and future are firmly embedded. Personality is an organized process extending through time. The past is not immutable; it changes as a past event acquires a new positional value in the biosphere. An experience which was terrifying when it occurred in childhood may be remembered later as merely a ludicrous incident. Consequently, the influence of the past on the present is continuously changing. The future is always active in the present as a potentiality or disposition. It, too, can change as the biosphere undergoes reorganization. New hopes supplant old ones as a person grows older.

The course of life is not merely a sequence of episodes in which tensions arise and are resolved; it also posseses an intrinsic design or purpose. For Angyal, this central design of life is the desire to shape one's existence into a meaningful, fully expanded whole which will give perfect coherence and unity to one's life. Development consists of forming a strong, extended, integrated pattern.

Development proceeds along the three dimensions of personality. In the depth dimensions, the person grows from a median position on the scale outward as well as inward. He develops deeper, more profound needs as well as more elaborate behavior patterns by which to satisfy the needs. In the progressive dimension, development means increased efficiency and productivity. He gets to his goals more directly and with less waste motion. In the transverse dimension, growth results in better co-ordination and a greater versatility of behavior. Harmonious growth in all three dimensions enriches and expands the personality.

The span of life is divided into phases in which each phase forms a relatively autonomous part of the whole temporal pattern. A phase is defined by a particular problem of life which furnishes the theme for that period and gives to it its specific meaning. Thus, the theme of the first phase of life centers around eating and sleeping. Later, the opportunities and relevancies of the environment are discovered. During the early part of this phase the child does not recognize the independent nature of the environment and deals with it in an arbitrary and unrealistic manner. He tries to force the environment to be what he wants it to be. The limitations of this approach are soon realized, however, and the child gradually learns to accommodate himself to the objective properties of the environment. The uniformities of development throughout the successive phases are due to maturational sequences and to cultural standardization. However, it is impossible to predict with complete accuracy the course of a person's life because the influence of the environment cannot always be known beforehand. Environmental events are pretty much independent of and beyond the control and foresight of the person; they are fortuitous and unpredictable. Predictions may be made on the basis of the laws of personality development but such predictions are merely approximate. One can predict with reasonable accuracy that a young man will eventually enter some vocation, but to foretell exactly what vocation it will be involves considerable guesswork. However, as a person grows older, he becomes more rigid and set in his ways and less open to influences from the environment, so that his behavior is easier to foretell.

Although Angyal acknowledges that regression can and does occur, he feels, like Jung, that regression often serves the forward-going tendency of personality growth. That is, an individual may learn something from regression that enables him to return to his present problems and wrestle more effectively with them.

Angyal also believes that the symbolic functions of the organism, for example, thinking, develop with age and that "the center of gravity of life shifts more and more toward the psychological realm" (1941, p. 77). As a person grows older he tends to satisfy more and more of his needs by means of instrumental psychological processes. That is, he spends more time thinking and less time acting.

Angyal does not espouse or enunciate any theory of learning. He is content to use such terms as differentiation, reorganization, shifting, and the like, most of which are borrowed from the vocabulary of Gestalt psychology.

MASLOW'S HOLISTIC-DYNAMIC THEORY

Abraham Maslow, professor of psychology at Brandeis University, has in his numerous writings, a selection of which has been brought together in his recent book *Motivation and personality* (1954), aligned himself closely with an organismic, or as he calls it, a holistic-dynamic point of view. We shall single out for discussion some of the extensions that Maslow has made to organismic theory.

Maslow upbraids psychology for its "pessimistic, negative and limited conception" of man. He feels that psychology has dwelled more upon man's frailties than it has upon his strengths; that it has thoroughly explored his sins while neglecting his virtues. Psychology has seen life in terms of man making desperate attempts to avoid pain rather than in his taking active steps to gain pleasure and happiness. Where is the psychology, Maslow asks, that takes account of gaiety, exuberance, love, and well-being to the same extent that it deals with misery, conflict, shame, and hostility? Psychology "has voluntarily restricted itself to only half of its rightful jurisdiction, and that the darker, meaner half." Maslow has undertaken to supply the other half of the picture, the brighter, better half, and to give a portrait of the whole man.

He writes as follows.

Now let me try to present briefly and at first dogmatically the essence of this newly developing conception of the psychiatrically healthy man. First of all and most important of all is the strong belief that man has an essential nature of his own, some skeleton of psychological structure that may be treated and discussed analogously with his physical structure, that he has needs, capacities and tendencies that are genetically based, some of which are characteristic of the whole human species, cutting across all cultural lines, and some of which are unique to the individual. These needs are on their face good or neutral rather than evil. Second, there is involved the conception that full healthy and normal and desirable development consists in actualizing this nature, in fulfilling these potentialities, and in developing into maturity along the lines that this hidden, covert, dimly seen essential nature dictates, growing from within rather than being shaped from without. Third, it is now seen clearly that psychopathology in general results from the denial or the frustration or the twisting of man's essential nature. By this conception what is good? Anything that conduces to this desirable development in the direction of actualization of the inner nature of man. What is bad or abnormal? Anything that frustrates or blocks or denies the essential nature of man. What is psychopathological? Anything that disturbs or frustrates or twists the course of self-actualization. What is psychotherapy, or for that matter any therapy of any kind? Any means of any kind that helps to restore the person to the path of self-actualization and of development along the lines that his inner nature dictates (1954a, pp. 340–341).

In a further statement of his basic assumptions, Maslow has added this important one:

> This inner nature is not strong and overpowering and unmistakable like the instincts of animals. It is weak and delicate and subtle and easily overcome by habit, cultural pressure and wrong attitudes toward it. Even though weak, it never disappears in the normal person, perhaps not even in the sick person. It persists, even though denied, underground (1954b).

In this eloquent passage, Maslow has made a number of striking assumptions regarding the nature of man. Man has an inborn nature which is essentially good, and is never evil. This is a novel conception since many theorists assume that the instincts are bad and must be tamed by training and socialization.

As personality unfolds through maturation, the potential goodness of man manifests itself ever more clearly. When man is wicked or miserable or neurotic, it is because the environment has made him so through ignorance and social pathology. The good man is made bad by a bad environment although some men may remain good in spite of the influence of a corrupting environment. Of course, the environment can also play a benign role by assisting man in his efforts to fulfill himself, but this assistance is not absolutely required. It is enough to ask of the environment that it stand to one side and not interfere with man's self-actualization. Aggression and destructiveness, for example, are not indigenous to man. He becomes pugnacious and destructive when his inner nature is twisted or denied or frustrated. As soon as the frustration is removed, aggression disappears.

Maslow has propounded a theory of human motivation which assumes that needs are arranged along a hierarchy of priority or potency. When the needs that have the greatest potency and priority are satisfied, the next needs in the hierarchy emerge and press for satisfaction. When these are satisfied, another step up the ladder of motives is taken. The hierarchical order from most potent to least potent is as follows: physiological needs such as hunger and thirst, safety needs, needs for belongingness and love, esteem needs, needs for self-actualization, cognitive needs such as a thirst for knowledge, and finally aesthetic needs such as the desire for beauty. Hunger and thirst always take precedence over a desire for approval or recognition, but the latter are prepotent over the need for beauty. It will be observed that no place has been provided in this hierarchy for antisocial or harm-producing needs. Man may become antisocial only when society denies him the fulfillment of his inborn needs.

Maslow believes that if psychologists study crippled, stunted, neurotic people exclusively they are bound to produce a crippled psychology. In order to develop a more complete and comprehensive science of the human person it is also incumbent upon psychologists to study people who have realized their potentialities to the fullest. Maslow has done just this; he has made an intensive and far-reaching investigation of a group of self-actualizing people. They are rare birds as Maslow found when he was securing his group. After finding suitable subjects, some of whom were historical personages, such as Lincoln, Jefferson, Walt Whitman, Thoreau, and Beethoven, while others were living at the time they were studied, like Eleanor Roosevelt, Einstein, and friends and acquaintances of the investigator, they were investigated clinically to discover what characteristics distinguished them from the ordinary run of people. These turned out to be their distinguishing features: (1) They are realistically oriented. (2) They accept themselves, other people, and the natural world for what they are. (3) They have a great deal of spontaneity. (4) They are problem-centered rather than self-centered. (5) They have an air of detachment and a need for privacy. (6) They are autonomous and independent. (7) Their appreciation of people and things is fresh rather than stereotyped. (8) Most of them have had profound mystical or spiritual experiences although not necessarily religious in character. (9) They identify with mankind. (10) Their intimate relationships with a few specially loved people tend to be profound and deeply emotional rather than superficial. (11) Their values and attitudes are democratic. (12) They do not confuse means with ends. (13) Their sense of humor is philosophical rather than hostile. (14) They have a great fund of creativeness. (15) They resist conformity to the culture.

It appears that Maslow's unique contribution to the organismic viewpoint lies in his preoccupation with healthy people rather than sick ones, and his feeling that studies of these two groups generate different types of theory. Both Goldstein and Angyal, as medical specialists and psychotherapists, have come into contact with defective and disorganized people, yet in spite of this biased sample each has fashioned a theory that embraces the whole organism, and one that applies to the sick as well as to the healthy. Maslow has chosen the more direct course of studying healthy people whose wholeness and unity of personality are readily apparent. As self-actualizers, these people whom Maslow has observed are the embodiment of organismic theory.

LECKY'S THEORY OF SELF-CONSISTENCY

Although Prescott Lecky did not develop a comprehensive theory of personality, his ideas have so much kinship with organismic theory that some brief consideration of them, as set forth in his little book, *Self-consistency* (1945), is called for. Gardner Murphy in his foreword to Lecky's book (p. 1) says that "Lecky had in his own way developed . . . the conception that the individual must *define for himself the nature of that totality which he is*. He must throughout life assimilate new experiences in such fashion as both to *be* and to *appear* a living unit."

For Lecky, personality is the central, unifying concept of psychology. All psychological phenomena are considered to be expressions of a unified personality. All of man's activities serve the sovereign aim of personality, to maintain self-consistency.

Personality is conceived of as an organization of values which are consistent with one another. Behavior is an attempt on the part of the person to maintain the consistency and unity of these values in an unstable environment. Accordingly, there is only one source of motivation, namely, the necessity to maintain the unity and integrity of the organism, and one developmental goal, namely, the achievement of a unified and self-consistent organization. Lecky believed that the person craves a sense of unification, rather than pleasure, but that as a result of attaining unity the person derives pleasure therefrom. Pleasure is only a by-product and not the actual goal of life.

In general, the individual resists experiences that do not fit his structure of values and assimilates those that do. He always tries to adjust himself to his environment in a manner that will be harmonious with his structure of values. Sometimes, however, a problem or conflict created by an unsympathetic environment may exert so much pressure upon him that in order to reestablish his stability he has to give in to a change in his value system. Development, therefore, proceeds in the direction of assimilating stimuli from the outside world that are consistent with one's values or of reorganizing one's values in order to fit the demands of the environment.

Personality develops as a result of actual contacts with the world and the organization of experiences gained from these contacts into an integrated whole. The problems of life become increasingly difficult as the child grows older. The most constant factor in the individual's experience after himself is provided by the members of his family. By identifying himself with his parents, the child tries to bring himself and them into a unified and consistent relationship. By the age of five, the child has usually assimilated the customary home situations and he is then ready to begin meeting problems outside the family. During adolescence the need for unity is most acute because this is the great transition period of life when the young person is forced to revise his childish values and take on mature ones.

Lecky, like Maslow, is optimistic about man and his ability to develop a healthy, self-consistent personality. And like all organismic theorists, Lecky places great emphasis upon the potentialities of man. Left to his own powers of growth, Lecky believes that man has the ability to create a unified personality.

CURRENT STATUS AND EVALUATION

Organismic theory as a reaction against mind-body dualism, faculty psychology, and stimulus-response behaviorism has been immensely successful. Who is there in psychology today who is not a proponent of the main tenets of organismic theory that the whole is something other than the sum of its parts, that what happens to a part happens to the whole, and that there are no separate compartments within the organism? What psychologist believes that there is a mind which is separate from the body, a mind which obeys laws different from those pertaining to the body? Who believes that there are isolated events, insulated processes, detached functions? Very few if any psychologists subscribe any longer to an atomistic viewpoint. We are all organismic psychologists whatever else we may be.

In this sense, organismic theory is more of an attitude or orientation or frame of reference than it is a systematic behavior theory. It says, in effect, that since everything is related to the whole, true understanding results from the correct placing of a phenomenon within the context of the total system. It directs the investigator to take into account a web of variables rather than pairs of variables, to consider the event which he is studying as a component of a system rather than as an isolated happening. To understand the laws by which the total system operates *is* in fact the ultimate concern of any scientist; it is the ideal towards which he constantly strives. The organismic viewpoint as applied within the province of human psychology asserts that the total person is the natural unit of study. Since the normal, healthy human being, or any other organism for that matter, always functions as an organized whole, he should be studied as an organized whole.

While recognizing that present techniques of research and quantitative analysis may not permit the psychological investigator to realize the organismic goal of studying the whole person, it urges psychology to find the means for doing so. If quantitative methods are not available then qualitative methods should be used. Meanwhile, psychology should address itself to the task of developing methods that will bring it closer to the organismic goal of understanding the whole person. Organismic theory in this sense is much more of a set of directives than it is a system of facts, principles, and laws.

There is not one official organismic theory of personality; there are many. An organismic theory of personality is defined by the attitude of the theorist, not by the contents of the model of personality that is constructed. If the theory focuses upon the whole organism as a unified system rather than upon separate traits or drives or habits then the theory may be called an organismic one. Goldstein, Angyal, Maslow, Lecky, Allport, Murray, Murphy, Rogers, Freud, Jung, and virtually all other contemporary personality theorists adopt an organismic orientation yet there are radical differences among these theories. What Goldstein finds in the organism is not precisely what Allport or Freud finds there, although all three may be classified properly as organismic in their general orientation.

There is little to find fault with in the organismic approach because it is so universally accepted. One can, however, evaluate a *particular* organismic theory such as Goldstein's or Angyal's. Perhaps the most serious charge that has been made against Goldstein's version of organismic theory is that it is not sufficiently holistic. Goldstein treats the organism as a segregated unit which is set apart from the rest of the world. The skin is the boundary between the organism and the world; exchanges take place across the boundary but the organism and the environment are treated as separate realms. A thoroughgoing holistic approach would make no such arbitrary division between what takes place within the skin and what takes place outside of it. The organism should be regarded as a differentiated component of a larger system, a system which includes the whole universe. Goldstein, while acknowledging the truth of this criticism, would reply that the whole universe is much too large a chunk for any scientist to study. The holistic theorist has to be realistic about what can and what cannot be taken into account. It is conceivable that events in outer space affect our behavior but we just do not possess the means of including such events within our scientific ken. Tennyson's flower in the crannied wall, could he but know it "all and all, I should know what God and man is" is a moving poetic truth, but it is scarcely an attainable goal. Although everything is related to everything else, Goldstein believes that many of the strands making up the total cosmic web are so distantly connected with one another that they can be ignored without doing any serious injustice to our understanding of personality.

Where is one to draw the line, however, and say "Beyond this boundary the effects are virtually zero"? If everything is a component in the grand scheme of nature, how can it be known without making a test what is and what is not relevant? The answer obviously is that it cannot be known. W. A. Hunt in reviewing *The organism* (1940) calls this the organismic paradox. The organismic theorist denies the validity of partitive concepts yet he is forced to use them. If Goldstein is justified in treating a part, the organism, as a segregated whole, then why is another psychologist not justified in considering learning or perception or emotion as holistic processes? Angyal's biosphere is one attempt to broaden the holistic base of organismic theory. According to this conception, the organism and the environment are poles of a larger system. If by environment Angyal means everything in the universe other than the organism, then the total biospheric system is identical with the universe, and the paradox is resolved.

That the question of deciding where to draw the limits of one's system is not an academic one is indicated by the diverse hypotheses that have been put forward to explain man's conduct. For example, serious attempts have been made to show that the course of the stars influences human behavior, that remote historical and prehistorical happenings as well as future events have a bearing upon present behavior. If clairvoyance and mental telepathy should prove to be true—and there are many today who believe that they are authentic phenomena—the limits of the holistic system to which a person belongs would be greatly extended. In the light of these considerations Goldstein's critics may well ask: Why stop at the skin, or even at the boundary of the near environment?

A number of more or less specific criticisms have been raised regarding Goldstein's theory. He has been criticized for not distinguishing sufficiently between what is inherent in the organism and what has been put there by the culture. Kattsoff (1942), for example, has raised this question. Goldstein's concept of self-actualization has been regarded as being too general in character to be useful for making specific predictions. Skinner (1940) considers self-actualization a metaphysical concept because it cannot be put to an experimental test. Some psychologists object to Goldstein's apparent disregard of statistical analysis in favor of a qualitative approach in his role as an investigator. These psychologists feel that qualitative analysis is highly subjective and that it is difficult to repeat an investigation when it is couched in purely qualitative terms. Other psychologists do not see eye to eye with Goldstein's strictures regarding the use of psychological tests. They feel that tests should be administered and scored in a standardized manner and that they should not be changed to meet the needs of the individual case. Goldstein has been criticized for placing too much emphasis upon maturation and not enough upon learning, and for exaggerating the importance of the abstract attitude in psychological functioning. Finally, there have been objections to trying to understand the normal personality by studying brain-injured patients. In spite of these specific criticisms, the prevailing attitude among psychologists toward the theoretical formulations of Goldstein is a highly favorable one. In conjunction with the holistic psychologies of the Gestaltists, of Lewin, and of Tolman, Goldstein's views have had great influence upon contemporary psychology and his significance as a theorist can hardly be overestimated.

When we come to evaluate Angyal's work our task is more difficult than is the case with Goldstein. Angyal's volume, *Foundations for a science of personality* (1941), received little critical notice when it was published and there has been little public response to his views during the last fifteen years. This is surprising not only because it is a very provocative and in many respects a highly original piece of theoretical reasoning but also because Angyal made a serious effort to formulate a theory of personality, something that Goldstein never essayed. The reason for this neglect may be due to Angyal's failure to heel in his theoretical speculations in the fertile soil of clinical observations and experimental investigations. Although Angyal has published a number of research papers, they do not seem to have much connection with his systematic position. Goldstein, on the other hand, has rich data from the clinic and the laboratory with which to support and illustrate his general theory. Whatever the reason may be for psychology's failure to react to Angyal's book, the fact remains that it has not received the critical attention that it merits.

In 1941 Rapaport had occasion to comment in a review of a book by Heinz Werner (1941) that organismic theory had not developed a theory of personality. He proposed at that time a merging of the organismic and psychoanalytic systems which would provide psychology with a comprehensive theory of personality. Although Angyal's theory does not embrace psychoanalysis in any substantive way, it is an organismic theory of personality.

The concept of a biosphere which includes both the organism and its environment is not entirely successful in solving the problem of how to bring the person and the world into some kind of holistic union. In reading Angyal one is puzzled by his tendency to treat the two not as poles of a single globe but as distinctive entities that interact with one another. In spite of his concept of an all-inclusive biosphere, Angyal writes as though it were still a matter of an organism versus an environment. The environment does things to the person and the person does things to the environment; they do not seem to behave as components of a single system. Whereas Lewin gets himself trapped in a purely psychological world, Angyal seems to be lost in the whole universe. Whenever Angyal discusses concrete problems dealing with personality organization, dynamics, and development, he has to put aside the notion of a cosmic whole and deal with the organism and the environment as separate but interdependent and interacting systems.

Some of Angyal's concepts, notably those of self-determination and self-surrender, have a somewhat mystical aura surrounding them, although probably no more so than some of the concepts proposed by other theorists. Angyal endows the person with capacities for either mastering the environment or submitting to it, but he does not say what the determiners of these capacities are or why a person does one rather than the other. Although Angyal does not go so far as to reintroduce the concept of a soul or other vital principles of the order of Bergson's *élan vital,* some of his ideas resemble fairly closely these metaphysical notions.

In conclusion it may be said fairly that organismic theory for all of its weaknesses has tried to right the wrong committed by Descartes three hundred years ago. It has conscientiously insisted that the organism is not a dual system of mind and body, each with its own motors or driving principles, but that it is a single entity consisting of many part-functions. For promulgating and promoting this cardinal conception, the organismic point of view richly deserves the esteem in which it is held.

BIBLIOGRAPHY

PRIMARY SOURCES

Angyal, A. *Foundations for a science of personality.* New York: Commonwealth Fund, 1941.

Goldstein, K. *The organism.* New York: American Book Co., 1939.

Goldstein, K. *Human nature in the light of psychopathology.* Cambridge: Harvard Univ. Press, 1940.

Lecky, P. *Self consistency.* New York: Island Press, 1945.

Maslow, A. H. *Motivation and personality.* New York: Harper, 1954.

REFERENCES

Angyal, A. *Foundations for a science of personality.* New York: Commonwealth Fund, 1941.

Angyal, A. The holistic approach in psychiatry. *Amer. J. Psychiat.,* 1948, *105,* 178–182.

Angyal, A. A theoretical model for personality studies. *J. Pers.,* 1951, *20,* 131–142. (Reprinted in D. Krech and G. S. Klein (Eds.). *Theoretical models and personality theory.* Durham, N. C.: Duke Univ. Press, 1952, pp. 131–142.)

Bertalanffy, L. von. An outline of general system theory. *Brit. J. Phil. Sci.,* 1950a, *1,* 134–165.

Bertalanffy, L. von. The theory of open systems in physics and biology. *Science,* 1950b, *111,* 23–29.

Coghill, G. E. *Anatomy and the problem of behavior..* London: Cambridge Univ. Press, 1929.

Dewey, J. The reflex arc concept in psychology. *Psychol. Rev.,* 1896, *3,* 357–370.

Dunbar, H. Flanders. *Emotions and bodily changes.* 4th Ed. New York: Columbia Univ. Press, 1954.

Freiman, I. S. Kurt Goldstein—an appreciation. *Amer. J. Psychother.,* 1954, *8,* 3–10.

Gelb, A., and Goldstein, K. *Psychologische Analysen hirnpathologischer Faelle.* Leipzig: Barth, 1920. (Partially translated in W. D. Ellis (Ed.). *Source book of Gestalt psychology.* New York: Harcourt, 1938, selections 26–30.)

Goldstein, K. *The organism.* New York: American Book Co., 1939.

Goldstein, K. *Human nature in the light of psychopathology.* Cambridge: Harvard Univ. Press, 1940.

Goldstein, K. *After-effects of brain injuries in war.* New York: Grune and Stratton, 1942.

Goldstein, K. *Language and language disturbances.* New York: Grune and Stratton, 1948.

Goldstein, K., and Scheerer, M. Abstract and concrete behavior: an experimental study with special tests. *Psychol. Monogr.,* 1941, *53,* no. 2.

Goldstein, K., and Scheerer, M. Tests of abstract and concrete thinking. A. Tests of abstract and concrete behavior. In A. Weider (Ed.). *Contributions toward medical psychology.* New York: Ronald Press, 1953.

Hanfmann, Eugenia, Rickers-Ovsiankina, Maria, and Goldstein, K. Case Lanuti: Extreme concretization of behavior due to damage of the brain cortex. *Psychol. Monogr.,* 1944, *57,* no. 4.

Hilgard, E. R. *Theories of learning.* New York: Appleton-Century-Crofts, 1948.

Hunt, W. A. Review of K. Goldstein's *The organism. Psychol. Bull.,* 1940, *37,* 637–639.

Jackson, J. H. *Selected writings of John Hughlings Jackson.* J. Taylor (Ed.). London: Hodder and Stoughton, 1931.

Kantor, J. R. *Principles of psychology.* 2 vols. New York: Knopf, 1924.

Kantor, J. R. *A survey of the science of psychology.* Bloomington, Ind.: Principia Press, 1933.

Kantor, J. R. *Problems of physiological psychology.* Bloomington, Ind.: Principia Press, 1947.

Kattsoff, L. O. Review of K. Goldstein's *Human nature in the light of psychopathology. J. gen. Psychol.,* 1942, *26,* 187–194.

Krech, D. Dynamic systems as open neurological systems. *Psychol. Rev.,* 1950, *57,* 345–361.

Lecky, P. *Self-consistency.* New York: Island Press, 1945.

Maslow, A. H. *Motivation and personality.* New York: Harper, 1954a.

Maslow, A. H. Personality problems and personality growth. Unpublished manuscript, 1954b.

Meyer, A. *The commonsense psychiatry of Dr. Adolf Meyer.* A. Lief (Ed.). New York: McGraw, 1948.

Rapaport, D. Review of H. Werner's *Comparative psychology of mental development. J. genet. Psychol.,* 1941, *59,* 429–434.

Rennie, T. A. C. Adolf Meyer and psychobiology; the man, his methodology and its relation to therapy. *Pap. Amer. Congr. gen. Semant.,* 1943, *2,* 156–165.

Scheerer, M., Rothman, Eva, and Goldstein, K. A case of "idiot savant": An experimental study of personality organization. *Psychol. Monogr.,* 1945, *58,* no. 4.

Skinner, B. F. Review of K. Goldstein's *The organism. J. abnorm. soc. Psychol.,* 1940, *35,* 462–465.

Smuts, J. C. *Holism and evolution.* New York: Macmillan, 1926.

Werner, H. *Comparative psychology of mental development.* Rev. Ed. Chicago: Follett, 1948.

Wheeler, R. H. *The science of psychology.* 2nd Ed. New York: Crowell, 1940.

9.

Sheldon's

Constitutional Psychology

For the man on the street physical characteristics of his fellow humans illumine manifold aspects of personality. It is "well known" that fat men are jolly and indolent, that lean individuals are shy and morose, that red hair betokens a swift and violent anger. A large dictionary of such diagnostic statements could be compiled and this is precisely what early investigators such as Lavater (1804) and Gall and Spurzheim (1809) did. More recently other students of human behavior (Rostan, 1824; Viola, 1909; Sigaud, 1914; Naccarati, 1921; Kretschmer, 1921) have advanced similar findings and have frequently attempted to introduce empirical control into the demonstration of such relations. Thus, the layman and many scholars of the past share the belief that behavior is related in important respects to observable aspects of the individual's physical make-up. In surprising contrast, we find few psychologists in this country who show much interest in this problem.

Acceptance of a theory or body of evidence is not solely dependent upon the empirical findings that can be summoned to substantiate it. There are many overriding considerations including the extent to which the formulations fit with the guiding preconceptions or convictions of the time and culture. The difficulty encountered by Galileo in his attempt to develop a concept of the universe that reversed the church-supported, Aristotelian view is merely a dramatic instance of a process that goes on continually in a milder form among all empirical

disciplines. Various scholars have written persuasively about the reluctance of most contemporary psychologists to give a fair hearing to
the extrasensory research (parapsychology) of Rhine and his collaborators. To this instance could be added many others, perhaps including constitutional psychology. The resistance of most American
psychologists to considering the possibility of an intimate tie between
body and behavior seems linked to a number of factors. One important by-product of American democracy, the Protestant ethic, and
the dogma of the self-made man has been the rejection of formulations
implying that behavior may be innately conditioned, immutable, a
"given." Because it is commonly accepted that physical characteristics
are linked closely to genetic factors, the suggestion that physical and
psychological characteristics are intimately related seems to imply a
championing of genetic determinism. It is not surprising that such a
conception has been unable to muster much support in the face of the
buoyant environmentalism of American psychology. In general, it
seems fair to say that American psychologists have largely neglected
the study of that important class of variables having to do with the
physical description of the body.

In the face of this indifference or hostility to the possibility of important associations between structural and behavioral characteristics
the work of William H. Sheldon stands as a unique contribution on
the contemporary scene. In the present chapter we shall attempt to
place Sheldon's work in brief historical perspective and then describe
his formulations and investigations. In some respects it may seem
unwise to focus so heavily upon the work of a single man when over
the years so many have worked in this area. However, Sheldon's
work is empirically far superior to that of his predecessors and for the
contemporary psychologist it is largely the research of Sheldon and
his collaborators that makes this a topic of significance.

A word should be said concerning the sense in which we intend
to use the term constitutional. There are two definitions frequently
encountered in psychology. In the first, the term is used to refer to
those factors that are given, or present, at birth. Here, constitutional
is simply a shorthand means of referring to the contributions of genes
plus the uterine environment. The second usage equates the term to
the most basic "make-up of the body." Thus Sheldon suggests that:
". . . constitution refers to those aspects of the individual which are
relatively more fixed and unchanging—morphology, physiology, endocrine function, etc.—and may be contrasted with those aspects
which are relatively more labile and susceptible to modification by

environmental pressures, i.e., habits, social attitudes, education, etc."
(1940, p. 2). As this definition implies, constitutional psychology then
becomes ". . . the study of the psychological aspects of human behavior as they are related to the morphology and physiology of the
body" (Sheldon, 1940, p. 1). It is clear that these two usages have
much in common because both physical structure and biological function are commonly assumed to be closely related to prenatal determinants of behavior.

For the purposes of this chapter we shall naturally adopt the definition proposed by Sheldon. There remains the question whether the
term constitution implies an equal emphasis upon physical structure
and biological function. Logically it should include both. Thus, the
individual who studied the relation between behavior and measurable
aspects of the autonomic nervous system or the endocrine system
should be considered a "constitutional psychologist" just as much as
the student of physique. In point of historical fact, however, the term
is ordinarily used to refer to those theorists or investigators who have
emphasized the relation between structural aspects of the body
(physique or body build) and behavior. Thus, for present purposes
the *constitutional psychologist is one who looks to the biological substratum of the individual for factors that are important to the explanation of human behavior*. Since more is known about morphology than
about the other aspects of this substratum, our discussion will perforce
dwell mostly on the dependence of behavior upon physique or body
build.

Before examining the formulations of Sheldon, let us look at some
of the important work that preceded his. Our historical account necessarily must be very brief; however, the interested reader will find excellent supplementary accounts in Allport (1937) and Sheldon (1940,
1944).

CONSTITUTIONAL PSYCHOLOGY OF THE PAST

Theories that suggest a relation between physique and behavior
antedate by many centuries the birth of academic psychology. Not
only did these formulations begin in the dim past but more surprisingly many of them show a remarkable correspondence to formulations that are still popular. The individual who is generally credited
with having begun work in this area is Hippocrates who suggested not
only a typology of physique but also a temperament typology and a
conception of humors that is highly congruent with the current emphasis upon the importance of endocrine secretions as determinants

of behavior (cf. Hoskins, 1941). He suggested a twofold classification of physiques, dividing subjects into those who were short and thick and those who were long and thin. Although this division may sound rudimentary, it is nevertheless not far removed from many of the classifications that have been proposed during the past century. He also suggested that these body types were accompanied by characteristic disease afflictions. The short and thick body build was especially prone to apoplexy; the long and thin build was frequently accompanied by tuberculosis. Here is the birth of constitutional medicine, a field in which Sheldon is currently active. Further, Hippocrates suggested that men could be divided into four basic temperament types that corresponded to Empedocles' four basic elements— air, water, fire, and earth. There were also four humors (liquid substances) within the body, the relative predominance of which determined the temperamental type to which the individual would belong. Thus, we have here the suggestion of classifying individuals in terms of temperament, and further the implication that liquids within the body (endocrine secretions?) have a determining effect upon the temperament an individual will display.

Following Hippocrates there were many scholars and speculative writers who dealt with this topic but, for our purposes, the next important contribution seems to have been made by Rostan (1824), a French investigator. Rostan's principal importance lies in his recommendation that physiques be classified in terms of a fourfold typology. His types were respectively the digestive, muscular, cerebral, and respiratory. His scheme incorporated Hippocrates' typology and added certain important dimensions. Actually, his digestive, muscular, and cerebral types represent the core of most modern-day schemes for typing or measuring physiques. Somewhat later Viola (1909), an Italian anthropologist, simplified Rostan's schema and proposed that physique be classified in terms of three types: microsplanchnic, normosplanchnic, and macrosplanchnic. The microsplanchnic was characterized by a small body and long limbs, the macrosplanchnic had a large body and short limbs, and the normosplanchnic represented a point between the two extremes. Viola's special contribution lay in the fact that he was more concerned with the details of measurement than most of his predecessors and he proposed a large number of specific bodily measurements that could be used in classifying an individual.

With Ernst Kretschmer (1921) constitutional psychology embarked upon its modern course. Kretschmer is a German psychiatrist whose contributions to European psychiatry are of first magnitude, although he is best known in this country for his studies of the relation between physique and mental disorder. In his psychiatric practice he became convinced that there were important relationships between physique and manifest behavior, especially the type of behavior displayed in the two major forms of mental disorder: manic-depressive psychosis and schizophrenia. Schizophrenia is the most common of all psychotic disorders and is characterized by a loss of affect or emotional responsiveness and a withdrawal from normal interpersonal relations, and is frequently accompanied by delusions and hallucinations. The manic-depressive psychosis in its extreme manifestation is characterized by mood swings such that an individual in one phase may be so overactive and excitable (manic) that he has to be forcibly restrained to prevent his harming himself and others, yet at another time he may be so inactive, lethargic, and depressed that he has to be cared for as though he were an infant.

Given this general pattern of interest, Kretschmer set out to accomplish three things: (1) to devise a means of objectively classifying individuals in terms of a limited number of physique categories; (2) to relate physique, as measured by the pre-established categories, to the two major forms of psychosis, schizophrenia and manic depression; (3) to relate physique to other forms of behavior falling in the normal range.

In the measurement of physique Kretschmer was surprisingly systematic and painstaking. In an effort to achieve repeatability and consistency of measurement he devised an elaborate check list representing the major parts of the body, with a cluster of descriptive phrases for each of these areas. This check list was then filled out with the subject standing naked in front of the investigator. As the result of a complex analysis of these ratings and objective measurements Kretschmer arrived at a conception of three fundamental types of physiques.

The first type is called *asthenic* and refers to a frail, linear physique. In Kretschmer's words:

> . . . there is typically . . . *a deficiency in thickness combined with an average unlessened length.* This deficiency in the thickness development is present in all parts of the body,—face, neck, trunk, extremities—and in all the tissues—skin, fat, muscle, bone, and vascular system throughout. On this account we find the average weight, as well as the total circumference and breadth measurements, below the general value for males . . . a lean narrowly-built man, who looks taller than he is, with a skin

poor in secretion and blood, with narrow shoulders, from which hang lean arms with thin muscles, and delicately boned hands; a long, narrow, flat chest, on which we can count the ribs, with a sharp rib angle, a thin stomach . . . (1925, p. 21).

The second physique type is the *athletic* which is a muscular ⟨ℓ⟩ vigorous physique.

The male athletic type is recognized by the strong development of the skeleton, the musculature and also the skin. . . . A middle-sized to tall man, with particularly wide projecting shoulders, a superb chest, a firm stomach, and a trunk which tapers in its lower region, so that the pelvis, and the magnificent legs, sometimes seem almost graceful compared with the size of the upper limbs and particularly the hypertrophied shoulders (1925, p. 24).

The third type is the *pyknic* physique which is characterized by ⟨♌⟩ plumpness and corresponds to Rostan's digestive type. Kretschmer suggests that:

The pyknic type . . . is characterized by the pronounced peripheral development of the body cavities (head, breast and stomach), and a tendency to a distribution of fat about the trunk . . . middle height, rounded figure, a soft broad face on a short massive neck, sitting between the shoulders; the magnificent fat paunch protrudes from the deep vaulted chest which broadens out towards the lower part of the body (1925, p. 29).

In addition to the three types outlined above an additional type was added—the *dysplastic.* This includes the small group of cases where there are strikingly deviant aspects to the individual's build so that they appear to even the casual observer as "rare, surprising and ugly."

Given this system of physique classification, Kretschmer set out to compare psychiatric patients. He studied 260 psychotics made up of 43 manic-depressive men and 42 manic-depressive women, and 125 schizophrenic men and 50 schizophrenic women. When these patients were classified according to his scheme Kretschmer found the distribution presented in Table 1. From these findings Kretschmer concludes that there is a "clear biological affinity" between manic-depressive psychosis and the pyknic body build and a similar association between schizophrenia and the asthenic, athletic, and certain dysplastic body builds.

Kretschmer also makes plain his conviction that psychotic states are directly continuous with normal behavior. He suggests that in addition to schizophrenia there is a schizoid state which is borderline

TABLE 1

INCIDENCE OF PHYSIQUE TYPES IN TWO TYPES OF PSYCHOSIS

Number of Cases

	Manic-Depressive	Schizophrenic
Asthenic	4	81
Athletic	3	31
Asthenic-athletic mixed	2	11
Pyknic	58	2
Pyknic mixture	14	3
Dysplastic	—	34
Deformed and uncategorized	4	13
	85	175

(Adapted from Kretschmer, 1925, p. 35.)

and a schizothymic state which is normal but nevertheless resembles the schizophrenic. Similarly, there is the cycloid personality which represents a mildly disturbed state related to the manic-depressive psychosis, and the cyclothymic state which is normal but still related to the psychotic state. Given the relationship between physique and psychosis, and given also Kretschmer's assumption of continuity between normal and abnormal, it is easy to see that Kretschmer would expect a relation between physique and patterns of behavior in normal subjects. This relationship remains merely an assertion, however, for Kretschmer provides no direct evidence to support his contention.

Although it is evident that Kretschmer made a considerable contribution to constitutional psychology, it is also evident that his work is not beyond criticism. The most important objection is that he failed to control adequately for differences in age between manic-depressives and schizophrenics. Thus, the common observation that with increasing age most of us increase in weight and are more likely to resemble pyknics, and the further evidence that manic-depressive psychosis typically occurs later in life than schizophrenia, might account for the relation he observed between physique and psychosis. In addition, various investigators have encountered considerable difficulty in assigning physiques to Kretschmer's categories in an objective and repeatable fashion.

The work we have described, especially that of Ernst Kretschmer, provides an indispensable backdrop against which Sheldon's formulations and procedures evolved. Although it is true that Sheldon's work is vastly superior in many respects to that of his predecessors, it is unlikely that his achievements could have been accomplished without the imaginative and painstaking efforts of these earlier figures. Let us turn now to a consideration of Sheldon's background, his theory, and his investigation.

WILLIAM H. SHELDON

Sheldon was born in the year 1899 in Warwick, Rhode Island, where he grew up in a farm setting. The rural atmosphere of his early life and his close relationship with his father, who was a naturalist and animal breeder, have had a lasting effect upon his values and upon his view of human behavior. Even today his writing shows clear evidence of his interest in the animal world and many of his ideas concerning determinants of human behavior seem to have grown out of a close familiarity with the ways and the breeds of animals. He was educated in public schools and attended Brown University where he received his A.B. in 1919. Subsequently he received an A.M. from the University of Colorado and a Ph.D. in psychology from the University of Chicago in 1926. In 1933 he received his M.D., also from the University of Chicago. From 1924 to 1926 he was an instructor in psychology at the University of Chicago and then was an assistant professor for one year at both the University of Chicago and Northwestern University. He was next an assistant professor at the University of Wisconsin from 1927 until 1931. After securing his medical degree he interned at a children's hospital in Chicago and secured a fellowship that enabled him to spend two years in psychiatric study abroad. Much of his time during this period was spent in Zurich with Carl Jung but he also visited Freud and Kretschmer. On his return to this country in 1936 he went to the University of Chicago as a professor of psychology. In 1938 he moved to Harvard University where he remained for a number of years and where his collaboration with the distinguished experimental psychologist, S. S. Stevens, developed. Following a period of wartime Army service, Sheldon accepted in 1947 a position as Director of the Constitution Laboratory, College of Physicians and Surgeons, Columbia University, where he has remained. In this position he succeeded George Draper, a pioneer in constitutional medicine; and like Draper he has been actively studying the relation between organic disease and physical structure.

Sheldon's professional writings follow a remarkably consistent main stream. With only two interesting excursions, they represent an attempt to identify and describe the major structural components of the human body (*The varieties of human physique,* 1940), the major components of temperament (*The varieties of temperament,* 1942), and the application of these findings to the area of delinquency (*Varieties of delinquent youth,* 1949). More recently Sheldon has returned to the problem of description of physique in his *Atlas of men* (1954). His first book (*Psychology and the Promethean will,* 1936) is a provocative essay on the role of religion in modern life. He also outlines in this volume what he considers are the principal sources of conflict in modern man. The other book not closely related to constitutional psychology is a technical volume that deals with the taxonomy of coins (*Early American cents, 1793–1814,* 1949), in which Sheldon proves himself as adept at classifying old coins as human physiques. At present Sheldon is actively working on an "Atlas of Women," an "Atlas of Children," and a volume concerned with physique and organic disease.

The breadth of Sheldon's training makes it difficult to isolate specific figures who have influenced his professional development. However, in both writing and investigation he shows clearly his indebtedness to predecessors in the field of constitutional psychology, especially Kretschmer and Viola. Furthermore, although he has pungently expressed reservations concerning the nature of Freud's impact upon psychology, there is evidence of some influence from this quarter and from the work of Carl Jung. The writings of William James, who was Sheldon's godfather, have exerted a detectable influence upon him. Sheldon's medical training and early interests in animal breeding are clearly reflected in his professional concern over biological and hereditary factors in behavior. Finally, the procedural and measuremental sophistication of S. S. Stevens manifestly had its effects upon Sheldon during the period of their collaboration.

In Sheldon's theory we find a clear and vigorous exposition of the crucial importance of the physical structure of the body as a primary determinant of behavior. Moreover, he identifies a set of objective variables which can be used as a bridgehead for describing physique and behavior. In an area where the use of types—what Whitehead has referred to as a "half-way house on the road to measurement"— has been the rule, Sheldon introduces and stoutly defends the notion of continuous variables. Furthermore, his techniques for assessing the structural characteristics of the body involve the use of standard photographs and a much more carefully specified and reproducible procedure than that of his predecessors.

Underlying this emphasis upon physique and its measurement is a strong conviction that biological-hereditary factors are of immense importance in determining behavior and a belief that the riddle of the human organism will be unraveled only with the aid of increased understanding of these factors. A fully rounded psychology cannot exist in a biological vacuum. Thus, in a psychological world that is focused upon environmental transactions we find Sheldon looking away from the external world and gazing instead at the physical structure that silently underlies all behavioral phenomena. It is his assumption that here, in the physique, the psychologist may find the constants, the firm substructures that are so desperately needed to introduce regularity and consistency into the study of human behavior. All of this is implied in the following statement:

> It has been growing increasingly plain that the situation calls for a biologically oriented psychology, or one taking for its operational frame of reference a scientifically defensible description of the *structure* (together with the behavior) of the human organism itself. This is perhaps tantamount to saying that psychology requires a physical anthropology for its immediate foundation support. More than that, it requires a physical anthropology couched in terms of components, or variables, which can be measured and quantified at both the structural and behavioral ends —the anthropological and psychological ends—of the structure-behavior continuum which is a human personality (Sheldon, 1949, p. xv).

In William Sheldon we observe not only a student of physical structure and a believer in the importance of biological factors but also a singularly provocative protagonist. His writing style is direct and unconventional. He is a scholar who delights in extreme statements and who can weave compelling word images to defend these statements. Thus, we have the desirable combination of a tireless investigator and a polemically oriented individual who is defending a position that is poorly represented in American psychology today.

THE STRUCTURE OF PHYSIQUE

One of the fascinations of Sheldon's theory of personality lies in its simplicity and specificity. In contrast to many personality theories, which provide an unlimited number of blank checks that can be written for puzzling behavioral equations, Sheldon defines a discrete number of physical and temperamental variables which he considers of primary importance in representing human behavior. Although he does not close the door to further elaboration or refinement, neither is he apologetic about the present fruitfulness of these variables.

Consistent with the approach of most other constitutional psychologists, Sheldon attempts to identify and provide suitable measures for the physical components of the human body. It is important to realize that he is not simply looking for a means of classifying or describing physiques. His goal is much more ambitious—to provide a "biological identification tag." He assumes that genetic and other biological determinants play a crucial role in the development of the individual. He believes also that it is possible to get some representation of these factors through a set of measures based upon the physique. In his view there is a hypothetical biological structure (morphogenotype) which underlies the external, observable physique (phenotype) and which plays an important role not only in determining physical development but also in molding behavior. The *somatotype* represents an attempt to assess the morphogenotype, although it must approach this goal indirectly, and in its derivation leans heavily upon measurements of the phenotype (physique).

We shall consider here Sheldon's approach to the measurement of the physical aspects of the individual, and following this we shall examine his efforts to identify the most important components underlying behavior.

DIMENSIONS OF PHYSIQUE. Although Sheldon was well aware of his predecessors' attempts to type or measure physique, he began his efforts inductively. The first problem he faced was to secure a large number of physiques that could be examined and re-examined. In order to make this procedure practical and efficient he devised a photographic technique that involved taking pictures from the front, side, and rear of individuals posed in a standard position before a standard background. This procedure has come to be called the *Somatotype Performance Test* and is described in full detail in Sheldon's *Atlas of men* (1954).

In his first important study of the human physique, Sheldon secured roughly four thousand standard photographs of male college students. These pictures were then inspected carefully by several judges with the intent of teasing out the principal variables that account for or form the basis of physique variation. Once a given characteristic was suspected of being a primary component, it was appraised in terms of the following criteria: (1) Was it possible to rank all four thousand subjects in terms of this characteristic? (2) Could different judges reach agreement independently in ranking physiques in terms of this characteristic? (3) Was it impossible to account for this variable in terms of some combination of the other variables that had already been identified?

Primary components of physique. After a considerable period of carefully examining and judging these pictures Sheldon and his associates concluded that, with a list of three, they had exhausted the possibilities of discovering new components. These three dimensions became the core of the technique for assessing the physical structure of the body, and their careful delineation and measurement occupied the next phase of Sheldon's investigation.

The first component was *endomorphy.* The individual who is high in this component and low in both of the others is characterized by softness and spherical appearance. Consistent with the softness and rounded quality is an underdevelopment of bone and muscle and a relatively low surface-mass ratio. Such an individual has a low specific gravity and floats high in the water. The fact that the digestive viscera are highly developed in this physique and that the functional elements of those structures develop primarily from the endodermal embryonic layer accounts for the use of the term endomorphy.

The second component was referred to as *mesomorphy.* A physique heavily developed in this component, and showing a decrement in both the other components, is hard and rectangular, with a predominance of bone and muscle. The mesomorphic body is strong, tough, resistant to injury, and generally equipped for strenuous and exacting physical demands. The athlete, adventurer, or professional soldier might best be endowed with this type of physique. The dominant portions of this physique have derived primarily from the mesodermal embryonic layer, hence the term mesomorphic.

The third component was labeled *ectomorphy.* An individual who is at the upper extreme in this component and low in the other components is linear and fragile, characterized by flatness of the chest and delicacy of the body. He is usually thin and lightly muscled. Relative to his mass the ectomorph has more surface area than the other types of physique; he shows a preponderance of mass over surface. He also has the largest brain and central nervous system in proportion to his size. From this, Sheldon reasons that his physique is made up, more so than the other physiques, of tissues that have derived from the ectodermal embryonic layer. The ectomorph, because of his large proportionate surface area, is overexposed to external stimulation. This is a physique poorly equipped for competitive and persistent physical action.

Intervening between a general definition of the primary components of physique and the final delineation of the somatotype are the details of an objective measurement technique. A suitable measurement procedure was derived from an intricate mixture of judges' ratings or rankings and an elaborate network of physical measurements. Each of the four thousand subjects was ranked and rated in terms of each of the primary components. It was possible to take a great many anthropometric measurements, most of them consisting of diameters of various parts of the body, and determine how effectively these measures differentiated between individuals who were high or low in the judges' rankings for each of the components. Those physical measurements that differentiated accurately between subjects the judges had ranked differently on the three primary components were retained, and all other measurements were rejected. This resulted eventually in the retention of a cluster of seventeen anthropometric measures, all of which were diameters expressed as ratios to the height of the individual. It was soon discovered that these diameters could be measured at least as accurately from photographs as from the body of the subject. Thus, the technique substituted measures derived from standard photographs for the previous practice of taking measurements directly from the subject's body.

At this point a total of four thousand subjects had been ranked by judges in terms of the extent to which each of the primary components was present in their physical make-up. In addition, all subjects had been assigned a score of from one to seven for each of the components. Thus, for every rating or score on each variable there existed a number of concrete illustrations in the form of individuals in the original sample who had been assigned this rating. In addition, for every individual there was a set of physical measurements that had been shown to differentiate between individuals with different ratings on the three components. It was then possible for Sheldon to develop a process whereby, given the seventeen physical measurements, the appropriate ratings on each of the three components could be objectively derived. At one point in the research a collaborator, S. S. Stevens, developed a machine, which, although it required a human operator, reduced the assignment of scores to a relatively simple, though numerous, set of manipulations. Using an operator who was unfamiliar with the somatotyping procedure, except for the instructions necessary to operate the machine, it was possible to demonstrate for one hundred cases a correlation of .94 between the ratings assigned by the machine and those arrived at by the more customary observational technique. Sheldon reports (1954) that, in general, individuals who were accustomed to somatotyping the college group customarily found correlations of .90 or above between their independent somatotype ratings.

The physical measurements not only lead to an over-all score for each of the components; they also provide *ratings for* these components for *five different areas of the body:* head-neck, chest-trunk, arms, stomach-trunk, and legs. A complete description of the process of somatotyping the male body is contained in Sheldon's recent *Atlas of men* (1954) which includes representative somatotype photographs of over one thousand men derived from a total sample of 46,000 such photographs.

Although the development of a machine for computing the somatotype served certain useful demonstrational purposes, Sheldon considers that such an approach to somatotyping is much too slow, mechanical, and inflexible. In practice the procedure most commonly used in arriving at the somatotype begins with tables providing the distribution of known somatotypes for the various ratios derived from dividing the subject's height by the cube root of his weight. These tables are available for five-year age groups from eighteen to sixty-five. Thus, if we know an individual's height, weight, and age it is possible to go to an appropriate table where we will find suggested a small number of somatotypes (usually not more than four or five) as most typical. It is then possible to select the most appropriate somatotype by examining the actual physical measurements or by simple inspection. This process of inspection can be facilitated by the file of photographs that appears in the *Atlas of men* where the pictures are conveniently ordered so that the user can quickly find photographs of any desired somatotype.

The *somatotype* of the individual is the patterning of the primary components of physique as expressed by three numerals derived from the seventeen measures mentioned above, or some equivalent set of operations, viewed against an adequate history of the individual. The first of these numerals always refers to endomorphy, the second to mesomorphy, and the third to ectomorphy. The numerals range from 1 to 7 with 1 representing the absolute minimum of the component and 7 the highest possible amount. Thus, an individual rated 7–1–1 is extremely high in endomorphy and very low in mesomorphy and ectomorphy. An individual rated 4–6–1 is about average in endomorphy and very high in mesomorphy but markedly deficient in ectomorphy.

In actual practice somatotypes are not only classified in terms of the seven-point scales but are also placed in the interval between these ratings. Thus a physique might be classified as a 1–1–7 indicating extreme ectomorphy and a very low rating on endomorphy and mesomorphy, or this physique might be given a somewhat lower rating in ectomorphy and a little higher rating in endomorphy and reported as 1–1–7—2–1–6 indicating that the rating for endomorphy was midway between 1 and 2 and the rating for ectomorphy was midway between 6 and 7. This has the same effect as assigning a rating of 1½ to ectomorphy and 6½ to endomorphy with the result that the ratings are placed on a thirteen-point scale rather than a seven-point scale.

To many readers it seemed that Sheldon implied in his early writing that the somatotype could be adequately derived from a single set of somatotype photographs. More recently, however, he has clearly indicated that information concerning the weight history of the individual and, ideally, a series of photographs separated in time are needed for a more precise measure of the somatotype (Sheldon, 1949, 1954). These recent qualifications seem related to a more explicit treatment of the underlying *morphogenotype*. As we mentioned earlier, the somatotype is viewed as a means of estimating or approximating the basic and unchanging biological determinants of behavior (morphogenotype) through measures in large part based upon the external observable body (phenotype). In Sheldon's words:

> The principal problem of constitutional research, to date, has been to try to throw a preliminary taxonomic illumination on the behavior of the morphogenotype in man. But you cannot deal directly with a morphogenotype. All you can see, or touch, or measure and weigh is a phenotype. The phenotype is the living body as it is presented to sensory perception at a given moment. The phenotype by definition has no fourth dimension, no continuance in time. . . . But to work directly with the genotype is impossible since at present the latter is but a conceptual abstraction. It was necessary therefore to introduce another concept, the somatotype, which is neither phenotype nor genotype but is the reflection of the continuity which apparently exists between these two aspects of organic life. . . . To somatotype is to try to reflect light on the *fixed* end of the continuum by repeatedly recording the *varying* end of it which is presented to the senses in successive examinations of the phenotype (1954, p. 19).

Thus, the somatotype is a compromise between the morphogenotype and the phenotype. It is more than the individual's present physique but it is clearly less than the biologically determined structure of the body independent of environmental influences. Sheldon suggests that if we are seriously interested in getting a best estimate of the underlying morphogenotype we should have, ideally, not only a complete history of the individual but also a record of his ancestors and descendants. Further, the somatotype photographs should be taken at regular intervals throughout the individual's life in addition to as many biological tests as are feasible. The ordinary somatotype does not, of course, approach this ideal; but presumably it does move in this direction and away from a simple static description of the present physique. Consistent with this view is Sheldon's most recent definition of the somatotype:

> The somatotype is by definition a prediction of the future succession of phenotypes which a living person will present, if nutrition remains a constant factor or varies only within normal limits. We define the somatotype more formally as a *trajectory or pathway through which the living organism will travel under standard conditions of nutrition and in the absence of grossly disturbing pathology* (1954, p. 19).

In the four thousand cases that Sheldon first studied he was able to identify 76 distinct somatotype patterns. Although he admitted the probability that additional patterns would be discovered, he did not expect the frequency of these to even approach the 343 that were theoretically possible. His acumen in this particular instance is documented by the fact that after examining over forty thousand male physiques he was able to report a total of only 88 different somatotypes.

Sheldon is clearly aware of the extent to which the somatotype is an abstraction from the full-blown complexity of any concrete physique. The primary components serve to set limits upon a classified physique but within any single somatotype classification there is still room for tremendous variation. This variation is in part intercepted or accounted for by a series of secondary components. Sheldon considers the primary components to anchor the physique and permit an adequate classification, but there remain additional dimensions that will be of interest to the investigator who wishes to describe physiques more fully. It is to these additional components that we turn now.

The secondary components. One of the most important of the secondary components is *dysplasia.* Borrowing the term from Kretschmer, Sheldon uses it to refer to "any inconsistent or uneven mixture of the three primary components in different regions of the body" (1940, p. 68). Thus, it is a measure of disharmony between different areas of the physique, for example, head and neck of one somatotype and legs of another. The measure of dysplasia is arrived at by taking the separate somatotype ratings for the five regions of the body and summing the differences for each of the components among the five areas of the body. In other words, it represents the amount of discrepancy in the somatotype as computed for each of the five areas of the body. One can derive separate dysplasia scores for each of the three components as well as a total score. Preliminary findings indicate that there is more dysplasia associated with the ectomorphic component than with either of the other two components, and also more dysplasia observed in the female physique than in the male physique. Sheldon (1940) also reports that there is more dysplasia among psychotics than among college students.

Another secondary component is called *gynandromorphy*. This represents the extent to which the physique possesses characteristics ordinarily associated with the opposite sex and is referred to as the "g index." The male individual who is high in this component possesses a soft body, broad pelvis, and wide hips as well as other feminine features including long eyelashes and small facial features. The theoretical range on this variable is from 1, no sign of characteristics of the opposite sex, to 7, hermaphroditism. In his study of delinquency Sheldon (1949) distinguishes between primary and secondary gynandromorphism. The primary measure represents the physique as "seen at a distance" or as inferred from the somatotype photograph. The secondary measure is inferred from a physical examination or direct observation of the person and includes physical movement, voice, and facial expression.

Perhaps most important of all the secondary components, and certainly most elusive, is the *textural aspect.* Sheldon indicates his conviction that this component is of great significance and likens the person who is high in this dimension to a purebred animal. He suggests,

> . . . within each somatotype there is a fairly clear gradation from very coarse to very fine physical texture . . . there is a high correlation between the *t*-index and the fineness of the hair of the head . . . coarseness of texture might correlate with the gross size of the individual cells of various parts of the body (1940, pp. 76–77).

In a later publication he suggests that this is simply a measure of "aesthetic pleasingness," and in attempting to answer the question "pleasing to whom?" he suggests:

> High *t* component is structure pleasing to any person of average aesthetic perception or of average appreciation of beauty of form and of proportion. Beyond this simple statement, objectification of the definition of *t* is difficult in the same way, and possibly for the same reason, that the definition of delinquency is difficult. In the final analysis, it is *you* to whom delinquency must be a disappointing performance . . . and to whom high *t* must be pleasing (1949, p. 22).

Sheldon reasons that the *t* component is an evaluation of the "aesthetic success of that particular biological experiment which the individual himself is" (1949, p. 21), and concludes that this kind of evaluation of humans cannot be avoided by a society that wishes to survive, or a social science that intends to deal with the most important of social problems.

There is an important distinction between primary and secondary *t* component which corresponds to the distinction drawn earlier between primary and secondary gynandromorphy. Primary *t* is inferred from the somatotype photograph itself whereas the secondary component is inferred from close and direct contact with the individual. The author provides (Sheldon, 1954) illustrations of somatotypes that have been rated as falling in each of the categories from 1 to 6 for both the textural aspect and gynandromorphy. In neither case has a physique been observed that deserves the highest rating on these variables.

We have not outlined all of the secondary components but those we have described are the most important. They will suffice to illustrate for the reader the manner in which Sheldon is able to supplement and enrich the description of physique provided by the primary components.

Female somatotyping. The bulk of the initial work that was done with Sheldon's physical dimensions was carried out with males. It is evident that in our society the sanctions against studying the naked human body are more stringent in the case of the female than in the case of the male. Consequently, it is quite natural that the initial work in this area should have been executed with male subjects. In his first volume on physique Sheldon (1940) states that the evidence then available indicates that the same seventy-six somatotypes seemed to occur among women as had been observed among men, although probably with different frequencies. He also suggests that endomorphy, and endomorphy combined with ectomorphy, are more common among women; while mesomorphy, and mesomorphy combined with endomorphy, are more common among men.

In a recent publication (1954) the author states that considerable work has been carried out in the area of female somatotyping, and he reports that an "Atlas of Women" will be published in the future. The more extensive findings that he now possesses confirm his earlier observation that female physiques are much more endomorphic than male physiques. He also reports that women show less range on the components than men; nevertheless there are a small number of female somatotypes without parallel in the male series.

Constancy of the somatotype. One of the points where common sense and the generalizations of the constitutional theorist seem to diverge is in regard to the degree to which a classification or description based upon objective measures of the physique can be expected to remain constant. The usual changes introduced by aging and diet variation seem compelling evidence to most people of the changeability of the somatotype. However, Sheldon, in his early writings, along with other constitutional psychologists is equally firm in his conviction that ". . . apparently no nutritional change can cause the measurements of a person of one somatotype to simulate those of another somatotype" (1944, p. 540). It is possible for nutritional factors to produce changes in the individual measurements, but these will not change the actual somatotype. Instead, they will appear as deviations from the normal or original somatotype. This generalization is presented by Sheldon in the face of measurements that have been carried out before and after shifts in weights of as much as one hundred pounds. He summarizes:

> . . . it has been possible to follow the development of several hundred individuals over a period of about a dozen years, and while many have shown sharp fluctuations in weight, we have discovered no case in which there has been a convincing change in the somatotype. In order for the somatotype to change, the skeleton must change, as well as the shape of the head, the bony structure of the face, the neck, wrists, ankles, calves, and forearms, and the relations of stature to measurements made at places where fat does not accumulate. The deposit or removal of fat does not change the somatotype, for it does not change significantly any of the measurements except those where the fat is deposited. . . . It can be said that the case has yet to occur in which a nutritional disturbance has caused a physique either to become unrecognizable or to simulate another somatotype strongly enough to cause any justifiable confusion (1940, p. 221).

Sheldon suggests that just as a starved mastiff does not become a poodle, so a starved mesomorph does not become an ectomorph. Only in certain diseases, such as acromegaly and muscle-wasting diseases, does the actual structure of the body change, and such disorders are readily identifiable through inspection and thus should not lead to unexpected changes in the somatotype. The constancy of the somatotype is so general that Sheldon maintains that even the index of dysplasia does not fluctuate with weight changes.

One type of physique that frequently leads to the belief that there has been a dramatic change in somatotype is the PPJ or Pyknic Practical Joke. Here we have an individual endowed with a rating, say a 4, in the endomorphic component, and a slightly higher mesomorphic component, a 5 let us say. Given such a physique, the individual is likely to appear lean and athletic in late adolescence and early adulthood, but with the passage of years the first component asserts itself, and the joke becomes evident as the person becomes very heavy and round. In spite of the anthropometric change in the physique the somatotype has remained the same. Another factor that makes it difficult to assess accurately the constancy of the somatotype is the much greater skill that is required to measure the somatotype in late adolescence or early adulthood. By the time the individual is thirty his somatotype is vividly revealed, but earlier in life it takes a more skilled observer to detect it, although the signs are nonetheless objectively present.

Some evidence in favor of the hypothesis of constancy is provided by the similarity in the distribution of types of somatotypes found in different age groups. For example, Sheldon (1940) reports that men forty years of age show roughly the same frequencies of the various somatotypes that college students display. It seems probable that if age led to systematic changes in the somatotype these would be reflected in shifts in the frequency with which the various kinds of somatotypes are observed in different age groups.

More recently, Sheldon (1954) seems to have modified, or at least elaborated, his views regarding the constancy of the somatotype. As we have already noted, the most recent definition of somatotype includes a provision of nutritional constancy as well as absence of pathology; furthermore, there has appeared a heavy emphasis upon the importance of an adequate history of the individual focused about his weight during development, especially just before pubescence, for an adequate somatotyping. Thus, the former impression of a somatotype derived from three standard photographs that is impervious to environmental change has been replaced by a more general and explicit conception which recommends that the somatotype be derived from successive photographs in conjunction with a history of the individual and which leaves open the question of the extent to which this somatotype may be modifiable. Sheldon's position on this topic is well summarized by the following quotation:

Is there a degree of dependability (or predictability) in the somatotype as in practice it is actually gauged? That is to say, when we have to depend on only two or three adult phenotype presentations, and a good history, can a predictive somatotype be assigned which will "stay put"? Some would like to answer that question in the categorical affirmative, fearing that any other answer might elicit an unhealthful complacency among "environmental determinists," a few of whom perhaps come near to believing, as they proclaim, that the somatotype is "nothing but nutrition." But only a good longitudinal study, carried on for at least one human lifetime, would adequately document such an answer (1954, p. 20).

THE ANALYSIS OF BEHAVIOR (PERSONALITY)

Given a stable means of assessing the physical aspects of the human build, the constitutional psychologist must still devise or borrow some method of assessing behavior if he is to explore the relation between physique and personality. In the present case, Sheldon began with the assumption that although there were manifold surface dimensions or variables in terms of which behavior could be described, underlying these was a small number of basic components which could be expected to account for all the surface complexity and variety. He set out to devise a technique for measuring these basic components that would borrow from the wisdom of past investigations of personality and combine with this his own clinical knowledge and inductive experience.

DIMENSIONS OF TEMPERAMENT. Initially the literature of personality, especially that having to do with specifying human traits, was carefully inspected, and a list of 650 traits was extracted. This list was increased by adding variables derived from the investigator's own observations and then was sharply reduced through combining overlapping dimensions and eliminating those that seemed of no significance. In the end Sheldon and his co-workers had a total of 50 traits which seemed to them to represent all of the specific phenomena that had been dealt with by the original 650 traits.

The next step was to select a group of thirty-three young men, for the most part graduate students and instructors, who were studied for one year through the medium of observation in their everyday professional activities and in clinical interviews. Each subject was rated by the investigator on a seven-point scale for each of the fifty traits, and the resultant scores were intercorrelated with the intent of discovering clusters of positively correlated traits that could be considered to represent the same underlying variable. It was decided arbitrarily that in order for a trait to be included within a cluster or component it must show a positive correlation of at least .60 with each of the other traits in the cluster and show a negative correlation of at least − .30 with all traits found in other clusters.

PRIMARY COMPONENTS OF TEMPERAMENT. The results of the correlational analysis revealed three major clusters or groups of traits which included twenty-two of the original fifty items. The first group included traits of relaxation, love of comfort, pleasure in digestion, dependence on social approval, deep sleep, need of people when troubled. The traits spanned by the second cluster included assertive posture, energetic characteristic, need of exercise, directness of manner, unrestrained voice, quality of seeming older, need of action when troubled. Finally, there was a third group of traits, including restraint in posture, overly fast reaction, sociophobia, inhibited social address, resistance to habit, vocal restraint, poor sleep habits, youthful intentness, need of solitude when troubled.

At this stage Sheldon was satisfied that at least tentatively he had identified components of behavior sufficiently basic to warrant further study. He set about improving and enlarging the lists of traits for each component in order to devise a sensitive and reliable measure for the three components. He attempted to add traits that reflected the constitution of the individual and thus were not highly variable in the face of environmental or cultural variation. A series of eight trial studies of various combinations of the old and new traits was completed before the investigator arrived at the last stage. A final intercorrelation study with one hundred subjects, using seventy-eight traits, resulted in the selection of twenty traits for each of the three clusters (a total of sixty traits), all of which met the criteria of correlating at least .60 with all other traits in the same cluster and showing a negative correlation of at least −.30 with all traits in other clusters. The traits that were finally selected are summarized in Table 2.

The first component of temperament was named *viscerotonia*. An individual high in this component is characterized by general love of comfort, sociability, and gluttony for food, people, and affection. He is relaxed in posture, reacts slowly, is even-tempered, tolerant in his relations to others, and is generally an easy person to interact with. Sheldon suggests: "The personality seems to center around the viscera. The digestive tract is king, and its welfare appears to define the primary purpose of life" (1944, p. 543).

The second component was called *somatotonia*. A high score on this component is ordinarily accompanied by love of physical adventure, risk-taking, and a strong need for muscular and vigorous physical activity. The individual is aggressive, callous toward the feelings of others, overmature in appearance, noisy, courageous, and given to claustrophobia. Action, power, and domination are of first importance to such an individual.

TABLE 2

THE SCALE FOR TEMPERAMENT

Viscerotonia	Somatotonia	Cerebrotonia
( ) 1. Relaxation in posture and movement	( ) 1. Assertiveness of posture and movement	( ) 1. Restraint in posture and movement, tightness
( ) 2. Love of physical comfort	( ) 2. Love of physical adventure	2. Physiological overresponse
( ) 3. Slow reaction	( ) 3. The energetic characteristic	( ) 3. Overly fast reactions
4. Love of eating	( ) 4. Need and enjoyment of exercise	( ) 4. Love of privacy
5. Socialization of eating	5. Love of dominating. Lust for power	( ) 5. Mental overintensity. Hyperattentionality. Apprehensiveness
6. Pleasure in digestion	( ) 6. Love of risk and chance	( ) 6. Secretiveness of feeling, emotional restraint
( ) 7. Love of polite ceremony	( ) 7. Bold directness of manner	( ) 7. Self-conscious mobility of the eyes and face
( ) 8. Sociophilia	( ) 8. Physical courage for combat	( ) 8. Sociophobia
9. Indiscriminate amiability	( ) 9. Competitive aggressiveness	( ) 9. Inhibited social address
10. Greed for affection and approval	10. Psychological callousness	10. Resistance to habit and poor routinizing
11. Orientation to people	11. Claustrophobia	11. Agoraphobia
( ) 12. Evenness of emotional flow	12. Ruthlessness, freedom from squeamishness	12. Unpredictability of attitude
( ) 13. Tolerance	( ) 13. The unrestrained voice	( ) 13. Vocal restraint and general restraint of noise
( ) 14. Complacency	14. Spartan indifference to pain	14. Hypersensitivity to pain
15. Deep sleep	15. General noisiness	15. Poor sleep habits, chronic fatigue
( ) 16. The untempered characteristic	( ) 16. Overmaturity of appearance	( ) 16. Youthful intentness of manner and appearance
( ) 17. Smooth, easy communication of feeling, extraversion of viscerotonia	17. Horizontal mental cleavage, extraversion of somatotonia	17. Vertical mental cleavage, introversion
18. Relaxation and sociophilia under alcohol	18. Assertiveness and aggression under alcohol	18. Resistance to alcohol and to other depressant drugs
19. Need of people when troubled	19. Need of action when troubled	19. Need of solitude when troubled
20. Orientation toward childhood and family relationships	20. Orientation toward goals and activities of youth	20. Orientation toward the later periods of life

Note: The thirty traits with parentheses constitute collectively the short form of the scale.

(From Sheldon, 1942, p. 26.)

The third component was labeled *cerebrotonia*. An elevated score on this component implies restraint, inhibition, and the desire for concealment. This individual is secretive, self-conscious, youthful in appearance, afraid of people, and happiest in small enclosed areas. He reacts overquickly, sleeps poorly, and prefers solitude, particularly when troubled. Such an individual consistently attempts to avoid attracting attention to himself.

The three general dimensions, together with the twenty defining traits for each dimension, make up the *Scale for Temperament* which is an elaborate rating procedure for arriving at scores for each of the primary components. Sheldon recommends in using the Scale that where possible:

> Observe the subject closely for at least a year in as many different situations as possible. Conduct a series of not less than twenty analytic interviews with him in a manner best suited to the situation, and to the temperaments and interests of the two principals. . . . After each interview . . . turn to the score sheet and assign a rating on as many of the traits as possible. . . . Repeat the observations, interviews, and revisions of ratings until reasonably satisfied that all of the sixty traits have been adequately considered and evaluated (1942, p. 27).

Thus, after a long period of observation the investigator assigns ratings of from 1 to 7 for sixty specific traits each of which Sheldon defines in detail. The total score for the twenty traits within each component is then computed by adding the individual ratings, and this is converted to an over-all rating for each variable by consulting a table (Sheldon, 1942, p. 95) or averaging the ratings. For a particularly careful analysis it is possible to assign half scores, thus expanding the seven-point range to a thirteen-point range.

There are also secondary components for describing behavior although these are not so numerous or so carefully worked out as those for the assessment of physique. For this reason we shall omit their description here. The interested reader will find the most complete account of these components in Sheldon (1949).

THE RELATION OF PHYSIQUE TO BEHAVIOR (PERSONALITY)

We have now seen how Sheldon identified what he considered to be the basic components of physique (structure) and temperament (function), and we have also observed how he devised instruments to measure these components. It remains to survey his attempts to relate these two classes of variables.

In one sense we might consider the earlier studies simply preliminary steps to the more significant goal of estimating the degree of relationship between physique and temperament. In another sense, it is obvious that the measures of somatotype and temperament possess an independent value not derived from the outcome of the study to be reported here. An adequate means of measuring physique is of value to many investigators who may have no interest in constitutional psychology as such; for example, physical anthropologists, applied psychologists, physiologists, pathologists. Similarly, a set of objective and sensitive measures of important dimensions of behavior would be a boon to almost all psychologists, whether or not they are interested in the relation between physique and behavior.

Most of Sheldon's research revolves around the question of how much association exists between physique and personality. However, we shall limit ourselves for the present to the description of a single representative study that related physique and temperament among normal college students. We shall discuss briefly, in a later section of the chapter, studies bearing on delinquency and mental disorder.

Over a period of five years Sheldon (1942) carried out a study of two hundred male, white subjects who were college students or college graduates involved in academic or professional activities. These subjects were rated on the temperament dimensions, as defined in the Scale of Temperament, after a long period of observation. Following this the subjects were somatotyped according to the procedure already described.

The most significant findings in this study concerned the degree of association between the temperament variables and the physique variables as estimated by a correlation technique. The results in Table 3 indicate very clearly that the correlation between the parallel physique and temperament dimensions is significant and surprisingly high, while the correlation between all other combinations of the physique

TABLE 3

CORRELATION BETWEEN PHYSIQUE COMPONENTS
AND TEMPERAMENT COMPONENTS

Somatotype	Viscerotonia r (n = 200)	Somatotonia r (n = 200)	Cerebrotonia r (n = 200)
Endomorphy	+.79	−.29	−.32
Mesomorphy	−.23	+.82	−.58
Ectomorphy	−.40	−.53	+.83

(Adopted from Sheldon, 1942, p. 400.)

and temperament variables is significantly negative. These results are unambiguous in suggesting that *there is a close correspondence between temperament as measured by observer ratings and physique as derived from measures taken from somatotype photographs.* Sheldon suggests:

> These are higher correlations than we expected to find, and they raise some questions of great interest. If we were to regard the product-moment correlation as a measure of the degree to which two variables are made up of common elements, correlations of the order of +.80 would suggest that morphology and temperament, as we measure them, may constitute expressions at their respective levels of essentially common components. . . . If we *have* already reached basic factors in personality, the correlations are not higher than should be expected, for then with the two techniques we are but measuring the same thing at different levels of its expression (1942, p. 401).

Sheldon concludes that if these measures, on further study, prove to have the basic status that he hopes for, they will provide a frame of reference in terms of which psychology can contribute to the study of individual differences in all areas of behavior. Such a possibility would facilitate the interpenetration of psychology with both biology and the social sciences.

We find, then, that Sheldon's research has led to a surprisingly strong confirmation of the constitutional psychologists' expectation that there is a marked continuity between the structural or physical aspects of the individual and his functional or behavioral qualities. In fact, the magnitude of the correlations observed between the physique and temperament components is sufficient to dwarf the correlations reported in similar studies attempting to relate personality and environmental or experiential determinants. Let us turn now to the interpretation of this relationship.

SOME THEORETICAL FORMULATIONS

It is important to realize that constitutional theory is more inductive and less of a theory than many other brands of psychological theory. Much more central to the position than a set of axioms are the primary components which have been described and the empirically derived relations among them. Sheldon himself seems to be essentially a naturalist with a taxonomic bent. Thus, he is at his best in making shrewd observations concerning regularities in behavior and in trying to group together or classify individuals who are similar in some important respect. He has shown little interest in formaliz ing or systematizing his viewpoint and this may well be a self-conscious choice as the following quotation seems to imply:

> If we seem to overemphasize the constitutional factor throughout this book by largely omitting the factor of environmental influence, it does not mean that we consider the latter unimportant. It means only that we are presenting here the neglected side of the picture, without which a general psychology seems fatuous or anomalous. The problem of synthesis lies on beyond. In these two volumes [1940, 1942] . . . we have attempted to do no more than write in the foundation for the constitutional side of this structure as a whole. That, in itself, has been sufficiently difficult.
>
> Constitutional psychology we regard as only a contribution to general psychology, not a substitute. Its place in the total scheme is possibly comparable to the description of the skeleton in anatomy. If such a point of view does not seem to have been maintained dispassionately in all of the sections of the present book, let the shortcoming be charged (in the reader's generosity) to counteremphasis (Sheldon, 1942, p. 438).

FACTORS MEDIATING THE PHYSIQUE-TEMPERAMENT ASSOCIATION. We accept here the existence of a marked relation between measures of physique and measures of important behavioral attributes, and inquire into what has led to this striking congruence. One may reason that an individual who is endowed with a particular type of physique is likely to find certain kinds of responses particularly effective while an individual with another type of physique will find it necessary to adopt other modes of response. This conception suggests that *the success or reward that accompanies a particular mode of responding is a function not only of the environment in which it occurs but also of the kind of person (type of physique) making the response*. The individual with a frail ectomorphic body cannot successfully adopt a bluff, aggressive, domineering manner in relation to most people, whereas it may be perfectly possible for the oversized mesomorph to do so. Further, the child with a small stomach, or low thresholds for pain, may be exposed to characteristic experiences that are strikingly different from those typical for individuals of different physical characteristics. Given a particular physique and a normal environment, the individual finds certain kinds of responses are relatively often rewarded and certain other kinds of responses are usually punished. This implies that the individual will develop patterns of behavior which will show similarity to the behavior of other people, who because of sharing the same kind of physiques have had similar sets of experiences.

Another possibility is that *the relation between physique and tem-*

perament is mediated by commonly accepted stereotypes existing within the culture in regard to the sort of behavior to be expected of individuals with different kinds of physique. Thus, we may suggest that the individual with a particular physique occupies a social role which includes a set of behavioral specifications and in the normal course of events the individual will conform to these specifications. Such expectations on the part of the culture will lead the individual with a distinctive physique to show distinctive patterns of behavior and this behavior will tend to be shared by other individuals with the same type of physique who have been exposed to similar expectations. This formulation does not account for the origin of the stereotype, nor does it have much to say concerning the individual whose physique is in the mid-range and fits no convenient stereotype.

Still another means of explaining the observed relation is in terms of experiences or _environmental influences that tend to produce particular kinds of physique and at the same time produce certain behavioral tendencies._ Thus, we might reason that exposure of the child to an overprotective mother would predispose the child to obesity and at the same time would produce identifiable personality characteristics. Likewise, it could be suggested that active participation in athletics would have a pronounced influence upon the physique and, at the same time, would expose the individual to unique group-membership influences which would tend to produce distinctive personality manifestations. This formulation avoids the notion of biological determinism and suggests that both physique and behavior are largely determined by environmental influences.

A final alternative is to account for the relation between body build and behavior in terms of _the joint operation of genetic factors._ Thus, one may argue that both physique and behavioral tendencies are largely determined by hereditary factors and among these hereditary factors there are certain associative links so that particular kinds of physical characteristics are tied to particular behavioral attributes. Just as there are sex-linked characteristics, so too there are body-linked characteristics. The individual who possesses particular physical characteristics may be expected to display certain behavioral tendencies because of _gene linkage._

It is primarily the first two modes of explanation, selective experience and cultural determination, which Sheldon appears to emphasize although he is also willing to acknowledge the operation of genetic determination. The third formulation, implying that both physique and behavior are the outcome of environmental factors, is least compatible with the assumptions of constitutional psychologists, Sheldon included.

BIOLOGICAL AND GENETIC ORIENTATION. Many personality theorists have chosen to place a heavy emphasis upon the psychobiological nature of human behavior (Murray, Murphy, Freud); however, few have shown much willingness to adapt their procedural methods to this assumption. In many respects the details of Sheldon's position may be considered to stem from a conviction that biological factors are of overwhelming importance in accounting for human behavior and his consequent decision to attempt the measurement of important elements of this biological foundation of behavior. As we have seen from his distinction between the somatotype and the morphogenotype, the measurement of physique is merely a means of estimating the underlying biological factors that have such a heavy influence upon the course of life. All things considered, it seems safe to say that Sheldon's position revolves more closely about biological determinants of behavior than does that of any other contemporary personality theorist.

Although our discussion of the possible factors mediating the association between physique and behavior made clear that Sheldon does not overemphasize the potential role of genetic factors in the determination of behavior, nevertheless he is hopeful that somatotype measurement may permit a more accurate measurement of some genetic factors and thus enable us to estimate realistically the indirect effect of genetic factors upon behavior.

ORGANISMIC AND FIELD EMPHASIS. Sheldon seems consistently concerned with the problem of context and, as one would expect of a devoted naturalist, he is reluctant to examine any one aspect of behavior to the exclusion of all (or most) other aspects. In general, his concern over considering all aspects of the total organism is much greater than his concern over the environmental context within which behavior occurs. Such a position stems quite naturally from his great interest in biological determinants of behavior.

Although Sheldon succeeded in isolating and measuring dimensions for describing physique and temperament, he does not believe that it is fruitful to examine these dimensions one by one. The *pattern* of relations between the variables is much more important than the absolute level of any single component. He is constantly aware of the essential uniqueness of each individual in both behavior and physical appearance. In spite of his willingness to fracture this unique totality with his component measurements, he still considers the outcome of such measurement only a first step toward describing the organism. It is his conviction that the sensitive, globally oriented observer is capable of contributing knowledge that the skillful and objective psychometrist cannot yet hope to unearth. A fundamental concern over the dangers of premature quantification and too heavy an emphasis upon objectivity run through all of Sheldon's writings.

DEVELOPMENT OF THE INDIVIDUAL. In view of what has been said concerning Sheldon's interest in biological determinants of behavior, it should come as no surprise to discover that Sheldon has shown somewhat less concern over the details of development than most other personality theorists. While he freely admits that early childhood events of a particular kind may presage certain types of adult adjustment, he is not convinced that the childhood event plays a causative role in such relationships. It is quite likely, he suggests, that there may be biological predispositions that lead to particular kinds of childhood or infantile experience, and further that these same predispositions may lead to specifiable forms of adult behavior. In other words, the apparent relation between early events and subsequent behavior may be largely a reflection of the consistent operation of biological factors over a long period of time.

Sheldon is interested in the developmental process, at least to the extent of expressing his conviction that it could be made much more efficient and less frustrating for the participants if those who were guiding the child would take the trouble to consider the child's somatotype. In this manner one could avoid instilling in the child aspirations and expectations inconsistent with his physical and temperamental potential. This view makes it clear that Sheldon does not consider the development of the individual to be completely fixed by his biological inheritance as represented in the morphogenotype. Rather, he sees the person as endowed with potentials that set limits upon and mold the possibilities for future growth. However, the particular experiences to which the person is exposed will have a crucial role in determining whether he eventually realizes the full extent of these potentials.

UNCONSCIOUS PROCESSES. The importance of unconscious determinants of behavior is accepted by Sheldon but he is inclined to equate these determinants to underlying biological factors. Presumably if the individual knew more about the structure of his body and the biological factors at work within it, he would be more conscious of the forces that impel his behavior. Sheldon (1949) suggests that the unconscious *is* the body and implies further that the reason there is so much difficulty in verbalizing the unconscious is simply because our language is not geared to systematically reflecting what goes on in the body. Thus, he considers that the psychoanalyst who is exploring the unconscious is approaching obliquely, and in a rather inefficient manner, the same thing that Sheldon attempts to reach more directly and objectively through his somatotyping.

CHARACTERISTIC RESEARCH AND RESEARCH METHODS

More than most personality theorists Sheldon's formulations are embedded in empirical studies. We have already gained a rather representative view of his investigations in the process of noting how he set about the formulation and measurement of physique and temperament. In the present section we shall deal briefly with two further studies in which he investigated mental disorder and delinquency against the background offered by somatotype measurement.

PHYSIQUE AND MENTAL DISORDER. Constitutional psychology not only gives promise of providing new vistas of understanding in the study of normal human behavior; it also offers the possibility of understanding better, and perhaps alleviating or preventing, various psychological and social abnormalities. Consistent with this conviction are Sheldon's studies of mental disorder which are reported in one brief paper (Wittman, Sheldon, and Katz, 1948) and in a chapter contained in his volume dealing with delinquency (Sheldon, 1949). After examining the state of psychiatric diagnosis he concluded that it would not be possible to approach the study of physique in relation to mental disorder without first providing a measure of mental disorder that was more objective and sensitive than the customary diagnostic techniques.

In the same manner that Sheldon had introduced continuous variables in place of discrete categories in the measurement of physique, so too in the measurement of mental disorder he proposed to substitute dimensions in place of disease entities. On the basis of observation of many psychiatric patients over a number of years he developed a conception of mental disorder as subject to description in terms of three primary dimensions. These three dimensions correspond roughly to three of the diagnostic categories frequently used in psychiatric diagnosis: the first psychiatric component (affective) at its height represents extreme manic-depressive psychosis (fluctuation between extreme elation and depression); the second psychiatric component (paranoid) at its height represents paranoid psychosis (strong delusional system marked by ideas of persecution and self-reference); and the third psychiatric component (heboid) represents the hebephrenic form of schizophrenic psychosis (extreme withdrawal). The three psychiatric components represent respectively a deficiency in the temperament components of cerebrotonia, viscerotonia, and somatotonia.

Sheldon frankly admits that his work in this area is still in a highly tentative state but promises that a future volume will give a full report of his research on this problem and describe a measurement technique and findings that are more definitive than those presently available. He has reported one study that is suggestive of the value of this approach to mental disorder. The research was conducted at the Elgin State Hospital in Illinois in collaboration with Phyllis Wittman (Wittman, Sheldon, and Katz, 1948; Sheldon, 1949). Wittman collected a large amount of descriptive material from the psychiatric files in this hospital, and after refining and pruning the material arrived at a list of 221 behavioral items that appeared to be important in the psychiatric description of patients. She then classified these items in terms of the three psychiatric components mentioned above and called the resulting list of items the *Check List of Psychotic Behavior.* A group of 155 male psychotic patients were then selected and were independently somatotyped by Sheldon and rated on the items on the check list by Wittman and a staff psychiatrist, neither of whom actually saw the patients. Average scores for the three psychiatric variables were derived from the check list for each of the raters and intercorrelated. These rater reliability correlations ranged from +.78 to +.91 indicating that the ratings were being made with reasonable objectivity. Wittman's ratings for the psychiatric components were then correlated with Sheldon's independent ratings for the physique components with the results summarized in Table 4.

TABLE 4

CORRELATIONS BETWEEN SOMATOTYPE AND PSYCHIATRIC COMPONENTS ($n = 155$)

	1st Psychiatric Component (Affective)	2nd Psychiatric Component (Paranoid)	3rd Psychiatric Component (Heboid)
Endomorphy	+.54	−.04	−.25
Mesomorphy	+.41	+.57	−.68
Ectomorphy	−.59	−.34	+.64

(From Sheldon, 1949, p. 69.)

Sheldon's exploratory work had led him to expect that there would be only moderate intercorrelations between the two sets of variables and this, of course, is what he observed. In general, the results confirm the expected relations although out of the nine correlations three reversed the direction that he would have predicted in advance of the study. The correlation between the first, second, and third components of the somatotype and the corresponding psychiatric components are, however, all positive and moderately high. These findings appear to imply that psychiatric diagnosis and somatotype are definitely associated, although the nature of this relationship seems somewhat more complex than that observed between physique and temperament.

Sheldon suggests that the components he devised for representing psychotic behavior have their parallels in less severe forms of maladjustment and may even be reflected in an obverse or superior form of adjustment. Thus, he discusses in a hypothetical vein the manner in which various kinds of exceptional achievement can be considered to represent unusually rich development of the potentialities implied by the various patterns of the psychiatric components. The psychiatric components are seen as a supplement to the somatotype and temperament ratings and serve to increase somewhat the spectrum of behavior that these components can adequately represent. Sheldon believes that eventually customary methods of psychiatric diagnosis may give way to a method of description and classification that leans more heavily upon objective techniques including the *Somatotype Performance Test*. This will imply a close linkage with biological determinants of behavior.

PHYSIQUE AND DELINQUENCY. Sheldon's eight-year study of delinquent youth was conducted to provide a kind of background against which to compare his findings from the study of normal college youth. The investigation was carried out at the Hayden Goodwill Inn, a resident rehabilitation home for boys in Boston, Massachusetts. During the three years from 1939 to 1942 approximately four hundred young men were studied by Sheldon and his collaborators and, from this sample, two hundred were selected for a follow-up study after the war on the basis of completeness of information and clear evidence of delinquency. All of the subjects were examined by means of the Somatotype Performance Test and assigned somatotype ratings as well as ratings on the secondary components of physique. They were also rated in terms of the psychiatric components and in addition detailed life histories were compiled which included information about their mental and educational performance, family background, medical history, delinquent behavior, and characteristic behavior.

The core of Sheldon's report of this research is a series of what he calls psychological biographies, which represent thumbnail sketches of the life history of the individual, together with somatotype photographs. These biographies are arranged in terms of a classification that divides the young men into groups according to mental deficiency, psychopathy, alcoholism, excessive femininity, and degree of criminality. In addition to these classified biographical sketches, which leave the task of generalizing largely upon the shoulders of the reader, Sheldon presents diagrams of the distribution of somatotypes for his delinquent population in comparison to the group of college students. It is clear that while the college students show a clustering around the mid-range somatotypes (4–4–4) with a scatter fairly evenly divided over the remainder of the diagram, the delinquents are heavily bunched in the "northwest region"—they tend to be endomorphic mesomorphs. There is obviously a much greater elevation of mesomorphy in the delinquent group and a marked absence of individuals high on the ectomorphic component. Sheldon also presents similar diagrams for each of the subgroups into which the delinquents had been divided. These plots suggest that although the characteristic delinquent physique is endomorphic mesomorphy, there is considerable variation among the delinquent subgroups in somatotype. The various subgroups of delinquents are also compared in terms of the secondary components, the psychiatric components, and a variety of demographic and life history data.

Sheldon at the culmination of his study appears convinced that there are important behaviorial and constitutional differences not only between delinquents and normals but also between the subvarieties of delinquents. Further, he speculates concerning the possible role of asthenia (weakness), dysplasia (uneven distribution of somatotype), and burgeoning (gross and nonfunctional enlargement of the physique) as biological determinants characteristic not only of delinquents but also of their parents. This observation leads him to relatively pessimistic conclusions concerning what is happening to the biological stock of this nation as a result of selective differences in reproductive rates favoring social and economic groups that typically display asthenia, dysplasia, and burgeoning.

As we have mentioned earlier, Sheldon is now working in a medical setting and is actively concerned with the relation between constitutional factors and organic disease. He has reported very briefly

(1949) on some preliminary findings concerning such disorders as cancer, gall bladder disease, and duodenal ulcer, and has also indicated some of the procedural problems encountered in studies of this sort. However, the bulk of these findings is to be reported in a book on constitutional medicine planned for the future.

CURRENT STATUS AND EVALUATION

Few psychologists have shown the singleness of purpose and the dedication that Sheldon has displayed in pursuing empirical paths all of which lead from a core idea. He has now published a consistent and integrated set of four volumes with several more related volumes in preparation. Thus, Sheldon himself has already shown remarkable energy and persistence in his attempts to arrive at a means of representing biological factors through the description of physique. The remainder of his career will undoubtedly be devoted to extending and clarifying the formulations and findings we have already discussed. More significantly, his research has produced a host of related investigations on the part of interested or indignant psychologists, psychiatrists, and anthropologists. The reader will find references to a representative group of these studies at the end of this chapter. Although few of these investigators have been much concerned with the theoretical formulations that could or should accompany these findings, they have nevertheless made valuable empirical contributions.

In any attempt to appraise the over-all significance of Sheldon's work it is necessary to consider it in the context of existing psychological theories. As we have already suggested, American psychology has been singularly insular in regard to the contribution of biological or hereditary factors as determinants of behavior. Even though some personality theorists have chosen to dwell upon these factors, they have, in general, shown little inclination to implement their theoretical assertions with procedural techniques for assessing the crucial biological factors. Thus we may largely credit Sheldon with reminding psychologists that the behaving human has a physique, and further that this physique provides valuable cues to an underlying set of determinants, which in the end may prove quite as coercive and pervasive as environmental factors.

Aside from the matter of general emphasis upon biological factors and the role of heredity, there is the further fact that Sheldon seems to have isolated and demonstrated a set of empirical relations that are important data for any theory of personality. One may quarrel over the degree of relation between physique and personality, or even over the factors that mediate this relation, but present evidence leaves little doubt, at least in the authors' minds, that something important is afoot here. Prior to Sheldon's forceful appearance on the scene, such a relationship was customarily dismissed in this country as representing little more than superstition or speculation.

In addition to contributions that are directly in the domain of personality theory, it is clear that Sheldon's somatotyping procedure exists as an important contribution to the person who would study the human organism. It not only serves as an admirable link between the anatomical, potentially biological, and the behavioral; it also provides a measuring technique for the individual who is solely interested in the structure of the human body. The human engineer, the physical anthropologist, and others who are not psychologists may derive from this technique unique assistance in their problems.

It is clear that the substitution of continua for dichotomies, or variables for categories, represents an important measurement advance. For the individual interested in measuring physique, things are likely to go more smoothly when he can provide values for a number of components rather than force an individual into one of three, four, or five categories. Likewise Sheldon's development of the dysplastic index as a quantified measure of somatotype discrepancy between the different areas of the body represents an advance over the "wastebasket status" it enjoyed in the system of Kretschmer. In this same area, his development of the photographic technique made it possible to introduce a degree of precision and control that could never have been hoped for when measurements were derived directly from the human body.

The positive contributions of Sheldon's work are evident and can be stated simply. Likewise the negative. Perhaps the most frequent criticism leveled at Sheldon's constitutional theory is that it is no theory at all. Indeed, if we adopt even very minimal standards of formal adequacy it is evident that this implication is completely justifiable. Yet we have already found that personality theories are in general a somewhat inchoate bunch, and it is a unique personality theorist who can raise the criticism of formal adequacy without baring a vulnerable flank. Granted the general state of personality theory, is not constitutional theory still a poor relative in terms of formal criteria? Yes! It is almost impossible to deduce propositions from the theory; in fact, as we have already discovered, the theory consists largely of one general assumption (the continuity between structure and behavior) and a set of descriptive concepts for scaling physique and behavior. In fairness to Sheldon we must remember that he has occasionally indicated that his position is not to be considered an attempt at a general theory but rather it is intended to account for a limited range of variables and perhaps to offset certain biases that are generally operative among individuals studying human behavior. Thus, he has suggested that it is the task of a more general theory to embrace the variables and findings of his work. It is hard to argue with this point of view although one may regret that such an attitude is not more consistently present in Sheldon's writings.

A further criticism that psychologists level against Sheldon's work has to do with the procedural flaws inherent in his investigation. Many aspects of his work are open to such attack, but these criticisms have usually focused about the inordinately high correlations he has reported between physique and temperament variables. Although Sheldon considers at great length the problem of rater bias and contamination of data (1942, pp. 411–425), no amount of discussion will eliminate the fact that in his study of temperament the same individual (Sheldon) made the somatotype and temperament ratings. More important, Sheldon, with his experience in this area, could undoubtedly classify the individual quite accurately in terms of somatotype while making the temperament ratings. Thus the magnitude of his correlations may reflect the strength of the investigator's preconceptions rather than an actual association between physique and temperament. In defending himself against this criticism, Sheldon has pointed out that his temperament ratings were made prior to his physique ratings. As we know that the physique ratings are highly objective, this reduces somewhat the likelihood of one set of ratings having been contaminated by the other, although the possibility remains of implicit physique ratings having influenced the temperament ratings. Further, he insists that it is ridiculous to ask an individual to perform temperament ratings without having seen the person he is rating. The very nature of the temperament ratings demands that the observer have a deep and intimate knowledge of the person being rated, and if he cannot observe this person how can he make sensitive ratings? In Sheldon's view, his critics insist that in order to avoid the possibility of bias he must introduce sufficient ignorance to destroy the likelihood of unearthing significant findings. It is clear that there is something to be said for both sides of this argument and it is also evident that there is little chance of Sheldon and his psychologist critics reaching agreement on this issue.

This criticism leads directly to a further objection to the temperament study. Correlations of the magnitude reported by Sheldon are simply not consistent with all that is known and generally assumed about human behavior. The measurement error inevitable in the type of instrument he used to assess temperament, and the complexity of the factors that *must* have some role in determining behavioral phenomena, combine to make it seem unlikely to most psychologists that behavior and physique should be so closely linked as these findings seem to imply. In replying to this assertion, Sheldon points out that he conceives of behavior as falling on a continuum ranging from those aspects that are most clearly determined by environmental or experiential events to those aspects that are most closely related to the biology and structure of the individual. In his study he deliberately selected aspects of behavior that seemed to him close to the constitutional or biological and therefore it should come as no surprise that there was a close relationship between his behavioral and structural measures. Naturally the magnitude of this relationship might depreciate if other aspects of behavior were related to physique. Sheldon's point is well taken, but it still leaves him open to criticism for having failed to make this sufficiently clear in his publications and thus having omitted certain important limits that should be placed upon the generality of his findings.

Frequently critics have insisted that the somatotype is not invariant in the face of nutritional or other environmental changes and there is some evidence to support this contention (Lasker, 1947; Newman, 1952). As we have seen, Sheldon's recent distinction between the somatotype and the phenotype, and his insistence upon the necessity of successive measures and nutritional constancy to permit adequate diagnosis of the somatotype, take much of the sting from such criticisms. Nevertheless, by giving up the invariance of his physique classification Sheldon detracts somewhat from its potential utility.

Psychologists who value quantitative methods highly look upon the results of several factor analytic studies of physique (Eysenck, 1947; Howells, 1952; Thurstone, 1946), which have produced factors different than Sheldon's primary components, as raising serious questions concerning his findings. Actually, these studies have generally used as their basic data physique measures that differ in important respects from those employed by Sheldon, making comparison of these findings very difficult. Further, there is sufficient disagreement concerning factor analysis as an empirical tool (see Chapter 10) to make it unwise to decide the status of Sheldon's work on this ground alone.

Many observers feel that in spite of appearing to follow an inductive path in developing his concepts and measures, Sheldon shows heavy evidence of having been influenced by preconceptions. Thus, his physique variables show a surprising correspondence to those characteristically employed by his predecessors and, more important, it is a genuinely remarkable coincidence that his temperament variables should turn out to mirror these physique variables so exactly. These critics feel that bias in the observer accounts for this correspondence rather than the natural state of things. They suggest further that some of his temperament ratings come dangerously close to the physique in the aspect of behavior to which they refer. We have already seen that Sheldon accepts this close parallel between physique and temperament ratings in his explanation of why the relation between these measures should be so high.

What has been the outcome of the empirical research stimulated by Sheldon's work? Have the numerous studies provided results which, in general, confirm or disagree with Sheldon's reported results? A careful summary and appraisal of these investigations would take more space than we can afford, particularly since most investigators have introduced sufficient variation in their procedures so that it is difficult to make a simple comparision with Sheldon's research. Thus, all we can hope to present here is a global impression. We believe that if the reader will examine carefully the numerous studies cited at the end of this chapter he will come away convinced that Sheldon is eminently correct in his assertion that there is a highly significant association between physique and personality. However, it will also be apparent that virtually none of these investigators has found an association between physique and personality which approaches the magnitude reported by Sheldon. Even accepting the fact that the lower correlations reported by almost all other investigators may be partly due to less sensitive measurement techniques, the difference between these findings and Sheldon's is so large as to suggest that "truth" lies in a moderate position. Thus, our belief is that an over-all appraisal of the many studies conducted since Sheldon began his work will lead the reader to accept the existence of a significant and interesting relation between physique and personality, but will leave him unconvinced that the relation is so close as Sheldon seems to imply.

In any final evaluation of Sheldon's theory it is important to consider the wealth of empirical studies that have been conducted by Sheldon and stimulated by his writings. Ultimately the value of a theory can best be measured by its empirical impact and who can deny that Sheldon's findings and formulations have provoked dozens or perhaps hundreds of related studies. Although few if any of these studies represent attempts to test derivations from a set of postulates, this is indeed a pallid criterion compared to the more vigorous query of how many such studies provide findings of ultimate significance. On the latter score it seems safe to say that Sheldon's work is of assured interest to posterity, for whatever its shortcomings may be it has led to findings that the future will have to reckon with.

BIBLIOGRAPHY

PRIMARY SOURCES

Sheldon, W. H. (with the collaboration of S. S. Stevens and W. B. Tucker). *The varieties of human physique: an introduction to constitutional psychology.* New York: Harper, 1940.

Sheldon, W. H. (with the collaboration of S. S. Stevens). *The varieties of temperament: a psychology of constitutional differences.* New York: Harper, 1942.

Sheldon, W. H. (with the collaboration of E. M. Hartl and E. McDermott). *Varieties of delinquent youth: an introduction to constitutional psychiatry.* New York: Harper, 1949.

Sheldon, W. H. (with the collaboration of C. W. Dupertuis and E. McDermott). *Atlas of men: a guide for somatotyping the adult male at all ages.* New York: Harper, 1954.

REFERENCES

Allport, G. W. *Personality: a psychological interpretation.* New York: Holt, 1937.

Child, I. L. The relation of somatotype to self-rating on Sheldon's temperamental traits. *J. Pers.,* 1950, *18,* 440–453.

Child, I. L., and Sheldon, W. H. The correlation between components of physique and scores on certain psychological tests. *Character & Pers.,* 1941, *10,* 23–34.

Coffin, T. E. A three-component theory of leadership. *J. abnorm. soc. Psychol.,* 1944, *39,* 63–83.

Eysenck, H. J. *Dimensions of Personality.* London: Routledge & Kegan Paul, 1947.

Fiske, D. W. A study of relationships to somatotype. *J. appl. Psychol.,* 1944, *28,* 504–519.

Gall, F. J., and Spurzheim, J. G. *Recherches sur le Systeme nerveux.* Paris: Schoell, 1809.

Hoskins, R. G. *Endocrinology: the glands and their functions.* New York: Norton, 1941.

Howells, W. W. A factorial study of constitutional type. *Amer. J. phys. Anthrop.,* 1952, *10,* 91–118.

Janoff, Irma Z., Beck, L. H., and Child, I. L. The relation of somatotype to reaction time, resistance to pain, and expressive movement. *J. Pers.,* 1950, *18,* 454–460.

Kline, N. S., and Tenney, A. M. Constitutional factors in the prognosis of schizophrenia. *Amer. J. Psychiat.,* 1950, *107,* 432–441.

Kline, N. S., and Oppenheim, A. N. Constitutional factors in the prognosis of schizophrenia: further observations. *Amer. J. Psychiat.,* 1952, *108,* 909–911.

Kretschmer, E. *Physique and character.* New York: Harcourt, 1925. (Translated by W. J. H. Spratt from *Körperbau und charakter.* Berlin: Springer, 1921.)

Lasker, G. The effects of partial starvation on somatotype. An analysis of material from the Minnesota Starvation Experiment. *Amer. J. phys. Anthrop.,* 1947, *5,* 323–341.

Lavater, J. C. *Essays on physiognomy: for the promotion of the knowledge and the love of mankind.* London: Whittingham, 1804.

MacKinnon, D. W., and Maslow, A. H. Personality. In H. Helson (Ed.). *Theoretical foundations of psychology.* New York: Van Nostrand, 1951, pp. 602–655.

Naccarati, S. The morphologic aspect of intelligence. *Arch. Psychol.,* 1921, no. 45.

Newman, R. W. Age changes in body build. *Amer. J. phys. Anthrop.,* 1952, *10,* 75–90.

Paterson, D. G. *Physique and intellect.* New York: Century, 1930.

Rostan, L. *Cours élémentaire d'hygiene.* 2nd Ed. Paris: Béchet jeune, 1824.

Sanford, R. N., Adkins, Margaret M., Miller, R. B., Cobb, Elizabeth A., et al. *Physique, personality and scholarship. Monogr. Soc. Res. Child Develpm.,* 1943, *8,* no. 1.

Seltzer, C. C. The relationship between the masculine component and personality. *Amer. J. phys. Anthrop.,* 1943, *3,* 33–47.

Seltzer, C. C., Wells, F. L., and McTernon, E. B. A relationship between Sheldonian somatotype and psychotype. *J. Pers.,* 1948, *16,* 431–436.

Sheldon, W. H. *Psychology and the Promethean will.* New York: Harper, 1936.

Sheldon, W. H. (with the collaboration of S. S. Stevens and W. B. Tucker). *The varieties of human physique: an introduction to constitutional psychology.* New York: Harper, 1940.

Sheldon, W. H. (with the collaboration of S. S. Stevens). *The varieties of temperament: a psychology of constitutional differences.* New York: Harper, 1942.

Sheldon, W. H. Constitutional factors in personality. In J. McV. Hunt (Ed.). *Personality and the behavior disorders.* New York: Ronald Press, 1944, pp. 526–549.

Sheldon, W. H. (with the collaboration of E. M. Hartl and E. McDermott). *Varieties of delinquent youth: an introduction to constitutional psychiatry.* New York: Harper, 1949.

Sheldon, W. H. *Early American cents, 1793–1814.* New York: Harper, 1949.

Sheldon, W. H. (with the collaboration of C. W. Dupertuis and E. McDermott). *Atlas of men: a guide for somatotyping the adult male at all ages.* New York: Harper, 1954.

Sigaud, C. *La forme humaine.* Paris: Maloine, 1914.

Smith, H. C.   Psychometric checks on hypotheses derived from Sheldon's work on physique and temperament. *J. Pers.*, 1949, *17*, 310–320.

Smith, H. C., and Boyarsky, S.   The relationship between physique and simple reaction time. *Character & Pers.*, 1943, *12*, 46–53.

Thurstone, L. L.   Factor analysis and body types. *Psychometrika.*, 1946, *11*, 15–21.

Viola, G.   *Le legge de correlazione morfologia dei tippi individuali.* Padova, Italy: Prosperini, 1909.

Wittman, Phyllis, Sheldon, W. H., and Katz, C. J.   A study of the relationship between constitutional variations and fundamental psychotic behavior reactions. *J. nerv. ment. Dis.*, 1948, *108*, 470–476.

10.

Factor Theories

Precisely what method is used in the analysis of psychological data has become a matter of considerable importance as psychologists have developed greater quantitative sophistication. Perhaps only in the case of factor analysis, however, has a quantitative technique attained a significance which has led to the development of theoretical systems explicitly linked to the technique. Proponents of such systems propose that a rational and largely objective procedure be substituted for the intuitive and usually unspecified manner in which most variables within the domain of personality have been formulated. The essence of such theories is customarily a set of carefully specified variables or factors that are seen as underlying and accounting for the broad complexity of behavior. These variables have usually been derived from large-scale studies of behavior involving numerous subjects and using multiple measures that permit easy quantitative scoring. Thus, the personality theories we propose to discuss here might be said to derive their unique features not from the therapists' chambers or the animal laboratory but rather from a particular statistical technique.

The development of these positions belongs in the main stream of the psychometric tradition. Commencing with the pioneer efforts of J. McKeen Cattell to study individual differences, there has developed an influential group of American and English psychologists whose approach to the study of human behavior has centered about the use of objective tests. Most of the work of this group has focused upon the study of intellectual ability, although recent years have seen an increased concern with personality variables. This interest in objective measures which lead to numerical results has naturally been accompanied by a growing skill in the statistical analysis of quantitative data. One of the outcomes of this interest in quantitative analysis was the development of factor analysis.

The essential ideas of factor analysis were introduced by Spearman (1904), a distinguished English psychologist who is best known for his work with mental abilities (Spearman, 1927). He suggested that if we examine any two related tests of ability we may expect to find two types of factors contributing to performance on these tests. First, there is a general factor (for example, verbal fluency, general intelligence, educational level) which is important for both tests. Second, there is a specific factor (for instance, visual memory, spatial perception, specific information) which is unique to each test. The method of factor analysis was developed as a means of determining the existence of such general factors and aiding in their identification. Spearman's technique for isolating single factors was revised with Thurstone's (1931) introduction of multiple factor analysis. This opened the way to studying much more complex problems and has since remained the principal method of factor analysis. The cogency of Thurstone's arguments, coupled with findings from Spearman's own laboratory, led almost all workers in this area to accept the fact that there were not only general factors, common to all tests or measures under scrutiny, and specific factors, which were limited to a single test, but also group factors, which were involved in more than one test but at the same time were not completely general. Factor analysis today places particular emphasis upon these group factors.

A detailed understanding of factor analysis is not necessary for purposes of the exposition involved in this chapter; however, it is essential that the reader appreciate the general logic lying behind the technique. The factor theorist begins the study of behavior with a large number of scores for each of a large number of subjects. These scores may be derived from questionnaires, ratings, situational tests, or any other source which provides a significant and quantifiable measure of behavior. Ideally these measures should deal with many different aspects of behavior. Given these surface indices, the investigator then applies the technique of factor analysis to discover what the underlying factors are which determine or control variation in the surface variables. Thus, he hopes to identify a small number of basic factors whose operation accounts for most of the variation in the very large number of measures with which he began.

The outcome of the factor analysis not only isolates the fundamental factors but also provides for each measure or set of scores an estimate of the extent to which this measure is contributed to by each of the factors. This estimate is customarily referred to as the *factor loading* or *saturation* of the measure and is simply an indication of how much of the variation on this particular measure is to be attributed to each of the factors. The psychological meaning of a factor and the name or label that is attached to it are largely determined by the nature of the particular measures which have high loadings on this factor. Having identified the basic factors to his satisfaction, it is conventional for the factor theorist to attempt to devise means of measuring these factors more efficiently than he can by means of the original measures.

Thus, the factor theorist commences with a wide array of behavioral measures, identifies the factors underlying these measures, and then attempts to construct more efficient means of assessing these factors. The factors of the factor analyst are in conception little different from the components or underlying variables of other personality theorists. They are merely attempts to formulate variables that will account for the diverse complexity of surface behavior. It is in the technique employed in deriving these variables that the novelty of this approach lies.

The reader should remember that although group or common factors are of particular interest to the factor analyst these are not the only type of factors. Burt (1941) has provided a widely accepted description of the kinds of factors that can be derived from the application of factor analysis. He suggests that there are universal or *general factors* which contribute to performance on all measures, and there are also particular or *group factors* which play a role in more than one but not in all measures. Further, there are singular or *specific factors* which contribute to only one of the measures, and finally there are accidental or *error factors* which appear on a single administration of a single measure and are to be attributed to faulty measurement or a lack of experimental control.

Like any other procedure factor analysis can be abused and the wisest investigators in this area emphasize the fact that it is no substitute for good ideas or detailed knowledge of the phenomena under investigation. Thus, Thurstone (1948) in discussing the work of his psychometric laboratory states:

. . . we spend more time in designing the experimental tests for a factor study than on all of the computational work, including the correlations, the factoring, and the analysis of the structure. If we have several hypotheses about postulated factors, we design and invent new tests which may be crucially differentiating between the several hypotheses. This is entirely a psychological job with no computing. It calls for as much psychological insight as we can gather among students and instructors. Frequently we find that we have guessed wrong, but occasionally the results are strikingly encouraging. I mention this aspect of factorial work in the hope of counteracting the rather general impression that factor analysis is all concerned with algebra and statistics. These should be our servants in the investigation of psychological ideas. If we have no psychological ideas, we are not likely to discover anything interesting because even if the factorial results are clear and clean, the interpretation must be as subjective as in any other scientific work (p. 402).

An excellent paper by Guilford (1952) serves an important cautionary function in pointing to the many conditions under which it is not advisable to use factor analysis. The reader who wishes to examine factor analysis in more detail may consult Cattell (1952), Guilford (1954), Thomson (1951), or Thurstone (1947).

So much for the logic of factor analysis. What of its application in the area of personality research? What are the theories or sets of variables that it has produced? Many have made contributions here, including L. L. Thurstone, J. P. Guilford, and W. Stephenson. However, the most important of such contributions, judged by explicitness and extensity of application, are the schemes of Hans J. Eysenck and Raymond B. Cattell. We shall summarize the position of each of these theorists and then consider the merits and shortcomings of this general approach to personality. The reader who is interested in the work of other contributors in this area will find an outstanding summary in a chapter by MacKinnon (1944) and a more recent survey by French (1953).

EYSENCK'S DIMENSIONS OF PERSONALITY

The work of H. J. Eysenck is characterized by a tough-minded disdain for existing preconceptions and convictions concerning personality and a readiness to study behavior on a large scale, using techniques in areas where they have not customarily been applied. He combines the traditional excellence of British psychologists in the use of quantitative techniques with an interest in the study of phenomena of personality in a psychiatric setting. This attempted synthesis of the procedural sophistication of the psychometrician with the insights of the clinician represents a valuable and distinctive emphasis. Eysenck has shown a preference for conceptions of behavior that are simple and relatively operational. He is convinced that in the long run theory and experiment must go arm and arm, as theories which carry the excess baggage of undefined terms must eventually perish. Further, he has demonstrated a highly developed critical sense which he has not hesitated to employ against the strongest of contemporary theoretical and empirical strongholds. To all of these qualities he has added the capacity to attract, stimulate, and coordinate a large group of able collaborators and students so that the volume of work he has turned out during the past decade is quite remarkable even by prolific American standards.

The core of Eysenck's view of psychology derives from his conviction that measurement is fundamental to all scientific advance and his further belief that in psychology we are not yet sure what we should be measuring. His conception of how this state of affairs can be improved is revealed in the following quotation:

> If our main task is to provide at least a provisional solution to the taxonomic problem in personality research, then we are involved automatically in the problem of finding appropriate *dimensions of personality*. And for a method to aid in the solution we must turn to factor analysis, because in spite of the acknowledged difficulties and weaknesses of this method there does not exist, at the present stage of our knowledge, any other method which could aid us in our quest (1952, p. 42).

Thus, we see clearly an investigator who believes that taxonomy or classification of behavior is a crucial first step and who is convinced that factor analysis is the most useful instrument for pursuing this goal. It is true that Eysenck has employed other techniques such as discriminant analysis (Eysenck, 1955a) but we shall see that the bulk of his work has involved factor analysis.

Eysenck was born in 1916 in Germany where he received his early education. In 1934 under the impact of the Nazi movement he left Germany and eventually came to England where he completed his studies, securing his Ph.D. in psychology at the University of London in 1940. During the war years he served as psychologist at the Mill Hill Emergency Hospital and following the war was appointed reader in psychology at the University of London and director of the Psychological Department at the Institute of Psychiatry, which includes Maudsley and Bethlem Royal Hospitals and where much of his research has been carried out. He came to the United States in

1949–1950 as a visiting professor at the University of Pennsylvania and during the summer of 1954 he taught at the University of California. In 1954 he was appointed professor of psychology at the University of London. In a general sense it is clear that Eysenck's work owes much to Spearman, the father of factor analysis, but it is more directly related to the contributions of L. L. Thurstone as Eysenck has acknowledged. On the theoretical side his writings show most in common with the work of European typologists such as Jaensch, Jung, Kraepelin, and Kretschmer. The writings of Carl Jung and Ernst Kretschmer seem to have been particularly influential and Eysenck considers his investigations to be closely linked to their theoretical formulations. In recent years his writings (Eysenck, 1954, 1955b) have shown the influence of Clark Hull's theory.

Although Eysenck's research has been largely centered in the clinical-personality area, he has also conducted investigations concerned with attitudes, humor, aesthetics, and many other areas. His unusual productivity has led to some seventy journal articles and five books. Three of his books are concerned with the study and description of personality: *Dimensions of personality* (1947); *The scientific study of personality* (1952); and *The structure of human personality* (1953a). A fourth volume, *Uses and abuses of psychology* (1953b), deals with the utility of psychology in man's everyday affairs. His most recent work is concerned with political behavior and is entitled *The psychology of politics* (1954).

THE STRUCTURE OF PERSONALITY

Eysenck's conviction that most personality theories are overloaded with complex and undefined variables, coupled with his use of factor analysis, has resulted in a personality system that is characterized by a very small number of major dimensions which are defined with great care. In this section we shall summarize his general conception of personality and then turn to the specific dimensions he has proposed.

THE NATURE OF PERSONALITY. Eysenck's over-all view of personality is quite consistent with various definitions we have already examined and appears to be particularly congruent with Allport's definition. Personality is defined as:

. . . the sum-total of the actual or potential behavior-patterns of the organism, as determined by heredity and environment; it originates and develops through the functional interaction of the four main sectors into which these behavior-patterns are organized: the cognitive sector (intelligence), the conative sector (character), the affective sector (temperament), and the somatic sector (constitution) (1947, p. 25).

Perhaps the most unusual feature of this definition is the explicit inclusion of the "somatic sector." This interest in the constitutional is reflected in Eysenck's empirical work where he has frequently employed body build as a relevant personality variable.

Central to Eysenck's view of behavior are the concepts of *trait* and *type*. He defines trait very simply as an "observed constellation of individual action-tendencies." In other words, a trait is simply an observed consistency among the habits or repeated acts of the subject. A type is defined as an "observed constellation or syndrome of traits." Thus, the type is a more generalized and inclusive variety of organization and includes the trait as a component part.

His recent studies of political behavior (1954) have led Eysenck to place considerable emphasis upon the concepts of *attitude* and *ideology*, which appear to have a status in the intellectual or cognitive realm which is roughly equivalent to the status of the type and trait in the personality sphere.

Explicit in Eysenck's writing is the conception of personality as composed of acts and dispositions that are organized in a hierarchical fashion in terms of their generality and importance. At the highest level of generality and inclusiveness are the types and at the most specific and least general level are the specific responses. Intermediate between the two are habitual responses and traits.

The specific response is nothing more than an observed act or response that occurs in a single instance. The habitual response is somewhat more general as it implies a recurrent response that is characteristically elicited under the same or similar circumstances. Certain of these habitual responses are related to one another and tend to exist within the same person and this organization is referred to as the trait. Finally, there is the organization of traits into a still more general structure and this is the personality type. These four levels of description correspond to the four types of factors we have already mentioned as derivable from factor analysis, that is, the personality type corresponds to the general factor, the trait corresponds to the group factor, the habitual response corresponds to the specific factor, and the specific response corresponds to the error factor. Exactly the same form of organization is proposed in the cognitive sphere with ideology as the most general concept followed in turn by attitude, habitual opinion, and specific opinion.

Let us turn now to a more detailed examination of the concepts of trait and type.

TRAITS OF PERSONALITY. Although Eysenck is quite explicit in his definition of traits he shows little detailed interest in them, at least by that name, in the report of his investigations. The bulk of his attention is directed toward his basic dimensions or personality types. However, consistent with his original definition the items or tests that make up the intercorrelation matrices out of which, by means of factor analysis, he extracts his dimensions must be considered to represent traits. If types represent regularities or clustering among traits and if his types are based upon regularities among these individual ratings or tests then the latter must be traits.

Thus, if we examine the original study of seven hundred neurotic soldiers (Eysenck, 1947) we find that the fundamental dimensions of neuroticism and introversion-extraversion were extracted from the factor analysis of thirty-nine items selected from a personal data sheet that included personality ratings as well as factual information concerning the subjects. Although some of these measures seem difficult to conceive of as traits of behavior, such as age above thirty, married, and unsatisfactory home, the majority of them fall easily into this category, for example, dependent, little energy, cyclothymic, schizoid, obsessional, apathy, anxiety, and depression. In subsequent studies, where Eysenck (1947, 1952) has introduced specific experimental measures designed to measure attributes that on *a priori* grounds seem likely to relate to one of his basic dimensions, it again seems clear that these measures are assessing variables that have the logical status of traits within his system.

For Eysenck then, the trait must be operationally defined, or accompanied by a specific measurement procedure, to be of any interest or utility. Beyond this, the trait derives its importance initially from its contribution to the general identification of the underlying dimensions or types of personality and subsequently from its use in further delineating these types. As we shall see, the delineation of his types is accomplished primarily by means of a detailed trait description. In spite of his focus upon the problem of typology Eysenck is willing to concede an independent importance to the study of traits and his own investigations of suggestibility provide evidence of this (Eysenck, 1943a, 1943b, 1943c; Eysenck and Furneaux, 1945; Eysenck and Rees, 1945).

PERSONALITY TYPES. In an important sense all of Eysenck's research is aimed at the ultimate goal of identifying primary dimensions of personality, which in turn will permit the establishment of a uniquely powerful typology. His investigations have followed the theoretical leads of Kretschmer and Jung, producing results which appear to substantiate many of Jung's formulations while, for the most part, failing to confirm predictions derived from Kretschmer's theory.

In his first major study carried out during the war years on a group of roughly ten thousand normal and neurotic subjects (Eysenck, 1947), he was able to discover two fundamental variables. This study began with the study of seven hundred male, neurotic soldiers who were rated on a large number of traits by attending psychiatrists and for whom there was also a good deal of life history information. These ratings and classifications were subjected to factor analysis and two underlying factors were extracted and identified as introversion-extraversion and neuroticism. Having isolated these two variables Eysenck and his collaborators proceeded to explore them in a large number of subsequent investigations so that they could characterize the dimensions more accurately. This usually involved comparing individuals high and low on the two primary variables in their performance on various independent measures or assessment situations. From these studies evolved a rather full and complex statement concerning the attributes of the individual who was extreme on the neuroticism or introversion-extraversion variables.

The first variable he isolated represents a bipolar contrast between *introversion* and *extraversion*. He considers his findings in this area to represent an essential confirmation of theoretical ideas advanced by Carl Jung.

At the end of Eysenck's program of studies he was able to produce the following descriptive statements concerning the "introvert" and "extravert:"

> . . . we find that (neurotic) introverts show a tendency to develop anxiety and depression symptoms, that they are characterized by obsessional tendencies, irritability, apathy, and that they suffer from a lability of the autonomic system. According to their own statement, their feelings are easily hurt, they are self-conscious, nervous, given to feelings of inferiority, moody, daydream easily, keep in the background on social occasions, and suffer from sleeplessness. In their body-build vertical growth predominates over horizontal growth; their effort response is poor, and their choline esterase activity is high. Salivary secretion is inhibited. Their intelligence is comparatively high, their vocabulary excellent, and they tend to be persistent. They are generally accurate, but slow; they excell at finicking work (Tweezers test). Their level of aspiration is un-

duly high, but they tend to underrate their own performance. Withal, they are rather rigid, and show little intrapersonal variability. Their aesthetic preferences are towards the quiet, old-fashioned type of picture. In aesthetic creation, they produce compact designs, often having a concrete subject. They do not appreciate jokes very much, and sex jokes in particular are not much favored. Their handwriting is distinctive (1947, pp. 246–247).

In comparison, (neurotic) extraverts show a tendency to develop hysterical conversion symptoms, and a hysterical attitude to their symptoms. Furthermore, they show little energy, narrow interests, have a bad work-history, and are hypochondriacal. According to their own statement, they are troubled by stammer or stutter, are accident prone, frequently off work through illness, disgruntled, and troubled by aches and pains. In their body-build, horizontal growth predominates over vertical growth; their effort response is quite good and their choline esterase activity low. Salivary secretion is not inhibited. Their intelligence is comparatively low, their vocabulary poor, and they show extreme lack of persistence. They tend to be quick but inaccurate; they are bad at finicking work (Tweezers test). Their level of aspiration is low, but they tend to over-rate their own performance. They are not very rigid, and show great intrapersonal variability. Their aesthetic preferences are towards the colourful, modern type of picture. In aesthetic creation, they produce scattered designs, often having abstract subjects. They appreciate jokes, and are particularly fond of sex jokes. Their handwriting is distinctive (1947, p. 247).

If we accept the validity of most or all of Eysenck's measures there is little doubt that the two types he has isolated represent rather different kinds of people. Not only are the two groups demonstrably different but the wealth of objective description that Eysenck has provided for delineating and further understanding these types is remarkably full. In contrast to many of his predecessors, who were content to speculate concerning useful types, and then to illustrate their speculations with examples drawn at convenience from the everyday world, Eysenck has provided a large number of objective measures, possessing psychological significance, which may be used to characterize his types. Eysenck suggests that these types bear at least an analogical relation to Freudian mental anatomy in the sense that the id appears to dominate in the case of the extravert while the superego seems strongest in the case of the introvert.

The same program of studies that led to a detailed description of the introvert and extravert also produced a profile of results for the individual who is high on the *neuroticism* dimension. Eysenck summarizes these results as follows:

. . . the neurotic soldier, on the average, is a person defective in mind and body; below average in intelligence, will, emotional control, sensory acuity and capacity to exert himself. He is suggestible, lacks persistence, is slow in thought and action, unsociable, and tends to repress unpleasant facts (1947, p. 260).

Eysenck indicates his belief that hereditary factors probably play some role in the development of this type but is frank to confess that the experimental findings from this set of studies do not lead to any firm inferences in this area. He also suggests that just as intelligence may be considered a general factor in the cognitive area and introversion-extraversion a general factor in the emotional area so neuroticism may be considered a general factor in the area of motivation or striving. Thus, Eysenck believes that, at least in part, neuroticism may be considered to represent a defect of the will or of the capacity of the individual to persist in motivated behavior.

Recently Eysenck (1955b) has developed a theory of anxiety and hysteria which draws heavily upon the work of Pavlov and Hull and which leads to some specific predictions concerning the variables of introversion-extraversion and neuroticism. As predicted by this theory, it was found that the ease with which conditioned responses could be developed in human subjects and the resistance of these conditioned responses to extinction was related to the variable of introversion-extraversion but unrelated to the variable of neuroticism. Predictions derived from the theory concerning performance in several other experimental situations were also confirmed. These studies reveal Eysenck's interest in examining the dimensions he has established in new settings and also suggest his intent of embracing them within a more general theoretical framework.

In a subsequent program of research Eysenck (1952) conducted a number of studies employing normal and mental hospital subjects. These studies extended to three the fundamental dimensions leading to personality types. The new variable was *psychoticism* and he describes the individual high on this dimension in the following terms:

> We find then that psychotics are less fluent, perform poorly in continuous addition, perform poorly in mirror drawing, show slower oscillation on the reversal of perspective test, are slower in tracing with a stylus, are more undecided with respect to social attitudes, show a poorer concentration, have a poorer memory, tend to make larger movements and to overestimate distances and scores, tend to read more slowly, to tap more slowly and to show levels of aspiration much less reality adapted (1952, p. 217).

He points out that these differences between psychotics and normals cannot be attributed simply to the tendency on the part of the psychotics to be poorer in performance than normals in all areas, as there were many tests where there was no difference in the performance of the normal and psychotic group.

Thus, Eysenck's research has led to the identification of three primary dimensions (introversion, neuroticism, psychoticism) which afford the basis for a discriminating typology of human subjects. This remarkably simple dimensional scheme is, of course, perfectly consistent with his pleas for theoretical parsimony.

CHARACTERISTIC RESEARCH AND RESEARCH METHODS

We have already noted that much of the uniqueness of Eysenck's work derives from his capacity to apply methods in areas where they have hitherto not been used and further the remarkable energy and orderliness with which he has approached problems of interest to him. Perhaps the most original contribution he has made to research methods is what he refers to as criterion analysis. In this section we shall discuss briefly the method of criterion analysis and follow this with an outline of a study employing this method to explore one of Eysenck's major dimensions—neuroticism. Before embarking upon this task, however, we shall consider briefly certain aspects of Eysenck's convictions concerning how personality research should proceed.

THE STRATEGY OF PERSONALITY RESEARCH. Altogether consistent with prevailing tides in American psychology is Eysenck's preference for large-scale research carried on by a team of psychologists who have united their efforts for a prolonged attack upon a given problem area. Somewhat more unique is his conviction that the main task of the fruitful theorist is pruning rather than extension or extrapolation. Both of these sentiments are clearly revealed in the following quotation:

> In my view, the time has come when the preliminary surveys of isolated traits, and the exploratory studies of small groups, must give way to work planned on an altogether larger scale; while small-scale exploratory studies will, of course, always retain their value in opening up new fields, such exploration must ultimately lead to consolidation if its full fruits are to be reaped. Similarly, while the large number of theories which has emerged in the past few decades has done much to stimulate interest in the scientific study of temperament and personality, these theories have been so divorced in the main from operational definition

and experimental control that simplification and ruthless discarding appeared more necessary than an attempt to add to the confusion (1947, p. ix).

Nevertheless Eysenck fully accepts the importance of theory and this conviction, together with his view of how theoretical advances are to be made, is clearly adumbrated in the following quotation from a paper presenting what he characterizes as a "hypothetico-deductive" theory of anxiety and hysteria:

> This type of theory is characteristic of scientific endeavour which attempts to go beyond pure empiricism and simple induction to the postulation of laws and general theories, and the deduction from these of both observed and, as yet, unobserved consequences. Such a theory in its early stages is almost inevitably a gross oversimplification of the very complex relationships included within it. Nevertheless, from the point of view of science, it is more useful than more complex and more sophisticated theories, which do not enable one to make clear-cut and testable deductions. It is only in making such deductions and testing them that the value of a theory can be assessed, and it is only through experimental procedures of this type that improvements can be made and greater complexity achieved without loss of rigour (Eysenck, 1955b, p. 47).

We have already alluded to Eysenck's interest in combining the methods of the psychometrician with the problems and procedures of the clinician. Integrally involved in this conviction is the belief that those who have used factor analysis have relied too heavily upon questionnaire and rating measures of behavior with a resultant dependence upon "subjective" data. On the other hand, he feels that those people who have used experimental measures of behavior have observed too little of the total organism they would understand. He proposes using experimental measures to avoid the dangers of subjectivity but employing them in such large numbers, in conjunction with factor analysis, as to avoid the narrowness of the experimentalist. Although Eysenck labels himself an atomist, and is firmly convinced of the essential importance of securing clear and objective dimensional measures of human behavior, he also insists that the investigator must use a wide variety of data sources if he is to learn much about personality.

> . . . work in the field of personality should not confine itself to a small sector, but to be convincing should embrace personality in all its aspects. The doctrine of the "total personality" appears to be entirely justified in so far as it declares that partial approaches are liable to lead only to partial understanding. Investigations should be as broadly based as pos-

sible, including ratings, self-ratings, objective behavior tests, estimates of physique, autonomic and other relevant physiological measurements, biographical and other historical information, and, indeed, all and every type of factual and objective information which may be used to support or refute the hypotheses under investigation (1953a, p. 319).

THE METHOD OF CRITERION ANALYSIS. Eysenck considers the method of criterion analysis to be nothing more than a combination of proposition-testing, or the hypothetico-deductive method, with the technique of factor analysis. As he points out, many critics of factor analysis have objected to the largely descriptive use to which the technique has been put and further have maintained that the technique permits a good deal of arbitrariness in determining just which factors will be derived from a given matrix of correlations.

According to Eysenck's procedure, the investigator must begin with a conviction or a proposition concerning a specified underlying variable or factor and then proceed to secure a set of measures or test scores that are presumably related to this underlying factor. Further, he must secure these scores for two groups that are contrasted in the degree to which they possess this variable. In other words, the investigator must not only secure multiple measures on a number of subjects in the conventional manner but he must also secure criterion groups, groups that possess discriminably different degrees of the hypothesized variable. Each of the individual tests is then correlated with the dichotomy between the two groups, so that we have a measure for each test which indicates how closely this test is associated with the distinction implied by the criterion groups, that is, how sensitive the test is to this particular variable.

It is impossible to give a detailed picture of the following steps without an understanding of the computational procedure of factor analysis. However, the idea behind these steps is quite simple. Whereas before there were a number of different factors that could have been selected, there is now a single factor to be isolated so that the contribution of the individual tests to the chosen factor corresponds to the degree of correlation between the individual test and the criterion groups. In other words, the criterion groups impose a definite restriction upon the factor analysis and imply that the factor ultimately derived will lean most heavily upon those tests that discriminate most effectively between the criterion groups.

Whatever the technical acceptability of this refinement of factor analysis may be, it has the singular virtue of forcing upon the investigator prior consideration of his problem and at least a tentative conceptualization of the nature of the variable he proposes to investigate.

OBJECTIVE MEASUREMENT OF THE NEUROTIC DIMENSION. Having established to his satisfaction the existence of the neurotic dimension as a principal factor underlying performance on a wide variety of different personality tests and ratings of personality, Eysenck (1952) and his collaborators set out to devise a means for the "exact quantitative measurement" of this dimension. This study represents the first detailed report of the application of the method of criterion analysis.

The investigators began by selecting a normal group and a neurotic group to which they proposed to administer, consistent with the method of criterion analysis, a large number of measures which were believed related to the underlying variable of neuroticism. The normal group consisted of 207 male soldiers who had at least six months' service, and whose intelligence was at least normal. The neurotic group consisted of 215 male soldiers who were being discharged from the Army on psychiatric grounds. The normal and neurotic groups seemed relatively well matched on all variables except for intelligence where the normal group was significantly superior. Eysenck attempts to take this factor into consideration in his interpretation of the findings of this study.

During a two-day test period the subjects were given a large number of tests which led to over seventy individual personality measures all presumably bearing some relation to the underlying variable of neuroticism. Each measure was then examined in terms of its capacity to differentiate between the normal group and the neurotic group. As a result of this analysis it was found that a series of questionnaire measures differentiated very effectively between the normal and neurotic groups, as did a large number of measures derived from "objective behavior tests," but a group of measures based upon expressive movements failed completely to discriminate between the normal and neurotic group. Two measures based upon a projective test (Rorschach) successfully differentiated the two groups.

Having completed this form of analysis for seventy-six individual measures the investigators selected twenty-eight measures to submit to a factor analysis. These measures were intercorrelated and the resulting matrix of correlations was subjected to factor analysis with the primary factor derived in such a way that it maximized the contribution (loading or saturation) of those tests that were most effective in differentiating between the normal and neurotic groups. Actually, this factor is determined by selecting the factor which has the highest correlation between the amount of saturation of the individual measures on this factor and the degree of correlation of these measures with the criterion groups. The correlation between the extracted factor saturations and the correlations with the criterion groups is .40, which Eysenck considers ample evidence for the real existence of the underlying variable of neuroticism. He is further convinced that this correlation would have been much higher if it had not been for the unfortunate inability to control for intelligence which in this case entered into and contaminated the measure of neuroticism. After performing a series of additional operations on these data, including a multiple correlation between selected measures and the extracted factor, Eysenck reaches the following general conclusion:

> It seems reasonable, then, to conclude that the battery of tests here assembled has a validity of approximately .80 or thereabouts: it will be shown later that a similar battery has a reliability of at least .85, and probably above .90. These figures strongly support the argument advanced in *Dimensions of Personality* that in neuroticism we are dealing with a personality factor which can be measured as reliably and as validly as intelligence (1952, p. 155).

Having reached this encouraging conclusion Eysenck goes on to strengthen his argument by reporting similar results for a study carried out on normal and neurotic children by Himmelweit and Petrie (1951) and then reports a study (Eysenck and Prell, 1951) designed to test the hypothesis that the neurotic dimension is, at least in part, determined by genetic or constitutional factors. This study also relies upon factor analysis as the principal method of analysis and leads Eysenck to the conclusion that:

> . . . we have shown that identical twins show a correlation on neuroticism of .851, while fraternal twins show a correlation of only .217. From this it was concluded that individual differences with respect to neuroticism, stability, integration, or whatever we may wish to call this trait or factor, are determined to a very marked extent by heredity, and very much less markedly by environment. This conclusion, of course, applies only in the general type of environment from which all our twins came, and might not be applicable under conditions of more extreme environmental variation such as may obtain in other cultures (1952, p. 189).

CATTELL'S TRAITS OF PERSONALITY

In Raymond Cattell we find an investigator whose deep interest in quantitative methods has not narrowed the spectrum of his interest in psychological data and problems. For him, factor analysis has been a subsidiary tool which he has used to enlighten a variety of problems all of which have been ordered within a systematic framework. His theory represents the most comprehensive attempt yet made to bring together and organize the major findings of sophisticated factor analytic studies of personality. He also pays considerable attention to the findings of investigators using divergent methods of study, although the core of his position revolves around the results of factor analysis, as it is here that he derives the variables which he considers most important in accounting for human behavior. He resembles Gordon Allport in that his position may accurately be labeled a "trait theory." On the other hand, he is like Eysenck in his conviction that large-scale studies hold the key to future advances in psychology, his interest in taxonomy, and also in the attention he has paid to the procedures through which data may be collected for the study of personality. In fact, he has developed a number of specific instruments for the measurement of personality and has had a great deal to say in the way of appraisal and admonition concerning the major measurement options currently available in this area. The principal difference between Cattell and Eysenck in their use of factor analysis derives from the fact that Eysenck typically employs the method of criterion analysis, which we have just discussed, while Cattell employs the more conventional method of "simple structure." It is also true that Eysenck customarily extracts only two or three factors in his studies whereas Cattell extracts a much larger number.

Cattell was born in Staffordshire, England, in 1905 and received all of his education in England. He secured his B.Sc. from the University of London in 1924 and his Ph.D. in psychology from the same institution in 1929. He was a lecturer at University College of the South West, Exeter, England, from 1928–1931 and director of the City Psychological Clinic at Leicester, England, from 1932–1937. This unusual combination of an academic post followed immediately by extensive experience in a clinical setting undoubtedly provides a partial explanation for Cattell's subsequent breadth of interest. In 1937 he was awarded a D.Sc. by the University of London for his contributions to personality research. He served as research associate at Teachers College, Columbia University, during the year 1937–1938 and following this was the G. Stanley Hall professor of psychology at Clark University until moving to Harvard University as a lecturer in 1942. In 1944 he accepted a position at the University of Illinois as research professor of psychology where he has remained since.

Like all other theorists who emphasize the method of factor analysis, Cattell is deeply indebted to the pioneer work of Spearman and the extensive developments by Thurstone. His theoretical formulations seem most directly related to McDougall's, whose interest in ferreting out the underlying dimensions of behavior and emphasis upon the self-regarding sentiment are seen in modern dress in Cattell's writings. The details of many of his theoretical ideas, especially those related to development, are quite intimately related to the formulations of Freud and subsequent psychoanalytic writers.

Over a period of twenty-five years Cattell has published an amazing number of articles which not only span the field of personality research and mental measurement but also touch upon topics within the traditional fields of experimental psychology, social psychology, and human genetics. He has published five books beginning with a manual entitled *A guide to mental testing* (1936, Rev. Ed. 1948), followed by *General psychology* (1941), an introductory text. His next two volumes are most important from the point of view of this chapter. The first is entitled *Description and measurement of personality* (1946) and attempts to outline from a cross-sectional point of view a descriptive foundation for an adequate theory of personality. The second is called *Personality: A systematic, theoretical, and factual study* (1950) and tries to build upon the foundation established in the earlier book a synthetic view of the major phenomena of personality, including both a developmental and a cross-sectional perspective. His most recent volume, *Factor analysis: An introduction and manual for psychologist and social scientist* (1952), is an attempt to introduce the reader to the principal research technique employed by Cattell and place this technique in a suitable perspective for the investigator interested in human behavior. He is also the author of numerous tests including *The culture free test of intelligence* (1944), *The O-A personality test battery* (1954), and *The 16 personality factor questionnaire* (with D. R. Saunders and G. F. Stice, 1950).

THE NATURE OF PERSONALITY: A STRUCTURE OF TRAITS

The system of constructs proposed by Cattell is among the most complex of any of the theories we shall consider. Although these concepts derive their characteristic flavor and, in many cases, their empirical definition from studies using factor analysis, some of them represent derivations from experimental findings or simple observational studies of behavior. This state of affairs is considered by Cattell to be only an expedient, however, as the following quotation reveals:

> Our knowledge of dynamic psychology has arisen largely from clinical and naturalistic methods and secondarily from controlled experiment. "Findings" of the former, and even of the latter, are in process of being placed on a sounder basis by the application of more refined statistical methods. In particular, experiments and clinical conclusions need to be refounded on real conceptions as to what traits (notably drives) are really unitary, and this requires a foundation of factor-analytic research (1950, p. 175).

Cattell considers that the detailed task of defining personality must await a full adumbration of the concepts that the theorist plans to employ in his study of behavior. Thus, he deliberately provides only a very general definition:

> *Personality is that which permits a prediction of what a person will do in a given situation.* The goal of psychological research in personality is thus to establish laws about what different people will do in all kinds of social and general environmental situations. . . . Personality is . . . concerned with *all* the behavior of the individual, both overt and under the skin (1950, pp. 2–3).

It is clear that this emphasis upon personality study including "all" behavior is not an attack upon the necessary abstracting or segmenting that takes place in the usual empirical study. It is simply a reminder that the meaning of small segments of behavior can be fully understood only when seen within the larger framework of the entire functioning organism.

A more detailed specification of the nature of personality is presented by outlining the major concepts employed by Cattell. When we have examined the meaning of such terms as *trait, erg, metaerg, self,* and *specification equation* we will have a relatively complete picture of Cattell's conception of personality.

TRAITS. The trait is by far the most important of Cattell's concepts. In fact, the additional concepts that we shall examine are for the most part viewed as special cases of this general term. If we except Gordon Allport, Cattell has considered this concept and its relation to other psychological variables in greater detail than any other current theorist. For him a trait is a "mental structure," an inference that is made from observed behavior to account for regularity or consistency in this behavior. The term structure is not meant to imply physical or neural status although Cattell is relatively explicit in pointing to the physical and physiological concomitants that underlie behavior.

Cattell agrees with Allport in suggesting that there are _common traits_ which are possessed by all individuals, or at least by all individuals who share certain social experiences. Moreover, he would agree that there are _unique traits_ that apply only to a particular individual and can be found in no other person in just that form. However, he goes one step further and suggests that unique traits may be divided into those that are _relatively unique_ and those that are _intrinsically unique_. In the former, the uniqueness derives from a slightly different arrangement of the elements making up the trait; in the latter, the individual possesses a genuinely different trait which is possessed by no other person.

Central to Cattell's point of view is the distinction between _surface traits_, which represent clusters of manifest or overt variables that seem to go together, and _source traits_, which represent underlying variables that enter into the determination of multiple surface manifestations. Thus, if we find a number of behavioral events that seem to go together we may prefer to consider them as one variable. In a medical setting, this would be referred to as a syndrome but here it is labeled a surface trait. Source traits, on the other hand, are identified only by means of factor analysis which permits the investigator to estimate the variables or factors which are the basis of this surface behavior.

It is evident that Cattell considers source traits more important than surface traits. This follows not only because the source traits promise greater economy of description, as there are presumably fewer of them, but more importantly because:

> . . . the source traits promise to be the real structural influences underlying personality, which it is necessary for us to deal with in developmental problems, psychosomatics, and problems of dynamic integration . . . as research is now showing, these source traits correspond to real unitary influences—physiological, temperamental factors; degrees of dynamic integration; exposure to social institutions—about which much more can be found out once they are defined (1950, p. 27).

Surface traits are produced by the interaction of source traits and generally can be expected to be less stable than factors. Cattell admits that surface traits are likely to appeal to the common-sense observer as more valid and meaningful than source traits because they correspond to the kinds of generalizations that can be made on the basis of simple observation. However, in the long run it is the source traits that prove to have the most utility in accounting for behavior. Clearly, any single trait may represent the outcome of the operation of environmental factors, hereditary factors, or some mixture of the two. Cattell suggests that while surface traits must represent the outcome of a mixture of these factors it is at least possible that source traits may be divided into those that reflect environmental conditions and those that reflect heredity, or more broadly, constitutional factors. The traits that result from the operation of environmental conditions are called _environmental-mold traits;_ those that reflect hereditary factors are called _constitutional traits._

> If source traits found by factorizing are pure, independent influences, as present evidence suggests, a source trait could not be due both to heredity and environment but must spring from one or the other. . . . Patterns thus springing from *internal* conditions or influences we may call *constitutional source traits.* The term "innate" is avoided, because all we know is that the source is physiological and *within the organism,* which will mean inborn only in a certain fraction of cases. On the other hand, a pattern might be imprinted on the personality by something external to it. . . . Such source traits, appearing as factors, we may call *environmental-mold* traits, because they spring from the molding effect of social institutions and physical realities which constitute the cultural pattern (1950, pp. 33–34).

Traits may be divided in terms of the modality through which they are expressed. If they are concerned with setting the individual into action toward some goal they are *dynamic traits;* if they are concerned with the effectiveness with which the individual reaches the goal they are *ability traits.* Or they may be concerned largely with constitutional aspects of response such as speed, energy, or emotional reactivity, in which case they are referred to as *temperament traits.* Any isolated act of behavior will, of course, express all three varieties of trait but, from the point of view of analysis, it is important to maintain the above distinction. For the student of personality the dynamic traits are of much greater importance than ability or temperament traits, for they are the most modifiable or plastic and consequently they introduce most of the variability into behavior. For this reason most of our remaining discussion of traits will focus upon dynamic traits.

Empirical derivation of source traits. There are three major approaches to personality measurement: the life record, the self rating, and the objective test. The *life record* is concerned with behavior in everyday situations and may employ behavioral ratings as a means of assessing such behavior. The *self rating* provides a "mental interior" to the objective observations of the life record method. Such responses may be treated either at their face value as valid reflections of the subject's true behavior or as items of behavior whose significance must be empirically determined. Objective tests involve observation of the individual in a specifically created situation in order that predictions can be made concerning his behavior in other situations. Although potentially any of these sources of data could be used for the basic derivation of source traits, Cattell prefers to use the life record method, as he considers such data to be of assured significance and importance because of their origin in real life situations. This preference for life record data in determining his basic variables places Cattell in mild contrast to Eysenck who has chosen to emphasize somewhat more heavily objective personality tests.

In identifying the source traits Cattell's basic procedure is to secure a large number of behavioral ratings of different dimensions for a group of individuals and then subject these sets of scores to a factor analysis. By this means Cattell hopes to extract the variables that underlie or contribute most of the variability to the large number of initial measures. As a result of investigations by himself and others Cattell asserts that fourteen or fifteen source traits have been identified with some degree of confidence but only six of these "are repeatedly confirmed and unmistakable" (1950, p. 57). These are: cyclothymia versus schizothymia; general mental capacity versus mental defect; surgency versus desurgency (anxious melancholy); adventurous cyclothymia versus withdrawn schizophrenia; socialized, cultured mind versus boorishness; Bohemian unconcernedness versus conventional practicality. Presenting these factors by names is rather misleading as Cattell himself places little confidence in the labels and actually suggests that at the present stage of psychological development it may be better to simply refer to the variables by means of the index numbers he provides. The essence of the definition for each trait is a list of the items or measures that were most highly loaded with this factor, that is, the items to which this factor contributed most.

In addition to the source traits that have been derived from life record sources, Cattell (1946, 1950, 1955) also presents comparable lists of traits that have been extracted from self ratings and objective test results. These trait lists are assigned code numbers that permit an immediate comparison with the traits derived from other sources. There is considerable duplication or overlap between the various lists but still there are unique factors to each list. Recently Cattell has devoted considerable energy to examining the relation between factors derived from different origins and attempting to arrive at an over-all formulation (Cattell, 1950; Cattell and Saunders, 1950). As a result of his investigations Cattell has been able to develop a number of objective personality tests for measuring the principal source traits (Cattell, 1954; Cattell and Beloff, 1953; Cattell, Saunders, and Stice, 1950).

Empirical derivation of surface traits. As the result of an extensive investigation that began with all of the traits mentioned in the unabridged dictionary, Cattell (1943) arrived at the conclusion that there were fifty or sixty clusters of traits that could be considered to represent surface traits. In this study, the measures were examined not through the use of factor analysis but simply through ordinary correlational methods. Those that seemed to covary or go together were considered to represent a single surface trait. Cattell (1946) also showed that the large number of surface traits could be further reduced to about twenty *sectors by bringing together those surface traits that shared something in common.*

These surface traits are presented (Cattell, 1946) with an identifying index number, a brief descriptive title, and a list of the items or variables that comprise the cluster making up the trait. Illustrative of these traits are the following: integrity-altruism versus dishonesty, undependability; infantile, demanding, self-centeredness versus emotional maturity, frustration tolerance; gentlemanly, disciplined thoughtfulness versus foolish, extraverted lack of will; crude social assertion, exhibitionism versus obedience to authority, modesty.

Thus far, we have examined Cattell's conception of the trait and we have seen how he derives the two major classes of traits. It remains for us to discuss certain further distinctions which are concerned with the determinants or origins of the trait. Further, we shall consider the manner in which he represents the interaction among traits. As the reader will notice, almost all of the subsequent discussion is concerned with dynamic, source traits.

Ergs. In simplest terms an erg is a constitutional, dynamic, source trait. It is this concept that permits Cattell to give adequate representation to the importance of innately determined but modifiable impellents of behavior. His heavy emphasis upon ergic motivation reflects his conviction that hereditary determinants of behavior have been underestimated by contemporary American psychologists. He defines an erg as:

An innate psycho-physical disposition which permits its possessor to acquire reactivity (attention, recognition) to certain classes of objects more readily than others, to experience a specific emotion in regard to them, and to start on a course of action which ceases more completely at a certain specific goal activity than at any other. The pattern includes also preferred behavior subsidiation paths to the preferred goal (1950, p. 199).

As Cattell indicates, this definition has four major parts which refer to perceptual response, emotional response, instrumental acts leading to the goal, and the goal satisfaction itself. If the last two parts are combined the definition consists of a cognitive, affective, and conative component, just as in McDougall's famous definition of instinct. Actually, the erg serves a function within Cattell's theory of personality that is almost identical to the function that the concept of instinct or propensity fulfilled within McDougall's theory.

Cattell has not yet published a specific list of ergs because the evidence which exists at present concerning the nature of innate patterns of motivation has been derived principally from naturalistic and clinical observation and is in need of empirical refinement before it can be accepted with much confidence. He does consider the problem of how "innateness" can be empirically determined and discusses the means by which the strength of ergs can be measured. He also outlines the manner in which ergs develop or mature and uses the example of the sex drive to illustrate his discussion. Here his ideas follow rather closely the formulations of psychoanalytic theorists. The physiological and biochemical substrate of ergs is a matter of considerable interest to Cattell and he surveys in some detail available evidence concerning the relation between ergic behavior and biological processes (Cattell, 1950, Chapters 10 and 11). Unpublished research has led him to propose a tentative list of ten ergs: sex, self-assertion, escape (fear, anxiety), protectiveness (parental behavior), gregariousness, rest-seeking (sleep), exploration (curiosity), narcistic sex, appeal, construction.

METAERGS. A metaerg is an environmental-mold, dynamic, source trait. Thus, it is parallel to the erg except that it is the result of experiential or sociocultural factors, not constitutional determinants. Ergs are, to a considerable extent, given at birth but metaergs appear only with development. Included in this category are all derived motives such as attitudes, interests, and sentiments.

The *sentiment* is the most important of the metaergs in Cattell's theory. In his words sentiments are:

. . . major acquired dynamic trait structures which cause their posses-
sors to pay attention to certain objects or classes of object, and to feel
and react in a certain way with regard to them (1950, p. 161).

Again both the definition and the use of the concept are highly congruent with the parallel concept in McDougall's theory which was
also called the sentiment. The reason that sentiments are more important than many other metaergs is that they are more permanent and
stable and often appear earlier in development than attitudes or interests. Actually, the distinction between the various classes of
metaergs is not sharp and sentiments shade into attitudes which in turn
are only roughly distinguishable from interests. Again there is no
published list of sentiments but his investigations have enabled him
to identify a small number of important sentiments including: interest
in career, sports and games, religion, mechanical interests, patriotism,
superego structure, self sentiment.

THE CONCEPT OF SUBSIDIATION. One manner in which the interrelation among dynamic traits can be explored is through examining them
in terms of some purposive schema. Thus, if we study a number of
related traits we may expect to find that there is generally a final goal
which is approached by means of a series of subsidiary or instrumental
goals. Those traits which have to do with attaining a preliminary goal
are subsidiary to those which have to do with attaining a final goal or
one that is closer to the final goal. The distinction between erg, sentiment, attitude, and interest can thus be made simply in terms of the
subsidiation chain. All are dynamic traits but interests are in general
subsidiary to attitudes, which in turn are subsidiary to sentiments,
whereas sentiments are ordinarily subsidiary to ergs.

Actually the interaction among dynamic traits is more complex
than the above analysis implies, for examination of any given act will
ordinarily reveal a multitude of subsidiation chains involving specific
ergs, sentiments, and attitudes. In order to represent this complexity
Cattell suggests the use of a *dynamic lattice*, which shows the inter-
weaving and overlapping of the many subsidiation chains as in Figure
1. This diagram represents the subsidiation chains as paths moving
from specific attitudes and interests on the left through specific objects
at the level of sentiment in the center toward ergic goals on the right.
Thus, any specific object may be subsidiary to a number of ergic goals
and at the same time many attitudes and interests will ordinarily exist
that are subsidiary to the object.

The path which the individual follows in his attempts to reach
an ergic goal is by no means always direct. Cattell refers to the process

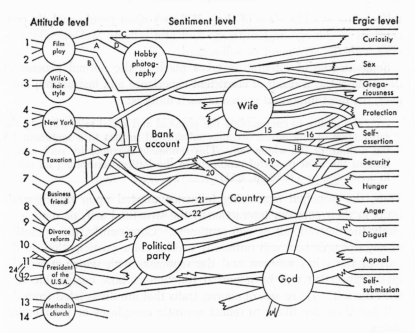

Figure 1. Portion of a dynamic lattice illustrating subsidiation. Reproduced from Cattell (1950), p. 156.

whereby a direct route to the goal is given up for a less direct one as *long-circuiting*. Most of the derived forms of motivation represent long-circuits, and are the consequence of barriers of frustrations that interfere with an innately preferred, direct means to the goal. The continuous modifiability of all traits, including the ergic, is emphasized throughout Cattell's writing but he points out that there is nevertheless a tendency for the organism to be conservative or resist change. This tendency is labeled *disposition rigidity* and is assumed to vary between different traits as well as among different individuals. In general, those forms of behavior that are acquired first are most resistant to change (show most disposition rigidity) so that ergs are usually more durable and persisting than subsequently derived dynamic traits.

THE SELF. Given the complex structure of traits and their interaction in the dynamic lattice, it is still necessary to introduce a further concept to account for the stability and organization which are so pervasive and important in human behavior. It is at this point that Cattell introduces his differentiated concept of the *self* and the *self sentiment.* His view of the self draws upon psychoanalytic conceptions of the ego and superego and also reflects McDougall's concern with the sentiment of self-regard.

Some degree of integration takes place in the normal process of development as a result of consistent experience and instruction; however, the most important source of such unity is:

> . . . the ability to contemplate the physical and social self, whereby the satisfaction of any desire becomes subsidiated in part to a sentiment for the welfare of the whole self. This sentiment becomes by such contributions the most powerful sentiment in the lattice, controlling all others in some degree (1950, p. 654).

Thus, the principal organizing influence exerted upon the dynamic traits in their complex interaction is the structural self, or more precisely the derived self or ego sentiment. Consistently, the operation of any dynamic trait will ordinarily involve some participation on the part of the self sentiment and the readiness with which it will be given expression will be a partial function of how compatible it is with the self. There are, of course, traits that are dissociated from the self but these are likely to reflect neurotic complexes or pathological states.

Not only is there a structural self but also there is an *ideal self* and a *real self*. Both of these selves depend upon the process of self-observation. The real self is the individual as he would have to admit himself to be in his most rational moments, and the ideal self is the individual as he would like to see himself. Thus, at least in the beginning of development, the real self is an imperfect reflection of the ideal self and may be seen as subsidiary to it. However, the passage of time and normal development may lead to an integration of these two selves within the dictates of the self sentiment.

> Normally the subsidiation of the actual to the ideal self tends to pass in time into a single self-sentiment, through abandoning of the symbols and behavior representing rewards which cannot be attained (or attained without too great a countervailing ergic deprivation) or through the elevation of the actual self to the aspired performance level (1950, pp. 656–657).

THE SPECIFICATION EQUATION. Under ideal circumstances where the psychologist knew what the relevant variables were that controlled behavior and also had precise means of measuring them, the individual's behavior in a given situation could be exactly predicted through substituting the appropriate scores or values in the following equation:

$$P_{ij} = S_{1j}T_{1i} + S_{2j}T_{2i} + \cdots + S_{nj}T_{ni} + S_jT_{ji}$$

where P represents the behavior or performance of the individual in a particular situation, T the various source traits that operate in this situation, and S the significance of this particular situation for each source trait. For present purposes it is not necessary to deal with the subscripts. Thus, if we have scores that represent for a given individual the extent to which he possesses the various source traits (they may be source traits that are common to many situations or unique to this one; further they may be common to many individuals or unique to this person) and also have a score that typifies the effect of this particular situation upon each of the source traits, we can enter these values in the specification equation and derive an exact quantitative prediction of how this individual will behave in this situation.

Needless to say, the above equation is a schematic device at the present time and has no immediate practical utility. It does serve, however, to illustrate the direction in which Cattell's research is leading. In an important sense, one might say that he is primarily concerned with identifying the important T's (source traits), devising means of measuring them accurately, and specifying the important S's (situational indices) or the contribution of the environment to the operation of these source traits.

THE DEVELOPMENT OF PERSONALITY

Cattell has considered the process of personality development so extensively in connection with the introduction of his structural concepts, as well as in connection with his discussion of behavior at various age levels (Cattell, 1950), that it is extremely difficult to give an adequate picture of his views. Here we can hope only to outline his treatment of the learning process and consider in a very schematic fashion his principles of personality formation.

It seems fair to say that in his developmental psychology Cattell has drawn heavily from both psychoanalysis and learning theory but has inserted many of his own ideas into this synthesis. For him the process of development consists primarily of the modification of ergs, the elaboration of metaergs, and the organization of a self structure. The ease and extent to which this kind of modification and growth takes place is a function of intelligence, amount of disposition rigidity, and strength of memory.

PRINCIPLES OF LEARNING. In representing the learning process Cattell has chosen to focus upon a series of choice points, or as he calls them *dynamic crossroads,* which represent events that follow the activation of some ergic pattern of behavior. That is, when the relatively innate pattern of adjustment is set into action this tendency, in combination with the particular environmental conditions that are operant, must result in one of several outcomes. Cattell has attempted to systematize these outcomes in terms of a sequential pattern of choices or crossroads.

Before outlining these crossroads, let us consider briefly Cattell's position in regard to the "laws of learning." Although he accepts the operation of both contiguity (classical conditioning) and reinforcement (law of effect), he clearly views the most important law to be the *dynamic law of effect.* According to his formulation responses tend to be learned that shorten the distance between the individual and the goal, but he implies further that the trial-and-error responses are elicited according to the principle of contiguity or association.

The *first dynamic crossroad* occurs when the individual makes an initial attempt to secure satisfaction of a given erg. There are four alternative outcomes that may follow upon instigation of the erg. First, the individual may secure gratification as a result of the innately determined pattern of behavior. Second, the individual may fail to secure gratification because of the ineffectiveness of the innate patterns of perceptual and motor response in the face of the particular environmental factors present. Third, the ergic pattern may be modified or superseded through the activation of another erg to which it is subsidiary. Fourth, the individual may fail to reach the goal because of the operation of a barrier, although the path to the goal is otherwise appropriate and is clearly perceived. Particularly important here is the distinction between the second (deprivation) and the fourth (frustration) alternatives. Cattell considers the characteristic reaction to deprivation to be *response dispersion.* In this case, the individual simply does not know what to attend to or how to respond in order to reduce the ergic tension and this leads to his responding in a more varied and indiscriminate manner. By contrast, the individual who encounters frustration feels rage and responds with aggression or pugnacity.

Cattell considers the further consequences of all four paths presented by the first crossroad, pointing to the importance of *confluence* or the development of response patterns (sentiments) that permit the simultaneous satisfaction of two or more ergs. He also points to the crucial role that response dispersion plays in conjunction with the dynamic law of effect in leading to the development of new patterns of behavior (sentiments). It is upon the fourth path, the ergic response faced with a barrier, that he focuses his further analysis. In fact, it is here that we encounter the *second crossroad.* The paths open to the individual at this point are: increased activity which leads to gratification, rage which overcomes the barrier and leads to gratification, and rage which proves to be ineffectual in the face of the barrier. The first two responses complete the behavioral sequence and necessitate no further comment, but the third response must be analyzed further.

Thus, the *third dynamic crossroad* is encountered when the individual reacts with rage to a barrier but is unable to surmount it. Here there are four paths of response: despair or giving up, fear and withdrawal, persistent ineffective pugnacity (aggression), and fantasy satisfaction. If the individual continues to respond in the manner implied by the second and third alternatives he will eventually either escape from the field, break through the goal, or else he must return to the first path and attempt to deny the source of stimulation. The fourth path is not crucial at this point, as it is likely to represent only a partial mode of response, and further it is seen as operating simultaneously with many of the paths of response yet to be outlined. Thus, the first alternative becomes the focus of our attention here.

The *fourth dynamic crossroad* is concerned with giving up the erg and with this step we move away from adjustments that are primarily external and visible to the observer toward adjustments that are primarily internal and only to be inferred. Cattell considers anxiety to be the key factor in denying or giving up the erg and further the development of this anxiety is intimately connected with the fear response that characterizes the second path of the third crossroad. (For a detailed account of Cattell's ideas concerning the origin of anxiety see Chapters 8 and 9 in Cattell, 1950.)

In the face of this anxious necessity of abandoning the ergic tendency the individual has four paths open to him. He may respond by suppressing the erg, that is, by voluntarily denying it and refusing to act out the relevant impulses. Second, he may attempt to repress it, repression being an involuntary process whereby unacceptable material is warded off from consciousness. Third, he may consciously sublimate the erg, that is, he may establish an acceptable substitute goal with full awareness of what he is doing. Fourth, he may return to persistent nonadaptive behavior or else resort to delinquency or some other socially unacceptable substitute goal.

Of these alternatives it is the attempted repression that captures our special attention and this represents the *fifth crossroad.* The individual is here presented with four alternative responses. He may resort to unconscious fantasies which occasionally may become conscious. Second, there is the possibility of successful repression, in which case the ergic impulses are maintained dependably at an unconscious level. Third, there may be unstable repression in which case the erg is maintained precariously at an unconscious level, usually with indirect consequences or effects upon the remainder of the individual's behavior. Fourth, there is the possibility of unconscious or involuntary sublimation.

The *sixth crossroad* is presented by the state of unstable repression. Here, the repression is not maintained successfully and the individual must resort to additional defensive maneuvers. Under these circumstances Cattell suggests that there are a total of ten different paths open to the individual. These paths correspond roughly to the defense mechanisms as they have been described by psychoanalytic theorists. These are: fantasy, reaction formation, projection, rationalization, further repression, restriction of the ego, other defense mechanisms, regression, displacement with symptom formation, and other symptom formation. The first seven paths are considered by Cattell to represent responses in which the ego is actively determining the mode of response; in the last three the id is the dominant force.

In our discussion of the dynamic crossroads we have used ergic motivation as our model throughout. Actually the same analysis can be carried out with derived motives, metaergs, as well as with those that are more closely linked to innate determinants.

In Cattell's system these six crossroads, in conjunction with the psychoanalytic concepts of id, ego, and superego, are used to represent both the path of normal development and also the manner in which neurotic, psychotic, and other deviant forms of behavior develop. The reader will find an account of the application of these concepts to such phenomena in Cattell's most recent book on personality (1950).

THE SOCIAL CONTEXT. Thus far, we have focused upon the individual and his development in interaction with the immediate environment. Here we shall suspend this restriction and consider the efforts Cattell has made to give adequate emphasis to sociocultural determinants of behavior.

Cattell suggests that objective dimensions may be used to describe groups in much the same manner as traits are used to describe individuals. These dimensions represent the group *syntality* (Cattell, 1948) which is the equivalent of the individual personality. Thus, an

important task for the individual who would study personality in relation to the sociocultural matrix is the description of the syntality
of the various groups that influence the individual personality. It is
only through an adequate representation of *both* the individual personality and the group syntality that he can hope to gain detailed
knowledge concerning the interaction between these two structures.

There are many social institutions that exert a molding or modifying
influence upon personality but by far the most important of these is
the family. In addition to this primary source of influence there are
other institutions whose role is worth consideration such as: occupation, school, peer group, religion, political party, and nation. Such
institutions may produce effects upon personality in one of three
ways. First, there may be a deliberate intention to produce a particular kind of character or personality. That is, the definition of socially
desirable behavior may include specification of personality traits and
the institution may involve a self-conscious attempt to produce these
characteristics. Second, situational or ecological factors may produce
effects that are not intended by the society or the institutions within
it. Third, as a result of patterns of behavior established through the
first or second processes, the individual may find further modification
of his personality necessary in order to express or gratify important
motives.

Thus, an adequate understanding of personality development must
include a specification of the contribution of various social institutions
ranging from the family to the nation or cultural group. Further, this
step can be taken only when the appropriate dimensions for describing and differentiating these groups and institutions have been isolated. We find that factor analysis plays just as crucial a role in the
description of the syntality as it did in the description of the individual
personality. Although work in this area has only begun, Cattell reports the results of one study of small groups (Cattell and Wispe,
1948) that led to seven factors or dimensions which he considers
promising for the description of the family syntality. These factors
are: extravert responsiveness versus withdrawal; intelligent *esprit de
corps;* realism, dependability versus instability, evasiveness; informed,
realistic relaxedness versus industriousness, rigid aggressiveness; practical shrewdness, doggedness versus autism, dynamic lability; forti-
tude versus easy verbal activity; friendly urbanity and *savoir-faire*
versus lack of group self-possession. Given these variables and means
of measuring them objectively, it is possible to proceed to plot the
relation between families whose structure varies in terms of such vari-

ables and individual personalities as described by the source traits we have already considered.

Cattell (1949) has also provided a set of dimensions for describing the syntality of nations. In this case, ten factors were derived from the study of seventy nations by means of seventy-two diverse measures. Of these ten factors only eight seemed to possess clear significance and these were: size; cultural pressure; enlightened affluence; thoughtful industriousness; vigorous, self-willed order; bourgeois-Philistinism; Buddhism-Mongolism; and cultural integration and morale.

In addition to the position we have summarized, Cattell (1950) has a great deal to say about the details of how the specific institutions interact with the individual personality. Here, it suffices for us to recognize the considerable role he assigns to such sociocultural variables, and to see that his approach to the empirical study of this interaction is consistent with his approach to the study of the individual personality in relative isolation. In both cases, delineation of the basic variables through the use of factor analysis occupies a crucial introductory step.

PRINCIPLES OF PERSONALITY FORMATION. After presenting his complex set of personality concepts, and at the same time discussing a wealth of empirical evidence bearing upon the development of personality, Cattell generalizes these concepts and findings in a series of seventeen principles or laws. These laws are concerned with such topics as the single drive, learning with the single motive, the maintenance of long-circuited structure, the self structure, personality integration, and personality and the larger context. To a considerable extent these generalizations represent a somewhat more formal statement of views that we have already summarized. Because of this redundancy we shall merely present the first three of these generalizations in order to give the reader their general flavor. The interested person will, of course, find a complete exposition in Cattell (1950).

Law 1. The law of innate goal tension patterns: An innate drive may be analyzed into an over-all goal tension and a series of subgoals (means-end) tensions. Any tension is manifested and measured by attentiveness to a particular kind of stimulus and a tendency (variously measured) to a particular kind of action. The main goal tension disappears as the main goal is reached, and the particular goal tension ceases as a particular intermediate goal is reached. The strength of action is a function of the total innate goal tensions (in their given appetitive state) and the strength of the stimulus situation (p. 633).

Law 2. The law of satisfaction in rigidity. Even when a dynamic gain exists from changing a trait, the change in behavior may be either resisted, i.e., may occur very slowly, or may not occur at all, due to factors of disposition rigidity (p. 635).

Law 3. Law of dispersion with excitement and deprivation. Continued stimulation of ergs, with deprivation of the goal, produces increasing variation in the stimuli to which attention is directed and increasing variation of response behavior (as well as introspectively, increased "excitement") (p. 635).

CHARACTERISTIC RESEARCH AND RESEARCH METHODS

In this section we shall mention very briefly certain distinctive aspects of Cattell's views concerning personality research. In addition, we shall summarize briefly an investigation of his that has applied the fruits of factor analytic studies in an investigation of the hereditary determination of personality. The reader will recall that we already have a considerable familiarity with Cattell's research as a result of frequent references to his empirical work in discussing his theoretical concepts.

RESEARCH METHODS. We have mentioned earlier Cattell's conviction that *large-scale research* will produce the most significant advances of the future in this area. Coupled with this is his belief that most psychologists have unwisely shunned the necessity of *careful description* of personality in favor of moving toward impressive generalization and the study of developmental phenomena. Much of his work, particularly that concerned with identifying source and surface traits, can be considered simply an attempt to fulfill this task of description and provide a firm base upon which future investigation and generalization can build.

One of the most novel features of Cattell's writing has been his consistent emphasis upon the different types of correlational studies that the investigator may pursue. First, he points out, there are *R-technique* studies which represent the customary approach of the psychologist. Here, a large number of individuals are compared in terms of their performance on two or more tests. The fundamental question is whether individuals who score high on one test tend to do so on the other test, and the resulting coefficient represents the extent to which scores on the tests covary or go together. Second, there is the *P-technique* where scores for the same individual on a number of measures are compared for different occasions or at different times. Here we are asking how consistent the individual's behavior is, and the resulting statistic is an index of how closely different samples of the same individual's behavior covary or go together. Third, there is the *Q-technique* where two individuals are correlated on a large number of different measures. In this case, the resulting coefficient represents a measure of similarity or covariance between two individuals and if such correlations are carried out on a number of persons the investigator may secure a typology or a clustering together of persons who are similar on these measures.

THE INHERITANCE OF PERSONALITY. As we have seen, Cattell has shown a steady interest in the role of hereditary determinants of behavior and this theoretical concern is mirrored in research activity. His interest in psychological genetics and his conviction that it is a crucial area of research are clearly reflected in the following passage:

> Psychological genetics is a sadly neglected crossroads embarrassing the main highways of psychology and genetics. In genetics this neglect involves nothing worse than a failure to meet the challenge of unusual methodological difficulties; but in psychology its causes are less reputable and its consequences more devastating. For a psychology lacking any dependable or precise knowledge of innate organizations and influences is bankrupt in its theoretical structure and a charlatan in its clinical and educational practices (1953, p. 76).

A number of his studies are concerned with the influence of genetic factors upon personality and intelligence (Cattell, 1945; Cattell and Molteno, 1940; Cattell and Willson, 1938), but his most interesting approach to this problem is contained in two recent papers.

The first of these papers (Cattell, 1953) contains an attempt to develop a means of studying the contributions of genetic determinants to behavior that is superior to the methods used customarily. Cattell asserts that psychologists traditionally have employed research designs and modes of statistical analysis that are adequate only to answer the question of whether there is *any* influence of hereditary factors upon the psychological characteristic under consideration. He argues that this is not a reasonable question to ask, for what we need to know is something about *how much* influence is exerted by heredity and, in particular, how much influence relative to the influence of environmental factors. As a means to this goal he outlines a multiple variance procedure that will permit the investigator to make inferences about the relative contributions of hereditary and environmental factors to specified dimensions.

In the second paper, Cattell, Blewett, and Beloff (1955) report the results of a study that followed the advice offered in the first paper. In this research data were collected from a large number of subjects consisting of 104 identical twins, 64 fraternal twins, 182 siblings reared together, 72 unrelated children reared together, and 504 children in the general population. Each of the subjects filled out the *Junior Personality Quiz* (Cattell and Beloff, 1953) which provides a measure of twelve personality dimensions identified through earlier factor analytic studies. Thus, Cattell secured measures for individuals of varied hereditary and environmental similarity on twelve personality factors which earlier research had established as significant.

The over-all findings of the study suggest that for five of the factors environmental determinants appear to play a dominant role. These factors are: tender-mindedness, general neuroticism, surgency-desurgency, will control, and somatic anxiety. In the case of two of these factors (general neuroticism and somatic anxiety) hereditary influences seem quite important in determining between-family differences although within-family differences seem to be largely environmentally controlled. Four factors seem to be equally influenced by heredity and environment in terms of differences within the family although the role of heredity is greater as a determinant of differences between families. These factors are: energetic conformity, dominance, socialized morale, and impatient dominance. Finally, there were three factors (cyclothymia versus schizothymia, adventurous cyclothymia versus submissiveness, and general intelligence) where the role of hereditary factors seemed generally most important. For each factor or variable Cattell is able to provide a tentative ratio that indicates the relative contribution to this variable of hereditary and environmental determinants.

These findings are clearly of a preliminary nature; nevertheless they provide more illumination than has hitherto been available concerning the inheritance of personality. The study illustrates Cattell's ingenuity in approaching problems that have been a source of concern and interest for psychologists and demonstrates how once the variables of personality have been identified to the investigator's satisfaction it is then possible for him to approach a host of significant problems that rest upon or assume the isolation of such variables.

CURRENT STATUS AND EVALUATION

Theories of personality based upon factor analysis reflect current psychological emphasis upon quantitative methods and in turn are reflected in large numbers of specially designed personality studies. Eysenck and Cattell, as well as others working in this area, have shown a ready inclination to convert their theoretical ideas into empirical steps. In contrast to other personality theories there is no tendency for theory to develop as an armchair abstraction while the empirical appraisal lingers far behind. In fact, there is scarcely any clear separation of theory and experiment. This empirical vigor seems assured for the future not only because of the demonstrated talents of those working in the area but also because individuals attracted to these formulations will almost certainly possess a similar orientation. In other words, the nature of the position guarantees that individuals who occupy it will be highly empirical. Further, the contemporary fascination of psychologists with the quantitative makes it unlikely that there will be any dearth of scholars interested in advancing and developing this body of thought and empirical finding.

In an area of psychology that has been characterized by sensitivity and subjectivity, factor theorists have introduced a welcome aura of tough-mindedness and emphasis upon the concrete. Where many personality theorists have been content to elaborate concepts and assumptions to a point where the investigator is trapped in a morass of conflicting and unclear implications, the factor theorist is inclined to put forward his faith in terms of a simple and lucid set of dimensions or factors. Thus, simplicity and explicitness are cardinal virtues of this brand of theory.

Not only is the factor theorist economical and explicit in his formulations but also he is operational. More than almost any other brand of psychological theory this position has included a detailed concern for clear and unambiguous empirical definition. The factor theorist has borrowed much of the traditional skill of the psychometrician in devising adequate means of measurement and has tended to ask embarrassing but important questions concerning unidimensionality, internal consistency, and repeatability which surely have had a beneficial effect upon colleagues who are less concerned with the details of measurement.

Whereas most personality theorists have arrived at their conception of the crucial personality variables through a process that is largely intuitive and unspecified, these theorists provide an objective and replicable procedure for the determination of underlying variables. Although one may quarrel with the assertion that the variables are determined by the factor analysis rather than by the tests that are inserted into the factor analysis, there is no possibility of objecting to the claim that factor analysis at least provides a test of whether the variable that had already been conceived of, and was represented in the initial measure, actually exists. In other words, even if factor analysis depends upon prior ideas, and surely it does, it provides a means of assessing the fruitfulness of these ideas. In contrast, many personality theorists have originated hosts of personality variables without ever submitting them to the empirical crucible.

Consistent with the last idea is the assertion that one particularly important function of factor analytic studies is to provide a completely independent means of confirming or denying the variables that have been inferred or intuited out of experimental and clinical observation. That is, when there is congruence between the underlying variables of the clinician and the factor theorist, the highly divergent paths followed in arriving at the similar sets of variables provides a reassuring promise that the investigator is dealing with real and important consistencies in behavior.

Most personality theories owe more to the clinical setting than to the computation room. Consequently, it is not surprising to find that many psychologists have treated factor theory as an interloper on the personality scene. One of the most frequent and vigorously voiced criticisms alleges that factor theorists create systems of artifacts that have no true relation to any single individual and consequently distort and misrepresent reality. This point of view is stated effectively by Allport (1937):

> An entire population (the larger the better) is put into the grinder, and the mixing is so expert that what comes through is a link of factors in which every individual has lost his identity. His dispositions are mixed with everyone else's dispositions. The factors thus obtained represent only *average* tendencies. Whether a factor is really an *organic* disposition in any one individual life is not demonstrated. All one can say for certain is that a factor is an empirically derived component of the *average* personality, and that the average personality is a complete abstraction. This objection gains point when one reflects that seldom do the factors derived in this way resemble the dispositions and traits identified by clinical methods when the individual is studied intensively (p. 244).

The essence of this objection is that the derived factors are not psychologically meaningful and consequently that they do not fit with the observations of other students of human behavior. Thus, most psychologists simply do not find the factors of the factor analyst useful in describing individual behavior. The reader should note that the factor analyst is in a rather precarious position here, for if his factors fit closely with prior observations of human behavior he is accused of having labored long and hard to produce the obvious. If his factors do not show this correspondence, he is accused of adding confusion to an already confused scene. Our discussion of Cattell's surface and source traits make clear that the factor analyst does not necessarily anticipate that his factors will show any exact correspondence with the results of simple observation of behavior. Indeed, it is the intent of such theorists to go beyond simple observation and dredge up variables that have not yet been inferred. Furthermore, the factor theorist would assert, with the passage of time and the accumulation of additional empirical findings these factors will become as meaningful and more useful than those psychological variables that are now in common use. Whether this will prove to be the case remains to be seen.

Another popular criticism is that what comes out of factor analysis is no more than what is put in. The factor analyst objects to subjectivity and eliminates it in the place where it is usually encountered, but actually he is simply moving subjectivity or intuition back to the point where he decides what tests or measures will be introduced into his matrix of correlations. This criticism seems clearly valid where the theorist maintains that the method of factor analysis, unaided by prior hypotheses, suffices to produce the fundamental dimensions of personality. However, this would not be the stand of many factor theorists. For example, Eysenck's method of criterion analysis makes very explicit the fact that the individual must have hypothesized the nature of the psychological factor before embarking upon his study.

Other critics point to the inevitable subjectivity involved in naming the factors that result from factor analysis. Particularly if the elements composing the factor are very diverse, as is often the case, the investigator may have to resort to as much imagination and ingenuity in arriving at an over-all caption for the variable as a clinician would ordinarily employ in describing a single intensively studied case. The last two points may be generalized as a claim that the concern for rigor and empirical control, professed by the factor analyst, is not evenly spread over the research process. Thus, these critics assert that whereas the factor analysis may be carried out with great care and attention to detail, the same amount of attention is not always paid to the steps that have led to the scores from which the factors are derived or the process by means of which the eventual factor is interpreted.

The many disagreements among factor analysis concerning the computational or interpretive steps involved in factor analysis provide a ready target for the detractor. If this method is so objective and rational, why is it that those who know most about it are least agreed as to just how the process should go? If the factor analysts cannot agree, why should the less sophisticated public accept the word of any single factor theorist as definitive? Perhaps more serious is the dissatisfaction that mathematicians display with the mathematical reasoning that lies behind factor analysis. A quantitative technique that involves mathematical flaws is more vulnerable than a qualitative technique that makes no pretense of being completely rationalized.

Many psychologists have felt that factor theories are not theories at all. Some of the systems simply specify important variables or factors but with no indication of the developmental process or provision of the detailed assumptions concerning behavior that would be necessary to permit predictions concerning unobserved data. As we have seen, this criticism does not apply to Cattell's position and Eysenck is moving in a direction intended to meet this criticism.

The necessary emphasis upon quantitative scores reduces the kinds of problems and variables that the factor analyst can presently deal with. Thus, many personality theorists would argue that early stress upon quantification results in artificial and premature congealing of an area that is still in an exploratory stage. Such critics assert that although factor analysis purports to be concerned with discovering the underlying dimensions of personality in a completely general sense, in fact the kinds of data that must be employed place tremendous restrictions upon the nature of the variables that may be derived.

Whatever the shortcomings of factor theories may be, it is clear that their emphasis upon explicitness and adequate standards of measurement represents a very healthy influence. One might contend that the *content* of factor theories may or may not make a fruitful contribution to future theories of personality but the *style* or mode of approach of these theorists will surely have an impact upon the way in which future theory will develop.

BIBLIOGRAPHY

PRIMARY SOURCES

Cattell, R. B. *Description and measurement of personality.* New York: World Book Co., 1946.

Cattell, R. B. *Personality: A systematic, theoretical, and factual study.* New York: McGraw, 1950.

Eysenck, H. J. *Dimensions of personality.* London: Routledge and Kegan Paul, 1947.

Eysenck, H. J. *The scientific study of personality.* London: Routledge and Kegan Paul, 1952.
Eysenck, H. J. *The structure of human personality.* New York: Wiley, 1953a.

REFERENCES

Allport, G. W. *Personality: A psychological interpretation.* New York: Holt, 1937.
Burt, C. L. *The factors of the mind.* New York: Macmillan, 1941.
Cattell, R. B. *A guide to mental testing.* Bickley, Kent, Eng.: Ohio, London Press, 1936, Rev. Ed., 1948.
Cattell, R. B. *General psychology.* Cambridge, Mass.: Sci-Art, 1941.
Cattell, R. B. The description of personality: basic traits resolved into clusters. *J. abnorm. soc. Psychol.,* 1943, *38,* 476–506.
Cattell, R. B. *The culture free test of intelligence.* Champaign, Ill.: Inst. Pers. and Abil. Test., 1944.
Cattell, R. B. The cultural functions of social stratification: I. Regarding the genetic basis of society. *J. soc. Psychol.,* 1945, *21,* 3–23.
Cattell, R. B. *Description and measurement of personality.* New York: World Book Co., 1946.
Cattell, R. B. Concepts and methods in the measurement of group syntality. *Psychol. Rev.,* 1948, *55,* 48–63.
Cattell, R. B. The dimensions of culture patterns by factorization of national character. *J. abnorm. soc. Psychol.,* 1949, *44,* 443–469.
Cattell, R. B. *Personality: A systematic, theoretical, and factual study.* New York: McGraw, 1950.
Cattell, R. B. *Factor analysis: an introduction and manual for psychologist and social scientist.* New York: Harper, 1952.
Cattell, R. B. Research designs in psychological genetics with special reference to the multiple variance method. *Amer. J. Hum. Genet.,* 1953, *5,* 76–93.
Cattell, R. B. *The O-A Personality Test Battery.* Champaign, Ill.: Inst. Pers. and Abil. Test., 1954.
Cattell, R. B. The principal replicated factors discovered in objective personality tests. *J. abnorm. soc. Psychol.,* 1955, *50,* 291–314.
Cattell, R. B., and Beloff, J. R. Research origins and construction of the IPAT Junior Personality Quiz. *J. consult. Psychol.,* 1953, *17,* 436–442.
Cattell, R. B., Blewett, D. B., and Beloff, J. R. The inheritance of personality. *Amer. J. Hum. Genet.,* 1955, *7,* 122–146.
Cattell, R. B., and Molteno, E. V. Contributions concerning mental inheritance: II. Temperament. *J. genet. Psychol.,* 1940, *57,* 31–47.
Cattell, R. B., and Saunders, D. R. Inter-relation and matching of personality factors from behavior rating, questionnaire and objective test data. *J. soc. Psychol.,* 1950, *31,* 243–260.
Cattell, R. B., Saunders, D. R., and Stice, G. F. *The 16 personality factor questionnaire.* Champaign, Ill.: Inst. Pers. and Abil. Test., 1950.
Cattell, R. B., and Willson, J. L. Contributions concerning mental inheritance: I. Of intelligence. *Brit. J. educ. Psychol.,* 1938, *8,* 129–149.
Cattell, R. B., and Wispe, L. G. The dimension of syntality in small groups. *J. soc. Psychol.,* 1948, *28,* 57–78.

Eysenck, H. J. Suggestibility and hypnosis—an experimental analysis. *Proc. roy. Soc. Med.*, 1943a, *36*, 349–354.

Eysenck, H. J. Suggestibility and hysteria. *J. Neurol. Psychiat.*, 1943b, *6*, 22–31.

Eysenck, H. J. Suggestibility to a visual illusion, as related to primary and secondary suggestibility and other functions. *Brit. J. Psychol.*, 1943c, *34*, 32–36.

Eysenck, H. J. States of high suggestibility and the neuroses. *Amer. J. Psychol.*, 1944, *57*, 406–411.

Eysenck, H. J. *Dimensions of personality*. London: Routledge and Kegan Paul, 1947.

Eysenck, H. J. Criterion analysis—an application of the hypothetico-deductive method to factor analysis. *Psychol. Rev.*, 1950, *57*, 38–53.

Eysenck, H. J. *The scientific study of personality*. London: Routledge and Kegan Paul, 1952.

Eysenck, H. J. *The structure of human personality*. New York: Wiley, 1953a.

Eysenck, H. J. *Uses and abuses of psychology*. Harmondsworth, Middlesex: Penguin, 1953b.

Eysenck, H. J. *The psychology of politics*. London: Routledge and Kegan Paul, 1954.

Eysenck, H. J. Psychiatric diagnosis as a psychological and statistical problem. *Psychol. Reports*, 1955a, *1*, 3–17.

Eysenck, H. J. A dynamic theory of anxiety and hysteria. *J. ment. Sci.*, 1955b, *101*, 28–51.

Eysenck, H. J., and Furneaux, W. D. Primary and secondary suggestibility: an experimental and statistical study. *J. exp. Psychol.*, 1945, *35*, 485–503.

Eysenck, H. J., and Prell, D. B. The inheritance of neuroticism: an experimental study. *J. ment. Sci.*, 1951, *97*, 441–465.

Eysenck, H. J., and Rees, W. L. States of heightened suggestibility: narcosis. *J. ment. Sci.*, 1945, *91*, 301–310.

French, J. W. The description of personality measurements in terms of rotated factors. Princeton, N. J.: *Educ. Test Serv.*, 1953.

Guilford, J. P. When not to factor analyze. *Psychol. Bull.*, 1952, *49*, 26–37.

Guilford, J. P. *Psychometric methods*. 2nd Ed. New York: McGraw, 1954.

Himmelweit, Hilda T., and Petrie, Aneseth. The measurement of personality in children. *Brit. J. educ. Psychol.*, 1951, *21*, 9–29.

MacKinnon, D. W. The structure of personality. In J. McV. Hunt (Ed.). *Personality and the behavior disorders*. Vol. 1. New York: Ronald Press, 1944, pp. 3–48.

Spearman, C. "General intelligence" objectively determined and measured. *Amer. J. Psychol.*, 1904, *15*, 201–293.

Spearman, C. *Abilities of man*. New York: Macmillan, 1927.

Thomson, G. H. *The factorial analysis of human ability*. 5th Ed. Boston: Houghton, 1951.

Thurstone, L. L. Multiple factor analysis. *Psychol. Rev.*, 1931, *38*, 406–427.

Thurstone, L. L. *The vectors of mind*. Chicago: Univ. of Chicago Press, 1935.

Thurstone, L. L. *Multiple factor analysis: a development and expansion of the vectors of the mind*. Chicago: Univ. of Chicago Press, 1947.

Thurstone, L. L. Psychological implications of factor analysis. *Amer. Psychologist*, 1948, *3*, 402–408.

11.

Stimulus-Response Theory

We shall present here the personality theory that is most elegant, most economical, and shows the closest link to its natural science forebears. Stimulus-response (s-r) theory, at least in its origins, can accurately be labeled a laboratory theory in contrast to the other theories with which we have dealt where the role of clinical or naturalistic observation has been much more important. Consistent with these origins is the position's explicitness, economy of formulation, and the serious efforts made to provide suitable empirical anchoring for the main terms of the theory.

Actually there is no single s-r theory, but rather a cluster of theories all resembling each other more or less, but at the same time each possessing certain distinctive qualities. These systems began as attempts to account for the acquisition and retention of new forms of behavior that appeared with experience. It is thus no surprise to find that the learning process is given predominant emphasis. Although innate factors are not ignored, the s-r theorist is primarily concerned with the process whereby the individual mediates between his array of responses and the tremendous variety of stimulation (internal and external) to which he is exposed.

Although there is no need to engage in a detailed discussion of the complex origins of s-r theory, it would scarcely be appropriate to introduce this theory without mentioning the contributions of Ivan Pavlov, John B. Watson, and Edward L. Thorndike. The distin

420

guished Russian physiologist Ivan Pavlov (1906, 1927) was able to demonstrate that through the simultaneous presentation of an unconditioned stimulus (meat paste) and a conditioned stimulus (sound from a tuning fork), the conditioned stimulus would eventually come to elicit a response (salivation) which originally could be elicited only by the unconditioned stimulus. The response of salivation to the sound of the tuning fork was referred to as a conditioned response (reflex). This process of conditioning became, in the hands of a number of American psychologists, a means of conceiving of behavior so that the dangers of subjectivity could be avoided. Here, for the first time, it seemed possible to build an objective psychology that dealt only with observables. J. B. Watson (1916, 1925) was the leader of this assault upon subjectivity and intuition. He seized upon Pavlov's principle of conditioning and, combining this with ideas he had already developed, presented to the world a position he called "behaviorism." This objective and environmentalistic point of view quickly came to typify American psychology and even today it is closely linked with the most distinctive features of psychology in this country. At the same time that these developments were proceeding, Edward Thorndike (1911, 1932) was demonstrating the signal importance of reward and punishment in the learning process, and his "law of effect" has become one of the cornerstones of modern learning theory. In spite of the crucial nature of Pavlov's contributions, s-r theory with its heavy stress upon objectivity, its emphasis upon careful experimentation, and its strong functional flavor exists as the most singularly American theory of all the positions we shall consider.

Psychologists have devoted more thought and activity to the construction of learning theory than to any other contemporary theoretical enterprise. As a result of the ideas and investigations of Edward L. Thorndike, John B. Watson, Edward C. Tolman, Edwin R. Guthrie, Clark L. Hull, and others, the dominant theoretical interest of American psychologists shifted during the third decade of this century toward the learning process. During the intervening years most major theoretical issues in psychology have been debated within the framework of learning theory. It is true that not all of these developments can correctly be called s-r formulations. In fact, one of the main issues within learning theory is concerned with just this question. Much of this controversy has centered about Edward Tolman's seminal contributions which have derived from the attempt to develop a theoretical position that does not conceive of learning as a process of developing s-r connections. Lewin also made sallies in this direction, although he was not deeply and continuously concerned with the learning process. This distinction between theories such as Tolman's and Lewin's on the one hand, and Hull's or Guthrie's on the other, is usually labeled an opposition between cognitive and s-r theories. As the title of this chapter implies, we are here concerned only with the latter formulations. The interested reader will find an excellent summary of all the major types of learning theory, including cognitive theory, in Hilgard (1956).

Among those theories that may accurately be called s-r theories, there remains another distinction important for our discussion. We find that some of these positions adopt as their leading assumption a principle concerned with reinforcement or reward, whereas others strongly emphasize contiguity or association. That is, some theories consider the essential condition for the formation of new s-r connections to be reinforcement or reward accompanying the response. Other theories consider the simultaneous occurrence (contiguity) of the stimulus and the response to be the mediator of the new s-r bond. Edwin Guthrie's position is the best-known example of the contiguity or association type of theory and Clark Hull's theory is the best-developed example of a reinforcement position. Again the focus of our chapter is restrictive, as it is only with reinforcement theory that we shall be concerned. More specifically, we shall be primarily interested in attempts to generalize or apply the theoretical position of Clark Hull (1943, 1951, 1952) to phenomena of interest to the personality psychologist.

What are the reasons for narrowing our interest to the cluster of formulations emanating from Hull and his writings? First of all, this theoretical position is by far the most elegant and highly developed of all theories of learning. The viewpoint has been stated more explicitly, has been more adequately formalized, and there has been a greater wealth of related empirical investigation than in the case of any other theory of learning. Second, and most important, it is largely the students of Hull who have made serious and systematic attempts to apply their laboratory-developed theories to the understanding of personality. There are many who feel that Tolman's theory offers at least as much promise as Hull's for application to personality and social phenomena but this promise for the most part remains to be demonstrated. Thus, our emphasis is determined not by any conviction that reinforcement theory is necessarily the most fruitful version of learning theory but rather by the fact that it is currently the most highly developed and therefore provides the largest amount of clear and unambiguous formulation and research. It remains the task of the future to sort among the formulations of Guthrie, Hull, Skinner, Tolman, *et al.*, for that single system of constructs that will be most uniquely fruitful.

Contrary to the theories we have already discussed, the rudiments of this position were developed in connection with data that possess little seeming similarity to the data of major interest to the personality psychologist. It may be an overstatement to say that the white rat has had more to do with shaping this theory than have human subjects, but it is certainly true that members of lower species have had infinitely more to do with the theory's development than in the case of the other theories we have considered. One must not, however, overemphasize the importance of the place of origin of this theory. A theory should be evaluated in terms of what it does rather than where it comes from. Hull, the intellectual father of this position, made explicit his intent of developing a general theory of *human* behavior at the very beginning of his theoretical strivings. It was only for reasons of strategy that he chose to develop his initial ideas against the relatively stable background provided by animal behavior in carefully controlled experimental situations. Thus, the essence of this theory did not develop from the study of lower organisms because of any conviction that all behavioral problems could be solved in this manner. Rather, it was hoped that the simplicity of the lower organism would permit the establishment of certain fundamentals which, when elaborated through the study of complex human behavior, might prove to be the core of a satisfactory theory of behavior. This readiness to change and extend the peripheral part of the theory, at the same time maintaining certain core assumptions and concepts, is clearly demonstrated in the work of many of Hull's students. Consistent with this point of view we shall make no effort here to outline the details of Hull's theory but rather will focus upon attempts that have been made to modify or elaborate the theory so as to deal with behavior of crucial interest to the personality psychologist. The outstanding example of such a derived theory is contained in the work of Dollard and Miller, and our chapter will give predominant attention to this position. Also of importance here are the writings of Mowrer and Sears, although space limitations will permit us to deal with their contributions only in passing.

Before turning to the details of these theories, a word should be said concerning the Institute of Human Relations at Yale University.

This institution was established in 1933 under the direction of Mark May in an effort to bring about closer collaboration and integration among psychology, psychiatry, sociology, and anthropology. The Institute embraced all of these traditionally separate departments. The first decade of its existence represents one of the most fruitful periods of collaboration in the behavioral sciences that has occurred in any American university. Although Clark Hull provided the theoretical underpinning for this group, its activities were by no means focused primarily on experimental psychology. Indeed, social anthropology, the study of the social aspects of man in nonliterate societies, contributed an important element to the intellectual framework of this group and there was an intense interest in psychoanalytic theory which contributed to many of the theoretical and research ideas of members of the group. During this ten-year period a remarkable group of young men received training either as graduate students or young staff members and upon all of them this experience seems to have exerted a powerful and enduring influence. Among the outstanding members of this group are John Dollard, Ernest Hilgard, Carl Hovland, Donald Marquis, Neal Miller, O. H. Mowrer, Robert Sears, Kenneth Spence, and John Whiting. It was the Institute of Human Relations, directed by Mark May, infused with the ideas of Clark Hull, and vitalized by the productive scholarship of the individuals just mentioned, that resulted in the developments with which we are concerned in this chapter.

THE REINFORCEMENT THEORY OF DOLLARD AND MILLER

This theory represents the efforts of two individuals, sophisticated in both laboratory and clinical investigation, to modify and simplify Hull's reinforcement theory so that it can be used easily and effectively to deal with events of major interest to the social and clinical psychologist. The details of the theory have been shaped not only by the formulations of Hull but also by psychoanalytic theory and by the findings and generalizations of social anthropology. As we shall see, the concept of habit, which represents a stable s-r connection, is crucial to this position. In fact, most of the theory is concerned with specifying the conditions under which habits form and are dissolved. The relatively small number of concepts that are employed for this purpose have been used with great ingenuity by the authors to account for phenomena of central interest to the clinician, for example, repression, displacement, conflict. In many instances the authors have attempted to derive from psychoanalytic writing and clinical observation substantive wisdom concerning behavior which in turn they have incorporated within their s-r concepts. Thus, a good deal of the application of the theory consists of the translation of general observation, or vague theoretical formulation, into the more aseptic terms of s-r theory. Although translation is not in itself a particularly important goal, this effort has frequently made possible new insights and predictions concerning unobserved empirical events, and these functions represent the highest order of theoretical contribution.

As we have agreed, the core of this position is a description of the learning process and Miller and Dollard clearly express their general view of this process and its constituent elements in the following passage:

> What, then, is learning theory? In its simplest form, it is the study of the circumstances under which a response and a cue stimulus become connected. After learning has been completed, response and cue are bound together in such a way that the appearance of the cue evokes the response. . . . Learning takes place according to definite psychological principles. Practice does not always make perfect. The connection between a cue and a response can be strengthened only under certain conditions. The learner must be driven to make the response and rewarded for having responded in the presence of the cue. This may be expressed in a homely way by saying that in order to learn one must want something, notice something, do something, and get something. Stated more exactly, these factors are drive, cue, response and reward. These elements in the learning process have been carefully explored, and further complexities have been discovered. Learning theory has become a firmly knit body of principles which are useful in describing human behavior (1941, pp. 1–2).

In some respects John Dollard and Neal Miller provide striking contrasts, whereas in other regards their backgrounds show great similarity. They are different in that Miller has advanced important ideas and findings primarily within the domain of experimental psychology, and Dollard has made significant anthropological and sociological contributions. However, both have been influenced heavily by their experiences at the Institute of Human Relations and consistent with this is their indebtedness to Hull and Freud. Perhaps the fruitfulness of their collaboration has derived from this common core of conviction upon which each has erected unique empirical and theoretical strengths.

John Dollard was born in Menasha, Wisconsin, on August 29, 1900. He received an A.B. from the University of Wisconsin in 1922 and subsequently secured his M.A. (1930) and Ph.D. (1931) in sociology from the University of Chicago. From 1926 until 1929 he served as assistant to the president of the University of Chicago. In 1932 he accepted a position as assistant professor of anthropology at Yale University and in the following year became an assistant professor of sociology in the recently formed Institute of Human Relations. In 1935 he became a research associate in the institute and since 1948 has been a research associate and professor of psychology. He was trained in psychoanalysis at the Berlin Institute and is currently a member of the Western New England Psychoanalytic Society. Dollard's convictions concerning, and personal dedication to, the unification of the social sciences is reflected not only in his publications but also in the remarkable fact that he has had academic appointments in anthropology, sociology, and psychology all at the same university. It should be noted that this interdisciplinary activity occurred at a time when the individual disciplines were much less cordial to integration than they are at present. Dollard has written numerous technical articles in the social sciences which have ranged from ethnology to psychotherapy. He has authored a number of books which reflect this same wide-ranging interest. *Caste and class in a Southern town* (1937) is a highly regarded field study concerned with the role of the Negro in a southern community and represents one of the early examples of culture and personality analysis. This was followed by a related volume, *Children of bondage* (1940), which was coauthored with Allison Davis. He published two volumes concerned with the psychological analysis of fear: *Victory over fear* (1942) and *Fear in battle* (1943); and a significant monograph concerned with the use of life history material, *Criteria for the life history* (1936). Most recently he has published jointly with Frank Auld and Alice White *Steps in psychotherapy* (1953), a book presenting a method of psychotherapy which includes the detailed description of an individual in treatment.

Neal E. Miller was born in Milwaukee, Wisconsin, on August 3, 1909, and received his B.S. from the University of Washington in 1931. He received his M.A. from Stanford University in 1932 and his Ph.D. in psychology from Yale University in 1935. From 1932 until 1935 he served as an assistant in psychology at the Institute of Human Relations and in 1935–1936 he was a Social Science Research Council traveling fellow during which time he secured a training analysis at the Vienna Institute of Psychoanalysis. From 1936 until 1940 he was an instructor and subsequently assistant professor at the Institute of Human Relations and in 1941 he became a research associate and associate professor. From 1942 to 1946 he directed a psychological research project for the Army Air Force and in 1946 returned to Yale University. Since 1950 he has been the James Rowland Angell professor of psychology at Yale University. Aside from his collaboration with John Dollard, Miller is best known in psychology for his careful experimental and theoretical work on the acquisition of drives, the nature of reinforcement, and the study of conflict. This work is presented in detail in journal publications although much of it is summarized in two excellent handbook chapters (Miller, 1944; Miller, 1951a).

In 1939 several staff members of the Institute of Human Relations including Dollard and Miller published a monograph titled *Frustration and aggression.* This was an early and interesting example of the kind of application with which we are concerned in this chapter. The authors attempted to analyze frustration and its consequence in terms of s-r concepts and in their monograph present a systematic formulation of this position, together with a considerable amount of new investigation and predictions concerning yet-to-be-observed events. This work not only illustrates the integration of s-r concepts, psychoanalytic formulation, and anthropological evidence but it also provides evidence for the fruitfulness of this union, as it has led to a host of related empirical studies. Miller and Dollard have written jointly two volumes representing the attempt to apply a simplified version of Hull's reinforcement theory to the problems of the social psychologist (*Social learning and imitation,* 1941) and to the problems of the clinical or personality psychologist (*Personality and psychotherapy,* 1950). It is primarily the contents of these volumes, particularly the latter one, which will form the basis for the exposition to follow.

THE STRUCTURE OF PERSONALITY

Dollard and Miller have shown a great deal of interest in learning and the process of development. Consistently they have shown much less interest in the structural or relatively unchanging elements of personality. Granted that these structural aspects are not emphasized, what concept do they employ to represent the stable and enduring characteristics of the person? Habit, one of the key concepts in s-r theory, occupies this role.

Habit. A habit is a link or association between a stimulus (cue) and a response. As we shall discover, the bulk of this theory is concerned with specifying the conditions under which habits are formed and broken or replaced. However, little or no attention is devoted to specifying classes of habits or listing the major varieties of habits thus far observed. Although personality consists primarily of habits, their particular structure will depend upon the unique events to which the individual has been exposed. Further, this is only a temporary structure, as the habits of today may be altered as a result of tomorrow's experience. Dollard and Miller are content to specify the principles governing habit formation and leave to the individual clinician or investigator the task of specifying the habits which characterize any particular person.

It must be pointed out that habits are not the only enduring portion of the personality, as there are also primary drives and secondary or derived drives as well as response hierarchies. All of these can be considered a part of the structure of personality. However, these concepts are better discussed in subsequent sections.

THE DYNAMICS OF PERSONALITY

Dollard and Miller are explicit in defining the nature of motivation and they specify in considerable detail the development and elaboration of motives; but there is again no interest in taxonomy or classification. Rather, they have focused upon certain salient motives and in their analysis of these have attempted to illustrate the general process that can be expected to operate for all motives.

Drive. A drive is simply a stimulus strong enough to impel the individual into activity. It energizes behavior but, by itself, does not direct it. Any stimulus may become a drive if it reaches sufficient intensity. While this statement is conceptually accurate it is also true that there is a small range of stimuli (largely internal) which characteristically reach sufficient intensity to serve this impelling function, and these are generally referred to as the innate or primary drives. These drives are usually linked to physiological processes and reduction of the drive stimulus is frequently necessary for survival of the organism. Examples of the primary drives are pain, hunger, thirst, and sex. The importance of such drives in the behavior of any individual will, of course, depend upon their intensity, and this in turn is related to the availability of opportunities for free gratification or reduction of the drive stimuli. Thus, if the individual has constantly available an adequate food supply the hunger drive will not be an important determinant of the behavior of this individual. The fact that most human environments provide more or less automatic means for the reduction of certain primary drives, such as thirst and air-getting, means that the operation of these drives is not normally easy to observe.

In general, then, a drive is a strong stimulus which impels the individual to behave or respond in some manner until the stimulus is reduced or eliminated. Learning consists primarily of developing efficient means of reducing drive stimuli. ✱

SECONDARY DRIVE. The effect of drives on the human subject is complicated by the large number of derived or acquired drives that eventually make their appearance. In the process of growth the typical individual develops a large number of secondary drives that serve to instigate and direct his behavior. "These learned drives are acquired on the basis of the primary drives, represent elaborations of them, and serve as a façade behind which the functions of the underlying innate drives are hidden" (1950, pp. 31–32).

In the typical modern society secondary drive stimulation largely replaces the original function of primary drive stimulation. The individual does not wait for the onset of the primary drive (stomach contractions or changes in chemistry of the blood) before engaging in the appropriate adaptive responses (eating). Rather, he responds to the secondary drive stimulation which may be linked to time, place, or verbal command. As this implies, the importance of the primary drives in most instances is not clear from casual observation of the socialized adult. It is only in the process of development, or in periods of crisis (failure of the culturally prescribed modes of adaptation), that one can observe clearly the operation of primary drives.

In order to understand the derivation of the secondary drives from the primary we must understand the learning process and this leads us to the general question of the development of personality. We shall have more to say about secondary or learned drives later.

THE DEVELOPMENT OF PERSONALITY

The transformation of the simple infant into the complex adult is a matter of little interest to some theorists, but this process is fully elaborated by Dollard and Miller. We shall present their treatment of this problem beginning with a brief consideration of the innate equipment of the infant and following this with a detailed discussion of the learning process and its application to the acquisition of motives and to thinking. In addition we shall briefly consider the importance of the social context of behavior and of developmental stages. In conclusion we shall illustrate the application of these concepts to the phenomena of repression and conflict.

INNATE EQUIPMENT. At birth and shortly thereafter the individual is endowed with only a limited array of behavioral equipment. First, he possesses a small number of *specific reflexes*, which are, for the most part, segmental responses made to a highly specific stimulus or class of stimuli. Second, he possesses a number of *innate hierarchies of response*, which are tendencies for certain responses to appear in particular stimulus situations before certain other responses; for example, it may be innately determined that when exposed to certain noxious stimuli the child will first try to escape from the stimuli before crying. This assumption implies that so-called random behavior is not random at all but is determined by response preferences which early in the organism's development are largely the result of innate factors but with development are influenced by a complex mixture of experience and these innate hierarchies. Third, the individual possesses a set of *primary drives* which, as we have already seen, are in the typical case internal stimuli of great strength and persistence and usually linked to known physiological processes. These drives impel the individual to act but, in general, do not guide or direct this action, so that prior to learning it is only the specific reflexes and the response hierarchies that give any directedness to behavior.

Thus, we have initially an individual who is capable of a few, relatively segmental, or differentiated, responses to specific stimuli. He also possesses a group of primary drives which under certain organic conditions impel him to act or behave but which do not direct this activity. The only initial guidance of responses stems from an innate hierarchy of response tendencies which imposes a gross or general control over the order in which particular responses will appear in specified situations. Given this initial state our theory of development must account for: (1) the extension of present responses to new stimuli or stimulus situations; (2) the development of new responses; (3) the development of new or derived motives; (4) the extinction or elimination of existing associations between stimuli and responses. The learning concepts to be outlined below are designed to provide a basis for understanding these developments.

THE LEARNING PROCESS. Dollard and Miller suggest that there are four important conceptual elements in the learning process. These are drive, cue, response, and reinforcement (reward). We have already considered drive in a provisional manner; let us now turn to the remaining concepts.

A *cue* is a stimulus that guides the response of the organism. Drive stimuli set the individual into action; cues direct or determine the exact nature of the response. "Cues determine when he will respond, where he will respond, and which response he will make" (Dollard and Miller, 1950, p. 32). Cues may vary in kind or in intensity. Thus, there are visual cues and auditory cues, but there are also weak flashes of light and blinding flashes of light. Or, there are auditory cues associated with the ringing of a bell and auditory cues associated with the human vocal cords, but there are also gentle, barely detectable, ringing sounds and there are shattering, clanging, ringing sounds. The cue function of stimuli may be associated with variation either in intensity or kind, although in most instances it is variation in kind which serves this function. Any quality that makes the stimulus distinctive may serve as the basis for the cue and in the usual case distinctiveness is more easily based upon variation in kind than intensity. Stimuli may operate as cues not only singly but also in combination. That is, the distinctiveness may depend not upon the difference in individual stimuli but rather upon the pattern or combination of several different stimuli, for example, the same individual letters may be used in different combinations to spell two or more words which will have completely different effects upon the reader. We have already suggested that any stimulus may become a drive if only it is intense enough; thus the same stimulus may have both drive and cue value—it may both arouse and direct behavior.

An exceedingly important part in the learning process must be assigned to *response* factors. As Dollard and Miller point out, before a given response can be linked to a given cue, the response must occur. Thus, a crucial stage in the organism's learning is the production of the appropriate response. In any given situation certain responses will be more likely to appear than others. This order of preference, or probability of response, when the situation is first presented is referred to as the *initial hierarchy of responses*. If this initial hierarchy appears to have occurred in the absence of any learning it may be referred to as the *innate hierarchy of responses*, which we have already mentioned as part of the primitive equipment of the individual. After experience and learning have influenced the individual's behavior in this situation, the derived order of response is labeled the *resultant hierarchy*. These concepts simply remind us that in any environmental setting the potential responses an individual may make have a different probability of occurring and can be ranked in terms of this probability.

With development, the hierarchy of response becomes intimately associated with language because particular responses become linked to words and consequently speech may mediate or determine the particular hierarchy that will operate. Thus, the same situation referred to as "dangerous" or as a "frolic" will evoke vastly different response hierarchies. The particular hierarchy displayed is also heavily influenced by the culture in which the individual has been socialized as the prescriptions of all cultures include notions of what the preferred or most likely response is to situations of social importance.

Once a response has occurred its fate is determined by its subsequent reinforcement or lack of reinforcement. Events which strengthen the connection between a given response and a particular cue are called *reinforcements* or rewards. It is generally assumed that reinforcement takes place only where there is an appreciable reduction in the drive stimuli operating at the time of the response; however, this is not always directly demonstrable. The classical definition of what constitutes reinforcement is clearly circular as the existence of reinforcement is inferred from the fact that learning has taken place or that the s-r bond has been strengthened. Dollard and Miller concur with Meehl (1950), however, in arguing that this definition is not completely circular, for once a given event has been demonstrated to reinforce (strengthen a s-r connection) it is commonly assumed that this same event will reinforce or promote learning in other situations. This transsituationality of the reinforcer or reward means that once the original demonstration of effect has been made, it is possible for the investigator to define reward independently of the particular s-r bond he wishes to study.

The view adopted by Dollard and Miller assumes that reward cannot take place except when drive stimuli are operating and further that there is always a reduction or lowering of the drive stimuli in the process of rewarding. As this implies, unless some outside factor is introduced to increase the strength of the drive stimuli, successive rewards will eventually reduce the strength of the drive stimuli to a point where they cannot be reduced further, and reward thus becomes impossible. This accounts for the fact that the individual does not endlessly repeat the same rewarded response.

A given response may be reinforced through reduction of primary drive stimuli, for example, hunger, thirst, pain; or it may be reinforced through reduction of secondary or acquired drive stimuli, for instance, anxiety, shame, conformity. It is obvious that most of the reinforcements in the ordinary life of human subjects are mediated by reduction of learned or secondary drive stimuli. *Secondary reinforcement* is, of course, derived from and dependent upon primary reinforcement. We have already pointed out that secondary drives represent derivations from primary drives and it remains only to indicate that the effects of secondary drive reduction will not continue to sustain learning indefinitely in the absence of any primary drive reduction. This point will be made clearer in our discussion of extinction and our return to the learning of motives.

Dollard and Miller are personally convinced that learning takes place only under conditions of drive reduction, but they suggest that if one wished one could embrace their theory without making this assumption. If the investigator is willing to admit that drive reduction serves as *a* reinforcement he need not assume that *all* reinforcements consist of drive reduction. Nor is it necessary to assume that the effects of reward or reinforcement are consciously mediated. The individual may or may not appreciate the role of reward as a determinant in his learning.

Situations in which the responses the individual can make readily are not drive-reducing, or reinforcing, play a crucial role in the development of new responses and a wider range of adaptive behavior. These *learning dilemmas,* as Dollard and Miller term them, necessitate new responses, or invoke responses that are more distant on the hierarchy of response, and this is the crux of learning new responses. If the individual's old responses are perfectly adequate to reduce all of his drive tensions there is no reason for him to produce new responses and his behavior remains unmodified.

We have just learned that habits or cue-response bonds are formed as the result of drive reduction or reinforcement. Consistent with this is the formulation that habits cease to operate or become weaker as a result of the absence of reward or reinforcement. This weakening of the habit or lowering of the response tendency is referred to as *extinction.* According to this principle, the more often a given response is made in the presence of a given cue and a particular drive state with no reduction in the drive stimuli, the less likely that cue is to elicit this response in the future. Of course, if the habit is very strong it may take many repetitions in the absence of reward to extinguish the response. This is a highly functional or adaptive principle for it implies that responses not leading to the desired state of reinforcement or reward become progressively less likely to occur as they are repeated without reward. As we have implied, extinction is a gradual process and the length of time it will take for a given habit to extinguish will depend upon its initial strength and also the strength of the drive during the extinction process.

If an extinguished response has not been evoked for a period of time, and the appropriate cue is presented once again, the individual will often produce the response that had previously been extinguished. This tendency for the habit to reinstate itself following extinction, without additional reinforcement, is referred to as *spontaneous recovery*. If the extinction process is carried on for a sufficiently prolonged period the organism will reach a state where spontaneous recovery disappears.

One may defend the proposition that no individual is ever confronted with just the same stimulus situation on two or more occasions. There are always small but specifiable changes between any two stimulus presentations separated in time. The cues presented on the second occasion are always slightly different than those that appeared on the first occasion. The concept of *generalization* is given the important function of accounting for the tendency on the part of the individual to display the same response even though there has been variation in the cue situation. In simple terms, this concept implies that habits learned in one situation will tend to be transferred or generalized to other situations to the extent that the new situations are similar to the original situation. The more similar the cues are to the original cues, the stronger the tendency to generalize to the new situation. This variable tendency to transfer the learned response to new and different situations is referred to as the *gradient of generalization*, and it implies that stimulus situations can be graded or ordered in terms of their similarity, and that this similarity will determine the likelihood that a response learned in one situation will be evoked by the new stimulus situation. In general, the stronger the drive that evokes the response, the greater the tendency to generalize to new cues; for example, a very hungry individual will salivate at the sight of objects which would not ordinarily evoke salivation.

Not only must the individual learn to respond consistently to situations that are somewhat different but also he must learn to respond differently to situations that are similar. Thus, the environment places conflicting demands for generalization and particularization upon the individual. In our society the person ordinarily must make similar responses to individuals who are in positions of authority even though there may be virtually no physical similarity among them; on the other hand, he would have to respond to identical twins who were in different relation to him, for instance, marriage, in a highly individual manner. By successive reinforcement of a given response to one set of cues and no reinforcement for the same response to a closely similar set of cues, it is possible to set up a *discrimination* between the cues so that the tendency to generalize is inhibited. Discrimination involves an increase in the specificity of the cues adequate to evoke a response whereas generalization decreases this specificity. Obviously the more distinctive two cues are the easier a discrimination will be learned.

Responses occurring immediately before a reinforcement are learned more rapidly, or become more strongly associated with the cue, than responses that occur at a time more remote from the reinforcement. There is a spread of effect, or a *gradient of reinforcement, which favors those responses that are temporally contiguous with, or im-mediately prior to, the reward.* Thus, if there is a series of responses elicited by a given cue and this series of responses leads to a reinforcement, the last of these responses will be more strongly linked to this cue than the responses that occurred earlier in the chain. Given this concept, it is clear why a shorter route to the goal is preferable to a longer—the responses in the shorter route are closer to the reinforce-ment and thus have a stronger tendency to be elicited by this particular cue situation.

As a result of generalization and the gradient of reinforcement the individual who has learned a sequence of responses leading to a goal will often produce *anticipatory responses*, that is, responses that hap-pen sooner in the sequence than they did in the original learning. These anticipatory responses have the function of eliminating the unnecessary or ritual steps on the path to the goal. Of course, in many instances the omitted response may turn out to be essential to producing the reward, in which case the individual must learn not to "anticipate." Again, it is important to realize that this process of inserting anticipatory responses into learned sequences of behavior is not ordinarily voluntary but takes place without conscious decision or awareness on the part of the performer.

At this point, we have examined the basic conceptual tools with which Dollard and Miller analyze and represent behavior. Of course, in the application of these concepts many additional assumptions are necessitated and some of these will become explicit as we proceed.

SECONDARY DRIVE AND THE LEARNING PROCESS. We have already seen that the infant is born with a limited range of primary drives which with growth and experience become elaborated into a complex and varied set of derived or secondary drives. Let us return to consider the development of these acquired drives in the light of the learning concepts we have just discussed. This presentation focuses about the learning of fear simply because this motive is more thoroughly understood than many of the other secondary drives. We assume that the learning process is in general the same for this motive as for any other motive.

Fear, at least in part, is a learned drive for the fear response can be attached to cues or stimuli which are not fear-producing for the naïve individual. Fear may legitimately be considered a drive because it impels the organism to behave and reduction of fear serves as a reward or reinforcement. In buttressing these assertions Dollard and Miller rely chiefly upon an animal investigation in which rats were exposed to shock in a white compartment and permitted to escape to a black compartment where there was no shock. After a certain number of trials the white compartment (originally a neutral cue) came to evoke fear. At this point, the animals learned instrumental acts such as pressing a bar or turning a wheel in order to escape from the compartment (reduce the drive stimuli) even though the primary drive (the shock) was no longer operant. As Dollard and Miller point out, there is a strong analogy between the white rat terrified by the harmless white compartment and the irrational fears and anxieties which can be observed in human subjects. If the observer has seen the learning process that preceded the fear of the white compartment there is nothing mysterious about the animal's fear; likewise, if the observer has seen the learning process preceding the neurotic symptom there is nothing surprising or inconsistent about the way in which the human subject behaves. It is only when the observer steps in at the terminal phase of a learning process that the subject's behavior appears strange and irrational.

Dollard and Miller assume that fear, and other secondary drives, are both responses and stimulus-producing. That is, the organism under certain circumstances produces a complex response which is called fear, and this response serves also as a stimulus or cue which may guide or control subsequent responses. Although the nature of the response and its stimulus properties cannot be precisely specified, it can be shown that fear follows the same functional rules as directly observable stimuli and responses. Consequently the assumption that fear is a cue-producing response seems justifiable.

The strength of a learned fear is a function of the same factors that determine the strength of other acquisitions of learning. Thus, the intensity of the primary drive involved in the reinforcement leading to the learned fear, and the number and pattern of reinforced trials, are important determinants of the intensity of the fear. If a weak shock and few trials are employed the rat will develop a much weaker fear of the white compartment than if a strong shock and a long series of trials are employed. The gradient of reinforcement and stimulus generalization also apply. Those stimuli most nearly adjacent to the reinforcement will be most strongly feared and the fear response will generalize to cues resembling the learned cue with those cues that are most similar being feared the most. Not only is fear learned like any other habit but it extinguishes in the same manner; although for complex reasons the extinction of fear responses is frequently more difficult than the extinction of less affect-laden habits. In general, situations in which the fear response is not followed by reinforcement will gradually lead to extinction of the fear response. Fear can also be eliminated through associating some response incompatible with fear to the learned cue more strongly than the fear response.

Acquired drives can serve as cues in the same manner as any other stimulus. The individual may learn to respond with the word "afraid" in fear-evoking situations, that is, label the secondary drive, and this response-produced cue will then mediate the transfer of responses learned in the original fear-producing situation to the present situation. This transfer, involving a response which serves as a cue, is called secondary generalization. Individuals can learn to discriminate different intensities of fear stimulation just as in the case of other stimuli, so that the cue value of the acquired drive may depend upon the intensity of the drive.

To summarize, fear may be learned or attached to new and originally neutral cues in which case these cues elicit an innate pattern of response or else an innate pattern that has been modified by subsequent learning. The fear response is a cue as well as a response. It is a complex response which may function as a cue to elicit those responses that have been learned in other similar fearful situations. Fear can serve as a (learned) drive in the sense that it will instigate or impel the organism to respond and its reduction will reinforce those responses associated with the reduction. In other words, it operates exactly like any other drive. One of the reasons for the central importance of learned fears is that when responses that are necessary to reduce other drives are punished, the individual may develop an acquired fear in association with these responses, so that an opposition or conflict will be set up between the original drive and the learned fear. For example, a child may be punished with sufficient severity and frequency while eating so that this response will come to evoke fear with the result that he will be suspended in conflict between the hunger drive and the fear of eating.

Our discussion of the learning of fear makes clear that acquired motives develop in accordance with the same learning principles that govern the formation and dissolution of habits. This analysis of fear can be duplicated for all other primary drives and thus account for their extension to new cue situations. Further, it is clear that mixtures of these drives will often be activated simultaneously, leading to acquired drives that do not have exactly the same properties as any single innate drive. In this way the individual's motivational structure is complicated and may come to show little resemblance to the original array of primary drives.

HIGHER MENTAL PROCESSES. The individual's interactions with his environment are of two varieties: those which are direct and guided by a single cue or cue situation and those which are mediated by internal processes. It is the latter class of responses which is of interest here, those mediated by *cue-producing responses*. Following Hull, Dollard and Miller distinguish between responses which are instrumental, possess some immediate effect upon the environment, and those which are cue-producing, whose main function is to mediate or lead the way to another response. Obviously language is involved in most cue-producing responses although it need not be spoken language.

One of the most important cue-producing responses is the labeling or naming of events and experiences. The individual may immediately increase the generalization or transfer between two or more cue situations by identifying them as having the same label, for example, by identifying two completely different situations as "threatening" the individual may greatly increase the likelihood that he will behave in the same manner in both situations; or he may build up a sharp discrimination between two similar situations by giving them different names, for instance, two individuals who are objectively very much alike may be labeled respectively as "friend" and "enemy" with the result that they will be responded to in a highly individual manner. Within any culture there will be critical generalizations and discriminations which are emphasized and thus made easier by the structure of the language. The often repeated examples of tribes where a given commodity, such as cattle or coconuts, is of great importance and where the language contains a tremendous number of differentiated labels for such objects illustrate this principle.

Not only may words serve to facilitate or inhibit generalization, they may also serve the important function of arousing drives. Further, words may be used to reward or reinforce. And, most important of all, they serve as time-binding mechanisms, permitting the individual to instigate or reinforce present behavior in terms of consequences which are located in the future but susceptible to verbal representation in the present. It is clearly the verbal intervention in the drive-cue-response-reinforcement sequence which makes human behavior so complex and difficult to understand and at the same time accounts for much of the difference between man and lower species.

Reasoning is essentially a process of substituting internal, cue-producing responses for overt acts. As such, it is vastly more efficient than overt trial and error. Not only does it serve the function of testing symbolically the various alternatives, it also makes possible the substitution of anticipatory responses which may be more effective than any of the overt response alternatives originally available. It is possible through the use of cue-producing responses (thoughts) to begin at the goal situation and work backward until the correct instrumental response has been identified, a feat which would not ordinarily be possible in motor learning. Planning is a special variety of reasoning, where the emphasis is upon future action.

In order for either reasoning or planning to take place the individual must first be able to inhibit or delay the direct instrumental response to the drive stimulus and cue. It is this inhibition that offers the cue-producing responses an opportunity to operate and this response of "not-responding" must be learned just as any other new response. It is also necessary that the cue-producing responses be efficient and realistic and finally that they lead to appropriate instrumental or overt acts.

The ability to use language and other response-produced cues is greatly influenced by the social context in which the individual develops. In the words of Dollard and Miller:

> The problem solutions painfully acquired during centuries of trial and error, and by the highest order of creative reasoning by rare geniuses, are preserved and accumulate as a part of the culture. . . . People receive an enormous amount of social training in putting words and sentences together in ways that lead to the adaptive solution of problems (1950, p. 116).

It is a rare and creative act to originate the Pythagorean theorem but it is not much of a trick to learn it at an appropriate time and place when it is already known. Thus, language provides the key by means of which wisdom from the past is transmitted to the present.

In view of the immense importance of language it is quite appropriate that the child should be trained to pay attention to and respond to verbal cues and eventually to produce them. The use of verbal symbols for communication with other people presumably precedes their use in thought and a great deal of the child's interactions with his environment are concerned with how to produce these cues under appropriate circumstances as well as how to understand those that are produced by others.

Language, as we have implied, is a social product and if we grant significance to the language process it seems reasonable that the social milieu within which the individual functions must be of importance. Let us turn now to a consideration of this factor.

THE SOCIAL CONTEXT. It is very likely that any theory or theorist influenced by social anthropology will highlight the role of sociocultural determinants of behavior, and the present theory is no exception to this rule. Dollard and Miller consistently emphasize the fact that human behavior can be understood only with a full appreciation of the cultural context within which behavior occurs. The psychology of learning provides us with an understanding of the *principles of learning* but the social anthropologist or his equivalent provides us with the *conditions of learning*. And one of these specifications is as important to a full understanding of human development as the other.

> No psychologist would venture to predict the behavior of a rat without knowing on what arm of a T-maze the feed or the shock is placed. It is no easier to predict the behavior of a human being without knowing the conditions of his "maze," i.e., the structure of his social environment. Culture, as conceived by social scientists, is a statement of the design of the human maze, of the type of reward involved, and of what responses are to be rewarded. It is in this sense a recipe for learning. This contention is easily accepted when widely variant societies are compared. But even within the same society, the mazes which are run by two individuals may seem the same but actually be quite different. . . . No personality analysis of two . . . people can be accurate which does not take into account these cultural differences, that is, differences in the types of responses which have been rewarded (Miller and Dollard, 1941, pp. 5–6).

As this passage implies, the learning theorist enriches the data of the social anthropologist through providing principles that help to account systematically for the importance of cultural events, while the anthropologist provides the learning theorist with the information he needs in order to fit his principles with the actual experience of human subjects. In one sense, this viewpoint argues that the empirical definition of psychological variables is impossible without the wisdom and data of the anthropologist.

Thus, the position of Dollard and Miller cedes a kind of transcultural generality to the principles of learning (or at least some of them) but at the same time grants, and even emphasizes, that the exact form of behavior displayed by a given individual will be tremendously influenced by the society of which he is a member.

CRITICAL STAGES OF DEVELOPMENT. Dollard and Miller assume that unconscious conflict, learned for the most part during infancy and childhood, serves as the basis for most severe emotional problems in later life. They agree with psychoanalytic theorists in considering experiences of the first half dozen years of life crucial determinants of adult behavior.

It is important to realize that neurotic conflict is not only learned by the child but it is learned primarily as a result of conditions created by the parent. This unfortunate capacity of the parent for impairing the child's development stems in part from the fact that cultural prescriptions concerning the child are contradictory or discontinuous and in part from the fact that the child during infancy is not well equipped to cope with complex learning demands even if they are consistent. Thus, society demands that the child learn to be aggressive in some situations and submissive in other very similar situations, a difficult discrimination at best. Worst of all, this demand may be made at a time when the child does not have at his command all the symbolic functions contributed by language so that such discriminations may simply overreach his learning capacity with resultant frustration and emotional upheaval. A similar set of overwhelming conditions may occur in adulthood under exceptional circumstances such as war. As might be expected, such conditions frequently lead to neurosis.

A crucial aspect of childhood experience is the extreme helplessness of the child. It is chiefly in infancy that he is more or less unable to manipulate his environment and thus is vulnerable to the depredations of tearing drive stimuli and overwhelming frustrations. In the ordinary process of development he will devise mechanisms to avoid situations which are severely frustrating. In infancy he has no choice but to experience them.

It is not surprising, then, that acute emotional conflicts occur in childhood. The infant has not learned to wait, not knowing the world's inescapable routines; to hope, and thus to assure itself that the good moment will return and that the evil occasion will pass; to reason and plan, and thus to escape present disorder by constructing the future in a controlled way. Rather, the child is urgently, hopelessly, planlessly impelled, living by moments in eternal pain and then suddenly finding itself bathed in endless bliss. The young child is necessarily disoriented, confused, deluded, and hallucinated—in short, has just those symptoms that we recognize as a psychosis in the adult. Infancy, indeed, may be viewed as a period of transitory psychosis. Savage drives within the infant impel to action. These drives are unmodified by hope or concept of time. The higher mental processes (the Ego) cannot do their benign work of comforting, directing effort, and binding the world into a planful sequence. What is gone may never return. The present pain may never fade. These are the tumultuous circumstances in which severe unconscious mental conflicts can be created. Only when the child has been taught to speak and think at a rather high level can the impact of the raw, drastic character of these circumstances be reduced (Dollard and Miller, 1950, pp. 130–131).

Consistent with this view is the prescription that during the early stages of life the parent's primary role is to maintain drive stimuli at a low level. The parent should be permissive, gratifying, and make few learning demands until the child's language skills have developed.

Granted the fact that every culture makes many demands upon the individual who is to live effectively within it, still there are certain of these demands that are particularly likely to produce conflict and emotional disturbance. Dollard and Miller identify four situations in which cultural prescription, as interpreted by the parent, is particularly likely to have disastrous consequences for normal development. These are the feeding situation in infancy, toilet or cleanliness training, early sex training, and training for control of anger and aggression.

Dollard and Miller suggest that their analysis of these conflict situations is a restatement of the formulations of Freud in terms of their own conceptual scheme. For this reason, we shall not attempt to reproduce here all that they have to say about these critical stages, but shall simply consider briefly their analysis of the feeding situation to illustrate the use they make of learning concepts in this setting. The important things for the reader to grasp are that this theory assumes events early in development to be of central importance in their effects upon behavior and, beyond this, that the operation of these events is seen as perfectly consistent with the learning process we have already outlined.

Drive stimuli associated with hunger are among the first strong activity impellents to which the individual is exposed. Consequently, the techniques the individual devises to reduce or control these stimuli may be expected to have an important role as a model for the devices used later in life to reduce other strong drive stimuli. In this sense, the theory proposes that the feeding situation serves as a small-scale model which in part determines the large-scale adjustments of the adult. Thus, Dollard and Miller suggest that the child who cries when he is hungry and finds that this leads to feeding may be taking the initial steps that will result in an active, manipulative orientation toward drive reduction. On the other hand, the child who is left to "cry himself out" may be laying down the basis for a passive and apathetic reaction to strong drive stimuli. Further, if hunger stimuli are permitted to mount without restriction he may come to associate mild hunger stimuli with the intensely painful, overpowering stimuli which he has subsequently experienced on so many occasions; and in this manner he may come to "overreact" to relatively mild drive stimuli, that is, the mild drive stimuli acquire a secondary drive strength which is equivalent to the very intense drive stimuli. Another dangerous consequence of permitting the child to be exposed to intense hunger drive stimuli is that he may develop on this basis a fear of being alone. If, when the child is alone, he is exposed to very painful hunger stimuli and if these stimuli are reduced only when the parent finally appears, it may happen that this strong reinforcement (reduction of hunger stimuli) will habituate the response that immediately preceded the appearance of the parent—a fear response. Thus, in the future when the child or adult is alone he will respond with this previously reinforced fear response and will show a typical pattern of fear of the dark or of being alone.

Perhaps the most important aspect of the feeding situation is that its relative success may be expected to have a great deal to do with future interpersonal relations. This follows from the fact that the feeding experience is associated with the first intimate interpersonal relation—that between mother and child. If the feeding is successful and characterized by drive reduction and gratification, the child comes to associate this pleasant state with the presence of his mother and this relation by a process of stimulus generalization comes to be linked with other people so that their presence becomes a goal or a secondary reward. If the feeding is unsuccessful and accompanied by pain and anger the reverse can be expected. Weaning and digestive disturbances are especially likely to have unfortunate consequences for the child as they introduce pain and discomfort into the situation and complicate a learning situation which is already taxing the full capacity of the infant.

UNCONSCIOUS PROCESSES. We have observed that Dollard and Miller represent language as playing a crucial role in human development. In view of this, it is quite natural that those determinants of behavior which elude language, or are unconscious, should play a key role in behavioral disturbances. The theory is quite consistent with psychoanalytic formulations in accepting unconscious factors as important determinants of behavior; however, the account offered by Dollard and Miller of the origin of these unconscious processes shows little similarity to the Freudian version.

Unconscious determinants can be divided into those that have never been conscious and those that although once conscious are so no longer. In the first category are included all those drives, responses, and cues learned prior to the advent of speech and which consequently were not labeled. Also in this group belong certain areas of experience for which our society provides only meager or inadequate names. Kinesthetic and motor cues and responses are generally overlooked by conventional labels and for this reason are not easily discussed and may be considered largely unconscious. In similar vein, certain areas of sexual and other kinds of tabooed experience are not usually accompanied by appropriate designations and thus are only poorly represented in consciousness. In the second category belong all of those cues and responses which were formerly conscious but which through repression have become unavailable to consciousness. The process involved in the first category is clear enough and it is to the phenomenon of repression that we shall devote our attention.

Repression is a process of avoiding certain thoughts and this avoidance is learned and motivated in exactly the same manner as any other learned response. In this case, the response of "*not-thinking*" of certain things leads to drive reduction and reinforcement, and thus becomes a standard part of the individual's repertoire. There are certain thoughts or memories that have acquired the capacity to arouse fear (secondary drive stimuli) and the response of "not-thinking" or ceasing to think of them leads to a reduction in the fear stimuli and thus the response of "not-thinking" is reinforced. Whereas in the initial learning the individual first thinks of the fearful act or event and then experiences the fear and gives up the thought with the consequent reinforcement, after experience the response of "not-thinking" becomes anticipatory and occurs before the individual has actually reconstructed the event or wish. "Not-thinking" as an anticipatory response not only keeps the fear-evoking thoughts from consciousness but it also interferes with the normal extinction process. That is, if the response does not occur it can hardly be extinguished even if the original source of reinforcement has since vanished.

Dollard and Miller clearly consider repression to exist on a continuum ranging from slight tendencies not to think about certain things to the strongest avoidance of threatening material. They also consider that this tendency can be traced largely to childhood training which often tends to produce fear of certain thoughts. Once the fear of the thought is developed, the process of repression is readily understandable in terms of the reduction of drive stimuli by "not-thinking." Children are often punished for the use of certain tabooed words; thus the spoken verbal symbol alone is sufficient to elicit the punishment without the act. Or the child may announce his intention of doing something wrong and be punished before any act has been committed. In other cases, the child may think certain things which he does not even express verbally but which the parent infers correctly from expressive behavior or other cues and for which the child is punished. Frequently the child is punished for acts that have been carried out in the past, so that the punishment accompanies the thought of the act and not the act itself. All of these and other experiences tend to build up a generalization from the act or overt behavior that leads to punishment to the mere thought or symbolic representation of this act. Not only can the individual generalize from the overt act to the thought but also he can discriminate between the two. In the well-adjusted individual this is an exceedingly important and efficient process. Such a person realizes that certain thoughts must never be expressed in certain contexts yet he will feel relatively free to think these thoughts privately.

The extensity and severity of repression depend upon many factors; among them are possible variations in the innate strength of the fear response; the degree of dependence upon the parents, and thus the intensity of the threat of loss of love to which the child can be exposed; and the severity of traumas or fear-producing situations to which the child has been exposed.

The crucial importance of consciousness has to do with the significance of verbal labels in the learning process, particularly in connection with the operation of the higher mental processes. We have already indicated that the processes of generalization and discrimination can be made more efficient by means of verbal symbols and if labeling is eliminated the individual clearly operates at a more primitive intellectual level. Thus, he must become more concrete and stimulus bound, and his behavior comes to resemble that of the child or lower organism where the mediating role of language is not highly developed.

CONFLICT. No human being operates so effectively that all of his tendencies are congruent and well-integrated. Consequently, all personality theories must deal directly or indirectly with the problems posed for the organism by conflicting motives or tendencies. Conflict behavior is represented by Miller and Dollard in terms of five basic assumptions which are extensions of the principles we have already discussed.

They assume *first* that the tendency to approach a goal becomes stronger the nearer the individual is to the goal and this is referred to as the *gradient of approach*. *Second*, they assume that the tendency to avoid a negative stimulus becomes stronger the nearer the individual is to the stimulus and this is referred to as the *gradient of avoidance*. These assumptions can be derived from the principles of stimulus generalization and the gradient of reinforcement which we have already described. The *third* assumption is that the gradient of avoidance is steeper than the gradient of approach. This implies that the rate at which avoidance tendencies increase with approach to the goal is greater than the rate at which approach tendencies increase under the same conditions. *Fourth*, it is assumed that an increase in the drive associated with the approach or avoidance will raise the general level of the gradient. Thus, there will still be an increase in the strength of approach or avoidance as the goal is approached but these tendencies will now have a greater strength at each stage of approach. *Fifth*, it is assumed that when there are two competing responses the stronger will occur. Given these assumptions, in addition to the concepts we have already discussed, Miller and Dollard are able to derive predictions concerning the manner in which an individual faced with the various types of conflict will respond.

One of the most important types of conflict is concerned with the opposition between approach and avoidance tendencies aroused simultaneously by the same object or situation; let us say that a young man is strongly attracted to a girl and yet finds himself embarrassed and uncomfortable (afraid) in her presence. As the first three assumptions above tell us, the avoidance response (getting away from the girl) falls off more sharply than the approach response as the subject moves away from the goal (girl). This is represented graphically in Figure 1, where the broken lines, representing the avoidance responses, are angled more sharply than solid lines which represent the approach responses. Therefore the avoidance tendency may be higher or more intense than the approach response near to the goal (girl) but when the subject has moved away a certain distance (in the diagram to a point beyond the intersection of the gradients) the ap-

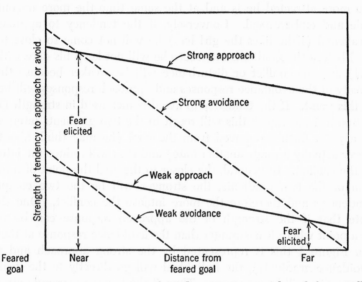

Figure 1. Graphic representation of conflict situations. Adapted from Miller, 1951b.

proach response will be stronger than the avoidance response (having left the girl he may call or write to arrange another date). It is at the point where the two gradients intersect (let us say, when the boy enters the same room with the girl) that the individual should show a maximum of hesitation and conflict, as it is here that the two competing responses are approximately evenly balanced. When the approach response is stronger than the avoidance response the individual will approach without conflict and vice versa when the avoidance response is stronger. It is only when the two are evenly matched in strength that the individual will have difficulty in mustering an appropriate response.

If either the approach or the avoidance response is increased in strength, this will have the effect of raising the entire level of that gradient as shown in the diagram by the upper gradients of approach and avoidance. This will naturally lead to a different point of intersection between the two gradients. Thus, if the approach tendency is increased in strength the two gradients will intersect closer to the goal and this implies that the individual will come nearer to the goal before he will hesitate in conflict. The closer he comes to the goal the stronger will be the avoidance response, and therefore the more intense will be his conflict. That is, the closer he approaches the girl the more attracted he is and at the same time the more uncomfortable and embarrassed. Conversely, if the tendency to approach is weakened (if he likes the girl less) he will not come so close to the goal before the gradients intersect (he will not keep his date with the girl) and his conflict or disturbance will be weaker because the intensity of the avoidance responses and approach responses will be less at this point. If the tendency to avoid is increased in strength (if his discomfort increases) this will result in the two gradients intersecting at a point farther removed from the goal (he may think about but never actually arrange another date) and thus will reduce the intensity of the conflict. In general, the closer to the goal the point of intersection of the two gradients, the stronger will be the two competing tendencies and therefore the more intense the conflict. One should note that if the strength of the approach response can be raised to a point where it is stronger than the avoidance response at the goal (in Figure 1 this is represented by the strong approach and weak avoidance gradients), the individual will go directly to the goal and the conflict will be overcome. Thus, if the boy is so strongly attracted to the girl that he is able to stay in close proximity to her even though uncomfortable the conflict will eventually be resolved.

A second type of conflict is encountered when the individual is faced with two competing avoidance responses, for example, a small boy may be afraid to climb and at the same time wish to avoid being called a coward by his playmates. Thus, the nearer he comes to the one goal (the higher he climbs), the stronger will be the avoidance response and the more likely he will be to retreat. However, as he retreats he comes closer to the other goal (being called a coward) and the second avoidance response increases while the first decreases. Thus, the individual should show vacillation, turning first from one goal and then from the other, that is, climbing to a certain height and then descending. If the strength of one of the avoidance responses is increased, this will change the point of intersection so that the place where the individual will turn back from this goal will be made more distant. It will also increase the intensity of the conflict as both gradients now will be stronger at the point of intersection. Again, if one of the responses is stronger than the other at the goal, the individual will simply continue to withdraw from the most feared situation until he is past the competing situation and the conflict will be overcome: he either climbs to the necessary height or accepts the fact that he is to be called a coward.

Miller and Dollard do not consider the competition between two approach responses to represent a realistic dilemma. They point out that once the individual has started to move toward one of the positive goals the strength of this response will increase (according to first assumption) and the strength of the competing response will decrease. Therefore, the individual will go directly to this goal. Even if the person begins exactly balanced between the two goals, variations in the stimulus situation or within the organism will upset this balance slightly and once this is done the individual will then continue to move toward the nearest goal. Where individuals appear to be in conflict between two positive alternatives there are always hidden or latent avoidance responses operating.

For a more detailed description of this theory of conflict the reader should consult Miller (1944, 1951b) where he will also find summarized a number of experimental studies which have tested various derivations from this position. In general, the result of these studies provide strong evidence for the utility of the theory.

CHARACTERISTIC RESEARCH AND RESEARCH METHODS

Miller and Dollard have reported a considerable quantity of investigation that illustrates or tests derivations from this theoretical position. In their volume *Social learning and imitation* (1941) a number of studies on human and lower animal subjects are summarized which represent attempts to confirm predictions derived from their theory. Miller, as we have mentioned, has conducted a number of experimental studies relevant to various aspects of the theory and many of these are summarized in his two handbook chapters (Miller, 1944, 1951a). Here we shall discuss a cluster of studies which deal with the concept of displacement. These investigations not only demonstrate an interest in bridging the gap between psychoanalytic theory and s-r concepts but they also provide experimental evidence for the operation of a number of the concepts we have already discussed.

The concept of displacement occupies a central position in psychoanalytic theory, where it is ordinarily used to refer to the capacity of the organism to redirect responses or impulses to a new object when they are denied expression toward their original object. In terms of the theory of Dollard and Miller, this phenomenon can be accounted for quite readily by the concept of stimulus generalization. Miller, in a series of experiments, has attempted to demonstrate the empirical phenomenon, show the continuity of stimulus generalization and displacement, and provide a theoretical account that will permit new predictions concerning these events.

An initial study by Miller and Bugelski (1948) attempted to demonstrate displacement with human subjects. These investigators administered a set of questionnaires that assessed attitudes toward Mexicans and Japanese to a group of boys who were attending a summer camp. While they were filling out these questionnaires, the boys were forced to miss a highly prized social event and a comparison was made of the attitudes expressed toward the minority groups before and after this frustration. The results showed that following the frustration there was a significant increase in negative attitudes expressed toward the two minority groups. This increase in hostility was interpreted as a displacement of the hostility aroused by the experimenters through their interference with the attendance of the boys at the social event. In psychoanalytic terms, the subjects were displacing the hostility felt toward the experimenters upon the minority group members; in s-r terms, they were generalizing a response from one stimulus object to a similar stimulus object. At any rate, the study showed that the phenomenon in question did occur among human subjects and could be produced experimentally.

This same process was subsequently demonstrated, using albino rats as subjects (Miller, 1948). Two white rats were placed in a compartment, the floor of which was an electrically charged grid. They were then exposed to a sufficiently strong shock to produce active motor attempts to escape from the shock. The experimenter observed the rats through a window and when they approached each other on their hind legs in a sparring position the shock was immediately terminated. This process was repeated until the animals had learned to quickly assume the sparring position when they were shocked. Next they were required to strike each other before the shock was terminated. These training sessions were continued until the animals had learned to stand on their hind legs and strike each other as soon as they were shocked. In the test trials the rats were placed in the compartment with a small doll of about the same size as the rat and the rats then clearly showed a tendency to strike the doll. However, when the other rat *and* the doll were present almost all of the rats struck the other rat rather than the doll. These findings imply that the response learned to one stimulus object may be transferred or displaced to another object but with a somewhat lower likelihood of occurrence than with the original object. This provides a clear instance of stimulus generalization and an analogue for what the psychoanalyst would call displacement.

Miller reasoned that both psychoanalytic theory and s-r theory assume that a given response may be generalized not only from one stimulus to another but also from one drive to another. Freud very early postulated a considerable amount of interchangeability or substitutability between drives or instincts and for the s-r theorist drives are only one kind of stimulus; therefore, it is perfectly natural that there should be drive generalization as well as stimulus generalization. In order to test this prediction, a group of rats was trained under the motivation of thirst, and with the reward of drinking, to run down an alley. These same animals were then divided into two groups, both of which were satiated on water, but one group was deprived of food and the other satiated on food. The prediction was that the response of running down the maze (which had been learned to thirst) would generalize or displace to the hunger drive. Consequently, the food-deprived rats should run down the maze faster than the non-hungry rats. The results of the study showed a clear confirmation of this prediction. It was also possible to show experimentally that the response of running down the maze, which was originally reinforced by reduction of thirst drive stimuli, extinguished when the animals continued to run down the maze with no reduction of drive stimuli. Likewise consistent with s-r theory was the observation that when the response had been partially extinguished, an interval with no trials produced spontaneous recovery, or a return to a higher level of response probability. The investigator also demonstrated response generalization from the drive of hunger to the relatively remote drives of pain and fear. The greater dissimilarity between fear and hunger made this appear a more stringent test of the prediction of drive generalization than the previous study.

Given these experimental findings, Miller incorporated them as derivations from a series of five assumptions which resemble very closely those we discussed in connection with the analysis of conflict. The principal difference between the two sets of assumptions is that those bearing on conflict concern the distance between the subject and the goal, whereas the present assumptions focus about the similarity between the original stimulus object and certain substitute objects.

This model accepts the fact that whenever displacement takes place there is a response competing with the direct response which is stronger than the direct response. Thus, the aggressive response of the child toward his father is not strong enough to overcome the fear response elicited by the same object. For this reason the child cannot express his aggression directly toward the father. Moreover, the model assumes that the direct response to the original stimulus generalizes to similar stimuli and that the competing response shows the same stimulus generalization. The more similar the new stimulus is to the original stimulus, the greater will be the degree of generalization. However, the gradient of generalization for the competing (inhibiting) response falls off or decreases more rapidly than the gradient of generalization for the direct response. Thus, while the competing response may be much stronger than the direct response in the face of the original stimulus, by the time the two responses have been generalized to stimuli of a certain degree of remoteness the order of strength may become reversed, that is, the child may show fear rather than anger to the father but show anger rather than fear to a fatherly doll.

These assumptions not only permit the derivation of the empirical phenomena we have already summarized, displacement or stimulus and drive generalization; they also lead to a number of additional predictions, some of them referring to relations that have yet to be tested under controlled empirical conditions. Miller has reported several studies that present further empirical evidence relevant to this theory, most of which is confirmatory (Miller and Kraeling, 1952; Miller and Murray, 1952; Murray and Miller, 1952).

Recently two of Miller's students (Murray and Berkun, 1955) have attempted to combine the theories of displacement and conflict and have tested certain consequences of this more general model. The authors suggest that attempts to apply the theory of conflict to complex human behavior suffer from the inability of the theory to account for displacement phenomena. Thus, Murray (1954) found that it was necessary to use *both* the theories of displacement and conflict in order to account for findings he obtained when he recorded the number of hostile statements made by a patient concerning his mother, aunt, and other (less important) people during fifteen successive therapy sessions. As a result of this observation, Murray and Berkun constructed a three-dimensional model which combined the attributes of the two s-r models previously described (conflict and displacement). Given this model, Murray and Berkun were able to predict correctly the behavior of rats who were first trained to run an alley with the reward of food, then exposed to shock while eating until they would no longer approach the food, and finally exposed to other alleys which possessed varying similarity to the original alley. In general, the rats came closer to the food in the substitute alleys and the details of their approach behavior corresponded roughly to the prior predictions made by the model. The authors also apply the theory in an illustrative vein to a protocol of a therapy session.

The empirical studies we have outlined above, and the theoretical reasoning that has accompanied them, demonstrate quite clearly how much tidier the formulations and investigations of these theorists have been than those of most personality investigators. We see revealed also the preference for paradigmatic studies involving animal subjects but with appropriate bridging studies carried out on human subjects. It is evident that these investigations not only make a contribution to the understanding of displacement or stimulus generalization but also lead to a large number of testable assertions which, when the appropriate empirical steps have been taken, may add weight to or challenge the effectiveness of this theory.

SOME RELATED FORMULATIONS

Our discussion thus far has omitted the numerous contributions in this area made by individuals other than Dollard and Miller. While we cannot hope to do justice to these many investigators and theorists, it would be highly inappropriate to leave unmentioned the distinctive work of Robert R. Sears and O. Hobart Mowrer.

Sears was a member of the early group at the Institute of Human Relations which pioneered in the application of Hull's theory to social and personality phenomena. He was one of the authors of the *Frustration and aggression* monograph and has conducted a number of empirical studies relevant to this problem (Sears, 1941, 1950; Sears, Hovland, and Miller, 1940; Sears and Sears, 1940). Further, he was one of the first to show a serious interest in the continuity between psychoanalytic concepts and s-r concepts. His monograph, entitled *Survey of objective studies of psychoanalytic concepts* (1943), and a similar handbook chapter (Sears, 1944) represent attempts to order and summarize empirical evidence relevant to psychoanalytic theory. These papers culminated a series of empirical studies in this area which he had carried out himself (Sears, 1936, 1937a, 1937b). During the years he served as professor of child psychology and director of the Child Welfare Station at the University of Iowa, and subsequently as professor of education and child psychology and director of the Laboratory of Human Development at Harvard University, he and his colleagues and students conducted a large number of investigations which centered about the socialization process, or the psychological growth of the child. These studies were conceived within the framework offered by s-r theory. The bulk of this work will appear in a forthcoming volume but some of it has already been published in the form of journal articles (Sears, 1948; Sears, Davis, *et al.*, 1948; Sears, Pintler, and Sears, 1946; Sears, Whiting, Nowlis, and Sears, 1953; Sears and Wise, 1950). This research is continuing at Stanford University where since 1953 Sears has been chairman of the Department of Psychology.

His research has been distinctive not only in the careful attention paid to child development but also in its continuity over an extended period of time, and its sophisticated intertwining of laboratory and field technique. Thus, his ideas have frequently been explored and developed within the confines of the experimental laboratory but at the same time there have been many investigations which involved large-scale community studies, frequently concerned with hypotheses sharpened within the laboratory.

In general, Sears' theoretical position is quite congruent with the theory of Dollard and Miller. Perhaps the most unusual emphasis in his theoretical writing appeared in his recent American Psychological Association presidential address (Sears, 1951a) which was amplified somewhat in a subsequent publication (Sears, 1951b). In these papers he has pointed to, and taken issue with, the preference of psychologists for limiting their focus of attention to the single individual. In Sears' words they are concerned with *monadic* units rather than *dyadic* units. He uses the term dyad here to refer to an aggregation of two or more.

Sears contends that psychology must deal primarily with action or behavior. Although perception, motivation, and other specialized processes may play a crucial role in the effort to represent and account for action, the psychologist must remember it is the action that is crucial and not the perception or other intervening process. Not only must the psychologist deal primarily with action but he also must be prepared to deal with social action—behavioral events involving two or more people interacting—for this includes the largest and most significant portion of all human behavior. This strategic necessity for dealing with the behavior of multiple actors simultaneously stems from the fact that the individual personality is influenced by the social setting in which it exists and at the same time this individual personality influences the social events in which it participates. This interactionist view implies that it is essential to devise means of bridging the gap between the concepts used to represent the individual personality and those used to represent the social environment.

It is at this point that the distinction between a monadic and dyadic unit becomes crucial. Students of behavior have, in general, failed in their attempts to link the individual to his social context because they have relied upon a unit for describing the individual which contained only the individual—a monadic unit. Properly they should have employed dyadic units which include simultaneous representation of the actions of two or more individuals. Having issued the challenge, Sears goes on to demonstrate the development of a dyadic unit employing conventional s-r concepts.

He begins with a conventional s-r paradigm of behavior for the single individual in which the actor, confronted with cues and drive stimuli, responds with instrumental acts, which have effects upon the environment, and in turn lead to the goal response and reduction of the drive stimuli. Sears points out that the environmental events that lead to the goal response often are responses on the part of another person or persons. Thus, the mother is confronted with a crying infant and engages in instrumental acts (picking up the baby and fondling it) which, if successful, will lead the infant to smile and thus reduce the mother's drive stimuli (fear, guilt). Likewise, if we view this situation from the point of view of the infant, the action of the mother is intimately linked to the infant's behavioral sequence, as it is the mother's response which permits reduction of the infant's drive stimuli. For Sears, then, a dyadic situation consists of any setting where the behavior of one person is functionally linked to the response of another person. Not only does the behavior of the other person enter into the sequence in connection with instrumental acts and their influence upon the environment; it is also an essential part of the initial drive and cue situation, for example, the sight of the baby crying had both drive and cue function for the mother in the example above. Thus, the responses of two or more persons may be, and usually are, linked in important respects from the initiation of the behavior all the way through to the successful completion of the behavioral sequence.

It is not sufficient to simply indicate that the response sequences of two or more people are associated. It is obvious that these relations in most cases have a structured or enduring quality which does not depend upon the fortunate coincidence of a particular instrumental act happening to produce a response on the part of the other person which by chance serves to reduce the drive stimuli of the actor. There is a consistent, patterned quality to these interactions which lends stability to interpersonal relations. In attempting to account for this dependability Sears suggests that in the typical situation the actor has developed an expectancy that if he behaves in a certain way this will lead to the desired environmental event (response of the other). Expectancies are viewed as simply a special variety of anticipatory goal response and they serve as response-produced cues which are involved in eliciting the appropriate instrumental act.

Thus, Sears makes the general assertion that an adequate theory of behavior must attend to both monadic and dyadic units of behavior and the two must in some way be integrated. He also indicates tentatively that dyadic units can be introduced into conventional s-r theorizing without undue difficulty. Finally, he provides illustrative evidence that certain empirical phenomena can be understood only when a dyadic conception of behavior is introduced. The development of such a view of behavior and its detailed application remains a task for the future.

Mowrer also was one of the early collaborators in the research and theory construction of the Institute of Human Relations Staff. Although he secured his Ph.D. from Johns Hopkins (1932), he went to Yale University shortly thereafter and remained in New Haven for six important years. In 1940 he accepted a position at Harvard University where he taught until 1948 when he became a research professor of psychology at the University of Illinois where he is at present. He too was one of the authors of the *Frustration and aggression* volume and he also shared with Sears an early interest in the union of psychoanalytic and s-r theory (Mowrer, 1940a; Mowrer and Kluckhohn, 1944). Although the bulk of his research during this period consisted of laboratory studies, he made at least one excursion into the clinical area in a study of the treatment of enuresis (Mowrer, 1938; Mowrer and Mowrer, 1938). His most important contribution within a reinforcement theory framework was his suggestion that the reduction of secondary drives such as anxiety might serve to reinforce responses in the same manner as the reduction of primary drives (Mowrer, 1939, 1940b). More recently he has shown considerable interest in the psychology of language (Mowrer, 1952, 1954a; Mowrer and Viek, 1945) and in various clinical problems, including psychotherapy (Mowrer, 1948, 1949). His interest in psychotherapy is most clearly reflected in a recent volume (*Psychotherapy theory and research*, 1953) which he edited and to which he contributed a number of chapters. Virtually all of the articles mentioned above and a number of other relevant studies are included in a volume of collected papers entitled *Learning theory and personality dynamics* (1950).

The historical importance of Mowrer's contributions to the learning of motives and the operation of these learned motives as reinforcers is unquestioned and the theory of Dollard and Miller owes much to his work in this area. Likewise his analysis of neurotic behavior in terms of s-r concepts is both original and intriguing. He suggests, among other things, that the seeming irrationality of neurotic behavior may be attributed to the point in time at which reinforcements and punishments are made following the neurotic response. Thus, if the individual engages in a form of behavior that leads to a small reward immediately and a large punishment subsequently the response may be retained because of the spread-of-effect, which results in those responses nearest to the reinforcement being reinforced most strongly. Or, the individual may have a small immediate punishment followed by a large reward at a later time, in which case the gradient of reinforcement will favor the immediate punishment and lead to the individual giving up the response. Thus, the dramatic unconcern of the neurotic for the consequences of his behavior is accounted for by the role of temporal factors and the gradient of reinforcement. As one might expect, secondary motives such as anxiety or fear play a very important part in this kind of learning situation.

Granted the importance of the contributions we have just men‹ tioned, it is the efforts that Mowrer (1947, 1951) has made to develop a dual theory of learning which are the focus of our attention here. We have already agreed that some learning theorists emphasize reinforcement while others stress contiguity, and Mowrer, as a student of Hull, originally fell in the first of these groups. However, with the passage of time he gave up this position, and since then has actively defended and developed an integrative or dualistic position.

For more than ten years I tried to make a monistic conception of learning work, but was forced to abandon it. There are clinical, experimental, logical, and common sense considerations which all suggest that there are two fundamentally different learning processes, which may be most simply referred to as *solution learning* and *sign learning*. In the one case the subject acquires a tendency to action, an action which is the *solution* to some problem, be that problem either a primary drive or a secondary one. In the other case the organism acquires what may be most inclusively referred to as an *expectation, predisposition, belief* or *set*. It is through the latter kind of learning that secondary drives, or emotions, become connected with new objects, thus *creating* "problems" where formerly there were none. In other words, solution learning is problem solving, drive reducing, pleasure giving; whereas sign learning, or conditioning, is often —perhaps always—problem making. In terms of the effector systems and neural tracts involved and the conditions under which they occur, these two forms of learning appear to be basically different (Mowrer, 1950, p. 5).

What Mowrer proposes is that there are two basic types of learning: sign learning and solution learning. The former is characterized by autonomic nervous system involvement, and usually entails stimulus substitution or associative shifting; the latter involves the central nervous system and implies response substitution. In the case of sign learning the primary condition is association or contiguity but in the case of solution learning the primary condition is reinforcement or reward. Limitations of space prevent our summarizing in detail the evidence and arguments that Mowrer puts forth in defense of his conception of the learning process. However, the focus of these arguments centers about the difficulties a monistic reinforcement theory encounters in dealing with avoidance learning.

The important thing for the reader to note is that Mowrer in contrast to Miller and Dollard has given up a theoretical position that rests squarely upon reinforcement in favor of a conception that incorporates both reinforcement and contiguity. This is not a completely new idea as both Skinner (1935) and Schlosberg (1937) made essentially the same suggestion earlier although they failed to elaborate and develop the idea to the degree Mowrer has. In his most recent writings Mowrer (1954b) has shown some evidence of a shift toward the position of the so-called cognitive theorists, as he has implied that learning is less a matter of forming stimulus and response bonds than it is the development of "attitudes, meanings and expectations."

The work of Mowrer and Sears is of particular interest to us because it provides some illustration of the multitude of different ways in which s-r theory may develop when confronted with new empirical problems and applications. At present the evidence is not available to permit a definitive choice between these various theoretical options and, further, the positions of Mowrer and Sears are not yet sufficiently elaborated to permit a fair comparison with the conventional reinforcement position.

CURRENT STATUS AND EVALUATION

The application of s-r concepts to behavioral events outside the laboratory has taken place, for the most part, during the past twenty-five or thirty years. In this interval a very large amount of relevant empirical research has accumulated. Furthermore, a number of able young psychologists have been trained during recent years, particularly at Yale and the University of Iowa, who possess the technical skill and theoretical conviction necessary to increase enormously the existing stock of such empirical evidence. The recent past has witnessed not only an empirical boom in this area but also the appearance of a large number of individuals actively concerned with extending and modifying the concepts we have discussed. In addition to Dollard, Miller, Mowrer, and Sears there are individuals such as J. S. Brown, Irvin Child, I. E. Farber, Ernest Hilgard, and John Whiting who have made and are making important theoretical contributions. Altogether it seems clear that this brand of personality theory is supported by an unusually vigorous group of adherents, and contrary to the belief or wish of many cognitive and holistic theorists there is little apparent danger that this theoretical school will vanish in the near future as a result of indifference.

Our discussion of the theory and research of Dollard and Miller has made manifest a number of virtues. The major concepts within this theory are clearly expounded and customarily linked, at least in a general way, to certain classes of empirical events. There is a real scarcity of vague allusion or appeal to intuition in the writing of these theorists. The hard-headed, positivistic reader will find much to admire in the works of s-r psychologists. Moreover, this evident objectivity does not prevent many s-r theorists from being ready and eager to embrace a wide range of empirical phenomena with their conceptual tools. Although their formulations began in the laboratory they have shown no timidity about advancing with them upon the most complex of behavioral phenomena.

A highly significant contribution of s-r theory to the personality scene is contained in the careful detail with which this position represents the learning process. Obviously the transformation of behavior as a result of experience is a crucial consideration for any adequate theory of personality, and yet many theories have largely overlooked this question or have brushed by it with a few stereotyped phrases. In this sense, s-r theory provides a model to be emulated by other theoretical positions.

The readiness of Dollard and Miller to extract wisdom from social anthropology and clinical psychoanalysis represents another attractive feature of their position. They make more explicit use of sociocultural variables than almost any of the other theories we have discussed and we have seen that their theory owes much to the impact of psychoanalysis. The readiness and sophistication with which sociocultural variables are introduced in the theory may be related to the fact that this theory has been applied by cultural anthropologists more widely than any other theory of personality except psychoanalysis.

The emphasis upon the function of a theory as a guide to investigation and the willingness to submit theoretical differences to experimental test, which s-r theorists have characteristically shown, represent a definite superiority of this group over most other personality theorists. In general, these theorists have a better sense of the nature and function of theory in an empirical discipline than any other group of personality theorists. In their writing there is less reification, less sterile argument over words, and more readiness to look upon theories as sets of rules that are used only when they are demonstrably more useful than other sets of rules, than can be observed among other theorists. This methodological sophistication is undoubtedly responsible for the relative explicitness and formal adequacy of the theory. It is probably fair to say that this position *looks* more the way a theory should than does any other personality theory.

In many ways s-r theory has come to typify an experimental, objective approach to human behavior. As such, it has been the prime critical target for those many psychologists who are convinced that an adequate understanding of human behavior must involve more than a slavish application of the experimental methods of physical science. These critics feel that although their personal theoretical positions may be vulnerable in that they rest upon empirical observation that is not adequately controlled, at least the observations are relevant to the events they purport to deal with. In the case of s-r theory, the bulk of the careful investigation is not only concerned with simple rather than complex behavior but, more important, it is carried out with an animal species that is phylogenetically far removed from the human organism, and manifestly different in many crucial respects. What good is rigor and careful specification in the experimental situation if the investigator is subsequently forced to make a tenuous assumption of phylogenetic continuity in order to apply his findings to important events? We have already seen that s-r theorists consider animal investigations only a step on the way to understanding human behavior and further they grant that these studies must eventually be justified with experimental studies employing human subjects. Thus, there is an essential agreement here concerning the importance of coordinating research and the only question becomes one of how much confidence can be placed in the theory until such studies are carried out in considerable quantity.

A related criticism frequently leveled at s-r theory asserts that most of the positive features of this position, including its careful definitions, explicitness, and wealth of research, exist only when the theory is applied to animal behavior or very restricted domains of human behavior. As soon as the theory is applied to complex human behavior it is on all fours with other theories of personality, with *ad hoc* definitions, and reasoning by analogy, representing the rule rather than the exception. This criticism suggests that the rigor and relative formal adequacy of the theory are illusory as they exist only when the theory is applied within a very limited scope. Once the theory is generalized, concepts which were crystal clear become ambiguous and definitions which were tight become flaccid. Actually a compelling critique of Hull's theory by Koch (1954) makes clear that s-r theory even in its home territory is not beyond criticism on formal grounds.

Perhaps the most important critical objection to this theory, and a point that embraces the criticisms we have already mentioned, is the assertion that it does not provide an adequate prior definition of stimulus and response. These two analytic terms operate quite well with a limited organism in a restricted environment, but with the adult human organism operating in a natural environment specification of the stimulus can come only after there is a relatively complete understanding of the behavioral event in question. It can be argued very cogently that if the psychologist can fully define the stimulus his task is virtually at an end, and if this is so it implies that the necessary definitions for s-r theory can be provided only after the fact. If the theory can operate effectively only on a *post hoc* basis, clearly its generality and predictive efficiency are greatly impaired. Roughly the same objection can be raised in connection with defining the response. In fairness to Miller and Dollard it must be admitted that they are well aware of this difficulty and have made attempts to improve upon the customary definitions of stimulus and response (Miller and Dollard, 1941; Dollard and Miller, 1950). Miller in a jocular vein has suggested that s-r theory might better be labeled hyphen theory as it has more to say about the connection between the stimulus and response than it has to say about either the stimulus or the response itself.

As we have seen, this theory has remarkably little to say about the structures or acquisitions of personality and this is undoubtedly why so many s-r theorists have found psychoanalytic theory useful in their thinking and investigation. This objection maintains that s-r theory is only a partial theory, as it deals with the process of learning but not with its outcomes; and the relatively stable components of personality are an essential element in any attempt to understand human behavior.

Certainly the most frequently voiced criticisms of s-r theory point to the simplicity and molecularity of the position. Holists feel that this theory is the very essence of a segmental, fragmented, and atomistic approach to behavior. They claim that so little of the context of behavior is seen that one cannot hope to understand or predict human behavior adequately. There is no appreciation of the importance of the "whole" and the patterning of the parts is overlooked in favor of their microscopic examination. In these objections it is hard to sort out the polemical and affective components from their legitimate intellectual accompaniment. In defense of the theory, it is certainly clear that there is nothing in the s-r position to imply that variables must operate singly or in isolation. Interaction of variables is perfectly acceptable, so at least this degree of holism is congruent with the theory, although it is not a point of particular emphasis. Further, so far as patterns of variables are concerned, if they can be specified adequately there is no reason why the theory would have to ignore such phenomena. Perhaps the core of this objection is the conviction that the set of variables employed by s-r theorists is too small and too ordinary to represent human behavior adequately. Again this is a matter of personal values. Whether progress will eventually stem most rapidly from a complex model that moves toward specificity and detail or a simple model that moves toward comprehensiveness and complexity is impossible to say at this time.

Some critics point to s-r theory as nothing more than a refinement of common sense. For the ordinary individual it is easy to view behavior as determined by a series of relations between stimuli on the one hand and responses on the other. Further, some of the key assumptions involved in these theories, particularly those having to do with the importance of reinforcement, also agree with the assumptions that most untrained observers make concerning the determinants of behavior. Still, this is hard to construe as a criticism because common sense is essentially a *non sequitur* so far as evaluating a theory is concerned. The evaluation of the theory must rest upon grounds of empirical fruitfulness, not upon its fit or lack of fit with usual conceptions of behavior.

In summary, s-r theory is a theoretical position that in many respects is singularly American. It is objective, functional, places a heavy emphasis upon empirical research, and is only minimally concerned with the subjective and intuitive side of human behavior. As such it provides a striking contrast to many of the theories we have discussed which are deeply indebted to European psychology. Undoubtedly its tough-minded, empirical strengths have made and will continue to make unique contributions to this area of psychology.

BIBLIOGRAPHY

PRIMARY SOURCES

Dollard, J., and Miller, N. E. *Personality and psychotherapy: an analysis in terms of learning, thinking and culture.* New York: McGraw, 1950.

Miller, N. E., and Dollard, J. *Social learning and imitation.* New Haven: Yale Univ. Press, 1941.

Mowrer, O. H. *Learning theory and personality dynamics.* New York: Ronald Press, 1950.

Sears, R. R. Social behavior and personality development. In T. Parsons and E. A. Shils (Eds.). *Toward a general theory of action.* Cambridge, Mass.: Harvard Univ. Press, 1951b, pp. 465–476.

REFERENCES

Davis, A., and Dollard, J. *Children of bondage.* Washington, D. C.: American Council on Education, 1940.

Dollard, J. *Caste and class in a southern town.* New Haven: Yale Univ. Press, 1937.

Dollard, J. *Criteria for the life history.* New Haven: Yale Univ. Press, 1936. (Reprinted, New York: Peter Smith, 1949.)

Dollard, J. *Fear in battle.* New Haven: Yale Univ. Press, 1943.

Dollard, J., Auld, F., and White, Alice. *Steps in psychotherapy.* New York: Macmillan, 1953.

Dollard, J., Doob, L. W., Miller, N. E., Mowrer, O. H., and Sears, R. R. *Frustration and aggression.* New Haven: Yale Univ. Press, 1939.

Dollard, J., and Miller, N. E. *Personality and psychotherapy: an analysis in terms of learning, thinking and culture.* New York: McGraw, 1950.

Hilgard, E. R. *Theories of learning.* Rev. Ed. New York: Appleton-Century-Crofts, 1956.

Hull, C. L. *Principles of behavior.* New York: Appleton-Century-Crofts, 1943.

Hull, C. L. *Essentials of behavior.* New Haven: Yale Univ. Press, 1951.

Hull, C. L. *A behavior system.* New Haven: Yale Univ. Press, 1952.

Koch, S. Clark L. Hull. In *Modern learning theory.* New York: Appleton-Century-Crofts, 1954, pp. 1–176.

Meehl, P. E. On the circularity of the law of effect. *Psychol. Bull.,* 1950, 47, 52–75.

Miller, N. E. Experimental studies of conflict. In J. McV. Hunt (Ed.). *Personality and the behavior disorders.* Vol. 1. New York: Ronald Press, 1944, pp. 431–465.

Miller, N. E. Theory and experiment relating psychoanalytic displacement to stimulus response generalization. *J. abnorm. soc. Psychol.,* 1948, 43, 155–178.

Miller, N. E. Learnable drives and rewards. In S. S. Stevens (Ed.). *Handbook of experimental psychology.* New York: Wiley, 1951a, pp. 435–472.

Miller, N. E. Comments on theoretical models: illustrated by the development of a theory of conflict behavior. *J. Pers.,* 1951b, 20, 82–100.

Miller, N. E., and Bugelski, R. Minor studies in aggression: II. The influence of frustrations imposed by the in-group on attitudes expressed toward out-groups. *J. Psychol.,* 1948, 25, 437–442.

Miller, N. E., and Dollard, J. *Social learning and imitation.* New Haven: Yale Univ. Press, 1941.

Miller, N. E., and Kraeling, Doris. Displacement: greater generalization of approach than avoidance in a generalized approach-avoidance conflict. *J. exp. Psychol.,* 1952, 43, 217–221.

Miller, N. E., and Murray, E. J. Displacement and conflict; learnable drive as a basis for the steeper gradient of avoidance than of approach. *J. exp. Psychol.,* 1952, 43, 227–231.

Mowrer, O. H. Apparatus for the study and treatment of enuresis. *Amer. J. Psychol.,* 1938, 51, 163–165.

Mowrer, O. H. A stimulus-response analysis of anxiety and its role as a reinforcing agent. *Psychol. Rev.,* 1939, 46, 553–566.

Mowrer, O. H. An experimental analogue of "regression" with incidental observations on "reaction-formation." *J. abnorm. soc. Psychol.,* 1940a, 35, 56–87.

Mowrer, O. H. Anxiety reduction and learning. *J. exp. Psychol.,* 1940b, 27, 497–516.

Mowrer, O. H. On the dual nature of learning—a reinterpretation of "conditioning" and "problem-solving." *Harv. educ. Rev.,* 1947, 17, 102–148.

Mowrer, O. H. Learning theory and the neurotic paradox. *Amer. J. Orthopsychiat.,* 1948, 18, 571–610.

Mowrer, O. H. Biological versus moral "frustration" in personality disturbances. *Progressive Educ.,* 1949, 26, 65–69.

Mowrer, O. H. *Learning theory and personality dynamics.* New York: Ronald Press, 1950.

Mowrer, O. H. Two-factor learning theory: summary and comment. *Psychol. Rev.,* 1951, 58, 350–354.

Mowrer, O. H. Speech development in the young child: I. The autism theory of speech development and some clinical applications. *J. Speech Disorders,* 1952, 17, 263–268.

Mowrer, O. H. *Psychotherapy theory and research.* New York: Ronald Press, 1953.

Mowrer, O. H. The psychologist looks at language. *Amer. Psychologist,* 1954a, 9, 660–694.

Mowrer, O. H. Ego psychology, cybernetics, and learning theory. In *Learning theory, personality theory and clinical research.* New York: Wiley, 1954b, pp. 81–90.

Mowrer, O. H., and Kluckhohn, C. Dynamic theory of personality. In J. McV. Hunt (Ed.). *Personality and the behavior disorders.* Vol. 1. New York: Ronald Press, 1944, pp. 69–135.

Mowrer, O. H., and Mowrer, W. M. Enuresis: a method for its study and treatment. *Amer. J. Orthopsychiat.,* 1938, 8, 436–459.

Mowrer, O. H., and Viek, P. Language and learning: an experimental paradigm. *Harv. educ. Rev.,* 1945, 15, 35–48.

Murray, E. J. A case study in a behavioral analysis of psychotherapy. *J. abnorm. soc. Psychol.,* 1954, 49, 305–310.

Murray, E. J., and Berkun, M. M. Displacement as a function of conflict. *J. abnorm. soc. Psychol.,* 1955, 51, 47–56.

Murray, E. J., and Miller, N. E. Displacement; steeper gradient of generalization of avoidance than of approach with age of habit controlled. *J. exp. Psychol.,* 1952, 43, 222–226.

Pavlov, I. P. The scientific investigation of the psychical faculties or processes in the higher animals. *Science,* 1906, 24, 613–619.

Pavlov, I. P. *Conditioned reflexes.* (Trans. by G. V. Anrep.) London: Oxford Univ. Press, 1927.

Schlosberg, H. The relationship between success and the laws of conditioning. *Psychol. Rev.,* 1937, 44, 379–395.

Sears, R. R. Experimental studies of projection: I. Attribution of traits. *J. soc. Psychol.,* 1936, 7, 151–163.

Sears, R. R. Experimental studies of projection: II. Ideas of reference. *J. soc. Psychol.,* 1937a, 8, 389–400.

Sears, R. R. Initiation of the repression sequence by experienced failure. *J. exp. Psychol.,* 1937b, 20, 570–580.

Sears, R. R. Non-aggressive reactions to frustration. *Psychol. Rev.,* 1941, 48, 343–346.

Sears, R. R. *Survey of objective studies of psychoanalytic concepts.* New York: Soc. Sci. Res. Council, Bull. No. 51, 1943.

Sears, R. R. Experimental analysis of psychoanalytic phenomena. In J. McV. Hunt (Ed.). *Personality and the behavior disorders.* Vol. 1. New York: Ronald Press, 1944, pp. 306–332.

Sears, R. R. Personality development in contemporary culture. *Proc. Amer. phil. Soc.,* 1948, 92, 363–370.

Sears, R. R. Relation of fantasy aggression to interpersonal aggression. *Child Develpm.,* 1950, 21, 5–6.

Sears, R. R. A theoretical framework for personality and social behavior. *Amer. Psychologist,* 1951a, 6, 476–482.

Sears, R. R. Social behavior and personality development. In T. Parsons and E. A. Shils (Eds.). *Toward a general theory of action.* Cambridge, Mass.: Harvard Univ. Press, 1951b, pp. 465–478.

Sears, R. R., Davis, H. V., *et al.* Effects of cup, bottle, and breast feeding on oral activities of newborn infants. *Pediatrics*, 1948, *3*, 549–558.

Sears, R. R., Hovland, C. I., and Miller, N. E. Minor studies of aggression: I. Measurement of aggressive behavior. *J. Psychol.*, 1940, *9*, 275–294.

Sears, R. R., Pintler, Margaret H., and Sears, Pauline S. Effect of father separation on pre-school children's doll play aggression. *Child Develpm.*, 1946, *17*, 219–243.

Sears, R. R., and Sears, Pauline S. Minor studies of aggression: V. Strength of frustration-reaction as a function of strength of drive. *J. Psychol.*, 1940, *9*, 297–300.

Sears, R. R., Whiting, J. W. M., Nowlis, V., and Sears, Pauline S. Some child-rearing antecedents of aggression and dependency in young children. *Genet. Psychol. Monogr.*, 1953, *47*, 135–236.

Sears, R. R., and Wise, G. M. Relation of cup-feeding in infancy to thumbsucking and the oral drive. *Amer. J. Orthopsychiat.*, 1950, *20*, 123–138.

Skinner, B. F. Two types of conditioned reflex and a pseudo type. *J. gen. Psychol.*, 1935, *12*, 66–77.

Thorndike, E. L. *Animal intelligence: experimental studies.* New York: Macmillan, 1911.

Thorndike, E. L. *The fundamentals of learning.* New York: Teachers College, 1932.

Watson, J. B. The place of the conditioned reflex in psychology. *Psychol. Rev.*, 1916, *23*, 89–116.

Watson, J. B. *Behaviorism.* New York: Norton, 1925.

12.

Rogers' Self Theory

Throughout the long history of man's curiosity about the causes of his conduct, and the shorter span of years since 1860 when psychology officially became a science, the question of a psychic agent which regulates, guides, and controls man's behavior has been repeatedly raised and discussed. Perhaps the most popular concept of an inner entity which shapes man's destiny is that of the soul. According to soul theory, mental phenomena are thought to be the manifestations of a specific substance which is entirely different from material substance. In the context of religious thought, the soul is considered to be immortal, free, and of divine origin. With the rise of scientific psychology, the idea of a soul or any other psychic agent such as a mind or an ego or a will or a self has tended to be firmly rejected.

Within recent years, however, there has been a resurgence of interest among psychologists in the concept of the self. William James in his famous chapter on the self in *Principles of psychology* (1890, Chapter X) set the stage for contemporary theorizing, and much of what is written today about the self and the ego derives directly or indirectly from James. James defined the self or the Empirical Me in its most general sense as the sum total of all that a man can call *his*—his body, traits, and abilities; his material possessions; his family, friends, and enemies; his vocation and avocations and much else. James discusses the self under three headings, to wit, (1) its constituents, (2) self-feelings, and (3) the actions of self-seeking and self-preservation. The constituents of the self are the material self, the social self, the spiritual self, and pure Ego. The material self consists of his material possessions, the social self of how he is regarded by his fellows, and the spiritual self of his psychological faculties and dispositions. James wrestled with the concept of the pure Ego and concluded that for the natural science of psychology the Ego can be defined as the stream of thought which constitutes one's sense of personal identity.

The term *self* as used in modern psychology has come to have two distinct meanings. On the one hand it is defined as the person's attitudes and feelings about himself, and on the other hand it is regarded as a group of psychological processes which govern behavior and adjustment. The first meaning may be called the *self-as-object* definition since it denotes the person's attitudes, feelings, perceptions, and evaluations of himself as an object. In this sense, the self is what a person thinks of himself. The second meaning may be called the *self-as-process* definition. The self is a doer, in the sense that it consists of an active group of processes such as thinking, remembering, and perceiving.

The two conceptions of the self are so distinctly different that it would be better to have separate terms for them. Some writers have adopted the convention of using the term *ego* when they wish to refer to the group of psychological processes, and to reserve the term *self* for the person's system of conceptions of himself. However, this convention is not universally followed. Sometimes the terms *self* and *ego* are employed in just the opposite sense from the one given above, or sometimes one of them, either the ego or the self, is used to designate both the processes and the object that is perceived.

It should be pointed out and clearly understood that no modern theory of the self holds that there is a psychic agent or "inner manikin" which regulates man's actions. The self, whether it be conceived as object or as process or both, is not an homunculus or "man within the breast" or soul; rather it refers to the object of psychological processes or to those processes themselves, and these processes are assumed to be governed by the principle of causality. In other words, the self is not a metaphysical or religious concept; it is a concept that falls within the domain of a scientific psychology. Self theory represents a serious attempt to account for certain phenomena and to conceptualize one's observations of certain aspects of behavior. In referring to the self as a doer, we do not wish to imply that it is anything other than a name for a group of processes.

In previous chapters we have seen that a number of personality theorists make some provision for the self in their systematic formulations. In the present chapter we shall focus more directly upon this concept and examine its role in current personality theory. For our specimen theory we have selected Carl Rogers' formulation because it is the most fully developed statement of self theory. Moreover, Rogers has buttressed his speculations with an imposing array of empirical supports. Before discussing Rogers, however, let us consider some of the ways in which the self and the ego have been employed by a representative group of psychologists. From this brief review, it will be apparent that there is no general agreement as to the precise way in which these two terms should be employed.

REPRESENTATIVE VIEWS OF THE SELF AND THE EGO

SYMONDS' SELF AND EGO

A good starting point is Symonds' little book entitled *The ego and the self* (1951). Following psychoanalytic theory he defines the ego as a group of processes, namely, perceiving, thinking, and remembering, which are responsible "for developing and executing a plan of action for attaining satisfaction in response to inner drives" (p. 4), and the self as the ways in which the individual reacts to himself. The self consists of four aspects: (1) how a person perceives himself, (2) what he thinks of himself, (3) how he values himself, and (4) how he attempts through various actions to enhance or defend himself. Symonds points out that the person may not be aware of these perceptions, conceptions, evaluations, and defending or enhancing reactions. Consciously a person may have one conception of himself and unconsciously he may have a contrary opinion. He may not be aware of the fact that he is being defensive when he perceives himself in a certain fashion. Symonds warns the reader against adopting the position that what a person says about himself is an accurate representation of his real feelings, and cites the experiments of Wolff (1933, 1935) and Huntley (1940) which show that conscious evaluations of the self do not necessarily agree with unconscious self-evaluations.

Symonds believes that there is considerable interaction between the self and the ego. If the ego processes are effective in coping with both inner demands and outer reality then the person tends to think well of himself. Also, if the person has a high opinion of himself his ego processes are more likely to function effectively. By and large, though, the effectiveness of the ego must first be demonstrated before the person can feel self-esteem and self-confidence.

SNYGG AND COMBS' PHENOMENAL SELF

Snygg and Combs consider themselves to be phenomenologists. They believe that "all behavior, without exception, is completely determined by and pertinent to the phenomenal field of the behaving organism" (1949, p. 15). The phenomenal field consists of the totality of experiences of which the person is aware at the instant of action. Awareness may vary between a low level and a high level, although presumably it never becomes completely unconscious. They believe that psychology must accept the common-sense idea that awareness is a cause of behavior, that what a person thinks and feels determines what he will do.

A *phenomenal self* is differentiated out of the phenomenal field. This phenomenal self "includes all those parts of the phenomenal field which the individual experiences as part or characteristic of himself" (1949, p. 58). On first glance it would seem that Snygg and Combs' phenomenal self is a variety of the self-as-object concept, but closer scrutiny reveals that the phenomenal self is both an object and a doer. It is a doer because it is an aspect of the phenomenal field which determines all behavior. Yet it is also an object because it consists of self-experiences. Apparently, then, Snygg and Combs' self is both object and process at one and the same time.

In a personal communication to the writers, Combs states his position on employing the self in the dual capacity of object and process.

It seems to me that this is quite possible, indeed is characteristic of everything we know of in the world of science; namely, that every organization is both composed of certain parts while at the same time it affects other organizations upon which it impinges. Thus, a rock is made up of certain molecules and is thus a product. It also, by its very existence, has an effect upon the world around it or upon the world in which it rests, and is thus also a process or a dynamic. In the same way, the self is composed of perceptions concerning the individual and this organization of perceptions in turn has vital and important effects upon the behavior of the individual.

LUNDHOLM'S SUBJECTIVE SELF

Lundholm (1940) has made a useful distinction between a *subjective self* and an *objective self*. The subjective self consists of those symbols, for example, words, in terms of which the individual is aware of himself, whereas the objective self consists of those symbols in terms of which other people describe the person. In other words the subjective self is "what I think of myself" and the objective self is "what others think of me." Lundholm points out that the subjective self-picture is not fixed but expands and contracts depending upon such factors as co-operation or conflict with others and the degree of effort required to accomplish a certain task. Lundholm does not mention the ego.

SHERIF AND CANTRIL'S EGO

In their encyclopedic book, *The psychology of ego-involvements* (1947), Sherif and Cantril define the ego as a constellation of attitudes of the type "what I think of myself, what I value, what is mine and what I identify with." Thus defined their ego is the self-as-object and not the working ego of psychoanalytic theory. They assert that "apart from the constellation of these ego-attitudes there is no such entity as the ego" (1947, p. 4). Yet by implication their ego is something more than a self-as-object, for if the ego becomes involved it motivates behavior. Their whole book, in fact, is replete with studies and examples of ego-as-motive. Sherif and Cantril maintain that when the ego (self)-attitudes are activated they energize, direct, and control the person's behavior. There are other nonego motives that do the same thing, but it is one of the main theses of their book that the ego-attitudes are more effective motivators of behavior than the nonego motives are. Thus, when a person is given a task to perform he will do it in a more or less perfunctory manner unless his ego-attitudes are aroused. If he feels, for instance, that his self-respect is at stake he will work much harder. It may seem regrettable, as it does to one reviewer of their book (Scheerer, 1948), that Sherif and Cantril did not differentiate more clearly between self-as-object and ego-as-process.

SARBIN'S SELF

Sarbin (1952) looks upon the self as a cognitive structure which consists of one's ideas about various aspects of his being. One may have conceptions of his body (the somatic self), of his sense organs and musculature (the receptor-effector self), and of his social behavior (the social self). These selves which are substructures of the total cognitive structure are acquired through experience. Consequently Sarbin speaks of them as empirical selves. He believes that the various selves emerge in a regular developmental sequence, the body self first and much later the social self. Sarbin uses the terms *ego* and *self* interchangeably and does not concern himself with developing a theory of the ego-as-process.

BERTOCCI'S SELF AND EGO

After criticizing Allport for using the term *ego* in the dual sense of process and object of knowledge, Bertocci (1945) advocates the use of different terms for the two senses in which Allport employs the single term, ego. Bertocci labels ego-as-process the *self* and self-as-object the *ego*, which is a direct switch in the customary meanings of these two terms. Bertocci's self is a complex, unitary activity of sensing, remembering, imagining, perceiving, wanting, feeling, and thinking. This is Freud's ego. Bertocci's ego, on the other hand, is a cluster of values, which may become embodied in the form of traits, with which the self identifies its success. Bertocci's ego is similar to Sherif and Cantril's ego.

HILGARD'S INFERRED SELF

In his presidential address before the American Psychological Association in 1949, Hilgard (1949) made a plea for the study of the self as indispensable to a complete understanding of the defense mechanisms of the Freudian ego. All of these mechanisms, Hilgard points out, imply a self-reference. "To feel guilty is to conceive of the self as an agent capable of good or bad choices. It thus appears that at the point that anxiety becomes infused with guilt-feelings, self-reference enters. If we are to understand a person's defenses against guilt-feelings, we must know something about his image of himself" (1949, p. 350). This is what Hilgard means by the self—one's image of himself.

Hilgard then poses the question as to how one can determine the nature of the self-image or self-concept. Hilgard rejects the approach of asking the person what he thinks of himself because he feels that the conscious self-picture can be distorted by unconscious factors. Hilgard prefers to infer the self-image from nonintrospective material, such as projective techniques, clinical interviews, and the like. The picture derived from such material is called the *inferred self*.

In his address, Hilgard gives a valuable clue as to the reason why there are two prevailing conceptions of the self: the self-as-process and the self-as-object. He says, in effect, that the person is prone to see himself as the active executor of his own behavior. What he intends or wills he does. To the man in the street behavior seems to be completely self-determined, and consequently he holds himself responsible for his actions. Hilgard reminds us that this lay person's picture of the self is inaccurate. Behavior is not the product of the self; rather it is the product of a complex of psychological processes aroused by proximal and distal stimuli of which the person is largely unaware. Yet even psychologists make the mistake of thinking that the self is an active, determining agent of conduct, and therefore confuse a self-as-doer with a self-as-object.

STEPHENSON'S SELF

In his provocative book, *The study of behavior* (1953), Stephenson introduces the reader to a new methodology for studying the person's notions about himself. Stephenson has little patience, as do other psychologists, with any concept which intimates that there is a psychic agent that determines behavior. He believes that a person can think and talk about himself just as he thinks and talks about other things, and that these self-reflections are as much a part of his behavior as anything else the individual does. Stephenson has provided a rationale and the basic tools, which he calls Q-methodology, for studying quantitatively a person's self-reflections, and this methodology has been widely used by self-psychologists. (See pp. 491–496.)

CHEIN'S SELF AND EGO

Stimulated by Allport's address on the ego in contemporary psychology (1943), Chein (1944) essayed to formulate a unified theory of the ego and the self. The self is not an object of awareness as the body is; rather it is the content of awareness and has no reality apart from such awareness. It is what we are aware of when we use the term self-awareness. The self does not do anything; that is left to the ego. The ego is a motivational-cognitive structure which is built around the self. The ego's motives and ideas serve the purpose of defending, extending, enhancing, and preserving the self. When the self is endangered, the ego comes to its assistance. However, not all of one's motives and thoughts are included in the ego; there is a nonego part of the personality which also determines action. Consequently, some activities are ego-involved and others are not.

Chein's view of the self and the ego appears to be in accord with the prevalent one that the self is what one is aware of while the ego is a group of processes. The distinctive feature of his viewpoint is that there are other processes which determine behavior apart from those included in the ego. Whether these processes are similar to those of Freud's id and superego or Jung's collective unconscious, Chein does not say.

MEAD'S SELF

One of the most influential social philosophers of this century, George Herbert Mead, set forth a conception of the self that has had a strong impact upon psychological thinking (1934). Mead's self is an object of awareness rather than a system of processes. It is developed in the following manner. At first, there is no self because a person cannot enter his own experience directly. That is, he is not innately self-conscious. He can and does experience other people as objects but he does not initially regard himself as an object. However, other people react to him as an object, and these reactions are experienced by the person against whom they are directed. As a consequence of these experiences, he learns to think of himself as an object and to have attitudes and feelings about himself. One responds to himself as others respond to him. Mead's self is a socially formed self. It can arise only in a social setting where there is social communication. "He becomes a self in so far as he can take the attitude of another and act toward himself as others act" (1934, p. 171).

Mead suggests that many selves may develop, each of which represents a more or less separate set of responses acquired from different social groups. For instance, the person may develop a family self which represents a structure of attitudes expressed by his family, a school self which represents attitudes expressed by his teachers and fellow pupils, and many other selves.

KOFFKA'S EGO AND SELF

For Koffka (1935), the ego is a segregated part of the total field. It is embedded within the behavioral environment which surrounds it and with which it interacts. The segregation of the ego from the total field results from experiences which are of a diverse or heterogeneous character. The person perceives himself as something that occupies the space between what is in front of him and what is behind him, and between what is above him and what is below him. One then has various kinds of experiences of this spatially segregated entity, and these experiences become welded together by the principle of proximity to form the ego. There may be unconscious experiences as well as conscious ones. The conscious experiences constitute the *phenomenal ego,* which is Koffka's name for the self-as-object concept.

However, Koffka makes it quite clear that the ego is a doer as well as an object. It consists of tension systems which interact with the environment. Changes in behavior are attributed to changes in "the great Ego-field gestalt." In this respect, Koffka's ego resembles Lewin's person, a resemblance that Koffka himself acknowledges. The ego as an organization of tension systems performs work. Koffka complicates the picture by introducing another concept, that of the executive. The executive controls behavior, yet it is separate from the ego. Koffka does not make it clear why it is necessary to postulate an executive as well as an ego.

In addition to an ego, which is both an object and a process, and an executive, which is a process, Koffka also recognizes a self. The self is the core or nucleus of the ego.

OTHER VIEWS OF THE EGO AND THE SELF

For other formulations of the ego and the self by personality theorists whose work has been presented in other chapters of this book the reader is referred to the following pages: Freud (pp. 33–35), Jung (pp. 85–86), Adler (pp. 124–125), Sullivan (pp. 138–139), Allport (pp. 268–269), Murphy (p. 508), Angyal (p. 319), Cattell (pp. 403–404), and Murray (p. 169).

This brief survey of some of the current notions regarding the self and the ego points up the fact that there is not too much consistency in the way in which these terms are used by various writers. One could wish that it were possible to establish by fiat standardized definitions of the self and the ego and make it illegal to use them in any other way. In the more or less free world of science, however, differences of opinion are not resolved by issuing fiats or passing laws. Agreement has to be reached by the slower but more democratic method of free discussion and mutual consent.

THE SELF THEORY OF CARL ROGERS

In the eyes of the psychological world, Carl Rogers is identified with a method of psychotherapy which he originated and developed. This type of therapy is called nondirective or client-centered. In the words of its originator, successful client-centered therapy conducted under optimal conditions

. . . would mean that the therapist has been able to enter into an intensely personal and subjective relationship with this client—relating not as a scientist to an object of study, not as a physician expecting to diagnose and cure,—but as a person to a person. It would mean that the therapist feels this client to be a person of unconditional self-worth; of value no matter what his condition, his behavior or his feelings. It means that the therapist is able to let himself go in understanding this client; that no inner barriers keep him from sensing what it feels like to be the client at each moment of the relationship; and that he can convey something of his empathic understanding to the client. It means that the therapist has been comfortable in entering this relationship fully, without knowing cognitively where it will lead, satisfied with providing a climate which will free the client to become himself.

For the client, this optimal therapy has meant an exploration of increasingly strange and unknown and dangerous feelings in himself; the exploration proving possible only because he is gradually realizing that he is accepted unconditionally. Thus he becomes acquainted with elements of his experience which have in the past been denied to awareness as too threatening, too damaging to the structure of the self. He finds himself experiencing these feelings fully, completely, in the relationship, so that for the moment he *is* his fear, or his anger, or his tenderness, or his strength. And as he lives these widely varied feelings, in all their degrees of intensity, he discovers that he has experienced *himself*, that he *is* all these feelings. He finds his behavior changing in constructive fashion in accordance with this newly experienced self. He approaches the realization that he no longer needs to fear what experience may hold, but can welcome it freely as a part of his changing and developing self (1955b, pp. 2–3).

(For another highly personalized discussion of client-centered therapy see Rogers, 1955c. The most complete account appears in *Client-centered therapy*, 1951.)

Nondirective therapy has enjoyed considerable popularity among psychological counselors partly because it is tied historically to psychology rather than to medicine. It is said to be fairly easy to learn and it requires little or no knowledge of personality diagnosis and dynamics in order to use it. Moreover, the course of treatment is relatively brief compared, for example, to psychoanalysis, and some clients are said to be benefited after a few therapy sessions.

However, psychotherapy is not our concern in this book, and we have mentioned it only because Rogers' theory of personality has evolved out of his experiences as a client-centered therapist. His therapeutic observations have provided Rogers with "a precious vein of observational material of unusual value for the study of personality" (1947, p. 358). The formulation of a personality theory has helped also to illuminate and elucidate Rogers' therapeutic practices.

Carl Rogers was born in Oak Park, Illinois, January 8, 1902, "the middle child in a large, closeknit family, where hard work and a highly conservative Protestant Christianity were about equally revered"

(1955a, p. 2). When Carl was twelve years old, his family moved to a farm and he became interested in scientific agriculture. This interest in science carried over to college where during his first years he was fond of the physical and biological sciences. After his graduation from the University of Wisconsin in 1924, he attended Union Theological Seminary in New York City where he became exposed to a liberal, philosophical viewpoint regarding religion. Transferring to Teachers College of Columbia University, he fell under the philosophical influence of John Dewey and was introduced to clinical psychology by Leta Hollingworth. He was awarded the master's degree in 1928 and the doctorate in 1931 by Columbia. His first practical experience in clinical psychology and psychotherapy was obtained as an interne at the Institute for Child Guidance which had a strongly Freudian orientation. Rogers observes that "the sharp incompatibility of the highly speculative Freudian thinking of the Institute with the highly statistical and Thorndikean views at Teachers College was keenly felt" (1955a, p. 3).

After receiving his doctor's degree in psychology, Rogers joined the staff of the Rochester Guidance Center and later became its director.

> The staff was eclectic, of diverse background, and our frequent and continuing discussion of treatment methods was based on our practical everyday working experience with the children, adolescents and adults who were our clients. It was the beginning of an effort, which has had meaning for me ever since, to discover the order which exists in our experience of working with people. The volume on the *Clinical Treatment of the Problem Child* (1939) was one outcome of this effort (1955a, p. 3).

During this period, Rogers was influenced by Otto Rank, the psychoanalyst, who had by that time broken away from the orthodox teachings of Freud.

In 1940, Rogers accepted an invitation to become professor of psychology at Ohio State University. This shift from a clinical setting to an academic environment proved to be a sharp one for Rogers. Under the stimulus provided by intellectually curious and critical graduate students, Rogers felt impelled to make his views on psychotherapy more explicit, which he did in his book *Counseling and psychotherapy* (1942). In 1945 Rogers went to the University of Chicago as professor of psychology and executive secretary of the Counseling Center, the position he now holds. He was president of the American Psychological Association in 1946–1947.

In assessing the influences on his thinking, Rogers places great emphasis upon

. . . the continuing clinical experience with individuals who perceive themselves, or are perceived by others to be, in need of personal help. Since 1928, for a period now approaching 30 years, I have spent probably an average of 15 to 20 hours per week, except during vacation periods, in endeavoring to understand and be of therapeutic help to these individuals. To me they seem to be the major stimulus to my psychological thinking. From these hours, and from my relationships with these people I have drawn most of whatever insight I possess into the meaning of therapy, the dynamics of interpersonal relationships, and the structure and functioning of personality (1955a, p. 5).

Rogers' theory of personality represents a synthesis of phenomenology as presented by Snygg and Combs, of holistic and organismic theory as developed in the writings of Goldstein, Maslow, and Angyal, of Sullivan's interpersonal theory, and of self-theory for which Rogers himself is largely responsible, although he acknowledges a debt to Raimy (1943) and Lecky (1945).

The principal conceptual ingredients of Rogers' theory are these: (1) the *organism* which is the total individual, (2) the *phenomenal field* which is the totality of experience, and (3) the *self* which is a differentiated portion of the phenomenal field and consists of a pattern of conscious perceptions and values of the "I" or "me." The organism possesses the following properties: (a) it reacts as an organized whole to the phenomenal field in order to satisfy its needs, (b) it has one basic motive, namely, to actualize, maintain, and enhance itself, and (c) it may symbolize its experiences so that they become conscious, or it may deny them symbolization so that they remain unconscious, or it may ignore its experiences. The phenomenal field has the property of being conscious or unconscious, depending upon whether the experiences that constitute the field are symbolized or not.

The self, which is the nuclear concept in Rogers' theory of personality, has numerous properties some of which are these: (a) it develops out of the organism's interaction with the environment, (b) it may introject the values of other people and perceive them in a distorted fashion, (c) the self strives for consistency, (d) the organism behaves in ways that are consistent with the self, (e) experiences that are not consistent with the self-structure are perceived as threats, and (f) the self may change as a result of maturation and learning.

The nature of these concepts and their interrelationships are brought out in a series of nineteen propositions formulated by Rogers. We will present and discuss these propositions in the order in which Rogers gives them in his book, *Client-centered therapy* (1951).

1. "Every individual exists in a continually changing world of experience of which he is the center" (p. 483). The "changing world of experience" is Snygg and Combs' phenomenal field although Rogers does not assume, as Snygg and Combs seem to, that all experiences are consciously perceived. In fact, Rogers states that "probably (only) a very small portion is *consciously* perceived" (p. 483). Experience refers to everything that is going on within the organism at any given moment, including physiological processes, sensory impressions, and motor activities. However, most of our unconscious experiences are capable of becoming conscious when the need arises. In psychoanalytic terminology they exist in the preconscious rather than in the unconscious. Consciousness for Rogers consists of that which can be symbolized; it is an attribute of the figure of the phenomenal field, of which the background is more or less unconscious.

Rogers believes that this private world of experience can only be known "in any genuine and complete sense" to the individual himself. The psychologist with his methods of identifying and measuring stimulus properties and his tests for assessing personality cannot know the person's phenomenal field as completely as the person himself is capable of knowing it. Of course, the person may never develop this self-knowledge although he has the potentiality for doing so. According to this proposition the person is the best source of information about himself. Since his verbalizations are symbolizations of inner experience the psychologist can learn what exists in the client's private world by listening to what he says. The client-centered therapy situation with its emphasis upon permissiveness and unqualified acceptance of everything that the client says provides an especially favorable atmosphere for obtaining free and candid self-reports.

2. "The organism reacts to the field as it is experienced and perceived. This perceptual field is, for the individual, 'reality'" (1951, p. 484). This proposition asserts that the person does not react to external stimuli or internal disturbances as such, but rather he reacts to his experiences of the stimulating or motivating conditions. Whatever he thinks is true, whether it is actually true or not, is reality, and it is this subjective reality which determines how he behaves. Consequently, a knowledge of the stimulus does not suffice for predicting behavior; one must know how the person is perceiving the stimulus. One could not predict, for example, that a person would put salt into his coffee unless he knew that the person thought it was sugar. This proposition also explains why people react in different ways to the same situation or in the same way to different situations.

Rogers admits that the person tends to check his experiences of the world against the world as it really is. This testing of reality provides him with dependable knowledge of the world so that he is able to behave realistically. However, some perceptions remain untested or are inadequately tested, and these untested experiences may cause him to behave unrealistically and even to his own detriment. Although Rogers does not deal with the issue of a "true" reality, it is apparent that a person must have some conception of an external or impersonal standard of reality, for otherwise he could not perform the act of testing an inner picture of reality against an "objective" one. The question then arises as to how the person can differentiate between a subjective image which is not a correct representation of reality and one that is. What enables the person to separate fact from fiction in his subjective world? This is the great paradox of phenomenology.

Rogers resolves the paradox by leaving the conceptual framework of pure phenomenology. What a person experiences or thinks is actually not reality for the person; it is merely a tentative hypothesis about reality, a hypothesis that may or may not be true. The person suspends judgment until he puts the hypothesis to a test. What is this test? It consists of checking the correctness of the information which he has received and upon which his hypothesis is based with other sources of information. For example, a person who wishes to salt his food is confronted with two identical shakers, one of which contains salt, the other pepper. He believes that the shaker with the larger holes contains salt, but not being dead sure he shakes a little of the contents on the back of his hand. If the particles are white rather than black he feels reasonably sure that it is salt. A very cautious person may even then put a little to his lips because it might be white pepper instead of salt. What we have here is a testing of one's ideas against a variety of sensory data. The test consists of checking less certain information against more direct knowledge. In the case of salt, the final test is its taste; a particular kind of sensation defines it as salt.

3. "The organism reacts as an organized whole to this phenomenal field" (1951, p. 486). The term *organized whole* is an organismic or holistic concept which has been popularized by Gestalt psychology, Goldstein, and others. By employing the term Rogers intends to set his viewpoint apart from any segmental approach to the study of the person. He disavows a stimulus-response type of psychology in favor of a psychology that stresses "total, organized, goal-directed responses."

"The organism is at all times a total organized system in which alteration of any part may produce changes in any other part" (p. 487).

4. "The organism has one basic tendency and striving—to actualize, maintain, and enhance the experiencing organism" (1951, p. 487). This proposition is borrowed from Snygg and Combs and agrees with a similar idea found in the writings of Angyal and Maslow. It rests on the assumption that the organism is a purely monistic dynamic system in which one drive suffices to account for all behavior. It also assumes that the personality unfolds along the lines dictated by the nature of the organism. On the one hand, there is a single motivating force; on the other hand, there is a single goal of life.

The organism actualizes itself along the lines laid down by heredity. It becomes more differentiated, more expanded, more autonomous, and more socialized as it matures. This basic tendency of growth—to actualize and expand oneself—is seen to best advantage when an individual is observed over a long period of time. There is a forward movement in the life of every person; it is this ongoing tendency which is the only force that the therapist can really rely upon to effect an improvement in the client.

Self-actualization is not accomplished without struggle and pain but the person engages in the struggle and stands the pain because the creative urge to grow is so strong. The child learns to walk in spite of his initial tumbles, the adolescent learns to dance in spite of his awkwardness and embarrassment.

Rogers adds a new feature to the concept of growth when he observes that the forward-moving tendency can only operate when the choices are clearly perceived and adequately symbolized. A person cannot actualize himself unless he is able to discriminate between progressive and regressive ways of behaving. There is no inner voice that tells him which is the path of progress, no organismic necessity that thrusts him forward. He has to know before he can choose but when he does know he always chooses to grow rather than to regress.

5. "Behavior is basically the goal-directed attempt of the organism to satisfy its needs as experienced, in the field as perceived" (1951, p. 491). This proposition, referring as it does to plural "needs," does not contradict the notion of a single motive. Although there are many needs, each of them is subservient to the basic tendency of the organism to maintain and enhance itself.

Rogers remains faithful to his phenomenological position by employing the qualifying phrases "as experienced" and "as perceived." However, in discussing this proposition, Rogers admits that needs may evoke appropriate behavior even though the needs are not consciously experienced (adequately symbolized).

6. "Emotion accompanies and in general facilitates such goal-directed behavior, the kind of emotion being related to the seeking versus the consummatory aspects of the behavior, and the intensity of the emotion being related to the perceived significance of the behavior for the maintenance and enhancement of the organism" (1951, p. 493). This proposition is based upon a view of emotion developed by Prescott (1938) and Leeper (1948) which states, in effect, that emotions are not disruptive but are beneficial to adjustment. The emotions of excitement, such as anger, help the person in his seeking and striving behavior, while the calmer emotions, like contentment, aid in the consummatory action on the goal object. Anger, for example, may make a person strive harder to get food, and contentment may facilitate digestion once the food has been eaten. The intensity of the emotion varies according to the meaning the situation has to the person. If his life is in danger, his fear will be great, but if the danger is trivial, his fear will be small. This view of emotion contrasts with those personality theories in which the harmful or disturbing effects of anxiety are stressed.

7. "The best vantage point for understanding behavior is from the internal frame of reference of the individual himself" (1951, p. 494). This statement underlines Rogers' faith in self-reports as providing psychological data *par excellence*. Trying to understand the person from an external frame of reference, that is, by means of inferences made from test data, observations, expressive behavior and actions, is less satisfactory than approaching the person through his internal frame of reference as revealed by the attitudes and feelings he expresses in the permissive, nonthreatening setting of client-centered therapy.

Rogers acknowledges that self-reports do not give a complete picture of personality nor do they divulge all of the determiners of behavior. The person may be conscious of the reasons for his behavior but not be able to translate them into words that will convey what he wants them to. Or he may not be conscious of all of his experiences in which case he cannot communicate them. Furthermore, he may be conscious of his experiences and be able to verbalize them but be unwilling to do so. If pressed for an answer he may intentionally deceive the listener. In spite of these shortcomings of self-reports Rogers prefers to try to understand personality and behavior from the person's own frame of reference as it becomes manifest in the favorable setting of client-centered therapy.

The foregoing seven propositions are primarily phenomenological in character and refer to the behaving organism. The eighth proposition introduces the concept of a self, and the remaining propositions elaborate this concept into a more or less complete self-psychology.

8. "A portion of the total perceptual field gradually becomes differentiated as the self" (1951, p. 497). Rogers follows Snygg and Combs when he asserts that a phenomenal self is differentiated out of the total phenomenal field. This self is the awareness of one's being and functioning. In other words, it is the self-as-object, a set of experiences that have the same referent, namely, the "I" or the "me." How does the self become differentiated out of the total field? The next proposition essays to answer this question.

9. "As a result of interaction with the environment, and particularly as a result of evaluational interactions with others, the structure of self is formed—an organized, fluid, but consistent conceptual pattern of perceptions of characteristics and relationships of the 'I' or the 'me,' together with values attached to these concepts" (1951, p. 498). Among the many discriminations that the baby learns are those which enable him to distinguish himself as an object from the environment. When he has learned this distinction, he then perceives that some things belong to him and other things belong to the environment. He also begins to build up a conception of himself in relation to the environment. These experiences become invested with value, which may be either positive in character ("I like it") or negative in character ("I dislike it"). The self-structure "is, then, the organized picture, existing in awareness either as figure (i.e. clear consciousness) or ground (i.e. hazy consciousness or unconsciousness), of the self and the self-in-relationship (to the environment), together with the positive or negative values which are associated with those qualities and relationships, as they are perceived as existing in the past, present, or future" (1951, p. 501).

Values not only accrue to the self-picture as a result of direct experience with the environment but they are also taken over from others and perceived as if the person had experienced them directly. Rogers considers this type of introjection or assimilation so important that he has made it the subject of a separate proposition.

10. "The values attached to experiences, and the values which are a part of the self-structure, in some instances are values experienced directly by the organism, and in some instances are values introjected

or taken over from others, but perceived in distorted fashion, as if they had been experienced directly" (1951, p. 498). The child finds pleasure in doing many things, for which he may be either rewarded or punished by the parents. The child who is punished for doing something he finds pleasurable is thrown into a conflict between the desire to obtain pleasure and the desire to avoid pain. In resolving this conflict he may have to revise his self-image and his set of values in such a manner that his real feelings and values are distorted. This is what happens in the following case. A boy has a self-picture of being a good boy, and of being loved by his parents but he also enjoys tormenting his little sister for which he is punished. As a result of this punishment he is called upon to revise his self-image and his values in one of the following ways: (a) "I am a bad boy," (b) "My parents don't like me," (c) "I don't like to tease my sister." Each of these self-attitudes may contain a distortion of the truth. Let us suppose that he adopts the attitude "I don't like to tease my sister," thereby denying his real feelings. Denial does not mean that the feelings cease to exist; they will still influence his behavior in various ways even though they are not conscious. A conflict will then exist between the introjected and spurious conscious values and the genuine unconscious ones. If more and more of the "true" values of a person are replaced by values taken over or borrowed from others, yet which are perceived as being his own, the self will become a house divided against itself. Such a person will feel tense, uncomfortable, and out of sorts. He will feel as if he does not really know what he is and what he wants.

Rogers points out that these conflicts between values can be ameliorated by parents who are willing to accept the values of the child although not necessarily approving of them. Under these conditions, the child is not made to feel insecure by being rejected, there is no threat to his self-picture, and the child can develop "a soundly structured self in which there is neither denial nor distortion of experience" (1951, p. 503).

11. "As experiences occur in the life of the individual, they are either (a) symbolized, perceived and organized into some relationship to the self, (b) ignored because there is no perceived relationship to the self-structure, (c) denied symbolization or given a distorted symbolization because the experience is inconsistent with the structure of the self" (1951, p. 503). This proposition states, in effect, that perception is selective, and the primary criteria for selection is whether the experience is consistent with one's self-picture at the moment. When one has a self-picture of being hungry he will select from the welter of

stimuli acting upon him those that are relevant to the satisfaction of hunger and ignore those that are not relevant. In other words, it is the contemporary self-structure that determines the kinds of experiences that will be accepted.

Denying an experience is not the same thing as ignoring it. Denial means falsifying reality either by saying it does not exist or by perceiving it in a distorted way. A person may deny his aggressive feelings because they are inconsistent with the picture he has of himself as a peaceful, friendly person. In such case, the denied feelings may be allowed to express themselves by means of a distorted symbolization, for example, by projecting them onto other people. Rogers points out that people will often stoutly maintain and enhance a self-picture that is completely at variance with reality. The person who feels that he is worthless will exclude from awareness evidence that contradicts this picture or he will reinterpret the evidence to make it congruent with his sense of worthlessness. For example, if he receives a promotion in his work he will say that "the boss felt sorry for me" or "I don't deserve it." Some people may even do poorly in the new position to prove to themselves and to the world that they are no good.

How can one deny a threat to the self-picture without first being aware of the threat? Rogers says that there are levels of discrimination below the level of conscious recognition, and that the threatening object may be unconsciously perceived or "subcepted"—to use a term introduced by McCleary and Lazarus (1949)—before it is perceived. The threatening object or situation, for example, may produce visceral reactions such as a pounding heart, which are consciously experienced as sensations of anxiety, without the person being able to identify the cause of the disturbance. Feelings of anxiety evoke the mechanism of denial or repression which prevent the threatening experience from becoming conscious.

12. "Most of the ways of behaving which are adopted by the organism are those which are consistent with the concept of the self" (1951, p. 507). This proposition is the theme of Lecky's little book, *Self-consistency* (1945), which is discussed in the chapter on organismic theory. If this proposition is true, then the best way to produce changes in behavior is first to effect alterations in the concept of the self. This is precisely what Rogers' client-centered therapy attempts to do. Client-centered therapy is a *self*-centered therapy.

13. "Behavior may, in some instances, be brought about by organic experiences and needs which have not been symbolized. Such be-

havior may be inconsistent with the structure of the self, but in such instances the behavior is not 'owned' by the individual" (1951, p. 509). This proposition is a necessary supplement to the preceding one because some behavior of the person is clearly inconsistent with his self-structure. When a person violates his self-consistency he is apt to say "I was carried away," or "that wasn't like me," or "why did I do that?" or "something must have got into me," or "I did it in spite of myself." In other words, he disowns the behavior in order to maintain an image of self-consistency.

Considering Propositions 12 and 13 together, it becomes apparent that Rogers recognizes two behavior-regulating systems, the self and the organism. These two systems can either work together harmoniously and co-operatively or they can oppose one another. If they oppose one another, the result is tension and maladjustment as set forth in Proposition 14, and if they work together the consequence is adjustment as set forth in Proposition 15.

14. "Psychological maladjustment exists when the organism denies to awareness significant sensory and visceral experiences, which consequently are not symbolized and organized into the gestalt of the self-structure. When this situation exists, there is basic or potential psychological tension" (1951, p. 510).

15. "Psychological adjustment exists when the concept of the self is such that all the sensory and visceral experiences of the organism are, or may be, assimilated on a symbolic level into a consistent relationship with the concept of self" (p. 513).

Like Freud's id and ego or Jung's conscious and unconscious, Rogers has his two systems, namely, the organism and the self, which may oppose one another. The organism may keep experiences from becoming conscious that are not consistent with the self, and the self is endowed with the power of selecting experiences that are consistent with its structure. The consequences of an organism-self dichotomy and the opposition between them are elaborated in the next proposition.

16. "Any experience which is inconsistent with the organization or structure of self may be perceived as a threat, and the more of these perceptions there are, the more rigidly the self-structure is organized to maintain itself" (1951, p. 515). The self builds up defenses against threatening experiences by denying them to consciousness. As it does so, the self-image becomes less congruent with organismic reality, with the result that more defenses are required to maintain the false

picture held by the self. The self thereby loses contact with the actual experiences of the organism, and the increasing opposition between reality and self creates tension. Consequently the person becomes more and more maladjusted.

How can this situation be ameliorated? The harmonious integration of the self and the organism can be effected by client-centered therapy which is the "certain conditions" of the following proposition.

17. "Under certain conditions, involving primarily complete absence of any threat to the self-structure, experiences which are inconsistent with it may be perceived, and examined, and the structure of self revised to assimilate and include such experiences" (1951, p. 517).

In client-centered therapy the person finds himself in a nonthreatening situation because the counselor is completely accepting of everything the client says. This warm accepting attitude on the part of the counselor encourages the client to explore his unconscious feelings and to bring them into awareness. Slowly and tentatively he explores the unsymbolized feelings which threaten his security. In the safety of the therapeutic relationship these hitherto threatening feelings can now be assimilated into the self-structure. The assimilation may require rather drastic reorganization in the self-concept of the client in order to bring it into line with the reality of organismic experience. "He will *be*, in more unified fashion, what he organismically *is*, and this seems to be the essence of therapy" (1955c, p. 269). Rogers admits that some people may be able to accomplish this process without undergoing therapy.

An important social benefit gained from the acceptance and assimilation of experiences that have been denied symbolization is that the person becomes more understanding and accepting of other people. This idea is presented in the next proposition.

18. "When the individual perceives and accepts into one consistent and integrated system all his sensory and visceral experiences, then he is necessarily more understanding of others and is more accepting of others as separate individuals" (1951, p. 520). A person who is defensive is inclined to feel hostile towards other people whose behavior, in his eyes, represents his own denied feelings. When a person feels threatened by sexual impulses he may tend to criticize others whom he perceives as behaving in sexual ways. On the other hand, if he accepts his own sexual and hostile feelings he will be more tolerant of their expression by others. Consequently his social relationships will improve and the incidence of social conflict will decrease. Rogers believes that the social implications of this proposi-

tion "are such as to stretch the imagination" (p. 522). It may even contain the key to the eventual abolition of international strife.

In his last proposition, Rogers points out how important it is for wholesome adjustment to maintain a continuous examination of one's values.

19. "As the individual perceives and accepts into his self-structure more of his organic experiences, he finds that he is replacing his present value system—based so largely upon introjections which have been distortedly symbolized—with a continuing valuing process" (1951, p. 522). The emphasis falls upon the two words, *system and process*. A *system* carries the connotation of something that is fixed and static, whereas a process signifies that something is taking place. For healthy, integrated adjustment one must constantly be evaluating his experiences to see whether they require a change in the value structure. Any fixed set of values will tend to prevent the person from reacting effectively to new experiences. One must be flexible in order to adjust appropriately to the changing conditions of life.

In this connection Rogers raises the question as to whether a continuing process of evaluating one's experiences in purely personal terms may not lead to social anarchy. He believes not. All people have "basically the same needs, including the need for acceptance by others" (p. 524). Consequently their values will possess a "high degree of commonality" (p. 524).

In concluding his discussion of the foregoing nineteen propositions, Rogers sums up his viewpoint in this concise way.

This theory is basically phenomenological in character and relies heavily upon the concept of self as an explanatory concept. It pictures the endpoint of personality development as being a basic congruence between the phenomenal field of experience and the conceptual structure of the self—a situation which, if achieved, would represent freedom from internal strain and anxiety, and freedom from potential strain; which would represent the maximum in realistically oriented adaptation; which would mean the establishment of an individualized value system having considerable identity with the value system of any other equally well-adjusted member of the human race (1951, p. 532).

In a recent restatement of his theory of personality which is as yet unpublished (1955a), Rogers has introduced three new unifying concepts. These are (1) the need for positive regard, (2) the need for self-regard, and (3) conditions of worth.

A need for positive regard by other people, which is assumed to be universal although not necessarily innate, develops as the awareness of self emerges. This need can become more compelling than the organismic valuing process so that the individual seeks the esteem of others more than he does experiences that are valued by the organism.

As a consequence of self-experiences with satisfaction or frustration of the need for positive regard the person acquires a need for self-regard. This need can function independently of interpersonal relations so that self-regard is experienced in relation to any particular kind of self-experiences.

Finally, as a result of the selective functioning of the need for self-regard, conditions of worth are acquired. A condition of worth is any condition which helps the person to avoid or find self-experiences that are less or more worthy of self-regard.

These three concepts are useful in helping to explain discrepancies between the self and experience, discrepancies in behavior, threatening experiences and defensive processes, and the process of reintegration.

CHARACTERISTIC RESEARCH AND RESEARCH METHODS

Rogers has been a pioneer investigator in the area of counseling and psychotherapy, and deserves a great deal of credit for stimulating and conducting research into the nature of the processes that occur during clinical treatment. Well-controlled studies of psychotherapy are exceedingly difficult to design and carry out because of the subtle and private nature of the psychotherapeutic setting. Therapists have been reluctant to subordinate the welfare of the patient to the needs of research by permitting any invasion of the privacy of the treatment room. Rogers, however, has shown that the electrical recording of therapy sessions, with the permission of the patient, is not injurious to the course of treatment. In fact, both patient and therapist soon ignore the presence of the microphone and behave quite naturally. The accumulation of a set of exact transcriptions of therapy sessions by Rogers and his associates has made it possible to study the course of treatment objectively and quantitatively. Largely through his efforts, we are beginning to learn something about the processes of psychotherapy. (See, for example, Rogers and Dymond, 1954; Seeman and Raskin, 1953.)

Although the empirical studies undertaken by Rogers and his associates have been aimed primarily at understanding and elucidating the nature of psychotherapy and evaluating its results, many of their findings bear directly upon the self theory of personality developed by Raimy (1943) and Rogers. In fact, Rogers' systematic formulation of a self theory was dictated by the research findings; it was not a preconceived viewpoint which determined the nature and direction either of the therapy or of the research. On this point, Rogers says, "The self has for many years been an unpopular concept in psychology, and those doing therapeutic work from a client-centered orientation certainly had no initial leanings toward using the self as an explanatory concept" (1951, p. 136).

Since the formulation of a self theory of personality Rogers has enlarged his therapy research program to include tests of inferences from his personality theory.

QUALITATIVE STUDIES. Many of Rogers' ideas about personality have been explicated by a qualitative, pointing-to procedure which consists of demonstrating by extracts from the record of the client's verbalizations what his self-picture is and what changes occur in it during therapy. The literature on nondirective or client-centered therapy is filled with examples of this type (Rogers, 1942, 1948, 1951; Rogers and Dymond, 1954; Rogers and Wallen, 1946; Muench and Rogers, 1946; Snyder *et al.*, 1947). Rogers himself seems to have a preference for this mode of presenting his ideas, although, of course, he does not regard excerpts from case records as proof of the validity of his personality theory. They are used more for the purpose of acquainting the reader with typical phenomena that occur during therapy sessions and to point out the kinds of experiences that are in need of explanation.

CONTENT ANALYSIS. This research method consists of formulating a set of categories by means of which the verbalizations of a client can be classified and counted. In a pioneer study, Porter (1943) laid the groundwork for much of the later work on the categorization of the recorded content of counseling interviews by showing that this method of analysis yields reliable results. In another early study by a Rogers' student (Raimy, 1948), an analysis of the characteristic changes in self-references during therapy was undertaken. For this purpose, Raimy used the following categories: positive or approving self-reference, negative or disapproving self-reference, ambivalent self-reference, ambiguous self-reference, references to external objects and persons, and questions. The transcribed records of fourteen cases who had had from two to twenty-one interviews were itemized and sorted into the foregoing six classes, and the number in each category at successive stages of counseling was counted. It was found that at the start of therapy the clients gave a preponderance of disapproving or ambivalent self-references, and that as counseling progressed fluctuations in self-approval occurred with mounting ambivalence. At the conclusion of counseling those clients who were judged to be improved were making a preponderant number of self-approving statements while those who had not improved were still being ambivalent and disapproving of themselves. Other investigators (Snyder, 1945; Lipkin, 1948; Seeman, 1949) have obtained substantially the same results.

In another group of studies employing content analysis an attempt was made to test the proposition that as a person becomes more accepting of himself he also becomes more accepting of other people. Categories of positive, negative, and ambivalent feelings toward self and others were formulated and applied to cases in therapy. In one study (Seeman, 1949), the number of positive self-references increased and the number of negative self-references decreased during therapy without any concomitant change in the feelings toward others. Another investigator (Stock, 1949), using a similar method of content analysis, could find no evidence that changes in self-feeling occur prior to and produce changes in feelings toward others. In a third investigation (Sheerer, 1949), some positive support for the proposition was obtained although the changes in attitudes toward others were neither as marked nor as regular as the increases in the acceptance of self. The most recent investigation of the proposition (Gordon and Cartwright, 1954) in which various tests and scales were employed in place of content analysis failed to support the hypothesis that increasing acceptance of self leads to an increasing acceptance of others.

It is of interest, however, that there is a fairly significant correlation, .51 in Sheerer's study and .66 in Stock's study, between conceptions of self and conceptions of others. This means that if an individual thinks well of himself he is likely to think well of others, and that if he disapproves of himself he is likely to disapprove of others. Correlations of about the same magnitude have been found by Phillips (1951) in an investigation of self-feelings and feelings toward others of various groups of people not in therapy.

Q-Technique Studies. The appearance of the English psychologist William Stephenson at the University of Chicago proved to be a great boon to Rogers and his associates. Although Stephenson is not himself a self-theorist, the methods of research that he has developed are uniquely adapted for investigating the self-concept by the single case method. These methods are referred to by Stephenson as Q-technique.

There is a difference between Stephenson's Q-technique and the logical basis upon which it rests which Stephenson calls Q-methodology. Logical hypotheses are derived from theory by Q-methodology and these hypotheses may then be tested by Q-technique. However, the investigator may employ Q-technique without using Q-methodology. This is what Rogers and his associates have done. The difference between the type of research fostered by Stephenson and that done under the influence of Rogers is brought out clearly by comparing the studies of Nunnally (1955), a student of Stephenson's, with those of Butler and Haigh (1954), students of Rogers'. Both of them investigated the changes in self-conceptions before and after therapy. Nunnally used Q-methodology in designing his experiment and the full complement of Q-techniques, including factor analysis, whereas Butler and Haigh used only the Q-sorting device and intrapersonal correlations. Moreover, Nunnally employed a single case, as Stephenson recommends, and Butler and Haigh employed a number of cases.

What is Q-technique? Essentially, it is a method of studying systematically the notions of a person about himself, although it can be used for other purposes as well. The person is given a packet of statements and is asked to sort them into a prearranged distribution along a continuum from those most characteristic of the person doing the sorting to those least characteristic of him. The distribution approximates a normal distribution and is exactly the same for all subjects in a given experiment. This constant feature expedites the statistical handling of the results since all sortings are forced into a distribution whose mean and standard deviation are the same.

Sortings may be made not only for how the person sees himself at the present time but also for how he would like to be, called the *ideal* sort, how he was at the age of fifteen, how his mother sees him, and so on. There may be as many different sortings or variates, as they are named, as the investigator chooses to use. Bowdlear (1955), for example, used twenty-five sortings in his study of an epileptic patient undergoing psychotherapy. The results of such a multivariate design may be analyzed by correlational methods, factor analysis, and analysis of variance.

The items for a Q-sort may be made up in various ways. They may be formulated so as to conform to a particular theory of personality of which many examples are given in Stephenson's book (1953) or they may be selected from a population of items obtained from therapeutic protocols, self-descriptions, personality inventories, and the like.

In order to illustrate the way in which Rogers and his associates have used Q-technique let us consider the study performed by Butler and Haigh (1954). These investigators set out to test the assumption that people who come for counseling are dissatisfied with themselves and that following successful counseling their dissatisfaction will be reduced. The Q-sort items for this study were chosen at random from a number of therapeutic protocols. They consisted of such items as "I am a submissive person," "I am a hard worker," "I am likable," and "I am an impulsive person." Prior to the beginning of counseling each client was asked to sort the statements in two ways, according to the following instructions:

Self-sort: Sort these cards to describe yourself as you see yourself today, from those that are least like you to those that are most like you.

Ideal-sort: Now sort these cards to describe your ideal person—the person you would most like within yourself to be.

The distributions of these two sortings were then correlated for each person. The average correlation between self-sort and ideal-sort for the group of subjects was zero, which shows that there is no congruence between the way a person sees himself and the way he would like to be. A control group of subjects who were matched with the client group but who were not interested in being counseled made the same two sortings. The average correlation for this group between self-sort and ideal-sort was .58, which proves that a nontreatment group is much better satisfied with itself than a group seeking therapy is. Following the completion of the counseling (there were an average of thirty-one sessions per client), the clients were again asked to make a self-sort and an ideal-sort. The average correlation between the two sorts turned out to be .34, a significant increase over what it had been prior to counseling although still short of the control group correlation. The control group was also retested after an interval of time equivalent to that for the client group and their average self-ideal correlation had not changed. Another group that had sought therapy but who were asked to wait sixty days before starting treatment showed no change in their self-ideal correlations during the waiting period.

As a check upon the permanence of the change that had taken place in the client's self-esteem during therapy, a follow-up study was made of the clients from six months to one year after therapy had been terminated. The average correlation between self-sort and ideal-sort was about the same as it had been at the close of counseling, .31 versus .34. The investigators conclude that self-esteem, which they define as the congruence between self- and ideal-sorts, increases as a direct result of client-centered counseling. It may occur to the reader that the increase in the average correlation from zero to .34 could have been the result of a change of the self-concept in the direction of the ideal, or of a change in the ideal in the direction of the self-concept, or of changes in both directions. In another study (Rudikoff, 1954), it was found that the ideal was somewhat lowered in the direction of the self-image during therapy, which suggests that both kinds of changes do occur.

It is of interest to note a few of the changes in individual correlations that occur between precounseling, postcounseling, and follow-up. Some of the correlations start out fairly low, increase markedly during therapy, and remain that way during the follow-up period. The following person, identified as Oak, exemplifies this pattern.

	Precounseling	Postcounseling	Follow-up
Oak	.21	.69	.71

Others remain low throughout as Baac's do.

	Precounseling	Postcounseling	Follow-up
Baac	−.31	.04	−.19

Still others start out low, increase following counseling, and then regress during the follow-up period.

	Precounseling	Postcounseling	Follow-up
Beel	.28	.52	−.04

For another type of person, the correlation starts out low, increases during therapy, and continues to increase after therapy has been concluded.

	Precounseling	Postcounseling	Follow-up
Bett	−.37	.39	.61

One might think that these different patterns of changes would be related to the amount of improvement shown during therapy. This is not the case. When the subjects were divided into an improved group and a nonimproved group, as judged by counselors and from projective test protocols, the two groups did not differ in respect to their self-ideal correlations at the termination of counseling, although at the time of the follow-up administration of the Q-sorts there was a tendency for the improved group to have somewhat higher correlations.

Butler and Haigh explain this failure to find a relationship between increased self-ideal correlations and improvement in terms of what they call "defensive sortings." A defensive sorting is one in which the person gives a distorted picture of himself so that it appears as if he is well-adjusted when actually he is not. For example, in another study the highest self-ideal correlation that was found, an extremely high .90, was secured by a person who was clearly pathological.

The question of defensiveness has received considerable attention from Rogers and his associates because it raises some serious problems regarding the validity of self-reports. Is it true, for example, that when a person says he is satisfied with himself he really is? Does the internal frame of reference give an accurate picture of personality? Haigh (1949) has made special studies of defensive behavior and finds that it may assume many forms, including denial, withdrawal, justification, rationalization, projection, and hostility. During client-centered therapy some clients show a decrease in defensiveness whereas others show an increase. However, Haigh tends to minimize the importance of defensive behavior. He assumes that most of it consists of intentional deception on the part of the client in order to save face. This view is in marked contrast to the psychoanalytic theory of defense mechanisms which assumes that they operate unconsciously.

A study undertaken by Friedman (1953) sheds some further light upon the problem of defensiveness. Three groups of white males classified as normal, psychoneurotic, and paranoid schizophrenic made self and ideal Q-sorts. The median correlation for the sixteen normal subjects was .63, for the sixteen neurotic subjects .03, and for the sixteen psychotic patients .43. In other words, the psychotic patients displayed considerably more self-esteem than did the neurotics and not a great deal less than the normal subjects. Friedman concludes that "to employ a high correlation between the self and ideal-self conceptions as a sole criterion of adjustment, however, would lead to the categorization of many maladjusted people, particularly paranoid schizophrenics, as adjusted" (p. 73).

Another study in which a measure of defensiveness was correlated with self-attitudes and the assessment of personality by outside observers was conducted by Chodorkoff (1954). Chodorkoff secured self-reports from thirty college students by having them sort 125 items into thirteen piles from most characteristic to least characteristic. Foui judges who had access to biographical information, Rorschach protocols and a summary of Rorschach scores, word association test data, and Thematic Apperception Test (TAT) protocols made a Q-sort for each subject using the same 125 items. A measure of perceptual defense was obtained by exposing threatening and neutral words beginning with a subliminal exposure speed and increasing it gradually until the subject was able to recognize all of the words. Measures of perceptual defense were computed by finding the difference between the recognition thresholds for the neutral words and the thresholds for the threatening words.

Chodorkoff was interested in testing the following hypotheses: (1) the greater the agreement between the person's self-description and description of him by others, the less perceptual defense he will manifest, (2) the greater the agreement between the person's self-description and an appraisal made by judges, the more adequate will be his personal adjustment, and (3) the more adequate his personal adjustment, the less perceptual defense he will show. Two measures of adjustment were employed: (1) the Munroe Inspection Rorschach check list and (2) ratings made by judges on eleven adjustment scales.

The results confirmed all of the hypotheses. The higher the agreement between self-descriptions and descriptions by others, the less perceptual defense there is and the better is the personal adjustment. The better adjusted subjects also displayed less perceptual defense.

These studies indicate that defensiveness is an important variable in the self-judgments of people, and that self-reports cannot be relied upon to give the same picture of personality as are obtained from outside judges.

OTHER EMPIRICAL APPROACHES. Although qualitative descriptions, content analysis of therapeutic protocols, and the use of Q-technique constitute the principal empirical approaches of Rogers and his associates to the study of personality, they have also employed a number of other methods. These methods consist of approaching the person from an external frame of reference. Such standard tests as the Rorschach (Muench, 1947; Carr, 1949; Haimowitz, 1950; Mosak, 1950; Haimowitz and Haimowitz, 1952), the TAT (Dymond, 1954; Grummon and John, 1954), the Minnesota Multiphasic (Mosak, 1950), the Bell Adjustment Inventory (Muench, 1947; Mosak, 1950), and the Kent-Rosanoff Word Association Test (Muench, 1947) have been used with clients in therapy. One of Rogers' students has also used physiological indices for measuring tension and emotion (Thetford, 1949, 1952). It is apparent that Rogers has not limited his investigative activities to the testing of hypotheses derived solely from self theory.

CURRENT STATUS AND EVALUATION

In attempting to make an over-all appraisal of Rogers' self theory, it should be borne in mind that his theory is not a completely formulated one. Because he prefers to keep his speculations rather closely tied to empirical data, Rogers has tended to be cautious and tentative in his theorizing and not to elaborate his theory much faster than the findings warrant. Consequently, any criticism of his theory should take into account the fact that it is unfinished and is constantly being revised and elaborated.

During the time that he was developing the method of client-centered counseling, Rogers did not concern himself with personality theory and, in fact, seemed to regard theory as an encumbrance to the performance of one's therapeutic activities. However, after his counseling methods and techniques were fully launched, Rogers began to see the need for developing a set of concepts and assumptions which would help to impose order and meaning upon the verbal reports of his clients and to increase his understanding of the client as a person. Consequently, the type of theory for which Rogers has shown a preference is one that fits the kind of data which have come out of a particular method of psychotherapy. It is well to remember this fact, that Rogers' view of the person has been shaped to a great extent by his therapeutic practices. Of course, now that he has formulated a theory of personality it would be surprising if his theoretical views did not influence his counseling practices, but this was not the case to begin with.

As we have already seen in earlier chapters, other personality theories have had their inception in the consulting room. Freud, Jung, Adler, Horney, and Sullivan were all primarily psychotherapists, and their views of personality emerged from their experiences in working with emotionally disturbed patients. Curiously, each of these theorists arrived at quite different formulations on the basis of much the same sort of observations, namely, those provided by the verbal reports of patients in a therapeutic setting. For the most part, the psycho-analytically oriented theorist has felt the need for interpreting what the patient said; he has been loath to take his patients' verbalizations at their face value. Behind the manifest content of the person's utterances he detects a rich, elaborate vein of latent content that runs deeply into the personality. This latent content is unconscious and can be reached only by inference, never by direct observation.

In contrast to the psychoanalyst's suspicions of the verity of what a person says and his tenacious searching and probing for hidden meaning, Rogers takes the position that self-reports are useful as direct sources of information about the person. There is no need to probe or interpret or to carry on extensive and intricate analyses of dreams or to excavate layer after layer of psychic strata because, in Rogers' eyes, the personality is revealed in what the person says about himself. The self-as-object, which is the central feature of Rogers' theory, is consciously experienced and these experiences it is assumed can be directly communicated to the investigator. The concept of unconscious motivation plays virtually no part in Rogers' thinking. The person is pretty much what he says he is. Such a viewpoint is not unlike the common-sense ideas regarding personality which are held by the average person. It might be expected, therefore, that self theory would be more popular with the public at large than with psychologists.

The chief criticism that many psychologists make of Rogers' self theory is that it is based upon a naïve type of phenomenology. (See, for example, Smith, 1950.) There is abundant evidence to show that factors unavailable to consciousness motivate behavior, and that what a person says of himself is highly colored and distorted by defenses of various kinds. Self-reports are notoriously lacking in reliability not only because the person may intend to deceive the listener but also because he does not know the whole truth about himself. Consciousness is not all there is to personality. Notwithstanding this evidence to the contrary Rogers maintains that "the best vantage point for understanding behavior is from the internal frame of reference of the individual himself."

The criticism of naïveté cannot be urged too strongly at this time because there is evidence in Rogers' recent writings that he is questioning and perhaps gradually abandoning the idea of an imperialistic phenomenal self which dominates the personality. Rogers is beginning to realize that a person may have defenses which seriously distort the self-picture; he recognizes the dilemma that defensive behavior places self theory in. "Some would have us resolve it by throwing overboard any attempt to make objective measurements of the phenomenal field" (1954, p. 430). However, Rogers is not ready yet to jettison a viewpoint which in his opinion has been so tremendously fruitful. "Consequently, we prefer to live with this dilemma until we understand it more deeply and perhaps can develop more sensitive theories as well as better instruments to deal with it" (1954, p. 431). Yet, he does not seem to be satisfied with this conclusion, either, because a few pages later he raises this question regarding the quest for the "real" personality.

> Is it possible that in place of this hypothetical single reality we shall have to substitute a recognition that there are various perceptual vantage points from which to view the person, one of these being from within the consciousness of the person himself. Certainly our evidence would suggest the lawfulness and internal order within each of these perceptual views.

There is also a suggestion of significant and perhaps predictable relationships between these perceptual systems. But whether there is *a* reality with which the science of personality may deal remains a question (1954, p. 433).

By "perceptual vantage points" Rogers means various ways of observing and describing behavior. One can, for example, study the person's responses in a standard test situation such as that provided by the Rorschach method, by the TAT, and by the Minnesota Multiphasic Test. One can also measure the physiological changes that accompany increased tension and emotion. Or one can observe another person's behavior in a natural life situation. Rogers in his role as a scientific investigator has not hesitated to employ these and other methods. He has by no means limited his observations to those of phenomenal self-reports, although such reports are favored by his theory.

Whatever the future of Rogers' self theory may be—whether its originator chooses to modify it to the extent that it is no longer primarily a self theory—it has served well the purpose of making the self an object of empirical investigation. Many psychologists have given theoretical status to the self but it is to Rogers' credit that his formulations regarding the phenomenal self have led directly to the making of predictions and to investigative activities. In this sense, his theory has been extremely useful.

BIBLIOGRAPHY

PRIMARY SOURCES

Rogers, C. R. *Counseling and psychotherapy; newer concepts in practice.* Boston: Houghton, 1942.

Rogers, C. R. Some observations on the organization of personality. *Amer. Psychologist,* 1947, 2, 358–368.

Rogers, C. R. *Client-centered therapy; its current practice, implications, and theory.* Boston: Houghton, 1951.

Rogers, C. R., and Dymond, Rosalind F. (Eds.). *Psychotherapy and personality change; co-ordinated studies in the client-centered approach.* Chicago: Univ. of Chicago Press, 1954.

REFERENCES

Allport, G. W. The ego in contemporary psychology. *Psychol. Rev.,* 1943, 50, 451–478.

Bertocci, P. A. The psychological self, the ego and personality. *Psychol. Rev.,* 1945, 52, 91–99.

Bowdlear, C. Dynamics of idiopathic epilepsy as studied in one case. Unpublished doctor's dissertation, Western Reserve Univ., 1955.

Butler, J. M., and Haigh, G. V. Changes in the relation between self-concepts and ideal concepts consequent upon client-centered counseling. In C. R. Rogers and Rosalind F. Dymond (Eds.). *Psychotherapy and personality change; co-ordinated studies in the client-centered approach.* Chicago: Univ. of Chicago Press, 1954, pp. 55–76.

Carr, A. C. An evaluation of nine nondirective psychotherapy cases by means of the Rorschach. *J. consult. Psychol.*, 1949, *13*, 196–205.

Chein, I. The awareness of self and the structure of the ego. *Psychol. Rev.*, 1944, *51*, 304–314.

Chodorkoff, B. Self-perception, perceptual defense, and adjustment. *J. abnorm. soc. Psychol.*, 1954, *49*, 508–512.

Dymond, Rosalind F. Adjustment changes over therapy from Thematic Apperception Test ratings. In C. R. Rogers and Rosalind F. Dymond (Eds.). *Psychotherapy and personality change; co-ordinated studies in the client-centered approach.* Chicago: Univ. of Chicago Press, 1954, pp. 109–120.

Friedman, I. Phenomenal, ideal and projected conceptions of self, and their interrelationships in normal, neurotic and paranoid schizophrenic subjects. Unpublished doctor's dissertation, Western Reserve Univ., 1953. See also Friedman, I. Phenomenal, ideal and projected conceptions of self. *J. abnorm. soc. Psychol.*, 1955, *51*, 611–615.

Gordon, T., and Cartwright, D. The effect of psychotherapy upon certain attitudes toward others. In C. R. Rogers and Rosalind F. Dymond (Eds.). *Psychotherapy and personality change; co-ordinated studies in the client-centered approach.* Chicago: Univ. of Chicago Press, 1954, pp. 167–195.

Grummon, D. L., and John, Eve S. Changes over client-centered therapy evaluated on psychoanalytically based Thematic Apperception Test scales. In C. R. Rogers and Rosalind F. Dymond (Eds.). *Psychotherapy and personality change; co-ordinated studies in the client-centered approach.* Chicago: Univ. of Chicago Press, 1954, pp. 121–144.

Haigh, G. Defensive behavior in client-centered therapy. *J. consult. Psychol.*, 1949, *13*, 181–189.

Haimowitz, Natalie R. An investigation into some personality changes occurring in individuals undergoing client-centered therapy. Unpublished doctor's dissertation, Univ. of Chicago, 1950.

Haimowitz, Natalie R., and Haimowitz, M. L. Personality changes in client-centered therapy. In W. Wolff and J. A. Precker (Eds.). *Success in psychotherapy. Pers. Monogr.*, 1952, *3*, 63–93.

Hilgard, E. R. Human motives and the concept of the self. *Amer. Psychologist*, 1949, *4*, 374–382. Reprinted in H. Brand (Ed.). *The study of personality.* New York: Wiley, 1954, pp. 347–361.

Huntley, C. W. Judgments of self based upon records of expressive behavior. *J. abnorm. soc. Psychol.*, 1940, *35*, 398–427.

James, W. *Principles of psychology.* 2 vols. New York: Holt, 1890.

Koffka, K. *Principles of gestalt psychology.* New York: Harcourt, 1935.

Lecky, P. *Self-consistency.* New York: Island Press, 1945.

Leeper, R. A. A motivational theory of emotion to replace "emotion as disorganized response." *Psychol. Rev.*, 1948, *55*, 5–21.

Lipkin, S. The client evaluates nondirective psychotherapy. *J. consult. Psychol.*, 1948, *12*, 137–146.

Lundholm, Helge. Reflections upon the nature of the psychological self. *Psychol Rev.*, 1940, *47*, 110–127.

McCleary, R. A., and Lazarus, R. S. Autonomic discrimination without awareness *J. Pers.*, 1949, *18*, 171–179.

Mead, G. H. *Mind, self, and society*. Chicago: Univ. of Chicago Press, 1934.

Mosak, H. Evaluation in psychotherapy: a study of some current measures Unpublished doctor's dissertation, Univ. of Chicago, 1950.

Muench, G. A. An evaluation of non-directive psychotherapy by means of the Rorschach and other tests. *Appl. Psychol. Monogr.*, 1947, no. 13.

Muench, G. A., and Rogers, C. R. Counseling of emotional blocking in an aviator. *J. abnorm. soc. Psychol.*, 1946, *41*, 207–215.

Nunnally, J. C. An investigation of some propositions of self-conception: the case of Miss Sun. *J. abnorm. soc. Psychol.*, 1955, *50*, 87–92.

Phillips, E. L. Attitudes toward self and others: a brief questionnaire report. *J. consult. Psychol.*, 1951, *15*, 79–81.

Porter, E. H., Jr. The development and evaluation of a measure of counseling interview procedures. *Educ. psychol. Measmt.*, 1943, *3*, 105–126, 215–238.

Prescott, D. A. *Emotion and the educative process*. Washington: American Council on Education, 1938.

Raimy, V. C. The self-concept as a factor in counseling and personality organization. Unpublished doctor's dissertation, Ohio State Univ., 1943.

Raimy, V. C. Self-reference in counseling interviews. *J. consult. Psychol.*, 1948, *12*, 153–163.

Rogers, C. R. *The clinical treatment of the problem child*. Boston: Houghton, 1939.

Rogers, C. R. *Counseling and psychotherapy; newer concepts in practice*. Boston: Houghton, 1942.

Rogers, C. R. Some observations on the organization of personality. *Amer. Psychologist*, 1947, *2*, 358–368.

Rogers, C. R. *Dealing with social tensions: a presentation of client-centered counseling as a means of handling interpersonal conflict*. New York: Hinds, 1948.

Rogers, C. R. *Client-centered therapy; its current practice, implications, and theory*. Boston: Houghton, 1951.

Rogers, C. R. A theory of therapy, personality, and interpersonal relationships, as developed in the client-centered framework. Unpublished manuscript, 1955a.

Rogers, C. R. The concept of the fully functioning person. Unpublished manuscript, 1955b.

Rogers, C. R. Persons or science? A philosophical question. *Amer. Psychologist*, 1955c, *10*, 267–278.

Rogers, C. R., and Dymond, Rosalind F. (Eds.). *Psychotherapy and personality change; co-ordinated studies in the client-centered approach*. Chicago: Univ. of Chicago Press, 1954.

Rogers, C. R., and Wallen, J. L. *Counseling with returned servicemen*. New York: McGraw, 1946.

Rudikoff, Esselyn C. A comparative study of the changes in the concepts of the self, the ordinary person, and the ideal in eight cases. In C. R. Rogers and

Rosalind F. Dymond (Eds.). *Psychotherapy and personality change; co-ordinated studies in the client-centered approach.* Chicago: Univ. of Chicago Press, 1954, pp. 85–98.

Sarbin, T. R. A preface to a psychological analysis of the self. *Psychol. Rev.,* 1952, *59,* 11–22.

Scheerer, M. Review of *The psychology of ego involvements* by M. Sherif and H. Cantril. *J. abnorm. soc. Psychol.,* 1948, *43,* 106–112.

Seeman, J. A study of the process of non-directive therapy. *J. consult. Psychol.,* 1949, *13,* 157–168.

Seeman, J., and Raskin, N. J. Research perspectives in client-centered therapy. In O. H. Mowrer (Ed.). *Psychotherapy.* New York: Ronald Press, 1953, pp. 205–234.

Sheerer, Elizabeth T. An analysis of the relationship between acceptance of and respect for self and acceptance of and respect for others in ten counseling cases. *J. consult. Psychol.,* 1949, *13,* 169–175.

Sherif, M., and Cantril, H. *The psychology of ego-involvements.* New York: Wiley, 1947.

Smith, M. B. The phenomenological approach in personality theory: some critical remarks. *J. abnorm. soc. Psychol.,* 1950, *45,* 516–522.

Snyder, W. U. An investigation of the nature of nondirective psychotherapy. *J. gen. Psychol.,* 1945, *33,* 193–223.

Snyder, W. U., et al. *Casebook of nondirective counseling.* Boston: Houghton, 1947.

Snygg, D., and Combs, A. W. *Individual behavior.* New York: Harper, 1949.

Stephenson, W. *The study of behavior.* Chicago: Univ. of Chicago Press, 1953.

Stock, Dorothy. An investigation into the interrelations between self-concept and feelings directed toward other persons and groups. *J. consult. Psychol.,* 1949, *13,* 176–180.

Symonds, P. M. *The ego and the self.* New York: Appleton-Century-Crofts, 1951.

Thetford, W. N. The measurement of physiological responses to frustration before and after nondirective psychotherapy. Unpublished doctor's dissertation, Univ. of Chicago, 1949.

Thetford, W. N. An objective measurement of frustration tolerance in evaluating psychotherapy. In W. Wolff and J. A. Precker (Eds.). Success in psychotherapy, *Pers. Monogr.,* 1952, *3,* 26–62.

Wolff, W. The experimental study of forms of expression. *Character & Pers.,* 1933, *2,* 168–176.

Wolff, W. Involuntary self-expression in gait and other movements: an experimental study. *Character & Pers.,* 1935, *3,* 327–344.

13.

Murphy's Biosocial Theory

Some theories of personality seem to have been born, like Athena, from the heads of their creators. They appear to have no psychological ancestry, to belong to no identifiable tradition within psychology, and to bear little resemblance at the time of their birth to other theories of personality. They are unique and original. Freud's theory of personality belongs in this category. Other theories borrow, to a greater or lesser extent, from a common stockpile of concepts, principles, laws, axioms, and assumptions which have accumulated over a period of years. These theories are readily identifiable in terms of their ancestry and the tradition to which they belong. They resemble each other to the extent that they have borrowed from the same storehouse. Their originality consists of a new organization or framework which is provided for the old ingredients, the addition of new material, and the relative emphases placed upon the various components of the theory. Many modern theories of personality are of this type. Perhaps the most vivid example of a theory which has borrowed heavily from the stockpile of psychology is one developed by Gardner Murphy. Murphy's biosocial theory, as he calls it, is an extremely eclectic theory. As presented in his book, *Personality: A biosocial approach to origins and structure* (1947), biosocial theory includes most, if not all, of the common and familiar concepts, principles, and postulates of modern psychology.

Murphy's eclecticism is intentional. As far back as 1932, when he and Friedrich Jensen wrote their book, *Approaches to personality*, Murphy argued persuasively for "a new sort of eclecticism." This "new eclecticism" differs from the patchwork type of eclecticism in which concepts and principles are torn from their original context and pieced together. It should use the contributions of various theories without robbing them of their vitality and it should be able to construct its own original hypotheses. Fifteen years later in his masterful effort to represent the intricacies of personality and to provide a polydimensional model of the person, Murphy still defended the virtues and values of a constructive, creative eclecticism.

> We have used jointly, or even simultaneously, the Gestalt doctrine of insight, the psychoanalytic principles regarding psychodynamics, especially unconscious drives, and the associationist doctrines regarding the gradual forging of mental connections, transfer of training, summation and dissociation. . . . Although the present venture may well be mistaken at many points, its aim is not to force together incompatible elements wrenched from different systems; it regards all the aforementioned principles as existing very compatibly in the organism (1947, p. 469).

Gardner Murphy is singularly well qualified for the role of an eclectic. Few psychologists today are as conversant with the whole domain of scientific psychology as Murphy is. His writings cover an extremely wide range of subject matter. In 1929 he surveyed the history of psychology in his highly respected book, *Historical introduction to modern psychology.* Two years later Murphy and his wife, Lois Barclay Murphy, published a comprehensive survey of the experimental work that had been done in social psychology. *Experimental social psychology* greatly influenced the development of social psychology as a branch of general, experimental psychology. The Murphys' credo is summed up in the following statement:

> This whole volume will make clear, we believe, that social psychology is rooted in general psychology, that its laws are psychological laws, that it draws constantly upon the psychological concepts and methods, and that whenever the time comes for social psychology to take its place as a systematized and exact science, it will take its place as a part of systematized and exact psychology (p. 37).

The following year saw the publication of *Approaches to personality* (1932) in collaboration with Friedrich Jensen, a book which revealed Murphy's grasp of the complexities of various personality theories. Finally, in 1933, Murphy's *General psychology*, a textbook for the introductory course, appeared. It would be difficult to find anyone who has matched this extraordinary achievement of writing four major books in as many diverse branches of psychology within a five-year period. It shows Murphy's encyclopedic knowledge of scientific psychology, his capacity for digesting, organizing, and systematizing a wealth of empirical and theoretical material, and his firm conviction that there is a basic unity among the diversities of psychological fields and viewpoints.

Three of these four books have been revised, *Experimental social psychology* in 1937 with an additional author, Theodore Newcomb; *Historical introduction to modern psychology* in 1949; and the general psychology under a new title, *Introduction to psychology* (1951).

Who is this prodigious writer and scientist? Gardner Murphy was born on July 8, 1895, in Chillicothe, Ohio, where his father was the rector of an Episcopal church. Three great universities contributed to his education. Yale awarded him the B.A. degree in 1916, Harvard the M.A. degree in 1917, and Columbia the Ph.D. in 1923. His studies were interrupted by the First World War when Murphy served with the American Expeditionary Forces. For almost two decades, from 1921 to 1940, he was a member of the faculty of Columbia University, and earned an outstanding reputation as a brilliant lecturer and inspiring teacher. He was awarded the Butler Medal in 1932 for his contributions to the university. He directed a number of dissertations, especially in the field of social psychology, and had a profound influence upon his students, a number of whom have since become prominent psychologists. During this period he and Rensis Likert wrote *Public opinion and the individual* (1938), a book which contributed significantly to the new field of public opinion polling and attitude measurement. In 1940 Murphy became chairman of the department of psychology at the City College of New York where he remained until 1952 when he was invited to become director of research at the Menninger Foundation in Topeka, Kansas.

Murphy is a highly respected member of the profession of psychology and has held many responsible positions within the professional organizations of psychology. He was president of the Society for the Psychological Study of Social Issues, 1938; president of the Eastern Psychological Association, 1942; and president of the American Psychological Association, 1944. Murphy's broad humanitarian and democratic values are reflected in his concern for world problems and the role that the psychologist can play in easing world tensions. He has written a number of articles in the area of international relations and world peace, and was largely responsible for planning, editing, and doing much of the actual writing of the yearbook of the Society for the Psychological Study of Social Issues entitled *Human nature and enduring peace* (1945a). In 1949 the Ministry of Education of India requested the United Nations Educational, Scientific and Cultural Organization (UNESCO) to send a consultant to India to organize research teams to investigate the causes of social tensions there. UNESCO asked Gardner Murphy to serve as the consultant which he did for six months during 1950. Murphy made a nontechnical interpretation of his impressions and the research reports of eight Indian social scientists which dealt with social tensions in India and the constructive forces working for national unity. This report was published under the expressive title *In the minds of men* (1953).

Murphy has also taken a great interest in the area known as psychical research or parapsychology and has made a number of investigations of paranormal phenomena, that is, clairvoyance and telepathy. He has served as president of the London Society for Psychical Research.

Although the seeds of Murphy's biosocial theory were planted in the first edition of *Experimental social psychology* and germinated to some extent in the revised edition of this work six years later, they did not come to full flower until 1947 when his large work on personality was published. This book represents the culmination of Murphy's apparently lifelong interest in the structure, dynamics, and development of personality. As we have said, it represents a highly eclectic approach to the understanding of personality. The dimensions of his theory are practically the same as those of the whole science of psychology.

Murphy calls his theory of personality a *biosocial* approach because he conceives of man as a biological organism which maintains a reciprocal relationship with its material and social environment. Personality is the product of a bipolar process, one pole lying within the body, the other pole in the outer world. In Murphy's words, "man is a nodal region, an organized field within a larger field, a region of perpetual interaction, a reciprocity of outgoing and incoming energies" (1947, p. 7). These outer and inner pressures acting within and upon the organic matrix form the adult personality. The adult personality is both biological *and* social.

Murphy's biosocial approach rests squarely upon field theory as its base. The person is neither conceived of primarily as a differentiated individual set apart from other individuals nor as a structured whole definable solely in terms of its own structural properties, but as a "structured organism-environment field, each aspect of which stands in dynamic relation to other aspects" (1947, p. 8). In this respect, Murphy's position is very close to the one taken by Lewin. Murphy differs from Lewin, however, in the emphasis that he places upon the biological foundations of personality. Lewin rarely mentions physiology whereas for Murphy the tissues of the body are hard facts of reality. Murphy's distinctive biological orientation was apparent as early as 1931 when he and his wife wrote *Experimental social psychology*. The facts and principles of genetics, embryology, and biochemistry are as central for Murphy as are the facts and principles of experimental psychology, sociology, and cultural anthropology.

THE STRUCTURE OF PERSONALITY

Murphy defines structure as the way in which the parts forming a whole are articulated or put together (1947, p. 997). This definition raises two separate questions. What are the parts? How are they put together? The first question involves the identification of the structural units of personality and the second question asks how these units are organized. Although Murphy uses the two terms, structure and organization, interchangeably, we shall discuss the components of personality under the heading of structure and the interrelationships under a separate heading of organization.

For Murphy, the principal basic components of personality are (1) *physiological dispositions* which arise from underlying genetic and embryological dispositions, (2) *canalizations* which are formed early in life, (3) *conditioned responses* which are deeply ingrained through repeated reinforcement, and (4) *cognitive and perceptual habits* which are the joint product of canalization and conditioning (pp. 714–715). Although these components are not immutable they do resist change and are relatively constant. In conjunction with a relatively stable environment they are what give continuity to personality.

The physiological dispositions are *organic traits*, of which there are three kinds. These are (1) the general dispositions of tissue such as metabolic rate, (2) the dispositions of specific tissues such as muscle tonus, and (3) dispositions that arise from the organization of differentiated tissues such as hunger. In other words, organic traits consist of tissue tensions.

Organic traits are reworked into *symbolic traits* by the process of conditioning. A person learns to react to a substitute stimulus or symbol as he did to the original tissue tension. Having learned, for instance, to associate the thought "I am hungry" with the organic state of hunger, the symbolic representation (the thought, that is) can by itself evoke food-searching and eating activities. However, these symbolic traits, unlike the organic ones, disappear if they are not reinforced periodically by some kind of gratification.

Organic traits can also be channeled by social directives into specific forms of behavior. For example, the society in which one lives dictates to a certain extent what foods will be eaten, how they are to be prepared, and the way in which they are eaten. Murphy calls this process *canalization* and defines it as a progressive shift "in differential response to the various means of satisfying a drive" (p. 981).

All personality traits are, in the final analysis, organic traits which have become conditioned to substitute stimuli or channeled into specific forms of behavior.

Murphy states that "the ultimate elements in personality structure are the needs or tensions" (1947, p. 641). A tension is a concentration of energy in a particular tissue or group of tissues. These tensions have functional connections with one another so that tension can spread from one region into other regions. "The result is a tension system whose lawful structure is expressed in terms of the relative strengths of tensions and the relative rigidity of barriers to their diffusion" (1947, p. 641).

A number of other structurelike components appear in Murphy's system. For example, he makes considerable use of the concept of *role*. A role is a more or less fixed way of behaving which is forced on the person by his culture. These roles, it would appear, are *in* the personality just as much as the tissue tensions are and they interact with one another just as needs do.

Another structural feature of Murphy's system is the *self* which is defined very simply as the person's perceptions and conceptions of his whole being, "the individual as known to the individual" (1947, p. 996). As it turns out, however, there are actually a number of selves. For example, Murphy discusses an ideal self and a frustrated self. Presumably these selves are interconnected dynamically just as one's roles or needs or traits are structured in the form of a total organization.

Murphy also employs the term *ego* which he defines as a system of habitual activities that enhance or defend the self, such mechanisms, for example, as rationalization, identification, and compensation. There may be in rare cases, as in multiple personality, two or more autonomous egos within the personality. Murphy's use of the terms ego and self follow that proposed by Chein (1944).

Finally, Murphy uses such concepts as habit, value, attitude, percept, conception, image, and character, all of which are structural because they are conceived to be components of the personality. However, they are all the products of canalized and conditioned tissue tensions. These tissue tensions, or organic traits as Murphy constantly reminds us, are the building blocks of personality, the irreducible structural units of one's psychological architecture. The concept of organic trait is one of the distinctive features of Murphy's viewpoint and occupies a cardinal position in his approach to personality.

THE ORGANIZATION OF PERSONALITY

There are three stages in the organization of personality: the global stage, the differentiated stage, and the integrated stage. In general, these three stages succeed one another during development in the order given.

In the global form of organization, there are no differentiated parts; everything is homogeneous. There are no nodes or gradients or traits or regions. Energy is diffused throughout the whole system, and the system functions as a totality in response to external stimulation. Such global behavior is usually referred to as *mass activity.* This is the primordial or earliest type of organization, the undifferentiated matrix which exists in the beginning of life.

In the differentiated form of organization, there are separate and distinct parts or regions. Instead of energy being diffused throughout the personality, it is parceled out among the various differentiated systems of personality. The responses of the person are specific rather than general and his perceptions, memories, attitudes, ideas, and values are discrete rather than unitary. Heterogeneity, separateness, and independence are the primary properties of the differentiated organization.

The third type, that of integration, represents the unification of discrete parts into an interlocking, intercommunicating, and interdependent system. Energy passes easily from one region to another so that there is a maximum of communication between the various components of personality. The behavior of the individual is organized and the adjustment of the whole person to his environment is the main consideration. Interdependence is the keynote of this mode of organization.

These three types of organization are merely convenient abstractions. Murphy does not believe that they ever exist in a pure state. Features of all three types can be found in the personality at any one time, although by and large, the adult personality is organized more according to the model of integration and the infantile personality according to the model of globality.

THE DYNAMICS OF PERSONALITY

"This whole volume [*Personality*] is about motivation; every aspect of personality is conceived in terms of the molding, the complication, the interpenetration, the concealment, the indirect expression of motives" (1947, p. 86). A motive is a tension gradient in a tissue; it has no definite beginning or end but rises and falls in a continuous series of energy changes. Tension represents a concentration of vital or organic energy in a particular tissue or group of tissues. When the concentration is lowered, the tension gradient goes down; when it is heightened, the gradient goes up. In general, tension reduction is equivalent to satisfaction; tension increase is equivalent to discomfort. We say "in general" because Murphy observes that sometimes satisfaction is associated with tension increase rather than tension reduction. The pleasure of mounting sexual excitement or the thrill of riding a spirited horse are cases in point. The association of pleasure with increases of tension has always been a problem for psychology and Murphy candidly admits that he is unable to solve this problem.

For Murphy, motives are not "levers" or "fuel supplies." "They are abstractions from an activity continuum, which may be identified only grossly in terms of their locus or their formal effects" (1947, p. 123). Anything that produces a concentration of energy in a particular region of the body, hunger, thirst, and sex, for instance, or that energizes the whole body, competition and love, for example, whether as a result of internal changes or outer stimulation, is a motive. It may be an inner deficit such as hunger; an activity tendency in a group of muscles; a sensory need for color, tone, touch, or taste; or an emotion. In Murphy's terminology, tension, need, and motive are interchangeable words.

Intercommunication among the various motives is achieved by the transmission of energy from one region to other regions of the body. As a consequence of this intercommunication a network of motivation develops. This network consists of "a system of nodes of varying levels of intensity and with networks or communication systems conveying energy to and from these tension centers, the general activity of the organism serving as matrix, and the specific responses to specific outer and inner stimuli serving as crystallization points" (1947, p. 120). There are no separate and distinct motives since every motive

(Freud — marginal note)

is a part of the total motivational structure or system. At the most, we can only speak of a particular motive as a node or differentiated region within the total organism. Nor does Murphy care to distinguish between biological and social needs because he considers that the biological and the social are not two separate spheres but one sphere. The biological is social, and the social is biological (1947, p. 769).

Murphy objects to the notion that complex activities result from the redirection of primitive forms of energy. Complex activities are produced by a complex motivational structure; they do not occur merely because simple energies form new channels. This view of the complexity of motivation is in agreement with Murphy's basic premise that all development progresses from a simple undifferentiated or global state through a stage of differentiation to the final culmination of integration. As the organization of tension systems becomes more complex, more complicated activities are required for tension reduction. Adult motives are not derivatives of infantile needs; they have their own emergent properties, based upon the factor of increasing complexity.

A distinctive feature of Murphy's theory of motivation is the emphasis which he places upon sensory and activity needs. The changes in tensions that have their locus in the sense organs and muscles are the basis for a person's delight in a beautiful sunset, a string quartet, a well-hit golf ball, and a multitude of other aesthetic and motor activities. Unlike other motivational theories which reduce artistic and manual interests to such drives as sex or hunger or achievement, Murphy believes that these interests are the direct result of tensions in specific regions of the body. Such things as music appreciation and a love of wrestling are actually organic traits. The implications of this feature of Murphy's motivational theory are far-reaching. It means, for example, that what other theories call acquired or learned drives may be in actual fact organic drives. If so, one does not have to depend upon a concept of secondary motivation or functional autonomy to explain the persistence of these motives. They persist because they are built into the organism by evolution and not by learning. One may love a certain type of music because it soothes or excites organic tensions, and not because it is associated with pleasant memories of being rocked to sleep or played with strenuously to the accompaniment of this preferred type of music. Although Murphy does not deny that there are acquired motives, his concept of sensory and activity needs greatly enlarges the domain of original, inborn tensions.

During the course of development, the dynamics of personality become more stable and rigid so that they either resist environmental pressures or they require these pressures to act upon one "in a more or less prearranged way" (1947, p. 730). That is to say, the person selects from his environment whatever is appropriate to his needs and remains relatively impervious to irrelevant features of the external world. If the outer world does not provide appropriate goal objects (privation) or if it forces itself upon the person in spite of his resistance (traumatic experience), the stability of the psychodynamics may break down. This is not likely to happen in a well-integrated person.

Since the distinction between mind and body is not a substantive one in Murphy's eyes, it is not necessary for him to distinguish psychic energy from physical energy nor to discuss the transformation of energy from one form into another.

THE DEVELOPMENT OF PERSONALITY

Murphy's biosocial viewpoint is primarily a genetic theory of personality. His major efforts are devoted to formulating precise yet comprehensive hypotheses regarding the way in which personality develops. "Personality is a flowing continuum of organism-environment events" (1947, p. 21).

STAGES OF DEVELOPMENT. Murphy's general position regarding the course of development is that it consists of three stages. The first stage is one of undifferentiated wholeness. The body reacts more or less as a whole to stimulation as typified by the squirming movements of the infant. During the second stage, separate functions are differentiated out of the global matrix. In the final stage, these differentiated functions are blended together into an organized, co-ordinated unity. Although this view of development is based upon studies of the growth of the body, Murphy believes that it applies equally well to the development of personality. These three stages, the global, the differentiated, and the integrated, are not sharply demarcated from one another in time. They overlap one another and there may be movement backward to an earlier stage (regression) as well as movement ahead to a later stage (progression). Some components of the personality may be further developed than others, and individuals differ widely with respect to the level of development attained. Finally, each stage manifests functions that are peculiar to it and which cannot be traced back to earlier stages.

ORGANISM AND ENVIRONMENT. Psychologists have long wrestled with the problem of the relative influence on behavior of heredity and

environment, or as it is often phrased, "nature versus nurture." Some
psychologists place more emphasis upon genetic determiners of behavior; others consider environment to be more important in determining human behavior. To this controversy Murphy brings a re-
freshingly sane point of view. He firmly rejects the popular notion that
heredity and environment are opposing terms, and regards the belief
in the inheritance of certain fully developed traits and the acquisition
of other traits through environmental conditioning as mere folklore.
What then does Murphy believe? Here is what he says.

> But if the organism is a tissue system undergoing changes partly because
> of its own dynamics, partly because of interaction with the outer world,
> it is "acquiring" new characteristics all the time, never by accretion but
> always _by modification of what it is_ [our italics]. No organism differently
> constituted could acquire in the same way or acquire the same tendencies.
> What is acquired is just as completely an expression of the inherited make-
> up of the organism as it is an expression of the outer forces. . . . New
> tendencies, habits, traits are not acquired, plastered on or stuck on as
> one affixes a postage stamp to a letter. The organism grows into new
> phases of behavior, under one form of pressure or another, as long as life
> continues. Similarly, to use the term "acquired traits" is to talk re-
> dundantly, for all traits are acquired by some kind of reaction with envi-
> ronmental forces. There was a time when any given trait was not there;
> and if one speaks precisely, no trait that is there will remain long in its
> present form (p. 51).

Murphy then goes on to say that "if it is true that nothing is acquired
in the popular sense, it is equally true that nothing is inherited" (p.
51) because from the moment of conception when the chromosomes
from the father are combined with those of the mother, forces external
to the germ plasm are shaping the development of the new organism.

LEARNING. Murphy's view of the learning process is that it involves
an interaction of an individually constituted organism with a specific
environment. As a result of this interaction, connections are formed
between needs and responses, between tensions and ways of behaving
that change tension. The connections between internal tissue conditions and specific forms of behavior are established by two processes.
These are _canalization_ and _conditioning_. Together they account for
all environmental modifications of behavior.

Canalization. Murphy borrowed the term _canalization_ from Pierre
Janet, the French psychologist and psychiatrist, but he has greatly
enhanced its conceptual significance. It is similar to the psychoanalytic
term _cathexis_, and also resembles fixation. Canalization is the process
by which a motive or concentration of energy finds a way of discharg-

ing itself in behavior. Like so many terms in psychology, canalization is a picture word, or in technical parlance, a trope or metaphor. In this case, the picture one is supposed to see is that of a canal or viaduct. It suggests, as Murphy intends it should, that there is a reservoir or concentration of energy located in one region of the body which passes by means of a channel into another region of the body, for example, the musculature, where it is used for performing work. An organism that has become canalized resembles a TVA project, in which the sources of energy (metabolic processes) are distributed throughout a large area and are utilized for a variety of purposes.

How is a specific canalization formed? To begin with, the person samples his environment and tries out various responses in a trial-and-error fashion. This trial-and-error behavior does not run off in a completely random manner because the predispositions of the person tend to orient or guide him in fairly specific directions. Thus, a child who has stronger auditory than visual needs is more likely to sample sounds then sights. When a response to a particular feature of the environment proves to be gratifying, the person tends to fixate upon that mode of discharging energy. Each time that he repeats the behavior with consequent satisfaction, the channel between need and response is deepened.

The strength of a canalization depends upon four factors: (1) the strength of the need, that is, the concentration of energy in the tissue, (2) the intensity of the gratification, that is, the amount of tension change, (3) the particular developmental stage of the person, and (4) the frequency of gratification. Although Murphy does not attempt to assess the relative contribution which each of these factors makes to the strengthening of a canalization, he does assume that they are functionally interchangeable. A person may have a weak need and weak gratification, but if the experience is repeated often enough the canalization can become fairly strong. On the other hand, if a strong, unfulfilled need is suddenly fulfilled, a strong canalization can be created then and there without further practice.

Murphy emphasizes the importance of canalizations that are laid down early in life. He believes that these remain influential throughout life. They may be overlaid by later canalizations but they are never likely to disappear completely. Under the proper conditions such as frustration, conflict, and anxiety they reappear in their original form. This accounts for many of the childish regressions that adults make under stress. More important than these regressions, however, is the fact that the early canalizations are the basis upon which later ones are formed.

It is not the bare wants or any interrelation of wants that makes the adult personality; it is not the adventitious pattern of connections between these inner wants and the conditioning stimuli of daily life. It is to a large degree the system of wants organized in a directed form toward familiar satisfiers; it is a system of anticipations and preparations for a round of experiences which have compelling value because they are the specific ways in which the diffuse and generalized wants have in the past been converted from tension to satisfaction. The process appears irreversible, as the life process moves forward, consolidating itself into more and more differentiated, firmly constructed patterns (1947, p. 170).

Since Murphy's view of motivation holds that there is an almost infinite number of needs and tensions, limited only by the number of tissues and the permutations and combinations of tensions arising from these tissues, the number of canalizations that a person is capable of forming during his lifetime is virtually limitless. Perhaps no other theory of personality has given a more satisfactory explanation for the versatility of man than has Murphy's. In many theories, man appears as a standardized and cramped figure, limited to a few basic motives which do all of the work of personality. Murphy endows man with versatility by recognizing a multitude of specific energies.

He points out that canalizations on one's own body are the basis for the emergence of a self-concept. The focusing of attention on the body and its differentiation from other objects in the world are brought about by the constantly recurring experiences of sensual pleasure which have their locus in the body. The self is originally nothing more than an image of one's body, an image that develops out of body-oriented canalizations. These canalizations are particularly resistant to change because they are so consistently satisfying. Observe, for example, how difficult it is to break a child of thumb-sucking. Murphy suggests that self-canalization may be the nucleus around which all other canalizations are formed.

Particularly important in Murphy's scheme of things are the sensory and motor drives. Instead of deriving the complex nature of adult canalizations from a few basic drives, as most personality theorists do, Murphy accounts for the elaborate system of adult interests, values, attitudes, and preferences largely in terms of their directly satisfying specific sensory and activity needs. A person eats because he gets hungry, but he prefers spaghetti to salmon because he likes the feel of spaghetti in his mouth better than the feel of salmon. His liking for spaghetti is sustained, not because it is linked with or derived from some other motive through conditioning but simply because every time he eats spaghetti the experience is pleasurable in and of itself.

The concept of canalization is broadly applied by Murphy and helps to illuminate a score of problems in psychology. Take, for example, the question of conflict. Murphy points out "that, in general, human conflict may be typically described as conflict between *drives in their canalized form*, e.g., love directed toward two individuals both of whom cannot be possessed, or conflict due to *ambivalent attitudes* . . . canalizations leading to contrary behavior toward a *single* object (including the self)" (p. 303). It is not difficult to see that many conflicts can be reduced to the common basis of incompatible canalizations, a simple yet effective conceptualization of an important aspect of human behavior. The concept of canalization is one of Murphy's most fruitful contributions to personality theory.

Conditioning. Murphy recognizes that canalization cannot carry the whole load of explaining the learning process. It is perfectly apparent that many forms of behavior which are learned are not directly satisfying to the person. They may even be quite painful or produce acute discomfort. Such activities, far from reducing tension, actually increase it. The saving of money is a case in point. Why do people develop habits of thrift and deny themselves the pleasures that spending would bring? Murphy's answer is that it is the result of conditioning.

The conditioned response, in Murphy's own words, "is a preparatory or anticipatory response of tissues that are ready for or are undergoing preparation for tension reduction" (1947, pp. 193–194). It is, very simply stated, "redirected drive." One's reaction to money is redirected from spending to saving, not because saving is inherently pleasurable but because it is a necessary antecedent for any large-scale spending. The more one can buy the greater is the pleasure. Saving is a conditioned response because it is a preparation for ultimate spending. If one saved solely for the satisfaction of accumulating money, as the miser does, it would be a canalization and not a conditioned response.

A canalization is always a consummatory response in the sense that the tension level is changed. A conditioned response is always a preparatory response for tension change but involves no change itself. Canalizations once formed do not disappear although they may be modified or suppressed. A conditioned response will completely disappear if that which is anticipated does not materialize. Bank failures or inflation tend to discourage thriftiness. Pavlov's dogs stopped salivating when the bell was not followed by food. If salivating to an auditory stimulus were really pleasurable to the dog, he would continue to salivate whether food were present or not. Conditioned responses may displace one another, for example, installment buying may take the place of saving, but canalizations cannot displace each other. A craving for sardines is not satisfied by a dish of tapioca.

Conditioned responses are easily generalized. This means that a particular way of responding to one environmental object can be transferred to other environmental objects. Saving money can lead to saving stamps. If the conditioned response diffuses to many objects, the person is said to possess a generalized behavior pattern or trait. For example, a person can develop a generalized acquisitive orientation towards his environment. He becomes a thrifty person, holding on to what he gets. All expressions of a generalized conditioned response are preparatory and not consummatory. The thrifty person practices thrift because it will help him reach some final goal that is rewarding. The thriftiness is not satisfying in itself; rather it is a means to satisfaction.

Conditioning has another important function in addition to that of preparing the person for some future gratification. A conditioned stimulus can arouse tensions that exist in a latent state. For example, a person who does not feel hungry may suddenly develop an appetite when he sees food. The reason for this is that the sight of food has been associated with hunger on previous occasions. When food appears it arouses the hunger tensions with which it is connected. However, this does not mean that a conditioned stimulus can create a drive. A satiated person will not respond to the sight of food by eating, nor will he feel hungry. There always has to be some tension present before a conditioned stimulus will have an effect. Murphy remains true to his major thesis that the energies of the body are the source of all motivation. Society can direct the expenditure of energy by establishing conditioned responses in the person and by encouraging or sanctioning the formation of specific canalizations, but it cannot implant new drives in the person nor can it eliminate old ones. Drives are inherent properties of the organism; they are the basic givens of personality. Of course, old drives may disappear and new ones appear as the result of organic processes such as maturation. But drives are never learned or unlearned.

Canalization and conditioning together account for all learned action patterns. If a person has learned to do something that gives him immediate gratification, that is canalization. If a person does something that is either neutral or negative in terms of immediate need reduction, but which leads eventually to a satisfying state of affairs, that is conditioning. In either case, the principle of reinforcement, as it is called in modern learning theory, or the pleasure principle, as it is called by psychoanalysis, is operative. Murphy's learning theory like so many others (Thorndike, Hull, and Freud) is a hedonistic one. We learn to do those things that give us pleasure. The big advantage of conditioning as an explanatory principle is that it explains why man endures discomfort and forms habits that are distinctly not pleasurable. He learns these things because they are, or he thinks they are, necessary for eventual gratification. The savings bank book is quite literally speaking a symbol of the automobile in one's future.

Perceptual learning. Canalization and conditioning have been considered up to this point in relation to the learning of actions or responses. The same principles of learning apply also to the development of what Murphy calls the "deeply ingrained habits of perception." "Based partly on the canalizations that give them anchorage, partly on the conditioned symbol system, these habits serve to structure the world, to give it meaning and stability, and to give the self meaning and stability in relation to it" (p. 715).

Perceptual development goes through the three stages of *globality*, during which the world is more or less of a blur to the infant, *differentiation*, during which figures emerge from a background, and *integration*, during which perceptual patterns are formed. In keeping with Murphy's insistence upon the functional properties of all psychological processes, perception is guided by need, or to use his own vivid expression, *"Needs keep ahead of percepts."* The motivational state exists first and exerts an influence upon the way in which the person will perceive the world. If the perceptual pattern is influenced by a need this is called an *autism.* "The perceived world pattern mirrors to a considerable degree the organized need pattern within" (p. 351). But it also reflects the world outside. Perception is in fact a bipolar process which is organized in terms of the inner world of tissue tensions and an outer world of external reality.

The pattern of perception is also more or less congruent with the pattern of action, so that what a person does reflects to some extent what he perceives. In other words, Murphy stresses the essential unity of motives, percepts, and actions. Needs, however, are in the driver's seat and guide and control the course taken by perception and action.

Earlier it was pointed out that the self as an identifiable aspect of personality grows out of the canalizations that become directed toward one's own body. These canalizations serve to bring the body and its various parts into perceptual focus, and in conjunction with conditioning to such verbal symbols as "me," "my," "mine," "myself," and "I" the self as an object becomes defined. When this takes place, as it does during the first two years of life, the self becomes a dominant perceptual figure around which one's perceptions and activities tend to become organized. Perceptions become "my" perceptions and actions become "my" actions. The "I" emerges as a pre-eminent unifying concept in Murphy's biosocial theory. The concept of the self also accounts for the continuity which every person feels in spite of his living in a changing world.

SOCIALIZATION. Murphy does not neglect the role of culture in molding personality. He sees society as influencing personality in four ways. First, a society has a traditional set of signals or cues to which the child becomes conditioned. He learns what leads to what in his particular society. If punishing a baby for crying is the accepted custom then the baby will learn to associate crying with an unpleasant consequence. In such a society, the incidence of crying will probably be small as compared with a society in which parents are expected to comfort babies when they cry. Learning the rules and regulations of a society is largely a matter of conditioning and perceptual learning. In the second place, society helps to form personality by prescribing certain outlets for drive energy while proscribing other outlets. In other words, society through its various agencies, chiefly the family, helps its younger members canalize their energies.

Third, Murphy believes that it is possible for the impulsive life of the organism to be changed qualitatively to some degree by rewarding some impulses and punishing others. However, a punished drive does not always disappear; it may be repressed and reappear later in a disguised form.

Finally, society can shape the perceptual and cognitive processes of its members so that they will learn to think in accordance with the norms of that society. They will tend to acquire common attitudes and feelings.

This brief account of the influence of culture on personality makes it appear that the two, culture and personality, are separate and distinct entities. Murphy disavows any such view. For him, nothing is separate and distinct, although it may be convenient for purposes of discussion and elucidation to create such a fiction. He believes it to be of the utmost importance to recognize that "the individual perceives himself as figure in the figure-ground pattern that is each social group, and that personality develops organically with this perception of the entire figure-ground system" (1947, p. 766).

ROLES. The concept of role and role interaction formulated by Bateson (1936) occupies a key position in Murphy's account of the socialization of the individual. The socialized person is seen as playing a repertoire of roles which have been defined for him by society in terms of his age, sex, race, occupation, religion, and other groups to which he belongs. A child is expected to play a role that is quite different from that of an adult. There is a role for males, and a different role for females. The role of a bartender is unlike the role of the banker whom he serves. The Catholic role is different from the role prescribed for Protestants, and both are different from the role of the Jew. A role, it seems, is a social function assumed by the person. It is contingent upon his being a member of a group.

The acquisition of a role requires no new principle of learning. Canalization, conditioning, and perceptual learning account for role learning as they do for all other kinds of learning.

A person's roles may conflict with one another and produce disturbances in the personality. A person may get pretty upset when he discovers that his role as a Christian is not entirely compatible with his role as a businessman. Not all roles are accepted willingly by the person, and society may often exert considerable pressure to get a person to perform a particular role. Concerted action by a group of people may succeed in changing a role, for example, the women's rights movement. Roles derive not only from the obligations that the person has to society; they also develop in response to the roles of other people. The role of the servant accommodates itself to the role of the master. A person's role system usually includes some that balance or compensate others in the system. An active role may be balanced by a passive role; a feminine role by a masculine role. One learns through experience what set of roles will yield maximum satisfaction.

SITUATIONISM. Murphy observes that by following the logic of role theory one arrives at a new approach to personality, that of situationism. "Situationism maintains simply that human beings respond as situations require them to respond; and that whatever their biological diversities, they will, if capable of learning, take on the attributes which the situations call for. . . . Given a changed situation, there is a changed role and consequently a changed personality" (pp. 867–

868). After exploring the values of this approach to personality and noting that American psychologists have tended to ignore the situations that people face, Murphy wisely concludes that situationism provides too narrow a screen upon which to project the whole panoply of personality. Murphy proposes instead that the personality theorist should make use of field theory in which both the structure and dynamics of situation and organism can be accommodated and integrated. For, as Murphy says, "We cannot define the situation operationally except in reference to the specific organism which is involved; we cannot define the organism operationally, in such a way as to obtain predictive power for behavior, except in reference to the situation. Each serves to define the other; they are definable operationally while in the organism-situation field" (p. 891) [italicized in the original].

CHARACTERISTIC RESEARCH AND RESEARCH METHODS

Murphy's empirical contributions have been made primarily in three areas: studies of attitudes during the 1920's and 1930's at Columbia University, studies of autism during the early 1940's at City College, and experiments in psychical research throughout the 1940's and continuing down to the present time. Since the research on autism has the most relevance for biosocial theory, we shall concentrate on those studies. However, because Murphy himself considers psychical research to be opening up new vistas for personality theory we shall devote a section to describing his endeavors in this area. In slighting Murphy's earlier work on attitudes and their measurement, we do not wish to convey the idea that these studies were unimportant. On the contrary, it is generally conceded that this sphere of Murphy's work had wide repercussions in the social sciences. Murphy and his co-workers were among the first to treat attitudes as embedded in personalities, and not as verbal responses or opinions dissociated from the whole man. Consequently, in their researches (see, for example, Murphy and Likert, 1938) they combined methods involving large-scale sampling and population trends with methods more frankly clinical in character. In the Murphy-Likert study, autobiographies were used to personalize the quantitative data and to provide insights into the underlying personality determinants of attitudes. This topic has been treated with great precision in the revised edition of *Experimental social psychology* (1937).

STUDIES OF AUTISM. One of the most active fields of research in psychology at the present time consists of investigations of the interrelationships among components of the personality and cognitive processes.

Numerous studies have demonstrated that perceiving, learning, remembering, and thinking are influenced by needs, values, interests, feelings, moods, and emotions (Bartlett, 1932; Blake and Ramsey, 1951; Bruner and Krech, 1950; Sherif, 1935, 1936). As a result of these studies, it is no longer conventional to draw a sharp line between cognition and motivation, between thought and affect, between reason and instinct.

Although the empirical propositions regarding the interrelationships between personality and cognition have been derived, either directly or indirectly, from a number of theoretical sources, for example, Rorschach, Murray, Bartlett, and Freud, it is widely acknowledged that Murphy's theory of personality is particularly congenial to this new empirical domain. In spite of the fact that many of the studies on perception and personality were done prior to the publication of Murphy's *Personality*, it is nevertheless true that Murphy's thinking from the early 1930's helped to provide the intellectual climate in which these studies flourished. Furthermore, in his 1947 book, Murphy provided a strong theoretical rationale for these studies by pointing out that perception is never an independent process but is always suffused with dynamic properties. That is to say, perception is always personal, and because it is, everything that the person is will participate in his perceiving. Moreover, Murphy and his students have made important experimental contributions through their studies of autism. It is these studies that we will review in this section.

The term _autism_ was coined by Eugen Bleuler, the Swiss psychiatrist. It is defined as the movement of a cognitive process in the direction of need satisfaction. A hungry person thinks about food. A thirsty traveler imagines he sees a pool of water in the distance. An old person reminisces about the pleasures of the past. An adolescent boy has conquering hero daydreams. These are all examples of autism. Cognitive processes are servants of one's needs.

In order to demonstrate under experimental conditions how a particular need, hunger, influences perception, Levine, Chein, and Murphy (1942) conducted the following investigation. Eighty pictures were displayed one at a time behind a ground glass screen, which caused the pictures to appear vague and blurred. The pictures as seen by the subjects were so ambiguous that they were susceptible of various interpretations. In this respect, the pictures were like Rorschach inkblots. Forty of the pictures were colored and forty were black and white. The subjects were asked to give one association to each picture.

The strength of the hunger drive was varied by testing the same subject after he had been without food for one hour, three hours, six hours, and nine hours. Five subjects were tested under these conditions. This was the experimental group. Another five subjects were tested on four separate occasions, subject 1 45 minutes after he had eaten, subject 2 1 hour after he had eaten, subject 3 1½ hours, subject 4 2 hours, and subject 5 2½ hours. These five subjects constituted a control group.

All five members of the experimental group showed an increase in the number of food associations (a food association was an article of food or an eating utensil) from the one-hour hungry trial to the three-hour hungry trial. Beyond the three-hour trial the results for the colored pictures differed from those for the black-and-white pictures. The number of food associations to the colored pictures decreased after the three-hour trial while the number of food associations to the black-and-white pictures increased on the six-hour trial and then went down on the nine-hour trial. These results are displayed in Figure 1.

The subjects of the control group showed no systematic variation in the number of food associations given on each trial.

The investigators explain their results in the following manner. Perception, they say, is influenced by two processes, an autistic process and a realistic process. The autistic process causes a person to see what he wants to see. In the present experiment, the autistic process

Figure 1.

causes the hungry subject to give food associations to ambiguous pictures. The realistic process causes a person to see things as they really are in the objective world, regardless of his wishes. The increasing number of food associations is due to the preponderant influence of the autistic process whereas the decrease in food associations is attributed to the greater influence of the realistic process. Apparently the realistic process acquires greater potency as the subjects become hungrier.

This conclusion is supported by other evidence from the experiment. When a subject could not give an association to a picture, that was called a rejection. The number of rejections increased from 41 on the one-hour hungry trial, to 49 on the three-hour trial, to 65 on the six-hour trial, and to 81 on the nine-hour trial. As the subjects became hungrier it was harder for them to imagine that they were seeing something meaningful in the ambiguous pictures. They were motivated to leave a situation that offered, on purely realistic terms, no opportunity for gratification.

The difference between the curves for the colored pictures and the black-and-white pictures is explained as follows. The colored pictures are less ambiguous than the black and whites. Less ambiguity favors the realistic process. Consequently there are fewer food responses to the colored pictures, 140 versus 232, and a more rapid falling off of the number of food responses with increasing hunger.

This experiment, it is felt, demonstrates the influence of a need upon perception, and confirms the earlier work of Sanford (1936, 1937) which Murphy calls the pioneer experiment on this problem.

In the next experiment on autism performed by Schafer and Murphy (1943) the following conditions prevailed. The need employed was the desire for monetary gain. Subjects were shown four profiles (Figure 2), one at a time, and they were told to learn the names of these profiles. The learning of the names had nothing to do with the experiment except to keep the subjects interested in looking

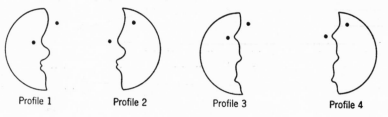

Profile 1   Profile 2   Profile 3   Profile 4

Figure 2.

at the profiles during the training period. The subjects were given a small money reward each time P1 or P3 appeared on the screen and a small amount was taken away each time P2 and P4 appeared on the screen.

Following this training period, the two profiles—P1 which had been rewarded and P2 which had been punished—were fitted together so that they shared a common profile. P3 and P4 were also combined into a single figure. See Figure 3. These figures were then shown to the subjects and they were asked to report what they saw.

Profiles 1 and 2
combined

Profiles 3 and 4
combined

Figure 3.

All of the subjects perceived the rewarded profiles more often than the punished ones during the first sixteen presentations of the combined figures. The results are presented in Table 1. After the six-

TABLE 1

Subject	Saw Rewarded Profile	Saw Punished Profile	Did Not See Either Profile
1	12	3	1
2	9	3	4
3	13	0	3
4	10	6	0
5	10	1	5
Total	54	13	13

teenth presentation, the response to the rewarded profile began to extinguish.

The findings of this experiment indicate that the way in which a person perceives an ambiguous figure, that is, a figure that can be seen in one of two ways, can be controlled by rewarding one of the perceptions and punishing the other. This experiment also demonstrates that an autism does not have to modify or distort or suppress any particular sensory element; it may only alter structural relationships in the perception. In this case, the structural relationship is the familiar figure-ground relationship discovered by Gestalt psychology. The rewarded profile becomes the figure and the punished one becomes background.

A similar experiment, although employing different material and different subjects, was conducted by Proshansky and Murphy (1942). During the first phase of the experimental procedure, which was called the pretraining period, subjects were asked to estimate the length of lines and the magnitude of weights. During the second phase, the training period, they were asked to look at the lines or feel the weights without making any estimates or other overt responses. Every time one of the longer lines or lighter weights was presented the subject was given a money reward; every time one of the shorter lines or heavier weights was presented the subject had some money taken away. For intermediate lines and weights the subject was sometimes rewarded and sometimes punished in a haphazard order. The purpose of these intermediate stimuli was to prevent the subject from consciously formulating a rule regarding the system of rewards and punishments used. During the third phase of the experiment, the posttraining period, the subject was again asked to estimate the length of lines and the magnitude of weights.

Another group of three subjects were treated in an identical manner except they were not given rewards or punishments during the second period. They merely looked at the lines or felt the weights.

All of the subjects who were given rewards and punishments for the longer lines and lighter weights increased their estimates for the lines and decreased their estimates for the weights, on the average, during the posttraining period as compared with the pretraining period. The control subjects showed no systematic shift in their estimates from the pretraining to the posttraining period.

These results bear out Murphy's contention that perception moves in the direction of need satisfaction. When a pleasant experience (the award of money) accompanies the perception of a particular type of stimulus, in this case longer lines and lighter weights, then one tends to perceive all lines and weights as being longer or lighter than they really are. Perception becomes modified by moving in the direction of a gratifying experience and away from unpleasant ones.

The influence of a need upon learning and forgetting was investigated by Levine and Murphy (1943). They made the assumption that it would be more gratifying (tension-reducing) for a person to learn and retain material that is congruent with his attitudes than to learn and remember material that is incongruent with his attitudes. The study was conducted in the following manner.

Two groups of students were identified as being procommunist and anticommunist. Both groups of subjects learned two prose passages, one favorable to communism, the other critical of communism. Each subject read one of the paragraphs twice and after fifteen minutes he was asked to reproduce it from memory. Following a short break, the second paragraph was learned in the same way. This whole procedure was repeated at weekly intervals for four weeks. Then once a week for five weeks the subjects were asked to reproduce the paragraphs without being given any opportunity to refresh their memory by reading them. The results were in accordance with the investigators' expectations. The procommunist students learned and retained the selection favorable to communism better than the anticommunist students learned and retained it. The anticommunist students, on the other hand, had the advantage over the procommunist students on the passage critical of communism. The findings are presented graphically in Figures 4 and 5.

Postman and Murphy (1943) conducted a similar investigation with eighth grade children to determine the influence of attitude upon memory. First, an attitude scale was devised and administered to the

Figure 4.

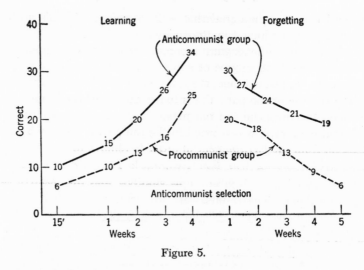

Figure 5.

subjects in order to find out how each child felt about the Nazis, the Japanese, and other participants in World War II. Key words were then taken from the attitude statements to make up a list of word pairs that were to be learned. For example, one such word pair was Nazis-honest. If a child agreed strongly with the statement that Nazis are honest, then the word pair was said to be highly compatible with the child's attitude and was given a weighting of +2. If a child disagreed strongly with the statement, then the word pair was said to be highly incompatible with the child's feelings and was given a weighting of −2. Less extreme positive and negative feelings were given weightings of +1 and −1. For each child, therefore, a compatibility score for each word pair was computed. The children then learned the whole list of words by the method of paired associates. They also learned another list of word pairs made up of words that had been selected and paired at random, for example, invite-peach, path-butter.

There were three major findings. First, word pairs that were either strongly compatible (+2) or highly incompatible (−2) with the child's attitudes were retained better than word pairs that were only mildly compatible or incompatible. Postman and Murphy's explanation for this finding is a double-barreled one. Highly compatible words stand out as meaningful, satisfying, and well-structured figures because they agree with the attitudes of the child. Then because they are such good figures, they are easily learned and remembered.

This explanation is in agreement with Murphy's general theory of autism which states that cognitive processes move in the direction of need satisfaction. The cognitive process in this case is memory and the need satisfaction is agreement with positive attitudes.

Why were the strongly incompatible word pairs remembered better than the more neutral ones? The incompatible pairs stand out because they challenge the values of the person and make him feel insecure. The need satisfaction in this case is self-protection. We pay attention to a threat from the environment in order to remove it.

The second finding was that compatible pairs were remembered better than incompatible ones. This suggests that the positive satisfaction of perceiving something that one likes has a greater influence on the retentive processes than the negative satisfaction of defending oneself against an environmental threat.

The third important result was that the control list made up of incongruous word pairs was retained better than the test list. Postman and Murphy offer the following explanation for this finding. Words like butter, school, peach, and path have more relevance and more interest for a child and therefore stand out more than words like Nazi, honest, Italian, Japanese, and cruel. Because they are better figures they are retained better.

These studies confirm Murphy's hypothesis that cognitive processes are saturated with motivational dynamics. It would be a mistake, however, to conclude that needs are the sole determinant of what will be perceived, learned, remembered, and thought about. Another major determinant, as Murphy takes pains to point out, is the nature of reality itself. Even a ravenously hungry person rarely mistakes a book for a meat loaf or a doorknob for a baked potato. The autistic factor shows up to best advantage when the stimulus object is ambiguous or when the person knows very little about the object. Under ordinary circumstances our perceptions are usually quite accurate.

Murphy's theory of autism and the experiments upon which the theory is based have not gone unchallenged. Pastore (1949) has subjected both the theory and the experiments to detailed criticism. His main point seems to be that Murphy and his collaborators have not distinguished between judgment or interpretation and perception. For example, in the Proshansky and Murphy experiment, it was not demonstrated that the subjects actually perceived, that is, had a visual experience of, the shorter lines as being longer. They may have merely thought they were longer. Pastore is making a distinction here between a pure perception and an interpretation or judgment of the perception. It is conceivable, Pastore points out, that the interpretation may be influenced by a need without the perception being altered in any way by the need.

In regard to the Levine, Chein, and Murphy experiment, Pastore says that it was not determined whether the ambiguous shapes were actually seen as food objects or whether they were merely judged to be food objects. In this case also Pastore is separating perception as some sort of direct sensory experience from judgment as a cognitive process. Murphy says the need acts upon the perception. Pastore suggests that it may not act upon the perception but upon the meaning that is attributed to the perception.

Murphy and his associates (Chein *et al.*, 1951) have replied to Pastore's criticisms by asking him how one should go about distinguishing between perception and interpretation, operationally as well as experimentally. They feel that interpretation and meaning are part of the perceptual process itself and that no distinction can be made between them.

Pastore has also raised the somewhat related question of the difference between perceptual distortion and perceptual selectivity. By distortion, Pastore means that the stimulus object is not accurately represented by the perception; for example, a line of three inches is perceived (not judged) to be four inches long. A vague picture is actually seen (not interpreted) to be a meaningful object. By selectivity, Pastore means those features of the environment that are perceived. A hungry person may perceive an apple lying on the ground and not perceive other objects lying close by. Everyone acknowledges that needs and interests have a lot to do with selective perception. The crucial issue is, Do needs and wishes distort perception? This, Murphy and his associates have not demonstrated, Pastore believes.

Murphy and his associates insist that selective perception as well as perceptual distortion can be used to indicate the influence of motivation upon perception. Moreover, they point out that selectivity and distortion are not independent of one another. A high degree of selectivity may produce stimulus distortion.

PSYCHICAL RESEARCH. Gardner Murphy is one of the few prominent psychologists who has taken an active interest in the area of investigation known as psychical research, a field which includes such phenomena as clairvoyance and mental telepathy. The name for the branch of psychology which includes psychical research is parapsychology (para = beyond). The importance of Murphy's contributions to parapsychology, which are both theoretical and experimental in character, is indicated by his election to the presidency of the London Society for Psychical Research.

It is not our intention to review the work that has been done by Murphy and his associates because limitations of space do not permit us to consider in any adequate fashion the many complexities in this very difficult and challenging area of research. Our reason for considering it at all is that Murphy's views regarding paranormal processes are a substantive part of his theory of personality and require consideration, brief though it may be, if we are to obtain a complete picture of his conception of personality. These views which are not incorporated in his *Personality* are presented in some detail in his presidential address (1949; see also 1945b).

Murphy feels that there is evidence to justify the hypothesis that all human personalities are capable of paranormal processes but that this capacity is often obscured by such factors as preoccupation with the immediate sensory world, motivation, intrapsychic barriers, and social climate. People who are able to dissociate themselves from the domination of their sense organs, who are motivated to succeed in parapsychological experiments, who believe in clairvoyance and mental telepathy, who are reasonably well adjusted, and who are tested under conditions that are compatible with their personality make-up often reveal paranormal capacities. For example, subjects who believe in clairvoyance make scores significantly above chance in a task requiring them to call off the names of simple geometrical designs arranged in random order and concealed from view (Schmeidler and Murphy, 1946). But subjects who do not believe in clairvoyance also obtain scores significantly different from chance, *only in the negative direction*. These results indicate that the "will to disbelieve" influences the person's performance as much as the "will to believe" does.

A follow-up experiment by Schmeidler revealed that socially well-adjusted (as measured by the Rorschach method) believers and disbelievers did significantly better and poorer than chance whereas believers and disbelievers who were not well adjusted socially made chance scores. These findings and others like them in which personality variables are correlated with the results of paranormal investigations suggest to Murphy that there are paranormal dimensions to the personality which probably obey the same laws as the normal dimensions do.

Murphy draws a very startling hypothesis from the findings relative to the effects of social climate upon the appearance or inhibition of paranormal phenomena. These findings indicate that the personality of the experimenter is an important factor in causing success or failure. An experimenter who does not believe in mental telepathy may obtain negative results whereas an experimenter who does believe may obtain positive ones. This is Murphy's hypothesis in his own words as he addressed them to the London Society for Psychical Research.

> I am asking you to consider a rather simple, naive and disturbing hypothesis, a conception which points not to the solitary grandeur and rugged independence of personality, as we like to conceive it, but to personality as a node or region of relative concentration in a field of vast and complex interpenetrating forces, in which none of us is completely individualized any more than he is completely washed out in a cosmic sink of impersonality (1949, p. 14).

Murphy is suggesting in this eloquent passage that there are psychological dimensions that transcend the individual person and which are transpersonal and interpersonal in nature. If this view is correct, then over and above the study of personalities as unique entities there stands the field of social psychology with its emergent principles.

In concluding this section, it should be pointed out that Murphy with his broad knowledge of psychological theory and research techniques has been able to make original and ingenious experiments in parapsychology. By helping to integrate personality research and psychical research he has extended the borders of both domains. Although some psychologists may frown upon these activities, Murphy continues to pursue them because he firmly believes that they are revealing new dimensions of personality. This may prove to be the most important work that Murphy has done.

CURRENT STATUS AND EVALUATION

To evaluate Murphy's biosocial approach to personality and to say what its status is in the contemporary scene presents some difficulties. He has no identifiable group of disciples to promote and publicize his viewpoint as many theorists have, notably Freud, Jung, Lewin, Sullivan, and Rogers. It is true that he has started a number of young psychologists on their way, some of whom, such as Rensis Likert, Abraham Maslow, Theodore Newcomb, and Leo Postman, have become professionally prominent, but these students are in no sense disciples. Murphy's position has not been held up to public scrutiny and criticism to any great extent. He has neither highly vocal proponents nor audible critics. Biosocial theory has not been a rallying ground, nor has it been a battlefield. Does this mean that biosocial theory is without influence, that it has been passed by, and that it is a dead theory which has been resuscitated for this book? Not at all.

It is our contention that the biosocial approach as formulated by Murphy is one of the most vital and influential movements in modern psychology. It does not need ardent proselytizers and it has few critics because it has been built into the sinews of psychology.

Our reasons for reaching this conclusion are these. Biosocial theory is eclectic, functional, holistic, and a field theory. These are all attributes that most psychologists value and that they desire in any theoretical formulation. Let us consider each of these attributes in relation to Murphy and to the current scene.

As we had occasion to point out earlier in the chapter, Murphy's biosocial approach is an eclectic system. It is eclectic not only in the sense that it borrows concepts, principles, laws, hypotheses, and axioms from other theories but also in the sense that it takes into account all aspects of the individual and his environment and all branches of psychology—child, physiological, social, clinical, and so forth. If the glands are important, well then so are the mores. Biochemical determinism is no less significant and no more so than economic determinism. Nature and nurture are given equal status, as are maturation and learning. The inner drives seem to be sovereign concepts until one reads Murphy's account of situationism. There is an organism but there is also a self. Everything that psychologists deem important for comprehending personality is there. Murphy rides no hobbyhorse, he has no strong appetites or aversions, no clichés or slogans, no newfangled vocabulary, no favorite techniques. He does not break with the past but gives a balanced treatment of the recurrent issues which have dogged psychologists for generations. For most psychologists, biosocial theory is just good common sense, at least a psychologist's common sense. It does not violate any of their basic values. They may not agree with everything that Murphy says, they may want to change an emphasis here and there, substitute some pet terms of their own for some of Murphy's, but these disagreements are strictly within the family. The average psychologist is strongly identified with Murphy's brand of personality theory because it is the sort of psychology that he is used to.

Murphy's eclecticism is no patchwork affair. He has shown taste and discrimination in what he has borrowed from others, he has been creative in fashioning a new organization for the borrowed material, and he has opened many new windows for viewing personality. At a time when the cultural or social-psychological schools of psychology seem to be in the ascendance it is refreshing to read Murphy's chapters on the organism. If a biological bias should return to psychology, one can turn to Murphy's chapters on the individual and the group to regain a more balanced perspective. Balance, proportion, organization, and creative synthesis: these are the salient features of Murphy's eclecticism.

The second aspect of Murphy's position which makes it attractive to many psychologists is its functionalism. Since the days of William James, John Dewey, and J. R. Angell, American psychology has viewed psychological processes as playing a functional role in helping man adjust to or master his environment. Psychological processes in the final analysis possess survival value. Although all current personality theories are functional to some extent, Murphy is consistently and emphatically functional in his orientation.

Biosocial theory as fashioned by Murphy is strongly holistic. As we have had occasion to remark several times before, there are no independent processes within the personality that can be studied for their own sake. Every process partakes of the whole. Perceiving implies a perceiver, and a perceiver is always a whole person with feelings, emotions, needs, self-attitudes, ego mechanisms, and all of the rest. When he perceives he does not stop feeling or needing or defending himself. Perception is saturated through and through with every other ongoing psychological process (Murphy and Hochberg, 1951).

When Wallach (Bruner and Krech, 1950) distinguishes between a primary perceptual process and a memory trace Murphy upbraids him for driving a wedge into the organism and creating an artificial and meaningless distinction. For Murphy, there are never isolated processes but a perpetual interflow of processes. In a similar vein he criticizes Klein for conceiving of attitude as a process which is independent of the biological individuality of the perceiver. "Why could not the common factor which holds these 'types' [of which Klein speaks] together prove to be a somatic predisposition molded through social living into a particular contour of formal process, thus reflecting both biological and social factors simultaneously and in their fullest interpenetration?" Murphy asks (Bruner and Krech, 1950, p. 52). There are no cleavages, no fissures, no dichotomies in Murphy's theory of the person. Interpenetration and dynamic wholeness are pervasive. The person is a unity.

Finally, Murphy is a field theorist. For him, the organism does not stand apart from the world but is, as he is fond of saying, "a node" in a field of interpenetrating forces. These forces may be categorized as physical, social, economic, and so forth, but they are all viewed by Murphy as being components of one unified field. Change any one of them and the whole field including the personality undergoes a transformation. The person is not the same person in a different environment. By the same field principle, when the personality changes, the interpenetrating forces of the external world also change. The hungry person and the satiated one, even though they may be standing next to one another, are not in the same field. Each is responding to situational forces appropriate to his inner dynamics. Murphy rejects the formulations of organism *versus* environment and organism *and* environment in favor of the formulation organism-environment. The hyphen represents inseparability and interpenetration.

A field theory approach to personality has been criticized because it seems to liken the person to a rudderless ship in a stormy sea, when it is plainly evident that there is considerable stability and continuity to personality. Murphy with his characteristic candor and insight has met this criticism face on. He points out there is nothing intrinsic to field theory that requires a perpetual kaleidoscopic shifting of the pattern of forces within the person or outside in the external world. The field can and does remain constant much of the time. There are, for example, the biological continuities which depend upon the germ plasm and maturational sequences. The organism is not in constant flux but has rather predictable patterns of growth. The early canalizations also provide for some degree of stability throughout the life of the person. Furthermore, as Murphy points out, "A large part of the continuity of personality is due to the reiteration of the same old demands, the same old pressures, upon the individual" (1947, p. 899). Finally, stability is provided for by the development of a tightly organized system of habits which becomes relatively impervious to change. Field theory as formulated by Murphy accounts both for the change and discontinuities in personality and for its stability and continuity.

This, then, is Murphy's biosocial theory—a wide-screen production of tremendous scope and deep perspectives. Murphy would be the first to acknowledge that the theory is unfinished, that it is more faithfully described by the word "approach" than by the word "theory," and that, in any event, theories whether finished or unfinished are highly expendable. Once they have served the purpose of spotlighting neglected areas of investigation, they should be put aside in favor of other theoretical spotlights. Writing as the skeptical psychologist Murphy says:

Despite all these lessons [of the past], we write and speak today as if at last the full context and stature of man were known. But like our predecessors, we shall rectify mistakes not primarily by the minor readjustment of the lines of the argument but by recognition of the fundamental limitations of the whole present system of conceptions. It is preparation for this destruction and rebirth of knowledge to which serious research should be directed (1947, p. 927).

BIBLIOGRAPHY

PRIMARY SOURCES

Murphy, G. *Personality: a biosocial approach to origins and structure.* New York: Harper, 1947.
Murphy, G., and Jensen, F. *Approaches to personality.* New York: Coward, 1932.
Murphy, G., and Murphy, Lois B. *Experimental social psychology.* New York: Harper, 1931. Rev. Ed. (with T. M. Newcomb), 1937.

REFERENCES

Bartlett, F. C. *Remembering.* Cambridge: Cambridge Univ. Press, 1932.
Bateson, G. *Naven.* Cambridge: Cambridge Univ. Press, 1936.
Blake, R. R., and Ramsey, G. V. (Eds.). *Perception: an approach to personality.* New York: Ronald Press, 1951.
Bruner, J. S., and Krech, D. (Eds.). *Perception and personality.* Durham: Duke Univ. Press, 1950.
Chein, I. The awareness of self and the structure of the ego. *Psychol. Rev.,* 1944, *51,* 304–314.
Chein, I., Levine, R., Murphy, G., Proshansky, H., and Schafer, R. Need as determinant of perception; a reply to Pastore. *J. Psychol.,* 1951, *31,* 129–136.
Levine, J. M., and Murphy, G. The learning and forgetting of controversial material. *J. abnorm. soc. Psychol.,* 1943, *38,* 507–517.
Levine, R., Chein, I., and Murphy, G. The relation of the intensity of a need to the amount of perceptual distortion: a preliminary report. *J. Psychol.,* 1942, *13,* 283–293.
Murphy, G. *Historical introduction to modern psychology.* New York: Harcourt, 1929. Rev. Ed., 1949.
Murphy, G. *General psychology.* New York: Harper, 1933.
Murphy, G. (Ed.) *Human nature and enduring peace.* Boston: Houghton, 1945a.
Murphy, G. Field theory and survival. *J. Amer. Soc. psych. Res.,* 1945b, *39,* 181–209.
Murphy, G. *Personality: a biosocial approach to origins and structure.* New York: Harper, 1947.

Murphy, G. Psychical research and personality. *Proc. Soc. psych. Res.*, London, 1949, *49*, 1–15.

Murphy, G. *Introduction to psychology.* New York: Harper, 1951.

Murphy, G. *In the minds of men: the study of human behavior and social tensions in India.* New York: Basic Books, 1953.

Murphy, G., and Hochberg, J. Perceptual development: some tentative hypotheses. *Psychol. Rev.*, 1951, *58*, 332–349.

Murphy, G., and Jensen, F. *Approaches to personality.* New York: Coward, 1932.

Murphy, G., and Likert, R. *Public opinion and the individual.* New York: Harper, 1938.

Murphy, G., and Murphy, Lois B. *Experimental social psychology.* New York: Harper, 1931. Rev. Ed. (with T. M. Newcomb), 1937.

Pastore, N. Need as a determinant of perception. *J. Psychol.*, 1949, *28*, 457–475.

Postman, L., and Murphy, G. The factor of attitude in associative memory. *J. exp. Psychol.*, 1943, *33*, 228–238.

Proshansky, H., and Murphy, G. The effects of reward and punishment on perception. *J. Psychol.*, 1942, *13*, 295–305.

Sanford, R. N. The effects of abstinence from food upon imaginal processes: a preliminary experiment. *J. Psychol.*, 1936, *2*, 129–136.

Sanford, R. N. The effects of abstinence from food upon imaginal processes: a further experiment. *J. Psychol.*, 1937, *3*, 145–159.

Schafer, R., and Murphy, G. The role of autism in a visual figure-ground relationship. *J. exp. Psychol.*, 1943, *32*, 335–343.

Schmeidler, G. R., and Murphy, G. The influence of belief and disbelief in ESP upon individual scoring levels. *J. exp. Psychol.*, 1946, *36*, 271–276.

Sherif, M. A study of some social factors in perception. *Arch. Psychol.*, 1935, no. 187.

Sherif, M. *The psychology of social norms.* New York: Harper, 1936.

14.

Personality Theory
in Perspective

W e have now reached the end of our tour through a dozen major types of personality theory. The reader who has faithfully completed the journey must surely be impressed with the diversity and complexity of these viewpoints. Each type has proved to have certain distinctive features and in each case we have found something about the position to approve or admire. It seems appropriate at this point to pause and attempt to identify general trends which exist in spite of the tremendous differences among personality theories. It is important that the student should have a sense of the individuality and distinctiveness of each viewpoint but it is equally important that he be aware of whatever common qualities may exist in the midst of this welter of conflicting assertion and individual expression.

In this, our final chapter, we shall return to the personality theories under consideration in pursuit of the goal of generality and our discussion will be organized around the dimensions proposed in the initial chapter as appropriate for comparing theories of personality. We shall also present a small number of issues that seem to us important in determining future developments in this area. As a concluding note we shall consider the advisability of attempting a synthesis of personality theories in order to arrive at a general theory that will be maximally acceptable to all persons working in this area and at the same time more useful than any existing theory.

538

THE COMPARISON OF THEORIES OF PERSONALITY

In comparing the theories we shall focus upon differences in content rather than differences in form. Our principal reason for overlooking formal differences derives from our conviction that at this stage of development there is little basis for choice among these theories on such grounds. All are in need of considerable improvement before they can be considered even minimally adequate in terms of formal criteria such as explicitness of statement and adequacy of definition. Although there are some detectable differences between the theories on these criteria, these differences are less interesting and important than the existing differences in substance or content. Something should be said, however, concerning the relative fruitfulness of the various viewpoints as generators of research and we shall return to consider this issue when we have completed our discussion of the substantive differences between the theories.

Our discussion of contemporary personality theory reveals that the importance of conceiving of the human organism as a striving, seeking, *purposive* creature is less central today than it was two or three decades ago. During the first third of this century this was an issue which provided a dramatic cleavage between various psychological theorists. McDougall, Watson, Tolman, and other leading figures focused much of their attention upon the question of whether man was necessarily purposive. While it is still true that some contemporary theorists, such as Allport, Murray, Goldstein, Rogers, Angyal, and Adler, place a heavy emphasis upon the purposive nature of behavior, there is little strong resistance to this point of view. Even theorists such as Miller and Dollard, Sheldon, Eysenck, and Lewin, who do not appear to view purpose as a crucial consideration in understanding behavior, make no attempt to pose this as a central distinction between their own position and other theories. One may suspect that the relatively general question concerning man's purposive nature has been replaced by a series of more specific questions concerning such matters as the role of reward, the importance of the self, and the centrality of unconscious motivation. In general, then, most personality theorists seem to conceive of man as a purposive creature but even where this is not taken for granted it does not seem to be a matter of hot dispute.

The relative importance of *unconscious determinants* of behavior as opposed to the importance of conscious determinants persists as a key factor in the distinction between the various theories of personal-

ity. Although this remains a central issue, the exact grounds for disagreement between theorists seem to have shifted considerably in recent years. Originally the debate focused about the reality or existence
of unconscious motivation but today the question seems to be less a
matter of whether such factors exist than a matter of under what
conditions and how strongly they operate. Clearly Freud's theory
gives the heaviest emphasis to unconscious factors and a variety of
theories influenced by the orthodox psychoanalytic position such as
Murray's and Jung's also give a heavy weighting to such factors. At
the other extreme we find theories such as Allport's, Lewin's, Goldstein's, and Rogers' where unconscious motives are de-emphasized or
ceded an important role only in the abnormal individual. It is true
that personality theorists have displayed a trend toward increased
acceptance of the role of unconscious motives but there remains a
great deal of variety among the theorists in the extent to which this
role is emphasized.

The centrality of *reward* or reinforcement as a determinant of behavior is most vividly emphasized in the reinforcement theory of
Miller and Dollard, in Freud's pleasure principle, and Murphy's concept of canalization. Cattell, Murray, and Sullivan also accept the law
of effect, with certain reservations, as a primary condition of learning.
In contrast Allport, Angyal, Goldstein, Lewin, and Rogers are relatively explicit in demoting reward to a secondary role. In general,
contemporary formulations seem less often than in the past to imply
that man is motivated by a conscious attempt to maximize pleasure
and minimize pain. They stress the function of reward as a determinant of behavior regardless of whether the individual is aware of its
role or not. There seems to be a growing tendency for personality
theorists to deal explicitly with the issue of reward, either assigning it
central importance or else subordinating it to other principles.

Association, the spatial and temporal linking of two events, is less
explicitly emphasized by most personality theorists than reward. In
spite of the tremendous historical importance of Pavlov's studies of
conditioning we find that of the theorists we have considered only
Mowrer appears to have made this factor one of the cornerstones of
his theoretical position. In contrast, Miller and Dollard clearly subordinate this principle to reward. Freud's theory appears to assign
some importance to association in the process of symptom formation
and symbolic transformation, as the nature of the symptom or symbol
may be partially determined by associative links in the past. For the
most part, however, personality theorists either do not deal explicitly

with association or else assign it a minor role in the determination of behavior. This state of affairs probably reflects the feeling of most of these theorists that association alone is not a sufficient explanation of behavior and that the operation of association as a minor factor in the determination of behavior is too obvious to need emphasis. It is also true that personality theorists are very much engrossed with the motivational process, and simple association without the binding effects of motives seems irrelevant if not heretical to someone focused upon motivation.

The considerable variation among theories in their concern with the *learning process* is anchored at one end by the detailed exposition provided by Miller and Dollard and at the other end by the absence of any specific treatment of learning in the theories of Sheldon, Jung, and Rogers. Allport and Cattell devote considerable attention to this process but for the most part their ideas represent attempts to pull together principles that have been developed by other theorists. Lewin has made some original contributions to the understanding of learning, but he has never centered his conceptual efforts in this area. Most personality theorists have been content to view development in terms of global principles such as maturation, individuation, identification, self-actualization, or the like, rather than attempting to provide a detailed picture of the learning process.

Although there may be some neglect of the learning process, there is an abundance of interest in the products of learning or the *acquisitions of personality*. One of the most distinctive features of personality theories is their numerous and distinctive schemes for representing personality structure. Among those who have been most detailed in their treatment of personality structure are Allport, Cattell, Eysenck, Freud, Jung, Murray, and Sheldon. Historically there has been a tendency for those theorists who were most concerned with the learning process to be least concerned with the acquisitions of learning and vice versa. At present, however, those theorists who are sharply deficient in their treatment of either learning or structure tend to compensate for this deficiency by borrowing a set of formulations from another theory whose conceptual focus includes this neglected area. The best illustration of this trend is provided by the efforts of Miller and Dollard to incorporate into their learning theory the structural concepts of psychoanalysis. There is no doubt that the sophisticated personality theorist today accepts a responsibility for dealing with both the process of learning and the outcomes of this process.

We have already pointed to the fact that as a group American psychologists have minimized the role of hereditary factors as determinants of behavior. Yet many of the theorists we have considered clearly and explicitly emphasize the importance of such factors. Sheldon is convinced of the centrality of genetic determinants and hopes that his approach to the study of behavior will shed light on the details of the relation between genetic and behavioral events. Eysenck and Cattell have displayed both theoretical and empirical interest in the role of heredity in behavior. Their investigations have actually tended to supply strong support for their theoretical convictions on this score. Jung's theory is deeply committed to the importance of the genetic and both Freud and Murphy consider hereditary factors of prime importance. Murray and Allport also accept the significance of heredity although they place somewhat less emphasis upon this issue then the previously mentioned theorists. Of the personality theorists we have considered it seems that Fromm, Horney, Lewin, Rogers, and Sullivan place the least emphasis upon such factors. We find, then, somewhat surprisingly, that the majority of personality theorists have accepted or emphasized the importance of heredity factors and several have coupled this theoretical emphasis with relevant empirical research.

The contrast between Freud's and Lewin's theoretical positions nicely illustrates the variation among personality theorists in their emphasis upon the significance of contemporary factors as opposed to the significance of events taking place early in development. The stimulus-response theory of Miller and Dollard, Murphy's biosocial theory, Murray's personology, and Sullivan's interpersonal theory resemble Freud's theory in their emphasis upon early experience, and Allport's and Rogers' theories resemble Lewin's position in stressing the contemporaneous. The real and important theoretical differences existing here are sometimes concealed by the implication that the theorists who emphasize early experience do so only out of a fascination with history or the past and not because of the predictive power or current significance of such events. The defenders of the importance of the ongoing present maintain that the past can be of significance now only through the operation of factors in the present. Thus, if we fully understand the present there is no need to deal with the past. Actually, there is no real disagreement over the fact that the past influences the present only through the operation of present factors, forces, or attributes (ideas, archetypes, memories, dispositions). The individual who emphasizes the importance of past events maintains, however, that the past is indispensable in order to understand development and also to provide information about forces that are operating in the present. The chief disagreement between these two theoretical camps centers about the question of whether factors influencing present behavior can be assessed adequately from viewing present behavior or whether knowledge concerning past events may not provide special information of a crucial nature. On this issue personality theorists seem rather evenly divided.

The most extreme emphasis upon the *continuity of development* appears in the theories of Freud and Miller and Dollard, although to a lesser degree the same theme is present in the theories of Adler, Angyal, Murphy, and Sullivan. These theories clearly imply that events taking place in the present are systematically linked to events that took place in the past and that development is an orderly and consistent process accountable in terms of a single set of principles. In contrast, Allport, Lewin, and to some extent Rogers, explicitly stress the lack of continuity in development and the relative independence of the functioning adult from the events of childhood or infancy. Jung too emphasizes the disjunctiveness of development although he sees the major discontinuity as occurring at middle age when biological motives are largely replaced by cultural and spiritual needs. All of these theorists suggest that somewhat different principles may be needed to account for what takes place at different stages of development. Not all theories of personality display much interest in the process of development but most of those which do seem to conceive of development as a continuous process to be represented in terms of a single set of theoretical principles.

We have already agreed that one of the features that distinguished personality theory historically from other varieties of psychological theory was an emphasis upon holism. Consistent with this observation is the fact that most contemporary personality theorists may be accurately classed as *organismic*. As a group they emphasize the importance of considering the individual as a total, functioning unit. Thus Allport, Angyal, Goldstein, Murphy, Murray, Rogers, and Sheldon all stress the fact that an element of behavior is not to be understood when studied in isolation from the remainder of the functioning person including his biological make-up. Only Eysenck and Miller and Dollard seem willing to resist convention on this issue and question the importance of studying the "total individual." The importance of the *field* is emphasized by Angyal, Lewin, Murphy, Murray, and Sullivan. Only Lewin and Murray, however, have attempted to provide a detailed set of variables in terms of which the field can be analyzed. This lack of interest in the details of analysis is a logical outgrowth of the holistic convictions of field theorists which lead them to be wary of specific sets of variables. Almost no one *denies* that the situation within which behavior occurs is important, although Allport, Eysenck, Jung, and Sheldon give this matter less explicit attention than other theorists with whom we have dealt. It is evident, then, that the usual contemporary personality theory places heavy emphasis upon the importance of studying behavior "organically" without attempting to isolate small segments of behavior for microscopic study. At the same time there is a growing tendency for the personality theorists to provide a full representation of the situation or context within which behavior occurs.

An individual who adopts a holistic position may be recommending one of two approaches to the representation of behavior. He may simply be suggesting that a successful theory must be complex, multivariate, and include reference to the situation within which a behavioral event occurs, as well as to other behavioral events of the actor. On the other hand, he may be suggesting that all of the individual's behavior is so tightly cemented together and, further, that it is so closely linked to its environmental context, that any attempt to abstract elements or variables for study is doomed to failure. The first point of view accepts the complexity of behavior and suggests that a reasonably complex model of behavior is necessary in order to achieve much efficiency in predicting behavior. The second point of view takes the complexity of behavior as a point of emphasis and insists that "all" aspects of the individual and his situation must be given their due before progress can be made. It is easily understandable that those theories representing the latter position have customarily placed a heavy emphasis upon the distinctiveness or *uniqueness* of the individual. As the theory insists that the observer consider more and more different facets of the individual, his behavior, and the context of his behavior, the distinctiveness of each individual and indeed each act must become obvious and a matter of concern. Allport's theory is by far the most thoroughgoing in its stress upon the importance of giving a full consideration to individuality. In fact, as we have seen, this emphasis led Allport to propose that more attention be given to the idiographic method of studying behavior. This same general point of view is given central emphasis in the theories of Adler, Fromm, Lewin, Murphy, and Murray. The theories of Eysenck and Miller and Dollard are most explicit in denying the crucial significance of the individuality of behavior. Although there are a number of personality theorists who deal centrally with the uniqueness of behavior, this seems less typical of modern personality theory than the organismic emphasis.

We have seen that there are several senses in which the *self* concept is employed by personality theorists. Either the self is seen as a group of psychological processes which serves as a determinant of behavior or else it is conceived of as a cluster of attitudes and feelings the individual has about himself. In one form or the other, however, the self occupies a prominent role in most current personality formulations. Not only are there specific theories such as Rogers' which are identified as self theories but a large number of other theories employ this concept as a focal theoretical element. Among the theorists who, in some way, make prominent use of the ego or self concept are Adler, Allport, Angyal, Cattell, Freud, Goldstein, Jung, Murphy, Murray, and Sullivan. Only Eysenck, Miller and Dollard, and Sheldon seem to conceive of behavior in such a manner that the self is not ceded an important role. It is true that many of the current formulations of the self have avoided or lessened the subjectivity which inhered in early conceptions. There has been a definite trend in the direction of providing operations whereby the self or aspects of it can be measured. One might say that in the early days of psychological theorizing the self tended to have mystical or vitalistic implications whereas the contemporary self seems to have lost these qualities as it gained at least a partial metric. Clearly personality theorists today are characterized by an increased interest in the self and attendant processes.

The significance of the *psychological environment,* or the world of experience as opposed to the world of physical reality, is accepted by most personality theorists and is a matter of focal emphasis for several. Lewin and Rogers are the most explicit and thoroughgoing in their development of this point of view. In fact, both have been accused of largely ignoring the world of reality as a result of their preoccupation with the world of experience. This point of view also receives considerable attention in all of the psychoanalytic theories, and in Murray's theory. Although no one questions that the manner in which the individual perceives a given event has some influence upon the way in which he will respond to this event, we find that this process receives little attention in the theories of Cattell, Eysenck, Miller and Dollard, and Goldstein. All in all, it is probably fair to say that personality theorists are more impressed with the importance of the psychological environment than with the importance of the physical environment.

The importance of *group membership determinants* of behavior is a matter for concerted emphasis primarily within those theories that have been heavily influenced by sociology and anthropology. Illustrative of this are the positions of Fromm, Miller and Dollard, Murphy, Murray, and Sullivan. Adler and Lewin also assign considerable importance to these determinants although the relation between their theories and social science developments is less clear. It is quite natural that those theorists who have stressed the "field" within which behavior occurs should also manifest an interest in the social groups to which the individual belongs. Consistent with this is the fact that all of the above theorists with the exception of Miller and Dollard may be considered field theorists. None of the theorists we have examined believes that group membership factors are unimportant although Allport, Angyal, Goldstein, Jung, Rogers, and Sheldon have chosen not to focus upon these factors. In general, it seems that there is a growing tendency for personality theorists to give explicit attention to the sociocultural context within which behavior occurs.

We have observed that it is customary for personality theorists to attempt some form of *interdisciplinary anchoring* of their theories. Most of these efforts center about the possibility of interpenetrating psychological concepts with the findings and concepts of the biological sciences. Illustrative of this tendency are the theories of Allport, Freud, Goldstein, Jung, Murphy, and Sheldon. None of the personality theorists we have discussed, except possibly Lewin, seems exclusively oriented toward linking his formulations with the disciplines of anthropology and sociology. However, Dollard and Miller, Murphy, Murray, and Sullivan show a balanced interest in establishing theoretical links with both biology and the social sciences. From this it is clear that personality theorists as a group are more oriented toward the biological than toward the social sciences. There is, however, a trend in the direction of increased interest in the findings and theories of sociology and anthropology.

The diversity and *multiplicity of motivation* in the human is given a full recognition in the theories of Allport, Cattell, Lewin, Murphy, and Murray. In each of these theories there is a firm emphasis upon the fact that behavior can be understood only with the identification and study of a large number of motivational variables. The theories of Cattell and Murray provide the only detailed attempts to translate this multiplicity into a set of specific variables. Angyal, Eysenck, Freud, Goldstein, Jung, Rogers, Sheldon, and Sullivan seem willing to approach the study of human behavior with a much more abbreviated set of motivational concepts. Thus, although personality the-orists share a detailed concern with the motivational process, they seem equally divided between those who choose to represent motiva-tion in terms of a relatively small number of variables and those who consider a very large number of such variables necessary.

Our discussion to this point has been quite general and little at-tempt has been made to assess each theory in connection with each issue. We have been more concerned with the over-all status of contemporary personality theory than we have with a detailed com-parison of the specific theories. Table 1 provides a partial correction for this generality through indicating for the individual issues whether each of the theories emphasizes, occupies a moderate position, or de-emphasizes this issue. Obviously these judgments are broad and ap-proximate. Their lack of precision is due to the extremely general categories used in the rating and also to the complexity of the theories which, in certain instances, makes it impossible to know with certainty just how a particular theorist stands on a given issue. In any case, the justification for these ratings has been presented in the preceding chapters along with appropriate references to the original sources. Consequently, there is no need for the reader to accept our judgments uncritically as he can freely make his own ratings using the same sources of data we have employed.

In Table 1 the symbol H indicates that the theory emphasizes the importance of this issue or this set of determinants, M indicates that the theory occupies a middle ground, L suggests that the issue or position is de-emphasized within this theory.

This brings us to the question of how well the various theories have functioned as *generators of research*. We have already agreed that this is the most important evaluative comparison that can be made among theories; unfortunately it is likewise the most difficult compari-son to make with assurance. All of the theories have had some func-tion as generators of investigation but the varied nature of the studies that have resulted, as well as the complexity of the relationship be-tween the theory itself and pertinent research, makes anything other than a rough judgment impossible.

Granted the subjectivity and the tentative nature of our verdict, we propose that theories may be divided into three clusters in terms of how fruitful they have been as stimulants to research. In the first group belong the theories that have led to a large quantity of investi-gation which has been carried out in a variety of areas by a diverse group of investigators. Here we place Freud's theory, stimulus-re-

TABLE 1
DIMENSIONAL COMPARISON OF THEORIES OF PERSONALITY

	Purpose	Unconscious Determinants	Reward	Contiguity association	Learning Process	Personality Structure	Heredity	Early Developmental Experience	Continuity of Development	Organismic Emphasis	Field Emphasis	Uniqueness	Psychological Environment	Self Concept	Group Membership Determinants	Biology	Social Science	Multiplicity of Motives
Freud	H	H	H	M	L	H	H	H	H	M	L	M	H	M	L	H	M	L
Jung	H	H	H	L	L	H	H	M	M	H	L	H	M	H	H	M	L	M
Adler	H	M	L	L	L	M	L	M	M	M	H	M	M	H	H	L	H	L
Horney	H	H	M	L	M	M	M	H	M	M	M	M	M	H	H	L	H	L
Fromm	H	M	M	H	M	M	L	L	L	H	H	M	H	H	H	L	H	M
Sullivan	H	L	L	M	M	H	M	H	H	H	H	H	H	M	H	L	H	H
Lewin	H	L	M	M	M	H	M	L	L	H	M	M	M	H	L	H	M	H
Allport	H	L	L	L	L	H	H	L	L	L	L	L	H	L	M	M	L	H
Murray	H	H	M	L	L	H	H	M	H	H	H	L	L	L	L	H	H	L
Sheldon	L	M	M	M	H	H	H	M	M	L	L	L	L	H	M	H	L	L
Eysenck	L	L	L	L	H	L	L	L	L	L	L	L	L	L	L	M	L	L
Cattell	M	M	M	L	H	L	M	M	M	L	L	L	L	L	M	H	L	M
Miller & Dollard	L	M	H	L	H	L	M	H	M	L	L	M	H	H	L	H	H	L
Angyal	H	L	L	L	M	L	L	L	M	H	M	L	H	H	L	H	L	L
Goldstein	H	M	L	L	M	H	M	H	L	H	M	L	H	L	M	M	L	L
Rogers	H	M	L	L	M	L	M	L	L	H	M	L	H	H	L	L	L	L
Murphy	H	M	H	H	H	H	H	H	H	H	H	M	H	M	H	H	H	H

Key: H high (emphasized). M moderate. L low (de-emphasized).

sponse theory, and Lewin's theory. In each case the message of the theory has transcended the bounds of one small group working in close collaboration so that issues related to the theory have been explored in a variety of different settings and by individuals who represent rather heterogeneous backgrounds. Psychoanalytic research is perhaps the best example of this, for the nature of individuals carrying out research which is conceived to be relevant to Freud's theory ranges from those who are directly in the main stream of the medical-psychoanalytic tradition to persons who belong to an experimental or biological tradition. There are numerous sources which document the very great quantity of such research, for example, Hall and Lindzey, 1954; Hilgard, 1952; Sears, 1943. The theory has not only had tremendous impact upon psychological research but has also had a considerable impact upon anthropological and sociological investigation as well as more limited influence upon the other social sciences, literature, the fine arts, and religion.

It is equally clear that Lewin's theory has led to a great deal of relevant research and that much of this has been carried out by individuals who have not been students of Lewin. Although the impact of this theory upon areas outside of psychology has been appreciably less than that of Freud's theory, within psychology its impact has extended to areas where Freud's influence has been little felt. It is evident that in both social psychology and personality psychology Lewin's theory ranks with the most influential in the quantity and quality of research that it has generated.

Hull's stimulus-response theory, as modified by Miller and Dollard and others, has clearly led to a very great quantity of research dealing with a broad range of topics. It has been applied in psychopathology, social behavior, and educational psychology as well as within the usual areas of animal and human learning. Even within social anthropology the theory has had more influence than any other theory except Freud's. Further, the amount of experimental investigation that has been carried out relevant to this theory is much greater than in the case of any other theory we have considered. It is true that there is somewhat more homogeneity of background among investigators here than in the case of Lewin's and Freud's theories. However, even here much of the research has been carried out by individuals who have had little direct contact with Hull.

The second cluster includes those theories which have been accompanied by a large bulk of studies which are either quite limited in scope or else have been carried out by individuals intimately involved with the theory and its development. In this group we would place the theories of Allport, Cattell, Eysenck, Goldstein, Jung, Murphy, Murray, Sheldon, Sullivan, and Rogers. As the individual chapters made clear, each of these theories is accompanied by, or grew out of, a large body of relevant research. In most cases, however, the research deals with a limited range of problems or else the application of a small number of techniques. Further, in the usual instance the research has been carried out by a small number of closely knit investigators. The third group consists of those theories where there is little evidence of accompanying investigation. Here we place Adler, Angyal, Fromm, and Horney.

It is reassuring that, in spite of the limitations of theories of personality as generators of research, the large majority of such theories has been accompanied by a considerable quantity of research. Whatever procedural limitations may inhere in these investigations, the fact remains that they document the interest of the theorists in examining the effectiveness of their theories in the face of empirical data. It is hard to believe that in the long run this attitude will not lead to progressive changes which will result in more effective theories.

SOME REFLECTIONS ON CURRENT PERSONALITY THEORY

What of the future development of personality theory? Are there qualities missing at present from the theoretical scene which should be added? Are there specifiable shortcomings in the theoretical approach of most psychologists? It seems to us that there are, although it must be admitted not all, or perhaps most, psychologists would agree with us as to their precise identity.

We believe the field of personality would benefit enormously from an *increased sophistication* on the part of psychologists *concerning the nature and function of theoretical formulation.* While there are many aspects to this sophistication, perhaps the most important has to do with understanding the central importance of theories as a means of generating or stimulating research. The psychologist should give up the idea that he has discharged his obligation if he provides a theoretical formulation that takes into account or makes consistent what is already known in a given empirical area. If the theory does nothing more than organize known facts we might as well remain at a descriptive level and forsake theorizing. The plea here is simply that theories be evaluated in terms of their capacity to generate new research. Psychologists should also show themselves more willing to accept the fact that assumptions concerning behavior that do not have eventual consequences for the kind of predictions to be made, or the type of data to be collected, are valueless and a waste of time, effort, and print. Let the theorist focus his attention upon formulations which have some meaningful relation to the business he is about—studying behavior.

Related to this need for increased sophistication in methodology is the need for more sensitive *discrimination between effective literary style and powerful theorizing*. It is obvious that from the point of view of the reader the more literately and interestingly a theorist can present his system the better. It should be equally obvious, however, that the elegance of presentation is of no importance as a measure of whether the theory will prove an empirically useful tool. At present many psychologists seem to evaluate a theory in terms of how compelling the creator of the theory is in his presentation of the theory. Although a vivid and effective style plays an important role in arousing interest in a theory, evaluation of the fruitfulness of the theory should rest upon uniquely different grounds. The essence of this point is that the value of a theorist should be equated to the research utility of his theory rather than to his literary brilliance.

Personality theory and research are in need of *an increase in both radicalism and conservatism*. One might choose to express this alternatively as an increase in both creative imagination and in critical evaluation. The successful theorist must develop a dispassionate willingness to do radical violence to common assumptions concerning behavior. He should, so far as possible, be able to free himself from common preconceptions concerning the nature of behavior. Once having displayed a capacity to innovate or create a theory which is not tied tightly to existing conceptions of behavior, the theorist should then display a rigid conservatism in extending, formalizing, applying, and testing the consequences of this point of view. In other words, the theorist should be a convention-breaker but once he has established a new set of conventions he should be willing to explore exhaustively the implications of these conventions. It is impossible to test the consequences of a theory unless the theorist is willing to remain in one position long enough for verification procedures to be instituted and completed. This does not mean that the person should cling to his formulations stubbornly in the face of empirical disconfirmation. It does mean that given a stable body of theory, change should be introduced as a result of controlled empirical evidence rather than because of whim or passing observation. It is of crucial importance that the theorist and his followers devote themselves to empirical investigation rather than polemic or verbal argument. It is of little significance which personality theorist is the most effective protagonist in a debate but it is of crucial significance which personality theory is most useful in generating important and verifiable empirical consequences.

It is high time that the personality theorist was *freed from obligation to justify theoretical formulations that depart from normative or customary views of behavior.* It is all too common to find that a given theory is criticized for the fact that it emphasizes too strongly the negative aspects of behavior or overemphasizes the importance of sexual motives. It is true that a common-sense view of behavior sees man as possessing both good and bad attributes and further considers him to possess not only sexual motives but other motives as well. This, however, is a complete *non sequitur* so far as the development of a theory of behavior is concerned. The theorist has complete freedom, as we have just emphasized, to depart from customary preconceptions about behavior and is required only to make statements about behavior that are empirically useful. The question of whether these statements please or offend the average individual is of no importance. It is quite possible that the most fruitful theories of behavior will prove eventually to be highly offensive to an average member of our society. Of course the opposite alternative is also perfectly possible. The point we are making here is not that the theorist must deny customary views of behavior or that he must accept such views. He is at liberty to do either. His position is neutral in regard to these views and he may conform or deviate as he wishes with the evaluation of his decision resting upon criteria altogether removed from the normative acceptability or deviance of his theory. Many other criticisms of theoretical formulations that are frequently encountered have an equally dubious status. Thus, the suggestion that a given theory is too molecular, too rational, or too mechanistic simply reflects preconceptions about behavior that the particular critic possesses. These remarks serve more to reveal the position of the critic than to evaluate the theory. In the final analysis *the only telling criticism of an existing theory is an alternative theory that works better.* If one says that a given theory is too molecular it remains for someone to demonstrate that an alternative theory employing larger units of analysis is able to do all the first theory can do and more besides.

One may argue that at present in psychology there is altogether *too little value placed upon empirical research that bears directly upon existing theories* and altogether too much value placed upon the contribution of new theoretical formulation or speculation provided after a given set of findings has been observed. There is more prestige associated in the minds of many psychologists with the creation of a new but trivial theory, possessing little demonstrated superiority over existing theories, than there is in the execution of research that bears crucially upon an important theory already in existence. Psychologists in their awe for theory and their failure to discriminate between after-the-fact explanation and before-the-fact prediction have created a set of conditions where there is a maximum of interest in developing new theories and a minimum of interest in examining the consequences of existing theories.

An annoying and possibly malignant characteristic displayed by some contemporary personality theorists is the tendency toward what might be called *theoretical imperialism.* We have reference here to the attempt, once a particular theoretical position has been developed, to try and persuade the reader that this is the only feasible manner in which a theory of behavior can be formulated. Thus, numerous psychologists assert that the only defensible theoretical mode is one that involves continuous interaction with physiological processes, others suggest that only "molar" formulations are fruitful, and still others imply that the social context must be the center of the theorist's attention. The point we wish to make is not that these theorists are necessarily wrong in their faith but only that theoretical formulation is a "free enterprise" if ever there was one. No theorist has the right to tell his fellow theorists their business. He is fully entitled to state his own convictions and link them with as much empirical evidence of their utility as possible. He may even wish to couple the theory and evidence with rational arguments which he finds convincing as to why this approach will prove in the end to be fruitful. But to imply that this is the way in which theoretical progress *must* be made is nonsense and can only serve to confuse the student in the field. Let the theorist present his theory in the most forceful manner possible but let him respect the fact that there is no such thing as theoretical certainty.

The reader should be careful not to construe what we have just said as indicating a sense of despair or discouragement with the present state of personality theory. It is true that there is much that can be presented in the way of criticism of current theories, particularly when they are compared with absolute or ideal standards. More significant, however, is the fact that when these theories are compared with theories existing three or four decades ago the signs of rapid progress are unmistakable. It was primarily during the past twenty-five years that the bulk of relevant empirical research appeared and it was likewise during this period that sophistication concerning the contribution of neighboring disciplines developed. At the same time, the theories have tended to become more explicit in their statement and much more attention is paid to the problem of providing adequate empirical definitions. Further, the range of ideas or conceptions concerning behavior has broadened immensely. In general, we believe that whatever the formal shortcomings of these theories may be, the ideas contained within them have had a remarkably broad and generative influence upon psychology. Nor does there seem to be any reason to expect that this influence will diminish in the future.

THEORETICAL SYNTHESIS VERSUS THEORETICAL MULTIPLICITY

We have seen that although there are similarities and convergences among theories of personality, the diversities and disagreements remain striking. In spite of the clustering about certain modal theoretical positions there has been, as yet, little progress in the direction of developing a single widely accepted theoretical position. One may indeed wonder at the apparently endless ingenuity of psychologists in devising new ways of viewing or ordering the phenomena of behavior. Sears in a survey of the personality literature was moved by this state of affairs to remark:

> Any theory is valid only to the extent that it proves useful in predicting or providing for control of behavior; there is no right or wrong in the matter, but only convenience. Since no theory yet has proved brilliantly efficacious in ordering the data of molar behavior for these purposes, it is perhaps not surprising that so many psychologists find themselves goaded into new attempts to construct a systematic set of personality variables (Sears, 1950, p. 116).

Granted that this theoretical multiplicity exists, and granted also that the factors leading to this state are evident, is it not undesirable to have so many conflicting viewpoints in a single empirical area? Would it not be better to provide a single viewpoint which incorporated all that was good and effective from each of these theories so that we could then embrace a single theory which would be accepted by all investigators working in this area? Surely many of the theories we have discussed contain strengths which are not present in other theories. Can we not combine these individual strengths so as to create a uniquely powerful theory which will give us added insight into human behavior and generate predictions concerning behavior that are more comprehensive and verifiable than those presently generated by any single theory of personality?

Although this line of reasoning is intriguing and finds much support among contemporary psychologists, there are, nevertheless, a number of serious objections which can be raised to it. First, this point of view assumes that the existing personality theories possess a sufficient degree of formal clarity so that their exact nature can be established and the synthesizer can then readily identify common components and disparate elements. As we have seen this is anything but the case. Many of the theories are stated so imprecisely that it would be extremely difficult to make any direct comparison of their elements with the elements of another theory. This suggests that synthesis of necessity must be a somewhat haphazard process as the elements involved in the synthesis are only dimly outlined. Second, the argument assumes that there are no unresolvable conflicts between the content of the various theoretical positions or, if such conflicts exist, that they can readily be settled through an examination of the "facts of the matter." It is evident that there are many points where the theories are in flat disagreement. Further, these points of disagreement are frequently related to empirical phenomena which are far from being adequately studied. In fact, many of these theoretical differences are concerned with empirical issues of the most elusive variety, so that the "facts of the matter" are by no means clear. Third, it assumes that all or most of these theories have a unique and positive contribution to make to a powerful theory of behavior. The truth of the matter is that some of these theories are a long way from possessing demonstrated empirical utility. If we except animal psychology, the amount of empirical testing of the derivable consequences of psychological theory is minute compared to the range of problems with which the theories purport to deal. Fourth, this point of view assumes that a state of theoretical harmony and agreement is healthiest at present. At a stage where the relevant empirical findings are so scanty, and where no single position seems to have a convincing superiority over all others, one may argue quite reasonably that, rather than investing all of our time and talent in a single theory, it would be wiser to explore actively the area through the simultaneous use of a variety of theoretical positions. When so little is known with certainty why place all of the future's hopes in one theoretical basket? Is it not better to let theoretical development follow a natural and unfettered course with the reasonable expectation that as stable empirical findings multiply, and the individual theories become more formalized, an integration may be arrived at naturally, and upon a firm empirical base, rather than as an artificially contrived process with personal taste and belief as the primary determinants of the process?

What of the didactic value of presenting to the student a single organized view of personality rather than the welter of contradictory ideas which we have seen presented in this volume? Presumably it is good mental hygiene to give the student a single clearly outlined theoretical position but it is certainly poor preparation for serious work in the field. If the student believes that there is only one useful theory, it is easy for him to feel that he has reality firmly in his grasp and consequently to overlook the importance of empirical study and the possibility of theoretical changes imposed by the outcome of such study. Why should the student be given a false sense of harmony? Let him see the field as it really exists—different theorists making different assumptions about behavior, focusing upon different empirical problems, using different techniques for research. Let him understand also that these individuals are united in their common interest in human behavior and their ultimate willingness to permit empirical data to make the final decision concerning theoretical right and wrong.

Related to the above argument is the compelling consideration that theories are useful chiefly to the person who embraces them and attempts in a sympathetic and sensitive manner to extract their consequences. The notion of a general synthesis or integration usually communicates to the student the need to be cautious, take all points of view into consideration, and to avoid emotional involvement with a particular, one-sided position. Before embracing any particular theory let us compare it with others, see that it is just as good in all respects, and read what the critics have had to say about it. Contrary to this conception, we recommend strongly that the student should, once he has surveyed the available theories of personality, adopt an intolerant and affectionate acceptance of a particular theoretical position without reservation. Let the individual be enthusiastic and imbued with the theory before he commences to examine it critically. A theory of personality is not going to say or do much for the individual who approaches it aloofly, with criticisms and reservation. It will dictate problems to the devotee and stimulate him to do research but it will not do the same for the cool and detached observer.

Let the student reserve his critical capacity and his detailed scholarly apparatus to make certain that the research he carries out is so well executed that the findings "fall where they may." If the individual does extract consequences from the theory and engage in relevant research, he will have ample opportunity for discouragement and despair concerning the adequacy of the theory and he may well end up convinced of its lack of utility. At least he will have had the opportunity of discovering just what the theory *can* do for him.

Our general proposal to the student is that he first acquaint himself broadly with the field of personality, and this is precisely what this volume is intended to do. Then let him immerse himself in one theory of personality. Wallow in it, revel in it, absorb it, learn it thoroughly, and think that it is the best possible way to conceive of behavior. Only reserve in one small corner of his mind the reservation that the final crucible for any theory is the world of reality studied under controlled conditions. After the romance is over and the student is seduced by the theory, he may set about the cold hard business of investigation in order to find out whether his theoretical marriage will withstand the ravages of reality.

It is our strong conviction, then, that this is not the appropriate time or circumstance for an attempted synthesis or integration of personality theories. In simplest terms we feel that it is unwise to attempt a synthesis of theories whose empirical utility remains largely undemonstrated. Why make a conceptual arrangement in terms of aesthetic reaction and internal consistency when the important issue is how these elements fare in the face of empirical data? Far more fruitful, we believe, than any attempt at a master theory is the careful development and specification of a single existing theory with simultaneous attention to relevant empirical data. The ultimate answer to any theoretical issue lies in well-controlled empirical data, and the nature of such data will be adequately defined only as the theories themselves are better developed. It is one thing to change a theory in the light of empirical data which force upon the theorist some essential change, and quite another to change a theory because of some conflicting rational or evaluative issue. Our faith is that almost any theory if it is systematically extended and coupled with extensive empirical research offers greater hope for advance than an amalgamation of existing theories some of which are poorly stated and precariously related to empirical data.

BIBLIOGRAPHY

Hall, C. S., and Lindzey, G. Psychoanalytic theory and its applications in the social sciences. In G. Lindzey (Ed.). *Handbook of social psychology.* Vol. 1. Cambridge, Mass.: Addison-Wesley, 1954, pp. 143–180.

Hilgard, E. R. Experimental approaches to psychoanalysis. In E. Pumpian-Mindlin (Ed.). *Psychoanalysis as science.* Stanford, Calif.: Stanford Univ. Press, 1952, pp. 3–45.

Sears, R. R. *Survey of objective studies of psychoanalytic concepts.* New York: Soc. Sci. Res. Council, Bull. No. 51, 1943.

Sears, R. R. Personality. In C. P. Stone and D. W. Taylor (Eds.). *Annual review of psychology.* Vol. 1. Stanford, Calif.: Annual Reviews, 1950, pp. 105–118.

Name Index

(Boldface numbers refer to the references cited.)

559

Subject Index